Mirabai

Mirabai

The Making of a Saint

Nancy M. Martin

OXFORD
UNIVERSITY PRESS

Oxford University Press is a department of the University of Oxford. It furthers
the University's objective of excellence in research, scholarship, and education
by publishing worldwide. Oxford is a registered trade mark of Oxford University
Press in the UK and certain other countries.

Published in the United States of America by Oxford University Press
198 Madison Avenue, New York, NY 10016, United States of America.

© Oxford University Press 2023

All rights reserved. No part of this publication may be reproduced, stored in
a retrieval system, or transmitted, in any form or by any means, without the
prior permission in writing of Oxford University Press, or as expressly permitted
by law, by license, or under terms agreed with the appropriate reproduction
rights organization. Inquiries concerning reproduction outside the scope of the
above should be sent to the Rights Department, Oxford University Press, at the
address above.

You must not circulate this work in any other form
and you must impose this same condition on any acquirer.

CIP data is on file at the Library of Congress
ISBN 978-0-19-515390-3 (pbk.)
ISBN 978-0-19-515389-7 (hbk.)

DOI: 10.1093/oso/9780195153897.001.0001

Paperback printed by Marquis Book Printing, Canada
Hardback printed by Bridgeport National Bindery, Inc., United States of America

*To my parents,
Ann and Russ Martin,
in love and gratitude*

Contents

List of Illustrations — ix
Acknowledgments — xi
Notes on Transliteration and Dates — xv

Introduction: In Search of Mirabai — 1

1. **Embodying Devotion in a Woman's Body: Mirabai among the Saints** — 21

2. **Participation and Transformation: Mira as Rapjut Renouncer, Varkari Devotee, and *Pativrata* of God** — 71

3. **History, Heroism, and the Politics of Identity: Mirabai in Nineteenth-Century Colonial India** — 109

4. **Weaver Woman and Lover Extraordinaire: Romance and Resistance in Rural Rajasthan** — 163

5. **Mobilizing Mirabai, Mobilizing Women in the Struggle for Independence** — 203

6. **Cultural Icon for a Nation in the Making** — 247

Conclusion — 289
Notes — 293
Selected Bibliography — 353
Index — 363

Illustrations

Figure I.1.	Painting of Mirabai in the Charbhuja Temple (aka Meera Temple) in Merta	4
Figure 1.1.	Map of Rajasthan	33
Figure 1.2.	The cup of poison being delivered to Mira in the illustrated manuscript *Mira ki Katha* (The Story of Mira)	36
Figure 2.1.	Mira and her cousin Jaimal worshiping Charbhuja, the four-armed form of Vishnu	74
Figure 3.1.	Portrait of Mirabai worshiping alone on display in the Udaipur City Palace	150
Figure 4.1.	Mira conversing with her mother depicted in the khyal script *Mira Mangal* (Mira's Marriage)	169
Figure 5.1.	Portrait of Mirabai displayed in the St. Mira School for Girls in Pune (1996)	234
Figure 6.1.	M. S. Subbulakshmi as Mirabai	277
Figure C.1.	Images of Mirabai and Krishna installed in the Meera Temple within the Chittor Fort	291

Acknowledgments

I have come to know Mirabai, who she was and has been and continues to be for so many, over some three decades of research. My understanding has been shaped by innumerable others, many of their names appearing across the chapters and filling the notes of this volume. I am deeply indebted to them all, for my work both draws on and flows into an ongoing and dynamic river of tradition and scholarship that surround the saint.

The seeds of this work lie in my undergraduate studies at University of Puget Sound, and I am grateful to Florence Sandler for fostering my interest in the power of myth and story; to Del Langbauer for introducing me to the study of the religions of the world, Hinduism, and so much more; and to Robert and Eileen Albertson, who made it possible for me to travel to India for the first time as a participant in the Pacific Rim Program. Wendy Doniger and Anthony Yu at the University of Chicago challenged and inspired me as these lines of interest coalesced, and I am immensely grateful to Clare Fischer for guiding my doctoral study at Graduate Theological Union and for her continuing support over the years as a mentor and friend. Linda Hess has profoundly shaped my understanding of bhakti (the devotional dimension of Hinduism) and guided my study at UC Berkeley, her extraordinary work on Kabir setting an unmatchable bar of excellence both in research and articulation to which I will always aspire.

My initial fieldwork in 1992–1993 was made possible by a dissertation fellowship from the American Institute of Indian Studies. Across the decades, my writing and research have also been made possible through the Graves Award in the Humanities, a National Endowment for the Humanities fellowship, and my tenure as an international fellow and now life member of Clare Hall, Cambridge University, as well as ongoing support from Chapman University both in funding and time. This volume was made possible through their great generosity.

So many in India facilitated the initial phase of my research as well as its continuation in subsequent years. For their assistance in the initial stage, I am deeply indebted to K. C. Shastri of Mira Kala Mandir and Ranchord Singh Ashiya at Bartiya Lok Kala Mandir in Udaipur, S. N. Samdani and Mira Shodh Sansthan in Chittor, and a multitude of others who offered me their time and wisdom as well as opportunities to interact with the wider community of

Mira scholars in India, most especially Kalyan Singh Shekhawat. The staff of Rajasthan Shodh Sansthan (Chaupasani, Jodhpur) and the Rajasthan Oriental Research Institute in Jodhpur opened their collections to me and offered much-appreciated assistance with manuscript sources from centuries past.

I am immensely grateful also for the generous hospitality and guidance of Sri Srivatsa Goswami and Robyn Beeche in Vrindavan, as I followed in the footsteps of Mirabai, sought and found women who "lived like Mira," and attended the lilas of her life performed there. I also remember Dominique Sila Khan with great fondness and gratitude. I always learned so much from our conversations, she so readily sharing her vast scholarly knowledge, her linguistic expertise, and crucial insights drawn from her many years of research in the field. The fieldwork we carried out together, joined by her husband and fellow researcher, Sattar Khan, was invaluable and their friendship an extraordinary gift.

I owe special thanks to Rajendra and Nirmala Joshi, who guided me in the difficult first months of my search for Mira, teaching me so much about so many aspects of life in Rajasthan, past and present, introducing me to scholars across the region, and offering me a crucial refuge on so many afternoons spent in their beautiful garden. Their daughter Varsha, too, became an invaluable colleague and friend in the years that followed. Words are insufficient to express how much their support and friendship have meant to me or the depths of my gratitude for Rajendra's mentorship.

Swami Om Anand Saraswati's invitation to stay at Padmini Arsh Kanya Gurukul in Chittor also transformed my work, he generously sharing both his extensive library and in-depth knowledge of Mirabai as a scholar of Hindi literature, and Seema Srimali and the girls at the ashram facilitating my conversational command of Hindi even as I assisted them with English. These were amazing days which also deeply impacted my understanding of life and relations in India, from the experience of the monsoon storms to the political tumult leading up to and following the destruction of the Babri Masjid in Ayodhya.

There are no words to express my gratitude and debt to Padma Sri Komal Kothari. Extraordinarily generous with his time and his home, he opened the world of oral traditions of Mirabai to me, including both materials from the archives of Rupayan Sansthan Folklore Institute and songs we documented together, he inviting singers from across the region and traveling with me so that we might record still more. His encyclopedic knowledge of all manner of folk traditions and aspects of culture greatly enriched my understanding of these dimensions of the saint, the songs sung in her name, and the people who perform them, and he provided me with access I could never have had without his entrée. His kindness and care as well as his wisdom were beyond compare, and he is deeply missed by all who knew him. I also offer my deepest appreciation to Manohar Lalas, who has been an invaluable partner in transcribing recordings and in long hours spent discussing the subtleties of meanings in so many songs, he, too, deeply steeped in the cultural life of Rajasthan. Having worked closely with Komalda for many decades, Manohar continues this important work of documenting all manner of Rajasthani folk traditions. I am grateful, too, for the ongoing support and friendship of Kuldeep Kothari, who has assumed the position of director of Rupayan Sansthan, and to the singers of *Mira Janma Patri* and *Kumbha Rana ri Bhat* and innumerable others who have shared their songs and stories and love of the saint with me.

My work would not have been possible without the contributions of a host of other researchers and colleagues. Foundational have been the studies carried out by historians and literary scholars in India who have scoured available manuscript collections and other sources to catalogue references to the saint across the centuries. The writings of Parita Mukta, Kumkum Sangari, and A. K. Ramanjun have been vital to my understanding of both Mirabai and bhakti. I offer special thanks also to Heidi Pauwels, Monika Horstmann, Winand Callewaert, Dan and Ann Grodzins Gold, Vasudha Narayanan, Julius Lipner, Keith Ward, Chakravarthi Ram-Prasad, Chris Chapple, David Lorenzen, Richard Barz, Frances Taft, Mark Juergensmeyer, and Lindsey Harlan in addition to Linda Hess for their own extraordinary scholarship and their contributions to and support of my work across the years in innumerable ways.

Most especially I must express my deepest gratitude to Jack Hawley, whose publications on Mirabai first inspired this study and who offered his immense knowledge and insight to me time and again in reading and commenting on my work, enriching my understanding and importantly introducing me to emerging new research and guiding me to new insight and away from errors. I will always be beholden to him for his unflagging support at each stage of my academic career—and also for being the one person with whom I could discuss minute details of my research who might share my enthusiasm.

I ask forgiveness from those I have not mentioned by name who have also contributed so much to what is valuable in the work herein. Any errors are strictly my own. It is my hope that this volume will add in some small measure to our understanding of this extraordinary saint, and I look forward to new materials and perspectives surfacing that will contribute further.

I must also express my deep appreciation to the anonymous readers of my initial manuscript and my immense gratitude to the editors at Oxford University Press; to Cynthia Read, who encouraged me across the years; and to Theodore Calderara, who embraced the project and brought it to fruition.

xiv Acknowledgments

Finally, none of this would have been possible without the unwavering love and support of my parents, Ann and Russ Martin, across the challenges, joys, and adventures of my life. I am immensely grateful to them and to my husband, Hawk Davila, whose belief in me allowed me to believe in myself and at last to send this work out into the world.

Notes on Transliteration and Dates

Transliteration of Hindi and Rajasthani terms and titles of texts has been done according to the system used by the Library of Congress, except that the medial or final *a* has been omitted where it is not pronounced in Hindi or Rajasthani (though it may be in Sanskrit). However, for certain words ending in conjunct consonants where pronunciation would be difficult for an English speaker without a final vowel, the final vowel has been retained (e.g., *bhakta, janma*).

To facilitate reading with ease for the nonspecialist, I have chosen to give non-English words, including place names and personal names, in common anglicized forms and/or those that best approximate pronunciation in English, defining terms as necessary with their initial usage. For example, *sh* has been used for both श and ष; *ch* for both च and छ. Non-English references are given with standard diacritics appropriate to the specific language in the notes and bibliography, and I have preserved diacritics in quotations per original texts.

All dates have also been given in the common era (CE). Vikram Sanvat (VS) dates have been converted by subtracting 57. Although this may not in every case be absolutely accurate, the dates themselves are tentative enough that no significant distortion is introduced.

Introduction

In Search of Mirabai

> "I choose to serve God," she declared.
> "Freely I take the servant's role."
> *Tying bells to her ankles, Mira danced away.*
>
> "Mirabai's crazy!" they said.
> Mother-in-law said "Family Destroyer!"
> *Tying bells to her ankles, Mira danced away.*
>
> The king of Mewar's gift, a poison cup—
> Laughing, Mira drank it down.
> *Tying bells to her ankles, Mira danced away.*
>
> Mira's Lord, that gallant One who raised the mountain high,
> So easily the Indestructible One was hers!
> *Tying bells to her ankles, Mira danced away.*

Stories of an extraordinary woman who lived some five hundred years ago in India come to us, passed from person to person, performed publicly and sometimes committed to writing across the centuries, printed, enacted, and broadcast in our time, telling of one who could not be turned from pursuing her heart's desire nor restrained from dancing and singing her love for God before the world. Haunting strains of impassioned poetry of exquisite beauty whisper from the past and gain force, building to an immense body of song, composed and performed in diverse languages and musical styles. So many stories are told about this woman called "Mirabai" or simply "Mira," so many songs sung in her name. Who was and is this woman who has captured the hearts and imaginations of so many people, throughout India and beyond?

Mirabai. Nancy M. Martin, Oxford University Press. © Oxford University Press 2023.
DOI: 10.1093/oso/9780195153897.003.0001

By most accounts she was the sixteenth-century daughter of a minor royal house in Merta, in the region now called Rajasthan in the deserts of northwestern India, promised to the ruling family of the kingdom of Mewar in southern Rajasthan in an arranged marriage of political alliance. Deeply devoted to God in the form of Krishna (whom she calls alternately "the Lifter of the Mountain," "Narayan," and the "Indestructible One" in the song quoted above), she refused to behave as a proper wife and woman of her caste and class should, rejecting the validity of an arranged marriage and its attendant privileges, refusing the seclusion required of royal *rajput* (warrior caste) women, and voicing and embodying her passion in the company of devotees from every walk of life, male and female, low caste and high. She resisted all attempts to isolate her and to silence her, standing her ground in the face of social condemnation, familial coercion, and feudal domination. She refused to break under the pressure or to die in spite of repeated attempts on her life, and she eventually left her marital home to become a wandering and widely recognized Hindu devotional saint.

Surely this dancing poet-singer must have been fearless, a free spirit and lover extraordinaire, to have risked so much, even her life, and to have remained so sure of her calling. She must have been revered by many outside her family, admired, but more than that—recognized as one whose power flowed from within, whose words and being were pure authenticity, and whose love for God was contagious. She faced terrible opposition, and yet she not only survived but thrived. Word of such a woman must have spread like wildfire, as one who dared to defy her family and caste, the ruler of the land, and the religious authorities, who dared to follow her heart at all costs and to love God with such fierce intensity. Sparks of story and song would have been carried from place to place by pilgrims and wandering religious teachers, by itinerant artisans, performers, and laborers, by soldiers mobilized for battle, by semi-nomadic herders on their seasonal migrations, by desert merchants moving out in search of investment and business opportunities, by women married into distant villages, and by travelers of every sort, going forth and returning home.

Intrigued, we want to know more about just who she was, and so we will in the coming pages. But this proves to be a challenge. There is at once too much information and too little. When we start to look for her in her homeland of India, we seem to find her everywhere, as her royal husband is said to have done when he had her locked in her chambers but still saw her dancing in every temple he visited. She is devotional saint but also romantic and nationalist heroine and ideal *satyagrahi* (practitioner of Gandhian nonviolence), her story recounted on the silver screen and television, on urban, village, and diaspora stages, and in oral epics, history books, literature texts, religious tracts, novels, and children's comic books. She is a prototype for women poets, dancers, film stars and film directors, spiritual leaders, and activists, her name a compliment to a woman of unusual talent, but also sometimes—even now—an ominous indictment of a woman's excessive independence or religiosity taken too far. Still, many a girl and young woman has participated in cultural performances, dancing and singing Mirabai's songs and acting out her life—this princess of their childhood imaginings. Festivals and international conferences are held in her honor, across India and in diaspora communities around the globe, and songs attributed to her performed in seemingly every musical style and venue. Her image graces greeting cards, postage stamps, and popular posters, and is available on plaques to be placed on personal altars and as figurines of marble, metal, plaster, or plastic, in temples and for purchase at popular pilgrimage sites, in market stalls, and on the internet (Figure I.1).

Outside of India, too, we find a multitude of references to her. Included in collections of great female mystics or poets of the past, her songs are now part of the canons of world literature and of an emerging global interreligious spirituality. They have been translated into English by the great American poet Robert Bly and others, from Andrew Schelling to Jane Hirschfield. And she has inspired still other American poets, such as Janine Canan and Daniel Ladinsky, to compose poetry about her and in her name, even as people in India have done for centuries and continue to do. She is cited as inspiration in books on spiritual journeying, by the likes of novelist Sue Monk Kidd, in self-help books on grief and anger management and finding your own poetic voice, and as a champion of everything from animal rights and deep ecology to feminist philosophy and theology. A number of notable women have either taken or been given her name by spiritual teachers, Sufi and Buddhist as well as Hindu, women like the interspiritual teacher, author, and translator Mirabai Starr and the cofounder of the Center for Contemplative Mind in Society Mirabai Bush. And there are Mirabai restaurants, Mirabai perfume, Mirabai chocolates, and much more.[1]

People have said and sung and written so many things about this wildly popular saint, some quite contradictory and many entirely irreconcilable. With such a dizzying array of portrayals and references, our first response may be to back away in confusion, as her royal husband is said to have done after he entered her chamber, sword in hand, ready to kill her when a spy reported her laughing and talking within as if with a lover. No man was there—only her image of Krishna stood before her—but he saw four Mirabais. Not knowing which one to strike, he froze in his tracks, backing out the door in bewilderment moments later. Isolating a singular "real" Mira will be equally

Figure I.1 Painting of Mirabai by S. K. Kumawat, commissioned by Om Prakash Modi of Merta in memory of Srimati Shakuthala Devi Agrawal in 1985 and prominently displayed in the courtyard of the Charbhuja Temple (also known as the Meera Temple) in Merta.

difficult for us. And though our reasons for wanting to do so may be quite different from those of the enraged king, it would be equally lethal to our understanding of the living reality of the saint were we to do so.

Our next impulse might reasonably be to look to the past to find the original seed of this abundance, to uncover the historical woman behind the stories, as Indian scholars began to do in earnest in the late nineteenth century, and we will indeed explore any and all evidence the past might yield. However, trying to find her in standard historical sources—dynastic chronicles, royal genealogies, and the like—we will come up empty-handed. In fact, we find next to nothing about her in verifiable documents of this kind until well into the nineteenth century. Had she been held in high esteem, as some members of her lineage would claim, we might expect to find some mention of her earlier. But women seldom make the chronicles of kingdoms except as the wife or mother of some great ruler, and the records of royal women that were kept have not been well conserved in any case.[2] If she had sponsored the building of a temple, as some allege, we might hope to find an inscription praising her as patron, as we do for other royal women of her time, but the stones too are silent.[3]

This absence might lead us to question whether she ever truly existed—might she not instead be the product of individual or collective imagination, as some have argued of the famed rajput heroine Padmini?[4] Yet though Mira may be absent from the royal records of her natal and marital families, we do find her very much alive in genres of hagiographic literature that recount the lives of great Hindu devotees, the earliest references to her dating to the latter half of the sixteenth century. These types of records are indeed all we have for many such popular saints, and there is every reason to think that there was an actual woman who inspired these tales, as we assume for so many other great figures of the past, religious or otherwise. But even these texts do not present a unified portrait of the saint, with their aim not history but hagiography in any case. We find ourselves moving instead through layer upon layer of narrative and song, but as with the proverbial onion, finding no kernel of verifiable facts or words at the center, no singular set of bones waiting to be unearthed, metaphorical or otherwise. Instead Mira seems to dance away from all attempts to pin her down decisively, a lively presence rather than a mere shadow cast long ago.

The Lives of Stories and of Saints

The available traces of Mirabai's life are found in the dynamic realm of story and performance. She is not the only or even the first great female exemplar of devotional Hinduism. The honor of being the very first remembered poet-saint goes to a South Indian Tamil woman, Karaikkal Ammaiyar, who composed her songs to Shiva in the sixth century CE. And there are many other great women saints who lived in the centuries that followed: Andal, Mahadeviyakka, Bahinabai, and so many more both before and after Mirabai, each with her own hagiography.[5] And yet Mira's story, seemingly more than that of any other saint, male or female, has proven to be one of those truly great stories that inspire and resonate with people so that they feel compelled to tell it again and again and to retell it in new ways, imitating but also playing off and countering earlier tellings, and translating it into new religious and cultural contexts.

We have grown accustomed to the notion, perhaps in India especially, that some great stories have no identifiable first telling but have instead an "always already" quality, as Mirabai's life story seems to have.[6] But, we might protest, Mira is not merely a story character but a historical person whom we want to get to know—a real person who lived in the sixteenth century (at least we think so). Yet is it not the case that in trying to get to know any person from the past, much of what we can learn about them does come from the stories others tell about their encounters with the person or knowledge people before us recorded, gleaned from others who knew them—some verifiable from multiple sources, some of it hearsay and rumor, fragmented remembrances or imaginings passed down from generations past? To get to know who Mirabai was and, perhaps more important, has been and is to so many, we too will have to listen to the multiple stories people tell and try to understand their particular relationships to the saint, the context and community in which they speak, and why they might choose to tell the particular stories they do.

In any case the narrative of Mira's life, like so many other great stories, seems to have a life of its own. Instead of a definitive original version or "urtext" of which all others might be classified as "variants," we find an ever expanding range of "tellings," as A. K. Ramanujan has suggested in regard to the *Ramayana*, the great Indian epic story of Rama, who must rescue his wife Sita from the demon king Ravana with the help of his brother Lakshman and the monkey warrior Hanuman.[7] Mirabai's life has similarly captivated people's imagination and been woven into the cultural landscape of India, her story about so many things beyond a life long past. We do well to remember, as Kirin Narayan and Kenneth George remind us, that "stories—like all genres of speech—are also practices intended to get things done... not only [to] conjure up other worlds, whether imagined or remembered, but... also a way to use words for social and political purposes in the immediacies of this world."[8] And the uses to which tellers will put Mira's story will indeed be multiple and divergent, generating an immense river of circulating narratives about her (as there are of Rama and Sita).[9]

Such a stubborn multiplicity, Julius Lipner suggests, reflects an "open-ended rather than closed mode of conceptualization" that is characteristic of Hindu traditions more generally, marked by an "instinctive ... understand[ing] that ... it is the very pliability of myth and narrative, their tendency to proliferate into variants, that allows their content to become relevant to one's present circumstances."[10] This fluidity and flexibility rather than fixity of form, the constant reworking of a story so that it has multiple registers of meaning, and the enjoyment and realization generated by a well-told tale that is at once familiar yet new are hallmarks of Indian narrative traditions, including those of Mirabai, and reflective of an underlying quality of orality that marks even written scriptural and teaching traditions in India.

The meaning of the tale told arises anew in each moment of encounter—writing, reading, telling, hearing, performing, seeing—and within communities of reception that bring shared and overlapping fundamental assumptions and strategies of interpretation to that meeting ground. The particular tale told does not originate solely with its author, for authors—known or anonymous, individual or collective—draw on a wealth of shared knowledge in such meaning creation, as performers and audiences also do. Authorial and performative intent remain significant but do not encompass the full import of any telling—even for a fixed literary work composed in writing by a known author, as Philip Lutgendorf has so clearly demonstrated with respect to the many lives of the saint Tulsidas's *Ramcharitmanas* (Lake of the Acts of Ram).[11]

Turning to Mira's case, even in the earliest records we have of her life story, it will be quite clear that there were diverse traditions already circulating about her from which the narrators were drawing, and she must have been known to their intended audiences, to some degree at least, so that they needed to make only brief reference rather than detail some aspects of her character and life. Intertextual references and reflexivity abound as stories are built on stories, expectations fulfilled and confounded, and recognition interwoven with delight and surprise. Each telling or performance occurs within this wider flow of circulating traditions, known in varying degrees to those experiencing the telling, and each new telling contributes further to this cultural flow.

Literary tropes and genres also impact structure and style, imagery and expectation, even determining types of episodes that must be included in the plot of the story and the ways certain events must be described, regardless of the tale's subject. Telling a story in a different genre, then, can dramatically transform the focus of the tale, as each comes with its own set of themes as well as specific performance contexts. Meter, rhyme, and rhythm add further constraints as well as structure and appeal, and translating the same story into different religious and social milieus will, at times, further necessitate telling a quite different tale to capture the same or at least similar meanings or alternately to deliberately counter and contest them.

It is also the case that the great stories people continue to tell, even when they are about a historical person like Mirabai, are not merely about preserving knowledge of the past. The tellers and performers, together with their audiences, are also engaged in "re-membering" the present and themselves—in the telling they participate in an ongoing creation, perpetuation, and transformation of culture, society, and self, of community and of the world as it is and/or as we might wish it to be. The stories remembered and retold are those that continue to speak to us and allow us to speak—to challenge as easily as reinforce values and worldviews, to explore fantasies and fears, possibilities and potentialities, to dare to hope and dream, to weep and mourn, and to rage against fate and circumstance—and that continue to speak about who we are as individuals and communities, our origins and our destinies. Fluidity of form facilitates this ongoing relevance for diverse and sometimes overlapping constituencies, whether those stories are "myth" or "history," great works of literature, hagiography, or a grandmother's tale. Mira's tale is one such powerful story that continues to be told across the centuries, with the Mira remembered also Mira "re-membered"—Mira as she lives and speaks to and for diverse peoples, past and present.

The "truth" of such stories lies not only, or often even primarily, in their fidelity to some allegedly objective and knowable facts of the past but also in the degree to which they articulate people's deepest understandings and experiences of the world and of themselves, together with their deepest questionings and yearnings. Myths are clearly such "stories about truth," as Wendy Doniger has defined them most fundamentally.[12] In our time, history has become a primary site where we tell the "true" story of who we are as peoples, based at least in part on evidentiary data with its claim to truth grounded in the certitude of scientific objectivity. Yet "truth" and "fact" are not necessarily equivalent, and history has proven to be a negotiated and contested terrain, its objectivity highly overrated. Historians remind us that there are multiple histories, histories told by those who are or would be powerful, victors in battle, colonizers and dominant classes, but also by subalterns, the oppressed and suppressed, the marginalized and colonized. Each marshals the "facts" of the past in different ways to reveal but also to conceal and to speak about the present in ways that may be interrelated but strikingly different and sometimes diametrically opposed. At the same time, it is also the case that traces of historical evidence, of past events and people, can be found in other narrative genres beyond dynastic chronicles and the like, even as some histories "are open to that dimension of reality that we call 'myth,' in the sense of being more deeply saturated with meaningfulness and also more creative of the reality that they purport to describe than are other expressive modes."[13]

Stories of Mira too speak of truth but also reflect complex "textures of time" present in many genres, with historical threads interwoven with experience and imagination in patterns of memory, that speak of the past but also to the present—telling of the challenge of loving God in the midst of the world, of the suffering and violence caused by caste and gender inequality and oppression, of the conflicts between individual desires and social norms and responsibilities, of shared cultural values and what it means to be "rajput" or "Indian," and of negotiating identities in changing times between tradition and modernity or between two worlds for those growing up in diaspora communities in alternate cultural landscapes. Told as "history" but also as hagiography, epic, and fiction, her life is further enacted in *khyal* (folk drama), *lila* (religious drama), film, and diaspora cultural performances. We will find many "Miras" within these texts and performances, in some cases so different from each other that the woman portrayed is scarcely recognizable as the same person; the Mira of the low-caste folk epic *Mira Janma Patri* (Mira's Horoscope) bears little resemblance to the Mirabai of nineteenth-century rajput historians or of Kiran Nagarkar's 1997 novel *Cuckold*.

How and why have so many people come to understand and speak of Mirabai so differently? Writing of the multiple "lives of Indian images," Richard H. Davis has argued that understandings are profoundly affected both by the frame in which an image is encountered—a museum versus a makeshift shrine—and by the assumptions that viewers bring to their interpretation of it as meaningful, suggesting that "[t]he viewer's frame is not just a set of interpretive strategies but something more global and diffuse: an outlook on the cosmos, on divinity, on human life and its possibilities, and on the role of images in a world so constituted."[14] In Mira's case, we do not have anything so tangible as the sculptured Didarganj Yakshi image unearthed in 1917 on the banks of the Ganges River with which Davis begins his study. Still, those who engage with the saint—who tell her story, enact her life, sing in her voice—experience her within different frames and bring equally divergent assumptions, some no less global and diffuse, to the encounter. Understanding something of these frames and assumptions will be essential to our coming to know who she has been and is to so many, as well as who she might become.

Even as a stone image may be encountered in a shrine or museum, so Mira's life story may be framed as hagiography or history or low-caste oral epic, and each of these frames has a tremendous impact on how she is both portrayed and received. When told as hagiography, the story of a saint among saints, then her life must include standard elements that demonstrate the sainthood of the hero or heroine and may be replete with miracles. When it is told as history, miracle is replaced with rational explanation and verifiable "facts" attached to the scaffolding of the tale. And while a hagiographic text may glorify a truly exemplary figure, an allegedly historical biography demands reception as the objective truth about the given person.

Yet when historians begin to write of Mirabai in the late nineteenth century, it is unquestionable in their minds that she was a good wife to her husband, ever obedient to male authority figures, and turned to serious devotion only after her husband's demise. It cannot be otherwise, it seems, to these male authors of rajput history, though it is primarily assumptions and other interests brought to the telling rather than documented sources that undergird this assertion. In contrast, when her story is framed as the tale of a woman devotional saint, marriage and devotion simply cannot mix; like oil in water, the saint must rise above and separate herself, escaping somehow from the trap of marriage, and so she does in hagiographic accounts.[15]

For low-caste singers of the epic *Mira Janma Patri*, Mira may not have wanted to get married, but she complies with her mother's request to protect her family, for the power of the ruler and of the ritual is too great to permit any alternative. While her devotion might be suspect in the eyes of her royal husband, this is potentially resolvable, but her discipleship to a leatherworker guru is decidedly not—and she is definitely his disciple in this telling. It is this association, rather than her public devotion to Krishna, that leads her husband to cast her out of the palace in fury.

Understanding something of the social, political, religious, and genre-related frames shaping such tellings will offer us insight in coming to understand these multiple Miras. Hagiographic tales will vary further with the differing theological and literary frames brought to the telling of the tale as well as the sociopolitical realities in which the tellers speak. Rajput and nationalist tales, in turn, are intricately connected to the politics of nineteenth-century India and the struggle to define caste, religious, linguistic, regional, and national identities in the face of changing times and colonial discourses and domination. Low-caste communities will have very different considerations and concerns and employ alternative genres. A host of other frames reflecting very different considerations, concerns, and genres are brought to bear on twentieth- and twenty-first-century tellings. In all these cases, tellers, performers, and audiences are also immersed in more specific circulating traditions about Mirabai herself, with comic books, films, television serials, novels, and Hindi textbooks added to earlier oral and written currents in the flow of story and song in our time, and varying knowledge of these circulating traditions too will influence performance and response.

There are other more "global and diffuse" elements that impact the telling and reception of Mirabai that are equally essential for making sense of who she was and is—understandings of an ordered world infused with the Divine, marked by samsara (the cycle of rebirth) and regulated by karma but also by a capricious fate, of the particular nature of humans in relation to the Divine and to each other, of the role of saints in this world, of social responsibilities and duties dependent on life stage, gender, and caste, of the nature of the feminine and the masculine and much more.

Mirabai is first and foremost identified as an Indian woman saint of the bhakti, or devotional, traditions of Hinduism. The world of bhakti to which Mirabai belongs (as do the majority of those who know and love her, to varying degrees) provides a shared interpretive frame that includes familiarity with a host of other devotees and their attendant stories and songs, a wide range of practices and theological perspectives, differing understandings of the nature of the Divine as well as stories of divine incarnations, and a highly developed religious aesthetic. Within this world, the nature of a "saint" differs dramatically from Christian conceptions of "sainthood" that would alternately frame Mirabai for some nineteenth-century British admirers.

And Mira's identification as an Indian *woman* saint further invokes a complex framing of the feminine in India, one which runs from the brahmanical law code of Manu, with its assertion that a woman should always be dependent on a man (father, husband, son) and should treat her husband as her god, no matter how he might act, finding her salvation through this wifely service, all the way to fierce and independent goddesses, or *devis*, like Durga and Kali, and women saints who will take only God as their husband. The power that drives the universe (*shakti*) as well as creative/illusory manifestation (*maya*) and material existence (*prakriti*) are also conceived as feminine, as is the ideal devotee and indeed the true self of all in relation to the Divine for many. The figures of the virtuous wife and the mother loom large, honored and powerful, coupled with the daughter as a guest in her parents' home, temporarily residing there until she joins her husband's family, and the sati, the woman whose virtue is so great that she may even reach the status of a goddess if she chooses to ascend her husband's funeral pyre, lighting it with the heat of her own inner purity and accompanying him into the next life. And there are innumerable tales of women's heroism, both military and domestic, and of romance and erotic pleasure, as well as cautionary tales of uncontrolled sexuality and the dangers posed by women whose virtue is compromised or lacking altogether. These complex understandings of gender are infused throughout the traditions that surround Mira.

Regional, local, sectarian, familial, and caste-specific practices that impinge on multiple dimensions of everyday life and relations, from birth to death, also find their way into tellings and songs, together with a menagerie of animals and a host of birds as well as diverse plants and foods, ornaments and articles of clothing, each with its own complex associations, second nature to those who live among them. Other understandings are even more diffuse—sensibilities and sensitivities—for example, the feeling of oppressive heat that precedes the longed-for monsoon rains, then the delight of standing outside as the first cooling drops begin to fall on the thirsty earth, until, soaked to the skin, all gather for tea and hot samosas in joyful celebration, as even the birds join in, opening their wings to let the rain wash away the dust and singing with abandon. And when the monsoon is in full swing, yellow-black clouds break open into torrential downpours that momentarily stop everything, offering blissful interludes of impassioned privacy to lovers fortunate to be alone together, or alternately seemingly interminable periods of intense longing for those far away.

Some will come to Mirabai without the benefit of many of these frames, yet she will equally capture their hearts and imaginations. British officers in the early nineteenth century and American writers searching for exemplary spiritual women in the late twentieth century will both write of her, though the differences in what they see rival the changing identities of Indian images documented by Davis. Even as those images "may find themselves carried off to new places, where they encounter new audiences, who may not know or appreciate their earlier significances . . . [o]r, even staying in their original locations, . . . take on new roles and meanings in response to the changing world around them . . . repeatedly relocated, reframed and reinterpreted by new communities of response in new historical settings," so too Mirabai is "made and remade in [her] encounters with differing audiences," both in India and beyond.[16] Yet Mira is more than a story, more than a hewn stone image, more than the portraits of her, drawn with words, on paper or in Technicolor, or embodied by actors and dancers.

Mirabai Sings: A Female Voice for Her Time and Ours

Mira, no less than the other saints of devotional Hinduism, is also known as a poet—the composer and public singer of songs in a distinctive and recognizable voice. Communal gatherings to sing *bhajans* (devotional songs) carrying the names of these poet-saints are a principal practice of this religious path, and Mira's songs are extremely popular, even as her story is. We find the first sporadic documentation of songs in her voice in the first decade of the seventeenth century, but by the nineteenth century manuscripts containing them multiply exponentially. And when we begin to listen, we also hear her voice everywhere, in every musical style—folk, filmi, classical, set to Western music, played from village loudspeakers or wafting from the cabs of trucks.

Her songs are sung in devotional gatherings in temples and homes, performed at concerts and on recordings, in films and on TV, even available as cell phone ringtones. As such, her voice and songs have become part of the soundtrack of many people's lives, especially in India.

Again we are intrigued. We would very much like to know what this sixteenth-century woman had to say in her own words, yet when we try to verify her authorship of a set of poems, again we will come up empty-handed (though some will claim otherwise) or, more accurately, with armloads of songs but no definitive way to sift through them. We find hundreds and hundreds, even thousands—far too many for a single person to have composed—and with tremendous variation rather than standardized forms. Some may reflect verses initially orally composed by this singular woman, but even for her they were probably not entirely fixed, shifting in the improvisational milieu of devotional performance and then picked up and similarly performed by others. But which might truly be her words and which someone else's—remembered, oft-invoked, imagined? What she would or should or could have said, perhaps, but to whose mind? And how fluid might the line between the two be?

As with the stories about her, we would need to examine the earliest available records of songs in her voice and explore why this particular voice might not have been formally included in the canons of the emerging institutionalized lineages of devotional Hinduism and thus not committed to writing in any systematic way in earlier centuries. However, we cannot identify originals of her own compositions any more than we can arrive at an urtext of her life story. What we would discover in these earliest records instead are most likely notes of and for performance, jotted down by singers to aid memory, verses pinned down in the moment of writing like butterfly specimens in a collector's box, no two identical, each beautiful in its singularity, but no longer alive as song and on the move. Other written records similarly document ephemeral "singings" frozen in time—whether recorded in a calligraphed manuscript preserved in a royal library or temple, printed in a textbook of Hindi literature, or translated to be brought to life in vastly different languages and cultural contexts for new audiences. And these too reflect editorial interventions carried out with a range of motives.

Different notions of authorship, authority, and authenticity need to be employed to understand what it means to associate Mira's name with such a collaborative body of song, as John Stratton Hawley has made clear with respect to bhakti songs more generally.[17] Instead of focusing on a single sixteenth-century woman's utterances as if they gave us direct access to her mind and heart, we would have to examine what makes the voice that she initiates recognizable and distinct as Mira's and what that voice makes it possible to say. We would need to explore also the ways others contribute to its profoundly intersubjective nature, for songs in this voice are largely without absolutely fixed forms, open for interpretation, poetic and performative license, enjoyment and emotional identification—a language to speak with, not only for Mira but also for others, to give voice to their own experiences of love and delight, of defiance and suffering, of longing and the dissolution of one into the other, words that continue to resound, a voice that cannot be silenced, compelling and articulate, strangely relevant, speaking to and from the hearts of so many in vastly different times and places, a collective voice, yet identified with this particular woman and with a distinctive recognizable character.

Even without the certitude of her precise words, Mirabai must have been extraordinary to have initiated such a voice in sixteenth-century India—a woman seemingly far ahead of her time. And yet something about this precise time and place allowed her to flourish and allowed this strong female voice to emerge. Even the rulers of the great kingdom of Mewar dared not kill her outright, it seems, though they might torment her. A poisoned offering delivered by another's hand, venomous snakes and scorpions, a hungry lion let loose—these might be risked as mortal dangers that lurked in this desert land. Or if she could be caught in the act of infidelity, she could safely be dispatched in the name of honor and her executioner held blameless. But such a woman could not simply be killed at the whim of a man, even the king. The warrior codes decry it. Famed hero of the *Mahabharata* epic, the Dharma King, Yudhishthira, cites the killing of a woman as among the worst of crimes, together with "surrendering to his enemies someone who has sought refuge . . . robbing a Brahmin, harming a friend . . . and abandoning one who has been devoted" to you.[18] And she was not only a woman but also a much-loved devotee of Krishna. Bhakti or loving devotion to God inundated this region as a principal form of communal religious practice, and great devotees arose from its deserts in the fifteenth and sixteenth centuries. Beloved of God and seemingly under divine protection, they achieved their status of saint through popular acclaim, as more ordinary devotees flocked to them to share in their songs and teachings. Mira would have moved among them.

It seems not by chance that such a female character and voice emerge at this time and place and come to be so powerfully embraced, in the wake of the solidification and assertion of a more unified rajput ruling identity and of the theological formalization and institutionalization of Krishna devotion. Even as a hereditary rajput warrior identity was taking shape and the kingdoms of Mewar and Marwar were becoming firmly established under Sisodiya and Rathor leadership, this female voice begins to speak, refusing to abide by notions of family and clan honor, rejecting the seclusion and political exchange of women, bypassing the dominant ideology to direct salvific loving service not to a husband or ruler but to its rightful recipient, God, and dismissing the material and social privileges of power and caste gained through violence and coercion to choose instead to live as the poorest of the poor must do of necessity.[19]

Concurrently, the land of Krishna's incarnation had been rediscovered allegedly almost simultaneously by Chaitanya, Vallabha, and followers of Nimbarka as the sixteenth century dawned, and the powerful *sampradays*, or teaching lineages, that would grow up around them were developing theologically and institutionally in the decades that followed.[20] At Chaitanya's direction, his key disciples Rup and Sanatan and then Jiv Goswami settled in this place called Vrindavan in the region of Braj, constructing the theoretical underpinnings of participation in the dramatic enactment, or lila, of Krishna's incarnation and proclaiming an ideal feminine spiritual identity, the devotee falling in love with the dashing young and imminently masculine Lord, as the cowherding *gopi* women of Krishna's adoptive community do. Yet Jiv Goswami's commentaries on his uncle Rup Goswami's work privileged the indirect experience of witnessing and facilitating Krishna's love play, becoming a vessel for emotion rather than direct experience.[21] In contrast, Mira's voice speaks not only in identification with the gopis and even with Krishna's beloved Radha but also of her *own* desire and her *own* encounter with God, in the not so subtle physical body of an actual woman.

Vallabhacharya would largely accept the theological formulations of Chaitanya's disciples even as he and even more his son Vitthalnath developed their own path, centered around Sri Nathji, Krishna in his form as the Lord of Govardhan who raised the mountain—as Mirabai so often also addresses him. No doubt her voice spoke to and for many affiliated with these developing lineages as well as the Nimbarka, Radhavallabh, and Ramanandi sampradays, her songs equally appealing to members of non-Krishna-oriented sampradays, including the Dadupanth and the Sikhs, who worship the Lord as ultimately transcending any form. Though much beloved, however, her voice and actions challenged emerging theological limitations and new religious hierarchies of privilege, as they did social and political ones.

Disciple to none by most accounts, save the low-caste saint Raidas, she would remain outside the boundaries of institutional control, her voice and life challenging attempts to limit and corral the spiritual aspirations and experiences of low-caste people and women, evincing the direct access and equality of all before God in this world and exposing the hypocrisy of those who would try to claim the spiritual identities, while degrading the embodied existence, of women and the marginalized. As such Mira's is a voice very decidedly female and of her time but one which also continues to speak to experiences and issues that are very specific to completely different circumstances, of our time as well as her own and all the centuries in between. It is a voice that seemingly also makes audible deep aspirations within many, a voice which declares unequivocally that the world as it is is not necessarily the world as it should be or must be. And it is a voice which people continue to actively co-create. To understand how this is so and what makes Mira's voice so distinct and yet so versatile, drawing people to continue to speak it, we would ultimately need to examine something of the range of songs composed in her name and listen wherever possible to who is saying what in her name and to whom. Such an expansive examination, however, is beyond the scope of the present study, as we seek first to meet the one to whom this powerful voice belongs. And it is clear that we cannot rely on this collective song tradition to give us direct access to what this particular sixteenth-century woman thought or said.

The Communities and Companions of the Saint

Mira is more than a great story to be told and more than a collective body of beautiful songs in a distinctive and powerful voice. She is a saint, experienced in presents past and in our time, playing a deeply meaningful role in the lives of those who have come to know and love her. She is present to multiple "publics," as Christian Lee Novetzke suggests in regard to the Maharashtrian saint Namdev, each constituted in part through the shared, public performance of stories and songs of the saint, in ways that address their specific historical circumstances and intersect with individual and communal identities.[22] Drawing on Benedict Anderson's work on the rise of nationalism, Parita Mukta writes of the "imagined community" of Mirabai, a virtual community of low-caste people in Rajasthan and Saurashtra bound together through identification and merger with the character, story, and voice of Mira in shared suffering but also dignity and resistance to structures of oppression.[23] Rajputs, nationalists, women renouncers, devotees of different religious persuasions, and others will constitute additional "publics" or communities for whom Mirabai figures in their imaginings and self-understanding, with varying points and degrees of identification and traditions of story and song. And in order to know Mirabai, we must necessarily come to know a number of them.

It is also the case that there are individual people who have particular and very personal relationships with the saint that transform their own lives and profoundly impact her wider reception—including key figures like the British officer and historian of Rajasthan James Tod. And there would be many more—for example, Rabindranath Tagore, who invokes her as a model for women's self-realization and emancipation; Mahatma Gandhi, who finds in her an exemplar of nonviolent resistance; Hindi poetess and social activist Mahadevi Varma, who would herself be called a "modern Mira"; advocate-turned-theologian Bankey Behari, for whom she was a visionary guru and guide; and famed Karnatic singer M. S. Subbulakshmi, who embodies her on the silver screen at the crucial moment of Indian Independence. For such individuals as well as for lesser-known members of her many publics, the saint has been experienced, in varying measure, as a living presence not confined to stories and songs of the past but rather continuing her love affair with God, embodying ideals and challenging complacency, instructing through word and example, even appearing to some in visions—known intimately as a fellow devotee and friend, a guru and guide. Many others will also speak of Mira as a "companion" across the decades of their lives. They come to know her in new ways and to understand their own experiences in relation to hers, with songs attributed to her seeming to speak directly to them at crucial crossroads, their meanings evolving over time and changing circumstances.

Her presence can be glimpsed in the records of these encounters, though the Mira we meet will be Tod's Mira, Gandhi's Mira, Behari's Mira, Subbulakshmi's Mira—each recognizable as the saint yet distinctive. We will see how she appears to individuals from their distinct perspectives and how she speaks to each in the circumstances of that person's particular life, desires, hopes, and needs. Such relationships can perhaps best be understood within Hindu frames of encounter—as *darshan* and *lila*—and are consistent with Hindu views of the nature of persons as constitutively relational. *Darshan* is to see but also to be seen, and one may receive darshan of God standing before a consecrated image in a temple or darshan of a holy or greatly respected person.[24] To do so is not merely to look on as an observer but to be recognized, seen, acknowledged in a two-way interrelationship, entering fully into the presence of the other to be touched and transformed in some way. Just so have many experienced Mira.

Lila is "play," encompassing both the creative playfulness of the Divine in manifestation and the play or drama of our samsaric lives and of divine incarnation. The enactment and visualization of the lila of Krishna's incarnation are important religious practices among his devotees, allowing them to receive darshan of their Lord, experiencing his presence and finding their true identities as characters in this eternal drama of the love affair between the self and the Divine. Imitation, identification, and transformation are woven together in this aesthetics of religious devotion with the goal of cultivating an ever-deepening capacity to experience and savor the full constellation of emotions that constitute "love" in all its many permutations. Mira's story will also take on this quality of lila, as a drama which can be entered, the saint encountered and identities merged, in a complex interweaving of temporal and eternal realities.

Nor does Mirabai stand apart as a static self-contained individual, popping in and out of such encounters like some kind of science fiction time-traveler. A key element of Mirabai's power is that she is understood to have been a real flesh-and-blood woman who lived centuries ago, who suffered yet could not be silenced or killed, a specific woman who chose to live against the grain and opened the way for others to do the same. But at the same time hers remains a relational self, as our own selves are: composite, multistranded, changing within and (from a Hindu perspective) across lifetimes, in varied and fluid interrelationships with others.[25] Her identity, like our own, is emergent and negotiated, a constant becoming rather than static being, in her time and ours. She is experienced as a living reality, and people continue to come into her presence, through story, song, vision, and identification, entering into deep and personal relationships with her, with profound effects on understandings of both who she is and who they are.

Robert A. Orsi, writing of Catholic saints and Italian immigrants in the United States, notes the intersubjective nature of all social, cultural, and religious identities and worlds, suggesting that religions generally are primarily networks not of beliefs but of relationships (that encompass also those who study them): "To be in relationship with someone . . . is not necessarily to understand him or her; but the relationship, which arises always on a particular social field and is invariably inflected by the needs, desires, and feelings, conscious or not, that draw on both parties' histories and experiences, become the context for understanding."[26] The context for our understanding of Mirabai will be such meeting places as we enter into relationships with those who have known and loved her as well as those who have found her irritating though sometimes also irresistible and those who continue to do so, who tell of her life and sing in her voice and for whom she is part of their cultural and religious imaginary, an intimate companion in their daily lives.

Much has been spoken and sung and written about the saint and in her name, including scholarly analysis. Instead of simply adding my voice to so many others, I invite the reader to join me on a journey of discovery, to get to know the saint as others have, those who have admired her and in some cases also feared her, who have sung and danced her, who have even become her, whether momentarily or in a more transformative way—experiencing her inner fierceness, fearlessness, and unshakable conviction or the overwhelming longing for relationships and for the world as it should be, or joining her in living as if it were thus with joyful abandon, daring to love, to dance, to laugh, to speak, to be in the face of all opposition. My aim is to introduce the reader to something of the vast streams of story and song that have continued to flow around the saint over some five hundred years and to individuals and publics who have participated in their creation and to whom the saint has meant and continues to mean so much.

The multifaceted portrait and voice of the saint I offer is necessarily shaped not only by what I have learned from all the accounts and individuals who have shared with me their understandings and love of Mirabai but also by my scholarly training and by my own experiences, needs, desires, and feelings as I, too, inevitably participate in the further shaping of Mirabai's identity, necessarily selectively drawing from and adding to the traditions that swirl around her and now circulate globally. I cannot do otherwise but have tried to proceed with as much respect, awareness, and openness as possible, and I invite readers to do the same, as together we seek to understand something of Mirabai's particular, even while intersubjective, identity and continuing appeal. Only by examining the artifacts of these complex relationships, circulating performance traditions, and imaginative innovations from the distant past, from the immediate present, and from everything in between can we begin to see who she was and is.

Accordingly, we will begin with the earliest available tellings of her life story, from the seventeenth and eighteenth centuries, situating her in the context of devotional Hinduism and those who tell her story in their own historical and religious milieus. As Patton Burchett reminds us, "*saints do not make themselves; saints are made.* For all the charisma, genius, good deeds, miracles, teachings, and hard work of any religious figure, he or she only becomes a saint when communally recognized and remembered as such by a group."[27] And so it is to the communal remembrances of divergent groups who have recognized her as a saint that we first turn. Though these hagiographic tales are diverse, they nevertheless reveal characters and key events that will be selectively and imaginatively recombined and expanded with innovation and borrowing across the centuries in subsequent tellings of the saint's life story. Committed to writing, these are our only traces of who she was before the nineteenth century, her songs and story belonging principally to the fluid and ephemeral realm of oral performance.

But in the nineteenth century, she will come to the attention of colonial British officers and scholars, who will find in the exotic impassioned princess persecuted by men in her family both fuel for their romanticization of the Orient and support for their domination. She will also be embraced by nationalists and their supporters as exemplary of women's education and respected status in India and as the preeminent poetess of the newly consolidated civilizational language of Hindi. Some will search for the historical Mirabai in earnest in the latter decades of the century even as others imagine the saint in alternative ways also consonant with the tales of Indian heroines. The allegedly historical biography they craft will continue to dramatically impact twenty-first-century understandings of the saint, yet there are clearly other tellings that they are seeking to overwrite and silence, stories enacted in folk drama and sung in epic form that challenge elite constructions of Indian womanhood, caste privilege, feudal politics, and much more. We will examine alternative tellings in turn, for without them we cannot fully know the saint, nor fully understand the interlocutors of Indian nationalists and scholars as they, like the ruler of Mewar before them, have sought to restrain the saint.

Having come to know the saint in this way, in the later chapters of this volume we will examine Mira's transformation into a pan-Indian cultural heroine in the decades leading up to Independence—in the writings of Gandhi, Tagore, and Mahadevi Varma but also in more popular cultural forms, including cinema and even colonial school textbooks. We will explore her place in the nationalist struggle, particularly with respect to issues around gender and women's education and equality but also in the projects of those seeking to foster Hindi literacy and to propagate a socially conservative Hindu orthodoxy. Subbulakshmi's cinematic portrayal of the saint, first in Tamil (1945) and then in Hindi (1947), released to coincide with Independence, is in many ways the culmination of this process, the singer-actress embodying Mirabai in the minds of many for decades to follow but also epitomizing the transformative power of the saint. As such this portrayal is a fitting culmination of our initial exploration of the life and character of the saint in this volume. An essential foundation, this is, however, by no means the end of her story.

Mirabai scholarship would burgeon and stories and songs of the saint continue to be told and sung, invoked and debated across the ensuing decades into the present, and not only in India but increasingly globally, by diaspora South Asians but also by others with diverse cultural, religious, and linguistic backgrounds. A thoroughgoing analysis of postcolonial and global invocations and incarnations of Mirabai is beyond the scope of the present volume, as is a detailed examination of her songs and voice, but to be able to comprehend either, we first have to get to know Mirabai as bhakti saint, Hindi poetess, and cultural heroine—the genealogy of the stories that shape conceptions and experiences of the saint from the sixteenth century into the present. And so we begin with the earliest records we have of her life in the literature of devotional Hinduism.

1
Embodying Devotion in a Woman's Body

Mirabai among the Saints

Mirabai is first and foremost a lover of God, a Hindu saint utterly devoted to Krishna. He is her *ishtadev*, the form of the Divine she chooses to worship, or more true to Hindu devotional understandings, the form through which the One Divine Reality comes to her as ravishingly beautiful Lord to steal her heart and claim her as his own. She expresses her love for him in intimate songs of great beauty and poignancy, and she pursues that love with heart, mind, and body. She dances out her love in ecstatic joy and suffers physically in the anguish of longing. And she does so in a woman's body, a body which becomes a site for theological reflection but ultimately also of murderous contention.

Devotion, or bhakti, is an integral strand within the practice of Hinduism, and Mirabai is one of its most beloved and revered saints. The earliest recorded narratives of her life and collections of her songs appear in its literature. Here Mirabai is portrayed as the virtual embodiment of bhakti, for whom devotion to God matters more than all else, including social expectations, family honor, and material privilege. She is unshakable in her love for God, though her behavior is scandalous to the wider world, calling into question all other sources of meaning and identity. She suffers greatly because of her choices but willingly embraces and shares the suffering that others must also endure—those who follow a religious calling at odds with the ways of the world, women who choose a life beyond the confines of marriage and motherhood, and others whose marginalized social status leaves them vulnerable to the abuses and exploitation of the powerful, religious or otherwise. And Mira does so with courage, conviction, and grace, as a beacon of hope and encouragement. She belongs to this devotional milieu, and her life story is irrevocably shaped by its conventions and values.

The World of Bhakti

The word *bhakti* has often been translated into English as "devotion," but this translation does not adequately capture the depth and emotional intensity of the human-Divine relationship that becomes the goal of many who embrace this strand of Hindu tradition.[1] *Bhakti* carries with it a much wider array of meanings, including not only reverence, submission, adoration, and loyalty but every possible dimension of love known in human relations, encompassing the totality of the love of parents for children and children for parents, of friends and siblings, of rulers and subjects, and of lovers. The connotations of the term include not only love but also partaking, experiencing, sharing, putting on (as with clothing), and both possessing and being completely possessed by another, as A. K. Ramanujan has detailed.[2] The English word "devotion" pales by comparison and cannot really do justice to the totalizing and embodied love which marks much of Hindu bhakti.

In this context, this Hindu concept might thus more accurately be described as "participation in" God rather than mere "devotion to" God, as Karen Pechilis has argued.[3] Indeed within bhakti characterizations, the devotee is both *in love with* the Divine and *a part of* the Divine, separate embodied existence making love possible but with an underlying paradoxical unity that stands in sharp contrast to the standard metaphysics of monotheism which posits a radical otherness between creature and Creator. The devotee is a manifestation of the One Divine Reality (as indeed are all things that exist) whose distinction arises precisely so that Divine Love may be actualized in the conjoining of lover, love, and Beloved.

The focus of the religious life in this strand of Hindu traditions is on developing one's capacity to love God and to embody the love which is God, a process involving the deliberate cultivation of emotion through disciplines of action and thought. The exemplars of the tradition in turn are those whose lives demonstrate the path to ever deepening love for the Divine and who are able to both express and draw others into that love, particularly through their composition and singing of devotional songs. The remembrance of these saintly figures' lives and the continued performance of the songs said to be composed by them are principal modes of religious practice within this strand of Hinduism, together with the recitation of the name(s) of God.

Regional traditions with this devotional and participatory orientation develop from the sixth century CE in the Tamil-speaking region of South

India and sweep across the subcontinent over the next millennium, with ideas, saints, texts, and practices circulating in fluid processes of mutual influence and sometimes competing sectarian identity formation. Though these various movements and sampradays (teaching lineages and the communities that develop around them) may differ considerably, they share the centrality of a loving relationship with the Divine as the heart of religious life and as the measure of religious authority rather than mere birth status or formal education. Spiritual authority is, at least theoretically, open to anyone, whether high or low caste, man or woman, and is validated only by others recognizing the depth of a person's love for and participation in God. Within these movements, God may be experienced primarily through a form (*sagun*) such as Shiva, Vishnu or one of his avatars (especially Krishna but also Rama), or one of the manifestations of Mahadevi, the Great Goddess (with devotees referred to as Shaivas, Vaishnavas, or Shaktas, respectively). Alternatively God may be experienced as being without and ultimately beyond any form whatsoever (*nirgun*), but in each case, there is an affirmation of a singular Divine Reality encountered and loved by all in these multiple ways. Even if one experiences God in a particular form, there is the paradoxical realization that God is all in all, transcending and incorporating all particularity.

The religious texts of these strands of Hindu tradition are principally the songs that their exemplary devotees composed in their mother tongues rather than the Sanskrit of the Vedas and Upanishads. This is the only language appropriate for such intimacy, and these compositions belong principally to the realm of oral performance, accessible to all, not only to the literate or to a hereditary priestly elite as texts in Sanskrit would be. These songs and the collected life stories of their saintly composers, both of which are recited and performed, are supplemented by theological treatises, more extended poetic works, and the mythic compendiums of the *puranas* which describe the exploits and adventures of specific divine manifestations.

The saints of these traditions achieve their status by popular acclaim rather than by the decree of any centralized or formal authority, and they are the first among equals, referred to by the generic terms *bhakta* (devotee) or *sant* (good person or sincere seeker of spiritual realization).[4] Yet they are also clearly revered as ideal practitioners of this spiritual path, their life stories recited and recorded in hagiographic texts and devotional songs continuing to be sung, and also composed, in their names in succeeding centuries. And they serve as spiritual teachers or gurus to subsequent devotees not only via song and story but also sometimes through dream and visionary encounter.

Mirabai belongs to this world of bhakti as one of its most popular saints, and we find her portrayed here in a variety of different and sometimes contradictory ways. Those who tell of the lives of saints in any religious tradition—the hagiographers—make no claim to be historians offering some evidentiary and "objective" rendering of the events. Rather they seek to present religious paragons, whose lives reveal the heights that human beings can achieve, sometimes as models to aspire to, sometimes as wholly exceptional and extraordinary, set apart to marvel at and celebrate.[5] At the same time, these hagiographers do claim to speak of individuals who existed in particular times and places, and this literature is the primary site of the historical traces of the lives of those particular people, who are remembered and honored therein.

This memory is neither univocal nor static, however, particularly in the Indian and bhakti context. It is not a fixed record of the past but rather a performative and lived experience of individuals and communities engaged in that remembrance, which is itself practiced as a *sadhana,* or religious discipline. Moreover, the stories told and performed of these saints are marked by their own underlying rationality, reflecting particular patterns that are characteristic of and confirm the identity of the subject as a saint, beloved of God. Consciously or unconsciously, listeners as well as tellers are familiar with these narrative patterns. Hagiographers present the particulars of individual saints' lives within this framework, and they deviate from standard forms to make specific points, deliberately playing off audience expectations. Mira's story is no exception. Tellers rely on these patterns and invoke stories circulating about Mira and other saints, by way of similarity or contrast, to craft their particular tales. Devotees, who may later also come to be known as saints, may consciously or unconsciously conform their lives to these exemplary patterns, or others may describe them thus, so that the lives of saintly individuals and hagiographic narratives converge.

The hagiographers themselves also belong to specific religious communities in specific times and places, and their tellings reflect and seek to reinforce and define the identities, practices, values, and beliefs of their communities in various ways. In doing so, hagiographers are participating in a highly sophisticated and intertextual tradition of employing narrative to speak about a wide array of issues, with a well-known story operating also as a second-order language, understood by all and used quite deliberately to speak in the complex ways that narratives make possible—through analogy, contradiction, inversion, and surprise and by mobilizing intricate networks of shared knowledge and placing unreconciled and sometimes irreconcilable values and desires in dynamic tension. The portrayal of Mirabai's life is impacted dramatically when it is deployed in this way, contributing to the richness of the hagiographic family of tales told about her.

The literature on the saints of devotional Hinduism is vast. Compendiums of the lives of multiple saints are sometimes limited by sectarian affiliation, and sometimes they incorporate a wider devotional heritage, as in the North Indian tradition of *bhaktamals* and their commentaries, appearing from the beginning of the seventeenth century.[6] These bhaktamals, or "garlands of devotees," join one poem after another like flowers in a garland, each recounting exemplary qualities and actions of a particular saint. These texts in turn generate commentaries that unpack the terse lines of their poetry, filling out the details of episodes alluded to in a word or phrase and narrating additional events, until we have full-blown life stories of the saints, from birth to death and across multiple lifetimes.

Still other texts take selected songs attributed to saintly devotees and link them together with narrative passages, contextualizing the composition and performance of the songs in the life of the saint. There are illustrated manuscripts as well and longer narratives in verse, telling of the miracles that surround a saint's life, and there are individual songs lauding individual saints or describing some significant event in their lives. References to Mira abound in all these forms and also in the songs of other saints. These latter songs often invoke the names of the great poet-saints of the past, who collectively form a supportive extended spiritual family for later devotees and serve as precedents for divine intervention or refuge. Even as the Lord came to the aid of each of these, so may the pleading singer's request be granted.

Within this extensive textual tradition, a set of interweaving stories about Mirabai emerges, stories that share conventional elements with those of other saints but offer portraits of a distinct and complex individual woman devotee. The earliest layer of this hagiographic literature of Mira confirms her place within the wider family of saints in devotional Hinduism, and her story reflects the challenges that not only she but other women, both saintly and more ordinary, must face who choose to pursue such a life of devotion in a woman's body.[7]

Early Invocations of Mirabai

It is from the latter half of the sixteenth century that the earliest references to this particular woman first come to us, and as the seventeenth century dawns, her life and character are enshrined in the compact verses of hagiographer Nabhadas:

> Abandoning worldly honor, shame, and family tradition,
>   Mira sang of the Mountain Bearer.
>
> Like a *gopi* she embodied love,
>   made manifest in this degenerate age.
> Without restraint, utterly fearless, her tongue sang the praises
>   of He who knows love's ways.
> Wicked ones found fault
>   and planned a murderous revenge,
> But not a single hair on her head was harmed—
>   She drank their poison as ambrosia.
> She beat the drum of devotion, ashamed before none.
>
> Abandoning worldly honor, shame, and family tradition
>   Mira sang of the Mountain Bearer.[8]

This brief account was composed in approximately 1600 CE, and Mira is one of hundreds of bhaktas (devotees) who receive Nabhadas's praise in this first bhaktamal—mythological figures as well as historical people drawn from many traditions and regions across North India, some described in more detail, others merely named or invoked in groups.[9] He portrays Mira as a fierce devotee of Krishna in the form of Girdhar Gopal, the cowherd boy holding aloft Mount Govardhan to protect the people and animals of his adoptive community from the torrential rains of the god Indra's wrath. They, like Mira, persist in their devotion to Krishna and arouse Indra's jealousy, but Krishna shields them. In this role, Krishna appears as a kind of protective little brother with divine powers, although the roots of the worship of the Lord of Govardhan reach back to earlier fertility festivals.[10] As such he embodies a divine willingness to shake the foundations of the world to open up a space for life and love and those who embrace it. In songs attributed to Mira, she will use a variety of other names for Krishna, but most often these songs end with the characteristic signature line, or *chap*: "Mira's Lord is Girdhar Nagar" (the clever, gallant, or sophisticated Lifter of the Mountain).[11]

In the verses that follow, Nabhadas compares Mira to Krishna's cowherding gopi lovers who were known to care nothing for social conventions or restrictions, captivated as they were by their young flute-playing cowherd Lord. Mira embodies this same type of love in an age that is far from the idyllic original time when people walked and played with Krishna in the forests of the land of Braj.[12] Fearless and uncontrollable in her devotion, she refuses the restrictions of family and social expectation and sings out in intoxicated love, in spite of the danger of doing so. That her devotion is opposed and that attempts are made on her life because of this is also clear. And the opposition she must face is named: it is the fetters of family (*kul*) and of traditional notions of shame and honor (*loklaj*) that she snaps. Poison cannot stop such love and instead miraculously becomes its opposite as she drinks it down.

The image Nabhadas draws in this poetic invocation is sharp, without sentimentality, and Mira is portrayed as a woman of great strength as he celebrates her defiance and recounts her poisoning. These key elements—her unswerving devotion, her disregard of social expectations, her fearlessness, and her persecution—will mark almost all tellings of Mira's life. Other issues that will concern later tellers find no mention here; for example, there is no indication of who her would-be persecutors are, only that they are wicked. Nor does Nabhadas mention family lineage, though her story is grouped with those of other royal devotees and patrons (including some Rathor rajputs), so this much of her alleged background may have been so well-known as not to warrant mention; in any case, it may not have been of key importance to the author.[13] It is her identity as a woman utterly immersed in God that he lifts up and the impossibility of silencing her as she sang her Lord's praise and publicly "beat the drum" (an instrument generally associated with those low in the hierarchy of caste) to call others to this highest of human pursuits in the face of which worldly concerns pale.

Who was Nabhadas, the author of this tale, and in what context did he compose his bhaktamal? He belonged to the Ramanandi sampraday, a Vaishnava sect devoted to Rama which traces its lineage back to the saint Ramananda and has a major monastic center in Galta (a gorge in the hills near Amer/Jaipur) established in the early sixteenth century by the devotee ascetic Krishnadas Payahari. According to his eighteenth-century commentator Priyadas, Nabhadas was abandoned as a small child by his widowed mother during a severe famine and rescued by Krishnadas's disciples Khildev and Agradas, who healed his blindness and initiated him into the sect. Though there are debates around Nabhadas's caste background and some later hagiographers identify him as a *brahman* or at least a brahman in a previous life, he is most often said to have been a *dom* (a member of a caste, likely of musicians and singers, with extremely low social status).[14] Priyadas reports that he followed his guru Agradas to Galta, becoming a servant of the Ramanandi renouncers (*sadhus*) there, and the culmination of his service was his composition of the bhaktamal, praising the devotees of the Lord, at the behest of his guru.[15]

In Nabhadas's time the Ramanandis would begin to trace their lineage through Ramananda back to Ramanuja, the great twelfth-century *acharya* (spiritual teacher) of the Shri Vaishnava sampraday of South India, though they did not follow the orthodox practices of that tradition, initiating members into their ascetic order who were *shudras* (from the lowest of the four levels in the caste hierarchy), even so-called untouchables, and women—classes of people generally excluded from renunciation.[16] Nabhadas's bhaktamal affirms both this lineage and this broad inclusivity in naming among Ramananda's twelve principal disciples the five low-caste saints Kabir, Raidas, Dhana, Sen, and Padmavati (a woman), as well as the brahman married couple Sursuranand and Sursuri. In being so named, they are recognized as full members of the guru-disciple lineage, even as Ramananda's role as the founder of the sect is reinforced by his having this requisite circle of twelve disciples.

Richard Burghart suggests that this inclusivity, which also extended to members of castes that had converted to Islam en masse (as did the *julaha* weaver community to which the nirgun saint Kabir belonged), gave the Ramanandi order an advantage over other ascetic orders as it was open to participation and support from a wider base of disciples, devotees, and patrons.[17] Examining the extensive writings of Nabhadas's lesser known guru, Patton Burchett makes a convincing case that the Ramanandis were indeed strategically pursuing just such an advantage and working to assure a respected position for their sampraday, particularly given the socially marginalized status of many of their adherents. In his writings Agradas sought to propagate a bhakti sensibility that was "transregional and transsectarian," inclusive across castes, affirming both sagun and nirgun devotion, combining yogic ascetic discipline with ecstatic devotion, and accommodating householders as well as monastics, while at the same time producing a literature and aesthetic that would appeal to the Mughal-rajput ruling elite, with clear resonances with Sufism and Gaudiya sampraday Krishna devotional practices.[18]

The Kachvaha rajput ruler of Amer (Jaipur), Maharaja Prithviraj (r. 1502–1527), had become a disciple of Krishnadas Payahari and patron of the Ramanandis of Galta, adopting an iconic image of Sita-Ram as the Kachvaha dynastic deity, even as other rajput rulers were also turning to Vaishnava devotion, though not necessarily with sectarian exclusivity or abandoning their dedication to clan goddesses (*kuldevis*).[19] An alliance between the Kachvahas and Akbar (r. 1556–1605) would be forged in 1562, with Maharaja Bharmal (fourth son of Prithviraj) offering his daughter in marriage to the emperor to cement the relationship in the first such marital alliance between rajputs and Mughals.[20] His grandson Man Singh (r.

1589–1614) would become both the highest ranking officer in the Mughal Empire and sponsor of numerous temples across North India, serving as founding patron of Govindevji Temple in Vrindavan—"the largest monument in India that had ever been designed as a single structure," housing the image worshiped by Rup Goswami—a testament to the close relationship of the Kachvahas also with the Gaudiya sampradaya (initiated by Chaitanya).[21] Having been "rediscovered" in the late fifteenth/early sixteenth centuries simultaneously by followers of Nimbarka and by Chaitanya and Vallabha as the site of Krishna's incarnation, Vrindavan would be effectively transformed under such joint Mughal-rajput patronage from a rural set of scattered villages into a city replete with grand temples by the end of the sixteenth century, even as these sampradays were being formalized.[22] And both these religious sampradays and the courts were participating in a growing "literization" and "literaturization" of the vernacular languages that would be the precursors to Hindi, with a concomitant embrace of such literature and the production and collection of manuscripts as a mark of power and prestige.[23]

In this dynamic time, Agradas sought to ensure the continued patronage of the Kachvaha rulers and access to Mughal largesse as well as diverse devotees and the flourishing of the Ramanandis and bhakti more generally, "expressing and mobilizing a distinctive set of aesthetic tastes, ethics and emotional values—a sensibility—common to a larger bhakti public."[24] And indeed the Ramanandis would become "the largest religious order in India,"[25] and such a broadly Vaishnava, inclusive bhakti sensibility and sense of belonging to a virtual bhakti community would be instantiated through the performance of the lives and songs of its many saints and the shared practice of the recitation of the name of God, even as Agradas advocated.

Nabhadas clearly shared a commitment to this Ramanandi project, praising a wide array of popular saints and thereby asserting the equality of all before God and their ready acceptance within the eclectic Ramanandi sampraday, as well as establishing a distinguished lineage for the sect and cultivating a larger vision of transsectarian devotional community (that included bhaktas of Rama and Krishna as well as nirgun sants, with some notable exclusions).[26] And in Nabhadas's characterization, the saints he praises are "not only . . . godlike and hence worthy of adoration, but the very act of singing their praises afforded a certain closeness to and filial dominion over God"—with community and God drawn into each other's presence in song.[27] And Nabhadas provided the verses to do just that.

Though not claimed as one of Ramananda's twelve primary disciples, Mirabai fits easily into this radically inclusive devotional milieu. Her intense devotion to God is readily recognizable regardless of sectarian affiliation and also effectively constitutes an alternative ascetic form of practice in her abandonment of worldly notions of honor and shame and of family tradition. Her playing a drum points to a disregard for caste and her survival of poison to the power of bhakti. Nabhadas's text would indeed be tremendously influential with respect to bhakti literature and practice as well as portrayals of the saint, inaugurating a tradition of imitation and commentary and continuing to be performed, recited, and read across regions and sects into the twenty-first century.

We find possibly even earlier references to Mirabai in two songs attributed to Hariram Vyas, a fellow devotee of Krishna living in Vrindavan and a disciple of Hit Harivamsh, whose followers would form the Radhavallabh sampraday, and also in the *Pipa Parchai* composed by another member of the Ramanandi sampraday, Anantadas. Heidi Pauwels has made a persuasive case that the two songs in question can reasonably be attributed to Vyas himself and thus would have been composed in the mid- to late sixteenth century.[28] In the first song Vyas speaks of Mirabai's death and wonders, now that she is gone, who else might "embrace devotees like [a daughter] her father," as she did (even as male ascetics were urged to greet women as their mothers).[29] In a second song, Mirabai appears in a list of members of Vyas's extended bhakti family with Sen, Dhana, Namdev, Pipa, Kabir, Raidas, Rup and Sanatan Goswami, Gangal Bhatt, Surdas, Parmanand, and Meha as one "who thought [only] of devotion."[30] As she was in Nabhadas's bhaktamal, here too Mira is included as a member of a very eclectic group, drawing together Vaishnava devotees with those of the Lord beyond form from different sampradays and regions across North India, suggesting that others too embraced this wider sense of devotional community.

Anantadas, also of the Ramanandi sampraday, was Nabhadas's contemporary in Rajasthan, composing and performing *parchai*, another genre of poetic telling of devotional saints' lives and teachings, in the decades leading up to 1600 CE.[31] Parchai offer an introduction (*parichay*) of sorts and a description of the miracles (*paracha*) associated with such figures, and Anantadas composed a series about the illustrious male saints Kabir, Raidas, Namdev, Dhana, Angad, Trilochan, and Pipa.[32] This genre tends to have a didactic character, leading Winand Callewaert to characterize parchais as "texts of subtle indoctrination," though in general "the purpose was always the same: to sing the praises of the saint and proclaim the supremacy of devotion (*bhakti*) to God (called Hari or Rām)."[33] Though Anantadas does not provide us with a life story of Mira as later parchai composers will, he does mention her in passing among a list of saints from different regions within his tale of Pipa, specifically as one who "showed great love for God (Hari)," a quality he also associates with Trilochan in the same verse.[34] These scattered early references together with Nabhadas's introduction are the only traces we have of the saint from the sixteenth century, this woman so seemingly ahead of her time but also of it: strong-willed, even headstrong, bent on a life beyond social expectations for such a woman, deeply devoted to God and pledging her allegiance to a larger notion of "family" among devotees, unashamed and fearless, publicly singing out her love, unrestrained and unstoppable even in the face of murderous violence.

It is not until a century later that we find more extensive narratives of Mirabai's life, in Priyadas's 1712 CE "commentary" on Nabhadas's bhaktamal and in a less comprehensive way in a slightly earlier and much less widely known text from the Punjab, the 1693 CE *Prem Ambodh*. These two accounts differ dramatically, and undoubtedly other stories, too, were being told about Mirabai in the sixteenth and seventeenth centuries without leaving written traces, particularly given that performance, rather than writing, was the principal mode of disseminating and experiencing such tales. Priyadas's work and the *Prem Ambodh* share this performative character, even as Nabhadas's bhaktamal and Anantadas's parchais do. We do well to keep this in mind as we gaze through these textual windows into the past.

Both Priyadas and the *Prem Ambodh*'s author were composing and performing their tales for specific audiences in particular times and places, some 100 to 150 years after the first mention of such a person we have been able to document. Though Priyadas's account would achieve a certain level of canonicity among a sector of later composers, there is no evidence to suggest that it should be privileged in any way as the "true" or "original" story of the saint, the urtext of which all others are variants, developing through some process of diffusion.[35] Rather these and successive stories clearly draw on already circulating traditions for inspiration and source material, and tellers seem to assume, and at times deliberately confound, their audiences' familiarity with these wider traditions for dramatic effect. Sectarian affiliations and theological agendas shape the tales told, as do individual authors' and communities' experiences, values, and imaginative flights of fancy, as Mira is drawn into their religious and social worlds. Moreover, there are standard episodes that tend to appear in hagiographic tellings of saints' lives, including Mira's. Not only do these standards govern the way tellers shape their tales, but the saintliness of the saint is also authenticated by the conformity of his or her life to these patterns.

Priyadas's Tale of Tragedy and Triumph

A disciple of the Gaudiya Vaishnava sampraday living in Vrindavan, Priyadas was undoubtedly a performer of Nabhadas's bhaktamal, but he does far more than simply reproduce this earlier work in his *Bhaktirasabodhini Tika* composed in 1712 CE.[36] With respect to Mira, he relates a discreet series of events in her life from birth to her demise that may reflect and certainly would become standard plot elements found in many tellings of Mira's tale. He tells of a woman of great conviction and courage who triumphs in the face of multiple threats coming from both within and outside her family and whose devotion never wavers in spite of it all—a tale meant (among other things) to awaken devotional sentiment, as the title of Priyadas's text implies.

Priyadas begins his particular account with Mirabai's birth, moving quickly to her marriage within the first verse:

> In Merta, the land of her birth, she was ecstatic,
>   and her gaze turned to love.
> Even in her father's house, she became immersed
>   in the Beloved Mountain Bearer.
> She was engaged to a *rana*—
> The wedding happened; but her mind,
>   absorbed in the sport of her indigo-ebony Lord,
>   did not attend.
> She circled the wedding fire, but her heart remained
>   with the true form of He whose face
>   is like the midnight sky.
> As if in a daze, she prepared to go to her husband's village.
> Her parents entreated her, "Please take these ornaments and clothes."
> "What value do these things have to me?"[she said],
>   her eyes filling with tears. (1)

This young woman of Merta (a town within the kingdom of Marwar in western Rajasthan) is clearly an unwilling participant in a marriage to an unspecified *rana* (a title specific to the ruler of the kingdom of Mewar in southern Rajasthan) (see Figure 1.1). But for Mira, the marriage never really takes place; throughout the ritual she remains absorbed in Krishna, whom she calls "Shyam," the dark one whose skin is the blue-black color of the midnight sky.

Her parents offer her traditional wedding gifts, but she has no use for such things and wants only the image of her divine Beloved that has been the focus of her daily worship and the locus of her experience of his presence:

Embodying Devotion in a Woman's Body 33

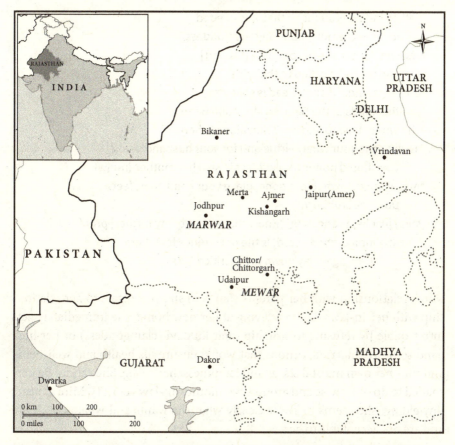

Figure 1.1 Map of Rajasthan, including Vrindavan and Dwarka beyond its borders.

"Give me my Mountain Bearer Girdhari,
    if you want me to be fulfilled,
Take away all these other gifts, this wealth."
Their daughter, so dearly loved, was in the full bloom of youth and love.
Having cried and cried, her mother came to her and said,
    "Take [this image] you have cherished."
Seated in a palanquin, her eyes meeting [those of her Beloved], she went,
Unable to contain her happiness [at] having obtained
    the love of the Lord of her life.
Reaching her husband's home, she was led by her mother-in-law
    to greet the Goddess at the family shrine.
Pleased, [her mother-in-law] said,
    "Tie the knot of love joining bride and groom." (2)

Mother-in-law brought all that was needed
>for the ceremony honoring the Goddess.
First she led her son to complete [his part],
>and then she called to the bride.
[But] Mira said, "If one's head is sold into
>the hands of the Beloved Mountain Bearer,
Who would bow to another? Him alone I cherish."
"To increase your wifely virtue and for your husband's sake,
>you should honor the Goddess," [said her mother-in-law].
"And when the worship is done, place your head at his feet.
>Don't be stubborn!"
[Mira] just kept repeating, "Know this without [any further] proof—
>[my indigo-ebony Lord] is the only prince for whom
>>I will again lay down my sacrifice." (3)

Mira's relationship with her parents stands in sharp contrast to her relationship with her in-laws. Upon arriving at her new home, she immediately gets into trouble by refusing to worship their kuldevi (clan goddess) or her husband so newly married, actions that would ensure his health and well-being and thus her own marital status and happiness, her *suhag*. She cannot be persuaded to do otherwise and arouses her mother-in-law's enmity. Mira appears unyielding; she seems to know clearly what she wants and what actions are and are not acceptable to her.

The stage is now set for her persecution to begin:

[Her mother-in-law] was furious,
>burning and fuming intensely.
She went to her husband and said, "This bride is worthless.
Even now she has answered back, dishonoring me.
Beyond this what more evidence is needed?"
>[she said], a bellows full of air.
Hearing this, the rana grew angry and nursed this rage in his heart.
He gave Mirabai a separate palace, and seeing it, his evil mind was pleased.
[But] loving the Dear One, she sang songs of praise and embraced Him.
And she delighted in the company of sadhus
>drawn to her indigo-ebony Lord. (4)

Here, the rana seems to be Mira's father-in-law, his rage ignited by his wife's complaints of their daughter-in-law's disrespectful speech, though Priyadas also says in the first stanza that she is betrothed and married to a rana, allowing an ambiguity to enter the tale in subsequent stanzas in which the rana plays a prominent role as her tormenter. (In other tellings the persecuting rana is definitively identified as her husband or her brother-in-law, and in still others he will be her own father.)[37] In this stanza her father-in-law orders a separate residence for her (readily pointed out by tour guides within the ruins of the Chittor Fort today), seemingly to isolate her from the rest of the royal household and to contain her insolence in some way, but Mira finds in it a freedom to worship as she pleases.

Mira persists in associating with devotees and holy men (sants and sadhus) even after her sister-in-law's warnings:

Her sister-in-law came and said,
    "Why don't you come to your senses, sister?
In devotion for sadhus, much disgrace accrues.
The rana—lord of the land—is shamed,
    and your father's family is brought down.
Accept what I say and end this association now."
[But Mira responded,] "Having dedicated my life to being with devotees,
    I have found unending happiness.
Find some convenient way of averting those who are disturbed."
Hearing of this, [the rana] sent a cup filled with poison.
[Mira] took it, and as she drank, behold,
    her face was aglow with the radiance of youth! (5)

She took upon herself the poison that was sent—
    she could not bear the far more lethal toxin of
        abandoning the company [of fellow devotees].
So the rana engaged a spy.
    "When she sits among holy men,
        tell me right away so that I may kill her . . ."
Caught in the net of love with her radiant Beloved Mountain Bearer,
    She could be heard laughing and talking as if with a lover.
[When the spy] reported what he heard,
    [the rana] came running.
Sword in hand, he burst through her door,
    [but] she was utterly alone. (6)

"The man with whom you were so immersed in pleasure,
    He's gone! Tell me quickly [where]."
"He sits right before you," [she said]. "There is no impropriety in this.

Seeing the Lord in all his beauty,
> let your eyes be opened that you may receive *darshan*."

Abashed, the rana froze like a painting on a wall.
Then he turned and went; he could not take it in at all.
He was completely shaken to the core.
Without Hari's grace, tell me, can anything be done? (7)[38]

Finding that isolating her has backfired, the rana begins to think about a more permanent solution to the problem that Mira has become. First, he attempts to poison her (see Figure 1.2). Poison appears to have been a weapon of choice

Figure 1.2 The cup of poison being delivered to Mira in the illustrated manuscript *Mira ki Katha* (The Story of Mira), c. 1750–1850 CE, from the private collection of Narendra Parson. A similar manuscript (30029) is found in the collection of the Rajasthan Oriental Research Institute, Jodhpur.

in familial disputes among rajput royalty, and references to the poisoning of family members also occur in Rajasthani women's songs describing more ordinary domestic quarrels.[39] In later tellings, she is told that the cup of poison is filled with water used to wash the feet of Krishna's image, *charanamrit*, "the nectar of his feet," a holy substance full of blessing that no devotee would refuse to drink. But the rana's poison is ineffective; in fact, Mira looks even more radiant after consuming it. Thinking to catch her in a compromising situation with some man that might justify her execution, the rana rushes to her room at his spy's report, only to find Mira alone worshiping before the image of her beloved Krishna. She invites him to have darshan of her Lord—to enter into Krishna's presence and to be recognized and touched by divine grace. The king is momentarily taken aback but ultimately absolutely uncomprehending.

The threats to Mira come not only from within her household but also arise from the public practice of her devotion. Priyadas goes on to relate:

> A devious, lustful man once took the guise of a sadhu
>   and played the following game [saying],
> "Please give your body over to mine.
> The Beloved Mountain Bearer himself has ordered it so."
> [Mira answered,] "Oh, then of course I will do it;
>   [But first let me] prepare something for you to eat—
>   please have some."
> Spreading a richly decorated bed in the midst
>   of the community of devotees, she said,
> "Before whom would you hesitate to act?
>   Fearlessly let yourself be drenched in pleasure."
> His face grew pale;
>   all his lustful feelings drained away.
> He came and bowed down at [her] feet [saying],
>   "Please give me the gift of devotion." (8)

Here keeping company with sadhus really does seem to cause Mira problems when this disreputable man disguised as a religious renouncer tries to seduce her, but she responds with wisdom, exposing his lust and his lie.

Other encounters do not correspond so directly to her in-laws' fears of what may happen to a woman who associates with men outside the family:

> The excellence of [her] beauty pleased the heart of
>   Emperor Akbar;
> Taking Tansen with him, he came to see.

> He was delighted at the Beloved Mountain Bearer's splendor.
> That very moment, swept up in a net of joy, [Tansen] offered up a song.
>
> Coming to Vrindavan, she was utterly delighted to meet Jiv Goswami,
> > Who abandoned his vow not to look upon a woman's face.
> In all the groves she saw her Dear Beloved
> > and holding this great joy in her heart,
> She returned to her homeland, composing [songs] and singing of it. (9)

The Mughal emperor Akbar and his court poet Tansen come for darshan, presumably of Mirabai—to enter her presence and to see and be seen by her—and they are overwhelmed by the experience, though in a very different way than the rana. During a pilgrimage to Vrindavan, Mira also encounters Jiv Goswami, one of the six direct disciples of Chaitanya who are the founders of the Gaudiya sampraday of Krishna devotion (to which Priyadas belonged), and in order to meet her he breaks his vow not to be in the presence of a woman.

When she returns to Mewar, however, the rana's mood seems little improved, and she does not remain for long. She leaves the palace for Dwarka, the city where Krishna established his kingdom after leaving Braj and another great Vaishnava pilgrimage center.

> Seeing that the rana's thoughts were tainted, she went to dwell in Dwarka,
> > [Where] passion for the dear Mountain Bearer is always cherished.
> Having grown eager, the rana came to know the true form of bhakti.
> [He] confessed great sorrow
> > [and] sent a group of brahmans to fetch [her].
> "Quickly get her and bring her back.
> > Give me breath and restore me to life."
> O, they went and sat at her door and recited [the rana's] entreaty.
> Hearing it, Mira went to take leave of Lord Ranchor.
> "Let me depart, protect [me]!" [she cried].
> > [Then] she disappeared—absorbed, no more to be found. (10)

The rana's change of heart comes too late, and Mira has no desire to return to him or her royal home. Her final merger with the image of Krishna, here addressed as Ranchor, closes the tale.[40]

In Priyadas's telling we find the basic outline of Mira's story that will characterize many tellings: her childhood devotion, her unwilling marriage to the rana, her insistence on bringing her image of Krishna with her to her new home, her immediate conflict with her mother-in-law over worship of the clan goddess, the rana's anger at her perceived impudence, her sister-in-law's efforts to persuade her to turn away from her association with holy men, the rana's plan to poison her, his angry outburst when he thinks she has a lover in her private chamber, the lustful false sadhu's attempt to seduce her, the visit of Akbar and Tansen, Mira's journey to Vrindavan and her encounter with Jiv Goswami, her travels to Dwarka, and her final merger with the image of Krishna Ranchor when the rana tries to get her to return to the palace.

Much of the narrative space in Priyadas's telling is given over to attempts made to sway Mira from her devotion by members of her marital family who do not fully understand the nature of the bhakti path. Mira refuses to live the life of a married woman of a rajput royal household, rejecting its decorum, rituals, and confinement. She escapes from multiple challenges coming from both inside and outside her family through the integrity of her devotion and the wisdom of her responses to her persecutors. Only her survival of the poisoning and her final merger with Krishna suggest possible direct divine intervention. She is somewhat vindicated when Jiv Goswami breaks his vow to meet her, evidently recognizing her as a fellow devotee of great merit, and the rana undergoes a conversion and begs for her return, but regardless of the circumstances she never wavers in her devotion to her Beloved Mountain Bearer.

Priyadas's Tale and the Grammar of Hindu Saints' Lives

We now have a sense of Mirabai the saint and the compelling quality of her life story. Such a woman would be an extraordinary individual without a doubt in any time and place, yet she also stands in the company of other saintly devotees, both men and women. How does her story compare to others in the larger genre of saints' lives in medieval India? Which elements will prove to be more standard and which unique to her? And how does Priyadas's particular telling compare to other traditions circulating about her in his time and in subsequent centuries? What choices might Priyadas have made in telling her story as he did? How might he have reflected and sifted through all the things people might have been saying about her? What narrative conventions was he constrained by and playing off, in addition to the requirements of poetic meter and rhyme? What expectations would audiences in his time and after have had for such a story, and what meanings might they have brought to and gleaned from the tale?

Priyadas and his contemporary and future audiences and performers would have been familiar with the life stories of other great Hindu devotees, as well as a range of material circulating about Mira herself. A number of shared elements found particularly in the stories of other women saints can be identified that speak to the distinctive challenges of embodying devotion to God in a woman's body, even as unique elements of the tale reveal Mira's particular character and something of the roots of her extraordinary popularity.

A. K. Ramanujan has developed a helpful fivefold typology of the life stories of Hindu women saints from across the subcontinent and across the centuries, to which Mira's story conforms in many ways. The essential common stages or elements in their stories he identifies as (1) "early dedication to God," (2) "denial of marriage," (3) "defiance of societal norms," (4) "initiation," and (5) "marriage to the Lord."[41] An additional element common to the life stories of many saints, both male and female, involves their encounters with kings or emperors, and this element also has a significant place in tellings of Mira's tale.[42]

Overcoming the "Trap" of Marriage

Like other Hindu women saints, Mira's devotion is traced to her childhood (without the kind of transformative originating experience to draw her into devotion that often marks the stories of great male devotees), and she faces her first serious challenge when forced to marry, according to Priyadas and many subsequent tellers.[43] Marriage, it seems, is incompatible with sainthood for women, though male saints have little problem practicing bhakti while being married. Their wives generally facilitate their practice by sharing their devotion and taking care of practical matters, or at worst they are an annoyance if they complain excessively, as Tukaram's wife is supposed to have done because he was not adequately providing for the family.[44] However, a woman seemingly cannot have the absolute devotion to a husband that is the cultural and dharmic ideal while at the same time fully embodying devotion to God. Or perhaps the problem is rather that husbands and in-laws will not tolerate such a perceived bifurcated loyalty.

Women saints, then, must somehow mitigate this conflict, preferably avoiding the trap of marriage altogether in their transition from childhood to adulthood. Their methods vary.[45] Some defy their parents' wishes (as Goggavve did), refusing to marry. Others undergo miraculous transformations to some unmarriageable state such as old age (Avvaiyar) or maleness (Tilakavve), or dispense with their husbands by leaving them (Mahadeviyakka, Lalla) or by terrifying them, however inadvertently, with their miraculous powers (Karaikkal Ammaiyar). Still others, like the Tamil Alvar saint Andal, leave this world by marrying and merging with the Divine when they reach marriageable age. Others find themselves widowed while they are yet children (Mahadamba, Akkabai, Venabai), freed of marriages contracted but never consummated, and transported outside of the realm of available women through their status as widows. Very few remain in the married state unless they are the wives of male devotees. The Varkari saint Bahinabai feels compelled to do so because she has a child, but her case is eventually ameliorated when her husband turns to a life of devotion. Even so she continues to speak of the difficulties that come with trying to follow the bhakti *marg*, or path, in the body of a woman subjugated by men and social expectation. Marriage and sainthood prove quite incompatible for most such women.

Mira is married in the vast majority of tellings of her story, and her "escape" most often comes through her refusal to consummate the marriage and her eventual departure from her marital home, both portrayed as self-conscious acts on her part. She is not rescued by divine intervention or some twist of fate and so is forced to marry. However, in Priyadas's account, her father-in-law promptly isolates her in a separate palace immediately after her arrival, effectively allowing her to avoid marital obligations. Elsewhere Krishna is credited with engineering this to protect his devotee in a realistic concession to the actual limitations of her agency under the circumstances.

In alternative later tellings, her husband is said to die a few years after their marriage, setting her free by default, as it were, and her defiance and persecution are said to take place only after his death, allowing for the assertion that she was a proper wife up to that point. This creates another problem, however. If she were a devoted wife and her husband died, then why did she not immolate herself on his funeral pyre in an act of *sati* to accompany him into the next life, as might be expected from such a virtuous royal rajput woman in her day?[46] Those who address the issue directly say that she refused to do so because, like the saintly women Gauribai and Venkamma, she did not consider herself a widow on the grounds that she was married to her Lord rather than the man others called her husband. There are still other tellings in which her whole story is set in her natal family and she never marries, thus avoiding the conflict, though her refusal to do so may lead her parents themselves to try to poison her.

Defying Social Expectations of Caste and Gender

In Ramanujan's third stage, the woman saint defies social expectations relating to gender and caste. In Mira's case, she struggles to overcome the limitations to and expectations for a rajput woman's proper behavior. She is clearly tormented by her family for this perceived deviance, though in Priyadas's account, as we noted, it is unclear whether it is only her father-in-law or both he and her husband who do so. The distinction appears not to have been especially important to Priyadas as Mira's behavior is presented as a general challenge to worldly notions of normative gender behavior and by implication also to rajput caste norms and conceptions of honor. The precise identity of her tormentor does come to be important in other narratives where he is specifically identified alternatively as her husband, his father, her husband's brother, or her own father, but always as a male family member who has power over her. Most great women devotees who seek a life outside the confines of marriage and widowhood encounter such familial resistance, as indeed do more ordinary women. It is not only family members who cause them grief, however.

In Priyadas's account we find a set of three additional stories involving Mira and men outside of her family—the lustful sadhu, Akbar and Tansen, and Jiv Goswami—that explore the challenges facing women who dare to step out of traditional roles and normative expectations. A woman outside of marriage has an ambiguous status which is constantly questioned and tested. Unless she has been transformed into some undesirable or asexual state, she must deal with the desires and aversions of men. The very fact of being a great devotee in a woman's body is problematic. To address this issue directly, some saints, like Mahadeviyakka and Lalla, are said to have chosen to give up clothing and to wander attired only in their long flowing hair. Such an act undertaken by a female devotee is vastly different from a male devotee's outwardly similar act of renunciation. That Mahadeviyakka still endured harassment from men as a result of her naked wandering is clearly articulated in poetry attributed to her.[47]

Though some, looking for exemplars of women's leadership in the past, have criticized Mira for not taking such a radical step,[48] she, too, discards the protective veils of domestic life as she sings, dances, and speaks in public and in the company of men outside of her immediate family. She, too, is exposed to the gaze of those who see her as an available object of desire, and she is stripped of that which would shield her from their advances. In Priyadas's telling, her wisdom and purity prove her strength, however. The lustful sadhu finds in her a wise teacher rather than a source of sexual satisfaction.[49] She, like Mahadeviyakka and Lalla, rejects the sexual attraction that modest dress and action may actually encourage and instead acts openly, without the need for any form of concealment.[50] Nevertheless she must still deal with men's lust, even as the saint Pipa's beautiful wife and fellow devotee Sita must also do.[51]

The second encounter between Mira and men outside her family involves the coming of Akbar and Tansen. Although the possibility of the rajput queen Mira talking directly to this particular Mughal ruler—an enemy of Mewar who would conquer their capital Chittor—is deemed historically improbable[52] and adamantly denied by some tellers of Mira's story, it has been incorporated as an essential element in a great many tellings of her life. Yet her encounter differs markedly from the reports of encounters with Akbar or other rulers found as a standard element in the life stories of a number of male saints, where these encounters often provide the occasion for demonstration of a saint's religious legitimacy.[53]

Reportedly, Akbar summoned the great Krishna devotee Surdas to court, moved by the beauty of songs attributed to him.[54] He challenged Sur, asking how he, a blind man, could sing of his eyes longing for the sight of the Lord. Sur wisely spoke of the inner eye that belongs to God and experiences perpetual darshan yet never ceases to yearn for the Lord. In response, the emperor offered him a boon: whatever he might request would be given to him. But Sur asked only for the removal of all obstacles to his devotion and to be released from the court. Akbar complied reluctantly, but he also began a collection of Sur's works. The emperor was said to be similarly impressed with all he had heard about the saint Dadu and his disciples' unflinching devotion to the Lord who transcends form.[55] He insisted that the saint come to his court, but Dadu did so only in obedience to God's command. Akbar and his Hindu and Muslim advisors were won over by this religious teacher of great wisdom, but like Sur, Dadu refused all gifts offered to him, being without desire and in need of nothing.

Mira's encounter with Akbar has a somewhat different flavor from those of Surdas and Dadu. First of all, Akbar's interest seems to be motivated by reports of her beauty rather than the artistry or profundity of her compositions or the spiritual strength of her disciples. Further, Akbar does not call her to come to the court but goes to her, his identity concealed in most tellings, though Priyadas makes no such caveat. Akbar was known for traveling about his realm in disguise and fraternizing with people of all levels of society in order to better know his subjects. That the youthful emperor might have come in this way to see this allegedly beautiful woman, so totally in love with her Lord, dance and sing before his image, carries a certain romantic flare. There is no mention of any verbal testing of Mira by Akbar and no report of any extended conversation between the two in these standard hagiographic sources.

Sometimes Akbar is said to have offered Mira a gift of a jeweled necklace to adorn Krishna, which she accepts. Akbar fulfills the role of an admiring royal patron in such a telling, as do other kings in the life stories of woman saints such as Gauribai.[56] Whereas a male saint's rejection of rulers and power is often lauded, power is seemingly not perceived as holding the same allure or danger of compromise for women saints. The stock character of the degenerate brahman priest who is a sycophant of the ruler and serves as a foil to the male saint in such episodes is also absent from this and other stories of women saints.

The danger for women saints encountering rulers is more often sexual. The relationship is not only one of ruler to subject but also man to woman, and the power differential is enormous when the two are combined. Mahadeviyakka had the misfortune of coming to the attention of King Kaushika, not because of her bhakti but in spite of it.[57] It was her beauty rather than her wisdom which made him want to keep her near him, and she was forced to marry him. Akbar poses no such threat to Mira (though the rana whom she must marry does), and she appears as a woman whose beauty draws others to the Divine rather than to herself.

Akbar is an exceptional ruler by all accounts, known for his appreciation of the arts and his inclusive religious outlook, and stories recounting his interest in Hindu bhaktas of all persuasion, Vaishnavas as well as aniconic nirgun bhaktas, reflect the fluidity of the religious milieu in this time, where Hindu saints (including Mira) and Muslim Ismaili and Sufi saints, or *pirs,* were honored by both Hindus and Muslims alike as great devotees of God. Yet even Akbar is said to have sorely tested lesser bhaktas, ordering Dadu's disciple Madhav Das placed in a lion's cage, for example.[58]

Other rulers come across in a far worse light in the stories of other saints, particularly those of very low caste. In the case of the saint Raidas, an unspecified king oversees a contest between him and brahman priests who are critical of his religious activities as a *chamar,* a member of an extremely low caste associated with leatherworking. Raidas easily wins and is then honored.[59] Oral versions of Raidas's story intensify the trials he must endure at the hands of the king, however, until they approach the extreme cruelty the emperor Sikandar Lodi shows toward the iconoclastic nirgun saint Kabir. At the insistence of both Hindu and Muslim religious leaders who chafe under Kabir's sharp critiques, Sikandar Lodi has him arrested. Angered by Kabir's perceived insolence, he tries to kill him in various ways, having the saint thrown into the Ganges River in chains to drown, bound and placed in a house set afire to burn, and placed at the feet of a wild elephant to be trampled. Unable to harm him, Sikandar Lodi eventually has to admit defeat and accept the truth of Kabir's Lord.[60]

The ever-present rana is such a figure for Mira, though the situation is somewhat more complex because he is also her husband, father-in-law, brother-in-law, or father. The rage directed at her seems as blind and brutal as Sikandar Lodi's anger toward Kabir, but it is not her transgression of caste restrictions and religious orthodoxy that spurs the king's actions. Instead it is her failure to live up to the propriety of her own high-caste birth and her transgression of gender rules. And if the rana is her husband, this is compounded by his own jealousy and obsessive drive to control and possess her, his treatment of her standing in stark contrast to the love of her indigo-ebony Lord.

The trials she reportedly undergoes at the rana's hand—not only poison but snakes, scorpions, and a hungry lion—are said to have been experienced by others. Madhav Das, at Akbar's insistence, faced such a lion, and Devara Dasimayya, a tenth-century saint of the Virashaiva tradition of South India, also found himself forced by an angry ruler to drink poison and confront a venomous snake.[61] Such trials become an opportunity for the Lord to intervene on his devotees' behalf and to demonstrate before skeptics that they are beloved of God. At the same time the ability to swallow poison, to handle snakes, or to pacify wild animals is seen as a mark of spiritual advancement (as these abilities are in other strands of Hinduism as well as other religious traditions).[62] Mira's survival of the rana's assassination attempts shows her Lord's care for her and her spiritual power and purity, while Akbar's chaste honor and respect for her devotion stands in dramatic contrast to the rana's murderous rage at her social transgressions. Akbar's appreciation of Mira and elsewhere her acceptance of his gift for Krishna further show that her devotion transcends the boundaries of religious traditions and that she cares little for distinctions between Hindu and Muslim when it comes to devotion to God (though in some later tellings this encounter will be politicized and prove to be the primary cause of her persecution, as we will see).

Mira's encounter with Jiv Goswami offers a third perspective on male-female relations, which is also mirrored in the stories of the lives of other women devotees. These women saints must deal not only with the direct lust of men and their murderous rage at women who do not follow the rules and whom they cannot control, but also with men's aversion as they project their own desire onto women. Women are then perceived as the embodiment of desire itself and as a destructive source of temptation, scapegoated for male lust and lack of self-control. From such a perspective, even though the ideal devotee might be conceived of as female before the male God, the ideal human being is still assumed to be male, and actual women are seen as fundamentally flawed and impure.[63] The stories of women devotees include episodes in which they challenge this view and in which they are confronted and tested by religious leaders because of their nonmale status.

For example, Mahadeviyakka is questioned about her nakedness by the spiritual leader Allama Prabhu after she tells him she is married to Shiva. If the point is to discard outward coverings that suggest artificial distinctions before God (of which gender is one), then why does she retain the veil of her long hair? She responds with a song acknowledging that her full nakedness might hurt others—that is, men—by providing a focus for lust, even though ultimately nothing can be hidden from God and gender has no relevance on the spiritual journey.[64] This test constitutes an initiation of sorts, and her answer wins her full acceptance into the devotional community. In a similar manner, the South Indian saint Kurur Amma meets Vilvamangal's challenge to her recitation of the name of God in a state of menstrual impurity, saying that if one could die at any moment, is it not better to do so with the name of the Lord on one's lips, whether in a state of purity or impurity?[65]

The meeting of Jiv Goswami and Mira is also often recounted as a kind of test she must pass before being admitted into the male world of religious authority. Priyadas simply relates that Jiv Goswami met Mira, although in doing so he abandoned his vow not to look at a woman's face. A more expanded story is widely told, however, sometimes with Rup Goswami (Jiv Goswami's uncle and the leading theologian of the Gaudiya sampraday) said to be the one she meets. In this more extended telling, the holy man refuses Mira's initial request to meet him because of his vow (though some will say that it was his disciples who tried to turn her away, rather than the great guru himself).[66] Mira responds by sending a message that as far as she knows, there is really only one male in Vrindavan—are not all, like the gopis, feminine in their love for Krishna? Hearing her response, he is pleased, and in some cases chagrined, and immediately comes to her.

In such tellings Mira clearly demonstrates her qualifications for acceptance into this male devotional world. Priyadas's account does not include such details, and it is understandable that he might not want to show his own community—much less one of its great leaders—in such a light, though equally possible that the more elaborate test episode comes from another strand of tradition and/or that he may be creating an intentional countertext, against his listeners' expectations of how such encounters usually go. Priyadas's simple description suggests a respectful meeting on equal ground (a radical suggestion in itself), without any humbling first encounter or assumption of male superiority (though Jiv Goswami's initial vow implies something less than a blind eye toward gender among the followers of Chaitanya).[67]

The overwhelming predominance of the test version of the episode supports the importance of such encounters in the life stories of great women devotees. Some rite of passage seems required, proving their worthiness and moving them from the position of "woman" to that of "bhakta," a category which Ramanujan has suggested may even constitute a kind of "third gender," as women cease to be women but men also take on the character of women in their devotion.[68] Though women do find a place in the world of bhakti, the voices of their male contemporaries still speak negatively of them as sources of temptation and distraction on the road to liberation, even while adopting a female persona in their devotion to God manifest in a male form.[69] Women need not go through any such gender transformation, nor do men offer this same sort of sexual temptation for them, if we are to judge by the songs attributed to women saints. Instead, it is the social and material privileges of the married state that these women renounce and that might tempt them away from their chosen path, as Madhu Kishwar and Ruth Vanita have observed.[70]

Implicit in Mira's encounters with the false sadhu, Akbar and Tansen, Jiv Goswami, and the rana is a defiance of social expectations for gender and of caste rules and distinctions. The saint Kabir's caustic and uncompromising style of verbal confrontation recorded in the *Bijak* is well known and aimed directly at religious and secular leaders of every ilk who are the guardians of the social and religious order.[71] In contrast, Mira's challenge is primarily articulated through her life choices and actions. Songs in her voice do not generally critique caste distinctions directly, but stories told about her show her breaking them by disregarding the rules of her own caste and associating with people from every level of society within the community of devotees, even in some cases becoming the disciple of the low-caste saint Raidas. Similarly, she does not critique false distinctions between Hindu and Muslim before God, but in her legendary encounter with Akbar and Tansen, she recognizes none.

She also does not explicitly protest the social limitations placed on women, and we would not necessarily expect her to do so, or furthermore expect those who tell her story and sing in her name in these centuries to do so, in the way nineteenth- and twentieth-century reformers might. But she refuses to live within these gender expectations, in most tellings rejecting her arranged marriage, seclusion and veiling, and all notions of honor and shame. She renounces the power and privilege of her own royal status as well, but without speaking explicitly against feudal political and economic structures. Mirabai's social protest is thus deeply grounded in her actions rather than radical verbal confrontation—actions that give reality to alternative possibilities. This is true in the stories of other devotees of marginalized status as well for whom to speak at all is a transgressive act, exposing them to potential violent repression by those in power. It is also the case, however, that Priyadas may have had his own additional reasons for portraying Mira in this way and that some songs attributed to Mira and stories told about her, especially by low-caste performers in the twentieth century, do contain more direct and biting critiques, a point to which we will return.

Initiation and the Taking of a Guru

Sometimes tests such as Mira must pass in her encounter with Jiv Goswami are also a precursor to a woman saint's formal initiation into a devotional community and/or discipleship to a male guru, Ramanujan's fourth stage. Formal initiation may be a concession to the dominant tradition which insists on the importance of a spiritual authority figure and on the necessity of a woman being under the control of a man at all times, or it may be a part of her defiance if she takes it from a low-caste guru, or both. Priyadas says nothing directly about Mira having a guru, and her meeting with Jiv Goswami shows only his respect for and acceptance of her, though the possibility of a guru-disciple relationship is certainly open and will be posited by others.

In many tellings of her tale, Mira neither meets nor takes initiation from any guru. Krishna is all in all to her: Lord, husband, and guru. Other renditions give her various gurus, often within the sect of the teller. For example, a late seventeenth-century Bengali Sahajiya Vaishnava text identifies her as Rup Goswami's tantric ritual partner, and a Rajasthani illustrated manuscript tradition portrays her as the disciple of Haridas of the Ramavat sampraday.[72] Such claims seem to reflect a desire to show Mira as one of their own by members of various sampradays who give her a high status within their community by associating her with key figures. Priyadas, as a follower of Chaitanya, may have wanted to lay claim to her for the Gaudiya tradition in a similar way with this episode.

Most often if Mirabai is said to have a guru, however, it is Raidas, the low-caste leatherworker identified as a disciple of Ramananda, who is respected by Vaishnava and nirgun devotees alike. Priyadas makes no mention of this relationship, but the slightly earlier *Prem Ambodh* clearly identifies Mira as his disciple.[73] Based on her inclusion in this latter text, she must have been popular in the Punjab as well as Rajasthan, Vrindavan, and Bengal by the late seventeenth century, with a clear association made here between her and Raidas, enhancing his reputation as her guru and hers as his devotee and also showing Mira unequivocally as one who disregards hierarchies of caste.

In the context of seventeenth-century Punjab, the connection may also have brought her more fully into the religious world of the Sikhs. Raidas—already recognized by Nanak's followers as expressing in his songs an aniconic theistic revelation in line with Nanak himself—legitimates Mirabai's inclusion as a member of their religious circle. Sikh assertions of caste and gender equality, institutionalized in the early establishment of communal kitchens and shared meals, are also confirmed in Mira's discipleship to Raidas and her inclusion as a woman among the saints.[74] One song attributed to Mira did appear in early recensions of the Sikh scriptural collection of songs of the gurus and related saints as early as 1604 CE, with her song positioned to follow songs of Raidas even as her story follows his in the *Prem Ambodh*. However, by the time the *Adi Granth* reached its final form in the 1680s, the Mira song had been removed.[75]

Given the association of these two saints by his time and possibly a century earlier, at least in the Punjab, we must ask whether Priyadas is simply unaware of this strand of tradition or deliberately excluding it. He does speak extensively of Raidas, appearing to draw on Anantadas's *Raidas Parchai* (c. 1588) as one source for his tale.[76] Both Anantadas and Priyadas do mention a *rani*, or queen, of Chittor who goes to Kashi (Banaras) to become Raidas's disciple, but they refer to her as the "Jhali Rani" and do not identify her with Mira. Might tales of Mira and this other rani of Chittor have converged in the Punjab and possibly elsewhere, or alternatively might a single tradition associating Mira with the chamar saint have been split to distance the popular saint from him? Or were these simply independent and perhaps regionally specific traditions, in existence by the end of the seventeenth century?

It is not unreasonable to conclude that in the Punjab region the identities of the unspecified rani from the Jhala clan and Mira might have been conflated—a queen from Chittor became a disciple of Raidas, Mirabai was the most well-known rani of Mewar as well as a greatly admired devotee, and her association with Raidas would bring her more fully in line with the theology of the growing Sikh community. Indeed in the *Prem Ambodh*, Mirabai does appear in the tale of Raidas, where she is said to have taken initiation from him in Banaras, an action which angered the local brahmans who then challenged his right as an extremely low-caste person to focus his worship on a *shalagram* (a sacred stone recognized as an aniconic form of Vishnu),[77] even as the Jhali Rani's similar action is said to have done by Anantadas and Priyadas.[78]

The *Prem Ambodh* tale of Mira then begins by noting that she is Raidas's disciple, the association providing a bridge to her story. However, her guru does not play any role in the specific episode recounted about her, even as she does not in the tale of her purported disciple Karmabai that follows hers. His absence could lend weight to the possibility that the association was independent from circulating traditions of Mirabai's life story and served primarily to legitimate her inclusion within this Sikh text. Peter Friedlander argues further that such an "amalgamation of hagiographies" might have been fostered by disciples of Raidas (also called Ravidas) and indeed is found in twentieth-century Ravidasi hagiographies in much the same form as it appears in the *Prem Ambodh*.[79] In any case such an alleged association might have been readily picked up by Sikhs and members of other nirgun sampradays as a way to integrate Mirabai as one of their own.

With respect to Anantadas and Priyadas and the Vaishnava communities in Rajasthan and Vrindavan to which they belonged, traditions associating Mira with Raidas could have been unknown, perhaps originating elsewhere, whether in the Punjab or in Banaras among Raidas's disciples. Neither Nabhadas nor his contemporary Anantadas mentions a relationship between the two. It is also the case that Nanak and subsequent Sikh gurus are not among the eclectic set of saints praised by Nabhadas, though it seems more likely that he excluded them intentionally as competitors of some kind or perhaps because of their exclusive nirgun stance rather than for lack of familiarity.[80]

Alternatively, since Anantadas mentions Mira only in passing, he could conceivably have been aware of the story of Raidas's royal female disciple from Chittor without realizing that this rani and Mira were one and the same. However, it is also possible that Anantadas and/or Priyadas after him might have been deliberately creating countertexts to any such association, given how widely Mirabai is associated with Raidas in later centuries and that popular traditions often identify her husband (when he is named at all) as the renowned Rana Kumbha, among whose wives was indeed a rani of Jhala rajput heritage, the mother of his heir Rana Sanga (whom others will come to identify as Mira's father-in-law).[81] For Anantadas's part, wider stories associated with Mirabai, if known to him, might have influenced his decision to make little mention of her within his works.

As Winand Callewaert observes, across his parchai, "Anantadas doesn't have a good word for women ... and he does not hesitate to load all the sins of the world on women," reserving his only praise for the faithful wife, obedient to her husband and uncomplaining, regardless of circumstances, epitomized by Pipa's wife and queen turned renouncer Sita.[82] As Anantadas and Priyadas after him present it, there is no reason to think Raidas's high-caste, royal disciple and patron, the Jhali Rani, might be anything other than an ideal wife either, her association with him further enhancing his spiritual reputation. But there is plenty of reason to think Mirabai might not have been, particularly given Nabhadas's roughly contemporary description—reason enough for Anantadas to fail to mention any equivalence even if others might posit one.

Composing a century after Nabhadas and Anantadas and in a quite different context, Priyadas associates Mira with the brahman Jiv Goswami of his own sampraday. In the later part of the seventeenth and first half of the eighteenth century, when Priyadas would have been living, Ramanandi and Gaudiya sampraday concerns came together, with key Krishna images associated with the sect of Chaitanya eventually making their way from Krishna's holy city of Vrindavan to the Amer (Jaipur) region of Rajasthan for safekeeping with their long-standing royal Kachvaha rajput patrons,[83] who were also patrons of the Ramanandis of Galta, as we have noted. Kachvaha ruler Jai Singh II (r. 1699–1743) took particular interest in the religious practices within his realm, reviving Vedic sacrificial rituals and working to harmonize orthodox social and ritual practices with the Vaishnava bhakti sampradays.[84] Vaishnava gatherings were convened in Galta in the early decades of the eighteenth century purportedly to establish orders of warrior ascetics to battle similarly armed Shaivite Dasnami ascetics for control of lucrative pilgrimage sites but also to enshrine the *chatur sampradays*, or four teaching lineages—traced back to Madhvacharya, Vishnuswami, Nimbarka, and Ramanuja and allegedly carried on by the Gaudiya sampraday, the Pushtimarg of Vallabhacharya, Nimbarka's sampraday, and the Ramanandis, respectively—as the four legitimate branches of a shared Vaishnava orthodoxy. Though both Nabhadas and Anantadas had affirmed these four sampradays a century earlier as important strands of a transsectarian Vaishnava tradition, the four increasingly became the measure of Vaishnava orthodoxy and legitimacy, particularly under the considerable influence of Jai Singh II, as he sought to reinforce his power and image as a distinctly Hindu king and protector of dharma, even as Mughal power began to wane.[85]

While Richard Burghart suggests that the Ramanandis effectively displaced the Shri Vaishnavas of South India as the legitimate followers of Ramanuja in this process, Monika Horstmann argues instead that the Ramanandis adopted more orthodox Shri Vaishnava traditions to place themselves more squarely within this lineage.[86] What is clear is that there was a shift in the Ramanandi tradition at this time, away from the radical inclusivity that characterized its earlier development and is reflected in Nabhadas's bhaktamal toward a much stronger caste consciousness, including the reaffirmation of rules of commensality and the assertion that the low-caste and female members of Ramananda's original twelve disciples were not initiators of legitimate sublineages within the tradition—an overall move toward conventional dharma consistent with the social agenda of Jai Singh II.

These saints were still recognized by Ramanandi ascetics, and women and low-caste people, or shudras, could still be devotees within the Ramanandi tradition, but they were not to be formally initiated into the guru tradition as carriers of the lineage. Raidas was among those who were demoted in this process (even as Nabhadas himself may have been because of his low-caste status, evidenced by Priyadas's description of him as a "servant" to the sadhus rather than spiritual heir apparent to his guru Agradas, as others would claim). These shifting notions of religious orthodoxy might have been reason enough for Priyadas, if he was at all aware of traditions associating Mirabai with Raidas, not to include this relationship in his story of her life.

As John Stratton Hawley points out, leaders within the Gaudiya sampraday in this period appear not to have been initially quite as concerned about legitimation through a South Indian lineage as the Ramanandis were, given their understanding that their founder Chaitanya was Krishna, or Radha and Krishna, incarnate.[87] Nevertheless, Kachvaha patronage remained important to them, particularly given Ramanandi rival claims, and Kyokazu Okita argues persuasively that the Gaudiyas were drawn into this "politics of genealogy" and Jai Singh II's religious and social reform agenda by 1719 CE.[88] Horstmann further notes that internal disputes within the Gaudiyas at this time and the influential presence of Vallabhites also in the court of Jai Singh II furthered both the affirmation of dharmic orthodoxy and theological innovation and collaboration.[89]

Priyadas was composing his *Bhaktirasabodhini* in the early years of this transitional era, and James Hare argues that his overall text reflects a similar redefinition of a still inclusive Vaishnava bhakti community, but with a stronger emphasis on sampraday membership, royal patronage, and the significance of caste identity within the religious sphere, as well as a subtle shift in focus in his praises of the saints from the devotee per se to God.[90] Hare makes his argument particularly through an examination of Priyadas's stories of Raidas and Kabir, comparing them not only with Nabhadas but also with Anantadas's earlier works, which Priyadas clearly used as sources.

Priyadas's tale of Mirabai, however, has no clear documented antecedents for comparison. He continues and expands Nabhadas's focus primarily on Mira's fearless devotion in the face of normative family and gender expectations, though he goes far beyond his predecessor with respect to political power and patronage in the contrast between the destructive rana and Akbar. The Kachvaha rulers were famous for having joined forces with Akbar, and Jai Singh II too was allied with the Mughals, having received the honorific title "Sawai" from Aurangzeb himself and remaining an official within the Mughal court. At the same time he continued Kachvaha patronage of the Gaudiya sampraday, his new capital, Jaipur, becoming an important Gaudiya center in the eighteenth century, with key images from Vrindavan installed there. Akbar's positive presence in Priyadas's tale of Mira reaffirms these relationships of patronage (as do his extended descriptions of patronage relationships between Krishnadas Payahari and Prithviraj and between

Man Singh and both Khildev and Agradas of the Ramanandis, far exceeding Nabhadas's accounts).[91] And Mira's journey to Vrindavan and encounter with Jiv Goswami legitimate the saint as a de facto member of one of the four orthodox sampradays—Priyadas's in particular—though not necessarily a formal disciple.

Associating her with brahman Jiv Goswami also precludes any issue of more radical breaking of caste rules in her taking a low-caste guru, consistent with the emerging ideas of Vaishnava orthodoxy in Rajasthan and Vrindavan. But did Priyadas even know of traditions associating Mirabai with Raidas, already clearly circulating among the Sikhs? If so, was he deliberately seeking to erase them or merely dismissing them in favor of his own sampraday? The connection between Mira and the chamar Raidas is certainly not limited regionally to the Punjab or to the past. It persists into the present as a widespread popular tradition and plays a particularly important role in the understandings of Mira among low-caste followers of Raidas centered in Banaras and more widely among low-caste communities in Rajasthan and elsewhere.[92] Within the logic of hagiographic narratives, to assert that Mira was Raidas's disciple not only fulfills the felt need that she must have had a guru and the legitimation that this brings, but it is a strong affirmation that she neither holds any prejudice based on caste nor recognizes any hard and fast distinction between Vaishnava and nirgun devotion—aspects of Mira's character that are essential in many people's experience of her and consonant with the envisioned wider nonsectarian, broadly Vaishnava, imagined community of bhaktas Nabhadas offers. Their guru-disciple relationship would also place her squarely under the guidance of a male religious authority and, for nirgun sampradays, under a guru ostensibly with their orientation (though Raidas's use of a shalagram in his worship makes him nominally Vaishnava as well). To assert that she was not Raidas's disciple, on the other hand, removes any taint of caste impurity or transgression from her and might keep her more fully in a more exclusively Vaishnava camp. But if she is not then said to be someone else's disciple, her independence from all male authorities, even religious ones, save God godself, is irrefutable—and so her discipleship to others will also be asserted.

Those who are aware of the distinct stories of the Jhali Rani and of Mira in more recent times deal with the identity of the two queens in a variety of ways. Hawley notes that some people, like the author of the *Raidas Ramayana*, affirm the existence of two queens from Chittor but claim that both became Raidas's disciples, with some asserting that the Jhali Rani was Mira's mother-in-law and in some cases that it was she who took initiation from Raidas rather than Mira, which would be consistent with Priyadas's account.[93] Twentieth-century historian Hermann Goetz will go further, speculating that the Jhali

Rani was indeed Mira's husband's grandmother (wife of Rana Kumbha) and that she recognized the image given to Mirabai as a child by the chamar saint who was also her own guru and thus became the young woman's protector in the palace.[94] All we can really say with certainty is that by the end of the seventeenth century at least two rather different strands of tradition were definitely circulating regarding who Mira's guru was and about Raidas's royal female disciple(s) from Chittor.

With respect to initiation either as the disciple of a specific guru or into a particular sampraday, Mira most often stands outside established lineages and remains unincorporated into the formal structures of developing religious institutions—a model of devotion but theologically wedded to none, her allegiance to Krishna undivided. Followers of many sampradays across the centuries seemed willing to accept and embrace Mira on these terms. As we have already noted, Hariram Vyas affirms her as a member of his eclectic spiritual family, as would Nabhadas for the Ramanandis and Priyadas of the Gaudiya sampraday. The seventeenth-century saint Tukaram is said to do the same for the Varkaris of Maharashtra, and there are many more such songs attributed to, among others, Eknath, Surdas, Narsi Mehta, Charandas, and even Kabir, who by all accounts lived in the century before her, confirming that Mira belongs to a broad nonsectarian devotional community that even transcends time.[95] There is one very notable exception to this wide embrace, however, among the disciples of Vallabhacharya who follow the Pushtimarg, or "Path of Grace."

In an important Pushtimargi text, we find Mira vehemently rejected not once but three times over the issue of her guru and of maintaining strict boundaries for the devotional community. This text, the *Chaurasi Vaishnavan ki Varta* (Acts and Sayings of the Eighty-four Vaishnavas), is attributed to Gokulnath, grandson of Vallabhacharya, and was compiled with commentary by Hariray. Gokulnath is said to have lived in the first half of the seventeenth century (sectarian sources give his dates as 1551–1640), and the first manuscript of this text lists 1640 CE as the year it was copied, so this text was likely composed some fifty to sixty years earlier than the *Prem Ambodh* and Priyadas's composition, and it emerges out of another of what would become the four "orthodox" Vaishnava sampradays. The text relates various incidents from the lives of eighty-four important disciples of Vallabhacharya and serves as a continuing source of spiritual guidance to the devotees of this sampraday, teaching by way of example the path from worldly life to supreme devotion and being read aloud regularly, even as the bhaktamals and their commentaries continue to be in a wide range of other communities.[96]

Three separate *vartas* or episodes relate to Mira.[97] In the first, Vallabhacharya's son sends a letter to a disciple named Govind Dube, who, he has learned, has been staying for some days with Mira and her community.[98] He berates him for exchanging an elephant for an ass by remaining in the presence of Mirabai rather than his own guru, who is in fact Krishna incarnate.[99] Govind Dube leaves immediately, in spite of Mira's requests that he remain. In the second varta, Ramdas sings a song in praise of Vallabhacharya in the presence of Mirabai, who then asks him to sing one for Krishna.[100] Her request implies that she does not accept Vallabhacharya as the incarnation of Krishna and thus equivalent to him. Ramdas is incensed, curses Mira, and leaves the village with all his relatives, again in spite of her entreaties and refusing her offerings.[101] Ramdas vows never to look upon her face again—how unlike Priyadas's description of Jiv Goswami's reception of her, and indeed the opposite of it. In the third varta, Krishnadas is passing through the village where Mira lives during a trip to collect offerings from Vaishnava pilgrims at Dwarka.[102] He enters her house but finds devotees gathered there belonging to various sampradays other than the Pushtimarg. He immediately announces his intention to leave. Disregarding Mira's appeals to stay, he also refuses her offered donation on the grounds that she is not a follower of Vallabhacharya, hoping that others will want to know more about his guru after observing his integrity.

The religious import of these passages is clear and consistent with many other passages in the *Vartas*: the path of devotion should be straight and narrow, without the distraction of conversation with those outside the purity of the Pushtimargi community and the teachings of Vallabhacharya. One should not be a religious dilettante, acknowledging spiritual authority only among the leaders of the Vallabha sampraday.[103] Not only should outsiders be avoided, but the teachings of one's own traditions should be kept hidden from them.[104] Mira seemingly is the most dangerous of outsiders: an admired devotee of Krishna but one who is neither formally a member of the sampraday nor a disciple of Vallabhacharya and who keeps mixed company.

There may be a number of reasons in this formative period of the Vallabha sampraday for such a vehement condemnation of Mira and refusal of her offerings. Hawley suggests that she might have represented a form of royal patronage which the Vallabhites wanted to reject in favor of support from the rising merchant class and that the inclusive type of bhakti she and others practiced might have been perceived as economic competition to the Pushtimarg in their collection of offerings. Further, with their reconception of temples as household shrines of the lineal descendants of Vallabhacharya or his closest disciples, Mirabai's rejection of her own familial lineage might also have been seen as particularly egregious, even as her assertion of religious leadership as a woman in her own independent household might have been.[105] No other narrative tradition of Mira speaks of her in this way as having such a household, giving further weight to Hawley's argument.

Given the religious politics of this period, it is also conceivable that these passages reflect a more general defensive posture of the Vallabhites in the face of perceived rivalry for influence in Vrindavan with the more well-established Gaudiyas and/or for orthodoxy and legitimacy in the emerging reification of the four sampradays in Rajasthan. A more local situation in Gujarat may also have impacted Mira's portrayal, arising from internal power struggles among the priests of the Dakor Ranchor Temple that was taken over by the Vallabhites during the period of the *Vartas*' composition, with Hariray initiating the transfer in 1625.[106] Pauwels raises this possibility, suggesting that the rejection of Mira could have served to reinforce allegiance to the newly installed Vallabha priests and to undermine loyalty to former priests who might have drawn authority from a connection between this particular temple and Mira.[107] All these factors may have come into play as Mira, the outsider, became a convenient "foil" for others from whom the Vallabhites wanted to distinguish themselves.[108]

It should be noted, however, that Mira is directly criticized in the texts only because she refused to acknowledge Vallabhacharya as guru and God incarnate and she associated with followers of other gurus and thus members of other sampradays, not for any other aspect of her behavior. Though it is possible that the audience of the *Vartas* would have found this portrayal of a lone woman devotee, surrounded by assorted devotees staying in her home, reprehensible in itself, without the need for further comment, the *Vartas* with Hariray's commentary do not shy away from reinforcing their didactic intent, and though her gender may have added weight to the evaluation of her practice of devotion as impure and her outsider status, there is no direct discussion of this. It is her lack of exclusive allegiance to Vallabhacharya that is clearly her most serious offense.

Though their intent is rejection, these accounts in some ways depict Mira in a rather favorable light as ever devoted to Krishna and practicing an inclusive form of bhakti, welcoming and supporting any devotee of Krishna, and indeed of God, as a member of her community. By comparison, the Vallabhites seem highly exclusivist in their sectarian allegiance or perhaps only equally uncompromising in their devotion to Vallabhacharya. They place a high value on the sampraday as a community of truth that must be protected from the incursions of the samsaric world and that provides a refuge of purity, facilitating spiritual realization.[109] For her part, Mirabai is not wounded by the Vallabhites' rejections, for even after they insult her, she entreats them to remain as recognized members of a wider *satsang* (gathering of true devotees).

The fact that not one but three such stories are told also suggests that Vallabhacharya's followers may have felt they had to deal with Mira and what she represented for them in some serious way. Surely she had to have been widely known and held in high esteem to be perceived as such a danger and/or to be such an effective and immediately understandable foil to their own tradition, as Hawley suggests. Because her ishtadev, or chosen form of the deity to worship, is the same Lord of Govardhan who is at the center of the worship of the Vallabha sampraday, it is possible that ordinary members readily embraced her songs.[110] Yet she did not follow Vallabhacharya, and as a result, though she might be loved and respected, she would be perceived as a corrupting influence and would have to be kept at a distance, however reluctantly. These expressions of rejection thus seem to contain both a recognition of Mira's great devotional power and popularity and an overwhelming disease. And so, at least rhetorically, for these early followers of Vallabhacharya, she remains uninitiated and unincorporated, ever the outsider, standing in emblematically for all outsiders, whether they be theological, economic, or ecclesiastical.[111] And during this formative and volatile period of changing understandings of the orthodox practice of Vaishnava bhakti in North India, her story and character as both insider and outsider—to family and society and to bhakti, sampraday, and guru lineage—would become a locus for the assertion of conflicting and converging claims by others as well.

Marriage and Merger with the Lord

The final stage in the woman saint's life (after her defiance of social and religious norms and her possible initiation by a guru) is, according to Ramanujan, "marrying the Lord." Such a final marriage goes far beyond the understanding of many that the Lord is their true husband, culminating in a complete merger with God that ends earthly existence. The South Indian Virashaiva saint Mahadeviyakka was Ramanujan's prototype.[112] She finds union with her Lord at the young age of twenty-two at Shrishaila temple when the intensity of her devotion comes to fruition.[113] For the Shri Vaishnava saint Andal, marriage and merger converge even more directly when she is but sixteen and goes to meet her Lord in the full attire of a bride at Shrirangam temple.

For Mira, however, marriage and merger with the Divine are more distinct. She sings of her wedding to Krishna happening in a dream in one seemingly autobiographical song (though we have no way of knowing whether she actually composed it), suggesting that her bonds to her Lord are formal and irrevocable and her vows witnessed by countless beings.[114] In another tale, which we will examine in detail in the next chapter, Krishna answers Mira's pleas for rescue on the eve of her earthly wedding by coming to marry her himself, and she is miraculously adorned with the marks of a bride.

Merger comes later in a Dwarka temple when she vanishes in the embrace of Krishna's image. Other saints also are said to disappear into images at the moment of death as they join with the Lord to whom they had been so devoted in life.[115] Such a death communicates the fundamental oneness of the devotee with the Divine and the transience of physical embodiment. Mira's final union with her Lord, described in this way, involves her entire being, in a merger that is at once spiritually and physically transformative.

Stories of the miraculous demise of so many speak of their ultimately being somehow different from other humans, neither living nor dying in an ordinary way, and being indistinguishable from or transparent to the Divine. For women saints particularly, this merging union with their Lord seems to speak both of God as the final and only refuge in this world and of the passing away of the self in the absolute reality of the Divine, an act of loving union and of annihilation such that only the Beloved remains. Priyadas ends his tale of Mira's life with her disappearance in just this way.

Alternative Tellings of Mirabai's Story: The *Prem Ambodh*

Priyadas clearly situates Mirabai within the family of Hindu devotional saints, and his account is our earliest record of what become standard forms of many of the specific events that mark later *written* narratives of Mira's life, at least within devotional literary circles in Vrindavan and Rajasthan. The tale of Mirabai that Priyadas tells, however, is a particular one, composed in 1712 CE and clearly shaped by his own religious background and his association with the traditions of Chaitanya. The contrast Priyadas develops, between the rana as a flawed human man (especially if he is Mira's husband) and Krishna as the perfect divine lover, is appropriate where the relationship of devotee and Lord is conceived of primarily as that of female devotee to male God and particularly that of lovers, as it is among the followers of Chaitanya. Priyadas emphasizes and explores dimensions of the relationship of male and female—the ideal Divine-human love of Krishna and Mira; the rage and jealousy of the controlling rana, who would dominate her or kill her; the lust of the sadhu, who would lie to get the object of his desire; the chaste respect of Akbar and Tansen, who come for darshan of Mira; and the humble admiration and egalitarian spirit of Jiv Goswami, who abandons any vow to eschew the presence of women in meeting her. The year of the composition of Priyadas's *Bhaktirasabodhini* is also significant given the political and theological debates of his day, as we noted particularly with regard to the place of Akbar and Jiv Goswami and the absence of Raidas within his telling. An accompanying critique of moral corruption among the celibate leadership of the sampradays and push by Jai Singh II for the marriage of ascetic leaders also resonates with the episode of the lascivious sadhu.

The story of Mirabai told in the *Prem Ambodh* stands in sharp contrast to the story told by Priyadas, not only in identifying her as a disciple of Raidas but also in offering a dramatically different description of her marriage, naming her father as her persecutor, and including an encounter with a lustful sadhu but not with either Akbar or Jiv Goswami. In discussing this alternative telling, I am indebted to John Stratton Hawley and Gurinder Singh Mann, who provide detailed information about the overall work and have made the episode about Mirabai readily accessible, translating it in full into English, providing contextual background, and offering their own insightful comparative analysis.[116] Though the earliest available manuscript of the *Prem Ambodh* is dated 1702 CE, this and other manuscripts claim to be direct copies of a 1693 CE manuscript, thus predating Priyadas's work by some two decades. The text includes parchai of sixteen saints: Kabir, Dhana, Trilochan, Namdev, Jaidev, Ravidas (Raidas), Mirabai, Karmabai, Pipa, Sen, Sadhana, Balmik (Valmiki), Sukhdev, Badhak, Dhruhi (Dhruv), and Prahlad. And like Anantadas's earlier works in this genre, the narratives include extended explanatory sections detailing the unidentified author's theological agenda.[117] Though composed in the language of Braj Bhasha,[118] the author incorporates many Punjabi idioms, and all known manuscripts are written in the Gurumukhi script used in the Punjab and among the Sikhs.

If even the Vallabhites, who were fellow Vaishnavas, seemingly rejected Mira on theological grounds, we might wonder how a woman so obsessed with her mountain-lifting Lord could find a home in the aniconic nirgun devotional world of the Sikhs, a community which also shares with the Pushtimarg, to some degree at least, an emphasis on the importance of their particular line of gurus. And yet the author of this text, writing for the court of the tenth and final Sikh guru, Gobind Singh, does find a way to bring Mira into this realm as the disciple of Raidas and as an embodiment of love for God, using her story to impart theological understanding but also clearly to entertain.[119] Indeed, the three-act narrative he weaves is more akin to later dramatic performances than to the tight structure of women saints' hagiographies outlined by Ramanujan. The question of how to be a devotee in a woman's body and to reconcile marriage and devotion occupies the *Prem Ambodh*'s author as well, but these challenges take on a vastly different character.

According to Hawley and Mann, the title of this text might best be translated "The Ocean of Love," with its focus on the One Divine Reality as Love.[120] The world and all that exists make possible the manifestation and actualization of divine love, and yet lover, love, and Divine Beloved are not separate but one reality, the relationship much like that of waves to a divine ocean. The stories of the saints found here, Hawley and Mann suggest, "are told in such a way as to demonstrate how the manifold undulations that connect lover, beloved, and love express the oceanic reality of all existence" and explore "how the feeling of love arises in the hearts of these exemplary persons and . . . the dramatic effects it has on their lives and on their families—the conundrums, the messes, and the eventual successes that make these saints the object of praise and affection."[121] Mira certainly embodies impassioned love in her relationship to Krishna, but this more aniconic understanding of love is a far cry from Vaishnava descriptions of the love play of Krishna among the gopis or of Mira's love for Krishna in the form of her gallant mountain-lifting Lord.[122]

Yet the author (whom we can reasonably assume to be male, given the context) draws Mira into this world in an ingenious way. First, he quickly establishes that she is a disciple of Raidas, a saint accepted within the Sikh tradition as we have noted but whom the *Prem Ambodh*'s author also presents as far more focused on love in his teachings than other sources do.[123] The author then jumps right into Mira's marriage—a marriage which has already happened between Mira and a rajput prince whose name just happens to be "Giridhar." In one stroke, husband and manifest Divine Beloved are conjoined. Her husband Giridhar is in fact God (referred to as "Ram" or "Hari"— more general names for the Divine beyond the specifics of avatars or myth). Giridhar inwardly knows this, but outwardly he appears enchanting but ordinary, his inner reality hidden. And is this not, in some sense, the case for all people, who appear so different even though "the Highest Teacher, the Highest Self, Ancient Person" resides in every heart?[124]

For her part, the *Prem Ambodh* suggests, Mira's devotion to God was "like the edge of a double-edged sword" (an image with clear connotations of cutting both spiritual and temporal ways for Sikhs, as Hawley and Mann note)— "a love without a shore" that could love the Divine in all but also could not love a man who did not love God. Because her husband would not say the name of Ram, she "took him for a beast" and refused to consummate the marriage, though she is portrayed as wanting very much to do so. Indeed Mirabai "aimed her love of God toward her beloved" and wanted to offer him everything, but she did not comprehend that her husband Giridhar was in fact her Lord "Giridhar, God Himself." If only he would speak the name of Ram and show devotion, then their love could manifest divine love, but he does not. She prays to Hari, sure that her past karma must have led to this disastrous marriage, "that's neither union nor true separation." She is portrayed as suffering terrible longing and hoping against hope that her husband will speak the name of Ram, even waiting night after night to hear if he should "babble the name of Ram as he dreams."[125]

Marriage does present a problem for Mira here, but only because she thinks that her husband (who is in fact God) is not even a devotee of God. The message is clear that marriage and bhakti are compatible, if both husband and wife are devotees and recognize each other as one with and inseparable from the Divine. With this realization, the Divine Beloved may be loved through the form of the human beloved. Equating devotees with the divine is not uncommon in devotional literature, and Nabhadas, too, frequently does so, but here this realization is applied directly to marital relations.[126] Devotion is primary—her husband must be a devotee in order to unify human and divine love in this way—but marriage and sexual pleasure are also thereby affirmed.

The way in which this all plays out in the *Prem Ambodh* is both clever and humorous, as Hawley and Mann detail. Mira is completely uncomprehending (even as the rana is of her love for Krishna in Priyadas's telling), and she learns the truth only after she finally hears her husband speak Ram's name in his sleep. She is delighted, and an explicit description is given of her arousal and joy, though she is too modest to wake him and spends the rest of the night gazing at him. This virgin Mira is all too ready to plunge into the pleasures of love-making once her conditions are met. In the morning she sounds a drum (as Nabhadas has her doing, but for a decidedly different reason), "calling Brahmans and ascetics as guests." Giving away her ornaments and "everything she owned," she tells her husband what she has heard him say. But when Giridhar hears that he has said the name of Ram, he is stunned to realize he has said the very words that a dying person should say before leaving this world. He immediately goes into a meditative state, and reaching liberation, he dies.[127]

Mira is beside herself. She realizes her error in not recognizing him and cannot believe her loss, shutting herself away in her room and refusing to speak to anyone. Not only does she not commit sati as her relatives expect, but she will not even attend the funeral rituals. No one can persuade her to snap out of it, and she sits locked away in an unwavering unconscious yogic pose until "the Friend of the World," the "Nondual Highest Person," finally comes to her door and asks her to open it. She returns to consciousness, and after expressing her anger at his deception, entreats him to take the form of Giridhar again. He does so, and she opens the door joyously. They engage in "the wondrous play of love" throughout the night. In that love, "[h]e stole away her ego, her consciousness of self, and showed himself as Self of All Three Worlds," and they were "as if two wicks burned in a single cruse." "One and two," the author writes, "that is just a way to tell a story," for "through love the many became one." Though Giridhar leaves at dawn, Mira is now fulfilled.[128]

As the second act begins, she becomes an ecstatic devotee and teacher (*pujari*), letting the ocean of love, which she has experienced and which she has become, flow out to those around her. Gone is the longing that had earlier characterized her life, and now she is a fully realized person, essentially assuming the role of a guru herself. As in Priyadas's account, she must still face the dangers that all women devotees do from men who see them as objects of desire and who feign religiosity, once again depicted through her encounter with a lascivious false sadhu. Reflecting what Mann identifies as "the Sikh emphasis on a strict ethical code for communal living," her actions, which may be outwardly condemned as immodest but are inwardly pure, are juxtaposed with the supposed external religiosity of this priestly figure who is inwardly corrupt and filled with wanton desire.[129] He approaches Mira burning with lust and entreats her, "For the love of Vishnu put out the fire." Because he asks in the name of God, Mira does not refuse, but when he steps forward to pursue his desire, his inner corruption is outwardly manifest as he collapses, his body "decompos[ing] like a leper." His own actions and character condemn him. Mira responds only with love, healing him and filling him with illuminating knowledge merely by looking at him, and he becomes her disciple.[130]

In the third act, the rana, her father, already angry at her immodest behavior, is further enraged hearing about this incident and tries to poison her, but to no avail—miraculously nothing seems to harm her. Her persecutor here is clearly identified as a ruler of Mewar and her father. People of all four castes keep coming to her home, their fevers, physical or otherwise, cooled and their wishes fulfilled. Infuriated by this breach of caste dharma, the rana enters her chamber with a raised sword only to be brought up short by a vision of Krishna in his four-armed form, *chakra* (Vishnu's spinning discus) in hand, listening to his daughter sing. He is captivated and remains completely absorbed in the beauty of sight and sound as the Lord accompanies Mira on his flute. Finally he flees, overwhelmed and filled with fear, unable to fully comprehend what he saw, either the first time or when he returns again to the threshold. In the end, these experiences lead directly to her parents' conversion, the tale closing with them repenting of their persecution of their daughter and saying, "Now you are no longer our daughter, [y]ou are Hari's servant, and Hari himself." In the story of Mira's disciple Karmabai that follows her own, Mirabai is said simply to have lived in Udaipur (the capital of Mewar established by Udaisingh in 1559 after the city of Chittor fell).[131]

Clearly the Mira of this Sikh text from the Punjab is quite different from the Mira of Priyadas's Vaishnava Vrindavan tale, though the intensity of her love is key to both. Here her love for God in the form of Girdhar Nagar, the gallant Mountain Bearer, is superimposed on her love for a human husband. This *pati* who is both husband and Lord is understood to be a manifestation of the one "Nondual Highest Person," as his lover Mira is, and their immersion in the play of love is simultaneously an affirmation of embodied pleasure and intimacy and a quite nirgun realization that true love for any manifest reality is, in the final analysis, love for the One Divine Reality, as all sense of separateness of self or God dissolves in the ocean of love that is that Reality.

Even so Mira is portrayed humorously as a woman of very human passions, and in the first act, the story takes on the character of a romantic comedy. Devotion to God is shown as fully compatible with devotion to a husband (or wife, presumably), with human love-making manifesting divine love—when the two are both devotees, that is. The lust of the false sadhu in act 2 stands in stark contrast to the purity of this marital desire, his hypocrisy exposed as the audience is again warned that things are not always what they seem on the surface. The Mira portrayed is indeed "more friendly to 'family values,'" as Hawley and Mann suggest, never coming into conflict with in-laws or arousing her spouse's anger, though it is clear that she does insist on "subordinating marital practice to a higher dharma" in her initial testing of her husband.[132]

Did the author and those initially listening to the *Prem Ambodh* know other stories of Mira similar to Priyadas's telling? They must have, as the *Prem Ambodh* narrative gains much of its amusement and appeal from this contrast with what might be otherwise expected, not only in Mira's attitude toward her worldly husband but also in many other details of the story.[133] The tension between the couple is caused by her rather than him; she rather than her princely husband is uncomprehending; she refuses to consummate the marriage, but for very different reasons; and she tests her husband's devotion rather than having to prove her own to Jiv Goswami or some other religious authority. She locks herself in rather than others confining her, and God asks her to open the door rather than the angry rana bursting in, his intent not murder but love.

The highly sagun character of Mira's devotion to Krishna sets the stage for its astonishing transformation into a devotion not only compatible with but exemplary of the nirgun Sikh tradition, her affiliation with Raidas suggesting its originating source (though in this narrative it is God who actually serves as her true guru, her Satguru, in bringing her realization, rather than Raidas). The details of her early life seemingly have no relevance here; knowing that she is a royal woman from Rajasthan is sufficient. There is no childhood origin alleged for her devotion or any indication of a marriage against her will. Her marital family plays no part, her persecutor clearly named as her father, and all the action takes place within the domestic sphere. There is no mention of Akbar, hardly surprising given that hostility rather than patronage marked Sikh-Mughal relations in this time.[134] Priyadas, composing several decades after the author of the *Prem Ambodh*, paints a very different picture, though both authors clearly draw from at least some of the same preexisting streams of traditions about Mira and other saints.

Priyadas might even have been countering elements like those found in the *Prem Ambodh*, but no definitive relationship can be established between these two texts. Further, the *Prem Ambodh*'s particular "test" episode related to Mira's marriage does not appear elsewhere in any currently known sources, and there is no evidence that this specific text circulated outside of the Sikh community and the Punjab, with all known copies in Gurumukhi script.[135] Was the *Prem Ambodh* portrayal of Mira in the first act simply too human for those outside this community and region to have wanted to repeat it? Was its description of Mira's erotic desire for her very human husband beyond the pale of acceptability or plausibility for the saint, straying too far from hagiographic norms for women saints' lives and undoing what for some is the linchpin upon which Mira's story turns? Some nationalist and rajput historians centuries later would proclaim her happily married, but they would discreetly say nothing more about this period of her life, save those who would declare her continued virginity with her husband's support. Indeed we do not see such an explicit portrayal of a receptive Mira resurface until international businessman, author, and public intellectual Gurcharan Das's avant-garde play *Mira* premiered to critical acclaim in New York City in 1970 and then in Mumbai, New Delhi, Ahmedabad, Chennai, and elsewhere—a very different time and context and decidedly not a bhakti telling.[136]

The *Prem Ambodh*'s author was composing for the court of Guru Gobind Singh, who was both the temporal and the spiritual leader of the Sikh community, and the drama clearly reflects both temporal and spiritual concerns—a nirgun theology coupled with a householder tradition affirming "family values." In Priyadas's telling (and the streams of tradition upon which he drew that were clearly familiar also to the *Prem Ambodh*'s author), Mira is not a ready advocate of either. It is also the case that even before the *Prem Ambodh* was composed, the one song attributed to Mira earlier included in the Sikh scripture had been removed from the finalized canonical version, as we have noted. Did this ejection make her fair game for a bit of fun by 1693? Moreover, was the *Prem Ambodh*'s author not only having a little fun with the saint for his audience's entertainment, but in fact, to some degree at least, making fun of her, perhaps at the expense also of more sagun Vaishnava theological formulations and their blatantly erotic descriptions of the love play of Radha and Krishna? In the next two acts, he then retrieves her, but only after her transformation through nirgun realization into a more "supernal" (Hawley and Mann's term) if rather generic figure and after her wifely responsibilities had ended.[137] Shadows of the sagun Vaishnava Mira who composed impassioned love songs for her flute-playing Lord remain, particularly in Mira's father's vision of Krishna listening to his daughter sing that culminates in his conversion. But even so, "one has the impression that the saint is less important than the sermon the author wants to give" (as Callewaert observes with regard to Anantadas's tales in this genre).[138] That the *Prem Ambodh*'s parchai of Mirabai might have gone over well within the Sikh community but not so well with those beyond it is evidenced by the existence of multiple manuscript copies but very limited circulation. Seemingly it was relished as an insiders' tale, but not necessarily meant for or finding traction with other audiences.

Nevertheless, the existence of Priyadas's and the *Prem Ambodh*'s very different tales suggest that Mirabai was already widely known by the beginning of the eighteenth century, with all kinds of stories about her readily moving back and forth across the boundaries of religious affiliation and language and marked by an intimate and playful familiarity and affection for the saint that allowed tellers to see her as a member of their own community, even to have fun with her, sometimes at her expense or that of their rivals.[139] Diverse traditions were clearly circulating associating Mirabai's natal family with Merta in Marwar when the persecuting rana was her husband or father-in-law and with Udaipur in Mewar when he was her father, lauding her guru as Raidas and depicting her as having no guru apart from Krishna himself, speaking variously of her travels to Vrindavan and Dwarka and of her encounters with a lustful sadhu, the Muslim ruler Akbar, and Jiv Goswami of the Gaudiya sampraday. Clearly also both the *Prem Ambodh* (with its emphasis on the oceanic oneness of Mira and God through love and on upright moral conduct) and Priyadas's *Bhaktirasabodhini* (with its contrasting male-female relations) reflect the religious milieus within which they emerged, so that from these earliest accounts we find those who tell Mirabai's story particularizing the tale. As a result what we have is Priyadas's Mira and the *Prem Ambodh*'s Mira, rather than any singular or originating presentation of the saint's life.

In spite of their differences, however, these two tellings do have much in common. Both present Mirabai as a woman who pursues devotion to God with her total being, fully participating in the Divine and in the devotional community and as the virtual embodiment of Love. And both portray the challenge to a woman who practices such complete and public devotion, from men in the outside world who see her merely as an object of sexual desire. Yet mortal danger comes not from an outsider but from men within her own family, whether it be her natal or marital kin. The values of bhakti and the norms of the social world come into conflict with each other, at least on the surface level. Ultimately bhakti is stronger—Mira does not die from the poison, her parents come to understand and embrace this path in the *Prem Ambodh*, and she cannot be forced to return to the court in Priyadas's telling but finds her ultimate home in Krishna. Other tellings will share many of these elements.

An Emerging Devotional Literary Tradition

These and other stories of Mira are not merely the creation of individuals but clearly partake of and contribute to a broad stream of circulating written and performance traditions. Even Priyadas's telling is in fact very compact; he appears to assume that his audience is already familiar with the episodes related, each in a few short lines. The *Prem Ambodh*'s author does not seem compelled to provide a backstory or every detail either; he too assumes his audience's familiarity with Mirabai and uses this both to teach and to entertain. As performed texts, both undoubtedly would have been elaborated in a variety of ways, and in the case of Priyadas's text, his condensed style invited further commentary and left considerable room for clarification and elaboration by later commentators with a variety of motivations, some of whose written compositions have been preserved.

For example, Priyadas's grandson Vaishnavdas is reported to have written such a commentary on his work, entitled *Bhaktamal ki Drishtant*, around 1750 CE.[140] Among other things, Vaishnavdas seems to have been disturbed by the possibility left open by Priyadas that Akbar and Tansen came for darshan of Mira (an understanding held by most subsequent commentators and many other tellers). In his commentary, Vaishnavdas seeks to correct what he evidently sees as a misconception, making very clear that Akbar and his court musician came inspired by Mira's songs but only to see the image of Girdhar Gopal. According to Vaishnavdas, Tansen composed his verse invoking Mira's name, not because they met her but because she is the quintessential devotee of

Krishna in this form. The perceived necessity for such a clarification suggests that he wished to discredit the far more romantic and popular story of Akbar's direct meeting with the royal rajput devotee, perhaps because such a story about Mira was offensive to his and others' devotional and/or political sensibilities. If the author and date of this work are accurate and the passage on Mira original to it, then his comments, at the very least, suggest that the more elaborate story was in circulation and that Mira's broad appeal to devotees of God, both Hindu and Muslim, was recognized in mid-eighteenth-century Vrindavan even as it may have been in Akbar's or at least Priyadas's time.

Nabhadas's bhaktamal of c. 1600 CE and Priyadas's 1712 CE commentary also directly inspired others to write bhaktamals and attendant commentaries styled after theirs, initiating an ongoing hagiographic literary tradition. Some relied very heavily on these earlier works, as did Dhruvdas, a disciple of Hit Harivamsh's son Gopinath and an instrumental figure in the formalization of the Radhavallabh sampraday. He acknowledges his debt to Nabhadas in his similarly inclusive *Bhaktanamavali*, composed several decades later, and his description of Mirabai largely mirrors Nabhadas's words.[141] He does, however, describe her as dancing with *kartals* in her hands—rhythm instruments of wood with metal jingles (resembling the edge of a tambourine in structure and also making a similar sound). Mira is popularly portrayed with this common devotional instrument in later paintings and images. And he further identifies those who gave her poison as "relatives" (not just "wicked ones"), who were filled with remorse after her miraculous survival.

Writing considerably before Priyadas, Dhruvdas also speaks of Mira wandering in the pleasure fields of Vrindavan. His poetic reference might be read in either of two ways: as describing a pilgrimage to a geographic location undertaken with a woman called Lalita (who is said in some later accounts to be Mira's maidservant and companion) or as describing an internal spiritual journey Mira takes in the company of the *sakhi* Lalita (Radha's girlfriend, who facilitates her friend's trysts with Krishna) into the eternal and transcendent realm of Vrindavan, where the heart dwells and embodied souls find their true identities, in accord with Radhavallabh teachings.[142]

Mira's travels become a standard part of hagiography, including Priyadas's account (though not the *Prem Ambodh*, as Hawley and Mann point out).[143] Indeed it is assumed that she must have gone to all the pilgrimage sites relating to Krishna (and some that are not), and there are stories of her travels not only to Vrindavan and Dwarka but also to Dakor, Nathdwara, Kashi (Banaras) or the Ganges River, Pushkar, and elsewhere.[144] Dhruvdas may be doing the same in making reference to such travels, but given his standing as a Radhavallabh theologian, he may also be portraying Mira as an ideal devotee of this sampraday, immersed in the eternal and transcendent realm of Vrindavan and experiencing the highest spiritual state as a sakhi herself, watching the sport of Radha and Krishna with pleasure in the forests of Braj.[145] And his account might even have been the seed for the growth of later tales of her travels and of her maidservant Lalita, just as easily as it might incorporate already existing traditions or carry the remembrance of her actual companion and a physical pilgrimage.

Raghavdas, a former Vaishnava who joined the nirgun Dadupanth, also writes of Mira in his bhaktamal some sixty years after Nabhadas and some decades still before the *Prem Ambodh*'s author or Priyadas.[146] Though his description is again similar to that of Nabhadas, he includes additional details, emphasizing Mira's acceptance of Vaishnava teachings and her fearless singing in the company of sants as the reasons that not just despicable people want her dead but specifically "the rana" (the ruler of Mewar), whom he identifies as "in all this great world . . . the enemy of Mirabai." Raghavdas's self-identification as a rajput and former Vaishnava might account for this greater specificity regarding her persecutor and his motives, as might his awareness of such a circulating tradition, even a memory, in rajput circles.[147] Further, he emphasizes that Mira not only abandoned social norms and family but also renounced the joys of the world (as he and his fellow Dadupanthi renouncers had done) and that she adored God as a wife would her husband. In describing her, Raghavdas refers to Mira's Lord not only as the Mountain Bearer but also as Ram and Hari (as the *Prem Ambodh*'s author would), thereby placing her story more fully within his larger agenda of lifting up the four aniconic nirgun *panths*, or paths, laid out by Dadu, Nanak, Kabir, and Haridas Niranjani, which he portrays as the fulfillment of the lineages first manifest in the Vaishnava four sampradays (to which Nabhadas and Anantadas make reference and which would become increasingly important in Priyadas's time).[148] Raghavdas classifies all the saints about whom he writes within this double fourfold rubric of panths and sampradays, and in doing so he assigns Mira, with Narsi Mehta, to the lineage of Vishnuswami and thus of Vallabhacharya (in distinct contrast to the *Vartas* composed in the same period). Perhaps, as Hawley suggests, this might reflect Raghavdas's awareness of the two saints' mutual association with Gujarat and the strength of the Vallabhites in that region by the mid-seventeenth century as well as his general need to find a place for the otherwise independent Mira.[149] One might also wonder, however, whether his designation might be evidence of an early Vallabhite affinity for the saint, one that might in fact have fueled the *Vartas*' need to distance her.[150]

Chaturdas comments (c. 1800 CE) on Raghavdas's text, following Priyadas's text closely, even as Raghavdas and others followed Nabhadas in composing their bhaktamals. However, he simplifies a number of difficult lines, seemingly resolving ambiguities by drawing on popular traditions or just deleting intractable phrases.[151] He, too, incorporates small additional details, including the fact that Mira's clothing was left behind draped across the image when she merged with Krishna at Dwarka. Mira's continued place in Dhruvdas's and Raghavdas's bhaktamals and Chaturdas's commentary further demonstrates the breadth of her popularity, not only among Vaishnavas of different persuasions but also among followers of more aniconic nirgun traditions, with their added details revealing the diversity of claims swirling around her.

A number of other bhaktamals and attendant commentaries would emerge in various regional languages by tellers with a broad range of religious affiliations and motives, the garland expanding as authors added selectively to the number and range of saints described but continuing to include Mira's tale.[152] Among them is Ram Soni's 1682 Afghan bhaktamal written in Persian, reflecting Islamic cultural influence and incorporating elements of *tazkira* (a Persian biographical genre employed by Sufis that may conceivably also have influenced Nabhadas).[153] For the most part Mira is not central to these authors' particular sectarian agendas, but as an immensely popular saint, her tale is included with subtle variations, seemingly in an effort to draw on her appeal (as well as that of Nabhadas and Priyadas) for each author's individual cause, her presence also reinforcing the inclusive rather than exclusive dimensions of their arguments and signaling a broader transsectarian shared bhakti sensibility and belonging.

Structural parallels and similarities in content regarding their presentations of Mira (and other saints) make it clear that Nabhadas's and Priyadas's tellings were widely known, familiar to the authors and at least to some degree accepted as a standard presentation of Mira's life within these literate devotional circles, and beyond. Nabhadas's and Priyadas's own works would continue to be reproduced, performed, and translated with an ongoing tradition of both oral and written explication and expansion across the centuries to the present day. Nevertheless, there would also be other narratives, of which the *Prem Ambodh* is merely the earliest of which we have documentation, that depart quite significantly from Priyadas and strike out in very different directions, reminding us once again that Priyadas's telling is by no means the first or original, its author clearly drawing at least in part on already existing traditions known also to the *Prem Ambodh*'s author. And no doubt these texts provide us with only a very limited slice of the traditions circulating about Mirabai in these early centuries in any case.

Even so, the available accounts do point to a remarkable woman who lived seemingly sometime before the end of the sixteenth century, a woman of such strength and authenticity that she caught people's hearts and imaginations, embodying devotion and defiance, suffering and survival, and so much more, and staking out a distinctly new terrain in the imaginary of the feminine. She is a figure who inhabits the margins of society and sampraday, or perhaps more accurately, her story plays out in centers of confluence—where sagun and nirgun devotion overlap and merge; where Hindu and Muslim, women and men, low caste and high might meet on equal ground as devotees of God; where individual desires and social norms, humanity and hierarchy collide; where renunciation and passion, enjoyment, and bliss are mutually valued; where hope and despair, violence and love coexist; and where pasts and presents converge. Hers is indeed one of those great human stories, at once universal and the tale of an individual woman in a distinct time and place, inspiring yet also troubling, compelling people to tell it again and again in new yet familiar ways.

2
Participation and Transformation
Mira as Rapjut Renouncer, Varkari Devotee, and *Pativrata* of God

Satsang, that is, the gathering of the good or virtuous people to cultivate devotion, is seen as essential to following the bhakti path, and the collective remembering of the lives of exemplary devotees of the past is a fundamental discipline, or *sadhana,* for further deepening love for God and embodying the love that is God. An overwhelming affection for Mirabai motivates many to want to participate in her life, both through the telling and performance of her tale and as fully engaged audience members. In this context such remembering—as Christian Lee Novetzke suggests with respect to the public memory of Maharashtrian saint Namdev—is not "marked by the logic of time and place, set in the language of proof and fact" but rather "makes connections freely, dips into shared pools of legend, and forms associations that are inherently social," its area of concern "the shape of the soul" rather than historical accuracy.[1] So it is with Mirabai. Playful, dynamic, entertaining, transformative—such remembrances of Mira's life connect past and present in the lives of communities, staking out and shaping identities, asserting and embodying values, and giving voice and meaning to experiences, religious and otherwise. Stories told and committed to writing in the latter half of the eighteenth and the early nineteenth centuries often depart significantly from the literary models initiated by Nabhadas and Priyadas, reflecting not only the narrative constraints of alternative hagiographic genres and the religious and social contexts and concerns of their own tellers and audiences (even as those of Priyadas and the *Prem Ambodh* do) but also the participatory nature of bhakti itself and the fundamental orality of Indian storytelling and religion.

Some tellers invite listeners to cultivate a Mira-like devotion by entering deep into her world, in much the same way that Vaishnava devotees across the centuries have entered into the mythic narratives of Vishnu's incarnations. In the songs of the ninth-century South Indian saint Nammalvar, for example, the poet-saint brings the listener into the story of Vishnu's dwarf incarnation Vamana at the point when Vamana has secured a boon from the demon Bali.

Bali has offered him whatever he desires as a reward for his faithful service, and Vamana requests only sovereignty over as much land as he can cover in three strides. Laughing at the foolishness of the dwarf, Bali readily agrees, and suddenly Vamana grows to cosmic proportions and strides across the three worlds. Having made the unbreakable offer of a boon, the demon Bali must surrender his dominance.

Nammalvar brings this story out of a distant past into the present moment, up close and personal.[2] Listening to his song, we find ourselves standing right there beside Vamana, experiencing the overwhelming power and immensity of God as he grows from diminutive dwarf to cosmic Lord. Those who hear Nammalvar's songs are also led into the pastoral world of Krishna's incarnation and into the presence of the ravishingly handsome youthful cowherd, as they and the gopis become one in the desire to be touched and possessed by him.[3] In a very similar way, some bhakta tellers of Mira's tale draw listeners into her story so that they, too, become participants in its dramatic unfolding. Listening, we are there, standing in the room with an intimate view of the happenings in her life, able to hear the inflections of her voice and to read the emotions on her face as well as those of the other characters, seeing what she sees and feeling what she feels.

Other tellers will draw Mira into their own world, telling her story in the vernacular of their own lives and religious practices. Even as bhaktas across the centuries have sung of God in their mother tongue and worshiped regionally specific forms of Vishnu, Shiva, and the Devi, so will devotees speak of Mira in the idioms of their own lives. As the embodiment of bhakti, she comes to embody *their* forms of bhakti, practicing in *their* specific ways and experiencing God as *they* do. And in the intimacy of this vernacular translation, she becomes a well-loved member of their devotional family, one who speaks their language and shares their struggles and their values, hopes, and dreams.

Still other tellers will expand Mira's story, lingering over and relishing each moment and detail of the story as they draw on material from a wide range of circulating written and oral sources and creatively imagine aspects of her life not covered in other tellings. There is so much that Priyadas, for example, does not tell us. Even in her father's house she was "immersed in the Beloved Mountain Bearer," but how did the little girl Mirabai act out that childhood devotion? And how did her mother and her playmates respond to her behavior? When she came of age, what did she think of the marriage arranged for her? Did she protest when her parents told her, ignore them, or accept their wishes? What kind of marriage ceremony took place? What were her thoughts and feelings? What of her husband? What was their relationship, and what did he think of her actions? What did she say to him and others she encountered and they to her? Under what circumstances did she compose her songs? And what previous life could have possibly led to the appearance of such a saint?

To ask and answer such questions, expanding the narrative, is an act of loving engagement, much like the questions raised by bhaktas about the epic *Ramayana*, answered and recorded in vast compendiums of "doubts," or *shankavalis*.[4] Though we might associate the raising of doubts with challenges to belief, the devotees who ask these questions about a wide range of characters' actions in the Rama story do so in a spirit of respectful devotion and out of desire for ever greater intimacy, wanting to know more as a way to prolong and enhance the experience and enjoyment of the text and to draw closer to the Divine. In Mira's case the explications of her life are not necessarily the result of direct doubts or questioning of seemingly problematic actions or contradictions, but they are equally ways of loving engagement in the narrative and devotion to the one about whom the narrative speaks, even while addressing aspects of her behavior as a woman, a rajput no less, that might be troubling to some.

In filling out these details and lingering over the tale, the tellers have the opportunity to offer reflections on a number of religious and social themes, even as the answers offered in the shankavalis do. In this way the telling of Mira's tale becomes an occasion for religious and social teaching, crossing over into the tradition of *katha* (didactic storytelling), a highly developed and respected form of popular religious preaching particularly in Vaishnava devotional gatherings in North India. The stories expounded in traditional kathas are most often those of Krishna's incarnation found in the *Bhagavata Purana* or of Rama and Sita especially as they are recorded in the *Ramcharitmanas* of Tulsidas, but Mira's story readily enters into this terrain.[5]

In the eighteenth and nineteenth centuries these ways of participating in Mirabai's life contribute to the burgeoning narrative traditions that surround her. The crowned prince, rightful king, and great devotee Nagridas would weave together song and narrative to comment on Mira's life from both a devotional and a royal rajput perspective. The great Maharashtrian hagiographer Mahipati would translate Mira's story into the Varkari religious milieu, and the Rajasthani author of miracle stories of the saints, Sukhsaran, would compose a tale which both describes Mira's miraculous life and offers more ordinary women advice on how to balance bhakti and domestic responsibilities. And many others would contribute further details of encounters, words exchanged, a glance or movement, creatively expanding the standard elements of saints' lives or adding something borrowed or something entirely new, each teller dipping into the characters, relationships, and events that mark Mira's story to tell a distinct and yet recognizable tale.

Figure 2.1 Mira and her cousin Jaimal worshiping Charbhuja, the four-armed form of Vishnu, in the temple associated with her natal family in Merta. Painting from the collection of Rajasthan Shodh Sansthan, Chaupasani, Jodhpur, undated.

Nagridas's *Padaprasangmala*: Rejecting Power and Privilege

The great devotee known as "Nagridas" (1699–1764 CE) is said to be the author of the hagiographic compendium the *Padaprasangmala* (Garland of the Occasions for Songs) in which Mira's story is featured.[6] In this text, rather than trying to present complete life stories, the author takes songs, or *padas,* of various saints and weaves them together with narrative, integrating song and story to distill the essence of each saint's character and devotion. In Mirabai's case, he draws six songs attributed to her into a series of vignettes that show her dedication, persecution, and renunciation, and he also includes a seventh song of Mira in the story of another saint, Narayandas Natava.[7] In his recounting of Mira's life, we hear her direct speech, revealing her passionate and intimate feelings, and Nagridas draws his audience into the place and time of the songs' composition, to witness these events as if firsthand and to share Mira's emotions—her deep longing, her defiant resistance to coercion, and her overwhelming love of God.

As Savant Singh, Nagridas ("Radha's servant") had been heir to the throne of Kishangarh (in central Rajasthan, roughly forty-five miles east of Merta), but after his father's death in 1748, his position was usurped by his half-brother Bahadur Singh. Though Nagridas eventually managed to win back a portion of his former kingdom, he turned this over to his son and abandoned his royal life to settle permanently in the vicinity of Vrindavan, the land of Krishna's youthful incarnation. Even as crown prince he had inspired and served as patron for a new school of miniature painting (identified as the Kishangarh style) in which devotional themes, particularly portrayals of Radha and Krishna, were prominent, and he had already begun to write devotional poetry in addition to anthologizing the poems of other saints. He was a Rathor rajput, belonging to the royal line of Mira's purported natal family, and has been alternately claimed as a member of the Vallabha and Nimbarka sampradays.

Nagridas begins his presentation of Mira in the *Padaprasangmala* at the death of her husband—an occurrence not mentioned in the bhaktamals and commentaries we have examined thus far, though it is an element of the *Prem Ambodh* story. In Nagridas's telling, his death rather conveniently separates Mira's radical devotion from her marital responsibilities and her husband from her persecutor. Nagridas is silent about her life before this time, however, except to say that her devotion to Krishna continued as before. The rana (who is explicitly said to be her husband's older brother, in contrast to other accounts) insists that Mira end her own life in an act of sati, immolating herself with her husband's body on his funeral pyre—but this is something she steadfastly refuses to do, answering her brother-in-law with a song she composes, writes down, and sends to him:

>   Mira's dyed in Hari's color,
>   blocking out every other hue.
>   I will sing for the One who lifts the mountain,
>   No sati will I be.
>
>   My mind is enchanted by the One named
>   for the storm clouds, heavy with rain.[8]
>   Ranaji, "husband's elder brother," "sister-in-law"—
>   these relations are meaningless.
>   I am his servant and he my Lord.

My bangles are only of auspicious grass;
>   Tilak and rosary, fasting and chastity my only ornaments.
> No other adornment pleases me, Ranaji;
>   The guru's knowledge is mine.
>
> Some condemn me,
>   Some praise me—
> I sing of the Cowherd's charms,
>   And walk the road traveled by the sants.
>
> Not by robbing or tormenting me
>   Can anyone make me do otherwise—
> One who has mounted an elephant
>   Won't climb up on an ass—
>   Such a thing cannot be!
>
> Those who rule are denizens of hell;
>   Pleasure seekers go to the God of Death.
> Those who engage in devotion win release;
>   Those who follow yogic discipline live.
>
> The Mountain Bearer is my husband [and Lord], my family;
>   The Mountain Bearer my mother, father, son, brother.
> Yours to you! Mine to me, O Rana! says Mirabai.[9]

Mira is strong and impassioned, and we hear her voice directly. Unintimidated before the king, she does not mince words in making clear what she thinks of those in power. She refuses to burn with her supposed earthly husband's body in an act of sati and admits no marriage to him and no widowhood. She rejects the outward marks of marriage, even as a widow of her caste would be required to do, but she does so because they have no value or place in her devotion. And she actively redefines her relationship with her brother-in-law, her identity no longer based on familial relations of any kind, either natal or marital, but solely on her relationship to God. By portraying her as taking this stand only after her husband's death, the challenge her behavior might offer to the normative behavior of a wife and thus family and rajput honor is mitigated, though not entirely erased, for she denies the validity of the marriage in the first place. Neither her critique of power nor of gender roles offers a true agenda for social revolution as presented here. Rather she proclaims a vision of the devotional life, pitted against the ways of the world, a world in which she wants no part and which she renounces utterly.

With the next song, Nagridas shows us how Mira responds to the rana's continuing harassment. She persists in associating with other devotees and refuses to cultivate relationships with those to whom she is related by ties of birth and marriage. Realizing this and knowing that he has no leverage over her, the rana decides to kill her. But instead of dying, Mira ties bells to her ankles, picks up a drum, and sings a new song of devotion:

> I knew it was poison the rana sent—
> I knew, but they said it was the nectar
>   poured over my Beloved's feet,
>   [so] I drank it knowingly—
>   I was neither crazy nor beguiled.
>
> Like gold tested on a stone,
>   My body pure, I lived!
> The Mountain Bearer himself was the judge,
>   separating milk from water.
>
> Rana, I'm sold into his hands
>   The One for whom I'd make a million sacrifices.
> Mira clings to the lotus feet
>   of that gallant Mountain Bearer.

Again the rana is shown as having no power over Mira, his violent intentions neutralized by her purity and the miraculous intervention of her Lord. She leaves the palace and begins a life of wandering first to the Ganges River, then to Vrindavan, where she meets Jiv Goswami, and then to Dwarka. On the way to Dwarka she composes another song, filled with longing and descriptions of her Lord, asking him to allow her to reside there with him. She appeals to him, for, having abandoned her former country and past identity, her honor now rests in his hands. Again Nagridas gives the full text of the song.

After she reaches Dwarka, brahmans who are said to be accompanying her insist it is time for her to return to the rana, suggesting that she is still nominally under his control and thus making her request that Krishna allow her to remain at Dwarka even more urgent. Mira turns again to her Lord in song, asking him to help her and reminding him—and perhaps also herself—that wherever there is sorrow, he feels the pain. Within this song, Mira draws on the examples of Krishna's protective intervention on behalf of Draupadi, Prahlad, and a drowning elephant in her request that he now save her (and other saints will add Krishna's miraculous protection of Mira when she drinks the poison to their list of rescued devotees in similar supplications).[10] In Nagridas's telling, Krishna does not disappoint her, but in the instant before he takes her into a final embrace, she sings one last song:

> Lover, you know how I feel—
>   Please remember me.
>
> Except you, I have no one—
>   O King, be kind to me.
>
> No hunger comes in the day, no sleep in the night;
>   this body destroyed as each second passes.
>
> Mira's Lord is the gallant Mountain Bearer;
>   Now that I have found you,
>   don't leave me behind!

Nagridas is careful to tell us just how these last two songs were recorded for posterity since Mira sang them when she went into the temple alone: her clever Vaishnava women friends (sakhis) standing near the door overheard, memorized, and later wrote down her words. In this song her divine lover, protector, and king stands in radical contrast to the all too human rana.

In a final song Nagridas invites his audience to listen to Mira sing of the agony that Krishna's absence brings her, as she transforms the language of separated lovers into the lamentations of an embodied soul longing for union with the Divine. A woman sent by the rana to betray her becomes her ally when she overhears Mira singing:

> Sister, sleep is destroyed.
> Gazing down the road for my beloved,
>   the whole night slips away.
> Friends come with advice,
>   but my mind hears nothing.
>
> Without seeing [my Beloved], I find no peace,
>   such is my heart's resolve.
> My body is weak, and I am restless;
>   my only words, "dear one, dear one,"
>   [echo the cuckoo's plaintive cry].

> Lifeless within, the agony of separation invisible from without.
> Like a *chatak* bird crying out again and again for the cloud
>   [and the raindrops that will quench its terrible thirst,]
>   or a fish out of water [dying on the shore];
> Mira, the distraught lover far from her Beloved,
>   loses memory, consciousness and sense.[11]

Nagridas identifies the listening woman as belonging to a different caste than Mira but says explicitly that for those in love with the Lord, caste is of no consequence.[12]

The songs Nagridas chooses to contextualize in this telling reflect Mira's deep love and longing for her Lord, her rejection of the rana and his world, and her vulnerability. The rana appears uncomprehending, worldly, and cruel, driven by desire and rage. Mira in contrast is a picture of strength, purity, and commitment to God, a woman who takes charge of her own life yet also depends heavily on God, who stands at the center of that chosen life. Nagridas presents the rana in a more negative manner than does Priyadas, perhaps influenced by his own royal background and his experience of the intrigues and viciousness of the power struggles within the court and between rival kingdoms. Yet he presents Mira's actions and words not only as an indictment of despotic kingship and the corruption that such power brings but also and even more as the renunciation of worldly values and the affirmation of devotional ones. His observation that caste means nothing in the context of devotion is part of a larger argument running through the text regarding the true nature of bhakti, though also perhaps reflective of his own intimate relationship with his courtesan mistress and companion in bhakti and poetry, Rasik Bihari. His overriding aim, however, is to draw those who hear his tale into Mira's presence, so that they, like the woman sent by the rana to betray Mira, may be touched and transformed by this intimate experience of her utter love for her Lord articulated in song.

That Mira's songs (and those of other bhaktas) have such power is also attested by another reference that Nagridas makes to Mira. In the tale of Narayandas Natava, this bhakta is dancing to a song of Mira, and in the midst of the song, he is so overcome with ecstasy that he freezes in the *tribhanga* pose of Krishna, his life ending as he is swept up directly into heaven.[13] Not everyone has sufficient love to experience these songs in this way, but if one enters fully into them, as Narayandas Natava does, the songs of the saints and particularly Mira's songs do have this liberative force. Nagridas in his *Padaprasangmala* invites his audience to experience Mira in this way through his interweaving of narrative and song, as will other tellers and performers of Mira across the centuries.

What more might we be able to say about Mira and the traditions that surround her based on this particular text and its author? We know that Nagridas was a Rathor rajput of royal heritage and thus Mira's natal kin (by most accounts), so we might reasonably conclude that, in the mid-eighteenth century, at least some members of Mira's natal family knew her story and admired her, in spite of her virtual absence in historical chronicles of their caste and kingdoms (with a possible exception of one reference in the seventeenth-century *Nainsi ri Khyat*, which we will examine in the next chapter and which does not figure in Nagridas's account). Yet the *Padaprasangmala* is undated and unsigned, appears in multiple and variable manuscripts with and without the section on Mirabai, and culminates with poems bearing the *chap*, or "signature," of Nagri but also includes other poems praising his works.

Heidi Pauwels has studied Nagridas's life and works in detail, and with respect to the *Padaprasangmala* she concludes that the stories therein likely "floated around among Nāgarīdās's entourage: some told by him, some by the [Vallabhan temple] priests, some perhaps by courtiers and visiting holy men [and that] Nāgarīdās may well have requested them to be anthologized."[14] The materials thus appear to have circulated orally for some time before being committed to writing, with the available manuscripts reflecting the fluid and participatory nature of performance. Internal references to Rupnagar, the portion of the kingdom Nagridas won back for his son, suggest that it must have been completed after his brother usurped the throne (1748) and likely after Nagridas had settled in Braj (1752), with the peace treaty being signed in 1756 dividing the kingdom.[15] The earliest dated manuscripts Pauwels located were from early 1792 and include colophons attributing the text to Nagridas, and it quickly became very popular judging by the proliferation of manuscripts.[16]

Is it likely the passages on Mira might be among those Nagridas himself composed? There is no way to know for sure, but he praises Mira as one of his "holy sages" in another work, clearly written by him—an anthology titled *Garland of Songs of Awakening*—confirming his appreciation of her by the time of his father's death.[17] He also includes one of her songs in another devotional anthology titled *String of Song-Pearls*.[18] Further, a painting in the Kishangarh Royal Collection from the latter half of the eighteenth century appears to show Mirabai engaged with others in worship in a temple.[19] Though admittedly precisely what is going on in this painting is a bit unclear, Mira is seated and dressed in white with a halo, setting her apart from other figures. She holds something in her outstretched hand, in an awkward gesture. Pauwels posits that she may be holding a cup upside down to show it is empty, the painting thus depicting her poisoning and possibly commissioned to illustrate the *Padaprasangmala,* as at least one other painting appears to have been.[20] This evidence suggests that the passages about Mirabai could indeed have been composed by Nagridas himself and potentially also indicates an ongoing tradition of honoring Mira among the Rathor rajputs of the Kishangarh Court and beyond. It must be admitted, however, that Nagridas's familiarity with the saint might have come to him through devotional sources quite apart from family heritage, though it is also the case that others among the Rathors, in addition to Nagridas, were widely recognized for their devotion, so the two may not be mutually exclusive.

What of the particular details that are not in known earlier devotional accounts: the placement of her radical devotion after the death of her husband, naming her husband's elder brother as her persecutor, the indication that she was properly accompanied by an entourage of brahmans in her pilgrimage, and the careful explanation of how some of her songs were written down by herself and her companions? Do these reflect a wider rajput memory of actual events or an idealized collective recollection of the past? Or might Nagridas's personal admiration and affection for the saint have led him to individually imagine her life as conforming at least in part to the values and ways of their shared lineage—heroically practicing devotion as a widow and properly escorted? Twentieth-century scholars say he was mistaken about the rana being her husband's older brother.[21] What of other details? Admittedly some have a "modern" feel, but as Pauwels confirms, this telling clearly dates from the latter half of the eighteenth century.[22]

If Nagridas composed this tale after he renounced his own royal inheritance to retire to Vrindavan, he might have identified with Mira precisely because she was known for having rejected (and possibly having been rejected by) this royal world, of which he also wanted no part. He mentions only once that she comes from Merta, and he does not speak of her Rathor lineage at all.[23] And in any case, she renounces all connection to her natal and marital families in the first song, suggesting that it is her renunciation of, rather than her belonging to, this world that mattered to the author as well as the saint. Indeed, in his own poetry Nagridas portrays the ways of the world and of bhakti as completely antithetical (though, as Pauwels points out, the Braj region to which he retreated was a cosmopolitan crossroads where military campaigns and pilgrimage might coincide and that was rife with religious debate of which he was highly critical—by no means a quiet backwater, though definitively a lively center of ecstatic devotional practice).[24] It is also the case that Nagridas's own sister Sundar Kunwaribai was a bhakta and poet, much like Mira, and Madhu Kishwar and Ruth Vanita report that she, too, suffered at the hands of family members, suggesting that such devotion but also such persecution was not strictly a thing of the past in eighteenth-century royal rajput circles.[25] Mira might have won the support of some great bhaktas among them, in her own time and in subsequent generations, but without there being any distinctively rajput tradition of remembrance or honoring her.

What of the Vallabhite connection? If Nagridas was indeed a member of the Vallabha sampraday, we might also reasonably conclude that the *Chaurasi Vaishnavan ki Varta* does not give us the whole story of Mira's reception within this community, with at least some members continuing to hold her in high esteem. The rulers of the Kishangarh kingdom were closely affiliated with the Vallabha sampraday, both before and after Nagridas. However, Pauwels found no convincing evidence of Nagridas having been formally initiated into the sampraday. Further, in her careful reading of the *Padaprasangmala*, she found clear influence from the *Vartas* (though not in Mirabai's case) but no particular Vallabhite bias to the overall work.

Similarly there is a long-standing relationship between the court and the Nimbarka sampraday, its monastery at Salemabad (between Kishangarh and Rupnagar) becoming its major center when leaders moved there from Braj even as major images from the region also made their way to Rajasthan. Again, though Nagridas's works show a familiarity with and appreciation of the Nimbarka sampraday, Pauwels found no discernable Nimbarkan influence on the *Padaprasangmala* nor any credible evidence of Nagridas taking initiation. After usurping the throne, Bahadur Singh would make a show of being associated with the Vallabhites, but this appears to be as much a political as a religious choice, designed at least in part to counterbalance the influence of local Nimbarka leaders, in Pauwels's analysis.[26] She raises the possibility that Nagridas may have been subtly but deliberately challenging the exclusivity of the Vallabha sampraday by bringing in Nimbarka and Ramanandi saints and songs (both with orders of warrior ascetics) into his works in a militarily motivated move to counter his brother's alliance.[27] The desire of both the Vallabha and Nimbarka sampradays to lay claim to this illustrious devotee speaks for itself.[28]

The bottom line is that the *Padaprasangmala* cannot reliably be read as a Vallabhite text, and thus cannot be said to document an alternative positive Vallabhite perspective on Mira. We might marshal other potential evidence, including Raghavdas's assignment of Mirabai to this sampraday as early as 1660 despite her slightly earlier rejection in the *Chaurasi Vaishnavan ki Varta* (as we noted in the previous chapter). Several more positive but less certain references to Mira are noted by Indian scholars in the *Do Sau Bavan Vaishnavan ki Varta* (The Sayings of the 252 Vaishnavas), a Vallabhite work also attributed to Hariray but likely composed in the eighteenth century, even as the *Padaprasangmala* was. Varta 15 speaks of "Jaimal's sister" as a disciple of Sri (Vitthalnath) who corresponded with him by letter because she kept *purdah* (taken by some as a reference to Mira, though she is more often identified as Jaimal's cousin and described as blatantly disregarding such restrictions as she is depicted in Figure 2.1), and varta 47 identifies Mira's husband's younger brother's wife, Ajab Kumarbai, as a disciple of Vitthalnath and the Pushtimarg, suggesting that the family (including Mira) all belonged to this sampraday.[29] A nineteenth-century text *Shri Nathji ki Prakatya-Varta* (The Story of Sri Nathji's Appearance) mentions Mirabai explicitly as accompanying her sister-in-law for darshan of Vitthalnath when the latter became his disciple.[30] It is clear that some would assume or seek to strengthen Mira's affiliation with this sampraday, their motives varied, but Nagridas and company do not appear to share this aim, nor is there any official rescinding of the *Chaurasi Vaishnavan ki Varta*'s threefold condemnation of her—a text that continues to have a vital place in this sampraday.[31]

Even as the *Padaprasangmala* imaginatively re-creates the context of the compositions of Mira's songs, we too can try to more fully re-create the context of its composition in order to better understand the intentions of its author(s) and performers. In the case of Nagridas we know far more about him than about many other hagiographers, in part because he was a prolific writer and great devotee and in part because he was of royal descent and so involved in the kinds of political dealings and military campaigns that are historically documented as well as being a patron of painting, performance, and scribing. The latter half of the eighteenth century in northwestern India was marked by shifting allegiances and alliances between rajput kings, Mughals, *marathas*, Afghans, *jats*, and others in a series of battles for territory, succession disputes, tribute relations, suicides, and assassinations. Ramanandi, Dadupanthi, and Nimbarka warrior ascetics were mobilized, and military campaigns readily combined with pilgrimage. There were also winners and losers in Jai Singh II's religious reforms and continuing intersectarian and intrasectarian conflicts in the years that followed his death in 1743, but equally an immense diversity and richness of devotional styles and lineages, with devotees, saints, and songs readily traveling across sectarian as well as social divides.[32]

Nagridas importantly authored a first-person pilgrimage account (completed in 1753), detailing not only his travels to holy sites but also his attempts to make alliances to help him recover his kingdom in this tumultuous time. Reading the *Padaprasangmala* side by side with this and other works by Nagridas, Pauwels argues that the *Padaprasangmala* is not only a "celebration of the power of the devotional song" but also constitutes a direct response to the reform agenda of Jai Singh II.[33] In contrast to Priyadas's early support, Nagridas eschews the tightened lineages of the four allegedly orthodox sampradays as marks of legitimacy, the Sanskrit philosophical wrangling and competition that this engendered, and the conservative *varna-ashrama-dharma* and emphasis on Vedic ritual that Jai Singh II embraced.[34] Instead Nagridas includes a wide array of bhaktas from multiple sampradays in his collection, with little attention to sectarian affiliation, among them not only Vaishnavas of many stripes, devotees of Rama as well as Krishna, but also nirgun saints like Kabir and Raidas (significantly without mention of their being disciples of Ramananda), and with stories privileging devotion over all else and lauding those who disregard the rules of commensality and caste purity.

Mirabai's strong critique of the rana's attempted interference in her devotion on the grounds of normative caste and gender dharma in the first song makes her an effective spokesperson for similar dissatisfaction with Jai Singh II's perceived meddling in seeking to "orthodoxize" bhakti. Further the cycle begins with the clear statement that Mira was "married off," her husband dying only days later and her devotion continuing as before.[35] Jai Singh II's similar insistence that the leaders of the chatur sampraday should marry met with opposition even in his day, with offending ascetics replaced. Mira's refusal to acknowledge the validity of her forced marriage, as one wholly devoted to God, might also carry an embedded critique of this policy (designed to affirm varna-ashrama-dharma and provide Jai Singh II with householder priests for the performance of Vedic rituals). Mira's lack of sectarian affiliation and appreciation for and popularity among all manner of bhaktas (as indeed the *Vartas* attest) would have been well-known. Nagridas, for his part, recounts her meeting with Jiv Goswami in Vrindavan (à la Priyadas) but also notes that she went on pilgrimage to the Ganges, thus leaving open the possibility of her encountering Raidas there. Yet instead of presenting her as the latter's disciple, he makes no mention of any formal affiliation while highlighting her disregard for caste in friendship as well as devotion in the final episode in relation to the woman sent to spy on her. Thus as Pauwels concludes, Mira appears an ideal spokesperson for this ecumenical and heterodox vision of bhakti and for Nagridas's primary "mission ... [t]o bypass all the sectarian concerns and simply enjoy songs of all denominations without bothering to establish their orthodoxy and without too much philosophical argument."[36]

To complicate matters somewhat, there are two distinctly different versions of the *Padaprasangmala*, the longer one including Mirabai and low-caste nirgun saints, the other, shorter version not (though the song of Mirabai in the passage on Narayandas Natava remains in both). There has been much speculation about which came first and who might have changed the text, for what reason, and when. Pauwels found both recensions in the Kishangarh Royal Collection and both already present in manuscript form dating from 1792 (twenty-eight years after Nagridas's death).[37] There is no clear indication of which might have been earlier, leaving open the possibility that the shorter version might have been censored to remove material objectionable to some (perhaps by Bahadur Singh or Vallabha priests or others sympathetic with Jai Singh II's agenda) or the longer one expanded to deepen the critique and/or to enhance inclusivity and enjoyment.[38] Again we find Mira inhabiting a potentially contested space, together with low-caste saints, standing on the side of a radically inclusive, egalitarian devotion to God.

These findings make clear the overwhelming importance of careful manuscript study of all hagiographic accounts of Mirabai's life, before we try to draw conclusions about how she might have been perceived in a given time and place. The texts are not as stable as we might be inclined to assume, emerging out of oral performance contexts, remembered in the dynamic participatory realm of bhakti, and subject to revision and the interventions of performers, scribes, redactors, and commentators with a variety of motives. Printed editions of such texts must equally be subjected to careful scrutiny because of both the variability in source materials and the specific circumstances attending their publication.[39] Further, as we examine the differences in these texts over time, it is essential that we also investigate how saints other than Mirabai are treated within them rather than looking only at the passages related to her, in order to accurately interpret the possible reasons for her removal or addition to a text and differences that may arise in her portrayal, as Pauwels has so clearly demonstrated with respect to the *Padaprasangmala*.

I concur with Pauwels's assessment, with her considerable caveats, that it is quite likely that Nagridas and members of his court did compose the *Padaprasangmala* and did have a deep admiration for Mira (particularly given the additional positive reference to her in the passage on Narayandas Natava), belying any comprehensive rejection of the saint or overt suppression of her memory by rajputs as a whole, as some have asserted,[40] and lending support to the possible existence of a tradition of honoring her at least among some rajputs in her natal family, a number of whom are also lauded for their great religious devotion.[41] Beyond this, the text presents us with a fundamentally bhakti view of Mirabai, highlighting the power of song, composed, heard, sung, and danced, as listeners and readers are drawn into the lila of Mira's life. The overall text is decidedly nonsectarian, offering a generalized and inclusive, though largely Vaishnava, vision of devotion and reaffirming the equality of all before God. Nagridas and his entourage were clearly not alone in this perspective. Indeed in his pilgrimage narrative he reports encountering many others like himself in the Braj-Rajasthan region who paid little heed to sectarian affiliation or orthodoxy in their recognition and ecstatic pursuit of devotion.[42] And they may arguably represent a significant pushback against Jai Singh II's attempts to define a restricted Vaishnava orthodoxy wed to Vedic ritual and socially conservative varna-ashrama-dharma, as Pauwels argues so persuasively.

Other seventeenth-century hagiographers would have other concerns and other motives for not embracing such an inclusive vision. The next telling we will examine, in contrast, is filled with details of the beliefs and practices of the teller's specific sampraday. And the outspoken, mature rajput woman Nagridas describes is nowhere to be found, replaced by a lively young girl in love with her Lord.

Mahipati's Mira: Precocious Child of God

Mahipati (1715–1790), a Maharashtrian brahman hagiographer of the Varkari sampraday, approaches Mira's story in a radically different way than the *Padaprasangmala* does, when he includes her in his *Bhaktavijaya* (Victory of the Devotees), completed in 1762 CE.[43] Before drawing his listeners into the world of Mira, he draws Mira into the world of Varkari devotion. For Mahipati and his audience, as for other bhaktas, Mira embodies the ideal of devotion, but their ideal differs substantially from that of Vaishnava traditions coming out of Vrindavan and Rajasthan, or the Sikhs for that matter. Mahipati was formerly an accountant and scribe turned *kirtan* performer, with a wealth of knowledge of circulating bhakti traditions that he drew on for this distinctly Maharashtrian form of devotional performance incorporating not only song but also dance, acting, and didactic preaching.[44] In composing the *Bhaktavijaya* he is concerned to establish the authority and authenticity of his tellings of saints' lives, assuring his reader/listener that the stories he writes and recites are not merely works of his own imagination or fancy but specifically based on earlier written and orally circulating accounts.[45]

He clearly knew of Nabhadas's and Priyadas's texts but apparently rejects these sources as not speaking the truth in reference to Mira. To tell the *same* story in two different times and places and in two different religious milieus may indeed entail telling a *different* story in order to properly contextualize the *same* or at least similar meaning. This is precisely what Mahipati does with respect to Mira, using a quite different vocabulary of devotion and claiming to draw on preexisting Maharashtrian traditions.[46] As S. G. Tulpule observes, "the writing of hagiographies was in itself a way of bhakti[, and a]s Mahipati says, what they sought in writing about the lives of the saints was their company, *satsanga*," to experience them as present members of their devotional community.[47]

Mahipati builds on past tradition, reportedly charged to write of the saints in a visionary encounter with the seventeenth-century saint Tukaram, and he produces a comprehensive Varkari hagiography that would achieve canonical status and to which he continued to add until his death, completing three subsequent volumes as well as shorter works. He was composing the *Bhaktavijaya* at the height of maratha expansion, a time also marked by dramatically increased religious patronage and "supra-regional pilgrimage . . . [with] Maharasthrians, both Brahmin and Maratha, replac[ing] Rajputs as the main patrons at Benares . . . [and t]housands ma[king] the pilgrimages to Benares," in addition to increasingly elaborate pilgrimages to Pandharpur and the popularization of other Varkari sites regionally.[48] The influx of songs, stories, and devotional traditions through the coming and going of pilgrims, soldiers, and other travelers and enhanced patronage may have fueled interest in reinforcing regional religious identity and Varkari perspectives, particularly with respect to saints like Namdev, said to have traveled extensively in the north but hailing from this land, as well as drawing popular figures like Mira, Kabir, and Raidas into the fold.[49]

As Mahipati tells her story, Mirabai is again said to be the daughter of a ruler of Udaipur, as in the Punjabi *Prem Ambodh*, but beyond this the stories diverge. In Mahipati's telling, Mira's father is portrayed as a great Vaishnava devotee, and observing his devotion to Krishna, the child Mira falls in love with this beautiful deity. When she comes of age, she insists that she will marry only Krishna. Her father confronts her, thinking at first that she is only a foolish child, but she speaks so wisely of the true meaning of bhakti that he is astonished and gives her an image to worship in her own chambers. Her devotional practice is elaborately detailed, and both her playing of the *vina* (a stringed instrument characteristically associated with Varkari kirtan performance and also typically present in pictorial representations of Mira) and her association with other Vaishnava devotees are described.[50]

Her father is indulgent, but outsiders criticize her shameless dancing during public devotional singing in the presence of male renouncers. Although he knows her critics are not good people, he is still concerned for the family's reputation and again insists on her marriage. Mira's mother is the go-between, bringing Mira her father's words and telling him their daughter's response. Mira says that the "pious and wise" applaud her for bringing glory rather than shame to her family name and that marriage is out of the question. Her mother's report is damning: Mira refuses to listen to anything regarding her duty as the daughter of a royal house.

Angry, the rana decides his daughter must die, and Mira's mother is dispatched to deliver the poison. All of these interactions, Mahipati emphasizes, occur in private, between Mira and her parents. Unwilling and weeping, her mother goes to Mira, and finding her in the temple, tells her exactly what she has brought. Mira reassures her mother, talking of the impermanence of all physical things and the inevitability of death. If her time has come, then she will go, even as the flower withers, the moon wanes, the mirage evaporates, and the fruit falls from the branch. As these things are not mourned, so her passing should not be. She belongs to Krishna, not to her parents or to this world.

Mira then prays to Krishna, anticipating the end of her physical separation from him but also concerned about who will worship him when she is gone. Her father neglects his worship out of anger with Mira. People will also revile her, saying that it is because she lived out her devotion that she was killed. Calling on other examples of Krishna's aid to devotees (in the same manner that we saw in Nagridas's account) and on his ability to stop the power of poison, she raises the cup to him as an offering and drinks it down fearlessly, his name on her lips.

The poison miraculously turns to nectar in Mira's throat, but the image of Krishna changes color for all to see. The king immediately repents, despairing that he has poisoned God. He begs Mira to pray to Krishna to right his wrong. She does so in an intimate prayer, trying to coax him to change back his color and asking how he could be poisoned. Has he not overcome poison repeatedly in the past, and does not his power extend throughout the worlds? Krishna responds to her loving entreaty and changes himself back, leaving only a small green patch at his throat. The king and all those who had reviled Mira are converted and glorify Krishna and Mira. She does indeed bring splendor to her family line, and Mahipati concludes by saying that even in his day beautiful images of Krishna could be found in the palaces of the kings of Rajasthan.

Mahipati's account is strikingly different from those of Priyadas, Nagridas, and the *Prem Ambodh*. Here Mira is a daughter not of Merta in Marwar but of Udaipur in Mewar (as she was in the *Prem Ambodh*), and gone are the interactions between her and her husband or her in-laws, her wanderings, and her encounters with anyone else outside her natal family, including any guru, low-caste or otherwise. The problematic nature of her behavior as a wife drops out, no lustful false sadhu appears, and her purity is absolutely preserved. Is this merely a sanitized version of the tale, or is it a translation of the story into a different religious and cultural milieu? I would suggest that it is predominantly the latter, though we cannot entirely rule out the former.

The central contrast in accounts coming out of Rajasthan and Vrindavan between the flawed men in Mira's marital family and her divine lover (particularly when her persecutor is understood to be her husband) has a particular logic when the relationship between devotee and deity is articulated in the language of male-female relations and erotic love. But this is not the primary metaphor used in the Varkari tradition of Maharashtra, nor is the merger of lover, love, and Beloved found in the Sikh tradition of the *Prem Ambodh*. Instead that relationship is most often described as that of a parent and child, and with this observation both the need for and the logic of the translation of Mira's story in Mahipati's telling begin to emerge.

Maharashtrian Varkari devotion is directed to Vitthal of Pandharpur, recognized as a manifestation of Krishna. In the simplest legend of his coming, Vitthal first arrives in Pandharpur from Govardhan to offer a boon to a man named Pundalik because of his devoted service to his parents.[51] But so complete is Pundalik's devotion that he will not attend to the deity until he has finished serving his parents, and he merely tosses Vitthal a brick to stand on while he waits. The deity is not insulted but rather delighted to see such love and decides to remain. Iconographically, the image of Vitthal appears to wear a *linga*-shaped crown (the phallic symbol so often associated with Shiva), and early stories speak of him as a hero who died protecting cattle. Though this manifestation of the Divine would become identified as a form of Krishna, Charlotte Vaudeville alleges that he had earlier been the focus of a Shaiva hero cult.[52]

Even as Vitthal comes to be equated with Krishna, differences remain between this tradition and Vaishnava traditions centered in Vrindavan. Vitthal has an innocence that the butter-stealing boy and precocious youth of Braj lacks, and his relationship with his devotees mirrors the deep compassion, caring, and attachment of a mother for her child.[53] And though in other regions also earlier Shaiva tantric allegiances gave way to Vaishnava devotion, in this Marathi-speaking region there is a clear blending rather than replacement still evident in text and practice.[54] The thirteenth-century brahman ascetic Jnanadev, a founding poet-saint of the sampraday, is identified as a Shaiva Nath yogi who also became a devotee of Krishna. In his famous Marathi work modeled on the *Bhagavad Gita*, the *Jnaneshvari*, he affirms the equivalence of Shiva and Krishna and advocates the devotional recitation of the name of God as a unifying salvific practice, with the names of either being efficacious and signaling "the invisible, all-pervading God-head," in a formulation that shares much with nirgun devotees as well as the aniconic understanding of the Divine common to the Naths.[55] Evidence of this blending of Shaivite and Vaishnava as well as sagun and nirgun elements can be seen in the tradition as a whole and embodied in practices. For example, during the pilgrimage to Pandarpur, "before entering Viṭṭhal's temple, Vārkarīs worship at Puṇḍalik's memorial (*samādhi*), an ancient and simple Śiva-*liṅga* temple half submerged in the Bhima river."[56]

In light of such information Mahipati's tale can now be read in a different light. The focus on parental relations together with the absence of any notion of Mira having married seem appropriate in a devotional tradition which has a strong emphasis on devotion to one's parents and models the human-Divine encounter on parent-child relationships and intimate friendship rather than the play of the divine cowherd of Braj with his gopi lovers.[57] In the Varkari milieu, where the Lord is envisioned as like a cow pining for her calf, the poisoner in Mira's tale becomes her parents, and the life-and-death conflict is situated in her natal rather than her marital family, with Mira's mother despairing at the anticipated death of her daughter even as she delivers the poison at her husband's command. Necessarily, the offending rana must be her father, and she born in Mewar rather than Merta, as the title of "rana" is specific to Mewar's ruler.[58] Krishna does not stand in opposition to an earthly husband in Mira's life but rather serves as a protector whose care for her contrasts with that of her earthly parents. For her part, Mira remains a child before such a deity, and he involves himself directly in her plight by taking the poison into himself rather than merely neutralizing it and responding to her entreaties to change his color back.

Varkari religious practices are also detailed in Mahipati's text. Elaborate descriptions of worship rituals are given, resembling the practices of other Vaishnava sects. Mira's offering of incense, light, and savories, of music and song are lovingly detailed, as is her rubbing her image of Krishna with fragrant oil and bathing it in milk, curds, butter, honey, and sugar and then the purest water, adorning him in jewels and the finest garments. The efficacy of the recitation of the names of God is emphasized, and Mira "performs kirtan describing the goodness [and good deeds] of Hari," reciting her own poetry, singing and dancing in the company of assembled devotees in this distinctly Varkari devotional performance style.[59]

Shiva also has a prominent but subordinate place in this telling of Mira's life, with Mira making references to him as a model devotee of Vitthal who requires Vitthal's help in times of difficulty. There is a further Shaiva twist to the tale, when Krishna appears iconographically as Shiva with the patch of color at his throat after the poisoning.[60] Shiva is marked in this same manner after he drinks the poison generated from the cosmic ocean, saving gods and demons alike, according to mythological accounts,[61] and this cosmic story of Shiva is embedded in that of Krishna's rescue of Mira, even as Shiva is incorporated into and subsumed by Krishna in Varkari tradition as a whole. Indeed in Mahipati's telling of the life of the goldsmith Narahari, this Shaiva devotee comes to the realization of the nonduality of Shiva and Krishna, recognizing his error and falling at the feet of Vitthal, with Mahipati concluding, "From this time forth, Pandurang held on his head the emblem of Shiva. For *Shrirang* (Krishna) never disappoints his servants."[62]

The tale which Mahipati tells of Mira shows a clear blending of Shaiva, Vaishnava, and aniconic elements and is thoroughly a product of the Varkari religious tradition, with Mira taking her place beside other saints from diverse backgrounds, as the author integrates traditions from further north with those of the region.[63] In part this portrayal reflects larger patterns, identified by Jon Keune, running through Mahipati's *Bhaktavijaya* that include an overarching Vaishnava framework, such that even Shiva is portrayed as a devotee of Vitthal/Krishna, with an emphasis on bhakti as the most efficacious form of religious practice and the portrayal of bhaktas as triumphing over all kinds of adversity, with God seemingly compelled to respond to their requests by the depth of their utter devotion.[64] Other patterns noted by Keune—a challenge to caste inequity without ultimately rejecting it and an ambivalence toward Muslims who generally come around to an appreciation of bhakti even if they are initially hostile—play no role in Mahipati's telling of Mira's story. They could easily have done so, but neither Akbar nor Raidas are mentioned here. This North Indian Rajasthani girl saint is simply portrayed as an innocent yet great Varkari devotee.

Even though there is a distinct logic to this translation of her tale, however, this obviously popular saintly figure does seem somewhat diminished in this telling, where she remains a child. For is it not the intensity of her mature conflict with established social norms and both the extended nature of her persecution and the strength of her conviction that make her story so compelling? Yet in Mahipati's telling, any possible critique of gender norms is transmuted into saintly exceptionalism for a virgin girl, and caste as an issue is completely erased from her story.

As Keune rightly observes, Mahipati opposed inequality but stopped short of radically challenging the caste system, instead evincing a "strategic ambiguity" that raises but does not resolve the issue, characteristic of bhakti in western India more broadly.[65] In his telling of Mira's tale, Mahipati does note that true devotees "are merciful to the lowly, and compassionate ... regard[ing] a common citizen as on equality with a king." And in his telling of the story of Rohidas (Raidas), he affirms generosity to others as the measure of human goodness regardless of caste, listing a whole series of castes and what each is able to give, with Raidas singled out for his generosity in repairing the shoes of pilgrims. He assures them all that those "who perform their accustomed task are without blame, and in performing acts of benevolence the Pervader of the universe is attained." Raidas speaks wisely to a brahman who challenges his right to worship the shalagram, asserting that because God is indwelling in all human beings, none is impure, and as all are bound by skin, then leather also cannot be impure. The brahman repents in the end, recognizing him as a great devotee but only after Raidas cuts open his own chest with a leatherworking tool to reveal his inner sacred thread. And even as he apologizes, the brahman also notes that his persecution of Raidas allowed the saint's true nature to be revealed.[66]

In Mahipati's view, even such mild refutations of caste oppression appear better left to male saints (even as many twentieth-century reformers would conclude). The story of the Maharashtrian servant girl Janabai shows Krishna disregarding caste and purity rules; he assists her in her work, shares food, wears her blanket, protects her from false accusations, and even writes down her poetry, but she herself takes no explicit stand, except to grieve when she is given no place when Krishna sits down to eat with Namdev and others, thereby eliciting her Lord's compassion.[67] The North Indian saint Mirabai's tale as told elsewhere offers a potentially much sharper critique of caste as well as gender oppression. Yet as much as she might be loved and admired, Mira's exemplary power, even as a woman, had to be reined in, it seems, to make hers an inspirational tale of exceptionalism. Only in this form, as a model bhakta girl child, could she be fully embraced by this Varkari hagiographer (and his sources and audiences, it seems). However, such a perceived need to contain the saint in some sense even while ostensibly praising her was felt not only in Maharashtra, as our next telling reveals.

Sukhsaran's *Mira ri Parachi*: Choosing Domesticity or Devotion

A much more extended story of Mirabai is lovingly recounted in the eighteenth- or nineteenth-century Rajasthani work *Mira ri Parachi* (The Miraculous Story of Mira) of Sukhsaran.[68] In this telling, Mirabai's childhood and even her previous birth are described in considerable detail, her thoughts and feelings are given voice as well as those of other characters, and a great many miraculous occurrences in the saint's life are recounted. Unlike the other texts we have examined so far, the persecuting rana here is unequivocally Mira's husband,

and this fact provides the teller with an opportunity to address the specific tensions between devotion and domesticity that many women face. In so doing, he outlines both the ordinary expectations for women's behavior and the alternatives offered by bhakti, upholding social expectations but severely relativizing them in the same stroke. His telling thus not only extols this great saint but also serves a didactic purpose, not unlike the kirtan and katha performance traditions of public preaching so popular in North India and in keeping with the parchai genre.

As one of the three most prolific composers of this genre (along with Anantadas and Jangopal), Sukhsaran tells of Mirabai together with other women bhaktas, including Muktabai, Kisturabai, Karmaitibai, Karmabai, Phulibai, and Ranabai, composing in the Marwari dialect of Rajasthani. C. L. Prabhat reports that Sukhsaran may have been a member of a Ramsnehi sect writing in the early half of the eighteenth century CE.[69] Four Ramsnehi sectarian lineages arise out of the Ramanandi sampraday in Rajasthan from the mid-seventeenth to the mid-eighteenth centuries, all focusing on loving devotion to Ram and practicing an eclectic and inclusive mix of nirgun and sagun devotion.[70] However, because neither Sukhsaran's religious affiliation nor the date of composition is stated directly in the text itself, others continue to report that the details of Sukhsaran's life are unknown. The published edition of his parchai of Mirabai is drawn from two manuscripts, dated 1877 and 1882.[71] Again, further investigation is needed to clarify the details of the text's composition.

Sukhsaran's tale is first and foremost a celebration of the life of this great saint, so that she might continue to guide others across the rough seas of samsara, the cycle of rebirth, onto the solid path of devotion. He includes many details about her not found in earlier written accounts (and sometimes also not in later ones). For example, he specifies that she was born into the house of the Rao Duda's son Ratan Singh of the village of Kurki and had a sister named Anaupa and no brothers.[72] That Mira was actually born in Kurki rather than nearby Merta is a popular tradition in the region of her birth, though Sukhsaran says in the next line also that she was born in Merta (and debates continue regarding her precise birthplace).[73]

In Sukhsaran's telling, Mira's life is marked by miraculous events and the intervention of the Divine at almost every step. On the occasion of her birth gold *thal*, or trays, ordinarily beaten to announce the birth of a son in the royal household, sound on their own. With this miracle all are sure that either a valiant hero or the *avatar*, or incarnation, of a saint has been born, and Mira's future greatness (which clearly transcends gender) is publicly proclaimed. *Tulsi* (sacred basil) plants, beloved of Krishna, sprout around her as she plays and fill Kurki, where they can still be found growing in Sukhsaran's time, he says. Mira appears here as an extraordinary being whose life, even in her childhood, is marked by miraculous signs.

When Mira grows older, she realizes that she will be forced to marry the rana and prays to Krishna to save her. Krishna comes to marry her himself, and in another miracle the outward signs of the marriage ritual appear on her body—her hands decorated with henna, a sacred thread at her wrist, her body perfumed. In contrast to this divine marriage, only one verse is given over to Mira's marriage to the rana (identified here as belonging to the Sisodiya rajputs); it happened, though she did not like it, and then she was taken to Chittor.

When the rana disregards initial suggestions that he place her in a separate palace and forget her and instead makes his way to her chamber, dressed in all his finery and proudly walking among his bowing subjects, she begs Krishna to intervene on her behalf and preserve her honor as a *pativrata*, a virtuous woman loyal to her husband. When the rana arrives, there appears to be a man sleeping in Mira's bed. Enraged, he goes to kill this interloper, but the man becomes a lion and lunges at the sword-wielding rana, who runs for his life. The parallel to Vishnu's incarnation as the man-lion Narasimha to protect his great devotee Prahlad is unmistakable. Witnesses immediately suspect Mira of dark magic, however, and consequently she is isolated and treated as a widow or a woman abandoned. The text is explicit that Krishna has liberated Mira from the bonds of the householder life by making the rana leave her.

When the rana goes to a temple, he sees Mira singing and dancing there. Then he goes to another temple, and Mira is also there and in the next and the next. Asking of her whereabouts at the palace, he is told that she is within her chamber deep in meditation. He sends word to Mira that she may do as she pleases within her chamber without fear of his interference but that she must not leave the palace. Distraught, Mira cannot bear to be blocked from darshan of her Lord in the temple or separated from the company of other devotees. The rana orders her chamber locked, but the doors open on their own, and she goes to the temple when she chooses.

She then miraculously survives a series of murder attempts by the rana. The *pundit* (religious advisor) who delivers poison is mentioned by name as Dayaram, and he lies coercively, telling her he brings this holy offering on Hari's (God's) orders and that if she refuses it, her bhakti will be destroyed. This encounter shares elements of Priyadas's tale of the lustful sadhu (not told here). The corrupt Dayaram is clearly an enemy of true devotion, as are structurally parallel corrupt brahmans in the stories of other saints. Popular tradition assigns Dayaram to the *vijavaragi* caste (traditionally purveyors of perfumes and drugs, with a stereotypical reputation for deception).[74] This caste has built a Krishna temple in the pilgrimage city of Pushkar in Mira's honor, with her image facing the main image of Krishna in the position usually occupied by a deity's associated animal vehicle, thus allowing her perpetual darshan. The temple is explicitly said to have been built and is maintained as an atonement for Dayaram's actions by his caste fellows.[75]

In Sukhsaran's tale, when poison fails, a cobra is sent in a beautiful gold box with the message that it is a jeweled necklace, and then poisonous scorpions in a bag said to be beautiful diamond toe rings. (Snakes and scorpions are common dangers encountered by women in more ordinary circumstances, for example, when going to the well to fetch water.) When Mira opens the box and bag, they do indeed contain sparkling new ornaments, which she wears to the temple, arousing the jealousy of the other queens until the rana feels compelled to confess that he had been trying to kill her rather than favor her. Mira's husband's older brother now tells her that he will kill her with his own hands if she does not remain in her chamber, accusing her of deceiving them all with her escapes, never crediting her survival to either her devotion or her Lord's intervention. But when he enters her chamber with a dagger ready to finish her off, he sees four Miras, and unable to tell which is the real one, he backs away.

When her sister-in-law Uda's attempts to persuade her to change her behavior fail as dismally as the rana's and his brother's attempts at violence, Mira prepares to go to Dwarka. To facilitate her going, Krishna sends a chariot decorated with precious gems. Everyone is again amazed, but this time the rana understands that Krishna has sent the chariot, and he appoints brahmans to accompany Mira, instructing them to bring her back after her pilgrimage.[76] Another miracle transports the whole entourage to Dwarka overnight. Mira visits the temples, bathes in the River Gomti, and prays.

She calls on Krishna, reminding him of a promise he made to her in a previous life that she could meet him when she chose. She invokes her Lord's intercession on behalf of Kabir, Sita, Prahlad, Draupadi, the *gujari* (cowherdess) in Gokul, and the monkey forces on their way to Lanka to defeat Ravana, as well as Namdev and Pipa. The examples of Kabir and Sita seem particularly pointed in this context. When Kabir's Muslim and Hindu devotees argued over his body, it disappeared and only flowers remained to be buried or cremated according to the practice of each group. At the close of some tellings of the *Ramayana*, Sita returns to the earth from which she came, rejoined with her divine mother, Bhudevi, and released from the social expectations and the notions of shame and honor that had been used to torment her. Mira, too, calls for such release. The temple fills with light, and she disappears.

The brahmans who have accompanied her demand to know where the people have hidden her. They threatened to kill everyone, but Mira reemerges from the image to stop this commotion, telling the priests precisely what has happened and to go away. So saying, she disappears again, and a piece of her garment that remained draped on the image (mentioned also by Chaturdas, c. 1800), Sukhsaran claims, could still be seen in his day. When the rana learns of Mira's fate, he is repentant and understands her true nature as an avatar. He orders a temple built in her honor, installing her image within. The whole kingdom rejoices that Mira has attained *moksha*, or liberation, and will continue to guide others along this path by her example. Here ends Sukhsaran's song of praise for Mirabai, whom he portrays as the incarnation of devotion itself, manifest in age after age.

Sukhsaran had begun his tale with the story of the saint's previous birth in which Krishna made this promise that she would be his devotee in life after life, and he uses the telling of the stories of both her previous and present births as an occasion to reflect on the relationship between devotion to God and embodied social existence, with all the attendant dharmic expectations related to caste, gender, and age. He identifies Mira in her previous life as a brahman woman of Barsana whose story appears in the *Bhagavata Purana*, and he recounts the episode.[77] To do so further places his telling on a continuum with Vaishnava traditions of katha performance which often draw on the same puranic narrative source in their preaching. In identifying Mira as the reincarnation of this brahman woman of Barsana, Sukhsaran is able to give her a brahman pedigree, to connect her to Krishna's incarnation in Vrindavan, to offer didactic reflections on the importance of embodiment and of conforming to caste rules within it, and to establish that Mira is not willfully rebelling against gender expectations in her current life but only fulfilling her destiny and the command of God laid down in a previous birth.

The story relates how Krishna's cowherd friends go first to the brahman men of Barsana (Radha's natal village) with a request for food for themselves and their Lord. Instead of being given food, however, they are severely beaten. When they return empty-handed, Krishna sends them back, this time to the brahman wives, to make the same request. The women, unlike their husbands, are delighted to comply. One woman's husband drags her home, verbally abusing Krishna and tying up his wife to stop her from going to serve him. Unable to free herself, she simply leaves her body and joins the other women.

These brahman wives beg Krishna to let them remain with him, motivated by both a desire to serve him and a fear of their husbands' retaliation. But Krishna sends them back. The woman who has left her body wants to stay immersed in him, but though he seems delighted with her desire, he tells her, too, to go back. The human body, though troublesome, is necessary for the practice of bhakti, Krishna reminds her, even as the texts of the Vedas and Puranas and the saints have always said. He wants her to return to an embodied state so that she may practice devotion and set an example for others. Krishna assures her that she can meet him at any time, however. This brahman woman from Barsana, Sukhsaran concludes, is reborn as Mirabai.

Sukhsaran frames this episode in terms of caste as well as gender. In this life Mira has been born into a kshatriya household of the Rathor rajputs to practice devotion in the Kali Yug (this final degenerate cosmic age before the world will be destroyed and then re-created anew). But in her former life she was a brahman. Similar brahmanizing stories are told to raise the status of low-caste saints. For example, Anantadas relates in his *Raidas Parchai* that Raidas was a brahman reborn as a chamar because he had eaten meat in his previous incarnation.[78] As an infant he refused his mother's milk as impure, and having seen his plight in a dream, Ramanand came to initiate the child and saved his life. Such a story may be told by brahmans to make their own association with this untouchable saint more palatable and to wrest him from his caste fellows. Certainly this seems to be the assumption of the low-caste followers of Raidas who reject this telling. However, we could also cite counterexamples of low-caste groups telling such stories to raise their own status or establish the legitimacy of their religious tradition by giving it a brahman stamp. This type of brahmanization can be seen among low-caste Kabirpanthis who describe Kabir as a virgin brahman woman's son who was adopted by the low-caste julaha Muslim weavers with whom he is traditionally associated (such a move making Kabir more thoroughly Hindu as well as raising his caste status).[79]

Sukhsaran's tale of Mira's past life may be a similar effort to brahmanize her, although her status as a member of a royal kshatriya family is not nearly as problematic as the extremely low-caste affiliations of Raidas or Kabir. In assigning Mira this role, however, she is also being given a specific place in the *Bhagavata Purana* and thus in the drama of Krishna's incarnation in the world of Braj, which is understood both as an occurrence in a specific historical time and as an ongoing eternal realm of human-Divine encounter. Though such a move might be understood as elevating her status, it also closes down claims made elsewhere (which some might consider overly extravagant) that Mira was an incarnation of one of Krishna's gopi lovers, the sakhi Lalita, or even Radha herself.[80]

The theme introduced here, exploring the relationship between devotion and embodied social existence, continues throughout Sukhsaran's telling of Mira's tale. At one point he suggests that those who are born in great houses (positions of social and political power) have a responsibility to cultivate devotion by way of example and that caste obligations, whatever they may be, are inescapable even for Krishna when he is adopted into a cowherding clan. If Krishna must follow the system, then what alternative do ordinary mortals have? If one is lucky enough to be born upper-caste, one should take full advantage of that birth and facilitate devotion for others less privileged than oneself.

In this episode from the *Bhagavata Purana* the women are told to return to their husbands, and marriage seems as inescapable as caste for women. Men's opposition to women's devotion within the marital bond is also clearly portrayed, though overcome at least temporarily. Bhakti does not automatically fit easily into domestic life. Yet Mira's ability in her previous life to leave her body to go to Krishna suggests that even abuse exercised upon the body cannot ultimately prevent one from encountering the Divine. Addressed to all who must struggle with the exigencies of life, such a message seems particularly tailored for women and low-caste people, encouraging devotion while reinforcing rather than challenging the social structures, and even violence, that keep them in their place.

Sukhsaran expands on the theme of bhakti's relationship to the householder life for women as he describes Mira's childhood. In no way did she resemble her peers, and each point of her divergence is spelled out, as is her peers' more ordinary behavior. We are left with no doubt about how upper-caste little girls should behave and with what they are expected to concern themselves. And Sukhsaran offers no particular condemnation of these norms. Mira's companions seek to beautify themselves and wear ornaments; Mira dances in the temple and wears a string of sacred tulsi wood beads.[81] They worship God in many forms and pray to Gangaur (Shiva's wife Parvati) for a good husband, while Mira worships only Krishna (Hari) and sits talking with sadhus.[82] She cares nothing for the world and learns none of the practical things necessary to being a wife in any household, royal or otherwise. Unlike her friends she will not do the *vrats*, or fasts, that are so much a part of women's orthodox religious lives, and she has none of the shyness a girl should have in the company of unknown men as she converses with holy men.[83] Her games are ones of devotion—imaginatively transforming an ordinary stone into a shalagram for worship, for example. The contrast between Mira and her peers shows her again as one who is extraordinary—fundamentally different from "normal" girls and women, and thus not necessarily one to be emulated.

Mira's strange and improper behavior leads to slander, and much space is given to her mother's and later to her sister-in-law's attempts to dissuade her from such behavior (her sister-in-law identified by name as "Uda.") Sukhsaran's narrative takes place almost entirely in the domestic sphere (as

Mahipati's does), and the conversations recounted predominantly address expectations for women's behavior and how bhakti and a woman's traditional dharma might be reconciled. There is no mention of Mira journeying to Vrindavan or encountering a lustful sadhu, Akbar and Tansen, or Jiv Goswami.

In addition to the usual arguments about upholding family honor, Mira's mother suggests that devotion is inappropriate at Mira's age—her concerns should be with household and husband. The simultaneous Hindu valuation of renunciation in the pursuit of spiritual liberation and of dharmic participation in the householder life (with its emphasis on both social responsibility and sensual enjoyment) is generally balanced by assigning them to different stages in life, and this is what Mira's mother is suggesting. Mira responds with an answer that is vastly beyond her years, saying that because death may come at any time, waiting until old age to practice devotion may be too late. Why should she become entangled in family relations that are but accidents of birth or lead to rebirth?

To soften any perception of willfulness on her part, however, she speaks of being addicted to Ram, unable to give up her addiction and ready to sacrifice all to maintain it (a theme in a popular song attributed to Mira). Her husband will not like her devotion to God, her mother counters, and whether she likes it or not, she will go to another's house and will be subjugated to their whims. Her mother is unmoved by her claims that she is protected by a higher power than the rana. She tells her daughter in no uncertain terms that she will be married and should answer back less because her in-laws will not like it. She must go, or the Sisodiyas will attack them. This conflict seems a universal one occurring between willful daughters and mothers who are more realistic about the possibilities and dangers of life in the world and want at least a modicum of happiness for their daughters and for themselves, even as they contribute to maintaining the very structures that confine and limit them both.

Mira's mother goes on to say that if a woman's heart is true, she can practice devotion within the householder life; one need not become an ascetic. Returning to this dynamic tension between renunciation and the householder life, she presents bhakti as a way of bringing the pursuit of liberation into the latter. Yet if the world is truly impermanent and ultimately illusory, then why should not all people take vows of *sannyas* and become wandering renunciants?[84] Further, can a woman be a true bhakta wholly devoted to God while being involved in marriage and family? For Mira, the world of domestic relationships is meaningless, but her mother assures her that the two can be reconciled (and Sukhsaran assures other young women through the telling of the tale).

Mira's sister-in-law Uda and all the other queens come to offer her advice after her marriage. A woman's husband is her supreme Lord, and the woman who treats her husband as God will attain moksha, while all other paths for women are false, they say, echoing the dharmic teachings of Manu.[85] Mira does not directly denounce their clear presentation of normative *stridharm* (the religious and social duty of women). She says instead that her husband is not the rana but the ruler of the three worlds. She proceeds with a glorious description of Vishnu, who is ultimately the husband and Lord of all, whether male or female. Why love a false husband who will die, in a relationship that is always tinged with the sorrow of impending separation? A true husband causes you to remember Ram (God) and remains with you in life after life. The first might be possible for a mortal husband, but the latter is more problematic. Mira is obedient only to her divine husband; at his command she practices devotion, and for this purpose alone he gave her earthly form. Why, she asks her sister-in-law and the other queens, do they praise domestic happiness when it is so uncertain and ultimately unimportant? Those who remember the name of God attain true bliss and merge with the Divine; those who seek worldly pleasures become mired in sin and sorrow and are trapped in eighty-four hundred thousand rebirths.

This is the lesson that Mira tries to teach the rana's wives before she leaves the palace. God alone is worthy of absolute devotion. Without that devotion, life is meaningless, an endless treadmill of sorrow and suffering with only temporary and pale satisfactions. But with devotion, life is filled with eternal joy. So ends Mira's teachings and the didactic portions of the poem. This is Sukhsaran's final word: ultimately bhakti transcends the relations and restrictions, the pleasures and the hopes of this samsaric world. Although it can be practiced within the structures of social expectations and should not necessarily disrupt these, they must not be assumed to be of ultimate importance. Embodied existence is the necessary site of this human-Divine love affair, but one must see clearly that this alone is the purpose of physical existence and the only ultimate source of meaning and bliss. Such a move relativizes the samsaric situation, suggesting that we should devote ourselves completely to God, conform to dharmic rules, and not waste our time further on worldly concerns.

Through these and other comments woven into the story of Mira, Sukhsaran both upholds stridharm and radically relativizes it. At one point he condemns male violence against women as demeaning to the man himself and his family, but he also instructs women to act in a way that does not displease their husbands, an injunction that applies also to their practice of devotion. In her actions, his Mira, too, upholds the pativrata ideal as Krishna's wife. When she calls for Krishna's protection from her erstwhile husband, she does so on these grounds. When she sets out to leave Chittor, the people of the palace try to stop her and the rana asks her to stay, pointing out that Dwarka is far away and when the gopis went to meet Krishna there, they were robbed even though the great warrior Arjuna was with them. Mira responds that they went without Krishna's permission, but she does not. She is not acting independently or choosing to abandon her domestic life, but rather acting in obedience to God that began in a previous birth. Mira's seemingly independent and rebellious behavior is thus recast as that of a pativrata or virtuous wife of God, and she offers not protest but rather a relativizing perspective on all social relations that partake of the impermanence of human existence.

Mira, so well-loved, becomes an ideal spokesperson for Sukhsaran's teachings. Her own intensity of commitment shows her to be no slave to the social order, but her incredible miraculous life, ordained and upheld by the Divine, sets her apart from ordinary women. Where her life meets theirs is in the struggles of familial relations and the suffering she must endure at the hands of the uncomprehending rana, and these provide points of identification such that she becomes exemplary of creative endurance and patient detachment rather than radical independence or renunciation in the style of an ascetic. And her status as a pativrata of God lends support to this normative ideal for those whose husbands are all too mortal.

Relishing, Embellishing, and Tailoring the Past Made Present

From these three tellings, we can see something of Mira's popularity in the eighteenth and nineteenth centuries, her story no doubt carried far by itinerant singers, storytellers, performers, and pilgrims, as well as members of pan-regional sampradays like the Ramanandis and Gaudiya Vaishnavas. From Mahipati we learn that her fame had spread to Maharashtra by the mid-eighteenth century, where she had been incorporated into the Varkari pantheon of saints, as it already had to the Punjab and Bengal.[86] And possibly by the eighteenth century and certainly by the nineteenth century, her lineage as a daughter of Merta and a daughter-in-law of Mewar was taken for granted in Rajasthan and inscribed in the landscape; one could go to Kurki to see the tulsi plants in the courtyard of her former home or to Dwarka to see the cloth that remained when Mira merged with Krishna, according to Sukhsaran. The temple said to have been where she worshiped in Chittor also appears in nineteenth-century travel guides.[87] With regard to Nagridas and the

Padaprasangmala, any conclusions we make must also be tentative, but these verses raise at least the possibility that in the mid-eighteenth century Mirabai was known and even greatly admired by at least some members of her natal royal lineage in addition to devotees affiliated with diverse sampradays. But apart from these details, we also learn much about the way in which people actively participate in the making of the narrative traditions which grow up around Mirabai and other saints.

In each of these three tales we find tellers drawing their audiences into Mirabai's life story, even as the composers and subsequent performers themselves participate in it through the act of telling, and her story becomes something much more than a tale about the past. The *Padaprasangmala*'s author invites us to stand in the room and listen directly to Mirabai's voice, to feel her emotions and cultivate the same strength and love she embodies and, ultimately, like her, to "lose memory, consciousness and sense" in our love of God, overhearing her words and songs and being transformed in the encounter in the same way that Narayandas Natava and the woman sent by the rana are.

Mahipati addresses his invitation to a more specific audience—members of the Varkari sampraday—inviting them to embrace Mirabai as one of their own, her story translated into the vernacular of Marathi and of their religious tradition. Mirabai pursues and experiences God as they do, participating fully in Varkari ways, thus becoming *their* saint, possessed by them and embodying their form of bhakti. Indeed he apparently refused to accept Nabhadas's and Priyadas's tellings as truthful; her story could not be as they say. Instead he claims the saint for his own community and performs her story, so that it is a present reality rather than a mere remembrance of the past.

Sukhsaran, too, enters Mirabai's story and invites participation but in a different way—like the proverbial fly on the wall, he seemingly observes all that Mira does, the conversations that ensue between her and her family members, and all the miraculous occurrences that signify her sainthood, even the events of her previous life and the intimate conversation between Krishna and the brahman woman of Barsana who would be reincarnated as Mirabai. These he duly reports, marveling at the miracles and relishing the details of description and conversation. As a precocious child and an impetuous young woman, Mira speaks words of great wisdom in these encounters, and in so doing both she and the other characters speak directly to the concerns of audience, particularly women bhaktas who like Mira must handle conflicting expectations as both devotees of God and wives. And it is the voice of the preacher Sukhsaran that we hear speaking through them.

In his telling, Mira speaks of ultimate truths, while the other characters offer much more practical advice on how to practice bhakti and live in the world, within the boundaries of social expectation and dharma. In this way Mirabai, like the gopis before her, is exemplary of devotion but not of life—after all, no one takes the gopis' scandalous behavior and adulterous love of Krishna as an injunction for women to act like this and to treat their own husbands this way. Just so, Sukhsaran does not encourage women bhaktas to do as Mira does. Let them take her wise words to heart—the domestic realm does not offer ultimate meaning to life—but let them, like the woman of Barsana, live in the world structured as it is by caste and gender dharma, to which they, not being extraordinary saints like Mira, have no choice but to conform.

In all three tales, we see a deep affection for Mira. She is portrayed as an inhabitant of the teller's world, reflecting the teller's experiences and values in important ways. In the *Padaprasangmala*, she suffers (as its attributed author Nagridas did) from the intrigues of the rajput court and embraces a life of devotion and renunciation, offering inspiration for others who must struggle against the world. For Mahipati, she models the childlike stance of the Varkari devotee in the presence of a loving and maternal Lord, upholding and exemplifying the religious practices and values of this tradition. And for Sukhsaran, she is a consummate devotee of Krishna deeply loved by her Lord and the masses yet immersed in the social and religious world of Rajasthan.

We also see elements of the wider tradition that might be problematic for each teller either missing or told in alternative ways. Nagridas's tale begins with Mira's husband's death, mitigating the possibility that her husband might have opposed her actions or that she defied him and thus that she might not have lived according to the norms for a married rajput woman of a royal household, regardless of how she might act as a widow. Mahipati shows Mira's persecution occurring only in her childhood and the private space of the household, shielded from the public eye and without any hint of scandal, and the tale ends "happily ever after" with her parents' repentance and embrace of their daughter's devotion. And Sukhsaran weaves a tacit and sometimes overt support for the caste system and gender norms into his story ostensibly about a woman who breaks them, particularly by having her act always in obedience to Krishna, who is clearly her eternal *pati*, she a pativrata after all. In none of the stories do we find any mention of the possibility that Mirabai might have taken the extremely low-caste leatherworker Raidas as her guru, though we know that this association dates back at least to the last decade of the seventeenth century in the Punjab. Drawing in varying measure on existing circulating traditions, the tellers of each of these tales actively shape the tales told, based on their own and their community's assumptions about how an admired saint like Mira would have (or should have) acted, the particular tale told also shaped by their individual and collective experiences and points of identification with the saint.

These tales attributed to Nagridas, Mahipati, and Sukhsaran are but three examples of the stories told about Mirabai that, by the latter half of the eighteenth century and the nineteenth, seem to multiply exponentially. Sukhsaran himself clearly drew material from other written and oral sources as he constructed his more extended tale and imaginatively created scenes and dialogue. Even so, his expansions as well as additional materials found in still other sources tend to add to Mira's tale by enhancing the descriptions of the specific stages identified by Ramanujan as characteristic of women saints' lives and expanding episodes present in earlier tellings (the *Prem Ambodh*'s act 1 notwithstanding).

Some develop the childhood roots of Mira's devotion. This is true of Sukhsaran's tale but also of other popular episodes. For example, the highly educated writer and patron of the arts and Ram bhakti Maharaja Raghuraj Singh of Rewa reports in his *Bhaktamal Ramarasikavali* (1864) that when Mira was a child, a sadhu came to her home, carrying with him a *murti* (image) of Krishna that she immediately adored.[88] She asked him if she might have it, but he refused. She was inconsolable. In a dream, Krishna came to the sadhu and ordered him to give it to her. Frightened and humbled, he went immediately to Mira and gave her the image. In tellings of this episode elsewhere, the sadhu who gives Mira this image is identified alternately as Raidas or as Jiv Goswami.

Another childhood incident drawn from circulating popular oral traditions is reported by Ram Gharib Chaube in "The Legend of Mirabai," published in *North Indian Notes and Queries* in 1893.[89] Chaube, a scholar with broad linguistic expertise, worked closely with William Crooke on this journal and in the collection and publication of Indian folklore and also with G. A. Grierson on his survey of Indian literature. He reports that the young Mira saw a wedding procession and, entranced, asked her mother who her own bridegroom would be. Her mother pointed to the image of Ranchor, saying he was her groom, and the child took her words to heart, considering herself married to Krishna from that point on. She refused to marry a second time, when the rana to whom her parents betrothed her arrived for the marriage ceremony. Another circulating tale, a variation on one consistently told of Namdev, relates how Mira's father thought his child was lying when she told him that the milk she had taken to offer to Krishna in the temple had been consumed by her Lord.[90] A trial was organized, and she begged Krishna to drink the milk before witnesses so that her devotion would be vindicated. Krishna complied, proving her purity and blessedness to all.

Other reported and often divergent details of Mira's life deal with the theme of her marriage to the rana, her defiance of social expectations, and her subsequent persecution as well as her possible subordination to male authority figures. Raghuraj Singh largely follows Nabhadas and Priyadas as he relates Mira's marriage and her encounters with her in-laws, the lustful sadhu, Jiv Goswami, and Akbar and Tansen, though he includes details about Mira's musical performance before the emperor and integrates many songs into his account in much the same way the *Padaprasangmala* does. He also gives other details. For example, in addition to reporting that Mira was the daughter of Jaimal (elsewhere her cousin), he reports that she was engaged to a rana of Udaipur at the age of twelve, but when it came time for the marriage ceremony, she brought her image of Girdhar Nagar to the wedding pavilion and went through the obligatory rituals with her attention focused solely on him rather than her earthly husband-to-be. In the wake of this and her refusal to worship the kuldevi (clan goddess), not only was the insolent bride banished to a separate residence, but the prince took a second wife (a further move that ensures Mira effectively escapes the marriage trap).

The rana sends Mira poison, but in Raghuraj Singh's telling it is Mira's mother-in-law who is given the job of delivering it (as in Mahipati it was her mother), and he also offers an alternative story of the poisonous snake in the basket sent to kill Mira. This time, Mira is told that the basket contains a shalagram, and indeed when she opens it, it does.[91] Other sources report other trials Mira had to endure at the rana's hand: a mattress of thorns which turn to flowers and a ravenous lion whom she treats as Vishnu's incarnation Narasimha and who lies down harmlessly at her feet. Elsewhere it is said that when the angry rana bursts into her room at the sound of her laughing and conversing with a man, she is in the midst of playing a game of draughts or checkers with Krishna, and just as the rana enters the room, the image reaches out its hand to move a game piece, stopping the rana in his tracks.[92]

Raghuraj Singh also records the popular tradition that when Mira had reached the limit of her endurance under the rana's persecution, she wrote to the poet-saint Tulsidas, asking for his guidance.[93] He answered, telling her that she should not remain with those who block her devotion—they were not her true family. The texts of both letters are given in full. Only with Tulsidas's encouragement did Mira make her way to Vrindavan and later to Dwarka, placing her seemingly independent decision to leave her marital home under the authority of this illustrious male saint, much as various types of initiation and tales of male gurus may subordinate other female saints. Though a variety of themes are woven through such tellings, standard hagiographic components still give structure to the overall narrative patterns, and these elements remain part of the popular traditions of Mira into the present.

Drawing on these many tellings we can identify a core of central elements and characteristics that consistently mark the figure of Mirabai across tellings: her absolute devotion, her royal birth and childhood dedication to God, her insistence on the public performance of her devotion and her association with holy men in direct opposition to societal norms for women's proper behavior and notions of honor and shame, public condemnation of her actions and her resulting persecution almost always by family members who attempt to murder her, and her survival and continued devotion. It is out of this struggle that her humanness and her strength emerge, and she captures people's imagination as well as their hearts as they see their own struggle and pain in her suffering and find hope and strength in her survival and triumph.

We could try to build a composite story combining these elements and all the other episodes drawn from the wide range of available tellings. It is possible that Sukhsaran may in part have been doing such a thing, although equally possible that he introduced a number of imaginative innovations into the story. Were we to try to do so, in the end we would not be able to reconcile Priyadas's and Mahipati's tales, or even those of Sukhsaran and Nagridas, to arrive at a single telling of Mirabai's story. And it seems likely also that these narratives may represent only a fraction of the stories that might have been circulating about Mira in earlier centuries but of which we have only this limited record. We do not, for example, have any known early tellings authored by women.[94] And there is no definitive authority to whom we can turn—neither "objective" historical documentation nor any "original" hagiographic telling or even an agreed upon authoritative one—of which others might be viewed as variants. Instead we have Priyadas's Mira, the *Prem Ambodh*'s Mira, Nagridas's Mira, Mahipati's Mira, and Sukhsaran's Mira.

The stories that surround Mira are the product of dynamic performance traditions, stubbornly multiple and intertextual, speaking not simply of a singular unified and shared memory of a woman of the past but of many different individuals' and communities' encounters with the saint as a living reality. This multiplicity of tellings directs us to examine the truths being articulated in each, from which we learn much about the tellers and their times as well as about the saint. People have not merely received or remembered past traditions but have actively participated in the performance of both narrative and song associated with Mira. The primary basis of this participation, as it is in bhakti, is love, a love which includes not only admiration or adoration but also the desire to possess Mira as their own, to try her on as with a set of clothes, sharing in her life and cultivating a Mira-like devotion (and/or defiance) themselves.

Love is not the only basis for such participation, nor is bhakti the only dimension of life in which tellers are active participants, however, and the tales have other agendas, as we have seen. Even as many tellers may love Mira, her story touches deeply on a variety of complex issues—social, religious, political, personal—and they draw on her power for their own ends. Storytelling is not an art of mere repetition but rather highly contextual and reflexive, as A. K. Ramanujan reminds us, such that tellings may "invert, negate, rework and revalue [one] another" and stand in relationships of "encompassment, mimicry, criticism and conflict," "constantly generating new forms out of the old ones."[95] And it is an active form of speech, meant "to get things done," to entertain and foster devotion and community, but also "a way to use words for social and political purposes in the immediacies of this world."[96] As for Mirabai, embraced by so many and manifest in the telling of her tale, she belongs at once to everyone and is the sole possession of no one, even as Krishna is not in the famed *rasa* dance in which each and every gopi experiences him as dancing only with her. Others, too, not so concerned about devotion, would begin to take an interest in Mirabai—as an exemplary sixteenth-century Indian woman and poetess as much as a saint.

3

History, Heroism, and the Politics of Identity

Mirabai in Nineteenth-Century Colonial India

In the first decades of the nineteenth century, Mirabai would catch the attention of British officers and scholars fascinated by India's culture and history but also engaged in the practical administration and justification of colonial domination. She would surface again and again across the century in lively debates about the status and education of women and about the nature and validity of Hinduism as a religion and of Hindi as a language. By the end of the century, she would be lauded by Indian nationalists looking for heroes and heroines to inspire the struggle against the British, and her life would become a subject for historians in Rajasthan engaged in modern, more objective historical writing but also in the assertion of a reinvigorated rajput identity.[1] Indeed Mirabai seems a likely candidate for those who would look to India's past for exemplary and distinctively "Indian" women of power and independence, and she would later be lifted up by Tagore, Gandhi, and others during the nationalist struggle and embraced by citizens of the new nation and diaspora communities after Independence as a unifying pan-Indian cultural heroine.

By the end of the nineteenth century, a family of tales was crafted by nationalists and rajput historians that has come to dominate many people's understanding and experience of Mira and popular portrayals of the saint in films, dance dramas, novels, and comic books as well as school lessons in Hindi literature through the twentieth century into the present. Claims for their rigorous historical accuracy, however, do not hold up under scrutiny, as we will see. Instead we find the pursuit of historical objectivity mixed with other concerns and coupled with an explicit attempt on the part of some to shut down alternative narratives and experiences of the saint. Despite their best efforts, diverse circulating traditions immediately flow back into this family of related tellings and into print, even as elements of this "historical biography" pass readily into performative and popular traditions.

Nineteenth-century writing on Mirabai in the English-language press drew primarily on devotional and oral sources, with most authors accessing these through the very limited works of select British officers of the East India Company, who clearly both admired her and romanticized the story of this exotic and impassioned princess from the deserts of Rajasthan. These British sources would in turn profoundly influence nationalist portrayals of the saint, as they would nationalist conceptions of the heroism of the rajputs, Sikhs, and marathas. Mira would be reimagined as a proper Indian and rajput heroine who could inspire similar heroism and serve the nationalist cause. Historians in Rajasthan would also seek to reclaim and correct their own history, embracing Mira in the process. The search for the historical Mira which they initiated would continue through the twentieth century in India and beyond, motivated, in part but not entirely, by a drive to know whatever objective facts might be recoverable about the saint.

We share this desire to know as much as possible about the actual life of this extraordinary, likely sixteenth-century woman—the flesh-and-blood person who inspired the devotional stories we have been examining and initiated the voice we have just begun to hear. Yet the kinds of historical sources privileged by nineteenth-century positivist historiography, such as written dynastic chronicles and inscriptions, provide little direct information about Mira's life. To be fair, the available written records—the *vamshavalis* (family histories) and *khyats* (state chronicles) of royal houses of Rajasthan—mention few women, royal or otherwise, especially if they were not the wives of famous men or the mothers of important sons. Without children, Mira is a genealogical dead end, though if she had married the illustrious Rana Kumbha, as some would claim, she might warrant mention. Generally, the primary historical traces we have of royal women of the past in this region are found in oral genealogies specifically about them, maintained by specialized professionals called *ranimanga* bhats.

The only apparent written reference to Mirabai Rathor in standard historical sources before the nineteenth century is found in the writings of Muhnot Nainsi (1610–1670), chief minister under Maharaja Jasvant Singh of Jodhpur.[2] *Nainsi ri Khyat* chronicles the history of the rajputs back to their mythic origins, though it focuses primarily on the history of Marwar (Mira's alleged natal kingdom), and it contains a wealth of detail about life and culture in seventeenth-century Rajasthan. In compiling his account, Nainsi clearly drew on a wide array of sources, including the oral histories of the ruling houses of the rajput clans, their traditional genealogies, and a range of other oral and written documents he would have had access to as chief minister, undoubtedly supplemented by the remembrances of many individuals, including both members and acquaintances of his influential family.[3] In his khyat we find Mira mentioned in a single line in a discussion of Mewar in relation to the son of Rana Sanga, Bhojraj: "it is said that Mirabai Rathor was married to him." This reference has been coupled with Bhojraj's alleged marriage date of 1516 CE to become the foundation for reconstructing the historical events surrounding Mira's life.[4]

Yet the reliability of this reference is questionable because of the explicitly hearsay quality of the statement, setting it apart from other material documented by Nainsi. The author himself seemingly records this information not as "fact" but as circulating tradition: "it is said that. . . ." There is also a larger reason for concern. We are unable to verify whether or not even this hearsay reference was actually part of the original text. As Frances Taft has noted, all currently available manuscripts of Nainsi's khyat appear to be based on a copy made in Bikaner in 1843, and without an earlier manuscript, it cannot be ruled out that this reference to Mira might have been added to the text at some later time, possibly even as late as the production of that copy.[5] It is also the case that Thakur Ram Narayan Singh, *raj diwan,* or chief minister, in the court of Bikaner, is credited with sponsoring the building of a temple in Mira's honor in Vrindavan in 1842 at the ostensible site of her meeting with Jiv Goswami.[6] His actions suggest interest in and perhaps devotion to the saint at that time in the Bikaner court—reason enough perhaps to make such an editorial insertion into the copying of Nainsi's text the following year. Taft's further broad search in the historical documents of Mewar and Marwar for earlier references to Mirabai as the wife of Bhojraj has yet to reveal any sources with copies that might be reliably dated before the 1830s at the very earliest.[7] The trail goes decidedly cold before this time. Yet despite this uncertainty, this singular reference in Nainsi's khyat continues to be used as the basis for historical biographies of the saint.

Bhojraj never actually became rana, though he was heir apparent. Nevertheless, as John Stratton Hawley and others have observed, his dates make him a reasonable candidate for the saint's husband if one accepts her Mertiya lineage and relation to Rao Duda, while Bhojraj's lack of significant accomplishments or children and his early death also make him a rather convenient choice.[8] There is another tantalizing genealogical reference to a woman called "Mirabai" allegedly from the sixteenth century reported by Richard Saran and Norman Ziegler.[9] This Mirabai was the daughter of Rani Bhatiyani Dharbai and Rathor Maldeo of Jodhpur (who would become the sworn enemy of the alleged uncle of the saint Mira, Viramdeo of Merta), and this Mirabai married into the family of the Bagriyo Chahuvan rajputs of Mewar. That there may have been more than one young girl named Mirabai in the Rathor royal houses during this period seems plausible, though the sources for this report have not been verified before the nineteenth century and warrant further interrogation. The existence of this record has been acknowledged by Indian scholars, but no connection to the saint has been suggested.[10] Still, the reference is intriguing, given that "Mirabai" does not appear to have been a common name, Maldeo comes to rule Merta, his daughter is married into Mewar, and there are no other specific references to the saint in such documents.

Historians, accepting Nainsi's reference and the date of Bhojraj's marriage as authoritative, have gone on to identify Mira's extended family and to hypothesize how well-documented larger political events and elements of social life in sixteenth-century Rajasthan might have impacted her life. Though they acknowledge that earlier hagiographic accounts and popular traditions are not strictly "historical" in nature, they accept these devotional texts as legitimate avenues of memory and information. That a devotee called "Mirabai" did indeed existed is not questioned, and need not be, I would argue, as these types of sources are the principal means by which we know about all such renowned saints of the past who lived outside of the realm of dynastic records and royal chronicles.

Deemed the culturally appropriate mode for remembering and recounting their lives, hagiographic sources thus bear the "texture" of history, if not the precise form, potentially recording unique details of individuals' lives, even as they are made to conform to hagiographic expectations and mobilized for instruction, entertainment, community building, patronage, politics, and more, lovingly embellished with creative imaginings.[11] Yet as we have noted, individuals become saints only as they are "communally recognized and remembered over time ... continuously constructed and reconstructed ... in a social process ... that is always political and in service of the historically contingent interests of particular groups."[12] In the available hagiographic references and tellings of Mira's life, this process of saint-making was already well advanced by the nineteenth century. But historians rely on these sources for the basic plot of their emerging biographies, presenting the outline of events therein as largely factual rather than fanciful. However, the uncertainty of Nainsi's reference and the nature of the majority of these sources, coupled with historians' highly selective use of them and their own "historically contingent interests," make any claims for the exclusive historical veracity of their accounts tenuous at best.

Even so, the emerging "historical biography" they initiate has largely been accepted and propagated in popular and scholarly works on Mirabai as "fact," for reasons we will explore. But though nineteenth- and twentieth-century historians can offer us considerable insight into the political and social context in which Mira might have lived, they, no less than other narrators, of necessity actively engage in a creative process as they selectively draw on both historical and nonhistorical sources and shape their data into a coherent life. As a result, their tellings need not and, I would argue, should not be accepted as the final word on who Mirabai was. Their tales, too, tell us at least as much about their own political, social, religious, and personal locations and concerns as they do about this particular woman supposed to have lived in the sixteenth century. We may well find additional references to Mira in as yet undiscovered historical records of earlier date to shed light on her genealogy or birth and death dates, but it is highly unlikely any more detailed evidence will come to light.

Finding the "historical Mira," then, proves to be an impossible task, with the saint always just out of focus and seemingly dancing away from every effort to pin her down definitively. In the absence of historical hard facts about Mira, it is this re-membering of her by different individuals and communities in different times and places that warrants further investigation, in this case the stories that Indian nationalists and historians (and others following in their footsteps) come to tell of Mira's life and why. It is in the performative present rather than in a static past that she lives and thus in presents past that we can know who she has been and becomes, for those who tell and write and sing of her and in her voice. Both the search for the historical Mira and the emerging nationalist heroic tellings of her life story have their roots in the colonial encounter, starting with early European accounts of Mira and of the history of Rajasthan. So it is here that we must begin to understand the genealogy of Mira's ostensibly historical and widely accepted biography.

Nineteenth-Century European Accounts of Mira

In the early nineteenth century Mirabai first caught the interest of Europeans writing about Indian religion, literature, and history, and across the century a series of interweaving concerns would lead British writers to return to her again and again. In 1827, when Tarinee Charun Mitra and William Price were compiling their *Hindee and Hindustanee Selections*, they chose to include her story among their limited selections from Nabhadas's bhaktamal, together with two poems attributed to her (identical to the third and fifth songs found in Nagridas's *Padaprasangmal*a that also appear in Vaishnavdas's *Bhaktamal ki Drishtant*) and a third poem included in another section of popular songs.[13] Horace Hayman Wilson, too, wrote of her along with other saints and sampradays in his 1828 study "The Religious Sects of the Hindus."[14] The copy of the bhaktamal Mitra and Price used they obtained from Wilson's library, and it included an anonymous commentary in addition to Nabhadas's and Priyadas's works.[15] Wilson in turn presumably draws on this same edition of the bhaktamal but also directly on Price and Mitra's collection. Colonel James Tod would also write of Mira in his groundbreaking work, *Annals and Antiquities of Rajasthan* (1829–1832), focusing British as well as nationalist and rajput attention on the saint, as he did more widely on the heroic heritage of the rajputs.[16]

Mitra and Price's and Wilson's works were both published in Calcutta during a time when familiarity with local languages and traditions became a part of the East India Company's administrative agenda as well as the passionate interest of a select number of those in its service. The British study of Indian languages was intimately connected to power and control and began with the study of Sanskrit and Persian (the language of the Mughal court). In the words of Bernard Cohn, this knowledge "was necessary to issue commands, collect taxes, maintain law and order," but also "to create other forms of knowledge about the people they were ruling ... to enable the British to classify, categorize, and bound the vast social world that was India so that it could be controlled."[17]

By 1772, the East India Company had transitioned from being strictly a trading company into a ruling political power with autonomous control of the region of Bengal, Bihar, and Orissa. The administration of the region now became its responsibility, requiring more than armies to ensure the continued orderly flow of revenue. Language facility became essential, and the collection, preservation, and translation of "native texts" was undertaken in earnest with the founding of the Asiatic Society of Bengal in 1784. Beginning in 1801, language requirements were instituted for judicial and revenue officers, and the College at Fort William was tasked with providing the necessary instruction.[18] British and Indian scholars staffed the College, working closely together in this educational mission and in the production of knowledge about India, with Indian scholars serving as "native informants" in the "transform[ation of] Indian knowledge into European information."[19]

William Price was appointed assistant professor of Sanskrit, Bengali, and Marathi at the College sometime before 1815 and was promoted to professor of Hindustani in 1824. By 1837 all staff officers were required to pass language exams. Grammars, dictionaries, and selections of literature for study were produced during this period, including Mitra and Price's collection.[20] Wilson too was involved in this project, becoming secretary of the Asiatic Society in 1811 and publishing a Sanskrit dictionary for the College, first in 1819 and then in expanded form in 1832, before leaving India to take up the post as the first Boden Professor of Sanskrit at Oxford University.[21]

Mira figures among these early literary selections and the presentation of religious traditions of India, presumably as someone so popular that familiarity with her was integral to understanding and appreciating but also ruling India. Was it Mitra or Price who selected her for inclusion in their popular instructional work, or did they both agree she should be there? Nabhadas's bhaktamal with Priyadas's commentary was clearly well known, considering the number and wide geographic distribution of manuscripts at the time and the subsequent proliferation of lithograph and print editions.[22] But why choose to include Mira from among the hundreds of saints therein? Mitra and Price give no reason.[23] Perhaps one or both had a fondness for her; it is equally possible that her story, character, and voice were implicitly identified as an essential part of the cultural vocabulary, widely used to talk about gender, devotion, social values and conflicts, and much more. In any case, Price and Mitra's selections would remain a standard resource for the study of Hindi for decades, introducing many to the saint.[24]

From a British point of view, Mira's compelling story and devotional sentiments may also have provided an engaging point of contact and recognition. Hers is simultaneously a wildly romantic tale from an exotic locale and a story with a familiar ring: the struggle of one utterly dedicated, whether to love (human or Divine), to beauty (art, music, or literature), or to knowledge (scientific or spiritual)—indeed the story of all those who would follow their calling without wavering, though to do so might require suffering fools and swimming against the stream of social norms and expectations into uncharted territory (as many of those who ventured to India from Britain might have seen themselves as doing). Recounted as the tale of an upper-class, educated, beautiful, and devoted woman in India, who was misunderstood at best or even persecuted by brutal men in her time, her story also conveniently lent support to emerging rhetorical justifications for colonial domination in part based on the alleged mistreatment of women in India.

Wilson tells Mira's story within his classificatory "Religious Sects of the Hindus" in the context of an independent sect or possibly a subdivision of the followers of Vallabhacharya in western India called "Mira Bais," identifying them as worshipers of Krishna in the form of Ranchor who considered Mira their leader.[25] Given the overwhelming rejection of Mira in the *Varta* literature of this sampraday, this is an unexpected claim, though perhaps there was a rapprochement between the sampraday and the saint in the eighteenth century or at least a continuing appreciation by some members of it. Wilson does admit that "except in the west of India, it does not appear that she has many immediate and exclusive adherents." Nevertheless, his claim of an independent Mirabai sect would be repeated by many subsequent authors and appears among the religious sects listed in the 1901 Census of India (although there are, interestingly, only six practitioners, all male, recorded in Bombay and only one adherent, again male, recorded in Central India).[26] No such sect or subsect has been independently documented by subsequent scholars, yet this assertion conveniently allows Wilson to include this extremely popular saint within his seminal work, establishing categories that would circumscribe "Hindu religion" for at least the next century.

Wilson goes on to describe Mira as "the heroine of a prolix legend in the *Bhakta Mala*" and the author of songs sung by "Hindu deists," especially followers of Kabir and of Nanak (particularly Udasis).[27] He identifies Mira as a daughter of a "petty raja" of Merta married to the Rana of Udaipur and a contemporary of Akbar, and drawing on Priyadas, he details her story as it appears there. The only three additions he makes are that (1) she was "expelled from the Rana's bed and palace" after refusing to worship the *devi*, (2) it was because of persecution of Vaishnavas in Udaipur that brahmans were sent to bring her back from Dwarka, and (3) her miraculous death happened in the following way: "[P]revious to departing, she visited the temple of her tutelary deity, to take leave of him, when, on the completion of her adorations, the image opened, and Mira leaping into the fissure, it closed, and she finally disappeared. In memory of this miracle it is said, that the image of Mira Bai is worshipped in Udaipur in conjunction with that of Ranchhor."[28] The final detail of the worship of Mirabai in Udaipur corresponds to Sukhsaran's account rather than Priyadas's, but may as easily reflect wider circulating traditions as any direct influence either way, particularly given the uncertain date of Sukhsaran's text and that Wilson recounts the information as being "said." And again there is no corroborating evidence of such an image or tradition of worship of Mirabai in Udaipur.[29] Wilson closes with translations of two Mira poems, drawn from Mitra and Price. He clearly notes Mira's wide appeal among members of diverse religious sects in his time, including Kabirpanthis and Sikhs, though he is also explicitly dismissive of her or at least of the "prolix" stories about her, reflective of his attitude toward the bhaktamal more generally.[30] Nevertheless, Wilson's account would become a primary source for writings on Mira throughout the nineteenth century and into the twentieth.

James Tod, too, began his service to the East India Company in Bengal in 1799 at the age of seventeen, becoming a member of the Second European Regiment in Calcutta in 1800, but he soon found himself traveling across the subcontinent and working as a surveyor and later mapmaker and intelligence officer.[31] Making his way rapidly up through the ranks, he was appointed political agent of western Rajputana in 1818, as the domination of the East India Company expanded with the defeat of the marathas and after treaties were ratified between Britain and the various rajput kingdoms. Among his principal responsibilities was the kingdom of Mewar, which was in disarray at this time, torn apart by war and debt, and Tod worked as an agent of the company to restore the maharaja to his former power and to act behind the scenes as an advisor, thus reinforcing (but also controlling) the existing indigenous political institutions to facilitate political stability and revenue collection.[32] His tenure was short, however. He gained a reputation for being overly sympathetic to the rajputs but also for being excessively interventionist, and he found his authority curtailed by his superiors, who, among many other things, "found Tod's objections to company imposed financial burden on Rajputs states unwarranted and insubordinate."[33] In poor health, Tod resigned his post in 1822 and returned to England in 1823.

Throughout his military service, Tod was a voracious collector of all manner of information about the geography, history, and culture of India and especially Rajasthan, and this encyclopedic knowledge would prove to be invaluable in securing British military objectives and a key to his rapid advancement. His position and respectful relations in the Mewar court allowed him to further his knowledge, providing great access to regional written and oral sources. He was fascinated by and greatly admired the martial culture of the rajputs, drawing in his letters a romanticized parallel between his own idealized Scottish martial heritage and that of the rajput past, lamenting their passing and longing for the restoration of these bygone days.[34] After returning to England, he traveled around Europe lecturing on India, assumed the position of the first librarian of the newly established Royal Asiatic Society, and wrote both his magnum opus, *The Annals and Antiquities of Rajasthan*, and a chronicle of his travels in 1822–1823 titled *Travels in Western India*. In the *Annals* Tod detailed the glorious deeds of rajput heroes of the past, and he is credited with ushering Rajasthan onto the national and world stage and with initiating modern historical writing on the region.

In writing the *Annals*, Lloyd Rudolph and Susanne Rudolph argue, Tod was influenced by "three interrelated metaphors and models—medieval feudalism, romantic nationalism, and civilizational progress."[35] He portrayed the kingdoms of Rajasthan as exhibiting the same "honor and heroism, the fealty and adventure that inspire sacrifice, service and noble deeds" that Henry Hallam attributed to Europe in his *View of the State of Europe during the Middle Ages* (1818) and as thereby representing a similar stage in India's civilizational development.[36] Deeply influenced also by romanticism, he underscored "integrity, sincerity, [purity of soul], readiness to sacrifice one's life to some inner light, dedication to some ideal for which it is worth sacrificing all that one is, for which it is worth both living and dying."[37] And he shared the Scottish romantics' glorification of "heroic youthful death" and their embrace of classical Greece as the foundation of European civilization.[38] The Greek nationalist struggle for independence from the Ottoman Empire, begun in 1821, characterized as a freedom struggle against despotic (Muslim) rule that all Europeans must join, no doubt also influenced Tod's depiction of the rajputs in their resistance to the Mughals and the direct comparisons he made between ancient Greek and rajput warriors and battles.[39]

When it came to Mirabai, she too captured Tod's imagination, readily illustrating such a romantic vision of medieval heroism, purity, and dedication. He writes in the *Annals* of the saint being the daughter of "the Rathore of Merta," Rao Duda, and the wife of Rana Kumbha (the grandfather of Bhojraj, with whom she is associated in *Nainsi ri Khyat*).[40] She is, he declares, "the most celebrated princess of her time for beauty and romantic piety," whose "history is a romance" and whose "excess of devotion at every shrine of the favourite deity with the fair of Hind" from Vrindavan to Dwarka "gave rise to many tales of scandal." He notes that her compositions, many still "preserved and admired," are better known to devotees than to "ribald bards" (a reference perhaps to popular singers who might sing of more ordinary love and heroism as well as those who might perform epic songs of local hero deities or recite the chronicles of rajput royal families). He adds that it is not known whether her husband influenced her "poetic piety" or she him in his writing of a commentary on Jayadev's *Gita Govind*. Elsewhere Tod writes of the temple in Chittor supposedly built by Mira for "the god of her idolatry, Shamnath," "the Hindu Apollo," and he describes her miraculous demise, presenting it in quotation marks, as if he were drawing the words directly from another (unidentified) source: "[T]he god descended from his pedestal and gave her an embrace, which extricated the spark of life. 'Welcome, Mira,' said the lover of Radha and her soul was absorbed in his!" He also attributes the commentary on the *Gita Govind* directly to her.[41]

In Tod's lesser-known *Travels in Western India*, he reveals his own deep affinity for Mira, identifying a temple allegedly built by her in Dwarka as his favorite among all he visited there.[42] Composed as a personal travelogue rather than history, in this text he identifies Mira as the wife of Rana Lakha (Kumbha's grandfather). With regard to her poetry, he praises it as unequalled by any other poet, filled with florid "descriptions of the spiritual charms of her divine lover" that fueled scandalous rumors (the most explicit of which he suggests may have been created by other poets jealous of her fame). He concedes, however, that she also brought this upon herself by her wanderings to pilgrimage sites and her dancing in the temples (perhaps echoing his own experiences in Mewar, leading to his resignation). However, he is clear that her husband, her "lord and sovereign," never "entertained any jealousy or suspicion," even when Krishna "descended from his pedestal and embraced his devotee," nor had he any reason to do so. Within Tod's conception of the rajputs, it could not have been otherwise, it seems. In this context, he identifies Lakha's son as Bikramajit (elsewhere son of Sanga), who he claims was also a great devotee, deeply influenced by his mother—the only maternal reference to Mira to my knowledge, but in keeping with Tod's view of rajputs and presumably with his own cultural ideals of womanhood.[43] The connections he makes between Mirabai, Lakha, and Bikramajit are inconsistent with his own historical writing as well as that of others, but this appears not to concern him here.

The accounts of Mira's life by the renowned Sanskrit scholar Wilson and the esteemed historian Tod become a major source for subsequent portrayals of Mira in survey works on Indian literature and religion in the decades that follow (notwithstanding internal inconsistencies therein). J. H. Garcin de Tassy cites both, directly translating much of Wilson along with applicable passages from Nabhadas and Priyadas in his presentation of Mira in *Histoire de la Litterature Hindouie et Hindoustanie* (1847).[44] Never having actually been to India, he assumed a chair in vernacular Hindustani at the École Spéciale des Languages Orientales Vivantes in Paris in 1828, and his French text—nonetheless "sponsored by British colonial authorities"—would be widely read.[45] Similarly George Grierson directly credits Tod and Wilson as the sources for his presentation of Mira in his important study *The Mediaeval Vernacular Literature of Hindustan* (1888), concluding with his observation, "Some idea of the popularity of her writings may be gained from the fact that I have collected, from the mouths of the people of Mithila [in Bihar in northeast India], songs purporting to be about her."[46]

Wilson and Tod clearly form the basis for presentations of Mira by many others as well, including Monier Monier-Williams (*Non-Christian Religious Systems: Hinduism*, 1882), Edward Balfour (*The Cyclopedia of India and of Eastern and Southern Asia*, 1885), John Murray Mitchell (*Hinduism Past and Present*, 1885), W. J. Wilkins (*Modern Hinduism*, 1887), and John McClintock and James Strong (*Cyclopedia of Biblical, Theological, and Ecclesiastical Literature*, 1887) as well as Bahadur Lala Baij Nath (*Hinduism: Ancient and Modern*, 1899). Even the presentation of Mira's life in Shiv Singh Sengar's influential poetic anthology *Sivsimh Saroj* (1878), which would become a principal foundation for subsequent study of the history of Hindi literature and enshrine the saint as its premiere premodern poetess, appears to have been influenced by Wilson and Tod, whether directly or through another source.[47]

Others, though clearly drawing on Wilson and/or Tod, embellish or misrepresent these sources. For example, Alfred Comyn Lyall cites Mira as an example in a discussion of the perceived Indian value of having the tomb of a holy person in one's village, claiming that she "vanished from earth through a fissure in a rock" (in what appears to be a conflation of Wilson's account of her demise and Sita's story and in keeping with Lyall's own wider characterization of Hinduism as superstitious, "disorderly," and marked by "discordant rites").[48] Seemingly more intentional distortions also enter as Wilson and/or Tod are quoted by one author who is referenced by another who in turn is referenced by yet another in a literary version of the mid-twentieth-century popular "telephone," but one belying the innocence of this childhood game. For example, the respected scholar Rajendralal Mitra mentions Mira in *The Antiquities of Orissa* (1880) within his discussion of the temple dancers and singers dedicated to Jaganath in Puri. Mitra's aim throughout the study is to explain and defend Hinduism against its foreign detractors, for whom grossly distorted accounts of the rituals attending Jaganath had become emblematic of all they abhorred about Hinduism from the early decades of the nineteenth century.[49] Mitra counters superficial assumptions that female ritual specialists are either mere entertainers or some kind of temple prostitutes, explaining their early dedication to a life of celibate purity and their marriage to the deity. In this context he reports, "In rare cases grown-up women betake themselves to the service of the temple and a notable instance of it is offered by Mira Bai, the daughter of Surya Rana of Jeypur, who devoted herself to the service of Rangchodji."[50] Mitra footnotes Wilson as his source in a clear appeal to his authority.[51]

Mitra's work is scholarly, with a multitude of citations, but when his description is popularized by William Simpson through his article "The Lord of the World," printed in *Fraser's Magazine* (London) and *Frank Leslie's Popular Monthly* (New York) in 1882, Simpson identifies Mira as a "nautch girl" (dancing girl) and offers her as an example of the fact that such women often came from distinguished families.[52] This characterization of Mira in the popular British and American press, particularly in the moral climate of the late nineteenth century and the anti-nautch movement which began in that same year, completely subverts Mitra's intent, and authors well into the twentieth century will still be defending Mira against this charge.

For other authors, Mira seems to have provided a small opening for appreciation of Indian religion and culture, even for those who wrote in the most scathing terms about India and Hinduism, particularly among

Christian missionaries. Despite her clear devotion to Krishna, Auguste Barth, William Samuel Lilly, and others recognized in her an uncompromising and singular love of God and a willingness to sacrifice even her life for it that they could not help but admire.[53] More sympathetic writers would compare Mira to Christian mystics such as Teresa of Avila and Saint John of the Cross.[54] Bhakti more broadly seems to have touched an emerging Victorian aesthetic religious devotionalism in this period, as Vijay Pinch argues, that led writers like Monier-Williams, Frederic Growse, Grierson, Max Mueller, and John Muir to sympathetically identify commonalities between Christian and Hindu devotion.[55] Despite her sagun devotion to Krishna, Mirabai appears to stand on this frontier, even more than many other saints, though there is also often an exceptionalism that clings to her in such portrayals.

New elements from popular traditions begin to enter English accounts of Mirabai in the latter decades of the nineteenth century, reflecting a growing Indian nationalist drive to celebrate and publish vernacular traditions as a primary "bearer of Indianness, of cultural identity," paralleled by a concomitant increased British focus on learning more localized and regional traditions to better understand (and control) their subjects in the wake of the Sepoy Rebellion of 1857.[56] But in addition, British officers and scholars like William Crooke, Richard Temple, Grierson, and Growse were "influenced by the folklorist revival of their native Ireland which also found echo in the English 'Arts and Crafts' movement" of the period, leading them to laud "popular cultures [as] resisting the 'artificiality' of the modern."[57] In so doing, as C. A. Bayly argues, British interest in and promotion of vernacular literature in this period "mirrored and stimulated north Indian nationalism, even as it sought to block and deny it."[58]

As the British drive for control combined with the search for "authenticity" converged with Indian concerns, diverse popular traditions of Mirabai were documented in print. A patron of Indian culture and arts and of Ram bhakti, Raja Raghuraj Singh of Rewa would record a wide array of circulating traditions surrounding her in his *Bhaktamal Ramarasikavali* (1864) which in turn would serve as a major source for later British scholars.[59] Working closely with Crooke on the collection of Indian folklore, Ram Gharib Chaube would also document additional popular traditions in "The Legend of Mirabai," published in *North Indian Notes and Queries* (1893). Nevertheless his account continues to draw heavily on Wilson and Tod, again perhaps as much for legitimating authority as for information, and he suggests that "though [Mira's] high birth and good education won her the respect of the Royal family, yet the Rana suspected her character," and so sought to kill her.[60] It would be this

Mira—high-caste, deeply spiritual, educated, and respected—who would be fully embraced by nationalist writers in the same year.

For the most part, these references to Mira are still fragmentary, drawn from hagiography, songs attributed to her, and popular circulating traditions, often accessed through Wilson's and Tod's accounts and/or drawing authority from them. Nainsi's reference appears unknown to these authors, and Mira's husband and the details of her life remain vague and fluid, although Rana Kumbha is most often reported as the one to whom she was married and she is said to be related to Rao Duda—both men remembered as great devotees. Her story is a romantic and somewhat scandalous tale of divine passion, she a pious, beautiful devotee and poet. She is generally invoked in a positive sense by both Indian and British writers but primarily in a tangential way in larger discourses on Indian history and literature, Hindu religion, and the position of women in India. In the latter half of the nineteenth century increasing attention would focus on Mira as these lines of discourse coalesced. And in the 1890s more complete stories of her life would take shape that differed dramatically from the hagiographic tales that preceded them and that were inextricably intertwined with the construction of Hindu nationalist and revitalized rajput identities in response to colonial domination.

Oriental Scholarship, Gender, and the Politics of Knowledge

The late 1820s—when Price, Wilson, and Tod first wrote of Mira—was a transitional era in British rule. Ashis Nandy, in his study of the psychology of colonialism, suggests that before 1830, the idea of empire had not yet taken hold in the minds of the British, nor had the "homology between sexual and political dominance... [become] central to the colonial culture."[61] After this time, however, both became operative as the British middle class entered colonial administration and British political and cultural dominance over India expanded. Justifications for colonial rule had to be constructed, asserting British intellectual, religious, cultural, linguistic, and moral superiority, and a simultaneous denigration of elements of Indian culture and religion was carried out in part through the production and framing of knowledge about India during this period. Linguistic study drew attention to the Indo-European roots of Sanskrit and fostered admiration for Sanskrit religious and philosophical texts, but these were disconnected from contemporary society in a vision of past glory, now lost, tied to a shared Aryan heritage originating outside India. Presented as the product of rational and objective study, British claimed superiority was naturalized and embedded in narrative as the inevitable culmination of an undeniable process of evolutionary social and historical development, while Indian culture was portrayed in a trajectory of decline.

The position of women was identified as a key measure of British superiority and a rhetoric of hypermasculinity generated that put the British in the role of dominant male, both rescuing vulnerable Indian women (who were perceived as victims of Indian male barbarism and ignorance) and taking care of those same men (who were alternately characterized as womanly, weak, and childlike, in need of guidance and discipline).[62] And Mira's story—with her upper-caste royal heritage, her romanticized devotion, her unwarranted persecution at the hands of unscrupulous and/or ignorant men, and her ultimate rescue by Krishna—could readily be drawn into this rhetorical strategy.

In the face of this type of rhetoric, members of the Indian elite set out to craft alternative narratives, rejecting much of the colonial portrayal of Indian culture and religion even as they accepted and responded to other aspects of it, largely embracing the notion of an idealized ancient past while initiating a number of reforms. Within this rhetorical battleground, Bayly suggests, "Oriental scholarship . . . was not a homogeneous mode of gaining power over India. It was rather an arena of debate in which the more powerful—the British and the Indian elites—attempted to appropriate themes and symbols [of indigenous and often popular origin] which suited their political needs and chimed with features of their intellectual culture. . . . They were distorted or modified as they were appropriated by the British, but they could also fragment in the hands of the colonial rulers and help subvert the very cause they were supposed to uphold."[63] India's past and the position of women would be key issues in this highly contested arena of public debate, as Uma Chakravarti, Partha Chatterjee, and many others have argued so compellingly, and Mira would be appropriated by all sides.[64]

Education for women and girls was at once a widely embraced and a highly controversial aspect of the reform agenda, with early resistance to missionary and coeducation overcome as Indians began opening their own schools for girls in the 1850s. But discussion about the precise nature of that education and its purpose would be ongoing. As Uma Chakravarti has noted, European women writers in this period also began questioning the dominant portrayal of Indian women as uniformly backward and oppressed. Some offered highly romanticized views of educated, strong Indian women and egalitarian gender relations but located them safely in the idealized golden age long past, showing women's education to be a deeply rooted indigenous practice and value but also not significantly challenging views of Indian women's oppression and degradation in their own day.[65] Others would turn to more contemporary women, Mirabai among them, to counter this rhetoric.

In 1855 an article titled "Eastern Indian Poetry—Female Poets" appeared in the *National Magazine*, an American monthly "devoted to Literature, Art and Religion," whose editor Abel Stevens aimed to provide high-quality educational yet lively reading material for the general public. Largely a translation of a portion of Garcin de Tassy's work, including his extended presentation of Mirabai, the article closes with an affirmation that these women's works were worthy in themselves of presentation as "expressions of universal passion" and as excellent poetry but also that the writer had another aim: "to show the development of Hindoo thought, supposed by very few among us to exist in that barbarous land, especially among its women, whose intellectual position is so generally degraded."[66] The author portrays Indian women, at least exceptional upper-class educated Indian women of the more recent past, like Mira, as admirable and to some degree at least "like us" for the American reader, though they might be beleaguered by living in such a distant and "barbarous land" where women generally were in need of educational opportunities as well as protection.

In the wake of the 1857 rebellion, Sangeeta Ray contends, there was a further shift in British rhetoric that may have accelerated a more positive portrayal of at least some Indian women, with "the discourses of imperialism and nationalism becom[ing] increasingly intertwined as each sought to gain control over the representations of the Indian woman."[67] The rebellion caught the British off guard, signaling widespread dissatisfaction with crippling revenue assessments and blatant British disregard and contempt for their colonial subjects, including regional rulers as well as those serving in their armies. In the aftermath of the violence and suppression of the rebellion, the raw reality of British political domination and economic exploitation was laid bare, largely dispelling any illusion of benevolent paternalistic rule but also yielding an increased sympathetic identification by the British with upper-caste Indian women who were viewed together with British women and children as vulnerable to and threatened by rebellious and violent Indian men. That identification may have opened the way for a more appreciative British portrayal of such women, but one which overlapped with growing nationalist claims that these same women were the embodiment of Indianness, thereby also subverting the colonial agenda, as Bayly noted, and adding another dimension of complexity to this contested terrain of gendered representation.

The rebellion triggered an intensification of British authoritarian control. The Government of India Act transferred authority from the East India Company to the Crown in 1858, while at the same time ensuring the position (and thus loyalty) of local princes and providing for at least a limited degree of Indian consultation in governance. To gather information and facilitate order and control, attention was brought to bear on vernacular and folk traditions, with attempts also made to limit freedom of speech in the growing vernacular press, and the Census of India was initiated, carried out for the first time in 1871. In the wake of sepoy involvement in the rebellion, the army was also reconstituted based on British "pseudo-scientific" conceptions of the Indian "martial races" with Punjabi Sikhs, jats, and rajputs identified as innately loyal and superior fighters—a racial characterization which included a parallel category of weak "feminine races," of which the Bengalis were deemed a prime example.[68] The colonial rhetoric of hypermasculinity and British superiority thus grew even more strident.

Countering this rhetoric and claiming the right to self-representation, Indian elites in turn began to draw on history and legend as well as on this same British conception of "martial races" to develop historical narratives that spoke of Indian heroism with the Sikhs, rajputs, and marathas valiantly resisting foreign domination (primarily portrayed as Muslim, though with obvious reference to the British). The works of Tod, J. D. Cunningham, and Grant Duff offered a wealth of raw material for this project.[69] This glorification of *kshatriya* (warrior and ruling caste) ideals was in full swing in the latter decades of the century, their origins traced back to the ancient Aryans and to the epic tradition of the *Mahabharata*. The rajputs especially were portrayed as having never bowed to foreign domination, preferring to die rather than submit.[70] The emerging Indian identity these increasingly nationalist elites began to craft was transregional and "Hindu," though in this period the term "Hindu" was used by both British and nationalist writers alike sometimes in its originating sense to indicate all the people of the geographic region who shared a common cultural heritage ("the people beyond the Indus") and sometimes in a more limiting sense to designate a set of interrelated religious traditions distinct from Islam, a usage dating back at least to the thirteenth-century Turkish and Afghan regimes collectively called the Delhi sultanate.[71]

This new Indian identity was being forged in narrative, consciously constructed through the reshaping of myth, legend, hagiography, and history and exercised in fiction. Heroes from the more distant past merged with those of the present, and even the deities were not privileged in this process.[72] Krishna was transformed under the pen of Bankimchandra Chatterji (1838–1894), a key figure in this nationalist endeavor to assert a reformed and unified Hindu identity.[73] In the words of Nandy, Bankimchandra "tried to build a historical and historically conscious Kṛṣṇa—self-consistent, self-conscious and moral according to modern norms . . . [and] rejected as latter-day interpolations—and hence unauthentic—every trait of Kṛṣṇa that did not meet the first requirement for a Christian and Islamic god, namely all-perfection."[74] His "restored" Krishna embodied the combined qualities of the military hero and the spiritual renouncer that would mark the newly envisioned ideal Hindu Indian man.[75]

The Search for Exemplars of a New Indian Woman

Mira enters this process of identity formation in part because a new image of the ideal Indian woman was needed to stand beside this ideal Indian man, and the search was on for exemplary women from the past as well as men. This ideal woman had to be both heroic and self-disciplined, ready to step out of the home in defense of the motherland yet also to remain within it, preserving Indian, understood as "Hindu," superiority over the British in the spiritual realm as the embodiment of all that was best in Indian culture and religion.[76] Indian history and legend included stories of heroic women, or *viranganas*, many of whom were rajputs (with the notable exception of the famous brahman Rani of Jhansi, Lakshmibai, whose battles with the British during the 1857 rebellion also made her an ideal figure to rally the Independence movement).[77]

These heroines moved beyond the normative gender constructions of their high-caste birth and were known for their martial skills and valor in battle. They took roles normally available only to men in administering kingdoms and leading armies in times of crisis, even dressing as men in many cases, riding horses, and wielding swords in defense of their homeland. Such strong women offered a stark contrast to British portrayals of Indian women as victimized, passive, and helpless, in desperate need of rescue. The bounds of this independence and strength had to be circumscribed, however, in order not to undermine the masculinity of the Indian man, under siege and weighed down by colonial subordination.

Nationalist and British characterizations converged in the *Calcutta Review*, which published a two-part extended essay in 1869 titled "Hindoo Female Celebrities" with the explicit aim of showing the historical strength of Indian women (at least "before the Muslim conquest," a dividing line embraced by both European colonial powers and many nationalists alike, that conveniently laid the blame for India's weaknesses at the feet of Muslims and reinforced an increasing identification of "Indian" as religiously "Hindu"). The intended audience of the *Review* was the English-educated Bengali middle class, the *bhadralok,* or "respectable people," with the editors in this period British and avowedly Christian.[78] The anonymous author begins the essay thus:

> Few subjects engage so much of the public attention at present time as the condition of Hindoo females. It is discussed in the legislature, in public assemblies, and in domestic circles. It is the fertile theme of philanthropists, reformers, and public lecturers. Affecting, as it does, the great question of the regeneration of India, it has well-nigh become the absorbing topic of the day.... But it is, in truth, far from having been exhausted. The opinions generally expressed, are too often the offspring of limited knowledge and superficial enquiry. Foreigners, judging only from what they see and hear, conclude that the women of this country are immeasurably inferior, both intellectually and socially, to women of other civilized lands, and, indeed, they are scarcely less degraded than women among savages.[79]

The author then takes up the task of countering this view, adding one more voice to the lively debates swirling around women's education, child marriage and the age of consent, widows' rights and remarriage, divorce, and the like, being carried out in vernacular as well as English print media, from newspapers and journals to domestic manuals and works of literature.

The author begins with Manu and then turns to the past to demonstrate the strength, dignity, and intellect of Indian women. The first half of the essay focuses on women found in scriptural, mythological, and epic sources, women like Gargi and Maitreyi from the Upanishads, Ahalya, Sita (who is compared to the Virgin Mary) and Shakuntala, Kunti and Draupadi, Yashoda, Rukmini and Radha, and many others. The second installment champions women of history and legend, heroines such as Padmini, Tarabai, Durgavati, Ahalyabai, and the Rani of Jhansi; the rajput queen and devotee Mirabai is mentioned, albeit in a short paragraph drawn entirely from Tod.[80]

In 1871 Keshub Chunder Sen, a Brahmo Samaji breakaway reformer and advocate of women's education, invoked a similar group of women, including Mirabai, in a lecture titled "Native Female Improvement," as evidence that "women of character lived in this country, who adorned and purified Hindoo homes and exercised an ennobling influence far and wide" and who would again do so through proper education.[81] Another article published in the *Calcutta Review* in 1872, "The Development of the Female Mind in India," takes up a similar theme, introducing Mira and other rajput heroines and lauding them for their intellectual, moral, and religious development, their fearlessness in the face of death, and their heroism, which placed them "on a par with the Greek and Roman women."[82] This same theme is picked up by John A. Weisse in his *Origin, Progress and Destiny of the English Language*

(1879) in which, though he ultimately argues for the supremacy of English and the cultures which speak it, he acknowledges these heroic and accomplished women in India—Sita, Gargi, Mirabai, and Ahalyabai among them.[83] But the emphasis for Weisse and even the most sympathetic of British writers during this period was generally on the exceptionalism and universal qualities of these women, their writings, and in Mira's case her religiosity, and thus on their similarity to women of Europe rather than their Indianness.

Nationalist authors would increasingly portray these same women as thoroughly Indian, countering British gender-based rhetorical justification of colonial domination but also asserting an Indian spiritual superiority in the face of European materialism. Concurrently Hinduism was being defined and defended as a distinctive unified religion on par with Christianity (employing a range of strategies, from monotheizing and/or "Vedic" reforms to an almost reactionary embracing of all things "Hindu" and the crafting of an overarching Vaishnavism or Vaishnava-advaita synthesis), and Hindi was being put forward as a civilizational and national language, derived from Sanskrit with an ancient Aryan pedigree and a storied literary canon, distinct from Urdu and purged of Persian and Arabic influences. Mirabai would be drawn into this contested ground as a saint and a poet, held up as a woman at once heroic and deeply spiritual, thoroughly Indian and decidedly Hindu, traditional yet also strikingly modern. Embraced as the greatest premodern Hindi poetess and as the embodiment of bhakti, she would also inspire some of the principal architects of this growing nationalism in deeply personal ways, including Bharatendu Harishchandra of Banaras, whose devotional poetry bears the distinct mark of her influence according to Vasudha Dalmia, along with that of the *astachaps,* the eight major poet-saints recognized by the Vallabha sampraday, of which he was a devoted adherent.[84] Lauded as the father of modern Hindi, he would also develop his own vision of an internally coherent Hinduism, marked at its core by a monotheistic Vaishnava bhakti that affirmed image worship and the puranic Krishna of Braj (in contradistinction to Bankimchandra's formulation as well as those of the Brahmo Samaj and Arya Samaj).[85]

It would be Bankimchandra who would provide a rhetorical justification for the conjoining of bhakti and nationalism, however, harkening back to the *Bhagavad Gita.* True Hindu dharma and religion, he would argue, consists of "devotion to God, love for mankind, and quietness of heart," grounded in control of the senses, inner purity, and the cultivation of all the faculties of the whole person (modeled by Krishna as the complete man) for the simultaneous benefit of oneself and others.[86] This defining devotion to God necessarily and inexorably led to the sacred duty to defend one's nation as the greatest practical unit of selfless concern:[87]

> The result of this *bhakti* is love for the world because God is in every being. There is no contradiction between love for the world and love for one-self, love for one's own people, love for one's own country.... [S]aving one's own people is a much greater duty than saving oneself, and saving one's own country is much greater than saving one's own people. When *bhakti* toward God and love for all people are the same thing, it can be said that, apart from *bhakti* toward God, love of country is the greatest duty of all.[88]

His transformed Krishna was the ideal toward which all men should strive, his actions the epitome of this universalized kshatriya dharmic duty/love.

In his watershed novel *Anandmath* (1882), Bankimchandra would further depict the transformation of this defining devotion to God into dedication to the motherland and portray the heroism of the ordinary woman as an everyday virangana who in a time of crisis could transcend both her sexuality (his heroine, Shanti, dresses as a male renouncer) and domesticity (she fights at her husband's side against both a degenerate local Muslim ruler and the British).[89] Still, crisis made this type of action acceptable, and in most nationalist constructions women were generally expected to continue to adhere to the pativrata ideals embodied by Sita—the long-suffering, self-sacrificing, virtuous, absolutely devoted wife of Rama—instilling in others the same sense of integrity, devotion, and self-sacrifice in the service of the nation. In this upper-caste, middle-class, Hindu reformulation, women who dared to challenge notions of stridharm (women's religious and social duty) were seen as betraying not only their men but also the nation. The other side of countering the British rhetoric of hypermasculinity was that "woman" had to remain the measure of the masculine by contrast and complementarity. The search for real women in the past who exemplified and could inspire this kind of heroism and "Indianness," coupled with the nationalist embrace of rajput martial culture, focused increasing attention on Mirabai in addition to more standard viranganas. Mira could conceivably become an ideal model for the feminine manifestation of Bankimchandra's dharmic duty/love for this nation-in-the-making, but like Krishna, she would need to go through a similar process of transformation/restoration.

Mirabai Revisioned: Ennobling Indian Religion, Society, and Self

In 1892, high court lawyer and acclaimed novelist Govardhanram Madhavram Tripathi (1855–1907) turned to Mira as the embodiment of Indian women's strength and independence, even as he laid claim to her for Gujarat as one of its greatest poets and praised bhakti as an endogenous source of progressive social ideals.[90] He did so in a lecture delivered to the Wilson College Literary Society in Bombay (subsequently published as *The Classical Poets of Gujarat and Their Influence on Society and Morals*).[91] Tripathi saw it as his patriotic duty to work for the transformation of his fellow Indians into "a people who shall be higher and stronger than they are, who shall be better able to look and manage for themselves than the present *helpless* generation of my educated and uneducated countrymen," and thus able and motivated to pursue freedom in an enlightened way.[92] Toward this end, he would write both fiction and history, leading Rachel Dwyer to dub him "[t]he Gujarati equivalent to Bengali's Bankimcandra."[93] He embraced fiction as "a powerful social force" that could captivate readers and join the ideal to the real in a way that offered "the ordinary reader subtler moulds and finer casts for the formation of his inner self,"[94] writing "the first great novel of real life in Gujarati," *Sarasvatichandra*, published to high acclaim in four volumes from 1887 to 1901.[95]

In the midst of writing this novel, however, Tripathi would turn to history as "the store-house of lessons as to what my people should be made to be, and how this is to be done, if at all, and what potent seeds be sown in what soil—in what season—by what implements—and by what husbandry."[96] His research would be wide ranging, and though he would choose to write about the classical poets of Gujarat, this meant also that he had to address religion, politics, social conditions, and much more, situating his study in broader Indian history. The finished work was, in the words of Sudhir Chandra, nothing short of a "radical remembrance of the past ... [that] counters the rulers' claim to represent a superior, progressive and liberal culture," offering "[m]odels of 'free and advanced societies' ... available at home" and "a tradition of the irrepressibility of human spirit and imagination in the face of everything designed to keep it in bondage."[97] It is in bhakti that Tripathi finds the articulation of such a homegrown progressive egalitarian vision and irrepressible spirit, and particularly in the poetry and lives of Mirabai and Narsi Mehta.

Acknowledging the paucity of available information about earlier centuries in the "present stage of historical ignorance," Tripathi was also intensely aware of the fictive dimension of the history of religion and reform. He states explicitly that people, particularly in India, have engaged in reforms through fictions, presenting their origins in and continuity with the past as "fact." The creation and acceptance of such fictive facts facilitated progressive change in a way that also ameliorated conflict, he argues, and he invokes legal fictions like adoption and ritual fictions that count as fulfillment of obligations in addition to religious reforms to demonstrate the ubiquitousness and utility of such social fictions.[98] Bhakti, as a religion of the masses open to all people, regardless of sex, caste, profession, or class, he presents as such a fictively Vedic and progressive reform in response to the challenge of Buddhism (though he insists its primary impulses also predate the Vedas, rooted in the most ancient layers of Indian culture, and he stops short of explicitly identifying his own work as being of this fictive nature).

The great bhakti poets, as Tripathi describes them, have combined philosophy and poetry, offering a utopian vision of an egalitarian and harmonious society with relationships of mutuality—where women have agency and independence in love and life, as his Mira does, and where caste and gender distinctions are no bar to respect and association—coupled with a spiritual path that readily accommodates diverse practices and conceptions of deity and leads ultimately to a realization of the true self and the indwelling Divine, out of which also naturally flows the highest moral behavior. Within Gujarat, Mirabai and Narsi Mehta (both of whom he dates to the 1400s) conveyed such a spirit, though in the century that followed, he claimed, Vallabhite priests blunted its effectiveness. Indeed Tripathi appears deeply suspicious of organized religion generally but particularly of the followers of Vallabhacharya, and he was not alone in this in the wake of the 1862 Maharaj Libel Case in Bombay over an exposé of corruption within the Vallabha leadership.[99]

Still, the songs of Mira and Narsi Mehta continued to be sung, and this progressive and elevating impulse resurfaced strongly in the seventeenth century in the poetry of Akho, Premanand, and Samal, in ways that maintained fictive ties to religion but which to Tripathi's mind moved beyond them, secular rather than sacred in intent and independently "work[ing] toward the emancipation, enlargement and ennoblement of the minds and aspirations of men."[100] Tripathi suggested that these poets maintained such fictive ties because to attack both religion and society simultaneously, calling for the radical reform of both, might have been too much for their audiences. But to portray dramatically different social relations and to draw people into empathy and appreciation of characters and actions that their own society would condemn, through the beauty of poetry and within the familiar frame of religion, was far more effective. He recommended the same strategy to those seeking change in his own time, given the religiosity of the populace in India.

The history of Gujarat from the fifteenth to the eighteenth century, as Tripathi details it, was one of alternating periods of domination (primarily by Muslims and marathas) and/or social upheaval. Still, the words of these great poets, religious or otherwise, continued to be sung and recited, offering "intellectual recreation, religious consolation, and moral strength" even in the worst of times. And these poets continue to raise people's consciousness, "to take their countrymen a step forward . . . in the line of progress . . . giving [them] nobler loves and nobler cares," into the immediate but seemingly vanishing past, with the power yet to inspire present and future transformation. Tripathi, as Chandra observes, "possessed the gift to create new transformative fictions" that might do the same, even in the guise of history.[101]

Tripathi's "heroes" in pursuing his self-conceived patriotic duty were poets, and Mirabai was among those he held in highest esteem. He lauded her innocent purity coupled with strength, her steadfast spiritual commitment, and her willingness to give up all for a higher cause, even as he emphasized her feminine character and India (most especially Gujarat) as a place of enlightened men where such women could flourish. In his telling, Mira is married to Rana Kumbha (whose virtues he describes in detail, including his skill as both a warrior and a poet), but she, "as ironic fate sometimes has it . . . did not find his roof congenial to her tastes and pursuits." She "proudly" announced to her mother-in-law that she would not worship their family deity, having chosen her own god and husband in Krishna, and she departed immediately for Gujarat to practice bhakti. Drawing on a popular Gujarati song attributed to Mira, Tripathi reports that the king sent a letter inviting her to come back to live with him, and she sweetly responded, asking him to abdicate his throne and join her community of sants and sadhus in devotion.[102] Tripathi describes Mira's rejection of the rana's world with all its material privilege and political intrigue as she prepares to leave the palace, and details her absolute devotion to her Lord Krishna, who had "taken possession of her heart" and of her love, so that "no living man on earth could claim it." He goes on to write of Mirabai as an ideal for all women, for "the heart of Mira was as pure and innocent and sweet and God-loving as the heart of woman should be."[103]

Tripathi is walking a fine line here, seeking to wed the progressive with the deeply traditional and renunciation with love in his portrait of Mira. Chandra suggests he tacks back and forth between radical and conservative stances in the text as a whole and in his larger body of work, reflecting the conflicted mindset of many English-educated elite Indians in this period, yet clearly asserting early, distinctly Indian sources for the most admirable of social and moral ideals. His Mira is sweet and demure, but she is also defiant and proud, with a mind of her own, capable of acting as she chooses and largely permitted to do so. Gujarat, he argues further, has been a place where women have long enjoyed considerable authority and freedom both within the home and outside. He makes no mention of any attempted poisoning or scandal around her actions, though Narsi Mehta's consorting with low-caste people is designated as such and Mira is said later in the text "to fly to Gujarat to escape both intrigue and persecution," the latter, however, specifically attributed to religious differences with her erstwhile in-laws.[104] Similarly caste plays no role in his presentation of the saint, with Raidas nowhere to be seen, and though it is true Tripathi has little sympathy for gurus and religious affiliation in general, Raidas's absence also keeps the focus of Mira's tale solely on gender relations and grounded in Gujarat.

Irrepressible, not cowed before a powerful political authority nor a slave to outdated social norms, unwilling to engage in intrigue and uninterested in the selfish pursuit of prestige or material wealth, unwavering in her commitment, Tripathi's Mira clearly embodies both the strength and the spiritual renunciation that would be so crucial to the new Indian identity under construction. While evincing distinctly "modern" sensibilities, she also upholds Indian ideals of a Sita-like womanhood of innocent purity and devotion, at least with respect to her self-chosen divine husband. Her relationships to the rana and Krishna mirror Tripathi's conviction that a woman cannot be made to love a man, but when she falls in love, she will stop at nothing to get what she wants (though on the practical level he also notes that in his time "a woman in Gujarat marries before she loves").[105] A woman "loves one who excels in some quality of body or soul, something æsthetical or intellectual, on which she has set her heart and for which alone she barters away and gives up her otherwise uncontrollable independence and turbulence of will."[106] Mira's love for Krishna, "the divine and invisible ideal of her soul," is such a love in Tripathi's telling, a willing submission to masculine superiority and mastery by a divine husband, chosen long before she came to the rana's palace. Her rejection of the rana becomes a renunciation of constricting social conventions that have no place in an ideal world even as it is also an assertion of wifely fidelity and a glorification of female subordination, for Mira's life remains entirely oriented around and fulfilled by her relationship with her husband, divine though he may be.[107]

Tripathi's portrayal of Mira is nevertheless imbued with progressive social ideals, particularly with regard to gender relations and qualities of independent will, self-confidence, fearlessness, moral strength, and an irrepressible freedom of spirit that he hoped to inspire his readers to find within themselves, securely anchored in Indian history and civilization and embodied in the person of a beloved saint. Clearly, she is one of his "heroes" on the frontlines of the struggle for inner transformation required for the citizens of a free and sovereign nation. Even so, Tripathi was avowedly not a political or social activist, and his Mira would not be sufficiently heroic for those who were, she having denounced "political activity and intrigue" for poetry and the ideals of the mind and heart (as Tripathi had) and "retired to Gujarat."[108] And her relationship with the rana, her erstwhile human husband, would be problematic for some as well; she may have been sweet, but she was decidedly not obedient or even obliging to him.

Tripathi is careful to depict the rana as an enlightened man only making a request and not appearing to oppose Mira's actions, and he couches her return invitation to him to abdicate and join her community as an instantiation of progressive social relations, whereby men and women might honorably join as equals to sing and dance and pray together in devotion to a singular God.[109] This portrayal and her identification as a pativrata of God notwithstanding, her independent and willful leaving for Gujarat is not consistent with the emerging new patriarchy, nor her rejection of even the water in the rana's kingdom with the glorification of rajput heroism and honor deemed so crucial to undergird the freedom struggle—however much his tale might appeal to and inspire Gujaratis. Mira's radical severing of relations with the world undercuts her ability to offer guidance to engaged activists, though many might follow in Tripathi's footsteps in embracing bhakti as an indigenous envisioning of a "free and advanced" egalitarian society.

Mira Transformed: The Heroic Pativrata Saint of Ind

In this last decade of the nineteenth century, an alternative and more extended story of Mira would take shape in Bengal, decidedly different from earlier hagiographic accounts, laying a firmer foundation for a broad nationalist embrace of Mira as a pan-Indian cultural heroine. In volume 2 of his *Gleanings from Indian Classics*, devoted to "the heroines of Ind" and published in Calcutta in 1893, renowned Sanskrit scholar and English translator Manmatha Nath Dutt unveiled this saintly heroine.[110] The published work gives Dutt as the editor but lists no author and employs the first-person plural pronoun throughout, suggesting a team of writers under Dutt's supervision and/or a collective nationalist persona. The volume begins with the assertion that all the heroines of India are good wives and all good wives are truly heroines, detailing the stages of a (middle-class, upper-caste, Hindu) woman's life and the events of the life of Shiva's first wife, Sati, who is presented as the inspiration of all such women, before turning to the specific life stories of heroines from Padmini to the Rani of Jhansi.[111] Mira's story is placed in a separate appendix, acknowledging a difference between her and these other heroines involved in "worldly matters" but affirming, "She was but one amongst many that have immortalized the holy land of Ind,—but she was perhaps the best amongst the best of them."[112]

History, Heroism, and the Politics of Identity 135

Dutt and his colleagues begin this essay noting Mira's extreme popularity:

> If you travel over the vast country, extending from the banks of the Ganges in the east to those of the Indus in the west, from the Himalayas in the north to the Vindyas in the south, you will notice a particular name mentioned in the most popular songs sung in the Hindi language. The cow-herd boys in their noon-day songs, the religious devotees in their devotional psalms, the celebrated songsters in their musical soirees, the dancing girls in their public entertainments;—all sing the name of Mira. . . . Mira is known to all,—young and old, men and women;—nay she is not only known, she is loved, admired, adored and worshipped as one of the angels of the Hindu race. . . . She was queen of the mightiest Principality in the land of heroic Rajasthan, but she assumed the garb of an ascetic, left her husband's royal palace and sang the name of her loving God in the sweetest strains that were ever heard in India.[113]

The tale they tell is no doubt influenced by Tod's and Wilson's accounts, which by this time had also been translated into Bengali, Wilson's articles "The Religious Sects of the Hindus" by Akshay Kumar Datta (in two volumes, published in 1870 and 1883) under the title *Bharatvaser upasak sampraday* and Tod in multiple versions, including Harimohan Mukherjee's *Rajasthaner Itihasa* (1884) and Gopal Chandra Mukherjee's *Rajasthana* (1884).[114] Both works were well known in intellectual circles and played key roles in shaping nationalist conceptions of rajput heroism and Hindu asceticism. Yet the story Dutt and company tell of Mira includes elements not present in these sources.

According to their account, Mira is born in Nerata in Rajputana and married to Kumbha of Chittor.[115] Husband and wife are both poets, but her poetry becomes more and more spiritual, and the couple drifts apart, with Mira spending more and more time in the temple. In spite of her increasing independence, Kumbha is supportive: "her loving husband and king allowed her all scope to gratify her wishes." Her behavior, though unusual for a woman of her life stage and station, is clearly sanctioned by her husband, and she conforms to the initial assertion that all heroines are pativratas, good Hindu wives. Her devotion to Krishna is described in quite monotheistic terms as love "of the Fountain of Love, the great God of the Universe" and her songs as focused "on God and on God made flesh,—the loving boy of Brindavana," propagating the message "that love of God is the only means of salvation."

Her fame reaches Akbar, who comes with Tansen to see her and hear her sing, but they do so in the guise of Hindu holy men. The writers assure the reader that Akbar was an enlightened Muslim ruler "who knew how to appreciate men . . . arts, science and learning," and he had no enmity toward Chittor though it had not submitted to him. Yet Akbar had a healthy respect for the rajputs, knowing that they had fought rather than allow a Muslim ruler to see their queen and that a rajput queen and her retinue would commit *jauhar* (mass ritual suicide) rather than be touched by a Muslim conqueror. He knew, too, "the pride of the Hindu race and their great sanctity for their women," so he comes in disguise and alone but for Tansen, to the temple where she worships daily. Overwhelmed at her singing, Akbar falls at Mira's feet, nearly ready to convert to Hinduism, but he recovers himself and gives her a diamond necklace to adorn Krishna. She asks how ascetics should come to have such a valuable item, and Akbar says he found it while bathing in the holy Yamuna River. She accepts his explanation and the gift, but Dutt and company note that it brings her only misery and the ruin of her marriage, "cost[ing] her the love of her dear husband."

The rana does some investigating, and the crown jewelers recognize the necklace as one sold to Akbar. Mira's royal husband orders her killed for dishonoring Mewar by allowing herself to be seen and touched by a Muslim, Akbar no less (who presumably would have touched her feet in a Hindu gesture of honor when he fell before her). But no one will carry out the sentence, so he sends Mira the death warrant, ordering her to kill herself. She asks to speak to him, but her request is denied, so she sends the officer who brought the order back with the message that "his wife will obey his command." Telling no one, she leaves under cover of darkness to drown herself in a nearby river.

She enters its swift current but has a vision of a brilliant being of light who tells her, "Mira, you have obeyed your husband and you have killed yourself. But you have a higher task to perform, a higher duty to do. You are to teach people the great love that makes mankind happy. Go and do it." The rana appears as one honor- and dharma-bound to uphold the state and social order, seeking Mira's death for this reason alone, and because her own actions leave him no choice, however inadvertent they may have been. Mira, in turn, is the heartbroken but obedient wife, willingly sacrificing herself but saved by God for a higher mission. The Muslim ruler, however enlightened, speaks falsely and is the cause of her suffering, and Hinduism's equality with Western monotheism and indeed superiority is revealed in his near conversion.

Mira wakes on the shore and begins a life of wandering, asking directions to Vrindavan from cowherds who give her milk and accompany her. On her way, people hear her songs and flock to her, offering her all manner of gifts, which she declines (as so many saints are said to do). Her followers grow exponentially as they learn of her presence in Krishna's holy city, this queen who has become a beggar woman, "full of the great love that gives mankind salvation and that makes this world a heaven on earth."

According to Dutt and company, she encounters Rup Goswami there (rather than Jiv Goswami, as Priyadas recounts). She hears of him, a great saint and man of learning but also an ascetic who does not look upon the face of women, adhering to the adage "Never see woman or coin if you want salvation." She sends a message, not asking to meet him but asserting that she knows of only one male in Vrindavan and if Rup Goswami has dared to enter the women's apartments of Lord Krishna, he had better flee for his life before any come to know of it. Pleased, Rup Goswami invites Mira to the temple, calling her "daughter" even as she addresses him as "father" (echoing the similar early reference to her in the sixteenth-century song attributed to Hariram Vyas). She asks to stay in the temple and learn from him, and he readily agrees. According to the authors, "people said *Rup Gosain* had become her desciple,—but *Mira* said she was a desciple [sic] of the great saint."

Mira's fame and her songs, even in her lifetime, reach every corner of the subcontinent, and the rana comes to hear people singing in her name. He realizes his error and that she has not brought shame to his house but rather the highest honor. He had banished her for fear of people condemning his family, and now no matter what he tries to do, he cannot please them—they are devoted to Mira. "All the world were loving his wife,—he must be a scoundrel not to go to her, ask her pardon and bring her back to her royal palace." In a reversal of the scene with Akbar, the rana now puts on a disguise and walks all the way to Vrindavan to find her. He begs from her, but she tells him to go to a rich man. He responds that an "honest beggar comes to a beggar for help." She asks what she can do for him, and he drops his disguise, asking for her pardon. A faithful wife, she falls at his feet and returns "to their happy home," living half the year in Chittor and half the year in Vrindavan. Mira did not, Dutt and company assure us, favor "a stern asceticism" but encouraged people to remain in their homes and to do their duty but always with love and devotion to God.

In this telling, Mira is a good wife from start to finish, who has her husband's complete support and whose religious message is pure love of the one God, couched in very Christian-sounding language. No condemnation is made of her singing and dancing in the temple or interacting with her many followers from all walks of life, but only of the dishonor she unintentionally brings to the kingdom of Mewar, her only fault that fame came to her unbidden and she failed to see through the emperor's deception. There is no angry mother-in-law, no murderous attempts to poison her by husband or in-laws, no lustful sadhu, and no low-caste guru. Other than her husband, only the highly respected brahman Rup Goswami and the chaste relationship of guru and disciple between these two saints remains, and it is Mira herself who willingly seeks to take her own life, in obedience to her husband and to uphold the rajput honor he is bound to protect. Only after she has dutifully carried out her husband's order and only by Krishna's direct intervention is she revived, her actions dictated by a male at all times, be he human or Divine. The details of her life before marriage are unimportant, her husband remains alive so there is no issue of her refusing to commit sati, and the denouement is the couple living "happily ever after."

Mira's relationship with her husband in Dutt and company's telling conforms precisely to developing ideals for the new Hindu woman and to the more nuclear and companionate model for domestic relations being crafted in Bengal at the time.[116] She is educated, and she and her husband are fellow poets, until they begin to drift apart because of her greater spirituality. Their relationship exemplifies the late nineteenth-century nationalist new patriarchy, in which a man may be more Westernized, a match for the British in knowledge and skill and able to move in that world, while his wife is expected to be educated and independent to a degree but no "memsahib," and to maintain family relations and Hindu spiritual practice and purity in the home. Mira's husband allows her independence which is fundamentally grounded in her spirituality, and she in no way attempts to disrupt their domestic tranquility. Her transgression is inadvertent but hints at the dangers of the outside world, especially for one so innocent and pure, acting on her own.

When her husband condemns her, she asks to speak with him; theirs is portrayed as a loving relationship of companions, so surely he would be willing to talk about this. But her actions, even if not deliberate, have gone too far, and she has compromised rajput and Hindu honor. When he refuses to discuss the issue further, she is obedient to his command and, heartbroken, sets out to end her life, her relationship to her husband of the utmost importance to her, above all things in her life, including her devotion to God. She does not ask for Krishna's help; it too comes unbidden, and she is saved only after she has actually killed herself and explicitly for a higher cause, one which is not chosen by her but given by God. Her husband comes to her when he realizes his error, and she, overjoyed, returns to marital bliss, and he grants her the relative independence to be able to return to Vrindavan for extended periods to be with her guru. There is no mention of her being a pativrata of God here, and the conflict between her and her husband is generated by others' deception and by misunderstanding and involves only the two of them, as does its resolution. She remains a paragon of spiritual virtue and ever the wife who yields to her husband's direction and command.

In the moral and political climate of the 1890s in Bengal, the home seemed to many in the upper and middle classes to be the last bastion of sovereignty, and it too was under siege by "reformist-cum-colonial-cum-missionary intervention into conjugality which had begun with renewed vigor from the 1870s—the Brahmo Marriage Act of 1873, proposals to introduce divorce in the 1880s and the Age of Consent Act of 1891."[117] In the homology of home and nation, Tanika Sarkar describes the complex antireformist arguments that would come to be made for nonconsensual marriage, including child marriage, as generating a stronger compatibility and "a complete spiritual union through perfect love," far superior to European conceptions of conjugality, with the chastity and austerities of the widow embraced as spiritual renunciation and the heroic self-sacrifice of the sati glorified as "a source of national inspiration and pride."[118] In such a context even silence with respect to Mira's attitude toward her marriage to the rana is insufficient—she must embrace it wholeheartedly. And even Nagridas's report of her husband's death and her refusal to commit sati (that would separate her radical devotion from her marriage) find no place in Dutt and company's telling; she must act with his full support or not at all.

Mira's encounter with Akbar receives considerable elaboration in this telling as well. The Mughal emperor's admiration of Mira's devotion and the praise the authors direct toward him as one who could appreciate learning and art evoke commonalities and mutual appreciation between Hindu and Muslim, yet there is also an implied Hindu superiority when Akbar nearly converts. And as a Muslim, he carries out a deception that destroys the heroine's life through no fault of her own, and he is thus still structurally cast in the role of the enemy other. In presenting him in this way, Dutt and company reflect the ambivalence toward Muslims within the nationalist movement during this formative period.

The founding of the Indian National Congress in 1885 in Bombay led to extensive debates over whether such an organization could adequately represent the concerns of both Hindu and Muslim communities in its declarations and petitions to the colonial government. The same year that the authors of "The Heroines of Ind" were composing their tale, Bal Gangadhar Tilak would champion the celebration of Ganesh's birthday as a national holiday, with organizers encouraging temperance and the boycott of British goods in favor of those produced in India but also rallying Hindus to cease their participation in the Muslim festival of Murraham and to actively work for cow protection. The latter would become an extremely popular but equally divisive rallying point, a touchstone for reformers to proclaim their Hindu religious orthodoxy and for those seeking higher status to embrace the high-caste practice of vegetarianism but one that was also fueled by Hindu fears of British favoritism toward Muslims and that in turn galvanized Muslims to stand up against the forced imposition of Hindu norms on their communities. It would lead to short-lived but widespread Hindu-Muslim riots in 1893 across North India and as far away as Rangoon, with more than a hundred people killed.[119]

Nationalist rhetoric was often contradictory. Many called for Hindu-Muslim unity as essential to the flourishing of the society. For example, "journalist, translator, poet and essayist" Pratap Narayan Mishra, whom Sisir Kumar Das identifies as "one of [the] makers of modern Hindi prose,"[120] wrote in 1889, "Hindus and Musalmans are the two arms of Mother India. Neither can exist without the other."[121] Yet these same writers elsewhere continued to identify the coming of Islam with the beginning of India's slide from its glorious past and equated Muslims with the British as foreign dominators whom heroic Indians (read: Hindus) must defeat, as the more radical Tilak would do in calling for a second national holiday to honor the maratha ruler Shivaji. And increasingly many, including Mishra himself by 1893, conflated and advocated commitment to the triple pursuit of "Hindi-Hindu-Hindustan."[122] Mira's story could encompass and articulate this wider ambivalence, though later tellers would also find in it the seeds of hope for transcending Hindu-Muslim animosity through shared love for God and mutual respect and in the recognition of common Indianness as well as humanity. Though every attempt is made to erase any ambivalence toward Mira's individual behavior in this account, ambivalence nevertheless resurfaces in the convergence of conflicting attitudes toward Hindu-Muslim relations and women's independence.

What were Dutt and company's sources for their tale of Mira? Are they drawing on earlier written accounts or circulating popular traditions, or are they primarily engaged in a conscious act of transforming Mira, or something in between? Without question, the overall work in which this story of Mira appears has an overt didactic and nationalist agenda, and yet the authors also seem to have a genuine appreciation of the saint, setting her apart in an appendix for special attention and praise. They would undoubtedly have been familiar with Tod and Wilson and perhaps others they influenced. But what of elements not found elsewhere: the rana's order to Mira to take her own life, Krishna's rescuing her from drowning, her encounter not with Jiv but with Rup Goswami, and the rana's coming to her in disguise in Vrindavan? Evidence of a Bengali tradition associating Mira with Rup Goswami, as we have noted, appears as early as the late seventeenth century in a Sahajiya Vaishnava text in which the two are portrayed as tantric partners, and in other Sahajiya texts under the title "Mira's Notebook" she is clearly described as his guru.[123] The authors may be drawing on a strand of this Bengali tradition for this association and their reciprocal guruship in their tale, and the characterization of their relationship as one of father and daughter may also be a refutation of any tantric implications.

However, attempts to trace other apparent innovations to earlier sources have so far yielded no precedents, though through them Mira is indeed transformed into a good wife and model heroine, a paragon of Hindu feminine purity, courageous self-sacrifice, and spiritual strength, who upholds rajput honor and the sanctity of Hindu women. Dutt and company provide no clues, and in the final lines of the essay they lament, "Pity it is that India had never historians! What little we know of Mira, we know from annals and tales. But her sweet songs will exist till the final destruction of Hindusthan. Her spirit will breathe over every Hindu home till the final collapse of the Hindu race."[124] Though they may indeed be drawing any number of elements from circulating tales or even a single other contemporary source, barring further evidence and given the context, it seems likely that Dutt and company are the principal architects of this nationalist heroic construction of Mira. As such, they follow a long line of others who have retold her story in varied ways, from Priyadas and the author of the *Prem Ambodh* to Mahipati and Sukhsaran. They make no historical claims for their telling; instead they lay claim to Mira as the best of the best of the heroic wives of the holy land of Hindusthan.

The publication of this story in English also seems to reflect a desire to speak to and for a nationalist audience—the English-educated elite across the subcontinent—and secondarily to British supporters and detractors alike. At the time of the publication of Dutt and company's tale and in its wake, heroic images of Mira were being quickly disseminated across the subcontinent in popular presses in Hindi and other regional languages. A Hindi journalist and novelist known for his Hindi translations of Bengali works and a key figure in the 1893 founding of Kashi Nagari Pracharini Sabha, Kartikprasad Khatri (1852–1905)[125] published his *Mirabai ka Jivan Charit*[126] that same year, as one of a number of short biographies of saints such as Tulsidas and Nanak and heroines like Ahalyabai and the Rani of Jhansi being published out of Banaras at this time. A series of dramas were also written and performed starting in this period, dealing primarily with social and political themes, with a small number focused on historical events and personages, such as Maharana Pratap and Amar Singh Rathor, though (as McGregor notes of both biographies and dramas in Hindi) these works, like that published under Dutt's editorship, generally made little attempt to take account of history per se.[127] Baldevprasad Mishra's Hindi play *Mirabai: Dharmamulak Aitihasik Natak* (1897) falls into this category and follows closely Dutt and company's portrayal of Mira's encounter with Akbar and Tansen and her meeting with Rup Goswami.[128] These types of biographies and dramas of Mira's life also appear in the decades that follow in Telegu, Tamil, Sindhi, Bengali, Urdu, and English—a testament to Mira's popularity and exemplary power and the perceived relevance and appeal of her story across the subcontinent.

The Historians' Mira of Rajasthan

In the face of such widespread attention and admiration for Mira being disseminated through print, the elite of Rajasthan could hardly ignore her, though they too might feel that she needed to be rehabilitated and alternative tellings of her story denounced. As she appears in hagiographic and many popular accounts, Mira does not fit the mold of an ideal royal rajput wife, even as she does not precisely fit the model of other Indian heroines—and rajput historians would tell her story differently even as Bengali nationalists had begun to do, with the virangana narrative structure used even more directly as a template. But their transformed Mira would be much more closely tied to her rajput roots, her life story conforming to rajput social norms and integrated into the events and personages of Rajasthani history, emerging as a part of the conscious self-representation of rajputs in this region through the medium of historical writing.

Similar moves were being made in other regions to take back Indian history from foreign scholars and political agents, in recognition of the ideological dimension of these historical formulations, despite their basis in evidentiary facts and claimed objectivity. For both British and Indian intellectuals during this period, in the words of Sudipta Kaviraj, "history [came] to be what myths explicitly are—stories that societies tell about themselves whose points, inevitably, are not in the past but in the present," "an order[ing] of facts," "never . . . free from a mixture, an undecided tension between what happened and what ought to have happened," and an "empowering discourse [that] gives reasons, justifications for practical initiatives."[129] Historiography became a key building block in the shaping of the nation, as well as a language to challenge and resist the present in the guise of the past while avoiding charges of sedition. Serious scholarly investigation of available historical records was undertaken in this process, with the resulting histories—the ordering of the facts—also serving nationalist and regional agendas, even as British historical studies served to reinforce, rationalize, and naturalize European claims of superiority and colonial domination.[130]

The first official recognition of Mira in this type of historical investigation associated with the royal family of Mewar is found in Kaviraj Shyamaldas's monumental work *Vir Vinod* (Heroes' Delight).[131] Nationalist interest in

Rajasthan had been fueled by Tod's tales of rajput warriors, and between 1872 and 1919 his work was translated in multiple editions not only in Bengali but also Gujarati, Hindi, Marathi, and Urdu as *the* foundational history of the region, a stature it has retained into the twenty-first century.[132] Tod's work inspired rulers in Rajasthan to commission the writing of their own history, seemingly as much to recover and disseminate a rajput identity of honor and valor as to forge a new national Indian identity. And they were encouraged to do so by political agents, as British enthusiasm for history and desire for information and modernization again converged with Indian elite concerns.

Shyamaldas belonged to a highly respected lineage of *charans*, the traditional bards of the courts, but he also developed a serious interest in the contemporary study of history. He was first assigned the task of writing a vernacular history of Mewar by Maharana Shambhu Singh, but this initial limited work was not yet completed when the maharana died in 1874.[133] After a five-year hiatus, his successor, Maharana Sajjan Singh (r. 1874–1884), reestablished a department of history, assigning Shyamaldas to the newly conceived position of "court historian" and providing him with financial resources and a team of scholars to work with him on this project.[134] In dramatic contrast to earlier bardic accounts, Sajjan Singh would declare emphatically, "[We] do not want eulogy in history."[135] Shyamaldas's more than two-thousand-page *Vir Vinod* would cover far more than the history of Mewar and would finally be completed (or nearly so) and printed under the rule of Sajjan Singh's successor, Maharana Fateh Singh (r. 1884–1930).

Only sixteen years old at the time of Shambhu Singh's death, Sajjan Singh acquired full power two years later and was recognized during his short reign for his social, judicial, and administrative reforms and his patronage of literature and history, hosting important nationalist writers from other regions, including Bhartendra Harishchandra.[136] Shyamaldas served not only as the principal historian of his court but also as a friend and close advisor to the maharana in multiple matters, including negotiating on his behalf during a Bhil uprising. He would continue to receive support from his successor, though in dramatic contrast to Sajjan Singh, Maharana Fateh Singh is remembered as a "staunch traditionalist," who rankled under British interference, notoriously not appearing when called to mandatory gatherings with other rajas and maharajas in Delhi.[137]

Shyamaldas traveled widely in his work on behalf of both Sajjan Singh and Fateh Singh as well as in his collection of information and materials, and he amassed a large library of contemporary literature as well as manuscripts, inscriptions, and the like. He corresponded and met with nationalists and European, American, and Indian historians, became a member of the Asiatic

Society of Bengal as well as the Royal Asiatic and Historical Societies in London, and published a number of highly regarded scholarly articles in their journals.[138] He was clearly impacted by Tod and others in his more objective approach to writing history than might be expected of someone sponsored by the rulers of a kingdom, and he also took on the task of correcting Tod's many errors, both in his *Vir Vinod* and, for example, in a journal article convincingly establishing a much later date for one of Tod's key allegedly twelfth-century sources.[139]

Yet Shyamaldas was also influenced by Tod's romantic and imaginative approach to historical events. Indeed Susanne and Lloyd Rudolph suggest, "There were, in a sense, two Shyamal Dases, the Shyamal Das who wrote the Mewar sections of *Vir Vinod* and the Shyamal Das who wrote for the professional journals of his time; the Shyamal Das who, like Tod, credited the imaginative truths of bardic poetry, and the Shyamal Das who zealously pursued positive history in the pages of historical societies. . . . The Shyamal Das of imaginative truth writes what we call docudramas about key events in Mewar history . . . writ[ing] the script as if he knew what the protagonists said and did . . . [their]perceptions and motives."[140] He eschewed legendary tales for which there was no evidence (with the full support of the maharanas), but where there was, he would analyze it thoroughly, importantly "includ[ing] the then prevailing social conditions and values and perception" in his evaluation.[141] He was also, however, a consummate storyteller as well as a professional historian, and where contemporary sources were limited, he wove a tale of heroism and intrigue, corresponding to known facts but also moving well beyond them into the imagined, subjective realms of motivation, thoughts and emotions, intimate conversation, and individual action.

In his portrayal of Mirabai, Shyamaldas seemingly employs both these positivist and imaginative approaches.[142] He begins by denying Tod's assertion that she was married to Rana Kumbha. She was in fact the wife of Rana Sanga's oldest son, Bhojraj, he asserts, and also was the granddaughter of Duda, daughter of Ratan Singh, niece of Viramdev, and cousin of Jaimal of Merta. His sources for identifying Bhojraj as Mira's husband are the histories of the Mertiya Rathors and Jodhpur, and he makes it very clear that Mira lived during the reigns of her brothers-in-law Vikramajit and Udaisingh and that it was they who caused her suffering, not her husband. In his portrayal, Mira was a very religious woman who honored devotees and holy men and composed and sang songs of renunciation (*virag*).

One might conclude from his brief portrait of Mira that he knew of Nagridas's text and Nainsi's reference at the very least, particularly given that, as Rima Hooja notes, he clearly drew much from Nainsi, Dayaldas, and

Bankidas as well as other Rajasthani sources for his larger work.[143] Frances Taft speculates that other sources "written by the Mertiyas" that Shyamaldas claims to have used may have been reports submitted to him by *thakurs* (regional rulers) of Badnor and Rupaheli, descendants of Jaimal (Mira's purported cousin who found refuge in Mewar after losing Merta to Maldeo).[144] Taft's suggestion is supported by Padmavati Shabnam's report that Keshari Singh of Badnor had composed a history of the lineage of Jaimal in 1884 and that his son published a second edition, though no copies of either have yet surfaced.[145] Nina Sharma and Indu Shekhar note that some (but importantly not all) of the vast material collected and produced by Shyamaldas during the writing of the *Vir Vinod* is now stored in the State Archives in Bikaner and the Rajasthan University Library.[146] A thorough study of these archives may yet yield further clues to his sources of information regarding Mira. However, Shyamaldas's own recorded conservative attitude toward women might well also have informed his "docudrama" imaginings.[147]

Shyamaldas's full work went far beyond the history of Mewar and was deliberately written not in the Sanskritized Hindi being promoted for academic writing but in Hindustani language as it was spoken, retaining commonly used Persian and Arabic words, so that it might be understood by all.[148] He drew on European and Persian historical sources in addition to bardic ones, following the style of "the Persian chronicles, classics by his time, and the Mughal gazetteer form as developed by Nainsi in his *khyats* (chronicles of states) and later in profusion by the British Raj," with immense detail starting from the history of the universe and moving through geography and contemporary politics on a global scale to then focus on Mewar and the other kingdoms with which it interacted, incorporating meticulous descriptions of life and culture in the region.[149] His approach was thus radically inclusive, placing the history of Mewar in this much wider context, emphasizing the multireligious nature and harmonious relations within the kingdom even as he embraced an "Indian" as well as "Mewari" identity.[150] In analyzing both the *Vir Vinod* and his published journal articles, the Rudolphs conclude, "this *charan*-turned professional, this *chela* (disciple) of the romantic Tod, can arguably be regarded as one of India's first modern historians."[151]

Though it was not made widely available for many decades, there is ample evidence that historians were able to access the *Vir Vinod* based on multiple citations in subsequent published works on the history of Rajasthan.[152] At the time of Shyamaldas's death in 1894, he had not finished his introduction and acknowledgments, with the printing of this monumental work well underway but not yet completed. Maharana Fateh Singh ensured its full printing by the end of that year, but the copies remained largely under his control, with access only by permission, as other items in the libraries of princely states were (and in many cases continue to be), until the text was finally made available for purchase in the 1940s.[153]

Within the *Vir Vinod* Shyamaldas acknowledged noted epigrapher and historian Munshi Deviprasad for his assistance; it was Deviprasad who would write the first more complete telling of Mira's life story attempting to take history into account, published in 1898.[154] He states his purpose explicitly within his introduction to *Mirabai ka Jivan Charitra*: to increase accurate knowledge about Mirabai because people either know little or have mistaken notions about her, with much misinformation drawn from devotional sources and hearsay, spread by word of mouth and widely disseminated in print. Tod and Kartikprasad Khatri are singled out for special criticism, but Deviprasad was also no doubt well aware of widely divergent song and narrative traditions about the saint circulating orally, particularly given that he served as assistant superintendent of the 1891 census in Jodhpur state and was largely responsible for the required extensive field data collection carried out between 1881 and 1891 and published in 1894.[155] His explicit goal of eliminating error marks much of the subsequent historians' presentation of Mira as well.

Deviprasad does not merely tell another story of Mira, as Dutt and company did, but rather seeks to present an accurate historical account of her life. In doing so, however, he operates under a similar assumption that she must have been an ideal wife who upheld the values of her rajput royal heritage. His approach to the saint mirrors the seriousness of purpose and critical awareness that Bankimchandra exhibited with regard to Krishna in the *Krishnacharitra*, as Sudipta Kaviraj has so clearly delineated it. Bankimchandra's underlying concern was nothing less than the moral regeneration of India (as Tripathi's was). As a Vaishnava, he understood Krishna as God godself, incarnate precisely "to show what perfection of virtue means in human terms," and he sought to remove the "deposits of interpretation" and excess to recover the historical and true Krishna.[156] He was fully cognizant of the way the Krishna tradition has come into its current form, "constructed through something like a massive collective sculpture, through a long series of texts and textual practices like retelling[, i]ts outlines, its emphases and inflections . . . thought, corrected and rethought through a collective historical process."[157] Underdeveloped narrative aspects of his life story had been filled in, episodes added, complex ideas cloaked in attractive metaphors that are all too easily literalized, in a process that continually reshapes the originating ideal. The resulting sculpted narrative can be read as the "self-representation of Hinduism, what Hinduism has thought of itself," but this self-representation was precisely what Bankimchandra found so objectionable.

He sought to recover the "true" Krishna—"the ideal of ideals in Hindu civilization"—from the excesses of folk accretions and interpolations, from "the entanglements of eroticism" and the "ordinariness" that would make God over to embody human fallibility and frailty rather than the perfected humanity and goodness to which people should strive and also from the multiplication and literalization of miracles that would make this ideal both inimitable and irrational, transgressing the laws of nature.[158] In this Bankimchandra rejected the puranic conception that "all constructions somehow contribute to an idea of what god is" in an abundance of poetic truth, and instead presumed "that one of these images of Krishna must be true and the others false."[159] He located the historical "true" Krishna (not unproblematically) in the earliest layer of tradition of the *Mahabharata* and sought to cut away or transform into allegory and metaphor later elements of the tradition (including the gopis and Radha) to arrive at a Krishna who is "calm, poised, rational, perfect and irreproachable," the warrior who upholds dharma and justice. In undertaking such an analysis, Bankimchandra was participating in a wider nineteenth-century scholarly subjection of religions to historical analysis and the rigors of science employing similar assumptions, as the concurrent quest for the historical Jesus and for the historical Buddha illustrate.

Deviprasad seeks to recover Mira in much the same way, the one and only true historical Mira but also one who cannot be other than the "ideal of ideals"—pativrata and bhakta, respectable in every way, intelligent, courageous, good, and, importantly, quintessentially rajput. Like Bankimchandra, he and others who follow him offer rational or metaphorical explanations for reported miracles and exclude what they identify as clear expansions of the underdetermined sections of the narrative (such as Mira's childhood conversation with her mother about who her bridegroom will be) and "folk" tendencies toward excess (like the multiplication of attempts on her life) and toward ordinariness (particularly Mira's alleged rejection of her husband) as well as any other elements that might be considered incongruous and out of character with *their* ideal. A few selected common elements that might fit, Deviprasad reports as hearsay, and in his allegiance to historical veracity, he explicitly sets aside several others. But by choosing to mention them at all he keeps them as vestiges within his narrative frame and leaves open their possible allegorical interpretation (in a manner not unlike Bankimchandra's treatment of Radha). His "restored" Mira is entirely in keeping with emerging rajput and nationalist identities and pasts; she is a superlative saintly heroine from their own lineage and region to stand beside the glorious rajput heroes who most truly embody the ideals of Bankimchandra's Krishna. (Indeed by the end of the next century the state of Rajasthan will be promoted as "the land of shakti and bhakti," with accompanying pictures of Rana Pratap and Mirabai prominently displayed.)

Deviprasad constructs his account first by taking the episodes related in the hagiographic narratives and the 1516 documented date for Bhojraj's marriage and then searching for all available historical facts that might impinge on Mira's life, weaving them together with selected threads of circulating traditions, both oral and written. He cites his sources, specifically stating that he has consulted Shyamaldas and his assistant Gaurishankar Ojha and the archives of Mewar, but also drawing on hagiography and song.[160] His resulting tale differs markedly from those of Tod and Dutt and from those of Raghuraj Singh and Priyadas before him.

Deviprasad begins by clarifying the lineage of both Mira and Bhojraj, important markers of her rajput affiliation and regional location. He details the long history of political squabbles and alliances forged through marriages between the Rathor and Sisodiya royal families, of which Mira's marriage to Bhojraj in 1516 is given as but one example. As Deviprasad tells the story, Mira was born in Kurki, one of twelve villages granted to her father, Ratan Singh, and as a child, she had an image of Krishna that she treated as a playmate. Her grandfather Duda, her uncle Viramdev, and her cousin Jaimal, all known to be great Vaishnavas, imparted their devotion to her. Her mother died when she was very young; her grandfather called her to Merta, where he saw to her education; and her father arranged her marriage to Bhojraj when she came of age. Deviprasad is silent about her married life and moves immediately to the death of her husband. Her father-in-law was killed shortly thereafter, as was her father while fighting as his ally. Mira is portrayed as turning to God as a result of the loss of so many people near and dear to her and as only at this point truly developing the devotion that began with her childhood games.

Her brother-in-law Ratan Singh (r. 1528–1531) came to power, and there was considerable turmoil within the kingdom during those years, from both internal strife and external threats. After Ratan Singh's short reign, the younger Vikramaditya (r. 1531–1536) (aka Vikramajit/Bikramajit) came to the throne, and Deviprasad says specifically that it was he who persecuted Mira because her association with saints and holy men led people to slander the family. The rana's sending of poison is recounted, on the counsel and with the aid of the sycophant merchant of the vijavaragi caste Dayaram, after which Mira returned to Merta to her uncle Viramdev and her cousin Jaimal.[161] She must have left Chittor before 1535, when the fort fell to Sultan Bahadur Shah of Gujarat and all the women and children within were consigned to jauhar (a mass ritual suicide by burning) as the men rode out to die fighting, clothed in the saffron robes of renouncers. If not, she too would have died.

In Deviprasad's telling, Mira's return to her natal home proves to be only a temporary solution to her problems, however, as her family was forced to flee from place to place after successive losses in battle to Maldeo of Jodhpur.

With respect to Mira's death, Deviprasad recounts the devotional tradition of her merger with Krishna's image as Ranchor in Dwarka, an image that he reports is now in Dakor (rather than Dwarka) in Gujarat, where the remaining bit of Mira's clothing could still be seen in his day.[162] He notes that a traditional genealogist of the Rathors reports the year of her death as 1546, but given that her place of death is unknown to this source and that others say she lived longer, he finds the evidence insufficient to conclude with any historical certainty when she died. Beyond this he reports that people say she went to Vrindavan and had her well-known encounter with an (unnamed) celibate renouncer and that she was supposed to have met Akbar and Tansen and corresponded with Tulsidas, both of which Deviprasad doubts could be historically possible because of the discrepancy of dates. Of Mira's poetry he adds that many songs were composed later in her name, and he closes with three very popular ones.[163]

The Mira who emerges from Deviprasad's telling is a woman whose life was marked by sorrow and loss and whose devotion flowered out of this soil of suffering—a very different image than we found in the devotional accounts, even that of Nagridas. She turned fully to Krishna only after she had been forced to realize the illusory nature of this world and its fleeting pleasures. In this way her devotion is rationalized and her rebellion becomes renunciation. Further, she was a widow whom fate and the world in a sense had renounced, rather than a passionate and beautiful young woman who renounced the world. Her behavior was somewhat extreme for a rajput widow, but the edge is taken off her infractions. Figuratively draped in white, she is an ideal for widowed women, strong in the face of opposition and absolute in her devotion to God *after* the path of wifely devotion was closed to her—an image in keeping with the nationalist lauding of widows' austerity and chastity as indicative of Indian superiority over Western cultural practices (as she is portrayed in Figure 3.1). Though almost every point in this version of Mira's story—her precise birth and death dates, her place of birth, even her father's and husband's identities—will continue to be contested across the century of scholarship that follows, a consensus view (with various disputed details) eventually emerges with the narrative structure laid down by Deviprasad at its foundation.

Details particular to this family of tellings of Mira's life seem to emanate from and are reinforced by a small group of men who acknowledge each other in their published works and in their correspondence with Purohit Harinarayan

Figure 3.1 Mirabai worshiping alone within the confines of the palace in a painting on public display in the City Palace, Udaipur.

Sharma, a renowned scholar of Hindi literature who himself spent forty years investigating Mira's life and songs.[164] They include Deviprasad, Gaurishankar Ojha, Jagdish Singh Gahlot, Chatur Singh of Rupaheli, and Gopal Singh of Badnor. Ojha had worked closely with Shyamaldas as a member of his team and subsequently became the preeminent historian of Rajasthan, publishing a number of volumes on various kingdoms from 1924 to 1940. Gahlot's extensive publications include histories of Rajasthan and of Marwar, and both these historians include Mira in their accounts.[165] Chatur Singh and Gopal Singh were members of Mira's natal family line through her purported cousin

Jaimal and the grandsons of those who, Taft has suggested, may have provided Shyamaldas with some of his information. Chatur Singh writes of Mira in his 1902 *Chaturkul Charitra*, and Gopal Singh in his *Jaymal Vansh Prakash*, published in 1932 (said to be a third edition of the family chronicles, building on earlier works by his father and grandfather).[166] These highly respected men were clearly in conversation with each other. Chatur Singh reports to Harinarayan that Deviprasad, Ojha, and Gahlot had visited him and Gopal Singh to discuss Mira.[167] Together with Shyamaldas, they come to be the primary sources for subsequent authors who claim the authority of history for their biographies of Mira.

Their accounts of Mira's life mutually reinforce and acknowledge each other. Gahlot adds that a brahman named Gajadhar was her childhood teacher (information he gleaned from Gurjargaur brahmans' khyats, where this relationship is mentioned in connection with a land grant given to Gajadhar by Mira).[168] Gopal Singh includes the detail that Mira's wedding to Bhojraj was accompanied by great celebration and that the Mertiya Rathors were proud of her.[169] Chatur Singh emphasizes in his account that Bhojraj was "the beloved husband of Mira" and that Rana Sanga treated her with the greatest respect when she turned back to her childhood devotion after her husband's death.

Chatur Singh gives the year of her birth as 1498, though he offers no source for this information and qualifies it as an approximation. If Mira were born in 1498, that would make her a respectable (by twentieth-century standards) eighteen years of age when her marriage is arranged in 1516, though others will report years ranging from 1498 to 1505 for her birth, citing traditional genealogists (Meritya bhats and Jodhpur ranimanga bhats) as their sources.[170] A 1504 or 1505 birth would make Mira a girl of eleven or twelve at the time of her marriage, arguably a more appropriate age in the sixteenth century for a rajput princess to be married and also a more likely date historically, Taft argues, based on the likely age of her father.[171] But in the end there is no conclusive evidence to choose one year over another, and all this speculation is based on the assumption that the available edition of *Nainsi ri Khyat* accurately reflects her family and marriage.

Harinarayan Sharma accepted Deviprasad's work as authentic, affirmed Ojha's and Gahlot's contributions of new material, and also assembled additional details from his conversations with Chatur Singh and Gopal Singh.[172] He reports that according to the Gurjargaur brahmans' khyats (drawing on Gahlot), Mira was well educated by her guru Gajadhar in reading, writing, music, and religious matters, and she was so intelligent that she was soon recognized for her wisdom, a point also made by Deviprasad, who credits her with such intellect and wisdom that she was able to help her father-in-law when none of his male pundits could. Further, based on conversations with Gopal Singh and Chatur Singh, Harinarayan reports that she appears to have lived happily with her husband for five or six years until he died, and only then, overcome with sorrow, did she turn completely to devotion. Sanga (her father-in-law) is portrayed as fully supportive of her religiosity, providing her funds to worship as she chose and to care for religious mendicants and giving her a great entourage of elephants, servants, and soldiers for her pilgrimages.

Because Mira refused to remain secluded within the confines of the household, Vikramaditya alone persecuted her. A temple was built for her by Udaisingh (r. 1540–1572) in Dwarka after her death (demonstrating that support by the male members of her marital family was uniform except for Vikramaditya). Harinarayan further reports that according to Chatur Singh, Mira never wore the saffron clothes of a renouncer, and the low-caste leatherworker Raidas was not associated with her in any way (in a correction/denial of this widely circulating tradition and Gahlot's earlier speculation that Raidas must have been her guru, based on his being mentioned in so many songs attributed to her).[173] Mira thus appears to challenge neither caste barriers nor women's traditional dharma, and she never steps out of the signification of a woman's identity in terms of marital status marked by dress.

Deviprasad, Gopal Singh, and Chatur Singh appear to be the chief architects of this more extended historical biography of Mira, ostensibly drawing on traditions preserved within this branch of Mira's natal kin for some of the unique details in their account. Did they, together with Ojha and Gahlot, have access to additional oral records preserved in the courts of Mewar and Marwar that allowed them to tell this more complete story? Or did they more actively and collectively create this narrative of Mira, adopting the conventions of the stories of other heroines as they imagined what her life must have been or should have been like and consciously or unconsciously transforming her into a proper national heroine even as they thoroughly "rajputized" her?

No corroborating sources have been uncovered for many of their details, nor is there evidence that the story they tell was known to rajputs or others in these regions. Nagridas's *Padaprasangmala* account, as we noted in chapter 2, suggests a possible tradition of appreciation and remembrance of her life among at least some of her natal kin. Like Deviprasad he places her persecution after the death of her husband, and even in her wanderings depicts her as traveling properly chaperoned by brahman priests from the court, so that she does not appear to significantly challenge rajput values but only to affirm devotional ones. Yet beyond this, his account differs significantly from Deviprasad's, both in terms of what is and is not included. A few elements also appear in Sukhsaran's parchai: Mira's lineage and birth in Kurki, the role of Dayaram, Mira's journey to Dwarka accompanied by brahmans, and the possibility of darshan of Mira's vacated clothing in his day. Otherwise, the texts diverge considerably. And as we noted, the date on Sukhsaran's text is uncertain, with the available published version drawn from manuscripts dated 1877 and 1882, so these may simply be late nineteenth-century circulating traditions.

Lindsey Harlan's work among rajput women in Udaipur almost a century later in the 1980s gives further weight to the suspicion that the unmitigated admiration for Mira expressed by these men might not have been shared by all rajputs in the past, nor was the precise story they told necessarily widely known and commonly accepted as authoritative in Mewar.[174] These women did clearly know about Mira, and there is little doubt that they would have had some familiarity with at least some aspects of these rajput historians' by then widely disseminated versions of her life. Yet in their tellings, Mira's behavior unequivocally enraged her marital family, although her husband was portrayed as alternately angry or supportive by different narrators. In every case, Mira refused to be a proper wife to the rana, denying her marriage to him by refusing to consummate it and claiming to be already married to Krishna. When she left her home and became a famous devotee (an action that they, too, presented as occurring after her husband's death), her marital family continued to be shamed by her behavior. They sent men to bring her back, but when they entered the temple where she worshiped, she was already gone, having merged with her Lord. The story of the lascivious holy man, found in Priyadas's account but largely absent from historical tellings, was included by these women, though the denouement occurred in private before the image of Krishna and the sadhu ran away rather than becoming Mira's disciple.

These women's tellings are definitely not the same story being told by Chatur Singh, Gopal Singh, Ojha, Gahlot, and Deviprasad. Mira's behavior was an insult to the Sisodiya rajputs of Mewar until she died and perhaps beyond, and there was no reconciliation. In Harlan's analysis, the women telling these tales simultaneously admire Mira's courage and dedication in facing social sanction and her in-laws' cruelty and question Mira's behavior as a pativrata or proper wife, suggesting that because she was married, she should not have taken up bhakti and renounced the world. Further, they focus on Mira's death, which somehow vindicates her life choices in their minds because she was willing to die for them, as a rajput heroine or sati would be, and because Krishna seemed to affirm in this final embrace the divine marriage that Mira claimed invalidated her earthly one. The miraculous nature of her demise separates her forever from ordinary women, and there is no suggestion that she was ever a pativrata of her earthly husband.

Her story thus again becomes something of a cautionary tale, reinforcing the value of the pativrata ideal and the rajput conviction that a woman should be willing to die to protect her honor, her *pati*, and her pativrata status, yet warning against excessive bhakti during marriage and divided loyalty. Harlan notes a latent potential for Mira to be mobilized in the dismantling of purdah by such women, but at the time of her research, though these norms were changing, Mirabai had not yet been tapped as an exemplar for this or any other social change within this community.[175] The differences between the tellings of these rajput women and those of the early historians no doubt in part reflect the gender of the tellers, but at the very least they belie any uniform memory and unequivocal admiration for the saint among rajputs in Mewar and verify the continuing presence of other "Miras" who do not so easily fit the nationalist mold for a heroine, even among rajputs.

Outright suppression of Mira's memory among the royal family of Mewar has also been asserted, most notably by Parita Mukta. Her evidence is primarily anecdotal, drawn from interviews carried out in 1986 and 1987, including the remembrance of a puppeteer who in 1971 inadvertently angered members of a Sisodiya rajput village by singing Mira songs to gather an audience for a performance; Mukta's own experience of hostility when she asked some Bhatti rajput women in a village near Chittor if they would name their daughters "Mira"; the testimony of a librarian in Udaipur, who assured her that Mira was reviled by the rulers and that no records would be found; the disparaging remarks of a rajput man in Chittor; and claims of a former employee of the princely state at Chittor that in past times no one would dare mention Mira for fear of losing his or her job, so despised was she.[176]

Further evidence might also be marshaled. In 1938, M. L. Menaria wrote to Harinarayan of Maharana Bhupal Singh's opinion of Mira: "Even the Maharana Sahib believes that Mira has been a black-blot on the fair page of the Mewar History and musicians are not allowed to sing the Padas of Mira Bai in the Palace."[177] Menaria asked Harinarayan not to mention this in any published work, but their correspondence has now been made public. Maharana Bhupal Singh's position may have softened by 1944, however, as he is reported to have provided support in the form of elephants and horses for the location shooting of Subbulakshmi's epic cinematic portrayal of Mira, after she performed for him (though there is no indication she actually sang any of Mira's songs in the palace durbar at that time).[178] Parashuram Chaturvedi (whose collection of Mira's poetry is a standard for Hindi literary studies) also said that in his travels to Udaipur he found little respect for the saint.[179]

In any case, as we have noted, the written historical records of the royal families of both Marwar and Mewar (with the possible exception of Nainsi) appear to have been silent with respect to Mirabai's existence until the nineteenth century, though admittedly there is a paucity of references to women generally in this type of documentation. Taken together, this limited evidence may be insufficient to definitively prove the deliberate suppression of her memory, but it certainly suggests at the very least great ambivalence toward her behavior as a woman and a wife and a range of attitudes from indifference to outright enmity toward her, in sharp contrast to the unbridled admiration espoused in the historical biographies of Deviprasad and company.[180]

Why these men might have been interested in presenting their particular version of Mira's story, quite apart from clearing up Tod's historical inaccuracies, is clear from Chatur Singh's correspondence with Harinarayan. He writes that people even in the smallest villages throughout the land do not know the names of Mewar and Marwar or even Rajasthan but everywhere are familiar with *Mira ka desh* (Mira's country) and the towns of Merta and Chittor.[181] When the great leaders of the nation (across the political spectrum) "sing the praises of the jewels of Indian womanhood," they inevitably mention Mira—Vivekananda, Bal Gangadhar Tilak, Lala Lajpat Rai, Chitta Ranjan Das, Madan Mohan Malaviya, Motilal Nehru, Rabindranath Tagore, and Gandhi all offered her the highest praise, he reports to Harinarayan.[182] Chatur Singh's pride in Mira is clear, as is the seeming necessity and efficacy of rajputs reclaiming her as one of their own.

These historians clearly sought to correct what they considered erroneous views about Mira even as they claimed her as a beloved rajput saint. As respected historians, they were no doubt pursuing evidentiary accuracy, particularly in the face of so many varied and often contradictory things being said and written about the saint. But were they only concerned about correcting her lineage and who her husband and persecutor were, or might they also have been attempting to silence alternative tellings, voices of dissent and challenge that might run counter to a carefully constructed idealization of rajput and Indian honor, feminine heroism, and patriarchal benevolence? Deviprasad is clear that he is seeking to override "mistaken" popular views. In this agenda, he and his fellow historians appear to be participating in larger trends across India in the late nineteenth century in the negotiations of language and power, as Bankimchandra was. Intellectual elites in Bengal sought to "purify" vernacular literature of what they considered the "vulgar" and "obscene" accretions introduced through the uneducated (including women), low-class and -caste traditions, and folk sources, a task made that much more difficult by the ready dissemination that inexpensive popular print publishing made possible.[183] Deviprasad and company, I would argue, were engaged in a similar campaign to make Mirabai "respectable," even as they asserted ownership of her for rajputs and Rajasthan.

Though not universally accepted in all its details, the narrative line of Mira's story put forth by Deviprasad and the others received further elaboration by later scholars and devotees and with time has become widely propagated as *the* truth about Mira, though often in combination with elements from Dutt and company's nationalist account. And this combined heroic Mira would indeed become a powerful cultural embodiment of Indian values and identity, especially among educated members of the middle and upper classes and castes, who it seems were only too willing to dismiss the miracle-filled tales of devotees and other popular renditions of her life that carried embedded critiques of social, religious, and gender hierarchies, even as they also longed for the confirmation of historical veracity and deeply admired the saint. Certain elements received more focused attention in the elaborations of this narrative line, such as Mira's education, her relationship with the men of her marital household, and a political awareness motivating some of her actions.

Two authors stand out as particularly significant in giving final shape to this historical family of tales of Mira's life: Hermann Goetz (writing in 1956) and Kalyan Singh Shekhawat (in 1969) with their politicization of Mira's actions.[184] Goetz was born in Germany in 1898, lived in India from 1936 to 1955, and was a respected scholar of Indian archaeology, precolonial history, and art history with an interest also in mysticism across religious traditions.[185] That Mira is deeply meaningful to him personally is clear, and the only person he deems worthy of comparison to her is Jesus.[186] But first and foremost he is a careful historian, combining a thorough study of history of the period with rational explanations for the seemingly miraculous elements of the tale. He is admired by many for his meticulous attention to historical details, though when these are absent, by his own admission he does not hesitate in "recreating" Mira's personality to weave a probable (and sometimes improbable) tale that will both inspire readers and reconcile a variety of narrative fragments.[187]

In his attempt to understand the motivations of the characters in Mira's life story, Goetz turns to politics as the most compelling explanation of events. Of Mira's early years in the home of her grandfather Rao Duda, he says, "Educated, together with a boy [her cousin Jaimal], by an old warrior, Mira was probably an excellent sports-woman. And educated with the heir to the throne of Merta by a successful old statesman, she probably was also well acquainted with the principles of politics and the affairs of her time."[188] As a result of this training, she was the one chosen for this marriage of political alliance between these illustrious kingdoms. He is also clear that Mira did not consummate her marriage to Bhojraj, instead continuing to "follow her vocation," something she was able to do in the polygamous court with the protection of her husband's grandmother, whom Goetz identifies as none other than Raidas's disciple, the Jhali Rani. For this reason alone she was not required to commit sati when Bhojraj died, and subsequently her deep religiosity was not only no longer a problem but was a model for widows of her station.

Goetz details the turbulent history of Mira's marital family in the years after her husband's death, suggesting that perhaps Mira earned her father-in-law's favor by warning him of an impending coup, but she may also have made enemies in the process. He suggests that the persecution of Mira was motivated by political concerns stemming from this incident. This is the only reasonable explanation for Ratan Singh's opposition to her, according to Goetz. Mira had no interest in politics or sectarian matters, but her integrity led her to speak the truth when she saw something unethical. Describing the lives of women in Mira's position, Goetz suggests that there was nothing unusual about her behavior except the intensity of her devotion—even taking care of wandering mendicants would have been a common activity.

When Sanga and her own father died, she lost their protection, and Ratan Singh went after her without anyone to stop him. He was suspicious of Mira's fraternizing with holy men because spies often took such a guise—clearly not an issue of honor or possible sexual impropriety here but a reasonable concern in sixteenth-century Rajasthan, where spies and mercenaries were known to move about in this way.[189] Attempts were made on her life, but she survived, not because of miracles but because she had supporters within the palace who replaced the poisonous snakes in the fruit basket sent to her with nonvenomous ones and who diluted or switched the poison said to be holy water.

When Vikramaditya came to power, he continued to torment Mira, ordering her decapitation. When no one would carry it out, he told her to drown herself (as she attempts to do in Dutt's account). She escaped somehow and joined her uncle Viramdev in Merta. Goetz's description of Vikramaditya is as degrading as he can possibly make it, portraying the young ruler's unmanliness in decidedly homophobic terms, describing him as "a wanton and coward, fond of strong young men, and subservient to older men who knew how to take him," despised by the rest of the court.[190] His nobles defected right and left, and his downfall was inevitable, according to Goetz. What more appropriate persecutor could there be for Mira than this man whom other historians would agree was an "unmanly" and despicable aberration in an otherwise noble line?[191]

Goetz goes on to speak of Mira as a revolutionary simply in the sense that she ignored the rules of the social order in the interest of spreading religion to the lower classes and to women. Her behavior was not tolerated by her relatives in Merta either, and she became a wandering mendicant, eventually reaching Dwarka. The Krishna of Dwarka, Goetz assures us, was the mature warrior prince rather than a cow-herding youthful lover, and Mira's attraction to him based on her own embrace of "the philosophy of duty and courage combined, in the Gita, with the message of Divine love and surrender" in a characterization that clearly echoes Bankimchandra's earlier portrayal of Krishna and the conjoining of dharma and bhakti.[192] Her disappearance when brahmans were sent by Udaisingh to fetch her is also rationalized: she must have left the temple by some hidden exit and continued to live out her life as a largely anonymous wandering devotee, in a further radicalization of her renunciation.

In the following years, he suggests, Man Singh must have become her disciple, later building a temple in Amer for her Krishna image, which he rescued when the Chittor Fort fell.[193] Goetz also affirms the adolescent Akbar met her, his disguise designed to protect her anonymity rather than hide his own identity, in an encounter which laid the foundation for his exceptional "pro-Hindu policy and his alliance with the Rajput princes." Indeed Goetz credits her with being "the inspiration for the first great attempt at bridging the gulf between Hindus and Muslims and at organizing an empire in which people were expected to find peace and justice"—an experiment that would fall apart and be "superseded by an orthodox Muslim course which ... led from discrimination to persecution, religious war and devastation until ... India was ripe for foreign rule."[194] Once more the blame for colonialism and interreligious violence is laid at the feet of Muslims in this post-Independence text, and Mira gets all the credit even for Akbar's exceptionalized "pro-Hindu" stance and his penchant for just rule.

Goetz's Mira is intelligent, strong, politically astute, and decisive, upholding social convention even as she pursues devotion. A religious reformer and active missionary (of a rather Christian-sounding sort), she preaches to the disenfranchised a gospel of love and of individual access to the Divine (in line with Tripathi's and other early twentieth-century characterizations of bhakti as a universal religion of the people and of love).[195] She is no *devadasi*, Goetz assures us, no intoxicated dancing lover of the Divine Cowherd. Rather she is one who, like Krishna in Dwarka, combines duty, courage, and devotion in a dignified religious calling and who is an ambassador for Hindu-Muslim unity and an active advocate for a just and peaceful society.

Kalyan Singh Shekhawat, a respected scholar of Rajasthani literature who has dedicated much of his career to the study of Mira, tells her tale yet again, drawing together the extensive hagiographic and historical scholarship on the saint and adding the results of his own conversations with genealogists of the Mertiya Rathors. But it is his politicization of Mira's motives for leaving

Chittor that is of greatest interest for our purposes here. Goetz had merely claimed that Mira was suspect because spies often took the guise of holy men to enter an enemy's territory undetected. Shekhawat suggests that when Mira learned that her actions might be endangering Chittor in this way, she chose to leave in order to protect the kingdom, even as her uncle Viramdev called her to him when he heard of her suffering at the hands of Vikramaditya.[196] Her actions in leaving Chittor thus become truly heroic.

This family of tales told by historians and scholars of Hindi literature from Shyamaldas and Deviprasad to Goetz and Shekhawat continues to be accepted by many as historically accurate and thus as the "truth" about Mira, based on its authors' claims and further authenticated by their scholarly reputations.[197] Though Madhav Hada (writing in 2015) contends that even their writings do not significantly challenge colonial presentations of Mirabai as an inimitable saint that obscure her humanity, his account mirrors these same venerable sources in presenting Mirabai's alleged "real" life, affirming her "happy childhood and marital life" and medieval Rajasthan as a place where such an independent woman could flourish (reminiscent of Tripathi's defense more than a century earlier).[198]

Joining the Ranks of Rajput National Heroines

Admittedly the oral nature of many of the historical records kept in Rajasthan in earlier centuries means that when searching for traces of a figure like Mira, the trail fades once we reach the earliest written copies of such information, and we have no way of verifying oral reports. Yet a number of the details are puzzling and do not seem to be based on any historical documentation, oral or written, including the hagiographic texts that have kept her memory alive. Why is Mira's mother said to have died when she was young, for example, when most other tellings of Mira's story clearly have her present at the time of her daughter's marriage? The logic for this and a number of other elements within this family of tales becomes clear through an analysis of narrative structure, quite apart from issues of historical data.

Other extraordinary women, as we have noted, find their way into oral traditions and legends, though they, like Mira, may not be mentioned in standard historical sources. The structure of historians' tellings places Mira squarely in the ranks of these legendary heroic women, as Dutt and company explicitly did—women whose sacrifice and devotion are for the sake of the kingdom and to uphold rajput honor. In these tales, heroic rajput and brahman queens, including Durgavati, Tarabai, Ahalyabai, and Lakshmibai, are broadly educated in the same way it is suggested that Mira was, well-versed in the arts of war and statecraft as well as literature and religion.[199] They are trained by older males—fathers and fathers-in-law—and there is no place for mothers in their tales, as there is not in Mira's story in this form. Only such a lack of maternal influence and a concomitant strong male presence in their lives could explain their future actions and their "manly" behavior.

Crises force these women to take positions of leadership usually reserved for men; either they fight side by side with fathers or husbands or they take over when their husbands die and their sons are too young to rule. Though Mira does not engage in such activities, her turn to extreme devotion is motivated by crisis, and Goetz and Shekhawat politicize her actions. She emerges as a strong and intelligent woman who exhibits fearless courage in the face of death and who has many characteristics of a man and moves in the world of men (though more often in the company of holy men than of warriors—a kind of masculinity defined by self-control rather than aggression, epitomized again by Bankimchandra's Krishna). No mere victim, she acts decisively and involves herself in the affairs of state in the name of truth. In Shekhawat's telling she even willingly gives up everything to leave Chittor for the good of the kingdom.

In general these heroines are portrayed both as having the strength, courage, and skills of men and as good wives as long as their husbands are alive. Ahalyabai decided to commit sati when her husband died but was deterred by her father-in-law and went on to rule the kingdom and lead armies into battle. Tarabai fought beside her husband to win back her father's kingdom, later immolating herself on her husband's funeral pyre after he was poisoned. Mira, too, takes on ostensibly masculine traits of independence and strength but exhibits characteristics of the pativrata during her husband's lifetime. This manly woman stands in dramatic contrast to the womanly man Vikramaditya, identified as the very opposite of the manly man Bhojraj and reviled by Goetz as an effeminate homosexual, the worst possible characterization in the larger residual colonial discourse of hypermasculinity of which such stories are a part. Yet Mira herself does not challenge the manhood of Bhojraj, acting as the perfect wife—in most of these historical tellings living in blissful marital union until his death, though in some she will offer him every wifely service while at the same time maintaining her chastity absolutely and thus transcending sexuality. Her husband cannot be said to have opposed her in any way, because as a pativrata she would never have contradicted his wishes. Mira's transformation into a rajput national heroine is complete, and the logic behind various elements of this family of tales falls into place.

Given the origins of these nationalist and rajput tellings of Mira's life, much of the aura of exclusive factuality of this ostensibly historical biography—so carefully cultivated and so widely accepted—begins to dissolve. In its place we find a fascination and engagement with Mira that moves beyond the religious sphere to other dimensions of experience and identity and into complex negotiations of autonomy and self-representation, gender and nation, tradition and modernity. This engagement will continue across the next century and into the present, as she becomes a truly pan-Indian cultural heroine and indeed a global saint. But it is clear that there were other tellings of Mira's life circulating in Deviprasad and Dutt's time (as there continue to be in our own)—and not only the familiar hagiographies or the new biographies and dramas in print. Even as Bankimchandra sought to cut away the "distortions of interpretation" and the excesses and ordinariness of folk accretions from the ostensibly historic Krishna, so too these rajput historians and elite nationalists felt the need to correct "distortions" surrounding Mira, even as they drew on the saint's immense popularity in championing her as a national and distinctly rajput heroine. Who else might have been telling and singing and performing Mira's life that they might have wanted to silence? And what might they have to say?

4

Weaver Woman and Lover Extraordinaire

Romance and Resistance in Rural Rajasthan

By the nineteenth century it is unquestionable that people across India knew of and loved Mira; there is ample evidence that there were many popular traditions in circulation about the saint, as even the early writing of Wilson and Tod demonstrate. Grierson had reported people in Mathila (Bihar) singing of her, and in Rewa (Madhya Pradesh) Raja Raghuraj Singh had drawn popular episodes into his bhaktamal commentary. By the end of the century her songs were integrated into Radha-Krishna bhajana communal singing led by S. V. Aiyer[1] in the southern city of Chennai (called "Madras" under the British), and in the east in Bengal Dutt and company would declare that she was known in every corner of the subcontinent and admired and loved by people at every level of society, "her spirit . . . breath[ing] over every Hindu home."[2]

Many in India would try to rein in and direct this unruly love of the saint, even as they sought to sort out and systematically define Hinduism as a religion and Hindi as a distinct language and literature, drawing from the dense weave of interrelated religious and linguistic currents that crisscrossed the subcontinent. In their self-appointed task of setting the record straight about Mira, nineteenth-century historians (and others who followed in their footsteps) discredited many streams of tradition as false or fanciful and attempted to overwrite them with their own nationalist and rajput heroic portraits of the saint, bolstered by claims of historical objectivity. Yet as we have seen, historical facts are hard to come by, and these tellings too reflect imaginative engagement and even introduce novel elements, drawn from alternative tales and genres. And though the "ordinariness" of "folk" tellings might have disturbed Deviprasad and others, even as it did Bankimchandra with regard to Krishna, had not these tellers themselves made Mira "ordinary"—a good middle-class, upper-caste pativrata in line with the new patriarchy and rajput heroism advocated by nationalists and rajputs alike? And had they themselves not in fact, to some degree at least, emptied her life story of the moral force to articulate and unmask power relations and to resist coercion and the injustice of caste and gender oppression even to the point of death and instead, at least in part, enlisted her to uphold rajput notions of honor and patriarchal and high-caste dominance and to serve their political ends?

What other tales and tellers might there be? Surely many among all those who have loved and admired the saint across the subcontinent must have imagined and experienced her far differently than did elite high-caste late nineteenth-century male rajput historians and nationalist writers (and their twentieth-century counterparts). As A. K. Ramanujan observes, "Where cultures (like the 'Indian') are stratified yet interconnected, where the different communities communicate but do not commune, the texts of one stratum tend to reflect on those of another: encompassment, mimicry, criticism and conflict and other power relations are expressed by such reflexivities[, and s]elf-conscious contrasts and reversals also mark off and individuate groups."[3] Who else might have been telling Mira's story, beyond the devotee composers and performers of the hagiographic texts we have examined and on whose works we know historians drew selectively?

Among their number must have been people like the tribal Dhangar shepherds of Pune district for whom "Mirabai" was among the most popular women's names, according to the 1885 *Bombay Gazetteer*.[4] It seems unlikely that they would have told the same story as the brahman Mahipati, any more than Lindsey Harlan's rajput women did that of Deviprasad and company a century later. Traces of such oral narrative traditions from centuries past are again very hard to come by. However, in rural Rajasthan in Marwar and Mewar, we can still find dramatically different stories of Mira's life, being lovingly told, sung, and performed, reflecting quite dissimilar themes, assumptions, and desires and yielding distinctly different portraits of the saint. The Mira found so alive here is decidedly not the Mira of Deviprasad or Dutt, or of Priyadas or Mahipati for that matter.

Across the twentieth century and into the present, Mira's life has been enacted as a romance in *khyal* (a form of Rajasthani folk drama) under the title *Mira Mangal* (Mira's Marriage). People also commonly sing a range of individual songs that describe particular events in Mira's life and recount possible conversations between Mira and the rana, her mother, her mother-in-law, and her sister-in-law.[5] But singers belonging to "lower"—formerly socially stigmatized and oppressed—caste communities also developed much more elaborate narrative traditions around Mira's life. One longer song tradition, under the title *Mirabai ro Byavlo* (Mira's Wedding), includes a detailed description of her marriage and of her becoming the disciple of Raidas,[6] while her life story reaches epic proportions in extended songs under the titles *Mira Janma Patri* (Mira's Horoscope or Mira's Birth Story) and *Kumbha Rana ri Bat* (The Story of Kumbha Rana).[7] The khyal of *Mira Mangal* has been performed in mixed-caste settings, while *Mira Janma Patri* and *Kumbha Rana ri Bat* have been performed predominantly by and for fellow caste members or at least those of lower caste standing. Raidas, as one might anticipate, plays a central role in many of these epics, which speak powerfully of caste and gender oppression and suffering but also of dignity and resistance.

Gender and caste, as key dimensions of identity and social relations, do play a crucial role in the unfolding drama of Mira's story across the board, though with starkly different consequences. Sukhsaran and rajput historians have effectively used Mira's story as a way to reinforce adherence to social norms within dharmic hierarchies, even when these are relativized within the wider horizon of devotion to God. But in the tales sung by lower-caste singers in rural Rajasthan, we find a raw and powerful articulation of coercion and suffering, renunciation and defiance, as the tellers explore the dynamics of caste from lower-caste perspectives and the struggles of women in positions of subordination. Here Mira is decidedly not the good rajput wife who acts only in compliant obedience to male authority figures and lives happily ever after, nor is she a mystic devotee lost in love of her Lord whose extraordinary life sets her apart forever from more ordinary women.

There is a realism within these alternative tellings, absent in many hagiographic and heroic accounts. Mira appears very down-to-earth, struggling with social and familial pressures, without the help of miraculous divine aid. She acts impetuously, as a woman of her age and social status might, even to the point of beating her servants—and of course she has servants as a woman of a royal household. Her all-consuming love cannot be contained and is instead portrayed as disruptive and dangerous to herself and others, shaking the foundations of familial and social stability and provoking violent repression.

How widespread such oral performative traditions may have been in the past we simply do not know. The roots of some may in fact be as old as the tales of our hagiographers. There are written traces of at least some Rajasthani folk dramas in the form of scripts going back to the nineteenth century, but even if we were to find corroborating references to these specific Mirabai performative traditions from a much earlier time, we would still have no way to examine how they might have changed across the decades or centuries of their performance. When a written textual tradition like that of the *Padaprasangmala* can appear in significantly different forms, how much more so narrative traditions in the improvisational realm of itinerant dramatic performance.

Their continuing existence today, however, suggests a wide, ongoing participation in the telling of Mirabai's story in this mercurial realm of popular culture and oral performance across a wide spectrum of society. No doubt such performances influenced the developing devotional literature and later historical constructions of Mirabai, even as these textual narratives have impacted subsequent oral performances. For just as there is no hard and fast dividing line between hagiographic, historical, and heroic tellings of Mira's story, so written, oral, dramatic, and now visual portrayals interact in myriad and complex reflexive and context-sensitive ways, recognized by tellers and audiences alike in varying degrees in something like "a verbal tent with three-ring circuses," as Ramanujan characterizes such cultural traditions in India.[8]

Like the hagiographers, nationalists, and rajput historians, their performers interact with and contribute to the diverse streams of tradition that swirl around the saint. They, too, will claim Mira as a member of their communities and imagine her in their own image, so that her story is imbued with their experiences, concerns, and values and told through the idioms of their lives. But theirs are very different worlds than those of upper-class rajputs, Bengali elites, and middle-class urban and diaspora Indians who might embrace nationalist and rajput heroic tales of the saint. And they do not necessarily share the historians' concern for exclusionary evidentiary truth, either as a goal or a mark of authenticity or authority for their accounts of Mira's life. In my experience, such performers do not seek to eliminate other possible tellings of Mira's story in favor of their own, nor do they seek to justify the stories they tell, sing, and enact of her life (even as Dutt did not). They do assert their right to tell her story, however, though their tellings may not necessarily be stable across performances and they may not always readily choose to perform them for outsiders.

Such stories speak truths that emerge out of their performers' particular lived experience of the world and of Mira, marked by their own deep regard for and varying identification with the saint, as those of other tellers do (including historians like Goetz, who says explicitly that the saint "helped [him] immensely in his own life").[9] Mira's story becomes a way to come to terms with and articulate these experiences and to address the shifting circumstances of particular audiences. Many of these tales reflect perspectives from the social position of the poor and the extremely low-caste, the Dalits—the "Broken" or "Crushed"—as some communities have named themselves, rejecting the "low" status and designation of "untouchables" imposed on them by the powerful and the attendant hierarchies of alleged purity and opportunity. In their tellings, when Mira renounces her world of privilege, she is choosing to live as they do, in solidarity with them, to share in their "common life," as Parita

Mukta has argued so persuasively.[10] In this context, Mira's character and life provide tellers and audiences with a language to affirm their dignity as human beings and to voice resistance and complex understandings of interweaving power relations, and many clearly draw inspiration and hope from Mira to live lives of integrity and meaning in the midst of sometimes terrible deprivation and suffering.

Even here, in rural villages, however, there is no singular vision of Mira, and thus no unified "folk" or popular portrayal of her. The "folk" of a village are diverse, and as Arjun Appadurai has observed, "any artificial homogeneity implied by the term *folk* masks many social diversities: of class, of gender, of region, of skill, of taste, and of temperament."[11] These vectors of difference (in both performers and audiences) intersect with the particular nature of given genres in varying ways and are played out anew in each performance context to shape the particular tale told. So here, too, we must be attentive to genre, to the social and religious positioning of both tellers and audiences, to performance contexts, and to regional specificity, tempered with a concurrent awareness of the improvisational, playful, and ephemeral character of actual performance. A comprehensive survey of popular tellings of Mira's life circulating throughout India would be fascinating but is far beyond the scope of the present study. We will focus our attention on two narrative traditions performed in mixed-caste and low-caste contexts in rural Rajasthan, the folk drama *Mira Mangal* and the epic song *Mira Janma Patri*, by way of example.

Mira Mangal: A Marriage against Her Will

Mira's story is a devotional and heroic story but also a love story, albeit a human-Divine one, as Tod observed, and it has been enacted as a romance in rural Rajasthan in the khyal, or folk drama, *Mira Mangal* for audiences that include members from the full range of castes and classes within a village. (Such dramas were targeted by late nineteenth-century nationalist reformers as unsuitable for "respectable ladies," and there has continued to be some stigma attached to watching them for upper-caste women.)[12] The basic plot of the drama dates back to at least the same general period during which Rajasthani historians were writing their heroic narratives, for the author of the earliest printed version available is Lacchiram of Kuchaman (1867–1937).[13] Though his telling of her story deals with the tension between renunciation and the householder life, love is the pivotal issue around which the plot turns in this drama exploring the problematic romance of Mira and her socially inappropriate (divine) lover and entering deep into the personal feelings of Mira and others when she is forced to marry.

The roots of this North Indian dramatic genre can be traced back to seventeenth-century religious plays, or *lilas*, of the lives of Krishna and Rama as well as secular forms of dramatic entertainment, including Nath jogi narrative performances, spontaneous and competitive poetic debates, and later court and Parsi theater, according to Kathryn Hansen.[14] The earliest available description of Rajasthani khyal appears in the 1866 report of the British district magistrate of Ajmer John Robson, in which he records that the form was said to have evolved out of poetic recitations in the court of Ram Singh of Jodhpur in the mid-eighteenth century when a clever bard began to employ costumes and act out episodes as he recounted them, in a manner that also poked fun at nobles of the court.[15] Since then khyal had become an extremely popular form of entertainment but was "not held in high esteem," the majority of the plays "immoral and even obscene," in Robson's (Victorian) judgment. He notes further that hundreds of scripts for such plays had been composed by the time of his writing, and shortly thereafter many were printed by local presses and later in Bombay, Pune, Delhi, and Calcutta as the form spread. As a regional form of folk drama, khyal has continued to be performed in Rajasthan into the present, with a corpus of as many as two hundred plays, some possibly dating back to the time of its origins.[16]

Mira's story, along with many other epic tales of romance, renunciation, and battle, entered this khyal tradition at some point. Lacchiram of Kuchaman was the leading proponent of what became known as the Kuchaman style in the Jodhpur region, and he is perhaps the most famous of the khyal authors. Lacchiram's own caste status has been a matter of some debate; some identify him as a brahman,[17] others as a *meghwal* (a community formerly considered very low in the caste hierarchy and identified with weaving and leatherwork).[18] Madan Mohan Mathur offers the clarification that he was "a 'Garuda Brahmin'—a priest of the Meghwal community."[19] Lacchiram composed a drama titled *Mira Mangal*, as did another author, Punamchand Sikhwal of Denda, following essentially the same plot line.[20] Whether earlier and/or different Mira khyals or other forms of folk theater might have been performed in this region is unknown, though later *nautanki* and *sang* folk dramas of her life in other regions are reported in the literature.[21]

Lithographed copies of the dramatic scripts by both Lacchiram and Punamchand Sikhwal were still available in markets in Rajasthan in the last decades of the twentieth century (see Figure 4.1).[22] The texts of the dramas offer only the bare bones of actual performance, although even these skeletal scripts are rich in narrative detail and intense emotion. Full performance

Figure 4.1 Mira conversing with her mother in an illustration from a printed edition of Lacchiram of Kuchaman's folk drama script *Khyal of Mira-Mangal* (n.p., n.d.), 72.

would include considerable improvisation—references to local people and events, to wider political issues, etc. might be added to an actor's set lines, and more recently a joker or clown figure has been added to the cast of characters in Kuchamani khyals, who is not mentioned in the script and whose words and actions are thus entirely improvised.[23] The familiarity of an audience with the lines of the text is assumed, and so it is performance style and innovation rather than the desire to know what comes next that defines excellence of performance in this genre. Audience members also sometimes make their own comments during the performance, particularly if they object to some aspect of it.[24]

Earlier such dramas were often enacted and sometimes also composed by villagers from a variety of castes for their own entertainment or some special occasion, particularly around the celebration of Holi, and then perhaps taken to neighboring villages.[25] Patronage would be from the village as a whole and took the form primarily of hospitality and goods rather than the exchange of money.[26] Actors who were recognized for their great skill might also be called by a village or town to perform, with a cast assembled for that particular performance, sometimes incorporating local talent. All actors were male and might come from a wide range of castes, including brahmans, though the drummers, playing the all-important role of calling people to the performance and providing accompaniment to the singing and dancing, were members of the *dholi* community.

Today, such spontaneous amateur performances have given way to professional drama troupes, hired by organizers and with regularized touring schedules, and the actors and musicians now come almost exclusively from lower castes and may include Muslim as well as Hindu professional caste musicians.[27] As Thomas Ault notes, "Professionals set performance standards unattainable by amateurs and assimilate all the best amateurs, thus destroying the base for community performance."[28] During the period when he was doing his ethnographic research in the 1980s and 1990s, Ault reports, such professional performances were still very common, both in towns and villages and at the major cattle fairs held annually across Rajasthan. However, in 2006, Mathur would note that there were only six professional Kuchamani khyal companies actively performing, and he appealed for increased government support for artists of this regional art form.[29] *Mira Mangal* has not figured among the most commonly performed khyals, past or present, which more often concern heroes like Amar Singh Rathor and the renouncer king Harishchand.[30] However, well into the 1990s the script was possessed by and familiar to drama troupes.[31]

A typical performance of a khyal may last into the early hours of the morning or throughout the night and may not include the full drama.[32] The actors are in costume with bells on their ankles, and small hand-held props are used. Sets are not elaborate. The lines of dialogue are largely sung, and there are generally only one or two characters on stage at any one time, accompanied by musicians. The actors do not speak in the first person but refer to themselves in the third person, in a style that suggests a direct continuity with epic performance even as many of the stories are shared by both genres.[33]

Performers have presumably always added considerably to the written text, even before the introduction of the clown character, and in these improvisations we would find the most stringent social commentary as the story is brought more fully into the specific world and concerns of the particular audience. In this way no two performances are ever the same, so that this genre, too, partakes of the character of oral tradition in spite of its textual base. In any case, like other dramatic scripts, their texts serve only as "a blueprint, a workman's plan drawn for a group of collaborating artists," and reading alone cannot bring this interactive dimension of the performance alive.[34] Nevertheless the scripts do offer continuity across the past century that threads through performances in various times and places in rural Rajasthan, and I will confine my analysis here to these texts.

When compared to the narratives we have examined so far, the khyal perhaps most closely approaches Sukhsaran's *Mira ri Parachi* in the primary place given to Mira's marriage and its discussion of renunciation versus the householder life, but the miracles that fill Sukhsaran's tale find no place in the khyal, and the two stories are vastly different in other ways. In the khyal Mira's marriage becomes *the* central issue, not as an event merely to be described but as an occasion to explore the intense and conflicting emotions surrounding arranged marriages and as a catalyst for the clash between Mira's individual desires and the need for familial, caste, and social cohesion.

Mira is largely a romantic heroine here (in spite of the fact that scholars have classified this drama as dharmic or religious rather than romantic).[35] She pines for a lover considered inappropriate by her parents, and her love threatens the honor and the very lives of her natal kin. Every possible argument for why she should marry, in both social and personal terms, is brought forth, and much of the discussion revolves around issues of propriety and a woman's proper behavior. It is her overwhelming love (of God) that threatens the social fabric and results in her banishment. Mira is less cooperative with the whole affair than in any other telling we have examined so far, even threatening to commit suicide in Lacchiram's account. She is also more theological (perhaps reflecting the influence on khyal of a debating style of poetic dialogue emerging first in the context of disagreements between members of religious sects in Maharashtra).[36] The tale is dharmic in the sense that much of this discussion deals with renunciation as a path to moksha, or liberation, a goal that does not generally find direct articulation in individual songs about renunciation attributed to Mira or in oral epics like *Mira Janma Patri*.

The play opens with an invocation to Sarasvati and Krishna and a brief history of the Rathor lineage of Duda, explaining how he came to rule Merta. Ratan Singh is named as Mira's father. Mira herself is but fourteen years old, though already well established in her devotion, serving a shalagram as well as dancing before an image of Krishna. She has given herself over completely to the company of the devotees (sants). The stage is now set for the action to begin.

Sadhus from Vrindavan who have been traveling to the great pilgrimage sites of India (Banaras, Haridwar, Ayodhya, Pushkar) stop in Merta on their way to Dwarka in order to meet Duda, renowned for his devotion and hospitality. When Duda hears of their coming, he rushes out to greet them himself and insists that they stay in the kingdom for the months of the rainy season. They refuse to stay in the palace—an inappropriate place for renouncers to reside—but agree to settle for some time in the gardens around the temple of Charbhuja, the four-armed Vishnu/Krishna.[37]

A temple to Charbhuja does exist today in Merta, which is said to be the temple where Mira worshiped as a child. An image of her stands near the entrance to the temple in a line of sight with the image of Charbhuja, and paintings of her along with texts of her songs adorn some of the walls. Historical sources credit Rao Duda with having built such a temple in Merta, but considerable expansion and renovation of the present temple was carried out in 1948 (vs 2004) by *jingar mochis*, a caste community who have the honor of making the first offerings in the temple and are publicly acknowledged as its patrons.[38] In the wake of Independence, this community also built a Charbhuja temple in the pilgrimage town of Pushkar with an image of Mirabai similarly placed, reflecting the central importance of the saint to these lower-caste artisans.[39] But there is also evidence that in the 1780s, there were attempts by local elites (brahmans and merchants) to bar them from worshiping at the Merta Charbhuja temple, though their customary right to do so was ultimately upheld by the Maharaja Vijai Singh of Jodhpur, indicating that their connection to this temple and Mira goes back centuries.[40]

In the khyal, the scene shifts from the sadhus and Duda to Mira's maidservant Mithula telling Mira about the leader of the sadhus Paramhams ("Great Swan" or "Great Soul").[41] Mira is excited—like a sister when her brother arrives, the text says—and she wants to go immediately to meet the sadhus. Mithula warns that her mother will object, so they go under cover of darkness. The holy man is startled when this young girl and her companion arrive in the night. He is concerned that people will talk and that the sadhus will be blamed. The issue here is not caste but rather the maintenance of an unblemished reputation of chastity and propriety for both the holy men and the virgin girls.

With childish innocence, Mira tells Paramhams that she wants to see God, to have him come and play with her. The sadhu replies that he can only direct her to the path, but then she must make her own way along it. To do so, she must leave worldly things and sit among devotees and sadhus. However, she is only a child, and this path is not yet for her, he insists, seeking to discourage her. His reasoning is much like that of Mira's mother in Sukhsaran's tale, but Mira is deaf to it and insists on being made his disciple. Their conversation ends with his telling her to worship the one God.

In the next scene Mira and her mother are engaged in an extended confrontation over her behavior, which is bringing condemnation down on the family. Her mother tries to be flexible, telling her daughter that she can do whatever she wants in the palace but begging her to stop going to the temple. Mira refuses, and her mother then invokes the specter of the Sisodiya rana's ire, saying he will come to kill them all if he hears of the way his betrothed is acting. For his part, Mira's grandfather refuses to intervene. He seems proud of Mira's devotion and does not see anything wrong with it. Nevertheless, Mira's mother is relentless in her pursuit of her daughter. Her arguments have a familiar ring, as she insists that Mira guard her reputation, prepare herself to be a daughter-in-law in a stranger's house, and protect the honor and thus the lives of her kin through proper behavior. Instead Mira runs around barefoot, letting her skin darken in the sun and staying out late at night, and she threatens to kill herself if her mother tries to force her to marry.

Yet her mother is not so easily defeated by her impetuous daughter, and the lively interaction continues. The arranged match is a good one—what better husband could she hope for than the rana of Mewar? Her family's status will be raised as well. Mira will have none of it (in an implicit refutation of this common practice of hypergamy—marrying daughters "up" for status).[42] She is of no use to the rana, nor he to her. She is concerned only for Girdhar Gopal, the Mountain-Bearing Cowherd Krishna. She has met her guru and renounced all. The householder life, the honor of the Rathors and of Merta mean nothing to her. What matters is liberation, moksha. In exasperation her mother protests to Duda. He must do something about Mira's outrageous behavior! In response he only comes to Mira's defense—what could possibly be wrong with such great devotion?

The marriage cannot be stopped whether or not Mira has Duda's support, however, because the matter has become one of ritual and rajput honor—such a pledge cannot be broken. Marriage songs are sung in the palace, and the preparations for a fabulous wedding described in elaborate detail. Mira is oblivious to it all. When Mithula tells her, she responds, "I am only for the Mountain Bearer. Who is this Sisodiya?" Mithula tries to talk sense into her, patiently explaining that the coconut exchanged in the betrothal ritual cannot be taken back—the marriage *will* happen. Everyone has been summoned, and the rana is on his way. A ritual process of transformation has been set in motion that is understood to be no more reversible than a caterpillar's metamorphosis into a butterfly once it has entered the cocoon.[43]

Mira prays to Krishna, but no miraculous intervention ensues. Instead her mother comes to get her dressed. Mira stubbornly resists. Duda also comes to reason with her. Why does he offer her poison, she counters, in forcing what she considers a second marriage? Finally he gets her to agree to go through with the ceremony if she can have the image of Krishna at her side rather than the groom. Duda goes to the sadhus to retrieve the image and implores them to try to persuade Mira to cooperate. Paramhams is indeed persuasive, and Mira moves another step closer to compliance, but she says that she will do the ritual only with the rana's sword and only after she has completed it first with her Lord's image.

Sword marriages were not unheard of among rajputs to cement alliances when the groom was unable to attend and perhaps also when the need for secrecy militated against his actual presence, and they appear in other Rajasthani epic traditions, including *Shri Devnarayanji ro Byavlo* (Wedding of Devnarayan)[44] When a rajput bridegroom's status was considerably higher than that of his bride, he might not attend the wedding himself but simply send his sword and then have the woman brought to him. But Mira's groom has arrived. There could also be an insult buried within Mira's request, for William Crooke (drawing on his collaborative research with Ram Gharib Chaube) reports that when a rajput woman married a man of lower caste, the ritual was also sometimes performed in such a manner.[45] And in the conventions of khyal, the sword is the visual mark of the power of a king, and "[t]he only time he appears without his sword is when he is disgraced or disabled in the action of the play."[46] Further Mira's insistence on carrying out the ceremony with her image of Krishna first effectively annuls her betrothal to the rana, a practice which also has precedents in parts of India where a betrothed but not yet married girl could escape the marriage if she managed to complete the marriage ritual around a fire in the jungle with a tree or particular sacred plants.[47]

Mira's limited acquiescence creates a flurry of activity in the drama, for the sword can be obtained only with the cooperation of someone in the groom's entourage. Mithula is forced to go to the other camp, though night is coming and she is afraid. One of the rana's maidservants gives her the sword and promises to make sure that the rana will not notice its absence too soon. The priest is summoned and somewhat reluctantly performs the unorthodox ritual. Still Mira refuses to go to the rana, but Mithula begs her and promises not to leave her alone with him.

When Mira is eventually persuaded, the rana is a bit confused about what has transpired but proceeds to shower her with flattering words. He tells her how he has longed for this moment and how he has been waiting to see her. Then he naturally enough invites his new bride into his bed. She will have none of it, although their conversation takes the form of a gentle banter rather than a vehement argument. She asks him to promise not to force her to do what she does not want to do. He tries to explain to her that no one will object to her devotion and bhajan singing in old age but that now she is young and this is a time for enjoyment and pleasure. His words do not move her, and she meets his every attempt to sway her with a clever retort, always culminating in a request that he not force her to comply. He tries another approach, offering her wine, but she responds by comparing their situation to that of Sita and the demon king Ravana in the *Ramayana*.[48] Eventually he realizes the futility of his efforts, and being an honorable man, he gives up for the time being (his "honor" here simple human decency rather than coercive and brutal male pride that, if affronted, requires violent retribution).

The story then proceeds along the usual lines. Mira goes with him to Chittor and wonders how she will know how to act properly as a wife and daughter-in-law since she always refused to learn such things. The thought is only passing, however. The rana tells her how to behave in a minimally acceptable manner and continues to try to entice her with the pleasures of the world that are now to be hers, but to no avail. She refuses the rana's reasonable request that she touch his mother's feet. "She is no relation to me," Mira says. Her new mother-in-law first takes Mira's side when her son complains, but says that if she is what he says, then he should get rid of the worthless girl—give her poison or put a snake around her neck. She goes to Mira to find out what kind of daughter-in-law has come to the house, and Mira is adamant in her commitment to bhakti and renunciation, refusing to listen to the entreaties of her mother-in-law.

Her new sister-in-law Uda is then sent to reason with her but with the usual results or lack thereof. Mira tells her explicitly that she carried out the wedding ceremony with both her *murti* (image) of Krishna and the sword and that she did the latter only so people would not slander the families. The rana talks of marrying another and leaving Mira, though Uda tries to dissuade him, and Mira ultimately decides to leave Chittor, going first directly to the pilgrimage town of Pushkar and then on to Merta. In a familiar song, she recounts the rana's attempts to kill her with poison and a snake and speaks longingly of wanting to take him to Vaikunth (Vishnu's heaven) and of his incomprehension. Finally she sets off for Dwarka (according to Punamchand Sikhwal) or settles in Vrindavan (according to Lacchiram), where she has darshan of Krishna daily, as the drama comes to a close.

Mira's story as it is told here is a romance, a tale of the purest form of love, albeit between a human woman and her Divine Beloved. She has fallen in love with someone her parents perceive as inappropriate, but her love is absolute, and she is willing to risk everything for it. In other romances within this genre of khyal the situation is much the same. Individual desires are pitted against communal allegiances, and love is portrayed as undermining structures of hierarchy but equally as a fundamental and positive aspect of human existence.[49] In this telling of Mira's tale, it is her *love* which is the foundation for every challenge she makes to hierarchy, whether based on caste, gender, or wealth, as all such distinctions crumble before this highest of human aims.

Of romances in this genre, Hansen suggests that "[t]he only place for romantic love is in an existence contrived beyond society's boundaries—in the barren wilderness, or in heaven," and such romances reflect the vehemence of social opposition to love in their often tragic endings, for "[s]ociety exacts its revenge on errant members not only by confining and exiling them, but ultimately by killing them."[50] If she had been writing specifically about Mira's tale, she could not have described the situation more accurately. Mira's love, religious though it may be, cannot be contained in the social realm, and she finds herself compelled to leave that world in the wake of multiple murder attempts (so well-known to the audience, it seems, that they need only be invoked in a single song). The khyal ends here, in Mira's social death though not precisely in tragedy, for she makes her way to the holy pilgrimage centers of Vrindavan or Dwarka, where her Divine Beloved resides and where such devotion might be allowed to flourish.

Further structural parallels exist between Mira's narrative enacted here and other romantic dramas. Like their heroines, Mira has trouble because men other than her lover desire her and because her family's overriding concern is honor.[51] The portrayal of love as a kind of renunciation and of the lover as a renouncer, a jogi or *fakir*, is also a common motif in such tales. Lovers may disguise themselves as jogis to search each other out and to meet without detection.[52] In light of such an observation, songs attributed to Mira describing Krishna and herself as wandering jogis take on a romantic resonance with more ordinary human experience and imagination. As the tale ends, Mira is such a renunciant lover, having left behind family and all else in her utter commitment to her true love.

In some romantic dramas, the pair of lovers come from different castes, creating the same kind of social tension that we will find in *Mira Janma Patri*. Raidas is absent from the khyal of Mira, however, not only because it is Krishna alone who must be Mira's focus in such a romance but also likely to keep the saint untouched by what some would consider "impurity" and avoid raising issues of caste-based oppression, given the drama's intended multi-caste audience. If something is to be said directly about caste, it would have to be inserted into the improvisational portions of the drama, having been given no essential place in the flow of this romantic plot. The stories of historical *viranganas* (heroines) are also told in this genre, and when they are, these stories, too, become strictly tales of romance, with heroism exercised on behalf of a lover or the maintenance of chastity rather than for the sake of a kingdom.[53]

Mira's story is not about a human love affair, but in its ideal form, love between human lovers seemingly most closely approaches the purest form of love for God and offers a language to speak about it (or even a mode to manifest it, as the *Prem Ambodh* suggests). Conversely, this story of human-Divine love resonates with and readily articulates feelings and experiences of human romantic love, both fulfilled and unfulfilled. Again Hansen writes of the love portrayed in such plays in words that may as easily have been written about the bhakti path as about more ordinary human romance:

> Running through this tremendous idealism and moral fervor surrounding love is a dark commingling of compulsion and tragedy. . . . The lover is compelled to love, driven by a destiny beyond conscious control. Commitment to the path of love allows no alternative, no turning back. Despite the travails of the most dedicated lover, separation remains as the unwavering condition of being in the world. . . . Love is in no terms an impossibility: rather it is the distinguishing mark of the human condition. It rages through human consciousness, demanding the ultimate in commitment, the best that is within us.[54]

Performed as khyal, Mira's tale explores these heights and depths of love, whether for a human or a divine lover.

Stepping back from such idealism, the tale enacted in *Mira Mangal* also explores the more everyday emotions and power relations that come into play in the conflict of individual and group values and the clash of impetuous and uncompromising youth with the more seasoned voices of elders who know the ways of the world and the precariousness of human existence. Embedded in this conflict is a questioning of and challenge to the practice of arranged marriage. The raw and unbridled quality of this "arrangement" is highlighted in Mira's case because the marriage is clearly a mode of political alliance between kingdoms and her individual wants and desires are completely overridden. The vulnerability of the young girl and the pressures exerted on her to conform are laid out in detail, as one after another mother, grandfather, religious teacher, husband, mother-in-law, sister-in-law, even companion and maid confront, cajole, and try to coerce her into compliance.

Mira resists, refusing to complete the ritual with other than Krishna's image and only secondarily with the rana's sword, asserting her love and marriage to her divine lover and carrying out the sword marriage merely as a token to satisfy others' superficial notions of propriety. And in the end she herself chooses to leave Chittor. But the specter of violence hangs over the drama with the Sisodiyas' potential to kill not only Mira but her family over honor tied to her behavior even before marriage and the clear message following the ritual that she is at the mercy of her husband and her in-laws. The rana can abandon her for another wife at any time, or they might even kill her. There is no one to protect her if they should turn on her. The young girl's recourse is in reality very limited: she can take her own life, as she threatens to do initially, or she can comply, however minimally. Yet there is no guarantee that her terms of compliance will be accepted or respected.

Further, though Mira's husband is portrayed here as understanding, engaging in gentle banter with his unwilling bride on their wedding night, the darker possibilities for such encounters run just below the surface. Twentieth-century novelists writing of Mirabai, such as Kiran Nagarkar and A. J. Joshi, and others writing of more ordinary characters named after her, such as Shashi Deshpande's namesake character in *The Binding Vine*, explicitly raise the specter of domestic violence and marital rape inherent in such a marriage against the woman's will, though the khyal performance does not step over the line overtly into that difficult terrain.[55]

Religious values of liberation and detachment also run up against those of householders and the world in this enactment of Mira's life, as they do in dharmic plays telling the stories of renouncer kings like Gopichand and Harishchand.[56] Mira will become a renouncer queen, as her pursuit of love and liberation merge, and she finally finds her home in Vrindavan or Dwarka, far from both her natal and marital families. All the reasons why Mira should not do what she is doing are articulated clearly in the play, and in this way the drama lends support to the network of social relations that love threatens. Love, religious and otherwise, is affirmed, but so is the social structure. Mira's khyal is not alone in this.

Out of the tension between these divergent and powerful values emerges a wealth of dramas marked by tragedy, compromise, and triumph in varying combination, true to the suffering and joy of human social life. These conflicting values and this beauty and pain mark Mira's tale as it is performed in khyal. Individual love and conviction run up against social stability and loyalty to one's group, and Mira comes out on the side of the pursuit of love and enlightenment, calling others if not to follow in her footsteps, at least to aspire to something greater than unexamined acceptance of social propriety and familial obligation—a compelling tale and a far cry from the Mira of Deviprasad or Dutt and unquestionably not a ringing endorsement of the nationalist new patriarchy or rajput notions of honor. The tale of Mira enacted here falls midway between those of hagiography and history on the one hand and low-caste epic renderings like *Mira Janma Patri* on the other, even as Hansen identifies this genre khyal itself as an intermediate one.[57]

Mira Janma Patri: Another Tale Told

In contrast to *Mira Mangal,* the intended audience of the epic song *Mira Janma Patri* (Mira's Horoscope or Mira's Birth Story) is primarily those who have suffered caste-based oppression, those of so-called lower castes, and the tale differs considerably, belying any assumption of a unified rural or popular "folk" view of Mira.[58] Raidas is a central character, as he is in other low-caste narrative traditions of Mira, and Mira's association with this chamar guru is identified as *the* cause of her greatest suffering. Her rajput identity is important only insofar as it lends authority to her embrace of low-caste people and her adoption of their ways of life. Her allegiance lies with those who also suffer at the hands of innumerable "ranas," and her narrative offers a language of dignity in which to speak the experiences of other lives and hearts as well as her own.[59]

Though this rather generic title is also used by tellers of other, often quite distinct tales of Mira, this specific epic *Mira Janma Patri* has a range across southern and western Rajasthan (and perhaps beyond) and is included in the repertoires of particular groups of low-caste singers. For the following account, I have drawn on recordings of one complete rendition sung by *bavari* singers from Borunda (1975), a nearly complete rendition sung by meghwal singers from Devdungri (1996), and fragments of the tradition performed by jat singers from the Chittor region (1993) and *garoliya lohars* from Udaipur (1993).[60] All the singers were male (with the exception of the husband-and-wife team of meghwal singers), reflecting the public context of this performance genre. I have asked many other singers in southern and western Rajasthan whether they knew this song. Many said they knew of it but could not perform it.

With respect to caste identity and status, the singers of this tale come from communities that have been considered very low to medium level in the social hierarchies of Rajasthan. Even with strong Indian constitutional guarantees of equal rights and initial remedial measures for "scheduled castes and tribes," coupled with the additional educational and employment reservations for "other backward classes" established in the 1990s, the legacy of caste-based oppression remains an ongoing concern and challenge in India and caste a flexible tool for asserting group identity and negotiating rights. The singers of this tale readily identified themselves by caste affiliation, and the social positioning that caste implies profoundly shapes the stories they sing, no less than it does our rajput and elite nationalist interlocutors.

According to the classificatory compendiums of peoples of India and of Rajasthan, the bavaris were known as hunters, their name allegedly derived from the *bawar*, or noose, they used to snare small animals and birds. Members of this community subsequently have primarily been cultivators who also engage in itinerant labor, including agriculture, masonry, and other services.[61] The meghwals were identified as leatherworkers and weavers and accorded very low status, though they also have engaged in agriculture and a wide range of other occupations and continue to do so. In the past they were treated as servants of the village and subjected to forced labor (as were people of other "low-caste" communities). Many have been and are worshipers of Ramdev (a hero deity of rajput descent who has had both Hindu and Muslim devotees and is identified with Krishna).[62] The garoliya lohars have traditionally been ironworkers. Many still travel from place to place offering their services, and they too worship Ramdev and practice Vaishnava devotion. They say that they took up their itinerant life the last time that the fort of Chittor fell, vowing not to live in a fixed place until the rana of Mewar again ruled from Chittor.[63] The jats are a midlevel agricultural landholding caste, the most numerous caste community in Rajasthan, and have had a higher status than the bavaris, meghwals, or lohars.[64] All such characterizations, particularly with relation to occupation, become less and less relevant particularly in urban centers and with continuing education and upward mobility, but remain pertinent to understanding this subaltern telling of Mira's life, generated and performed by and among these communities.

In performance, the epic story of Mira may be performed as a whole or portions sung as independent songs. Song alternates with speech as lines are repeated and narrative details added, and there is again much room for elaboration, making the description I offer herein exemplary of this dynamic epic tradition but by no means a definitive and always repeated fixed "text."[65] More widely circulating Mira songs are also often incorporated into its telling, especially as a way to end the performance.[66]

Though the episodes are quite distinct, a common refrain threads through them:

> Come Sanvariya, Girdhari come quickly;
> Having put her trust in you, Mira is alone.

This refrain marks the trajectory of the plot, away from the embrace of Mira's childhood family into an increasing isolation from and rejection by the social world. Half-lines are sometimes added: Mira asks her Dark Lover Sanvariya, the Mountain Bearer, to climb up quickly, promising that she will sweep the path before him with the edge of her red wedding *ordhni*, or veil, and to come immediately because her heart aches as if pierced by an arrow or cut by a saw.

A further refrain is also added in the latter part of the work. As Mira's situation becomes more desperate and the opposition to her actions more intense, she calls out to her Lord, asking why he has brought her into this world of death.

The narrative begins on a lighter celebratory note, recounting in great detail and with obvious enjoyment the events surrounding Mira's birth. The initial lines trace the passing months of the rani's pregnancy in Duda's palace.[67] Mira is born at an auspicious time. Gold trays are beaten, as is traditionally done to herald the birth of a son (as Sukhsaran reports, though here not miraculously but by human hands). Mira's umbilical cord is cut with a gold knife amid singing.[68] Her father's sister takes responsibility for making the necessary arrangements. Bringing a fine tray of pearls, she wakes the sleeping astrologer with a call to come to the window. Less than pleased at this disturbance in the middle of the night, he learns that he is being summoned to the palace of Dudaji of Merta where a daughter has been born. He comes, bringing his sacred texts and his charts to determine and record Mira's horoscope. These sacred texts are referred to as "*Ved* and *Puran*" (the Vedas and the Puranas) in the sung portion and as "*Ved* and *Kuran*" (Vedas and Qur'an) in the spoken section of one performance, reflecting the permeable boundaries between Hindus and Muslims in the singers' world. When her aunt asks what the name of the child should be, the astrologer says that her birth name is "Yashoda" (Krishna's adoptive mother's name) but that she should be called "Mira."

Mira's aunt next calls the carpenter, asking him to build a cradle for Mira. He, too, is sleeping and must be awakened to serve Dudaji of Merta. The cradle must be intricately painted with animals and peacocks, green-feathered parrots and black cuckoos. Only sandalwood will do for such a royal child, so the gardener must be summoned as well. When asked, he describes the trees that grow in his garden, including the *champa* with its delicate fragrant blossoms and the sandalwood tree. A deal is struck for the purchase of sandalwood. Gifts given in exchange for each service are also enumerated, including multicolored turbans and various items of jewelry and clothing for both husband and wife.

These verses are repetitive and expandable. Only the naming of Mira and the mention of Dudaji of Merta are specific to Mira's story. The initial portion of the song appears to be an abbreviated form of a type of song that follows the months of a woman's pregnancy: her morning sickness, her growing physical limitations, her desires, etc.[69] The characters of astrologer, carpenter, gardener, and father's sister in the next segment appear together in other songs as well, including a Gangaur song sung by Rajasthani women in which the divine bridegroom Shiva is greeted by each in turn as he moves from the outskirts of his bride Parvati's village into the ritual center of the marriage.[70]

The series of actions involved in calling each person for service in *Mira Janma Patri* and the need first to awaken them are also found in a Rajasthani wedding song in which a gardener is being called to make a wedding crown for a bridegroom.[71] It is ornamented with flying birds and peacocks, and the gardener's wife brings it from the market. Mira's cradle is similarly decorated and brought to the palace. Clearly the *Janma Patri* portrayal of Mira's birth partakes of images and structures from the traditions of birth and wedding songs. Parallels are also found in the epic traditions of Rajasthan. For example, in the story of Pabuji (another rajput hero deity around whom an elaborate and highly specialized epic performance tradition has developed), a carpenter is called to make a sandalwood cradle for a royal child and, at another point, to make a sandalwood spinning wheel carved with frogs and peacocks.[72] Such observations place *Mira Janma Patri* within a continuum of Rajasthani performative traditions from song to epic.[73]

Elsewhere Mira's birth is not described in such detail and with such obvious relish. Why should it be here? In part the answer would seem to be simply for the love of Mira, the pleasure of song, and the beauty of description. Mira's story is drawn into the world of the singers and audience as her birth is sung in common idioms, and she is claimed as a member of their circle of affection. The types of material included reflect the logic of oral epic traditions as well; particular types of events warrant particular types of descriptions and songs that have a formulaic quality. Yet in a dramatic reversal, the customary celebrations for the birth of a son are being carried out for the girl child Mira, without any claims that she is exceptional, only that she is a beloved daughter.[74] The welcoming of Mira into her natal family in this way also stands in stark contrast to her entry into her marital home and sets the stage for her renunciation in the next episode.

As the next episode begins, Mira goes to the garden with her girlfriends to meet a Nath *baba* who is specifically identified as Raidas. She is determined to become his disciple, although he initially refuses her (as Paramhams had in *Mira Mangal* but for different reasons). She is from a great house, he says, and Duda of Merta will complain.[75] However, in the face of her conviction, he eventually agrees. There is no doubt here that Mira is insisting on becoming the disciple of a low-caste guru, specifically identified as a chamar, and that Duda will complain because of this, as well as because of Mira's turn to a life of religious renunciation.

To call Raidas a "Nath baba" (a highly respected Nath) might not necessarily follow expectation, if this appellation is assumed to refer specifically to a Saivite tantric ascetic of the Nath sampraday, and such a guru would seem an unlikely choice for a fervent Krishna devotee.[76] However, in the past as well as the present, Naths have been both respected and feared in Rajasthan for their spiritual power. Raidas is also called a "jogi" here, and bhakti and yoga have often been conjoined in practice.[77] Seventeenth-century Dadupanthi texts confirm that "Nath" has equally been used as an honorific title for a master of yogic asceticism, "the perfected sadhu," regardless of religious affiliation, and Dadu himself is praised as such.[78] To address Raidas in this way would thus honor him as a widely renowned spiritual master, resonating also with songs sung in Mira's name in which she addresses and describes Krishna himself as a jogi of the Nath tradition.[79] Further, within the Nath sampraday, there have been those who also embraced Vaishnava devotion, and indeed in another narrative that appears to combine elements of the *Janma Patri* with portions of a second epic song tradition of Mira, she also asks her Nath guru to give her a Vaishnava *tulsi mala* (rosary of basil wood beads) at her initiation.[80] Such portrayals of Mira, Raidas, and Naths fit easily and logically into the pluralistic religious landscape of Rajasthan, particularly among low-caste communities, where devotion takes inclusive and noninstitutional forms, blending devotion to Ramdev with Vaishnava and Nath influences and much more.[81]

Raidas asks why Mira would want to take on saffron dress and a life of sorrow, but she is adamant. That she is still only a child is clear, however, as she is described playing on the far bank of a river with her friends. They build sandcastles with rooms and verandahs and then smash them. Mira builds shrines to God and, while playing, picks up a stone. Holding it close, she begins to worship it as a shalagram. This shalagram, rather than a murti given to her by some sadhu, stands at the center of her childhood devotional practice. This detail is again appropriate, given that the practice of worshiping the aniconic shalagram might be more open to women and people of lower caste who may not have been permitted to handle images (as well as being commonly associated with Raidas).[82] On one level Mira's actions are a child's imaginative play, but they demonstrate her ability to see God in all things, even an ordinary stone, and her uniquely religious orientation emerges from the comparison with her companions (much as it did in Sukhsaran's tale).

When Mira returns to the palace dressed in the saffron of renunciation, there is trouble. Her engagement to the rana has already been arranged, and the rana has been informed of the auspicious time for the wedding. A priest is sent to call him immediately. The only hope is to have the ceremony performed quickly before he finds out the true nature of his bride and before she becomes any more extreme in her renunciation. The rana comes with the wedding party, arriving first at the village border, then at the well, at the door of the bride's house, and finally at the wedding pavilion. Successively he encounters cowherds, water carriers, Mira's girlfriends, and the priest. Each admires his beauty, and each is given a conventional payment (*neg*). Again there is nothing specific to Mira's story about this wedding song, which belongs to the wider tradition of bridegroom songs.

The bridal clothes, given by the groom's family, are brought to Mira by servant women. They try to persuade her to take off her saffron and put on a traditional Rajasthani *ghaghara* skirt, an *ordhni* veil trimmed in gold, and the sixteen ornaments of a bride. They encourage her to put the vermilion powder in the part of her hair that is the mark of a married woman. She grows angry and, after calling the women to bring the clothes into her chamber, picks up a whip and begins to beat them. They run out, afraid of this crazy holy woman. Mira's mother intercepts them and asks what has happened. They call Mira a *samman*—a term for a renouncer but also a term of abuse—and recount the beating. Mira's mother tells them to speak softly; the rana has already arrived for the wedding and must not learn of her improper behavior. Her mother proceeds to the palace to try to persuade her wayward daughter to go through with the wedding.

Mira's mother implores her to uphold the "*murjad* (*maryada*) of the *palla*," the propriety of the married state, and to put on the clothes and ornaments of a bride. If she does not, Duda will complain, and dishonor and trouble will come to them. She reminds her daughter that although God has given her beauty, it is her mother who has given her birth in this world. Mira accepts her mother's request, having spent her anger on the maidservants and seeming to realize the futility of her resistance and the legitimacy of her mother's claim (made as it is in a characteristic posture of begging with the extension of her *palla*, the edge of her sari).[83] Mira says that she will put on the clothing, ornaments, and vermilion mark of a bride, listing for the third time all these outward marks of marriage.

Mira is indeed a beautiful bride, and she and her mother set off for the wedding pavilion, lest the rana become impatient. Halfway there, however, Mira realizes that she has forgotten her shalagram and the other things needed for her worship, and she insists on going back for them. Because this is a rajput marriage, she is not sure that they will let her do so after the ceremony. Her mother allows her to return—how can she refuse, when she knows that it is for her sake that Mira has agreed to the marriage at all? Having retrieved the necessary items, they proceed to the wedding pavilion, where the marriage takes place.

The emphasis in this portion of the story is on the relationship between Mira and her mother and the coercive nature of the marriage. In the repetitions of the refrain, her Dark Lover Sanvariya, the Mountain Bearer Girdhari, is called to come quickly and to help Mira in this time when she is alone. Neither her maidservants nor her mother seem sympathetic to her desires. In this telling, as elsewhere, Mira's marriage becomes a narrative occasion for exploring the emotions that surround arranged marriages especially when love for another intervenes. However, unlike other tellings and in a manner reminiscent of folk renditions of the stories of gods and goddesses, Mira appears as a flesh-and-blood woman of strong will whose anger leads her to beat her servants even though it is not their fault that she must marry.[84] She is neither passive nor sweet at this moment, and certain details—that she first calls the women into her room and that the whip she takes out has been soaked in oil—underline the harshness of her action. The marriage itself gets only a brief mention—a single line.

Afterward Mira's mother is still concerned that the rana's family will learn of his bride's true feelings, and so it is decided that the couple must leave immediately for Udaipur. Even before Mira reaches the home of her new husband, however, she runs into difficulties, but here the problem is not her mother-in-law and it is not a bride's proper devotion to the family goddess and her husband that is at stake. The rana has sixteen wives already, who come out to greet the new queen out of respect for the Rathor family and for Marwar, even though they are older than she is. Mira in turn hurries to greet them first as the youngest among them in an expression of deference. Unfortunately, the bag containing her shalagram and the other things she uses for worship falls open; a large stone and sixteen smaller ones tumble out before the ranis. They suspect Mira of some kind of sorcery—the larger stone representing the rana, the smaller ones themselves. Without saying a word to Mira or the rana, they leave and return to their palaces. The eldest queen pressures the others to agree that none will speak to the rana or to Mira or let either one enter her palace under threat of dire punishment.

The suspicion directed at powerful women whose devotion allows them to do miraculous things finds expression in many Mira stories, usually with reference to her survival of attempts on her life. In the *Janma Patri* this theme takes a more overt form, one more common to women's ritual contexts. Ann Grodzins Gold has reported similar episodes in "women's worship tales" where a woman's devotion and associated ritual practice are suspect in the eyes of her husband and the women in her marital household.[85] Gold examines one such tale she heard in Rajasthan—that of the "*jungli* rani" (the queen from the jungle, or the uncivilized queen)—contrasting this story with the dominant form of narratives within this genre, those of "clever-bride heroines."[86]

In Gold's analysis women tell such stories of suspicion to articulate their struggles with a cultural ideology that says independent, powerful women are dangerous and to affirm their own identities as both great devotees *and* virtuous wives. The jungli rani's problem seems to be that she does not use her miraculous powers (gained through devotion) in the direct service of her husband, as other wife heroines do. The bread and flowers she offers in her *puja* to the Sun God Surya miraculously turn to gold and to diamonds and pearls, her crazy mother is transformed into a golden image, and a palatial residence complete with a raft of relatives appears when her royal husband insists on visiting her natal home, even after she says she is from a poor brahman family with no resources. When the other queens accuse her of sorcery and her husband sees these things with his own eyes, he threatens to kill her, but the story ends with her explaining to him that her powers truly do come from devotion to the Sun God rather than some more sinister source.

Presumably he will accept what she says, and the jungli rani will take her place finally beyond suspicion as his wife, but the story does not state this explicitly. Her integrity maintained, her identity as devotee first but also as an exemplary wife is clearly portrayed and asserted as the tale ends, but there is no comforting closure of the king's positive response. Variants of this story are told in many parts of India with other complex resonances. For example, in the foothills of the Himalayas in Kangra, Kirin Narayan recorded tellers who stressed the changing relationship of mother and daughter and conflicting dharmas as well as practices of marrying daughters "up," with attendant feelings of inferiority, "bashful modesty," and perhaps even something scandalous to hide. In one telling the jungli rani even dies of shame when forced by her husband to reveal that in fact she had her crazy mother killed (though the Sun God had concealed her crime by transforming the mother's body into gold).[87]

In the *Janma Patri*, Mira's relationship with her mother is not so fraught, but her extreme devotion is definitely "something to hide" (at least from her mother's point of view), and it is when she seeks to show deference to the other ranis that her bag falls open and she finds herself under suspicion. Clearly the episode partakes of this genre of women's worship stories, raising similar issues of women's power and devotion in relation to the ideal of the virtuous wife, and additional parallels could be drawn between the character and situation of the jungli rani and the saint Mirabai more generally, particularly with both women continuing to maintain their premarital established and independent identities as devotees of God rather than being fully transformed solely into wives.[88] Gold closes her discussion of the tale suggesting, "Perhaps the implicit happy ending to the jungli rani's tale gives expression to women's visions of themselves as persons empowered by divine beneficence as well as maintaining familial bonds—stretched, but not split, by characterizations of female duplicity."[89] In the *Janma Patri* telling of Mira's life, there is no possibility of any such resolution, but the tragic turn is not due to her powerful devotion to Krishna and the shalagram but rather to her unforgivable embrace of a low-caste guru.

When the ranis suddenly leave without saying a word, the rana is puzzled. He goes first to one queen's palace, then to another's, but every door is closed to him and his calls go unanswered. The whole night passes in this fashion. Finally he realizes none will let him in, and he decides to go to Mira's palace. In the meantime, Mira has told her maidservants to watch for the rana's approach and to warn her if they see him coming. While they stand guard at the main gate, she takes off the garments of a bride and dons the attire of a renouncer, lets loose her hair, and applies the markings of a devotee to her forehead. The palace is new to Mira and her servants, and though they watch diligently, the rana enters through a back way and comes upon Mira without warning. He is shocked and confronts his bride, asking her whose name she takes and whom she worships. Guileless, she tells him that her guru is Raidas and that she serves the shalagram.

The suspicion surrounding Mira's devotional practice might have been dispelled through conversation as understanding presumably dawned on the jungli rani's husband—devotional power and wifely virtue can coexist, though the tension between them requires some active resolution. Mira's renunciation is even more problematic, but it is the alleged impurity caused by her association with a chamar that cannot be mitigated in the eyes of the rana. The situation is cut and dried for him: because of her association with Raidas, it is as if she herself were now equally an irrevocable source of pollution. She has defiled his golden palaces, and he wants nothing more to do with her. He orders her to leave the palace. She suffers the same rejection as her "untouchable" guru, and it is her transgression of caste rules rather than of gender roles that is pivotal. In this moment the broader range of interdependent and reciprocal relationships between people of different castes depicted at the opening of the tale, including the powerful rajput rulers' obligations to distribute specific gifts to members of other communities on such ritual occasions, is utterly eclipsed.[90]

Mira responds by begging the rana not to throw her out, something she does not do in any other telling of her story. She asks that he allow her to remain essentially as a servant. She will build a hut beneath the palace wall, and there she will spin thread and weave clothes (*dhotis*) for him. Here her voice merges with that of innumerable women who have faced abandonment. Pain flows from her words, and in the public singing of this song, private pain becomes shared sorrow, breaking isolation in the realization that no woman is alone in this experience and providing a basis for community.[91] To sing of such degradation is itself a courageous act, creating beauty in song and narrative out of the ashes of suffering and lifting the singer, the audience, and Mira above the devastating circumstances which are its cause.[92] Mira's story here clearly becomes a language for articulating women's experience, pain, and vulnerability. Her offer to weave the rana's dhotis also identifies her with members of weaver castes, and the rana himself refers specifically to her association not only with chamars but also with meghwals (both communities associated with leatherworking and weaving).

Parita Mukta notes this identification and the use of songs addressed to the rana as vehicles of expression for those oppressed by political and social elites.[93] However, in her reading of Mira traditions, the solidarity joining Mira and members of low-caste communities who sing of her is one of shared pain and suffering, but emphatically not shared subservience. For Mira to beg the rana as she does here is an act of self-degradation and out of character in Mukta's understanding of Mira, and so, it seems, she would prefer to exclude any such portrayal. At least some Dalit literary theorists would likely agree with her, insisting that truly authentic Dalit literature is not only composed by people who have suffered from caste-based oppression but also must be, in Sharankumar Limbale's words, "life-affirming and realistic," reflecting "Dalit consciousness," that is, "a revolutionary mentality connected with struggle," as inspired by Bhimrao Ambedkar's philosophy.[94] That struggle is both for self-representation—the articulation of an identity of dignity—and for "freedom from the tyranny of caste-based discrimination," a tyranny that led Ambedkar ultimately to reject Hinduism and convert to Buddhism along with millions of his fellow mahars in 1956 and that lingers despite its constitutional illegality and the political, educational, and economic reservations that have allowed at least some within these communities to prosper.[95] At this juncture in the *Janma Patri*, Mira appears to be struggling for neither dignity nor freedom, with no source of hope or possibility for positive change in sight.[96] It is true that the low-caste singers of this tale do not refer to themselves as "Dalits," claiming no such politicized consciousness, yet they will evince a profound understanding of the dynamics of oppression as the tale proceeds.

Mukta's and Dalit literary theorists' potential objections notwithstanding, this episode in the *Janma Patri* is sung and told in this way and poignantly deepens the identification of Mirabai with women and members of the meghwal and chamar communities. The rajput rani has become a weaver wife facing abandonment. In this moment she willingly embraces the identity that the rana would force upon her—that of being a meghwal/chamar woman, an "untouchable" and a servant—begging to be accepted as such. Yet the rana rejects her offer, saying he wants neither dhotis nor turbans woven by her hands and that she is of no use to him (echoing Mira's contention in the khyal that she would not be, nor he to her). In this moment his utter rejection of her dramatically exposes the impossibility of ever truly "winning" through acceptance of such imposed identities and subservience, which leave one completely vulnerable to the caprice and cruelty of the one to whom power is conceded.

That this image of Mira marks a nadir in her portrayal for the singers and the audience is also clear—her story simply cannot end here in devastation, for hers is indeed a tale of hope and of survival, not of annihilation. In all but a handful of tellings of Mira's tale, life and love simply cannot succumb to the forces of destruction; even for Dutt, Krishna's intervention must bring the ever-obedient pativrata Mira back to life and her alleged loving relationship with the rana must be restored. In the *Janma Patri* this agonizing interchange is a short one, and Mira quickly turns from supplication to defiance. She clasps a pillar (a tree, in the spoken portion) and shatters the ivory bangles that designate her marital status.[97]

She tells the rana to take back the clothing and ornaments of marriage, once more enumerating each item she had earlier been forced to accept. She rejects her caste privilege to wear such ornaments in the same move.[98] She dons black clothing and jewelry, climbs into a black chariot, and leaves the palace. Such a color choice is unusual and significant: she does not choose the auspicious red of marriage, the pure white of *brahmacharya* (sexual abstinence) and of celibate widowhood, or the holy saffron of renunciation. Instead she dons a color largely outside this whole system of signification of women's status with respect to men and marriage. Worn by widows in some castes (though decidedly without jewelry), black is generally considered to be bad luck ("ill-omened" and inauspicious) but also thereby to have the protective power to frighten away even evil spirits.[99] And it is also sometimes associated with renunciation; one popular Gujarati Mira song speaks of her exchanging the colorful clothes of marriage and love that fade for the black ascetic's blanket that cannot be stained.[100] But Mira had already donned saffron for this purpose when the rana surprised her.

A key to the deeper meaning of this act can be found in a ritual to banish the goddess of cholera from Kota, observed by James Tod in 1821.[101] The elaborate ritual included a sacrifice and a formal decree of banishment issued to the cholera goddess Mari. A black cart was prepared for her, drawn by black horses and driven by a man dressed all in black. Black bags of grain were loaded into it so that she would have food on her journey, and the cart was driven across the river and out of town as the crowds yelled and priests commanded that she never set foot in Kota again.[102]

Mira's exit from the palace conforms to this pattern of banishment and associates her with the cholera goddess of the region, widely worshiped by the poor and people of low caste. She herself seems to choose black, embracing the exile that the rana has ordered and making clear to all that she will never return and that she no longer belongs to this place. Mira's character invokes a respect and an ambivalence not unlike that evinced toward disease goddesses, who are seen both to cause disease and to offer protection from it. The "dis-ease" in this case is social—Mira's egalitarian and independent spirit is perceived as a threat to the social order (though also admired as a counter to injustice and a sign of her great devotion). Her transgression of caste boundaries cannot be contained in the normative social realm, even as her love cannot be in *Mira Mangal*. The scourge her rana husband perceives her to be will be removed by her leaving, or so he believes, yet the ritual formality of her banishment also implies recognition of her inner power, her shakti (the force that enlivens the universe, identified with the feminine Divine and with women).

A version of a defiant popular song is inserted at this point. Mira sings, "What can the Mewari rana do? The Lord's name is written on my heart. What can the Sisodiya rana do?" The snake in the basket and the cup of poison sent to kill her are mentioned in the song, though these common episodes are absent from the main body of the narrative itself (as they were in the khyal). There is evidently poison enough in the social system to make a physical source of venom unnecessary. The rana's inability to harm Mira is celebrated as she drinks the antidote of renunciation, dignity, defiance, and devotion. The rana may have physical and social power, but these cannot touch one for whom social sanctions and privileges have no meaning and who has the strength of inner conviction. He cannot erase the name written on her heart. The singer of this song is again the same high-spirited and passionate woman who might beat her servants in a fit of anger for bringing her wedding clothes.

The song continues with Mira passing Merta and going to Pushkar to bathe in its holy waters, then shifts back into the main line of the narrative. According to the rana's design, the chariot driver abandons Mira to die in the forest (as Sita is banished and abandoned in tellings of the *Ramayana*), and here it appears that it is indeed he who has sent her away. She is alone in the jungle—a dry desolate place, uninhabited except by animals yet also the realm of renunciation, spiritually fertile and free of human society with its distractions and restrictions. Mira's choice to be a devotee, especially of a low-caste guru, is necessarily and practically an act of renunciation. Nowhere in the tale is her isolation more complete; the refrain reaches its fulfillment here and resonates with deep sadness. "Come Dark Lover; Mountain Bearer come quickly; Having put her trust in you, Mira is alone."

It is now Mira's turn to complain. Addressing a parrot, she asks him to take her complaint to her guru.[103] She sings of a cow with two calves (one destined to be the bull of the sun and the father of sons, the other to be a slavish bullock endlessly circling a millstone to crush seeds for oil), a vine with two gourds (one to be used to bathe in the sacred Ganges River, the other to carry water to wash away excrement), and a king with two sons (one destined to rule the kingdom, the other to be a trader). Equally far apart are she and the rana—a mismatched couple if ever there was one. He does not understand her, though she has tried to explain and would take him to Vaikunth if she could (as she would in *Mira Mangal*). He is blinded to the truth. She tells the parrot to recite this complaint to her guru if it can find him. Mira, unafraid, simply sings to Krishna and worships her shalagram.

In a dream, her guru sees that she is alone, and he sets off at midnight, reaching her at dawn. He blames himself for her plight, but she asks, "What suffering is there in my life?" and calls herself blessed because she is in her guru's presence. After praising him, she again sings to her Lord. The story ends here, without any real closure but with an open invitation to participate. The audience seemingly joins Raidas, listening to Mira sing songs of great devotion in this wild place as the performers conclude with a number of popular Mira bhajans. Mira triumphs, but she does so ultimately by stepping out of the social world. Even within her private chamber, her devotion could not be accommodated. Finally only the forest of renunciation remains a plausible realm for the independent and powerful religious life of this "jungli rani."

Voicing Resistance and Suffering in Subordination

Within this tale, Mira is drawn deep into the lives of its low-caste singers and audiences. Her birth is celebrated in popular idioms, she belongs to a noninstitutional inclusive religious milieu, and she speaks directly as a woman and as a weaver. This portrayal lays claim to Mira as belonging to these groups and as choosing to be a member of their communities. Such a telling suggests an identification with Mira so complete that her story becomes their own, reflecting their lives and experiences of subordination and struggle.[104] In telling her story, those who sing also tell themselves, their oppression based on caste and gender both articulated and resisted within the narrative.

Although the public performances of the *Janma Patri* I have observed were sung by men and in one case by a married couple and the author of the tale is unknown (as is generally characteristic of such oral traditions), the genres from which much of the material in *Mira Janma Patri* comes generally belong to women—wedding and birth songs and women's ritual tales—and the story predominantly addresses women's concerns and relationships, giving voice to their experiences. That women played a role in shaping the tale seems highly probable. The narrative begins with the celebration of a daughter's birth, laying claim to traditions reserved for sons in a radical affirmation of femaleness—surely to the delight of little girls as well as women of all ages—in unspoken but stark contrast to their devaluation, and also to the specter of female infanticide.[105] The chief male characters, the rana and Raidas, are also less developed than the chief female, Mira, and there are more minor female characters with more active roles (Mira's aunt, companions, servants, and mother, and the ranis of Chittor) than male (Duda, the astrologer, the carpenter, the gardener, and the chariot driver). Raidas and the rana are seen primarily as sources of trouble or blessing for Mira. Raidas becomes the occasion for her transgression of the caste system, while the rana becomes the cause for her suffering, personifying those forces which uphold such a system and punish any who would contravene it. Women's relationships and women's negotiation of power structures defined by gender and caste are at the center of the tale.

The focus is not on Mira's violation of gender roles from the perspective of upper-caste men; rather the view seems to be that of a woman trying to negotiate an identity and life of her own choosing within structures of power that subjugate her and in relation to other women who must act within those same structures and who also actively participate in maintaining them. She marries to protect her mother from dishonor and from Duda's wrath, though she beats the maidservants over whom she has power when they would encourage her to go along with the marriage. She tries to establish relations of respect with the ranis of her marital home, but they are suspicious of her devotional activity, and her attempt fails, her isolation mirroring the experiences of innumerable young women sent off to the homes of their new husbands, far from their natal families and at the mercy of strangers in such patrilocal exogamous arrangements.[106] She sets her maids to watch for the rana so that she can pursue her devotion without angering him. The rana never really understands who Mira is or what has transpired between her and his other queens. At the end of the narrative she laments that he has not and so cannot see that she would bring liberation rather than disgrace and dishonor to him and his family.

Raidas also does not fully understand her, it seems, though he is her guru. Mira insists on becoming his disciple despite his reluctance and his fear of

Duda. Unlike the situation with her mother, the danger here seems primarily to herself and Mira is undeterred. In the end, Raidas is apologetic and sad, but Mira makes it clear that he has caused her no sorrow. Though he is a much more sympathetic figure than the rana, he, too, seems to be thinking in worldly terms. We hear nothing of his great spiritual teachings, and though he is praised and the necessity of a guru is acknowledged in Mira's initiation, the essential narrative meaning of this episode is to demonstrate Mira's choice of a religious life and to introduce the issues of caste and untouchability.

Mira herself seems to see clearly what is at stake and acts decisively, though under varying degrees of coercion (particularly with respect to her marriage and her leaving/banishment). By insisting that Raidas become her guru, she denies the validity of caste hierarchies but also suffers bitterly because of them. The perspective with respect to caste, as with gender, reflects a view from below rather than above. The elite position is clear in the rana's uncompromising reaction to Mira's revelation of who her guru is and in Raidas's reluctance to make Mira his disciple, but the rana's abrupt change in attitude also lays bare its baselessness—Mira has not changed in any way. The focus of the story is thus on the suffering which such assignations of caste impurity cause. As such it contests the naturalization of subordination based on heredity and association, opening up "fissures" in the dominant paradigm and offering alternative possibilities for self and society.[107]

That the telling of this tale is indeed perceived as an act of resistance and challenge to the system is made apparent when this performance is juxtaposed with a 1987 commercial release of the *Mira Janma Patri* (sung by Naina Ram, a jat from western Rajasthan)[108] and a more restricted epic song tradition of Mira from the Sirohi district, *Kumbha Rana ri Bat*. Recognition of this veiled yet very public critique seems implicit in the decision to release only the first two episodes of the *Janma Patri* in the commercial recording: Mira's birth and her becoming Raidas's disciple. The first episode offers a beautiful description of the joyous celebration of the birth of a beloved daughter and saint. In the second the relatively safe and popular assertion that caste means nothing before God and within the community of devotees is made. Admittedly even this much is absent from many other tellings of Mira's tale. But in this commercially released recording, the terrible violence directed at Mira because she challenges the system is not exposed. The troubling accusations of sorcery and Mira's plea not to be thrown out of the palace also find no place, just as her banishment does not.

One might claim that the first two episodes conveniently filled one tape, but the text can be expanded or contracted according to performance needs, and there is no indication that there were ever any plans to release tapes of further episodes. This truncated commercial telling, then, seems to have been deemed less problematic and more marketable than the full telling.[109] It might also be that these were the only episodes known to this higher-caste jat singer. If this is the case, however, then the lack of full transmission may mark the excising of the more troubling assertions by and/or for those who might be challenged by them, or a recognition of the potential danger of speaking them more publicly by those singing from positions of extreme subordination, or both.

In contrast, the articulation of resistance and defiance appears both stronger and less hidden in *Kumbha Rana ri Bat*, where anger over caste-based exploitation is portrayed in more graphic and violent terms.[110] This much more restricted epic tradition is performed by *turi bhat* singers for meghwal patrons and not readily for others outside these communities.[111] The epic follows Mira through two lifetimes; in the first she is the rajput rani Mirabai married to Raja Bhoj; in the second she is reborn as a low-caste potter woman, a *kumhar* named Deval, while her husband is reborn as Rana Kumbha (though he does not initially remember his past life).[112] In their first life, Mira and her guru Raidas undergo many trials before Raja Bhoj is finally converted, and Mira and Bhoj are husband and wife in name only.

Through a convoluted series of deceptions and lies, Raidas comes to be accused of stealing and is brought before Raja Bhoj. When the chamar saint sits on one corner of the carpet in the court, Raja Bhoj, enraged at his polluting presence, slices off the piece where he sits. But as others join Raidas, his small scrap of carpet expands until it is larger than that of the raja. In ensuing discussions between Raidas and the priests in the court, Raidas claims to have an inner sacred thread (*jama*) in contrast to the priests' merely external mark of "twice-born" status—a familiar element in stories of Raidas. Here Raja Bhoj orders him cut with a circular saw so that all may see this alleged inner thread. The saw, however, has no effect, and Raidas counters that a *neem* leaf will do the trick.[113] A leaf is brought, and he is cleanly severed, with milk rather than blood flowing forth.

Mira, imprisoned at the time, breaks the locks and demands that the king's brahman priests undergo the same trial, saying she will bring Raidas back to life and the raja can do the same for his priests. The priests protest, but Raja Bhoj proceeds accordingly with the saw, the neem leaf being ineffective on them. The result is bloody carnage. Raidas's two halves are brought together and his life restored (as are the lives of the priests, though not by the king). Though trials of saints before rulers are common in hagiographic stories, the results seldom turn out so badly for the brahmans who challenge them.[114] Raja Bhoj becomes Raidas's disciple, and Raidas tells him that he and Mira will meet again in another birth.

Such stories are public declarations of the unfairness and moral and religious bankruptcy of hierarchies of birth, including of both caste and gender. There is ample documentation to support the claim that these types of narratives and performances "signal sites of struggle" and serve to undermine the rhetoric of power and trouble the status quo, with the potential to create common ground for community, for resistance, and even for revolt.[115] It seems likely that such stories about Mira were among those that the early rajput historians and nationalists might have wanted to silence, even as they sought to create dramatic performances of her life and of those of other heroes and heroines that might get past British censors under the guise of "history" to fuel the nationalist struggle. The Mira of the *Janma Patri* or *Kumbha Rana ri Bat* is certainly not the companionate pativrata of Dutt or Deviprasad, the sweet and gentle spiritual guardian of Indian honor and the Hindu home. Raidas is front and center, and Mira high-spirited with a will of her own, disregarding caste rules and restrictions and in no sense "happily married." Such a Mira does indeed continue to be an affront to rajput honor and to patriarchies, whether "old" or "new" (or postcolonial, for that matter).

There may be multiple reasons why performers of such epic songs, especially *Kumbha Rana ri Bat*, might be reluctant to sing them before outsiders. Telling stories is profoundly relational, with individualized tellings of any given story tailored to specific people in specific contexts, and also sometimes tied to specific and even ritual occasions.[116] Whether a story is told depends on the time and place and who is asking to hear and why, with specialized cultural knowledge in some cases reserved, told only by specific tellers and/or within specific communities. There is the legitimate question of what outsiders intend to do with the knowledge they "take." And beyond such concerns, there is the clear and present danger of violent responses to stories that speak the truth of oppression and unmask the dynamics of power in public venues.

Some low-caste communities have employed and continue to employ narrative dramatic performances in overtly political ways, engaging in guerrilla street theater and song, as Kabir Kala Manch and Bhudan Theatre are doing in the twenty-first century.[117] Like others from formerly "untouchable" castes, the young members of Pune-based Kabir Kala Manch take the name "Dalit" and are courageously working to bring an end to caste and communal distinctions and the attendant social injustices and suffering of those of minority and low-caste status. Falsely accused of being terrorist Naxalites, a number of their members have been arrested and imprisoned, while others have been forced to go underground.[118] Their only real "crime," it seems, is to dare to speak the truth of their experience directly in public, to expose hypocrisy, and to advocate change, as their namesake, the "untouchable" saint Kabir, had done.

Similarly, Bhudan Theatre began within the Chhara community in Ahmedabad. Formerly labeled among the "criminal tribes" by the British in 1871 and interned in settlement camps for forced labor, the Chhara were officially "denotified" (along with similarly "criminalized" tribes and castes) and released from this incarceration in 1952. But they remain socially marginalized, with few economic and educational opportunities and legally vulnerable to police brutality, torture, and even murder, targeted as the "usual suspects" when a crime is committed, under the authority of the Habitual Offenders Act of 1959.[119] Engaging in theater performance "by and for the community," members seek above all to demonstrate that Chharas are not "born criminals" and to acquire the constitutional protections afforded others. Many have faced arrest and harassment, though the project has simultaneously begun to garner national and international attention to their cause.

Women activists have similarly employed street theater to raise awareness of women's issues beginning in the 1980s; engaged as both authors and actors, they have woven popular folk songs into the productions as a way to engage audiences and create solidarity.[120] In 2002 world-renowned dancer Mallika Sarabhai, recognized for her commitment to artist activism and her radical portrayal of female cultural icons like Sita and Draupadi, created a multimedia performance of Mirabai's life titled *An Idea Called Mira*, inspired in part by the low-caste *Janma Patri* we have examined.[121] The performance included two "Miras," one traditional and one modern. Video elements show Rajasthani villagers first happily celebrating Mira's marriage (as people today laud the saint) and then viciously turning on her. The rana's attitude too reflects the still prevalent assumption that women's individual self-actualization necessarily diminishes men and is destructive to family. Nandi Bhatia, in her comprehensive study of theater and politics in India in both colonial and postcolonial contexts, further details "the utter centrality of theatrical activity, in its varied forms, to subversive cultural practices."[122]

Though the performers of *Mira Janma Patri*, *Kumbha Rana ri Bhat*, and other low-caste oral narratives of Mira do not have an overtly activist agenda, the "unauthorized" stories they publicly sing of Mira similarly connect individuals and communities to the realities of their own lives, forge solidarity, and unmask brutality and injustice, with the potential to inspire individual and social transformation. Clothed in the story of a well-loved saint, these epic songs assert alternative visions of the world and social relations, as Mirabai is understood to have done in her time, over against received narratives and the worlds and ways of dominant others. Performed in more limited community settings rather than on street corners, they may not elicit the same degree of violent suppression as the performances of Kabir Kala Manch and Bhudan Theatre, but were it performed more widely and outwardly directed, the carnage visited upon the brahmans in *Kumbha Rana ri Bhat*, articulating outrage and a longing for justice, might indeed be deemed incendiary.

It is the undeniably realistic portrayal not only of relations of domination and exploitation and the violence and suffering they perpetuate but also of marginalized people's own lives and experiences, together with the alternative set of values articulated therein, that is the source of the potency and perceived threat of these tellings of Mira's life. After all, the "graded inequality"[123] of the caste hierarchy can be maintained only if "all the groups [accept] the values of the upper castes as the most respectable ones" and compete to maintain and raise their own status vis-à-vis each other rather than standing in solidarity against oppression.[124] Narratives that undermine those values and/or foster solidarity—as such tales of Mira decidedly do—have the potential to destabilize the whole structure of domination, as Phule, Ambedkar, and other low-caste leaders and activists have clearly understood, along with their elite contemporaries.[125]

In the late nineteenth century and early decades of the twentieth, when rajput historians were writing their histories in Rajasthan, there were repeated revolts by the Bhil tribal community as well as cultivators of middle to very low caste, being crushed by the exorbitant taxes on agricultural production, a wide variety of additional assessments arbitrarily imposed, and forced labor demands by rajput royalty and landed retainers in addition to the British.[126] Why rajput male elites might want to suppress these types of low-caste Mira stories and instead put forward one of their own, portraying rajputs as heroic warriors (rather than exploitative and violent overlords) and Mira not as a rebel but a devoted pativrata and widowed bhakta, beloved among rajputs, seems clear, given the saint's immense popularity. Nationalists, too, had a vested interest in fostering heroic rajput images and women in the mode of the new patriarchy, and focusing all eyes on the goals of God and nation in ways that would not challenge their elite status and power, either in society or in the home. Clearly their tellings reflect an awareness of stories of other "Miras," going all the way back to Nabhadas, against which they were intentionally producing countertexts to enlist this powerful figure for their own purposes.

The simultaneous existence of these radically different portrayals of the saint points to one of the most fundamental elements of this narrative language. Many can identify with Mira—women of diverse classes, castes, and cultures; devotees who face obstacles to their devotion, whoever or whatever might be its object; those who have fallen in love with a socially inappropriate person or whose individual desires have run up against those of family or society; those of low caste or class who see her as sharing their oppression because of her association with Raidas and standing in solidarity with them through her renunciation of privilege; and all those who have suffered under a "rana" of any kind—even colonial officers of Scottish descent and nationalist and rajput elite men.

Hers is, among other things, also a story of "making a way out of no way," of crafting a meaningful and dignified life against all odds.[127] As such it is an empowering tale which gives hope and inspiration to others to do the same, and as a result, the language generated by her narrative can always be used to speak resistance, challenge, and defiance, whether to domination and exploitation by religious, political, or familial authorities or to the restrictions of caste hierarchies or gender roles. It is not always used in this way, and indeed some would employ it in support of such norms, as we have seen, particularly by insisting on Mira's exceptionalism, the relegation of her devotion to widowhood and *viraha* (love and longing in separation, loss, or absence), and/or the portrayal of her relationship to Krishna as one of marriage, making her a pativrata of God. But because domination and opposition (carried to a murderous extreme), coupled with a refusal to succumb to them and the assertion of alternative ways to be in the world, are so fundamental to the identity of Mira from the very earliest renderings of her story, there is always the potential that resistance may be heard even if not intentionally spoken by the teller or resurface in the next telling from other familiar streams of the tradition that swirl around the saint, to be articulated quite openly under the protective guise of a well-loved saint's tale. Perhaps such an observation brings us closer to understanding why Mira's story has itself resisted the formation of a truly dominant "great" tradition while at the same time seeming to encourage a multitude of retellings. This narrative is used repeatedly to speak of resistance, of the oppression and suffering that generate resistance, and of the dangers of resistance, even as it is used to speak of multiple dimensions of human love and heroism, of devotion to God, of hope and dignity, and so much more.

In truth, neither those who wish to dominate nor those who would advocate total social revolution can entirely control the narrative or voice of this saint. Because of the potential for resistance and defiance within her story, in the end it has not proved entirely suitable for Hindu fundamentalist political rhetoric or conservative social agendas, nationalist and rajput formulations notwithstanding.[128] At the same time, in these narrative traditions of low-caste communities, though Mira herself may challenge the powerful and the hypocritical and refuse to comply with norms, she does not necessarily call directly for radical social change, and for those who accept the rajput-nationalist telling as historical fact, her character and story are even more problematic. Additionally, in her insightful analysis of songs attributed to Mira, Kumkum Sangari has argued persuasively that the repeated use of images of subordination, even though transposed to speak of the relation of human to Divine, leaves Mira's bhakti fundamentally contradictory, undermining its "radicalizing potential."[129] Yet Sangari also importantly questions whether Mira "[could] have disarticulated this [social] order in its entirety and remained intelligible or been allowed to exist," and we must ask the same question with respect to those who tell her story and sing her voice from positions of subordination.[130]

The narrative language of Mira in the *Janma Patri* is being used to speak of the complexities of power relations and of negotiating one's way through them, offering a keen "diagnostic of power," as Lila Abu-Lughod suggests of Bedouin women's songs.[131] As such it reflects what James Scott has called "the voice under domination" and inhabits the region between "overt collective defiance of power-holders [and] complete hegemonic compliance"—a realm of shifting alliances, collaboration, and compromise as well as resistance, where, as Douglas Haynes and Gyan Prakash put it, "domination is constantly being forged and fissured."[132] And indeed as Robert Orsi contends, though we might wish it were otherwise, rather than resistance per se, more often "[t]he opposite of compliance is creative engagement with what is given as reality in such a way that both self and the world are taken up and set in motion."[133] Mira's story, as told in the *Janma Patri*, does precisely this.

Further, this telling is marked by a realism essential to the survival of those in positions of extreme subordination who must of necessity be keen observers of human nature and cannot, it seems, afford fantasies of perfect princesses or "happily ever after" endings any more than they can outright sedition.[134] Mira, the heroine of this low-caste tale, beats her servants. There is nothing revolutionary or even egalitarian about this action—it is simply realistic, given the power differential between them, though also worthy of critique as the action of a desperate or crazed woman, as her servants articulate and her mother concurs. Yet Mira does what an upper-caste woman, or for that matter any person in a position of extreme stress might do, however unjustly, in relation to a subordinate or an intimate. To whom can she express her anger?

Ultimately, Mira gives in to the pleas of her mother, acknowledging the power which both her mother and Duda have over her. Her mother uses her emotional hold to pressure her daughter to comply with a system that denies her daughter's desires and to protect both herself and her daughter from the power of men who have control over them. Mira can act with complete freedom only within her private chambers (and even this has its limitations, as becomes clear when the rana enters through a passage unknown to her) and in her inner life ("What can the Mewari rana do? The Lord's name is written on my heart"). For the most part, she must act from a position of subordination to her mother, Duda, her husband, her co-wives, and even her guru. Sometimes she resists, sometimes she complies, at least minimally, and either way she pays a price. But she does not give up her dignity, and she remains true to her inner sense of herself and her convictions. Indeed Sumi Madhok suggests that it is precisely to such negotiated "self-shaping" in relation to coercion and imposed social norms that we should look to see women's agency in oppressive circumstances.[135]

Mira's story and songs provide a language and a context for articulating such experiences, including both suffering and protest, and for such "self-shaping." Songs attributed to her characteristically speak in the first person of her own life struggles, and her critique of hierarchies is embedded in the life she lives, consciously embracing an alternative reality, embodied in action and song.[136] The narrative language generated by this life story is ideal for articulating personal and communal experiences of pain and oppression, but also hopes and fears in the face of such a life, and defiance, resistance, and courage. In this, her story functions as other life histories do in epic ballads and folktales, "as a narrative strategy for truth-telling," as Stuart Blackburn observes.[137] Mira's tale becomes the story of other lives lived with dignity and sorrow but also joy under repressive hierarchies of caste and gender, race, religion, and class. And Mira's voice becomes a voice for those who would speak the truth of their own existence and unmask the injustice and violence perpetrated against them (when to do so directly might prove to be impossibly dangerous and not nearly as effective, with Mira both authorizing the speech and giving authority to the insights therein). Though hers may not be a language of direct confrontation in much of *Mira Janma Patri*, it breaks the silence of hegemonic acceptance of social hierarchies and facilitates the public articulation of an alternative relationship between "high" and "low."

These tellings of Mira's tale, including the *Mira Mangal* khyal, also reveal another vital dimension of her appeal and continuing relevance. Within them we find a complex interweaving of contested values and a tug-of-war of allegiances and identities: on the one hand practical compliance and compromise, grounded in a realistic and nuanced understanding of power relations; on the other, defiance and freedom, founded on an alternative vision of what truly is and what could and should be. Mira's story can hold both together, offering an example of how to live simultaneously according to a higher truth and in the midst of the world as it is, a choice which comes at considerable cost but which is possible. Participation in Mira's story then seems to offer a way to work through and express this wide range of experience and to move out in some way transformed and strengthened, having put together the narrative of one's own life and values, as a community or as an individual, in a new, more integrated way. As such Mira's story can be shared and draw people together, for its strength lies in this participation—something which nationalists and rajput historians implicitly understood and sought to restrict and channel to their agenda alone.

Yet in both *Mira Janma Patri* and *Mira Mangal,* Mira's conviction leads to her isolation and/or banishment, and there is no easy social incorporation of an all-encompassing love that grants no ultimate validity to the hierarchies of caste, class, and gender and accepts no compromise to its integrity. Such love underlies all of Mira's defiance and sustains her through all her struggle. What can the Mewari rana do with such a one, whose actions relativize every hierarchy established between human beings? Mira's banishment from society can be retold and reenacted again and again or her actions papered over with compliance, but it seems this voice which calls others to a life of integrity and unswerving commitment and to the highest love for God and for fellow humans cannot be silenced.

The narrative of Mirabai provides an avenue for such a call to be voiced and heard. Mira is willing to sacrifice everything for the truth and for love, and her will cannot be broken. Both this great love and this commitment and strength lie at the heart of many people's understanding of Mira's character and her tale, of their deep love and admiration for the saint, and of their multiple ways of identifying with her. Such a powerful and expansive character and story cannot be harnessed in any final sense to a singular limiting vision, whether social, political, or religious, and tellings of her tale continue to proliferate unabated into the twenty-first century, not only in oral epics and dramas ("folk" and otherwise) but also in newly emerging forms of popular culture, including fiction, film, and television.

Though the khyal *Mira Mangal* and other oral narratives (perhaps even this *Mira Janma Patri*) were undoubtedly being performed at the turn of the twentieth century and likely earlier, such oral alternative Miras would receive serious scholarly attention only after Independence, when regional and folk arts and literature came to be seen as a mark of the rich cultural heritage of the emerging nation, and later in the search to uncover subaltern, Dalit, and women's voices past and present. In earlier decades, as the Independence movement came into full swing, their contents were deemed potentially disruptive and dangerous and worthy of suppression—though as impossible to eliminate, it seems, as the saint herself. Elite nationalists and middle-class citizens might not share the rana's murderous intent, but they, as much as he, wanted the saint to behave like a proper rajput pativrata, one who could bring honor and inspiration to their cause and might serve as an invaluable resource for the crafting of Indian identities amid changing and conflicting values and for the controlled movement of women into politics and other public spheres. These processes would be facilitated by key individuals whose very personal engagements with the saint would profoundly impact her reception and transformation into a cultural icon for a nation in the making.

5
Mobilizing Mirabai, Mobilizing Women in the Struggle for Independence

With the dawning of the twentieth century, Mirabai would be an increasing focus of attention through decades of intense struggle and immense change leading up to Independence, as people looked both back to the past for continuity and forward into imagined futures. The saint would be called upon by both women and men to negotiate transformations of the normative performance of gender in private as well as in public spaces and to facilitate women's participation in both the constructivist and the political dimensions of the nationalist struggle. This revered medieval woman, in her life and character, seemed able to bring together ever-changing conceptions of the "traditional" and the "modern" in ways that were distinctly Indian, even as she embodied deep ambivalences and conflicting cultural values. Her story and example would prove to be a vital cultural resource for a very diverse range of people in vastly different circumstances—a resource to think with and to invoke as precedent to inspire and aspire to and to shape and authorize new yet culturally rooted selves, as women and men, as Hindus, as Indians, and as human beings. This fascination with Mirabai fueled an immense desire to know more about her, spurring scholarship as well as a wealth of new tellings, appropriations, and embodiments of the saint.

In the wake of Deviprasad's 1898 publication, scholars of Indian literature, religion, and history sought to integrate his work with Dutt's telling as well as devotional accounts and circulating popular traditions to produce a comprehensive life of Mira. M. A. Macauliffe's "The Legend of Mirabai, the Rajput Poetess," published in the *Indian Antiquary* (1903), epitomizes this synthesizing trend in its earliest stage. He draws heavily on both Deviprasad and Dutt without acknowledging either but also on Raja Raghuraj Singh of Rewa, Priyadas (in a manner consistent with Wilson), and Mahipati. While conceding that he is reporting the "legends" of the saint, in blending these different strands he grounds her devotion in her childhood and reinforces the sense that she is married to Krishna, but also portrays her as ever obedient to a male, with Tulsidas fully incorporated to join her father, husband, and Lord in directing her actions. He presents her final merger with Krishna in *advaita* (nondual) terms of dissolution in the singular reality of "the all-pervading Brahma, the knower of truth, the Eternal," and he draws Hindu-Muslim relations back into the tale with Akbar's coming, lending the patina of fact to the report by including the encounter alongside Deviprasad's history, which would exclude it. His final conclusion—that the rana loses his kingdom to Akbar "as a retribution for the ill-treatment of Mira Bai"—is a popular tradition but also resonates with British rhetoric, embracing an identification of the British and Mughals, this time from the British side, in a way that justifies the domination of both over Indian society on the grounds of moral degeneration and the mistreatment of women.

Other scholars would acknowledge the difficulty of untangling the multitude of often contradictory things said of Mira and the realities but also the limitations of historical inquiry. The details of her life would continue to be contested and largely a matter of speculation. Krishnalal Mahanlal Jhaveri, writing his *Milestones in Gujarati Literature* in 1914, would assert that who her husband was really was not important because she rejected him, and he would follow G. M. Tripathi in immediately turning to the period after she left her royal home and claiming her for Gujarat.[1] Others would revisit the issue of who her guru might have been. F. E. Keay theorized in *A History of Hindi Literature* (1920) that it was Mira's "frequent lavish expenditure in the entertainment of sadhus" that really upset her family, and she left in the face of her sister-in-law Uda's persecution to become Raidas's disciple.[2] Yet he questions why this devotee of Krishna Ranchor would have embraced such a guru and whether Raidas might have affected her religious views. In shifting the agent of Mira's persecution to her sister-in-law, this conflict becomes the petty interaction of women over material expenditures, further removing any possible taint from either Mira or the rajput men of her household (and potentially also critiquing such religious practitioners as hypocritical and practices as wasteful). But Raidas's significance remains unclear.

For others, like Sanskrit scholar Kshitimohan Sen (who would deeply influence Tagore's understanding and appreciation of bhakti), the chamar saint would take the role of a teacher who purifies her devotion into a more aniconic nirgun form, appropriate to what Sen views as the most original and highest form of Indian spirituality: a humanistic and universal religion of the people, marked by a mystical worldview grounded in experience and love and epitomized by nirgun poets such as Kabir, Nanak, Dadu, and Raidas.[3] Others would continue to characterize India's shared spiritual heritage as a Vaishnava *shudhadvaita* bhakti ("pure nondual" devotion to God who is all in all, immanent as well as transcendent, such that all that exists is real and a manifestation thereof), more accommodating of sagun devotion and supportive of the varna-ashrama-dharma system.[4]

These debates about the nature of India's religious heritage would be woven together with the project of developing a history for Hindi literature in which bhakti saints were credited with the early development of vernacular poetry and also by some with instantiating an indigenous egalitarian, humanistic social vision (as G. M. Tripathi had done).[5] In this context, in the words of Purushottam Agrawal, literature was conceived of as "the autobiography of the nation," integral to the articulation of its history as "a self description of the community's individuality struggling to realize its true self... its journey from the past on toward the future of realizing its inherent destiny as a self-confident, powerful, modern collectivity—a nation."[6] Much was thus at stake in this scholarly endeavor, with the crafting of this contested literary history in full swing across the early decades of the century, under the considerable influence of Ramchandra Sukhla of Banaras with his classic *Hindi Sahitya ka Itihas* (History of Hindi Literature), first published in 1929 by the Nagari Pracharini Sabha with a revised edition published in 1940, and the evolving thought of Hazariprasad Dvivedi from Tagore's Shantiniketan, culminating in his extremely influential *Hindi Sahitya ki Bhumika* (Introduction to Hindi Literature), also published in 1940.[7]

Though Mirabai would be lauded as the greatest poetess of early Hindi literature, she would remain largely peripheral in these debates, claimed by all but problematic, particularly given the dizzying array of contradictory things said about her then and in her name. Some deemed her poetry too sagun or too erotic,[8] though such songs often were denounced as spurious or attributed to sectarian interventions and/or serialized as sagun before and nirgun after her encounter with Raidas, as Sen would argue. Similarly with her behavior—her seeming independence, even defiance, might be denounced as an outright fabrication, or it might be cited as a sign of an early enlightened attitude toward women. Raidas was generally absent or minimally included to correct her sagun ways, with caste not a part of her story, in order, it seems, to eliminate any possible grounds for solidarity among low-caste people and/or women that might challenge an indigenous elite patriarchy. In general Mira received high praise but little sustained attention, with writers offering lip service to this "greatest" Hindi poetess and emphasizing her immense appeal to the populace, but turning especially to Kabir but also to Dadu, Surdas, Tulsidas, and other saints to develop their claims.

Though she might not be given a significant role in these larger literary histories, however, the production of knowledge about the saint through academic study would continue to develop across these decades. Many highly respected scholars of Hindi, Gujarati, and Rajasthani literature demonstrated an immense dedication both to the saint and to the research and continued to weave tapestries of her life incorporating popular, hagiographic, historical, nationalist, and rajput threads in patterns governed by a range of concerns and assumptions. Recognizing the paucity of available dedicated manuscripts, Kshitimohan Sen himself would collect songs of Mira he heard during his research trips to Rajasthan, though he reports having lost the completed manuscript of this oral collection just as he was about to publish it.[9] Harinarayan Sharma spent some forty years studying her life and songs and interviewing countless people, though his collection of 662 songs drawn from manuscripts and his extensive notes and correspondence were only published posthumously decades later.[10] Sets of poetry attributed to her together with introductions to her life would also be published, with U. N. Mukhopadhyay in Calcutta publishing a set of Bengali and English translations in 1901, and Belvedere Press in Allahabad issuing its first edition of Hindi poems in 1909.[11] Rajasthani scholar Narrotamdas Swami published his collection of her poetry drawn from a manuscript source in 1930, and Parashuram Chaturvedi followed with the first edition of his collection in 1932, the latter reissued and revised in multiple editions and becoming the standard for Hindi literature classes.[12] In 1934 R. C. Tandon published a set of English translations of Belvedere Press's collection, and Anath Nath Basu published a different set of poems translated into Bengali and then into English.[13] Other scholars would publish works in Hindi, Rajasthani, Gujarati, Marathi, Sindhi, and English dedicated to exploring multiple dimensions of Mira's life, religion, and poetry.[14] This scholarly community was and remains highly interactive. Its members readily acknowledge their interdependence and friendship, in many cases revising their works to take into account each other's new findings and publishing multiple editions. Divisions between academic, devotional, and popular publications were not sharply drawn, especially in these early decades, as researchers sought to find all available information about the saint.

But quite apart from these scholars, there were key individuals in these decades of the struggle leading up to Independence for whom Mirabai had a deep personal significance and who would come to have a profound influence on popular as well as scholarly perceptions of the saint and on her continuing development as a cultural icon and national heroine. Among them were Rabindranath Tagore, Mahatma Gandhi, and Mahadevi Varma. Tagore would turn to her as a precedent for women's emancipation and self-realization. Gandhi would find in her an exemplary practitioner of nonviolence, lifting her up as a model for women but also for men in her fearlessness and fidelity to truth. And the renowned poet Mahadevi would herself come to be called a "modern Mira," embodying wider possibilities opened up by the saint for twentieth-century women. Each would contribute to Mira's emergence as a pan-Indian cultural icon and national heroine in the twentieth century, as the saint was deployed time and again to disrupt and remake notions of Indian womanhood in a complex interweaving of heterogeneous strands of nationalism and the intricate negotiations involved in crafting Indian identities, both individual and collective, in this tumultuous period.

Tagore, Mira, and Women's Empowerment

Rabindranath Tagore (1861–1941) clearly had an affinity for Mirabai, naming his third daughter, born in 1894, after her. A prolific writer of both critical essays and literature from his youth, he was deeply engaged in debates about Indian social and religious issues and denunciations of colonial rule, in 1892 turning his attention particularly to the problematic nature of colonial education. He increasingly committed himself to a program of cultural education in Indian languages rather than English, designed to foster a holistic decolonization and freedom that would be at once intellectual, emotional, and spiritual as well as social, economic, and political, and it would be on Indian terms, marked by self-respect and equality and grounded in rural agricultural development and the needs of the masses. In 1901 he established Shantiniketan School on his family lands, and though he actively participated in protest and noncooperation in response to the 1905 British partitioning of Bengal, by 1907 he had broken with other nationalists over the use of violence and the fueling of Hindu-Muslim animosity. Tagore came to be recognized by Gandhi and Nehru as the "conscience" of the nation, and the three would continue to hold each other in high regard, though they might at times disagree considerably.[15]

In these turbulent years, Tagore arranged the marriages of his three daughters at very young ages, despite his explicit commitment to women's education before marriage and his opposition to child marriage, lamenting the impossibility of a relationship of mutuality with his own wife. It is not clear whether he was persuaded by senior family members, the need to provide for his daughters in a system that demanded dowry and in which his family's caste standing was considered inferior among fellow brahmans, or a desire to clear his responsibilities in order to focus on building Shantiniketan School, but he nevertheless did so, though with increasing anxiety, particularly with respect to his daughter Mira. He arranged her marriage in 1907 when she was only thirteen, immediately sending her husband Nagendranath Gangulee to the United States to join his son Rathindranath to study agricultural science. Tagore was very close to his daughter, as their correspondence reveals, and her marriage was a very difficult one, deteriorating to such a degree that by 1919 she was spending considerable time with her father at Shantiniketan.[16]

During this period Tagore wrote a number of stories that addressed the struggles of women in marriage, including "Letter from a Wife" (Streer Patra), in which the heroine specifically invokes Mirabai, published in 1914 (the year after he was awarded the Nobel Prize in Literature for his poetry collection *Gitanjali,* or *Song Offerings*).[17] Cast as a final letter from a wife to her husband, telling him she is leaving him, the heroine begins by remembering her own arranged marriage at the age of twelve, as a girl from a remote village selected by an urban family for her great beauty to make up for another sister-in-law's lack—a beauty she scarcely knew she had. Her intelligence proved to be a problem, however—she was too opinionated, too vocal, with a mind of her own—and they soon forgot her beauty in their condemnation. No one suspected that she secretly wrote poetry. With her first pregnancy, her daughter died in childbirth, robbing her of motherhood and this vital relationship. She would have merely endured, so accustomed to neglect that she was unaware of it until she witnessed the horrific mistreatment of her sister-in-law's sister, Bindu, orphaned and shuttled between family members, with neither beauty nor wealth, shunned as a servant even by her sister, who feared her husband's disapproval.

The heroine, Mrinal, offered the girl love in spite of family opposition, and Bindu saw in her a beauty that opened a space for Mrinal to see herself as something other than "the second daughter-in-law," allowing her for the first time to see herself "beautiful as a free human mind, in being [her] natural self."[18] The family was outraged that Mrinal should act on her own initiative and begin to speak out, challenging her husband and elders. Finally they found a way to get rid of Bindu by forcibly marrying her off to a man she had never met. But she ran away and returned after three days, frightened because her groom was insane, his mother a tyrant. Mrinal was appalled and spoke up for her, to the distress of the family, but even as she did, Bindu surrendered to her brother-in-law to avoid causing trouble for Mrinal. Mrinal makes clear that she is not writing to criticize any of them—she was sympathetic especially to the girl's sister who cried in secret and critical of herself for not having been assertive enough on the girl's behalf, seeing clearly the multiple ways women are constrained and become self-constraining.

Forced repeatedly to go back to her husband, Bindu finally kills herself by setting her clothes on fire, leaving a note for Mrinal, which Bindu's in-laws destroy so that she will never be able to read it. With Bindu's death, Mrinal is no longer afraid: "[T]he barbed wire fence of the rules and punishments for violating the rules dissolved ... all the measures for inflicting pain and insult, which the society devised to subdue ... [recognized as] the clamping of fake chains and the cracking of false whips."[19] Telling her husband that she will not return to his home, she invokes Mirabai directly, writing:

> Do not fear that I will kill myself. I am not going to play that old joke on you. Meerabai too was a woman like me, and her chains were by no means light, but she did not seek death in order to live. In her joyful rebellious songs, she said, "Meera is going to stick by you, my lord, even if she is rejected by her father, mother, by everybody else, no matter what their rejections may bring upon her." To stick to one's truth is to live. I am going to live. I have just started living.[20]

Tagore understands the saint Mirabai's potential for authorizing forthright speech, naming domestic abuse, exposing the ideological scaffolding of "exemplary wifehood," and embodying the fearlessness required to break out of it.[21] His heroine finds in Mirabai a guiding light, for the saint is a woman who understands her individual human destiny and place in a joyous and beautiful universe, as Mrinal comes to do, and who affirms hope and life rather than succumbing to the decay, despair, and death that come with the "bondage of trivialities."[22] This Mirabai, too, has known suffering, but she is not one who patiently endures abuse but rather is a joyous rebel who courageously steps out into the world to live by following her own truth, undeterred by the rejection of family.

Tagore writes this story as he is watching the destructive results of his decision to arrange his daughter Mira's marriage at such an early age and to a young man he had selected, it seems, primarily if not entirely on the grounds that he considered him a good prospect for his Shantiniketan project. In a letter to his son Rathindranath in 1919, his anguish is clear. His daughter has asked him whether she should go back to her husband, and he knows she will do so if he tells her to—something he refuses to do, having already ruined her life, he feels, by arranging her marriage in the first place. He writes, "How can I ask Mira to return, knowing what she is likely to face? How can she and her children spend their lives amidst insults and antipathy? ... [L]et Mira not think we want her to go back. I will not let her burn alive inside a circle of fire."[23] Her marriage would finally end in 1932, her husband leaving India to settle permanently in England, but she would suffer much in the intervening years.

Tagore's writings demonstrate that he was painfully aware of these realities for women even among the well-off and supposedly enlightened families of his day, and he acknowledged his own complicity. He was not alone in this guilt. Similarly progressive men committed to educating their daughters also succumbed to the pressure of elders, including Mahadevi Varma's father, who arranged her childhood marriage to fulfill the family patriarch's desire to complete the religious obligation of *kanyadan* (the giving of a daughter) before his death—a marriage the poet never accepted. Yet Tagore was also aware that women themselves must awaken to their own self-worth and break free of their own fearfulness and acceptance of bondage (something for which the saint could certainly offer encouragement).

Written entirely from a woman's point of view and in her words, Tagore's "Letter from a Wife" departed from his own and many other men's earlier writings for and about women.[24] The story was, in the words of Sabyasachi Bhattacharya, nothing less than "a manifesto of women's fight against a patriarchal society which allows neither agency nor voice to women in the family."[25] Tagore published it in *Sabuj Patra* (The Green Leaves), whose avowed purpose was "to jolt the reader's mind and shake it," as Tagore put it.[26] This avant-garde journal deliberately "forefronted . . . discontinuity and rupture with established relationships, a stance inimical to the preservation of tradition," and Tagore wrote a number of stories for it, "deal[ing] with women as individual subjects engaged in negotiating with problematic relationships in their marriages and with their husbands' households, but also women who created alternate lives, some of which involved being single."[27] And he wrote in a less Sanskritized, more colloquial Bengali to mark "the individual voice capable of asserting its distinctiveness against the authority of unjust tradition," doing so for the first time in "Streer Patra."[28]

The story's publication elicited a strong reaction in the nationalist press at the time from defenders of the new patriarchy who "predicted chaos and doom in the family and social life" as a result of such publications.[29] And Mirabai was in the middle of it. Seemingly not by chance, a counterinterpretation of the saint's final moments would also begin to circulate, alleging that she had escaped through a door of the temple and committed suicide, walking into the sea, in some tellings with her maid and companion Lalita following right behind her. Such an ending offers a rationalization of her miraculous disappearance, to be sure, but one seemingly designed to undercut precisely the exemplary power of her life and character that Tagore lifted up.[30] And it was an ending that would get little traction except among a limited set of her detractors.

At the time "Letter from a Wife" was published, the specter of women's suicide had been made very real with the widely publicized story of a young woman who took her life "declaredly to spare her father the burden of providing her dowry."[31] And Tagore remained haunted by his sister-in-law Kadambari Debi's suicide decades before, in 1884, revisiting this issue in stories written across his literary career.[32] In the minds of most, Mira simply would not have taken such a despairing action.[33] Some conceded she might seek to end her life, but only if ordered to do so by her husband (à la Dutt in nationalist tellings), and in such a case this would be an act of obedience, not desperation, and for the honor of clan and kingdom. And Mira is always saved, making this an occasion for miraculous divine intervention rather than her demise, and leading in Dutt's telling ultimately to her reconciliation with her husband. Indeed across its permutations, her life story refutes the narrowing of women's options to either conform or die, for she does neither in most accounts, despite repeated attempts on her life.

In Tagore's invocation of the saint in this story, there is no sense of Mira acting at the behest of anyone else, human or Divine, and she unquestionably chooses to live and to live boldly, even as his heroine Mrinal does, "aided only by her intelligence and the tragic awakening that comes to her through the death of the hapless Bindu."[34] At the time the story was written, as Kalpana Bhardhan has noted, Bengali middle-class women did learn to "read, write, and think" within the confines of the home, as Tagore's Mrinal does, their reading material including the nationalist-inspired biographies of heroes and heroines, Mirabai among them. Bhardhan and many others continue to share with Tagore a vision of "Mirabai's life [as] a truly revolutionary counterpoint."[35] Tagore's "Letter from a Wife" would come to strike a deep cord with feminist writers across the century, in the United States as well as India, as evidence of a universal striving for women's emancipation and self-actualization, with this cross-cultural impulse rooted in earlier centuries in India in the person of the saint Mirabai.[36]

As Tanika Sarkar importantly observes, it was "the new presence of women's writings in the public sphere that enabled Tagore to develop a fresh expressive form at this time," evident in "Streer Patra"—writings which demonstrated that women had "a critical mind, an intelligence, an authorial function of their own," just as men did, thereby constituting "a sign as well as a site of the dismantling of the basic opposition of the sexes, the transcending of the primal 'lack' that constructs sexual difference."[37] In this Tagore turns to Mirabai as cultural resource and precedent—as an Indian woman who can be construed as having such an independent critical mind and voice, despite the restrictions of her own time and standard nationalist/rajput portrayals of her.

He would turn to the saint again in the much darker and more nuanced 1927 *Yogayog*, "where," as Sabyasachi Bhattacharya puts it, "Tagore explores with a cruel scalpel gender relations in Hindu society, in particular, in conjugal life."[38] He wrote this novel in serialized form in the agonizing months of court proceedings and attempted reconciliations leading up to the final breakup of his daughter Mira's marriage.[39] The title is not easily translated into English, having multiple registers of meaning around the idea of "contact, connection ... communication ... coincidence," leading Supriya Chaudhuri to translate it as "Relationships" and Hiten Bhaya as "Nexus."[40] The novel recounts the loveless marriage of the aristocratic protagonist Kumudini, educated at home in relative isolation from the outside world and steeped in tradition, lovingly taught and cared for by her progressive elder brother, Bipradas, after her father's death. Her once wealthy family is now deeply in debt and her own unmarried state at eighteen a further source of shame. As the narrator describes this beautiful sheltered young woman, she lived "in the twilight zone between the old and the new ... [where] reality had no power to dispel the illusions created by dreams ... [and] there was no place for logic, there was only the observance of rules and taboos," one's fate as inescapable as it might be undeserved.[41]

Her marriage is arranged with her full consent to the holder of their debts, Madhusudhan, a crass, much older, but extremely successful businessman who wants to possess her as a trophy of social status and to humiliate her family, as they had earlier his own. She believes that the marriage is divinely ordained, her God coming to her in human form. Alone but for her new sister-in-law in the night hours after reaching her husband's home for the first time, she sings Mirabai's lines, "Mine is Girdhar Gopal, there is no other," taking the saint's absolute fidelity to Krishna and trying to will herself to see "the one eternal truth in everyone" manifest in her husband's form, as the only one for her, in a test of her faith.[42] Such a characterization brings to mind the *Prem Ambodh* but also reveals a disturbing latent potential within the structuring of Mira's devotion and voice that is profoundly conservative. As Tagore himself describes his heroine Kumudini in a 1928 letter, "She had installed in the figure of her deity the complete ideal of manhood that inwardly, unknown to herself, had attracted her mind on the threshold of adolescence. ... [S]he had given her womanly love in the guise of worship to that deity ... [and] caught up in the mist of her belief, imagined that it was her deity who had beckoned her through the proposal of marriage."[43] Having so deeply internalized the ideals of wifely devotion, she expects to be able to see the Divine Beloved of her youthful inner world in this hard, harsh man, as a devotee through faith "brings forth the form of Vishnu from [the] formlessness [of the shalagram's black stone]," and to be able to serve him with an "impersonal" dedication and love, offered to this ideal in the husband, irrespective of the individual characteristics or worthiness of the man.[44]

Indeed similar advice appears in one of the many late nineteenth- and early twentieth-century socially conservative Bengali domestic manuals, produced predominantly by men to school women on how to be ideal wives in the new patriarchy, though in this case the author was a woman.[45] In her turn-of-the-century *Women's Dharma*, Nagendrabala Dasi (1878–1906), a published author of both poetry and prose, advocates making a similar "choice," calling women to consciously devote themselves to their husbands with the same purity and intensity Mira directed to Krishna. Having first praised the "jewels of Indian womanhood" with the usual litany of goddesses and legendary women of the past and reminding her readers to "[r]emember how the fiery spirit of the Aryan women is linked to their love for their husbands," she invokes Mirabai as such a "jewel" and a quintessential "ideal wife," but decidedly not in the way that Dutt had.

It is Mirabai as a pativrata of God whom Nagendrabala invokes, first quoting the initial two lines in Hindi of the same familiar song: "Mine is Girdhar Gopal—there is no other; The one who wears the peacock crown, he is my *pati* (husband/Lord)." She then offers her own elaboration in Bengali:

> Mīrābāī has said . . . "Lord Krishna is my husband, and I have no one other than he" and saying that she became mad with love for him. When a human like Mirabai could surrender herself at the feet of a god she could not see, are we so weak that we can not dedicate ourselves at the feet of our own husband, a god whom we can see! If we cannot do even *that*, then what is the point of carrying on with such a useless life! . . . But it is not impossible if we try—if we first remember the gracious Lord with firm faith and set out along the path of duty, in time we too will be able to become true wives.[46]

She goes on to argue for the kind of spiritual relationship Tagore's Kumudini is imagining: an indivisible unity through the realization of the divine by the wife in the husband such that the couple become soul-mates in life after life. She advocates the wife's selfless devotion and surrender as the marks of this true love, with her husband as her god and she aspiring to be the Lakshmi of his home, and she condemns in the strongest terms women who complain of bad matches, a lack of love in marriage, and the like. Like Krishna to Mirabai, "[t]he husband is a woman's only god and serving him her highest dharma," she asserts, in a distillation of all her advice.[47]

In invoking Mirabai in this way, both Nagendrabala and Tagore acknowledge the ways stories of goddesses like Sita, legendary women like Savitri, and bhakti saints *including Mirabai* are deployed to school young girls, weaving sati-pativrata images of virtuous women and wives into their developing identities and channeling their emotions into selfless service and loving devotion to a divinized male, their very own Krishna/Shiva/Rama/husband enshrined in their hearts and in their imaginations and expectations. In an essay written at the request of Europeans wanting to understand Indian marriage customs, which Sabyasachi Bhattacharya suggests should be read as a kind of prelude to *Yogayog*,[48] Tagore notes this explicitly and its impact at marriage: "[F]rom their earliest years the husband as an idea is held up before our girls, in verse and story, through ceremonial and worship. When at length they get this 'husband,' he is to them not a person but a principle, like Loyalty, Patriotism, or such other abstractions which owe their immense strength to the fact that the best part of them is our own creation and therefore part of our inner being."[49] Kumudini has thoroughly absorbed all this, intensified by her isolation coupled with her memory of her mother's failure of her father despite their love for each other and her own determination not to make the same mistake. When she was only ten, her mother had gone to Vrindavan in an attempt to punish her father for yet again staying out all night carousing, an action with tragic consequences for them both, precipitating his untimely demise (he drank himself to death in her absence) and ultimately also her own, both consumed by guilt and remorse—something for which Kumudini never forgave her mother (even as her brother would never forgive their father for dishonoring their mother).

In her first moments of self-doubt, Kumudini calls on Mirabai to reinforce this scaffolding upholding her world and her identity. Yet Mirabai is not just another model pativrata, though this dimension in the traditions that surround her is undeniably there and troubling, critically undermining for some her "radicalizing potential," as we noted in the previous chapter. Yet Nagendrabala and Tagore, while acknowledging this pativrata dimension, will both find much more in the "ideals of Mirabai."

Nagendrabala invokes Mira from a very different vantage point than the still innocent Kumudini in the early pages of Tagore's novel. As a young woman of sixteen and seventeen, Nagendrabala had written scathing critiques in the women's journal *Bamabodhini Patrika* of child marriage, arranged marriage, and the abusive treatment of women in patrilocal extended families, having direct experience with all of this. But evidently her marriage improved under a Vaishnava guru whom both she and her husband had embraced, and *Women's Dharma* was written in 1900 with her guru's guidance and both his and her husband's support.[50]

She calls on Mira specifically as an example of women's agency, even within the confines of the "old patriarchy." If Mira could choose, then so can other women—they can choose to live within the system and to be happy and fulfilled doing so (as Nagendrabala evidently had). Yet at the same time she draws on Mira's singular and absolute devotion to Krishna to support the prioritizing of the relationship of husband and wife over all others, including those of family and in-laws, in a decided shift away from older norms. She is highly critical of mother-in-laws' interference and mistreatment of in-marrying women in particular, a theme not so overt in other advice manuals but common in women's story and song traditions, as well as in stories of Mira's life.[51]

Like other reformers and advice givers of the era, Nagendrabala also strongly supports women's literacy and education, though for the explicit purpose of reading religious texts, and she is highly critical of assertive "modern" educated women who selfishly pursue their own agendas.[52] Alleged to have taught herself to read Bengali, Sanskrit, Orissi, and English when her marriage blocked her further formal education, she grounds much of her understanding of women's dharma in "ancient" texts—the Shastras, Laws of Manu, *Mahabharata*, and *Ramayana* as well as tantras and Bengali literature.[53] Even so she makes her own selections and provides her own translations (as she did with Mira's bhajan), so that, for example, rather than choosing Manu's uncompromising statement of women's inherent dependent nature, she quotes the *Mahanirvana tantra*: "[I]n girlhood, on the father, in youth on her husband, in old age on the son or the husband, [a woman] should always be dependent on *those who wish her well*."[54] Significantly she also grounds the cause of women's degradation in the loss of their education and the abandonment of true Hinduism and Indian traditions and customs, tying her advice directly to the renewal of the nation.

Judith Walsh argues persuasively that what Nagendrabala is engaged in here is not a mere reiteration of either old or new patriarchy but rather a complex renegotiation, marked by recognition that women did not merely have to accept either the old or new formulations as they were given to them but could instead develop and assert their own understandings as she does so forcefully in *Women's Dharma*, and thereby actively participate in defining themselves, their relationships, and the nation. For her and other women of her time, Walsh suggests, "[d]evotion to one's husband and acceptance of the new patriarchy those husbands represent becomes a tactic deployed along one patriarchal axis to deflect the customs, controls and hierarchy of another."[55] Nagendrabala's work was thus recognizably "traditional" and nationalist but with a subterranean subversiveness. And it was immensely popular, selling out immediately on publication and deemed appropriate for school libraries.[56]

Apparently it is only in such a context that Mirabai might be invoked in turn-of-the-century advice literature, and then it is Mira's absolute dedication to Krishna as her god-husband and decidedly not her obedience to her earthly husband that finds resonance, in dramatic contrast to Dutt and Deviprasad. And significantly it is a woman who invokes her, asserting women's agency even while ostensibly remaining within and even reaffirming patriarchal restrictions but thereby opening up a larger space within which to negotiate relationships and to manifest "a critical mind, an intelligence, an authorial function of [her] own."[57] Nagendrabala died at the young age of twenty-eight of complications during childbirth, leaving us to wonder how her ideas might have evolved if she had lived through the decades that followed.

Writing some thirty years later, Tagore puts the relationship of husband and wife under a microscope in *Yogayog*, without the distraction of mothers-in-law and the like, and his protagonist Kumudini turns to Mira in approaching her marriage in much the way Nagendrabala recommends. She invokes these famous lines "*Mere to Girdhar Gopal, dusara na koi*" yet again as she is being led to her husband the next night, having fainted and clearly frightened but determined, as she thinks to herself, "Such is my tryst, all darkness outside, all light within."[58] The night is fraught with argument, her husband impatient, frustrated, and insulting, she utterly shocked, defensive, and withdrawn, and it ends in stalemate, without the expected "bridal consummation" and with her shattered expectations lying in ruins around her. Though she continues to try to exercise the kind of "choice" Nagendrabala advocates, the ideology utterly fails her in her encounter with the real man, for she is unable to see either her husband as her god or god in her husband and unable to will herself to love him or even overcome her revulsion and sense of shame and humiliation. For his part he alternately torments her and tries to win her over with lavish gifts, the fruits of his wealth which are meaningless to her, and as a man of power, he finds himself uncomfortably vulnerable for the first time with a woman.

She fails utterly to become a "true wife," and in her failure Kumudini loses her inner light, even ceasing the outward practice of her personal puja in the aftermath of her delayed first sexual encounter with her husband, in what Tagore describes as akin to "rape legalized by the institution of marriage" in the 1928 letter to Radharani Debi.[59] Though Madhusudan might be controlling and vindictive, however, he would not accept her mere obedience, refusing to order her to come to him—he wanted her affection as well as her submission, allowing her no easy way out as one self-aware, who herself could not accept the "degradation of surrender without respect" but who had equally built her identity around wifely ideals. Yet there is no victory in it for him, as subsequently in an unguarded moment he sees her loathing.

Finally, he banishes her to her beloved brother's house. Kumudini asks Bipradas, who has always also been her teacher and protector, whether it is a sin that she cannot "endear [her] husband to [her]self." Bipradas will make no such judgment, and it is then that she, and Tagore, again turn to Mirabai:

> Whenever the struggle between what is to be done and what is not to be done raged fierce in her mind she thought of Mirabai. She wished fervently for someone to explain to her the ideals of Mirabai.
> With some effort she overcame her hesitation and said, "Mira found her real beloved within herself, so she could sincerely give up her social husband. But have I got such a major right to relinquish my mundane household?"[60]

In this struggle between individuality and dharma, between self-respect and selflessness, it is "the ideals of Mira" to which she turns—not to Sita or Savitri or other oft-invoked pativratas or heroines. Yet the ideals of Mirabai do not provide her with a ready-made or definitive answer to her quandary. Her brother responds, "But, Kumu, I thought you already had your deity fully within yourself." She replies that she has lost all sense of this. She is clearly deeply constrained by her upbringing and internalized pativrata-sati ideals, over against "ideals of Mirabai," and also haunted by the memory of her mother's leaving her father.

Brother and sister leave the topic and turn to music, as she does across the novel, its beauty lifting her above her own circumstances and allowing her to experience a full range of emotions. Of Tagore's extensive use of music in the novel, Supriya Chaudhuri observes, "Music as the sign of an infinitude of feeling beyond language as such, is an integral and possibly untranslatable element in Rabindranath's construction of mental and moral worlds in *Relationships* . . . confirm[ing] the soul's capacity of achieving transcendence . . . suggest[ing] a space beyond the social, a space that can only be signified by music."[61] At this moment, as Kumudini specifically sings a Mira bhajan of Girdhar Gopal's arrival, bliss pervades her entire being, the Divine once again grasped as inner presence. As Mira's voice and her voice become one, she recovers some sense of self and reconnects to a wellspring of joy and love within. Singing Mira thus brings not merely compensatory solace but transformative restoration, a coming home to herself and indwelling divinity. Yet the external reality of her tortured marital life remains, and in contemplating returning, she considers the seductive oblivion of death. In the end, however, she concludes that life is perhaps bearable after all, with the promise of light and bliss as its culmination but also potentially available whenever the eternal breaks into the "now" in music and song. And so she resolves to go back to her husband.

But just as she does, brother and sister learn of Madhusudan's very public affair with his older brother's widow in Kumu's absence. Bipradas is outraged at the private torment and public humiliation of women condoned by Indian society and insists that they must stand against it or be complicit in the oppression of all women that is dragging the entire society down and indeed degrading all humanity. In his voice we hear the strident critique of progressive elite men, speaking against "blind reverence" in whatever form, religious, political, or marital, and identifying women themselves as part of the problem, having "put out their own light," embracing "the cozy retreat of deliberate, blind slavery, which men have long preserved under the cloak of high-sounding words."[62]

Kumu speaks the conflicted part of many an elite woman of her time, to the consternation of those men who, in their benevolent paternalism, would seek to educate them and end their servitude. She responds:

> What you call freedom, comes through knowledge and that is just not in our blood. We cling to men, and we also cling to our beliefs and we are unable to untie the knot. The more we are hurt, the more we go round and round and get enmeshed. You men know a lot and that liberates your mind, we women believe a lot and that fills the emptiness in our lives. When you explain things to me, maybe I can see my mistake. But to know your weaknesses is not the same as giving them up. Like the tendrils of a creeper, our possessiveness[, our tenderness,] clings to everything, good and bad alike, and then we can not let go of them.[63]

Her sister-in-law speaks in even deeper resignation and learned helplessness—whether men are bad or good, women must learn to live with it, as their lot in life: "If one does not accept this truth, the only way out is death."[64]

Her brother offers her refuge, recognizing his own responsibility in having parented her: "If you were like any other girl you would have had no problems. But today any place where there is no recognition, no respect for your own identity would be hell to you. Can I have the heart to banish you to such a place?"[65] (His words echo Tagore's own to his son with regard to his daughter Mira.) Yet Kumu's resolve never to return and to endure all manner of coercion and suffering that might result from her decision is called into question when she finds herself pregnant. She is compelled to go back to her "mundane household," with all its ignominy, bound by the inner compulsion of her own self-doubt coupled with pativrata-sati ideals, but even more by her brother refusing to tell her not to go. Ironically he is now unable to overcome his own weaknesses despite his knowledge and indeed insists that she must go back for the sake of the child. He even holds out the promise of coming joy in motherhood.

This is a much darker story than "Letter from a Wife"—a story not about leaving but about a woman walking back into a living hell, in adherence to both internal constraints and external circumstances and compulsion—though it ends without closure, the way left open for future possibilities and decisions. Nor is her situation meant to be exceptional or even peculiar to India, for Tagore concludes his essay on Indian ideal marriage with a condemnation of marriage as it is now practiced in all societies, calling it "a prison house for the confinement of women—with all its guards wearing the badge of the dominant male" and "one of the most fruitful sources of the unhappiness and downfall of man, of his disgrace and humiliation," depriving men, women, and society of enlivening feminine power, creative energy, and compassion—of *shakti* that is everywhere "so shamefully wasted and corrupted."[66]

Though Mrinal might have been able to break out of this prison-house in "Letter from a Wife," this short story also does not deal with what happens next. Even for an educated woman with a sense of her own identity coupled with a strong conviction not to accept "surrender without respect" like Kumudini, attaining freedom may in reality be extremely difficult, especially if she does not yet know how to fully "give up [her] weaknesses" and if she must still inhabit a world that itself is insufficiently "new" and "free." Tagore's daughter could spend more and more time with him and the work of Shantiniketan, but she too would ask his advice on whether she should go back to her husband. And what of other women, who might have children and other family members whose lives must also be considered and who might have neither supportive male natal family members nor a husband who might turn to devotion, as the saint Bahinabai's and Nagendrabala's do? When idealism seems to founder on the shores of survival, responsibility, or self-doubt—what then?

Yet Kumudini makes one last declaration to her brother as she prepares to return to her marital home:

> [M]ark my words, Dada, one day I shall be rid of them and I shall be free to come back to you. There is no point in being the Borrobou [senior daughter-in-law/wife] of that family if I can't be Kumu, my own self.... There lies beyond all this a space where the sun, moon and the universe are still turning—that is where paradise lies, that is where my god resides.... I have realized that there is a residue of your own even after you've lost all. And that is inexhaustible, that is my god. If I hadn't realized this truth, then I would have clung to you till my death and never entered that prison-house again.[67]

She has found "god," not in outward deities and practices or in her husband but within herself and in the universe around her, and she has discovered "a residue of... self" that exists apart from dharmic roles and relationships of blood and marriage, from all the doing and having, the assumptions and judgments of upbringing and habit—a part of her self that cannot be taken by another, a divinity within rather than an external religion of rules and obligations, all too easily weaponized to dominate, control, and destroy.

At the heart of the novel, in Chaudhuri's words, is a "truth" that "involves the tragic restriction of individual liberty in the frame of the domestic and the social: a restriction that must be fully experienced, felt in the body, before it can be transcended or undergone."[68] It is in such stark reality that the "ideals of Mirabai" finally come to fruition for Kumudini, as Tagore suggests they could potentially do for other women, making possible the imagining and crafting of individual selves not limited by cookie-cutter social norms and of a self-respect not grounded in judgments of superiority over others, the kind of selves and self-respect that are the seeds for living without fear and in true freedom. These "ideals of Mirabai," it seems, may allow one woman to walk away from the prison-house of marriage, another to live within it, in both cases with an irrepressible self-awareness and inner strength.

Many have found this novel unsatisfying, the device of Kumudini finding herself pregnant trite, and she narcissistic, arrogant, self-absorbed, and obstinate.[69] In dramatizing the play, actors and scriptwriters wanted to change the ending, turning the play into "advice to chaste and devoted wives," with Kumudini touching Madhusudan's feet and he asking Bipradas's blessing. Tagore objected vehemently to such changes and is reported to have said, "Do you want to make my Kumu a run of the mill Hindu? Rebellion is in her blood, shattering all her beliefs." He resisted pressure to "finish" what Chaudhuri describes as "his most sustained, most difficult and most serious treatment of human relationships ... its open ending ... a significant element of its structure."[70] Amartya Sen would see in Tagore's propensity for such open endings "a celebration of the unresolved and the incomplete," and Amit Chaudhuri "of contingency"; its openness was a mark of both its realism and modernity, according to Radha Chakravarty.[71]

Others would report that Tagore said if he had finished it as a saga of three generations, as its original title implied, Kumu would ultimately have rejected all her limiting beliefs and embraced the religion of humanity and her son would have rebelled against his father's materialism.[72] She would have reached the kind of full realization that Kshitimohan Sen attributed to the saint after her encounter with Raidas and which Tagore espoused: universal, interior, marked by a mystical realization of the "Eternal Spirit of human unity" that resides within all people and is experienced as Beauty, Truth, and Infinite Love, necessarily flowing out in service to all—articulated in the songs of nirgun bhaktas like Kabir and the Bauls but also by Vaishnava poets.[73] But Tagore left the story as it stands, with Kumu's having found an irreducible core of her being, a core of infinite value, and stepping out into the flow of life's uncertainty—perhaps not so unlike Mrinal after all, with the saint Mirabai acting as a vital catalyst in this transformation for both fictional women.[74] And as Tagore's heroines had, other men and women who found themselves "in the twilight zone between old and new" and in the midst of individual and social awakening and striving for self-determination and human rights and dignity in India, would continue to turn to Mirabai when "the struggle between what is to be done and what is not to be done raged fierce in [their] mind[s]," particularly with regard to women.

Gandhi's Mira: The Saintly Satyagrahi

Others would seek to draw the saint much more directly into the service of nationalism, as Dutt had, hailing her as a symbol of Indian women's strength and courage and highlighting her characteristic extreme dedication and willingness to undergo suffering for a greater good. Leading the way in this, Mahatma Gandhi would be tremendously influential in the popularization and propagation of a heroic Mirabai, lifting her up as a model for nonviolent resistance and women's political activism. References to her abound in his essays, speeches, and correspondence, from the beginning of his nonviolent campaign in South Africa in 1907, and he would honor Madeleine Slade, his devoted British disciple, by calling her Mira Behn (Sister Mira).[75] His affinity for the saint was deeply personal as well as practical and political. She epitomized his ideals of *satyagraha* (truth force), embodying fearless courage in the face of oppression, never turning to violence no matter what others might do to her and converting them through love and the rightness of her cause.[76]

The portrait Gandhi drew of the saint was consonant with Dutt's portrayal in many ways, but also diverged significantly in important aspects. In his more limited and fragmented telling, her husband, whom he identifies as Rana Kumbha, clearly opposed her devotion, setting the stage for her embodiment of Gandhian nonviolence. Gandhi's Mira endured her husband's torments and looked on her persecutor never with hatred or anger but only with love. In the end he became her disciple, as the rana essentially does in Dutt's account. In speaking of her, Gandhi appears to have been generally aware of circulating traditions, no doubt including elements from oral traditions of story and song and popular print biographies and plays as well as the emerging historical-nationalist synthesis, but there is no indication that he had read Dutt, Deviprasad, or Macauliffe. Indeed in 1926 he reports that he has just heard about her encounter with Jiv Goswami for the first time.[77] His association of Mira with Rana Kumbha might be traced to his childhood in a Vaishnava household in Saurashtra, given that their connection continues to be a popular tradition in Gujarat, reported by G. M. Tripathi in 1892 and Neelima Shukla-Bhatt in 2007 among others, as well as in oral traditions of southern Rajasthan, some of which also relate her eventual conversion of her husband, as we saw in the previous chapter.[78] It is undeniable, however, that this notion of a wife's ability and duty to transform her husband through her patient virtue, regardless of his behavior, is a refrain found widely in other nationalist conceptions of *stridharm* (women's religiously sanctioned ideal conduct and character).

Gandhi repeatedly compared Mira to Socrates (in addition to Jesus, Daniel, the great devotee Prahlad, and Buddha), because both she and the Greek philosopher willingly drank poison rather than abandon the truth. In this context he declared that she was a model wife, as Socrates was a model citizen and Prahlad a model son, yet he also lauded her as an example of women's independence, particularly in regard to moral conscience.[79] She set a precedent for women taking a stand even against their husbands if need be and holding fast to their convictions, even to the point of death, as she did. Indeed as Madhu Kishwar and Ruth Vanita have noted, "Gandhi frequently referred to Mira's having 'forsaken' her husband as a sign of the right to individual choice of a path," and he "wished the fearless Mira to be seen as a role model for all women."[80] The saint played a pivotal role in Gandhi's effort to mobilize women for social change and political action. And he invoked her as one who knew the world's condemnation but was undeterred by it and who willingly gave up the things of the world for love of God and truth.

Songs attributed to Mira were sung in his ashrams, along with those of other bhakti, Sufi, and Sikh saints and Christian hymns. For Gandhi, these devotional saints and their songs calmed, oriented, and "tuned" the heart to the Truth, offering "clarity of vision" and individual and shared experiences of beauty, bliss, and enjoyment of the Divine, providing moral guidance and inspiration and facilitating inner transformation and the formation of inclusive community (as Nabhadas had sought to foster centuries before).[81] Margaret Chatterjee writes, "When Gandhi tried to explain to inquirers what the essence of Hindu tradition was, it was to the hymns of the medieval saints that he appealed most often," for they were to him "beacon lights . . . [t]heir words illuminat[ing] his way, the encircling gloom . . . penetrated by their example, the lamp within . . . fueled to burn bravely even in the windy spaces of the twentieth-century world."[82] Shukla-Bhatt offers further detailed analysis of Gandhi's "devotional aesthetic" and the intimate and multifaceted role these saints and their songs played in the development of his emerging identity, thought, and action, particularly with respect to Narsi Mehta.[83]

Mira had an important place among them, and Gandhi often made reference to lines from songs attributed to her, particularly to the verse in which she allegedly sings:

> Hari has bound me to Him by a slender thread.
> As He pulls me so do I turn.
> My heart by love's dagger has been pierced.[84]

This slender thread showed, for Gandhi, the degree to which Mira had given herself over to God and aligned herself with Truth (as indeed for him God and Truth were synonymous). Her heart broken open by love, she was able to discern the inner voice of wisdom and would respond instantly, like a marionette enlivened at the puppeteer's slightest touch.[85] Gandhi contrasted the power of that slender thread of love to the chains that bound those arrested for nonviolently opposing the British, the binding power of love far stronger than any mere physical restraint or any form of violent coercion. That thread would also allow him to make a tenuous connection between Mira and spinning. He would personally draw great inspiration from her, and she proved a highly effective model for satyagraha, with pan-Indian appeal.

However, Gandhi's portrayal of Mira has been criticized by Parita Mukta and others as, in the end, a betrayal of all that the saint stood for, particularly in his insistence on Mira's love for her husband as her motivation to work to change his heart no matter what violence he might direct toward her.[86] Mukta argues that Gandhi misses the opportunity to invoke Mira's example in his condemnation of untouchability and falls short in his continuing support of patriarchal marital relations as well as his excision of critiques of marriage and widowhood from Mira's story in his telling and from her songs sung in his ashrams. Without a doubt, nationalist portrayals of Mira overwhelmingly do blunt and even erase these dimensions of her story and affirm women's heroism and independence only in the service of a "higher cause," determined and approved by these elite men and without disrupting domestic relations.

Gandhi is no exception, though the "higher cause" his Mira (and those inspired by her) might serve encompasses not only the nation but also truth, love, justice, equality, devotion to God, and the betterment of the lives of the poor and oppressed, and she is far more disruptive in her domestic resistance.

Indeed his is a lifelong and very personal engagement with the saint, and thus his portrayal of her is complex and multidimensional, reflecting "a coexistence of different tonalities, which push... up against one another," rather than a unified vision, as Tanika Sarkar observes about his position on untouchability.[87] Mira is his constant companion (even as Narsi Mehta also is). Her bhajans brought him courage and inspiration from his earliest days of engagement in nonviolent action and imprisonment and at least a measure of solace in his anguish over partition violence in the final months of his life.[88]

It is not insignificant that though in some instances he stresses Mira's long-suffering endurance, his emphasis on her active choice to do so and her inner strength and his repeated references to her leaving her husband meant that she could not entirely be confined within pativrata ideals of the past. Importantly Gandhi did not merely reinforce patriarchal relations (either in their "old" or "new" forms) but fostered the active public involvement of mass numbers of women in the political sphere and thus departed radically from earlier nationalists.[89] In the words of Sarkar:

> [U]sing a vocabulary of religious sacrifice, [Gandhi's] nonviolent activism recast politics—something still new and transgressive for most women—as worship, something that women were expected to do ... [and he] never tired of pointing out that their acquired habits of deference, acceptance, and patience made women ideal patriots, born satyagrahis.... [Yet t]his conjoining of female patriotism with female virtue was paradoxical. It eased the Indian woman into the public domain, into transgressive activities and spaces; it made her a valued political subject.... In equal measure, it rendered suffering and self-sacrifice privileged female qualities, it re-anchored her in them.[90]

For Gandhi, it seems, Mira provided an ideal model for such transgressive yet virtuous feminine behavior, facilitating this transition for women. In this context, however, any alleged "transgression" by the saint that might run counter to his conception of "virtue" and "purity" simply could not be acknowledged.

Gandhi's connection to Mira was deeply personal in other ways. In his talks to women at morning prayer meetings in 1926, he offered the following view of gender: "My ideal is this: A man should remain a man and yet should become woman; similarly a woman should remain woman and yet become man. This means that man should cultivate the gentleness and discrimination of woman; and woman should cast off her timidity and become brave and courageous."[91] Mirabai is such an ideal gender-balanced woman for Gandhi—she is above the passions of the flesh, living in celibate matrimonial purity (in her relations with both her human husband and with her true divine one), and she is utterly fearless, though also gentle and discriminating, never acting on selfish desires but only out of love. As such she is also Gandhi's ideal for the inner feminine characteristics that he strove to cultivate in himself and to embody: sensitive to the slightest touch of the Divine, able to discern clearly the inner voice of Truth, and following her conscience with absolute dedication at any cost, having transcended all sensual and material desires and facing suffering with equanimity, dancing with joy in the face of public condemnation and seeing God—in the form of the shalagram—even in the rana's violence (the poison snake that could harm only her body but not her soul becoming such a sacred stone when she opened the basket). Gandhi would continue to invoke the saint in myriad ways across the decades of his life.

With respect to marriage, though Gandhi embraced an ascetic lifestyle, he did not oppose the institution, upholding this dharma and a gender complementarity even as he did caste distinctions in some ways, though in his idealized view of marriage it should be a loving companionship and celibate, except for procreation. It should be a "spiritual union through the physical" with "the human love that it incarnates . . . a stepping stone to the divine or universal love." In this context he draws directly on Mira's authority to support this understanding and show its highest manifestation, in her claim "God alone is my husband—none else."[92] In the same essay he asserts that a woman should view marriage as "a means of realizing the ideal of selfless and self-effacing service by completely merging her identity in her husband's . . . [and] prov[ing] her satihood . . . by her renunciation, sacrifice, self-abnegation and dedication to the service of her husband, his family, and the country." It is hard to imagine a more thoroughgoing patriarchal presentation of stridharm, but he then goes on to claim that a husband should do the same in his relations with his wife, for "the wife is not the slave of the husband but his comrade . . . his better half, his colleague and friend . . . a co-sharer with him of equal rights and equal duties . . . [such that t]heir obligations towards each other and towards the world must, therefore, be the same and reciprocal."[93] Though he sought to revalue these normative feminine characteristics and make them universal with claims that men should also be as women, his glorification of them reinscribed women even more tightly into this box, as Sarkar observes, his addition of service to the nation and humanity notwithstanding. Yet even as he frequently encouraged women to follow the example of Sita in self-sacrifice and service, Mira appears a necessary additional vessel for his ideals, as one who could embody an essentialized femininity yet whose strength, renunciation, absolute commitment, and, above all, fearlessness could be harnessed to spiritualized political action.

This is a powerful but also limiting vision of the saint. As Parita Mukta rightly contends, there is no place in Gandhi's view of Mira for circulating traditions that challenge arranged marriage or the socially imposed deprivations of widowhood. For Gandhi, widowhood was a virtuous and honorable calling, further embodying self-restraint, and he vehemently denounced the disrespectful mistreatment of widows. But his Mira was necessarily not a widow, as she could not be for Dutt, though for different reasons. Her husband's intense opposition sets the context for her practice of satyagraha for Gandhi, her relations with him marked by patient endurance and equanimity rather than radical challenge even as she stands fast. Though her husband lives, she nevertheless epitomizes a self-restraint similar to that of a widow in her chastity and renunciation, both essential elements of Gandhi's ideal spiritual political activist. Given this conception of Mira, she logically also had nothing to do with his more practical campaigns against child marriage (largely on the grounds that it awakens lust prematurely) or against restrictions on child widow remarriage (on the grounds that widowhood becomes virtue only if consciously embraced, not forced).[94]

Neither does he invoke Mira in his campaign against untouchability, never mentioning Raidas as her guru. It is Mira's and other women's strategies of nonviolent resistance to "domestic tyranny" that spiritually prepare them to be ideal satyagrahis and thus are at the heart of Gandhi's portrayal of the saint.[95] Though he harshly forced his own wife to confront untouchability with his insistence that she clean an untouchable's chamber pot, it appears to be beyond the pale of his imagination that Mira as a wife—a "better half"— might confront her royal husband in a reciprocal way by taking a low-caste guru. Mira is his perfect satyagrahi, he himself acting more like the rana in relation to his own wife in this context, threatening to banish her if she did not comply.[96] Indeed though Gandhi would say that there should be no force in marital relations, his notion of the companionate marriage in practice was at times far less than an egalitarian spiritual partnership marked by the same rights, duties, and obligations to each other and the world.[97] His Mira would be strategically mobilized to get women out of the home to stand beside their menfolk, or even to stand without them, in working for the nation, but not to directly challenge those same men with respect to caste prejudice (or even domestic tyranny in any but nonviolent, gentle ways).

He does cite Mira as an example in one case in the context of a woman giving up the morally wrong practice of untouchability, but he does so only in the context of assuring her son that his father's pleasure or displeasure over her choice is not an issue: "Ultimately everyone is reconciled if we observe dharma" (even as his Mira eventually converted her husband and as Gandhi himself softened in response to Kasturba's love and obedience).[98] This in itself is a radical suggestion, going against deeply held internal as well as external constraints associated with pativrata ideals. Certainly neither Deviprasad's nor Dutt's Mira would have intentionally acted against her husband's wishes (though Tripathi's Gujarati Mira might have). However, nowhere does Gandhi invoke the saint as one who herself refused to practice untouchability and embraced a low-caste guru, even as she does not appear to denounce patriarchal structures of marriage (arranged or otherwise) and conceptions of widowhood.

Still, given Gandhi's conviction that it was the responsibility of those in the upper castes to eliminate practices of untouchability as the perpetrators of this sin, this rajput royal devotee would seem to have been an appropriate spokesperson at least to stand beside the brahman bhakta Narsi Mehta to whom Gandhi repeatedly turned in this regard.[99] In low-caste tellings like the epic *Mira Janma Patri*, she insists on becoming the disciple of a chamar guru (even in the face of Raidas's initial reluctance) and chooses to live in solidarity with the poor and those of the lowest castes, evincing a radical egalitarianism, transgressive of caste and class distinctions, even as her story exposes the terrible human suffering that results from them. It is possible that Gandhi's "top-down" approach may have prevented him from even being aware of the popular circulating traditions about Mirabai and Raidas among low-caste communities in Gujarat (documented in detail by Parita Mukta). But it is equally possible that he deliberately chose to ignore them.

As Joel Lee has persuasively argued, in the 1920s and 1930s, upper-caste nationalists, including Gandhi, turned to bhakti to draw people of the very lowest castes firmly into the Hindu fold through a shared devotion in which all stood side by side before God, thereby affirming a form of equality and inclusivity that was necessary for democracy even as they sought to increase their political base "by fundamentally redrawing the borders of Hindu society to encompass its erstwhile others, redefining the unruly religious traditions of the untouchables as Hindu."[100] Yet in relationships with each other, hierarchies were maintained, with "untouchables" cast as the passive and deferential recipients of upper-caste active initiative and largesse in this process, as women were expected to be in relation to men in the nationalist struggle (though Gandhi would also acknowledge that both would ultimately have to emancipate themselves).[101] Mira's absence in his repeated calls to women to give up the practice of untouchability is particularly striking, but perhaps to mobilize her in this way would have been perceived as introducing a much too radical and thoroughgoing notion of universal equality and perhaps also as potentially fostering coalitions between women and those of low caste that could destabilize elite male nationalist leadership. It must be admitted that issues of caste and untouchability are far more central to the hagiography and songs of Narsi Mehta, and as a male brahman he is perhaps a more appropriate but also less problematic exemplar, with gender and caste issues conveniently divided in Gandhi's thought between these two popular Gujarati saints.[102]

Mrinalini Sinha has argued persuasively that national women's organizations (including the Women's Indian Association, the All-India Women's Congress, and the National Council of Women in India) also contributed to maintaining a separation between issues of gender and caste oppression in this period, even as they actively shaped a newly emerging conception of a "modern Indian woman."[103] In denouncing colonialist critiques of Indian society based on the position of women and championing reform legislation on women's issues, they joined nationalist agitation for universal adult suffrage, opposing proposals to differentially award voting rights and representation along community lines. They thereby affirmed a solidarity of women across such distinctions (well aware that it would be difficult for women who critiqued patriarchy within their own communities to get elected otherwise) and "provided crucial ideological support for the construction of an allegedly neutral and unmarked citizen-subject."[104]

But in also refusing any special concessions for women, "offering the modern Indian woman as the model citizen," they effectively framed such an ostensibly universal "formal equality" as "modern," thereby marginalizing other and more critical voices, including the anti-caste Self-Respect movement, that saw gender, caste, and class inequality as inextricably linked and called for a more radical restructuring of society to ensure "substantive equality."[105] Such voices and demands thus were made to appear parochial, antimodern, and divisive, as was caste-based prejudice. If Mirabai were to be allied with these newly emerging "modern Indian women," she would seemingly also have to remain among them, standing in solidarity with women across caste, class, and religion to ensure smooth sailing, rather than rocking the nationalist boat by bringing up the issue of untouchability in an "old" way that might disrupt the ordered hierarchy of its crew.

But it was not only upper-caste, upper- and middle-class nationalists, both male and female, who failed to strategically deploy the saint's relationship with Raidas toward this end. Neither did the lower-caste Varkari saint and social reformer Gadge Maharaj (1876–1956) invoke Mira in this cause, if his last kirtan performance in November 1956 is representative, though he too worked tirelessly against untouchability and championed nonviolent resistance to the British even before Gandhi rose to prominence.[106] An illiterate member of a lower caste (associated with washing clothes), he was radicalized by his father's fall from a landholding successful farmer into drunken abuse of the family and wastefulness, including what Gadge Maharaj saw as useless expenditures on religious rituals while the family lived in desperate poverty. He became a *sannyasin* (renouncer) around the age of thirty, his only possessions a clay pot, or *gāḍge*, and a broom, and he spent the next fifty years as a kirtan performer, singing and preaching a combination of bhakti and social reform in his own brand of inclusive nationalism across Maharashtra.

Gadge Maharaj became a strong supporter of Gandhi; indeed in his kirtans, as Anna Schultz notes, "he deified Gandhi, but redefined divinity as extraordinary service to the nation" and "expounded on Gandhi's extraordinary human efforts to empower listeners to make practical changes in their own lives."[107] He and his followers would wed bhakti and politics in a pilgrimage that the British clearly recognized as protest, and he would take up a broom himself to sweep performance venues and other gathering places, encouraging others to do the same. He built the first *dharmshala* (rest house) for those who would come to call themselves Dalits at the famous Varkari pilgrimage center of Pandharpur in 1925, and in 1952 "founded the Shree Gadge Maharaj Mission with the purpose of abolishing animal sacrifice and educating [so-called] backward classes and tribals."[108]

In his final kirtan delivered in 1956 in his characteristic rough, earthy style, he does mention Mirabai, but only in connection with a socially conservative message directed at women to sing bhajans as Mirabai did while maintaining stridharm with respect to their husbands. (Sukhsaran suggested the same, though Gadge Maharaj also says that if a woman's husband comes home drunk, she should "worship" him by throwing a basket of hot ashes in his face!)[109] He describes Mira as one who gave up fine clothes (a laudable action encouraged elsewhere if undertaken to help the poor or to educate one's children), but he also tells women that their place is in the home (unlike Mira, who abandons her palace). The dedication to bhajan singing that Mirabai exhibits is extremely important in Gadge Baba's teachings and practice, not only as *the* premiere mode of devotion to God but also because, as Schultz argues, "the participatory performance structure of bhajan also modeled the democratic political and social structures Gadge Maharaj promoted and engaged listeners in an embodied experience of the nation."[110]

The saint Mira could offer strong support for this kind of devotional and communal engagement and "organic" nationalism, and indeed one of Gadge Maharaj's close circle of disciple kirtan performers carried her name—Mirabai Shirker—and it was she who was responsible for organizing their pilgrimage-protest march "at the height of the Quit India movement."[111] But it is also clear that both he and his audience associated the saint with behavior unbecoming of a pativrata, so that he encouraged ordinary women to sing bhajans like her but to serve their husbands, not to do what she did. Is it this behavior that might also have disqualified her for him from being a moral exemplar with respect to overcoming untouchability, though her exceptional devotion might be admired?

The Varkari hagiographer Mahipati, it is true, also does not mention Raidas or caste in relation to Mira, but neither does he say she left her home. Based on colonial reports we do know that she was popular among tribal communities in this region, as we noted in the previous chapter.[112] Might there have been oral traditions that associated the two here, as there clearly were in Rajasthan and Gujarat, sung particularly among the lowest castes? Gadge Maharaj does not draw on them if there are, at least in this final kirtan, though he himself was from a lower caste and by no means a member of a standard nationalist elite. Apparently, Mira (like the upper-caste, upper-class ideal woman of the new patriarchy) had to remain within the confines of gendered relations and spirituality in such nationalist discourses, whether because she was a good wife or because she wasn't.

Even for an "organic intellectual" and unconventional *kirtankar* like Gadge Maharaj, though he advocated radical social reforms, he stopped short of advocating women's emancipation. Indeed when he addresses caste prejudice in a lively back and forth with his audience, acknowledging a series of commonalities that all people share, he says "[t]here are only two castes of mankind ... male and female" (though of course women too share all these commonalities, from the number of teeth to how they are born). These "castes" it seems must remain in place. The majority of his advice is directed at men, encouraging them to "serve the world" and "have pity on the poor," to educate their children, to practice "cleanliness, economy, and the greatest thing—compassion," to eschew the eating of meat and drinking of alcohol, to eliminate untouchability, and to sing bhajans (very much in line with upper-caste nationalist "uplift" campaigns among the "Depressed Classes").[113] Women too might take this advice to heart, but when he actually addresses them directly, it is to tell them to sing bhajans, invoking Mirabai, and to take care of their children and husband in the home (even after he has just specifically told men that they must do more than just take care of their own children and wives or they are no better than animals who do the same).

So even for a great reformer like Gadge Maharaj from a very different social location than Gandhi, there appears to be no room for Mirabai as a woman to be invoked in the cause of eliminating casteism or even for working specifically for women's independence and emancipation.[114] A woman might work with men in pursuit of the social reforms he advocates and has, to his mind, the ability to choose to undertake such actions, as well as to choose to be devoted to her husband and sing bhajans. But the relationship between these "two castes" remains hierarchical, she serving and honoring him. The only exception he offers is if a man is destroying the family through drunkenness—then he is neither a true man nor a true father. Mirabai is decidedly a member of "woman caste"—honored and respected for her bhajan singing but otherwise a counterexample for more ordinary women. The all-important work of eliminating caste prejudice is, at least at the rhetorical level, deemed by both him and Gandhi the work of "man caste," though women's issues would play a far more central role and understandings of gender developed in far more nuanced ways in Gandhi's thought, with Mirabai in the thick of it.

Gandhi's Mira is in some ways highly idiosyncratic, as much an eclectic "maverick mix" as his religious ideas were more generally, as Akeel Bilgrami characterizes them.[115] He took liberties with her story as he did with those of a wide range of mythic and legendary heroes and heroines. In analyzing his interpretive strategies, Veena Howard concludes, "In his reinterpretation of ancient narratives, Gandhi appears to 'dig deep' and extract 'diamonds' of 'transcendent' Truth. . . . He is not confined to a literal reading of the text. . . . Rather, in his search for Truth, Gandhi is selective: he chose [those] that enhanced his message and inspired people and rejected those that did not . . . focus[ing] on stories that validated the theme of sacrifice and service."[116] When he spoke of Mirabai, too, it appears his interest was in mining the truth of her story and accessing the "living reality" of the saint, as he understood and experienced her. He makes it clear that it was in Mirabai and figures like her, whose stories are recounted in such enduring cultural narratives, that "he found the model for his personal and political strategy of self-sacrifice" in "the service . . . of the nation and humanity."[117] Thus when he talks of Mirabai as well as other narrative exemplars, he does so in the selective and evocative way of a "*kathakar* . . . dr[awing] on the traditions of a *sādhu* imparting teachings through an oral discourse," as Howard points out.[118] And Mira's relationship to Raidas, it seems, does not fit into his saintly satyagrahi model and the twin themes of self-sacrifice and service that are the focus of his Mira kathas (as it did not fit into the final kirtan of sadhu Gadge Maharaj).

Though highly personal in some ways, Gandhi's Mira does, nevertheless, remain largely consonant with the wider rajput/nationalist synthesis. The white homespun cotton, or *khadi*, that was the hallmark of the Gandhian renouncer/activist could easily be conflated with that of the widowed Mira of the rajput historians. His Mira, too, is the virtuous ideal wife who acts with courage and bravery in absolute allegiance to higher truth but with nonviolence, love, and discipline, as a pure but engaged embodiment of Indian spiritual values and upper-caste and -class notions of the feminine, all compatible with her being a perfect model for women's participation in the nationalist cause. Yet Gandhi's position on women was more complex; he asked them to act in transgressive ways in entering the political arena, even if he did spiritualize the action to redefine it as being within the realm of feminine virtue. Having interviewed women active in the Gandhian movement, Tanika Sarkar points out, "When women activists returned home, they were transformed human beings, prepared to renegotiate domesticity on new terms."[119] And Mirabai, it seems, contributed to facilitating that transgression, transformation, and renegotiation. These aspects of her story and character continued to run beneath the surface portrayal and, importantly, were still accessed by Gandhi and others as a wellspring of her inspirational power.

A limited but significant number of women chose, and indeed continue to choose, not to marry but instead to devote themselves completely to Gandhian goals and social uplift.[120] Gandhi's Mira provided a model and spiritual justification for such a choice, and as Madhu Kishwar notes, "during the freedom movement led by Gandhi, many male leaders exhorted women to follow the example of Meerabai, who chose to follow the call of conscience rather than the beaten track of matrimony."[121] Winning the support of male members of their natal families was generally essential for women in making this choice, and many continued to live under the protection of fathers and brothers or in Gandhian ashrams. For many theirs was and continues to be a life of simplicity, of *brahmacharya* (chastity), and of service and dedication to "a higher cause." But importantly it is a meaningful life of their own choosing, outside the normative gender roles of mother and wife but within the acceptable alternative of renunciation for the sake of service to humanity and the nation. Kishwar suggests that "under the prevalent social circumstances, brahmacharya had a very liberating potential for women ... [as] perhaps the only way women could free themselves from household drudgery and the burden of childcare to an extent sufficient for them to become active participants in social change."[122]

Gandhi's influence on twentieth-century perceptions of Mirabai has unquestionably been immense. His stature as a pivotal leader of the Freedom Struggle and a recognized "Mahatma," or Great Soul, meant that his words carried extraordinary power. And references to Mira were often among them. Further, the vast majority of those who would portray Mira in the first half of the twentieth century in new forms of mass media, from print to cinema, had met him and participated in his nonviolent campaigns. Gujarati painter and journalist Ravishankar Rawal (1892–1977) would become his disciple, working closely with him, and include Mirabai among his subjects, depicting her dressed in white, adorned only with tulsi beads, playing the *ektara* and *kartals*, seated before an image of Krishna, her eyes half closed as if in a trance.[123] Equally inspired by Gandhi, Rawal's pupil Kanu Desai's series of ten watercolors of the saint, again as an ecstatic and otherworldly mystic dressed in white, continue to grace the covers and pages of books and articles about Mirabai and to influence cinematic portrayals and people's imaginings.[124] Yet in this more mystical portrayal of Mira, Rawal and Desai were no doubt also heavily influenced by others, both Indian and British, from Tod to Tripathi, who had propagated such an image of the saint across the nineteenth century and into the twentieth. Both artists were directly impacted by the Tagores and the Bengali School of Art emanating from Shantiniketan, and some elements in Desai's series, such as Mira's departure from Mewar by camel, also appear in popular Gujarati Mira songs.[125]

Gandhi's Mirabai would also be called upon to rally support for the holistic vision of women's education developed by Gandhian nationalist Swami T. L. Vaswani (1879–1966), who established the headquarters of the nascent Mira Movement for Education in 1933 in Hyderabad, Sindh. Vaswani was a staunch believer that "education is [or should be] a thing of the Spirit and that the end of all knowledge is service—service of the poor and lowly, the sick and afflicted ones."[126] The headquarters of his movement was transferred to Pune after Partition, and St. Mira's School for Girls established there; the high school opened in 1950, followed by the primary school in 1952, and continued to expand as the decades followed, with St. Mira College founded in 1962. Vaswani would write his own story of Mira's life, and images of the saint continued to grace the school grounds, where young girls received both academic and spiritual training (see Figure 5.1).[127] He insisted that education at the school

> should not merely be associated with Mira's name, but should be rooted in the teaching of Mira's songs and Mira's life. Out of this root may, I fondly hope, rise up flowers, rich in beauty and radiance, to bless our community. Think of the stuff of which the heroic Mira was made! Her songs of faith filter through my very blood. She sings from the centre of life which the majority of our schools do not endeavor to touch. A heroic and a prophetic spirit was St. Mira. And in the Mira School an endeavour should be made to see that students grow in the heroic mold of life.[128]

The school's motto, "Simplicity, Service, Purity and Prayer," encapsulates its avowed goal to prepare girls of high moral character to serve humanity, girls modeled on Gandhi's spiritual activist Mirabai—heroic, dedicated to the Truth, without ego, filled with love, bringing beauty and radiance to society and reflecting the best of Indian spirituality and culture.

Figure 5.1 Portrait of Mirabai prominently displayed in Swami T. L. Vaswani's St. Mira School for Girls in Pune (1996)

Though Gandhi did not single-handedly make Mirabai over into this nationalist heroine, his devotion to the saint and his characterizations of her easily flowed alongside other currents in the growing nationalist-rajput synthesis and similarly did not take into account popular traditions that might have more radically challenged gender and caste hierarchies and oppression. Though how familiar Gandhi might have been with these other traditions is unknown, they certainly would have run counter to the image of Mirabai he sought to mobilize. At least some of the popular Mira songs sung in his ashrams do appear to have been selected or perhaps more actively improvised for a new public to more closely enhance his specific image of the satyagrahi saint. For example, Parita Mukta notes the excision of references to widowhood from a Mira song very popular in Gujarat even today, with the clear and pointed claim "I annihilate the fear of widowhood" replaced with the rather generic statement "[T]he happiness that the world gives is like a mirage."[129] Yet for Gandhi renunciation was essential to his conception of the "ascetic activist," as Veena Howard has argued, and neither was Mira a widow nor was widowhood something to fear, in his mind in any case, so the latter singing proves the more impactful and relevant to him and for his community.[130] The line about the world's happiness as illusory is consistent with Mira's renunciation as it is portrayed, for example, in many hagiographic tellings of her life and both fits with many other songs attributed to her and readily supports Gandhi's continuing challenge to women to give up wearing silk and jewels and to share their wealth with the less fortunate. Still many other people continue to sing the song with the alternative line in Mira's voice, as a powerful indictment of the tyranny of social understandings and practices that attend widowhood for so many women, as Shukla-Bhatt confirms.[131]

There seems little place in Gandhi's conception for the aspirational, more individual self-realization marked by the courage to live and to leave, to set out on a new life of one's own choosing, that Tagore's heroine in "Letter from a Wife" found in Mirabai, though Kumudini's rebellious willingness to shatter all her beliefs in the name of truth does find some resonance. Gandhi unquestionably contributed greatly to the formation and dissemination of a spiritualized and heroic nationalist image of the saint—one that left the varna-ashrama-dharma and pativrata ideals largely intact even as he advocated a complementary egalitarianism—adding his own particular take but also the weight of his considerable influence to the authentication of this family of tellings. Yet his Mira, who could transform women into political activists, could and did in fact also facilitate their renegotiation of women's traditional roles and relationships, as she did his own feminine transformation.

Mahadevi Varma: "A Modern Mira"

In the early decades of the twentieth century, individual women would carve out more independent lives, becoming powerful public orators and political leaders and achieving a hard-won respect and self-realization much more akin to that articulated by Tagore's Mrinal. Some would come to draw specifically but in varying measures on the twin authority of Gandhi and Mira in doing so. Chhayavad Hindi poet and champion of women's emancipation and education Mahadevi Varma (1902–1987) would be explicitly likened to the saint.[132] Highly acclaimed as the first woman poet of modern Hindi, Mahadevi was a respected educator, essayist, editor, painter, and literary theorist and a powerful advocate for Hindi language and literature. Though she was not a devotee of God in the traditional bhakti sense, her lyrical poetry brought to mind the intensity and purity of Mira's longing, and there were striking parallels between her own life and Mira's in other ways. Her association with Gandhian activism, her simple ascetic lifestyle, and the example of Mirabai made her choice to reject her arranged child marriage and to move in a literary world of men acceptable, if exceptional, and comprehensible, though she—like the saint—was subjected to intense criticism and scandalous rumors.

Mahadevi knew of Mira from her childhood and deeply admired her. She fondly remembers waking and going to sleep, hearing her mother sing Mira bhajans together with morning songs and lullabies.[133] From her mother she learned both to sing the songs of Mira, Kabir, Surdas, and others and to begin to compose her own verses. Her mother often sang Mira's "*Suni main Hari ki avaz*" ("I heard the sound/voice/call of Hari"), and one day Mahadevi asked if her mother could indeed hear that voice of God.[134] She said yes, but in order to hear it, one must have a tranquil and concentrated mind. Taking these words to heart, the young Mahadevi sat with eyes closed, sometimes for hours, but the sound eluded her. She complained to her mother, who assured her that sometime in the future, if she persisted, she would hear it. Mahadevi reported that with time her mind did become very still and focused, and in those moments she did hear. As she would come to realize, she had learned much from Mira, who played a crucial role in her developing inner life and sense of herself. Significantly, Mira songs were a language and vehicle through which Mahadevi's mother passed down to her daughter her own deep spiritual wisdom, teaching Mahadevi to cultivate an inner silence that would in time allow her to know an indwelling divine presence, in addition to facilitating her earliest poetic experimentation.

Rather than being an outpouring of devotional sentiment, Mahadevi's own mature poetry would be something else entirely, composed in the Chhayavad style, profoundly influenced by Tagore and marked by a dramatic shift away from earlier Braj Bhasha poetry of bhakti and courtly love and from the didactic rationalism, nationalism, and social reform and the formal poetic structure of the first wave of modern Hindi poetry led by Mahavirprasad

Dvivedi. In contrast, Chhayavad poety articulated a visionary subjectivity and sensuality in a freer lyrical verse form.[135] Mahadevi was the youngest and the only woman of the four major poets who pioneered this radically new style of poetry from 1918 to 1938.

Writing poetry, for Mahadevi, was a deliberate exercise in intellectual and spiritual growth, as Karine Schomer details in her insightful analysis of Mahadevi's life and work.[136] Those reading her poems recognized the emotional depths being explored, but in Schomer's estimation sometimes moved too quickly and simplistically to conclude that she was either a mystic or a repressed and lonely woman writing of sexual longing. Mahadevi saw herself as experiencing and telling a "love myth" that she entered imaginatively in the act of writing and which led to her own emotional transformation. She published five volumes of poetry: *Nihar* (Mist, 1930), *Rashmi* (Ray of Light, 1932), *Niraja* (Water Lily, 1934), *Sandhya-git* (Twilight Song, 1936), and *Dipshikha* (Lamp-Flame, 1942).

Her poetry and that of her fellow Chhayavad poets articulated, in her words, "a wonderous sense of the relatedness of all things that can give the heart a firm grounding, raise love above the worldly level, and create a harmony between the intellect and the emotions."[137] She would write of literature generally that through it "we are able to live at many deep and unfamiliar levels of life and in many unknown worlds of imagination. We broaden our lives, deepen our emotional experience, and thereby *intimately bind ourselves to the totality of life.*"[138] There is a deep spirituality articulated here, marked by a sense of cosmic relatedness and unity and the grandeur of nature, enhanced and intensified by the imagination rather than merely described.[139] There is a distinctive continuity with earlier poetic and religious traditions, including bhakti but also the Upanishads, reflective of "the attempt to make concepts, images and themes from the past personally meaningful and relevant, that characterized the Chhayavad poets' approach to their cultural heritage."[140] Mahadevi herself contended that modern Hindi (and the poetry she wrote) was deeply rooted in the songs and language of bhakti.[141] Yet though her poems spoke of impassioned and embodied love, often from the perspective of the *virahini,* or "separated lover," they were hardly a carbon copy of bhakti, nirgun or sagun, and the voice was decidedly her own.[142] Accordingly, Mahadevi fought the oversimplified identification of her poetry as a twentieth-century version of Mira's bhajans, even as she was honored by the comparison to the woman poet considered the measure of all others in Hindi literature.

It was her poetry that first led people to call her a "modern Mira," in particular her increasing adoption of the virahini persona in her second volume, but Mahadevi's life also paralleled that of the saint in striking ways. Born into a *kayastha* family, she was well-educated, precociously demanding to be allowed to study Sanskrit and the Vedas and Upanishads—something girls just did not do, though her progressive, English-educated father supported her in this endeavor, providing her with home tutors from the age of five.[143] At her grandfather's insistence, however, her father nevertheless arranged her marriage when she was only eleven.

As she recalls, she did not know what was happening when the groom's family arrived with great fanfare; she fell asleep before the ceremony and woke in the morning to find a knot in her sari which she quickly untied. She refused to go home with these unfamiliar visitors, and when forced to do so, she wept constantly and refused to eat until she was sent back to her parents. She never accepted this marriage or any other, in spite of all her mother's attempts at persuasion. Out of concern for her happiness, her father suggested that she convert to another religion, an act that would automatically nullify her first marriage so that she could marry again; he even offered to convert with her. But she was not interested in marriage. She had other things to do.[144]

Mahadevi began composing poetry from a young age, and her first poems were published in literary journals in 1922. She and her sister had been sent in 1918 to Crosthwaite College in Allahabad, a vibrant center of Hindi literary activity, second only to Banaras, and a nexus for progressive reform and nationalist agitation, home to the Nehrus.[145] Having been made the provincial capital of the Northwest Provinces after the 1857 revolt, "in the second half of the nineteenth century Allahabad became a city of reform movements, educational institutions, printing presses, libraries and journalism," with a growing educated middle class.[146] The tremendously influential Hindi literary magazine *Sarasvati* was inaugurated there in 1900, with poet Mahavirprasad Dvivedi stepping into the editorship in 1903.

In 1910 Allahabad was selected to be the home for the newly formed Hindi Sahitya Sammelan, designed to complement the Banaras-based Nagari Pracharini Sabha's scholarly publication agenda by fostering "the use of Hindi and the appreciation of Hindi literature among the general public."[147] The literary journal *Sammelan Patrika* was started in 1913 to support Hindi writers, and a series of literary prizes initiated in 1914, with a national curriculum and examination system developed in Hindi to parallel the English education system. Around 1920 students in the Hindu Boarding House at the University of Allahabad began organizing Hindi poetry readings, popular gatherings that quickly spread to other boarding houses, and in 1924 the university appointed its first professor of Hindi, with a department to follow.

The saint-poet Mira was embraced as one of the Hindi literary greats of the past, and accordingly her songs needed to be made available for the new Hindi reading public. Belvedere Press had been founded in Allahabad in 1900 by Baleshvar Prasad Agarwal, an influential member of the Radhasoami Satsang (a nineteenth-century reform movement that played an instrumental role in popularizing the works of nirgun saints).[148] The Press published a small set of Mira songs in 1909 and many subsequent editions, and in 1932 Hindi Sahitya Sammelan published the first edition of the enduring collection of Parashuram Chaturvedi, one of those students in the Hindu Boarding House who went on to become a professor of Hindi. It was in this vibrant Hindi literary community, particularly supportive of young writers, that Mahadevi would come into her own as a poet.

The young Mahadevi completed high school in 1925 and then her BA at Crosthwaite before going on to complete an MA in Sanskrit at the University of Allahabad. Dedicating herself to her education, and then increasingly to the cause of women's education and empowerment and to the development of Hindi literature, she also wrote with immense compassion about the lives of ordinary people, demonstrating a great empathy and respect for the poor as well as for women, as does the Mira of low-caste traditions. Mahadevi relished the opportunity to come to know all manner of people, volunteering her free time to teach in the villages of Jhusi and Arail from her college days until Independence, and in later years attending the communal bathing festivals of the Kumbha Mela and Megh Mela. The literary world in which she spent much of her time, however, was predominantly male, as was the leadership of the religious world the saint Mira inhabited, and though she would thrive in this milieu, she similarly had to overcome the dismissive attitudes of some men within it, even as she suffered from speculation about her morality and relationships.

She allegedly did consider becoming a Buddhist nun at one point during her undergraduate years, not in order to annul her marriage but because she enjoyed solitude and saw this as a way to live and move about as a woman alone and to continue her spiritual growth and social service. However, it is said that when she went for an interview with a Theravada Buddhist abbot, he covered his face with a fan while talking to her. She learned afterward that he never looked at the face of a woman as part of his religious discipline. Mahadevi was disillusioned by this, as well as by his less than spartan lifestyle. The parallel with Mira and Jiv Goswami is unmistakable, and Schomer notes that there is some doubt whether this encounter ever really took place, suggesting that it may have been generated by the identification of Mahadevi and Mira.[149]

Mahadevi never affiliated herself with any formal religious institution, though she lived a kind of monastic existence nonetheless. In answer to the call of Gandhi and Nehru, she gave up jewelry and put on white khadi in

1929, continuing to wear it throughout her life.[150] This, too, contributed to her Mira image, as did her beauty, intelligence, and outspoken independent character. Further inspired by Gandhi, she took a vow no longer to speak English but only Hindi, and she became a gifted and popular orator, able to "[make] her audience resonate with her at the deepest levels of Indian cultural identity."[151] She did much to foster the development of Hindi literature as well, thereby contributing to the nationalist project of promoting Hindi as the national language, though as Anita Anantharam argues, she advocated an inclusivist rather than exclusivist notion of language, resisting the communalist division of Hindi and Urdu. She wrote with nostalgia about her childhood experiences of the fluid ways in which people communicated across regional languages, readily using words and imagery of Sanskrit, Braj Bhasha, Awadhi, and Persio-Arabic/Urdu origins in her writings.[152]

In 1933 Mahadevi became the first resident principal of Prayag (Allahabad) Mahila Vidhyapith's newly established women's college, which she transformed from an examination center into a thriving institution of higher learning for women that combined "the self-respect of women . . . [with an] emphasis on Gandhian idealism and the cultivation of the arts."[153] In this period, higher education of women, particularly in Hindi and outside government institutions, was considered essential for the "constructivist" dimension of the nationalist struggle (and consequently viewed as potentially seditious by the British.) The wives and daughters of many Congress leaders were among Mahila Vidhyapith's students, and Mahadevi considered her first duty to be the continuation of the education of her charges and their protection. She refused to allow police to interrogate them, and she is alleged to have engaged in clandestine activities, including printing and distributing illegal Congress materials and aiding political fugitives.[154] Residing within the campus grounds as principal afforded Mahadevi the opportunity to receive all manner of visitors and to develop the kinds of "literary friendships and political camaraderie" with men newly possible for independent educated women, while still maintaining the required "strict code of chastity and respectability."[155]

Mahadevi also served for three years as editor of the Hindi journal *Chand*, the highly acclaimed public forum for women's issues and women's voices, that was founded in 1922 and changed the face of such publications. Francesca Orsini discusses in detail the impact of this and other women's journals in the period 1920–1940. Of *Chand*'s innovations she writes:

> [F]rom the very beginning the awakening and activities of women in the Hindi belt were seen as part of a countrywide, indeed a worldwide phenomenon. Though

most of the longer articles and special issues centered on north Indian women and society, the news section offered information, facts, and figures on women all over India and abroad as if they were part of the same, irresistible wave. This both legitimized women's initiatives and increased their self-confidence to go further. Also, while addressing the educated and newly literate women, *Chāṁd* did not limit itself to issues concerning them but as part of the same project of social and political regeneration that touched on those affecting peasants and workers: all kinds of oppression had to be denounced in the quest for *svarajya* [self-rule].[156]

Commanding a large readership, the journal "was soon recommended for public and school libraries by the Education departments of the United Provinces, Punjab, Bihar and Rajasthan," significantly not seeking "to 'teach' or reform women [as earlier journals had] but to reform 'society' on their behalf," and serving as an "important forum for women's self-awareness and an instrument of politicization" as well as "recognizing women as emotional beings, questioning their homebound existence, and envisioning new public roles."[157] But when its editor Ramrakh Singh Saghal serialized a blatantly nationalist history of British rule in India in 1929, the editor and the journal immediately came under intense pressure and censorship. Its recommended status was revoked, leading to great financial hardship and Saghal's eventual resignation.

Mahadevi took over the editorship a few years later, increasing the number of women contributors, giving a more literary focus to the journal, and more directly addressing the middle-class and elite educated women who were its primary readers.[158] Schomer discusses Mahadevi's insightful editorials written during these years, noting that Mahadevi took up the many specific challenges Indian women faced but also provided a sophisticated and cogent analysis of both the causes and repercussions of the current state of affairs and the kind of attitudinal and behavioral shifts required to effect real change.[159] As the first woman editor of any such journal, her focus was on the need for women to be able to define themselves, to develop as individuals, rather than remaining mere shadows of men or merely imitating them. She identified education as the key means for women to come into their own, individually, socially, economically, and politically.

In her oft-quoted essay "The Links in Our Chain," Mahadevi affirms the universal need for individual development: "In the human communities of the world, only those individuals are considered alive and capable of receiving a certain status and respect whose hearts and minds are properly developed and who are capable, by virtue of their personality, to forge intellectual bonds and emotional ties with human society. Everyone needs to develop an independent personality, because without it, a person can neither consider his willpower and resolve his own, nor can he gauge his actions on the scales of justice and injustice."[160] This egalitarian stance toward men and women is followed immediately by an affirmation that women do not need to become like men to do this. Instead she describes women and men as having different natures which are equally necessary to a harmonious society, to be equally valued, and in this she asserts women's emancipation on "women's" as well as "Indian" terms. Women need not give up being women as they develop their "individual, appropriate, and rational personalities," and indeed were they to do so, this would be like a prisoner slicing off his feet in the process of cutting through his shackles. She instead claims the right for women to determine what it means to be women, thereby allowing their unique energy and power as women to be set free as a source for change and justice and for beauty and harmony in society, in addition to the many contributions they may offer based on their individual talents.

In this she is seeking balance, acknowledging the value of the roles of wife and mother but insisting that women should not be limited to these. She is advocating conscious choice and, in Schomer's words, "a genuine equality of status in the performance of complementary duties ... [so that] the relations between the sexes could be reformulated without the social fabric being completely torn apart."[161] Social embeddedness and responsibility remain front and center, coupled with a love which should encompass family but also flow outward to humanity at large. In doing so, she is consistent with the constructivist, regenerative nationalist agenda even while radically challenging oppression and suppression of women at all levels, even equating marriage with slavery, as Tagore did and Keshub Chunder Sen before him.[162] And she is also keenly aware that once women awaken to their own selfhood and power, they cannot be expected to go back to sleep. She knows this will cause inevitable and considerable disruption to society—so be it. Some criticized her for being too radical, others for not being sufficiently revolutionary (as the saint continues to be criticized), but she was able to embody a respected Indian womanhood—decidedly not as a companionate pativrata of the nationalist new patriarchy but as a "modern Mira"—and as such she could advance her constructive agenda for the education and awakening of women *and* men. A number of her editorial essays were collected and published in 1943 and have been read by subsequent generations of Indian college women, inspiring them both to break the chains that bind them and to understand their place as vital links in the fabric of society and nation.[163]

Mahadevi's prose writing takes a hard-hitting analytical and objective approach to the problems facing women in India and what it will take to improve the situation on the part of both men and women and for the good of the collective society. The voice in her poetry is vastly different, though here too she proved highly inspirational. Mahadevi found prose entirely appropriate for analyzing the external social realm, but poetry gave expression to the inner world.[164] Yet to read her poetry as the direct statement either of her personal desire for God or of her loneliness as a single woman, Schomer argues, is to radically misunderstand it. Instead, "Mahadevi's poetry was the means by which she created within herself certain states of mind she wished to experience."[165] Though similar in its transformative intent to bhakti poetry, "[i]n Mahadevi's case . . . it was not religious devotion she sought to nurture in her inner self, but the emotional richness of a love relationship."[166] Like the other Chhayavad poets, she creates a poetic "I" different from the actual individual "I"—an imaginative subjectivity which Anantharam identifies as that of the ideal emancipated woman—through which she could envision and explore the depths and heights of love and relationship possible for such a fully individuated self-realized woman and express feelings in a way not necessarily revealing of individual ordinary relationships but rather of capacity and potentiality.[167]

In this, she took women's "right to feel" (advocated by women's journals in this period) into heightened realms of imagination, affirming love, sensuality, and an ecstasy merging on the mystical.[168] Though she was a dedicated Gandhian, her poetry evinced a sensuality and view of women's sexuality in dramatic contrast to Gandhi's ascetic activist ideal and not necessarily confined to marital relations. Given the imperfection of actual human relationships and the limitations of the era—when men's and women's interactions were so highly circumscribed and independent women had to maintain impeccable reputations in order to be accepted as respectable and to protect this option for women who came after them—this imaginative experience, Schomer concedes, may have allowed her to experience what ordinary life did not and "to live at many deep and unfamiliar levels of life and in many unknown worlds of imagination," as indeed she herself had written of literature's power, and thereby to achieve the transformation of emotion and intellect she sought in this crucible of inner experience.[169]

The independent lives of women such as Mahadevi did allow them more interaction with men and opened up at least "the possibility for love and sexual relationships, [though if these occurred, they] had to be kept away from the public gaze."[170] It is also the case that, as Orsini notes, "[t]he obliqueness of Chhayavad poetry was eminently suited for . . . [a] strategy . . . of voicing personal yearnings through a poetic 'I' and within a safely unspecified and circumscribed space, and many women poets at the time followed her on this path."[171] Though Mahadevi and those who write about her continue to make careful distinctions between her poetry and Mira's, it seems likely that songs sung and composed in Mirabai's name and voice—in a Mira "I"—have operated in similar ways and serve similar expressive and transformative functions.

Dvivedi and other supporters of the first wave of Hindi poetry and those who embraced the Progressive movement that followed would criticize Mahadevi and other Chhayavad poets for being disengaged from the political realities of the day and involved in a self-absorbed fantasy, "irrelevant and escapist," though Schomer contends that they were, in fact, "seeking to refashion an entire cultural identity," a task foundational and essential to the nationalist struggle.[172] In her own defense against Progressivist critics who insisted poetry should be about the grit and grime of real life, Mahadevi asserted of poetry and song, "When a poor woman grinding flour hums along as she works, her song is not about the grinding stone and the grain, but perhaps about swinging in a mango grove. We may call this escapism, but it could also be called enrichment of reality; and, beyond the question of definition, we recognize it as an essential human drive."[173] Songs attributed to the saint Mirabai have been similarly characterized either as compensatory and escapist or as inspirational, rebellious, and visionary, at times reflecting the world as it is, at other times as it should or could be.

In any case, with the publication of her fifth book of poetry in 1942 (the poems completed by 1938), Mahadevi would cease writing poetry for publication.[174] Why she did so is unknown and has been the subject of much conjecture. Was it because she had completed her self-appointed poetic intellectual/spiritual project; because Chhayavad had lost its edge in finally becoming accepted and widely imitated; because her poems generated excessive speculation about who her real-life lover might be, detracting from her social work; or because she simply had other things that demanded her full attention?[175] She did not say, but the Chhayavad movement effectively ended in 1938, though it would remain popular and increasingly appreciated as a crucial development in modern Hindi literature, and many subsequent women poets would be inspired and encouraged by Mahadevi's example.[176]

Mahadevi is also known for initiating another genre of Hindi literature, the life sketch, in which she did write lyrically about the realities of the external world.[177] She wrote a series of very compelling and popular short pieces about very ordinary people with whom she came in contact and who had impacted her life. She described their life circumstances and struggles and her interactions with them, in insightful and poignant ways that spoke to the heart as well as the mind. Her first set of such life sketches was published in 1941, though she began writing them in 1920, initially for personal remembrance. There is something here of the romanticization of the rural life found in other nationalist writings of the time. But more than this there is a keen awareness of the dynamics of relationships and of the tragedies great and small that mark the lives of the marginalized, as well as a respect for their individuality with all that that entails and for their resilience as they try to craft lives of dignity for themselves and their "families," whether by birth or association. In these accounts, Mahadevi appears as an "eloquent witness," her attention focused on her subject, resulting in what Orsini describes as "a dark private core in an otherwise fairly public life."[178] Orsini goes on to suggest that the more objective analytical style of her essays coupled with the poetic "I" of her poetry and the outward trajectory of these life sketches allowed Mahadevi, as "a woman alone, to have a *private* life, live independently and remain respectable," and to demonstrate to others that this was possible.[179] Her ability to do so turned on her Gandhian dedication to service and society and, I would argue, on the association of her life and character and of her sensual, erotic poetry with the saint Mirabai, in addition to these rhetorical strategies.[180]

Her association with the saint was multidimensional. Though she was not a Krishna devotee and at times was critical of organized religion, she had a deeply spiritual sensibility. Her poetry was highly praised and thematically similar to works attributed to Mira, with a continuity of passion and imagery. She did not hesitate to reject social prescriptions for women, and her strong sense of who she was challenged the definition of a woman solely in terms of her relationships with men, as her words did. To come to terms with her place in the cultural landscape, people compared her to Mira. Though initially resisting this identification, she later came to accept and even embrace it, delivering a series of lectures on the saint in 1975.[181] To a certain degree, she reinforced a version of Mira that appealed to the upper- and middle-class imagination and reflected elements of the rajput-nationalist synthesis—well-educated, beautiful, impetuous but dignified and cultured. Yet she also embodied rebellion against social restrictions that made her a "cultural hero" to some and opened her up to slander from other quarters.[182]

A kind of mystique arose around this "modern Mira," which Schomer describes thus: "What fascinated people about Mahadevi was her complex personality, attractive in its strength and independence, mystifying in its reserve and formality. . . . Above all, she was a 'woman alone' who had dared to rebel against her child marriage, yet insisted on being considered a respectable member of society—a symbol of woman's independence at a time when independent women were increasingly portrayed in literature but rarely found in real life."[183] Yet though she was admired, Mahadevi was also suspect, particularly with regard to her private life—precisely the sort of woman Tagore's critics so feared.

Of independent modern women such as herself, Mahadevi observed, "Old-fashioned men look down upon them with contempt; modern-minded men support them but are unable to help them actively and the radicals encourage them but find it hard to take them along."[184] Such women were in some sense also caught between the past and the future, and each had to find "a balance between her individual convictions and social expectations" in order to be able to act effectively while living authentically.[185] Though they might be dismissed as few in number and exceptional, Mahadevi asserted, "They may be exceptions, but it is only such exceptional people who are worthy of bringing forth new changes that oppose the traditional order. Without such individuals, we could not even comprehend how something seemingly impossible could be possible or normal."[186] Mahadevi was such a modern enlightened woman. She was no memsahib and no surrogate man but instead a woman at once Indian, independent, intelligent, and feminine, who with grace could and did hold her own in a man's world—a woman to be taken seriously who had found her own voice in multiple registers and did not hesitate to speak out and act publicly on a whole host of issues. In short, a modern woman like Mira.

The sixteenth-century saint clearly played a role in Mahadevi's becoming, helping to make it possible to conceive of such a life and in some sense authorizing her choices, her actions and her words within the larger society. Though the young Mahadevi may not have consciously chosen Mirabai as a model, the saint was clearly a presence in her life from her earliest memories and part of the gendered cultural heritage that would shape her and on which she would draw. Some would seek to limit Mahadevi with the identification, as they tried to limit the saint, reducing both to otherworldly mystics and their speech to a generic devotion. But neither Mahadevi nor the saint, it seems, would stand for this. Mahadevi embodied Mirabai for many in her time, demonstrating the potential and ongoing relevance of the saint—how she might act and speak and feel, what challenges she might offer to the powers that be, the actions she might inspire, and the "impossible" selves women might craft in her exceptional image, quite beyond Tagore's literary heroines and Gandhi's saintly satyagrahi. The saint made Mahadevi's unique and powerful personality and life recognizable within the broad spectrum of accepted and beloved Indian modes of being female, and she would come to be recognized and honored as an exemplar of Indian self-respect and cultural heritage, even as the saint Mirabai was, though in radically different guises. Yet some feared the explosive and disruptive potential of such an exemplar, and the saint's life and character continued to be a site of contestation among overlapping British and Indian constituencies, seeking to draw on, and in at least one case to destroy, her powerful appeal.

6
Cultural Icon for a Nation in the Making

As Tagore was writing of Mrinal, Gandhi's fearless satyagrahi Mira was taking shape, and Mahadevi was coming into her own as a quite different "modern Mira," others continued to propagate compelling stories of this heroic saint, who would play such a vital role in the crafting of emerging Indian cultural, national, and religious identities. Across the early decades of the twentieth century, dramas and biographies in print form multiplied in Telegu, Tamil, Hindi, Sindhi, Marathi, Gujarati, Rajasthani, Bengali, and English, combining elements from Dutt, Deviprasad, and other circulating traditions in various measure, as Macauliffe had, and also disseminating low-caste tales that challenged and contested upper-caste formulations of nation and caste. Written for popular consumption, many aimed explicitly to shape the minds of young audiences, informed by a clear nationalist agenda, and sought to instill moral rectitude and cultural pride and to motivate courageous self-sacrifice. Colonial educators, too, took up her tale, seeking to do just the opposite in the battle for control of those same young minds.

Other individuals and new forms of media would also have profound impacts on perceptions of the saint, reaching people across the subcontinent and beyond and into the twenty-first century. Retired lawyer and respected Krishna devotee and theologian Bankey Behari wrote an immensely influential biography of the saint, recognizing her as his guru and experiencing her incarnate in his sole disciple. His work was picked up by Gita Press and carried along with their larger program to promulgate a socially conservative Hindu orthodoxy and was widely disseminated in multiple languages and later in comic book form. The introduction of film, first silent and then with sound, provided still another avenue to propagate other Miras, to explore her exemplary potential, and to further her transformation into a cultural icon for the nation, most poignantly as she was portrayed by M. S. Subbulakshmi on the cusp of Independence.

Mirabai in the Battle for Hearts and Minds

Annie Besant (1847–1933) wrote of Mira in her *Children of the Motherland* (1906), a volume intended "to inspire Indian youths and maidens, on whom the future of India depends."[1] Well-known for her social and political activism in England and India, Besant was a tireless supporter of Indian self-rule and unity, social reform, Hindu revivalism, and universal education as well as the owner-editor of the Madras daily newspaper she renamed *New India* and president not only of the Theosophical Society (1907–1933) but also of the Indian National Congress in 1917.[2] She established the Central Hindu College (a predecessor to Banaras Hindu University, founded in 1913) as well as the Sons of India and Daughters of India, designed to reach out to younger children, the aim of her work "the inculcation of pride in being Indian and the virtues of Hindu civilization," in addition to disseminating "principles of nationalism."[3] She was the author of a number of works on politics as well as theosophy, including *How India Wrought for Freedom* (1914) and *India: A Nation* (1915), in addition to being the guardian and promoter of Krishnamurti (lauded by Theosophists as the anticipated next World Teacher).

Gandhi met her in his early years in England, where it was Theosophists who in some sense reintroduced him to the *Bhagavad Gita*, and he initiated one of his earlier nonviolent campaigns in India in 1917 to secure her release after she had been arrested for her role and that of *New India* and the Theosophical Society in agitation for Home Rule. Though Gandhi, Tagore, and other Indian nationalists might not always agree with her tactics and have reservations about the Theosophical Society, they respected her intellect, tenacity, and self-sacrifice and her devotion to India, and she played a vital role in nationalist and colonial politics as a prolific writer and an extraordinary organizer and orator, particularly in this period.[4]

In *Children of the Motherland*, Besant includes stories of Akbar, rajput heroes, Shivaji, and Nanak to foster a sense of a shared heroic past "wrought by children of the common Motherland," a past in which Muslim, Hindu, and Sikh could take pride. She included the stories of heroic women as well as men, Mirabai among them, drawing on Deviprasad (likely via Macauliffe) for dates and family relations but narratively following Dutt. Her Mira is one who cares only for God, is "clever and of exceeding beauty, yet humble and graciously tender to one and all." In her telling, Mira implores her mother not to force her to marry. Her wishes are disregarded, but she cares nothing for the world, living in utter simplicity even in her palace home. Her husband does become very angry with her, and the snake and poison cup are brought back into the tale, but she is sweetness, innocence, and humility throughout (as Tripathi had earlier characterized her), and the tale ends as Dutt's does, in reconciliation and "happily ever after." Besant's Mira, akin to the romanticized Mira of earlier British and Indian nationalist accounts, evinces the universal spirituality advocated by Theosophists, even as she fosters pride in a shared Indian spiritual heritage and the Hindu-Muslim unity seen by Besant and others as essential to India's wresting the right to self-governance from the British.[5]

Dutt's storyline would be repeated even more directly by Australian-born Theosophical Society historian and leader Josephine Maria Davies Ransom (1879–1960) in her *Indian Tales of Love and Beauty* (1912) focusing specifically on Indian women.[6] Ransom credits Besant with introducing her to the study of Indian women and portrays Mira with the same mystical sweetness, incorporating the snake and poison as Besant had. Her motivation, however, is to dispel the ignorance of people *outside* India and thereby win support for India's self-rule by showing (with some ambivalence) "that Indian women are not, as a rule, hidden, badly-treated and incomprehensible mysteries; but are mostly, delightful human beings, even if they do throb in their own special way to the pulse of life."[7] She details the stories of Maitreyi, Savitri, and a range of heroic Hindu, Buddhist, and Muslim women, including Mirabai, all in the style of pativrata viranganas. She goes on to conclude that "the truly great among them realised, as has every noble woman of whatever nationality that: The path of duty is the way of glory," in a universalization that both reaffirms dharma and highlights Indian women's heroism rather than victimization.

Irish poet and fellow Theosophist James H. Cousins (1873–1956), adding his voice to wider calls for national unity, wrote a play titled *The King's Wife* (1919), dramatizing Dutt's telling of the encounter between Mira and Akbar and stressing her embrace of a universal love of God that left no room for religious exclusivity or conflict between Hindu and Muslim.[8] Cousins came to India at Besant's invitation in 1915, accompanying his far more well-known wife, Margaret, who would play an instrumental role in working for women's suffrage in India and cofounding the Women's Indian Association. He is clear in the preface to his work that what he writes is not history; though Akbar and Mirabai could not have been contemporaries, he recounts an extended conversation between the two after Akbar unquestionably, even if respectfully, physically touches the rajput queen's feet. Rather than history, Cousins seeks to present "three types of religious expression (the spiritual adventure and breadth of Akbar, the simple devotion of Mira, the inquisitorial fanaticism of Kumbha) which are contemporaneous in all lands and ages."[9]

He readily admits to taking liberties with the saint's story, including ending it without miracles in her death; others could add those back as an epilogue if they choose, he concedes. In his telling it is the rana's jealousy and the corruption of power that drive a wedge between the formerly happy pair, yet Mira is ever the obedient "king's wife," taking her own life when no one else will obey his command. The story ends with reports of her demise in the flooded Jamuna, having fearlessly embraced death as the gateway to the inner Vrindavan, her spiritual home.[10] Mira thus becomes a spokesperson for the singular inner reality common to all religions, the particular details of her life rallied to support this rationalized spiritual realization. Indian spirituality is lauded (at least in its allegedly universal "simple devotion"), even as Mira's position as a wife at the mercy of a brutal, fanatical husband conforms to British characterizations of the moral bankruptcy of Indian society and women's victimization as well as romanticization. And having lent her authority to the Theosophist cause, it appears this Mira can be dispensed with: she commits suicide, however honorably.

Cousins reports that he drew his plot from "a tattered booklet" he came across quite by chance and incorporated songs he had heard performed into the dialogue of his play, yet the saint also got under his skin as well.[11] He had initially intended to write a fifth act in accordance with his source, but just as Tagore did not want his heroine Kumudini made over into a compliant wife in dramatic performances of *Yogayog*, so Cousins resisted reconciliation between Mira and his "fanatical" rana, as anticlimactic to such a tragic drama. He felt compelled to go to Rajasthan for authenticity's sake, and the opportunity arose when his work on behalf of universal education took him in that direction. Along the way, he agreed to give a lecture at Gandhi's Sabarmati Ashram if it might be followed by the singing of Mira songs, which he recalls "got into [his] memory to bloom," particularly the very well-known one in which Mira asks Krishna to make her his servant.[12] When Cousins finally reached the threshold of Mira's Temple in Chittor, he spontaneously entered a meditative state. He writes, "When I returned to outer consciousness I was alone, with silence, and half-light, and dimly seen pillars and a graven image, and a memory vivified by an inner reality and a certainty as to my effort to put something of the beauty and devotion of Mira's tragic but triumphant life into the purest verse I could command."[13] It was only after these experiences that he completed the drama, notably without a fifth act.

Margaret Cousins would also champion the saint, including Mirabai among other women of India "honored for their outstanding capacity in religion, statesmanship, rulership, philosophy, travel, imagination, courage, strength, gentleness, wise self-sacrifice, learning and beauty."[14] She promoted the production of her husband's play, insisting that the female roles be played by young women (though the idea of public production evoked extreme social opposition to women acting, mixed rehearsing, and the like and ultimately had to be called off).[15]

Based at Adyar, Madras, members of the Theosophical Society and its charismatic leader were extremely influential and their publications distributed across India and abroad. R. Srinivasan cited Besant as the inspiration and source for his earlier katha performances as well as his 1919 explicitly didactic play on Mira's life, originally published in serial form over a two-year period in the Tamil magazine *Poorna Chandrodhayam*.[16] Clearly Mirabai was already popular in Tamil Nadu before the Theosophists arrived.[17] However, they added to traditions swirling around her, as their widely distributed tellings along with many others continued to be published, read, and enacted across the 1920s and beyond throughout India.

Mirabai was also brought to Europe and the United States as representative of the best of a unified Indian cultural and spiritual heritage. Pir-o-Murshid Hazrat Inayat Khan (1882–1927), the extraordinarily talented Indian classical musician, was sent by his Sufi master to introduce Indian music and spirituality to the West. He arrived in the United States in 1910 and traveled, performed, and lectured there and across Europe for the next sixteen years, making France his home. He ultimately gave up his music, that which was most precious to him, and became the founder of the International Sufi Movement, a universal religious movement flowing from India to the West, in contrast to the Theosophists, though both found in Mirabai an ambassador for their universal teachings. At the age of twenty-one, Khan was given the title "Tansen of India" by the Nazim of Hyderabad in recognition of his extraordinary talent, and in 1916 he wrote a play about the illustrious musician, titled simply *Tansen*, in which Mira figures prominently.[18] Inspired by Parsi theater productions he had seen as a child, he embraced drama as an excellent means of introducing Western audiences to Indian traditions.[19] In his play, Akbar travels to the Himalayas with Tansen to hear his Sufi teacher sing, disguising himself as Tansen's servant, but it is his court singer who first encounters Mira on his own.

Consumed by the fires of mystic realization, he finds in Mira a healer, for when she sings, the rains gather and quench his burning. He pledges himself to her, moving to touch her feet, though she stops him out of humility. "He then, holding her hands, kisses them and places them to his breast," embarrassing the shy Mira and sparking the outrage of those gathered who berate Mira and try to kill Tansen, who in turn is rescued by Akbar's soldiers sent to find him and bring him back. In the next and final act, Mira is in Dwarka, having become a renouncer, and Tansen, not recognizing her, asks if she can direct him to Mira. She responds, "Mira is dead," and Tansen is distraught, saying that if this is so, then life is not worth living and he would prefer to die. Mira tells him that his life is not his own but belongs to God and gives him the robes of a sannyasi: "Come and adorn this garb of humility, may the rich ones of the world envy your poverty, may life's grandeur kiss the feet of thy simplicity. Live for God, and live forever. Thou art dead to the unrealities of life, but alive until the real and lasting. Mira is not far from thee, neither art thou separated from her. Raise thine eyes and behold, lo, here is Mira. The living dead thou could'st not have found hadst thou not been dead to mortal life."[20] Only now does Akbar arrive, as well as Mira's family members, to celebrate her sainthood and listen to her sing.

Here Mira is a prophet of a universal path to Love, with bhakti and the Sufi way one and the same. She is ever humble and reserved in the presence of unsolicited male attention yet undeterred by condemnation, and she is a spiritual teacher of great wisdom, able to instruct men and fulfilling the role of guru. Hindu and Muslim are portrayed as part of a unified spiritual and cultural heritage, with music readily transporting all to the realm of Love and both affirming a mystic renunciation. Mirabai embodies this unity and spiritual path. The play is addressed to Western audiences and also reflects Khan's own teachings, and she is a woman of substance who is honored and respected for her wisdom, strength, and humility.[21] Rather than passing away tragically as she does in Cousins's play, here she remains center stage, offering spiritual sustenance that might nourish seekers in East and West alike.

Back in India, however, Oxford University Press published a series of plays and dramatic dialogues "suitable for schools," including a series from Indian history, authored by educator Eleanor Lucia Turnbull and dramatist R. Watkins. (Turnbull wrote more than fifty children's books of history, legend, fairy tales, and folk tales from India, England, Wales, Ireland, Scotland, Scandinavia, Japan, and North America.) The vignettes for the first volume of the series, published in 1931, were drawn from the lives of Samudragupta, Mirabai, Sher Shah, and Shivaji.[22] Their tone and intent differed vastly from the work of Besant and her fellow Theosophists, Pir Hazrat Inayat Khan, and other Indian nationalists and devotional writers (and even from earlier British primary school vernacular textbooks).[23] Aiming to teach Indian students both history and English through the "entertaining and engaging" mode of drama, the authors hoped that the students might also "gain insight into the various types of character, and learn, almost instinctively to put themselves in the place of others"—a "priceless faculty" for improving the world (a vital role of literature in Mahadevi's view as well). However, the dialogue was moralistic, and the authors deliberately chose to focus on the more domestic side of historical characters' lives in the hope that "[t]hese scenes may remind the readers that war, administration and intrigue were not the sole occupations of the great, and may perhaps lead them to compare social conditions of the past with those of the present day."[24]

Turnbull and Watkins are clearly drawing from a synthesis of Dutt and Deviprasad but introduce Mira's story as a sad tale, their introduction beginning with clashing steel and "the smoke of the funeral pyre upon which some devoted wife had uttered her last prayer—that she might meet her hero-lord in paradise" (invoking the much-maligned practice of sati).[25] Mira's turn to Krishna is presented as a compensatory outcome of growing up in such a harsh world (rather than even personal tragedy). Though she minimally complied with the arranged marriage ceremony, she considered herself the "spiritual bride of Sri Krishna," and immediately alienated her in-laws, becoming "the object of steady persecution." When people slandered her because she was heard speaking as if to someone in her private chamber, the authors note, "She was only pouring out her unhappy heart at the feet of the god in those beautiful poems which the women of India sing today."[26]

"[N]o doubt angered by what he considered her defiance of his authority," her father-in-law sent her poison, but to no effect. When her husband died shortly thereafter, "[h]er position now, as a Hindu widow, was worse than before." She decided to drown herself in the river (now of her own accord and in despair), but even "death forsook her." She was saved by cowherds (not her Lord) who took her with them to Vrindavan. In conclusion, the authors write that she "was as good as she was beautiful, and . . . handed down the finest Hindi poetry ever written by a woman."[27] They recommend that this introduction be read by the class instructor before the dialogue, to set the tone and contextualize the episodes to be enacted.

In the first scene of the dialogue, Bhojraj, his father, Rana Sanga, his mother the rani, and Mirabai's cousin Jaimal are present. The rani is shrill and catty, Bhojraj a pouting, spoiled adolescent, and Sanga irritated and impatient, none of them sympathetic characters. Jaimal speaks on Mira's behalf but is powerless to do anything to help her. Sending the others away, the rana calls Mira in, telling her she must stop her "sickly habit" of worshiping Krishna, calling her brooding, defiant, and hysterical and telling her to busy herself with "new trinkets" and spend her time with other women and children, preparing to have her own. In the next scene, in her own apartments, Mira is childlike in appearance, "her eyes bright with mystic fire," flowers in her hair. But she insists on drinking the poison brought to her in a melodramatic scene, with her nurse and maidservant trying to intervene and sobbing uncontrollably—yet she lives.

One wonders what the reaction of the intended audience of thirteen- or fourteen-year-old Indian schoolchildren might have been to such a play. The dialogue has an overly dramatic soap opera quality, with only Mirabai a truly sympathetic character, but she is reduced to a vulnerable mystic child whose life will go down in a spiral of despair—a far cry from Dutt's or Besant's or Khan's tellings. The play seems a heavy-handed colonial intervention to counter any notion of the rajputs or Indian women of the past as heroic in any way and to undercut any possibility of Mirabai's inspiring women (or men) to self-respect and fearless resistance. Especially given that the students are to be "encouraged to learn and act out the parts," the dialogue appears instead intended to foster feelings of helplessness and self-loathing and to bring tears to their eyes on behalf of the poor girl-child Mira.

Turnbull and Wadkins's play was published in 1931, within a year after Gandhi's successful Salt March, so it is perhaps no great surprise that colonial educators might want to try to shatter this exemplary satyagrahi, as the rana had tried to do before them. It is also no wonder that Gandhi, Tagore, Mahadevi, and Besant were so committed to developing distinctly Indian educational institutions. Already by 1917 the British had conceded in principle to Indian self-rule, spurred by war rhetoric of freedom and sovereignty and the participation of Indian soldiers in fighting on behalf of others, and with the passage of the Government of India Act in 1919, some legislative authority was granted to Indians, though the country was still under tight British control. During the interwar period, nationalist agitation grew and became a truly mass movement under Gandhi's leadership, putting the British in a delicate situation internationally, with closer ties to the United States and attendant concerns about popular opinion of the Indian situation and the British Empire.[28]

In an Anglo-American collaboration, U.S. journalist Katherine Mayo's blatantly imperialist propaganda piece *Mother India* was published in 1927, infusing new life into colonial rhetoric. She portrayed India as a backward society incapable of self-governance and Indian women as victims, bolstered by graphic descriptions of the horrors of child marriage and early maternity. Mayo sought to undermine any image of a glorious Indian past when women were allegedly held in high esteem, situating women's oppression in "an irredeemably perverse Hindu culture" and succeeding at least initially in raising questions in the minds of those inclined to support Indian nationalism in the United States and Europe and pity from those concerned about the plight of women, including the League of Nations and newly enfranchised British women.[29]

Nationalists of necessity would have to craft a new response to present realities, beyond taking refuge in a bygone golden age. As Mrinalini Sinha has argued, Indian women's organizations played a key role in shaping this response, supporting reform legislation such as the Child Marriage Restraint Act, also known as the Sarda Act, that British authorities had been resisting, unwilling to upset orthodox Hindu and Muslim loyalists.[30] The result was that Indian nationalists, led by Indian women themselves, came out on the side of modernity, with British hypocrisy embarrassingly laid bare. The passage of the Act in 1929 signaled, Sinha notes, "a new nationalist consensus in which the woman question was redeployed to demonstrate that India was ready to take its place among the modern nations of the world."[31] In the same year, the Indian National Congress dropped its call for self-rule within the British Empire, now demanding complete independence, and thirty-two labor leaders were arrested for organizing a railroad strike in an alleged Bolshevik plot. Their trial, the infamous Meerut Conspiracy Case, took four years and ended up galvanizing the Communist Party in India and further fanning the flames of anticolonial sentiment.

In light of this international debate and intensifying nationalist agitation, the extreme nature of Turnbull and Watkins's portrait is perhaps more understandable, though no less reprehensible. It is not surprising that in such a climate, others might seek to reaffirm Mirabai once and for all as indeed a heroic Indian woman of the past, a great Hindu devotee of God who could be universally appreciated, and an accomplished Indian poetess—an authentically Indian woman who could be called upon in the service of a cultural nationalism, both traditional and modern in her sensibilities. Within a few short years a definitive integrated rajput-nationalist-devotional telling of Mirabai would emerge, authored by former advocate and recognized philosopher and theologian Bankey Behari, that would become the most popular telling of her life in print for adults as well as children (though it is worth noting that Turnbull and Watkins's didactic drama continues to resurface into the twenty-first century).[32]

Canonizing a Rajput-Nationalist-Devotional Mira in Print

Bankey Behari (1910–1975) composed his popular biography of the saint in 1935, his own personal engagement with Mirabai also running deep.[33] Raised in an educated eclectic religious household in Allahabad, he distinguished himself as a student (studying English, Persian, and Urdu as well as math and science) but also as a spiritual seeker from a young age, and he would come to know Shri Aurobindo, Krishnamurti, Maharshi, Anandamayi Ma, and other great saints and would study with Sufi and Vedanta teachers as well as embarking on an eight-year in-depth exploration of the world's major religious traditions.

As a young man he reportedly visited Gandhi and spent some time at his Sabarmati Ashram, trying his hand at spinning but driven by the desire for spiritual realization. It is reported that Gandhi asked him to stay on as editor of *Young India* because of his excellent command of English, but he declined, returning to Allahabad to study law. As a lawyer, he was involved in representing the defendants in the appeal of the Meerut Conspiracy case as well as other cases brought by the Raj against anyone considered threatening to British sovereignty in India.[34] He regularly held devotional kirtan sessions at his home, which Mahadevi is reported to have attended along with other renowned poets and devotees, and at some point, according to Chhaganlal Lala, he was initiated into the Radhasoami Satsang.[35] In these years he wrote a series of books, many on law but also on religion, including his biography of Mirabai, as well as works on Sufi poetry and the Upanishads. He never married, his sole focus, beyond his legal work, the pursuit of spiritual liberation.

Though he visited many great spiritual teachers, it was the saint Mirabai who ultimately became his true guru, eventually leading him to give up his legal practice and move to Vrindavan in 1940 and promising to meet him there, where he would finally achieve realization, according to Behari. He accepted only one primary disciple: a young woman, Shri Krishnaji (her name a feminine form of "Krishna"), whom he recognized as Mirabai incarnate. When I met Shri Krishnaji in Vrindavan some eighteen years after Behari's death, she spoke unequivocally of him as her guru and said she spent her days immersed in devotion, waiting for death to come so that she might rejoin him.[36] Their relationship seemed to mirror that of Mira and Rup Goswami as described by Dutt, both praising the other as guru, sharing a Mira-like all-encompassing devotion to Krishna, and espousing a deep love for the saint. Behari was very highly respected for both his scholarship and his devotion, and people came from great distances for his darshan and teaching (among them American poet Allen Ginsberg) as well as to hear Sri Krishna-ji sing.[37]

When Behari published *The Story of Mirabai* in 1935, Gandhi's deployment of Mirabai as a model satyagrahi was in full swing.[38] In Allahabad, Mahadevi had already been dubbed a "modern Mira" with the publication of her second volume of poems, *Ray of Light,* in 1932, and Parashuram Chaturvedi had published his collection of some two hundred songs of Mirabai with a short scholarly introduction to her life (drawn heavily from Deviprasad) that same year. Tandon's English translations of the Belvedere Press collection had come out in 1934. Behari acknowledged Tandon for his assistance with the translations of some of the songs that appear in his own volume (even as Tandon acknowledged Chaturvedi's assistance).[39] Behari mentions Tod and Macauliffe in his introduction as having written about traditions associated with Mira, as well as contemporary scholars, crediting them for "explod[ing] many established traditions, especially the one which ascribes maltreatment of Mīrā Bāī by her husband," and commending those studies to the interested reader. His aim in telling the story of his own beloved saint-guru is something else: to teach "the Path of Love." "Modern Science and Art might well mock at her poetic outbursts and call those emotional effusions as mere paroxysms of a maniac or the after-effects of an 'overheated' brain," but he dismisses such criticisms outright.[40]

The tale Behari tells is a seamless blending of Dutt's nationalist account and the rajput historians' presentation of Mira in a devotional story which at once lauds Mira's renunciation and purity *and* the universal nature of her love of God, coupled with her willingness to sacrifice all for it, manifest in a decidedly Hindu way but transcending distinctions between religions.[41] Behari makes it clear that he writes a truth about the saint that is (in his estimation) higher than that arrived at by historical and academic investigation, and he is reported to have written it in a single sitting, "as if it were revealed to him through supernatural agency."[42] His tale thus appears as *shruti*, "heard" or revealed truth, like the Vedas and Upanishads, rather than *smriti*, or "remembered," like the great epics of the *Ramayana* and *Mahabharata*.

His telling, like many of the hagiographic accounts we have examined, turns on Mira's triumph over opposition of various kinds. Some previously reported conflicts are reduced to mere appearance. Although Mira's mother-in-law feigned anger at her refusal to bow down before the Goddess, she was in fact deeply impressed with the girl's piety. At the same time, Mira begged forgiveness from her, even as she refused her mother-in-law's request. Nowhere in Behari's telling is Mira anything but the perfect wife. Indeed he writes, "[B]lessed is Mira who left no stone unturned to please her husband and see that his mandates were obeyed. She tried to give him no occasion for offense. She stood out a sublime figure of a devoted wife, an ideal that could be the boast of any Hindu lady."[43] The single exception was that "she stood adamant in her virgin glory, guarding her rights with meticulous care," and spent her nights ("after finishing her household work") worshiping Krishna rather than with the rana. Behari portrays her as very popular with the court as well as the people. Bhojraj is a sympathetic character, though a bit hot-headed—an unparalleled paragon of rajput valor who has nothing to do with Mira's persecution but who must come to terms with a wife madly in love with God.

Behari draws elements from the nationalist telling of Dutt and the rajput historian's portrayal of Mira as well as a few additions from popular traditions to enhance Mira's upholding of stridharm and rajput honor. Mira's encounter with Akbar and the rana's subsequent order follow Dutt, though it is Bhojraj himself who tells her to drown herself for having allowed a Mughal to touch her feet and Mira who is identified as the source of Akbar's "tolerant nature and liberal views" even as Behari judges him spiritually inferior for seeking God through the intellect rather than the heart (as indeed did Cousins). Mira goes to her death willingly, upholding that same honor that motivates her husband's order and obedient to his command. Behari laments the world's ignorance, likening her impending martyrdom to that of Jesus, but at the same time lauding Mira's surrender of all to God. Only Krishna's direct intervention saves her at the last minute, just as she is about to jump, and he releases her from the bonds of her earthly marriage, sending her to Vrindavan, where she dreams of her former life as Radha (a considerable step up from Sukhsaran's brahman woman of Barsana). The way is full of hardship and privation, but Mira is uncomplaining, entirely immersed in God and mindless of the difficulties of the journey, as Bhojraj is when on military campaigns, according to Behari.

As her fame grows and people flock to her, the news reaches Bhojraj, and, again following Dutt, he goes to find her, disguising himself as a holy man. Ever the good wife, she willingly returns to Chittor. But the story does not end with the couple living "happily ever after," as it does in Dutt's account. Unfortunately, Bhojraj dies soon thereafter, and his brother Ratan Singh, at the instigation of her sister-in-law Udabai, begins to torment Mira, "the persecution continu[ing] day and night." Behari includes the episode in which Mira, distraught at the interference with her devotion, writes to the poet-saint Tulsidas, who responds that her true family is the community of devotees and urges her to leave Chittor and live among them. She goes to Vrindavan, eventually encounters her true guru, Raidas, and finally, having grown old, she merges with Krishna's image in Dwarka in a state of ecstasy and in the midst of the community of devotees rather than in isolation and as a result of coercion.

In Behari's telling Bhojraj and Mira together uphold both rajput ideals and devotion, and Mira is the embodiment of feminine virtue and strength. She remains always obedient to men who control her destiny: to her father in accepting her arranged marriage without question, to her husband in conforming to his every request (except perhaps one, but surely he never asked), to Krishna in going to Vrindavan, to Tulsidas in finally leaving Chittor, and to Raidas, who is credited with leading her to a higher experience of her Lord. Within Behari's narrative, she manages to remain both a wife and a disciple, obedient to social and religious authorities as well as to God, who seems to reinforce these structures. Even her spiritual realization is ultimately mediated by her guru Raidas, who gives her the divine name, or *Shabd,* and shows her the way to return Home, though he never actually appears as a character in the narrative, instead standing in generically for the all-important guru. Behari is clear on this: "The Lord does not permit direct meeting. The devotee must meet through his preceptor."[44]

Even so, all may enter the divine presence, he assures the reader, regardless of "birth, poverty, age or sex," with love—bhakti—the only way to the highest realization and "the secret of all religions."[45] "Caste" is noticeably absent from this list, replaced by the more generic "birth," and no reference is made to Raidas's identity as an untouchable chamar. (The author's caste status similarly is rendered invisible in available biographical information; he is said only to "[belong] to a rich 'Zamindar' family (landlord) who had great landed property.")[46] Behari spends nearly half the book detailing the nature of this spiritual path: the movement of the soul away from its original state "merged in . . . and with the Lord"[47] into ignorance of its true nature and worldly distraction; awakened into love, the pain of separation, and the renunciation of all else; and ultimately guided Home by the guru who makes the divine call audible to the disciple, who cannot resist it. He closes his tale with Mira's final merger, she "the moth that burnt itself in the candle of love for Giridhara and for all times filled the Temple of Devotion with fragrance."[48]

Behari's book, written in English and reprinted in multiple editions to the present, seems to have done more than any other work to crystallize and propagate a thoroughly rajputized and nationalist image of Mira, even as she becomes the poster-child for a generic Hindu devotion that eschews "forms, formalities and dogmas" and readily crosses sectarian and even religious divides, Behari as readily speaking of "Satan" as of "maya" as that which deludes the soul.[49] His Mira is a demure devotee, obedient to father, husband, God, and guru, immersed in love of Krishna, without any hint of rebellion or wayward independence, her story reinfused with the albeit postmarital opposition and suffering that reveal her true strength, the emotional depth of her love and longing, and the thoroughgoing nature of her renunciation. Though she grows old by the end of the tale, Behari refers to her repeatedly as a child throughout, in relation to God and guru but also as one who might school little girls in the affective development of a valorized, internalized devotional orientation.[50] Composed by a man with impeccable credentials—educated in science and law, scholarly and fluent in English, cosmopolitan in his knowledge of the world's religions as well as deeply devotional and thoroughly Indian—his telling is compelling as story, *sans* academic debate, drawing the reader deep into Mira's world—a world at once distant and yet familiar—and providing a full backstory for the fragmentary invocations of the saint made by so many nationalist leaders, male and female alike. Her suffering and sorrow invoke sympathy but are wedded to her immense devotion to husband as well as God, and thus safely separated from the kind of real-world brutality and rebellion that surface in Tagore's fictional invocations and in low-caste epics.

Though initially written under the auspices of Behari's own Temple of Mysticism, the volume was immediately picked up by Gita Press, and this too contributed dramatically to its dissemination. This publication house had been established in Gorakhpur in 1923, initially to make the *Bhagavad Gita* more widely available, by Jaydayal Goyandka (1885–1965), a deeply religious member of the Vaishnava marwari trading community.[51] Hanuman Prasad Poddar (1892–1971) joined him in 1926 as disciple and editor of the press's journal *Kalyan*, a project initiated by the Marwari Agarwal Sabha (a voluntary association of the marwari community).

The journal has been published continuously on a monthly basis to the present (with more than sixty additional special volumes on a variety of issues), offering advice and religious instruction on all manner of subjects. The press is well-known not only for the journal but also for its inexpensive and widely available editions of Sanskrit texts and medieval devotional literature with Hindi translations and extended interpretive commentaries (most especially the *Gita* and Tulsidas's *Ramcharitmanas*) as well as for its innumerable didactic pamphlets on issues from dowry and Hindi films to the meaning of dharma (reprinted from and in *Kalyan*), of which a substantial number were written by Goyandka and Poddar themselves. They also produced an English-language monthly counterpart, *Kalyana-Kalpataru*, edited by Chimanlal Goswami beginning in 1934 (with a hiatus between 1974 and 1989) and designed for diaspora Hindu communities.

The aim of the press from its inception has been "to present and project a new, yet conservative concept of Hinduism which is easily acceptable and accessible to the general public," a universal *sanatan dharma* (eternal dharma) grounded in the teachings and authority of the *Gita* that encompasses all sectarian distinctions within the boundaries of India—with Sikhs, Buddhists, Arya Samajis, and other reformers, even tribal communities, included, but distinctly not traditions originating elsewhere, such as Christians, Muslims, Jews, or Zoroastrians.[52] In this project, Monika Horstmann argues, Goyandka and Poddar were as motivated by a cultural/religious nationalism as others were during this period and every bit as concerned about contemporary issues as Gandhi, Tagore, and Mahadevi, though their approach would differ radically.

Their publications reflect a fundamentalist "affirmation of traditional values in response to modern challenges and in the interest of a wider mission-oriented, universal and societally geared ethics" that could unify "Hindus" broadly defined, both at home and abroad,[53] "eradicat[e] social evils to establish a society ruled by religious principles,"[54] and "channeliz[e] . . . aggression against a group still more oppressed than the Hindus, namely the Muslims."[55] In his monumental work, Akshaya Mukul demonstrates the unequivocal role of Gita Press in the dissemination of an increasingly virulent Hindu nationalism and details Poddar's personal commitment to this agenda from his leadership in anti–cow slaughter campaigns from the 1920s and his opposition to both Ambedkar and Gandhi on caste issues to his later involvement in Hindu Mahasabha condemnation of Muslims post-Partition, the Ramjanambhumi agitation in Ayodhya, the Krishnajanambhumi project in Mathura, and much more.[56]

Nevertheless, *Kalyan*, in keeping with its universalizing and unifying aim, consistently included a wide range of voices across the spectrum of Hinduism from its earliest days, playing a crucial role in the shaping of a modern Hindu orthodoxy. Among its multitude of contributors were none other than Gandhi and T. S. Vaswani (founder of the Mira Movement for Education), as well as at least a few women and Muslim writers (though the topics they might address were carefully circumscribed by the editors), while Kanu Desai and a number of artists trained at Shantiniketan provided illustrations.[57] Indeed Poddar and Gandhi were on very friendly terms, as their correspondence reveals, though their relationship would break down over the widespread opening of temples to "untouchables" and the like that followed in the wake Gandhi's 1932 fast against separate electorates for the "Depressed Classes." Such changes were anathema to Poddar's staunch support of traditional caste hierarchies, enshrined in his own and Goyandka's writings, along with equally restrictive views on women's proper behavior and increasingly negative portrayals of Muslims.[58] *Kalyan* gained legitimacy through this wide participation. Mukul notes, "Writers like Rabindranath Tagore, Kshitimohan Sen, C. F. Andrews, S. Radhakrishnan, as can be discerned from their responses to Poddar, genuinely considered Gita Press and *Kalyan* as a spiritual, cultural, and religious intervention without subscribing to its communal dimension."[59] Nevertheless, the journal proved an effective vehicle for disseminating a profoundly socially conservative Hindu nationalist agenda and continues to be, with a high subscription rate and essays by Poddar and Goyandka regularly reprinted in current issues, though both passed away long ago.

Regarding their own spiritual qualifications, Poddar and Goyandka made another significant intervention, radically reformulating interpretive authority. Claiming ignorance of Hindu textual traditions and teaching lineages generally, they privileged the *Bhagavad Gita* as the culminating scripture, encompassing and superseding those that came before, and asserted that anyone who followed the rules of the sanatan/eternal dharma laid out therein was automatically authorized to preach it, including most especially themselves.[60] In so doing, Horstmann notes, "[t]he vocabulary of tradition gains a new function: to serve as the foundation of a newly self-assured, yet religiously legitimized cultural identity."[61] That cultural identity was avowedly Hindu (equated with Indian) and rested on varna-ashrama-dharma and the doctrines of karma and rebirth. Furthermore, though "hagiographic writings published after Poddar's death . . . all emphasize that his and Goyandka's writings are based on divine visions and interpretations," their works were distinctly nonsectarian, and they therefore claimed an unbiased impartiality and a grounding strictly in sacred text that lent authority not only to their translations and commentaries but also to their advice on all kinds of practical matters.[62]

Some of that advice, Monika Freier argues, was addressed to the specific circumstances of the transregional marwari community of the time. Diatribes against greed as destructive to salvation and society as well as to business interests, for example, clearly speak to scandals and anti-marwari riots in 1910, 1918, and 1926, resulting from "unscrupulousness in commodity speculation and hoarding" and the adulteration of foodstuffs and even ghee (used in ritual offerings as well as for cooking) by marwari traders.[63] Lack of devotion and lack of control of desires and emotions were identified as the cause. As Philip Lutgendorf notes, with their rising domination of trade across North India, increasing wealth, and acquisition of land, marwari traders were effectively displacing kshatriyas as the "rulers" in society, but without the same social standing, evoking jealousy and resentment from outside and an identity crisis within the community.[64] Their pan-Indian trading network notwithstanding, they remained closely connected to their ancestral villages in Rajasthan, engaging in charitable activities, both social and religious, and building luxurious homes there, where their wives tended to remain living in the midst of close-knit communities.[65] Yet as they sought greater recognition and status with their increased economic power, embarrassing fault lines were revealed on the domestic front.

In 1929, the woman's journal *Chand* (still under the editorship of Saghal) published a scathing exposé that "shook the Marwari world" (as Mukul puts it), alleging (among other things) the loneliness and promiscuity of marwari women and their illicit relationships with family members and sadhus. An article published eight years later was written by Sukhda Devi, the wife of a prominent member of the marwari community, who gave a firsthand account of the confinement and conditions of marwari women's lives despite their material wealth—uneducated, mired in trivial pursuits and gossip, married off at a young age often to older men, vulnerable to domestic violence, and forbidden remarriage if widowed—and she called on marwari women themselves to establish schools for the daughters of their community.[66] In light of these and other very public critiques, Poddar and Goyandka—the self-appointed "conscience-keepers of the community"—took up the task of reforming women as the essential preservers and propagators (but also potential destroyers) of an evolving honorable marwari self-identity founded on Hindu spiritual traditions, as women were seen to be for a broader Indian identity in the "new patriarchy" of other nationalists.

The reform Poddar and Goyandka would advocate, however, was a return to an idealized ancient patriarchy grounded in standard exemplary women of the past, coupled with a renewed cultivation of devotion and disciplining of desires and emotions (which they recommended also for men, though in a different form). In contradistinction to so many women's journals of the time, Freier notes, "[t]he Gita Press publications . . . put a strong emphasis on a highly hierarchical model, dominated by absolute devotion to the husband. In the Gita Press model, there was only one duty for every married woman—to serve her husband as befits a true *pativratā*. All her actions were to be centered on pleasing her husband. The enunciation of these norms was backed by frequent citations from the Manushastras and references to the 'sages and mahatmas of the east.'"[67] Obedience was above all else, even in a situation where religion and husband might come into conflict. At the same time, singing bhajans was affirmed as the "natural duty of mankind," so if a husband were to forbid this, then his wife was encouraged to sing them within her heart, as a universal (and universally Hindu) practice.[68] But "cultivation and control of the emotions" was essential "to uphold the community, and simultaneously . . . to pursue the highest goal in life—the attainment of spiritual bliss." Thus what was lifted up here was not women's "right to feel" (which Orsini names as a theme in women's journals of the time) but rather "right feeling," appropriate to the upright Hindu woman and man.[69]

As one might expect, in the drive to create this nonsectarian universal Hinduism, the extraordinarily popular saint Mirabai would need to be included, but in a form that also would fit their socially conservative agenda. In 1930 Poddar authored an essay on Mira for a Gita Press volume on "women devotees" (*bhakt nari*), drawing on familiar hagiographic sources for spiritual authority.[70] He opens with Nabhadas and loosely follows Priyadas, offering his own commentary and inserting a number of popular songs, so that he not only presents Mira as an exemplar of feminine bhakti but also provides a set of her bhajans for the devotional singing incumbent on all Hindus. Throughout, he emphasizes Mira's absolute and admirable devotion to Krishna, her composition and singing of bhajans, and her ability to arouse devotion in others, especially women.

A number of Poddar's commentarial interventions relate to her marriage, as one might expect. He highlights her completing the marriage ritual first with Krishna's image, thereby affirming her understanding of herself as married to her Lord, and notes that though Bhojraj was at first upset by her behavior, he came to understand and support her, swept up in bhakti himself by her singing and even building a temple for her. Mira, realizing that she is failing to fulfill his needs, encourages him to take another wife. She is delighted when he does and dedicates herself entirely to devotion to her Lord for the next ten years. With these added details, Madhav Hada observes, "Poddar ... present[s] her as a loving, considerate ideal Hindu woman, who, despite being divinely inspired, was not completely oblivious to her wifely duties and also felt a tinge of guilt, failing to carry them out."[71]

Following Bhojraj's death, Mira continues her all-consuming devotion to her husband-Lord. Poddar records a number of full bhajans, many presented as responses to her sister-in-law and women of the household who, though increasingly appreciative of her devotion, try to dissuade her from behavior unbecoming of woman and wife, and a rani no less. She is highly emotional, at times blissful, at others filled with tearful longing, but always and only in a devotional context. Mira's encounter with the deceptive sadhu is also elaborated, with clear resonances for the twentieth-century marwari community, as both a warning against unbridled lust and a triumphant example of the transformative power of womanly virtue. Akbar's coming, disguised as a Vaishnava, receives only the briefest mention. Vikramajit's attempts on her life are enumerated but deployed primarily to demonstrate God's miraculous protection of his devotee, and her letter exchange with Tulsidas authorizes her departure from the palace. Poddar notes her reported encounter with Jiv Goswami in Vrindavan and songs speaking of Raidas as her guru and, in an inclusive move, suggests that perhaps she had taken initiation from both. He recounts her miraculous merger in Dwarka and concludes by lauding Mira as a source of purifying holiness and blessing to India, the Hindu race, and all womenkind.

Mira was also featured prominently in the first issue of the English-language *Kalyana-Kalapatru* (God-Number) in 1934.[72] In this essay, respected educator and linguist Nalini Mohan Sanyal emphasizes the universal high regard for the saint, "woman though she is," and her exceptionalism and surrender to her Lord, whom she considered her husband. Overall the article is scholarly in approach, drawing on a wide array of sources and detailing their debates, thereby making much Hindi scholarship on the saint more broadly accessible to English-language readers.[73] However, with a nod to Tod, the author begins with a romantic tale about Kumbha hearing of her beauty and coming in disguise to see her, falling in love at first sight, and insisting on their marriage. He is understanding of Mira's devotion and is supportive until, seeing her singing in the temple before strangers, he becomes enraged. Having caused him such distress, Mira decides on her own to drown herself, but rescued by divine providence, she proceeds to Vrindavan and lives out her days in devotion to Krishna, "whom she began to conceive as identical with her husband the Rana," so that she is worshiping her God-husband after all.

Having drawn the reader in, Sanyal then declares this to be only a fanciful tale and proceeds to offer a far more sober, standard "historical biography," emphasizing Mira's turn to extreme devotion only after the death of her husband, "[h]er early convictions, now nursed and watered by sorrow settling on her head, one after another." Under Ratan Singh's and Vikramajit's persecution and, "[in] this critical condition, unable to judge for herself," she sends her letter to Tulsidas. Sanyal assures the reader that Mira was "a truly devoted and dutiful wife" during the life of her husband and that her devotion to Krishna made her life as a widow more bearable, even as her "persecution and the resultant resistance served to expand her character." Her "uncommon strength of mind and uncompromising spirit of independence" are noted, though balanced with "a full measure of Vaishnava meekness and humility." In her renunciation and "religious frenzy," she may have cared nothing about the world's judgment, though Sanyal reminds the reader, "To sing and dance before a promiscuous gathering of strangers was not, nay, it is not even now, considered fit conduct for a lady, much less a lady of rank." The article is illustrated with a picture from the earlier Gita Press volume of a young Mira, dressed in white, kartals and vina in hand, worshiping alone in the palace, her face illumined by a beam of heavenly light, in distinct contrast to such a public display. This popular portrait would be reproduced again and again, gracing the cover of multiple editions of Behari's biography of the saint and prominently displayed in St. Mira School for Girls decades later (see Figure 5.1 in the previous chapter).[74]

As befitting the theme of the issue, Sanyal goes on to place Mira within the context of Vaishnava devotion and then paraphrases and analyzes a series of popular bhajans, explicitly rejecting any criticism of the rana or mention of Raidas.[75] These songs offer a counterpoint to his rather heavy-handed presentation of her life, but in the final section he claims, "Our only road to salvation, Mira says, is repentance, resignation and prayer" (though he admits that no full bhajan carries such a message). Sanyal thus manages to praise Mirabai while at the same time diminishing her, allegedly rescuing her from "hav[ing] been done to death by her admirers," by showing her as conforming to more orthodox expectations for women even as she seems to violate them, worshiping and ever obedient to God-cum-husband, a proper wife and widow, if a bit childish and/or deluded in her excessive attachment to an image. And in the end, she becomes a voice for restraint and renunciation. Taken together, these essays introduce and lay claim to Mira but do not yet provide a sufficiently comprehensive and compelling makeover of this popular saint to adequately defuse in her disruptive potential.[76]

Behari's extended telling of her story, published a year later, would do just that, readily fitting into the larger agenda of the press. Here Mira appears as a quintessential Hindu bhakta, universally beloved across sectarian and nirgun/sagun distinctions; ever obedient, her emotions always positive and yielding as a wife's should be, regardless of her husband's behavior or her personal suffering, and deferential to her mother-in-law; the absolute embodiment of the twin devotion to husband and God that was to be at the center of every woman's life—thoroughly Hindu but also universal and on a par with the greatest saints of other traditions and indeed Jesus himself. And Behari claimed the same visionary revelation that allegedly marked Poddar and Goyandka's interpretations and advice and would himself publish a highly acclaimed commentary on the *Gita* that would earn him an honorary doctorate in theology.

Like those of Poddar and Sanyal before him, Behari's telling was a clear socially and religiously conservative response to other circulating Miras, manifest in the words of Gandhi and Tagore and the person of Mahadevi, but also in print biographies, plays, and academic works as well as colonial school readers and innumerable oral stories, songs, and dramas, and even the newest medium of popular storytelling: the cinema. With its expanded detail, it could also provide a backstory for other nationalist invocations of Mira as a heroic pativrata to inspire service and self-sacrifice as well as their use of bhakti to espouse a formal equality and draw low-caste communities into the Hindu fold and vote bank, without raising divisive issues of caste hierarchy and oppression within Hinduism and the elitism of the nationalist movement itself.

In selecting Behari's work for publication, the saint was fully integrated into the universal sanatan dharma and Hindu cultural nationalism advocated by Gita Press, in what was indeed a palatable form that would come to be seen as definitive and authoritative. Behari himself might not share all the views of the press's editors, importantly translating and publishing the works of Sufi saints and espousing a deep appreciation for the diverse spiritual traditions of India and the world.[77] He nevertheless champions a universal and unifying Vaishnava Hinduism informed by a social conservativism that readily allowed his Mira to join a pantheon of Hindu figures from the past who could indeed form "the foundation of a newly self-assured, yet religiously legitimized cultural identity" that the press promoted in the name of "traditional" Hindu orthodoxy.[78]

At a practical level, his was also a tale of Mira that could be read to young girls as well as newly married marwari women living in ancestral villages in Rajasthan or coming to join their husbands in new urban settings, in the attempt to supplant other, possibly more rebellious images of the saint and/or to draw on affection for her to reinforce proper wifely behavior and feeling, particularly in the absence of senior female relatives. That affection and familiarity with the saint existed among such women and reasons why a corrective might be needed are made abundantly clear in the case of one marwari wife-become-saint, Banasa, from the arid region of Shekhawati, who wrote her autobiography the year before her death in 1957 and whom some would even call "a modern *avatār* of Mīrābāī."[79]

Born in 1896, Banasa was married at thirteen to Narvadaprasad Lath of Mandrela, a highly successful businessman, supporter of Gandhian nationalism and social reform, widely read and religiously inclined, as his father was. Married into this wealthy and prestigious family, Banasa "was supposed to find fulfillment within the scope of her home and the religious pursuits available for a married woman," but she failed to do so.[80] With children, a comfortable life, and a supportive husband, she still longed for something more. She entered an extended period of psychological/spiritual crisis, during which she was restless, dissatisfied, and quarrelsome, often ill and in physical pain. Her family tried to address her state with pilgrimages and trips to resorts and even a stay in a sanitarium, and in her autobiography she expresses her own conflicted desires for detachment but also for family approval and her attachment to her children.

In January 1929, back in the family ancestral village, where it was hoped she might feel more at home and find solace, she accompanied other women to visit a holy man, the Ramavat sadhu Baldev, who lived naked in the village cremation ground and who was held in high esteem by the traditional rajput *thakur* (local landholder and ruler) as well as her own and other influential marwari families. This meeting changed her life, as she came to identify Baldev as her guru and as God manifest. Baldev himself initially resisted her devotion to him, and her family tried to reason with her, seeking to persuade her that she could do all her worship as a married woman and within the home, even accepting that Baldev should reside within the family compound. But this was an uneasy truce, she renouncing all but her service to him.

When people began to talk and slander the family, with rumors even reaching family business interests in Calcutta, the situation proved intolerable, particularly given that they had children whose marriages were yet to be arranged (no doubt exacerbated by scandalous accusations about the relationships of marwari women and holy men circulating in the press at the time). Family members brought her to Calcutta on the pretense of attending a wedding, but when they would not send her back, she repeatedly ran away. They resorted to tying her down and other forms of restraint, but she was undeterred. In her autobiography she writes, "As I did not do what my relatives wished, they inflicted all kinds of cruelty on me. In our society, a woman has enough power to look after the household and children. If she keeps her husband in [a] good mood, they may get along, but not otherwise. I wonder how many men leave their home to become sanyasi [renouncers], a woman has hardly enough authority to stop a man from doing so. A woman, however, can hardly do what she wants.... [W]here would a woman go who would do this?"[81] Further crisis led to her nearly dying, bringing both holy man and family around to accept and indeed support her devotion, taking Baldev in essentially as a member of the family and eventually building an ashram for the two of them in 1937. Both would come to be known as saints, and Banasa's daughter continued to foster devotion to them, though Baldev died in 1947 and Banasa a decade later.

Horstmann has translated her autobiography and interviewed family members and others who knew her. She describes the way Banasa negotiated a life of her own choosing, drawing on the triple authority of family patriarchs, rajput thakur, and respected holy man to ultimately confirm her choice—a negotiation in which Mirabai played a crucial role. Writing of her period of intense crisis, Horstmann observes:

> [S]he was in a condition that made her catch hold of a distinctly religious Rajasthani tradition to which she had natural access. This tradition was to give her words and guidelines for action. She was familiar with it prior to her encounter with Baldev,

and she was enabled by it to interpret her rebellion against the fate allotted to her by society in line with that tradition. It was as if that accessible store of tradition had lain dormant in her and was activated by the contact with Baldev and his congregation of devout followers, the *satsaṅg*, the community of the good and godly.... The persona she came to be was created on the model of the paragon of female bhakti, Mira Bai, and the way she would experience and articulate what she experienced was moulded by that tradition of female bhakti.[82]

Banasa quotes Mira songs repeatedly in her teachings and in writing about her life, particularly the now familiar song in which Mira declares that for her there is no other but Krishna and that she has abandoned all for him, watering the vine of love with her tears, and finding joy only in the company of his devotees, while the world brings her nothing but sorrow (the same song invoked by Tagore's Kumudini and Nagendrabala Dasi in her *Women's Dharma*). "Baldev was to Banasa what the Dark Lord was to Mira, or rather, this is how Banasa conceived and elaborated the meaning of her relationship with her guru."[83]

Banasa is not alone in drawing on Mira to craft an alternative religious life. Other women have taken the radical step of becoming renouncers, leaving domestic life entirely behind, some also explicitly drawing on traditions of Mirabai. K. M. Jhaveri writes in his *Milestones of Gujarati Literature* (1914) of a woman renouncer poet and singer named Radhabai who died in 1857, a Dakshini brahman from Baroda whose life seemed modeled on the saint and who traveled widely and composed a biography of Mirabai.[84] I have documented a number of rajput and brahman women who have taken up similar religious lives; hailing from Rajasthan and Madhya Pradesh and settling in Vrindavan, the oldest was born in the 1930s, perhaps earlier.[85] A community of women renouncers with a dedication to Mirabai was also portrayed in the 1950 popular film *Jogan* in a matter-of-fact way, and Horstmann reported meeting a similar group of Dadupanthi nuns from Nagaur District near Merta devoted to the saint in the early 1980s.[86] And female Dasnami and Nath sadhus in Mewar who invoke Mira as precedent for their life choices have been documented by Antoinette de Napoli in the early decades of the twentieth-first century.[87]

Widows, too, in this region have found the traditions of Mirabai and female bhakti to be a resource for creating respected alternative lives. G. N. Sharma reported that in his travels throughout Rajasthan in the 1940s as a school inspector, he encountered a number of mostly high-caste widows who embraced a life of renunciation and devotion, dressed in white, and took refuge in temples, and who were offered support and honor as holy women and compared to the saint in their choice of celibate religious life after marriage.[88] Banasa's case is somewhat unusual, as she remained so closely connected to her husband, children, and extended family in straddling these worlds (though others do continue to interact with natal and marital family members, especially when renunciation comes during marriage and even motherhood). Indeed Banasa writes with pleasure that her husband pledged to attire her at her death in the auspicious clothing of a married woman.[89] He kept his promise and lit her funeral pyre himself. However, while other women within Banasa's world might sing songs of Mira together and practice bhakti communally but then return to their householder lives (as Sukhsaran and Gadge Maharaj advised), Horstmann concludes that "Banasa, by strength or by weakness, lacked the capacity to accommodate the model of Mira to her ordinary life ... conceiv[ing] of herself as emulating Mira in her surrender to Baldev."[90]

We know of Banasa's case because she had some basic literacy and wrote an autobiography and because her highly respected family continued to revere her. Though documentation is limited regarding how other women might have drawn on the saint in these early decades of the twentieth century and before, there is sufficient ongoing evidence to suggest that traditions of Mirabai were widely known and accessed by women in constructive as well as disruptive ways with respect to women's normative behavior in marwari, brahman, rajput, and potentially other households. Marwari women would also have contributed to the circulation of traditions about the saint as they moved out to join husbands engaged in business across the subcontinent, traveled widely on pilgrimages, and returned to ancestral homes. Disseminating a Mira who was ever obedient to male authority, as Behari is so careful to present her, would undoubtedly have seemed an absolute necessity to the socially conservative within the marwari community and beyond, especially with "traditional" women's roles and identities being questioned under the perceived corrupting influence of Western and "modern" ideas.

Behari's particular telling of Mira's story continues to be deemed ideal for communicating Indian/Hindu cultural values to readers, young and old, male and female, in India and beyond. In addition to being reprinted repeatedly by Gita Press, this work was also picked up by Hindi Sahitya Bhavan as part of its "book university" and published under the title *Bhakta Mira* (1961 and 1971).[91] In this avowedly integrative context and in line with his own inclinations, Behari would add an introduction, drawing extensively on the work of his disciple Shri Krishnaji and making explicit comparisons between Mira and Christian mystics and Sufi saints (though subsequent Gita Press editions never incorporated this addition).[92] And it was Behari's telling that was selected as the storyline and illustrated for the popular *Amar Chitra Katha* comic book series in 1972, reprinted in multiple languages and distributed nationally to schools and also abroad.[93] Behari's formulation continues to play a dominant role in shaping people's perceptions of the saint today as the most widely circulating account of her life in print. His telling would be complemented by portrayals of Mira's life and character in the immensely powerful, new medium for telling, picturizing, and creating cultural narratives: cinema.

Mira on the Silver Screen

From the silent era, beginning with *Meerabai*, directed by Kanjibhai Rathor in 1921, Mira's story took its place in the genre of devotional saint films, many of which reflected political and social themes and explored issues of gender relations, caste, and economic disparity as well. Following the introduction of sound in 1931, films of Mira's life appeared in Hindi, Bengali, Tamil, Telegu, Punjabi, Gujarati, Marathi, and Malayalam, as had earlier plays, though many of the initial films have been lost, including Rathor's 1921 silent one. Early cinema, like other forms of narrative performance, drew on existing circulating stories, and as Kumkum Sangari notes, these films "were themselves continuously reabsorbed into oral and print narratives . . . viewed as ephemeral and transitory, preserved in popular memory through oral repetition (more than re-viewed as consolidated archives), and 'saved' in oral narrative as narrative vignettes and gossip."[94] These and subsequent films and later television serials would become another major avenue of encounter with and experience of the saint, particularly for those of the upper and middle castes and classes who might have less and less access to other streams of circulating traditions.

India entered the world of film from the inception of this technology, with the cinematograph publicly available for viewing in Bombay in 1896 and cinema halls in most major cities by 1910. Dhundiraj Govind Phalke, the undisputed leader of the silent era, was initially inspired by the religious potential of film after viewing *Life of Christ*, and his first films were "mythologicals"—*Raja Harishchandra* (1913) and *Shri Krishna Janma* (1918). Even from this early silent era, however, films were also marked by explicit political and social messages, particularly as the struggle for Independence gained momentum in the 1920s, and religious and political themes were overtly combined in films such as the banned *Bhakta Vidur* (1921). Melodramatic romance, slapstick comedy, and action stunts entered the mix in varying measure as well.

Cinema in India was influenced by international films but also by Indian performance traditions of classical, court, and Parsi theater; the musical, dramatic, and visual dimensions of epic performances; a wide range of regional folk drama forms and themes; the religious aesthetics of bhakti and the Vaishnava lila traditions of enacting the lives of Krishna and Rama; and other religious ways of seeing, including darshan (to see and be seen by the Divine), *jankhi* (a living tableau of the gods), and practices of inner visualization.[95] Like the folk and religious dramatic traditions before them, Indian films generally do not depend on suspense or surprise endings—the outcome is a foregone conclusion—but the way the story is told and wider contexts of meaning are what is relished.[96] Consequently remakes abound, and films invoke and play off all these other genres as well as plots, visual images, and music of earlier films in an "intertextual excess" that defies distinctions between classical and popular and between written and oral traditions.[97] With the introduction of sound, songs became a key element of Indian cinema, as they are in the folk epics and the devotional performance and textual traditions we examined in earlier chapters, and they often serve as a counterpoint to the visual and dialogue elements of the narrative.[98]

Plots interweave social and political commentary, with cinema becoming a primary zone of cultural contestation and debate[99] and, as Rosie Thomas has argued, "a central arena for the definition and celebration of a modern Indian identity, working to negotiate notions of traditional and modern India."[100] Further, cinema provided a venue for exploring diverse imaginings of the new nation, culminating in Mehboob Khan's 1957 epic *Mother India* (*Bharat Mata*).[101] Patronage, increasingly in the form of commercial viability, further compelled filmmakers to appeal to increasingly diverse audiences with spectacle and music, comedy and romance, as well as the beauty and innovation in the telling and picturizing of the tale.

The first film with sound was made in India in 1931, and the 1930s brought the rise of studios, of which New Theatres in Calcutta, Prabhat in Pune, and Bombay Talkies were the most significant. Even as Mirabai's story was visualized from the earliest days of the silent era, so too her story would quickly be depicted with the innovation of sound. Of the first films on Mirabai, *Meerabai* (Hindi)/*Rajrani Meera* (Bengali) released in 1933 by New Theatres is of particular note, directed by Debaki Bose (1898–1971), who also wrote the Hindi screenplay.[102] The two versions were big-budget films starring Durgadas Bannerjee and Chandrabati Devi in the Bengali one and Prithviraj Kapoor and Durga Khote in the Hindi one. Chandrabati Devi would go on to become a major Bengali film star, and Prithviraj Kapoor's career was launched with this film and Bose's *Seeta* (1934), in which he also starred with Durga Khote, the two becoming a famous on-screen duo.[103] In subsequent advertising New Theatres used the production of these Mirabai films as a mark of its self-described status as a "cathedral of culture."[104]

Analyzing cinematic portrayals of Mira brings its own challenges. The authorship of a film is unquestionably collaborative, with the directors playing decisive roles but studios, screenwriters, actors, cinematographers, and others contributing to the final product, which is further shaped by the restrictions and tropes of the genre, audience expectations, and commercial concerns. Such dynamic intersubjectivity, marked by multiple and sometimes conflicting messages infused with varying authorial intent, performative interpretation, and audience participation in the construction of meaning, has become familiar to us by now as a general characteristic of the performative narrative traditions that surround Mirabai—the process of making a film merely bringing this into high relief and adding its own genre-specific dimensions.

Each film is necessarily shaped by these multiple variables and influences, and Mira's role in the cultural and national debates taking place within them will vary considerably. The commercial success and critical acclaim of many of these films are a testament that they—and she—touch widely and deeply held sentiments and values, struggles and aspirations. It is also the case that specific individuals have had profound impacts on this genre, as they have on others, both with respect to the choice to portray Mira and the ways in which she is invoked and translated. Among these individuals are the directors Debaki Bose, Kidar Nath Sharma, and S. S. Gulzar and the singer-actor M. S. Subbulakshmi and her husband, Sadasivam.

Debaki Bose is recognized as a key innovator of character development in Indian cinema, praised for the lyrical quality and technical and artistic sophistication of his films and credited with making significant contributions to establishing the genre of saint films and the social and educational potential of cinema in India.[105] As a young man, Bose left university to join the freedom struggle in Calcutta and only later made his way into film, first as an actor, then directing New Theatres studio's first major hit, *Chandidas,* in Bengali and Hindi in 1932, with his *Meerabai/Rajrani Meera* released the next year. As Rachel McDermott observes, "It is no coincidence that the devotional [film] rose to such prominence during the 1930s when nationalism was one of the dominant public concerns in India and Gandhian nationalism was at its height" and with Gandhi so "closely aligned to bhakti in his everyday life and politics."[106]

Though Bose's Mira film is clearly highly regarded, information regarding it is limited, and unlike *Chandidas* scholars have given it little attention.[107]

According to an available summary, the Rajasthani princess from Chittor marries the rana of Mewar only to be "persecuted by her husband and brother-in-law when she abandons the world to become a devotee of Krishna. She undertakes a journey of penance and performs a miracle which the king attributes to the machinations of an evil army chief Abhiram. After being imprisoned, vilified and accused of infidelity, she dies and is united with her god."[108] Such a brief synopsis cannot possibly convey the complexities and nuances of the plot, dialogue, and picturization of a full-length feature, yet clearly the film takes liberties with devotional accounts of the saint's life, just as *Chandidas* did.[109]

Drawing on this limited "narrative vignette" (in much the same way that such films enter the wider circulating traditions, as Sangari has suggested) but also on the extensive analysis available for *Chandidas*, we can surmise that this saint film too must have been marked by the authentic devotional sentiment attributed to their common director.[110] Melding bhakti with popular chromolithographic-style images and melodrama, Bose's films are characterized by "[v]isual excess including ornamental sets, the key placement of figures and uses of strong focused light, along with the deployment of music and dance."[111] These last are essential to Mira's tale, which is readily told as a romance, with the psychological depth and realness of character, noted by critics in Bose's earlier film, already one of the strengths of her story (attested by the Rajasthani khyals and low-caste epic *Mira Janma Patri* we have already examined).[112]

The relationship of Mira to her husband and brother-in-law within the film might readily conform to nineteenth-century notions of gender, so much a part of *bhadralok* (English-educated Bengali middle-class) consciousness, heavily influenced by the extremely popular nineteenth-century novelist Surat Chandra Chattopadhyay, whom Ashis Nandy and others identify as the "principal literary inspiration and patron saint" of New Theatres.[113] Mira is clearly the strong but long-suffering woman, and her persecutors are easily made to conform to the corresponding image of the weak, vacillating male that haunted this bureaucratic class in varying measure, despite concomitant nationalist assertions of a heroic Indian masculinity.[114] And her enraging decision as a married woman to renounce the world for God parallels the real-life choice of Banasa. The story as it is told here also resonates with Gandhi's invocation of Mira as ideal satyagrahi—in her patient endurance in the face of domestic abuse, in her holding fast to her convictions at all costs, including imprisonment and even death, and in her abandoning sensual desires and material pleasures as a renouncer.

Notably the potential Hindu-Muslim conflict that Akbar's presence characteristically represents appears to be replaced in this bilingual film with an internecine rajput dispute, perhaps deliberately intended to mute other nationalist rhetoric that cast Muslims in the role of enemy. Neither Raidas nor issues of caste are mentioned, and whether the film might have commented more directly on gender roles, either by way of challenge or reinforcement, cannot be ascertained from the available fragmentary synopsis. It does appear that Mira is suspect here, however, in much the same way she was in the *Mira Janma Patri*, for powers associated with her devotion which are given a more sinister interpretation, and she is presented as undertaking acts of penance, suggesting that there was some error in her behavior that she herself acknowledges, perhaps tied to her decision to renounce the world while her husband is alive or perhaps simply to the fact that she has displeased him.

Bose made another film, *Apna Ghar/Aple Ghar* (Your Home), released in Hindi and Marathi in 1942, that invoked the saint in a more overtly nationalist context, but also challenged both arranged marriage and pativrata ideals and offered Mirabai as a model for twentieth-century women to follow their conscience into political action, even in the face of familial opposition.[115] Set in contemporary times, this is a "social" film rather than a "saint" film, describing the arranged marriage of a forest contractor to a woman named Meera. She is a social activist working among tribals who are threatened by his business practices, and she accepts the marriage only to please her ill father. Refusing her husband's demands that she stop her unionizing work and conform to the pativrata ideal of exclusive service to his personal needs, she vows to leave and never return. His attitude toward both his wife and the tribal people is radically transformed after she is presumed drowned in a river, though unbeknownst to him the tribals have rescued her. Even in this equally very limited narrative vignette, echoes of the rajput-nationalist synthesis of Mira's story are clear, particularly in her presumed drowning, as the film explores the more transgressive implications of invoking Mira as a nationalist heroine and of Gandhi's employing her example to motivate women's political activism and independent moral conscience. And it ends with the transformation of her husband, even as Gandhi insisted Mira's loving resistance had impacted hers.

Another Hindi film released in 1942, *Armaan* (a word meaning a heart-felt wish, desire, longing, or hope), also features a heroine named Meera, but in a dramatically different contemporary translation. This melodramatic "science fiction romance" written and directed by Kidar Nath Sharma was his first experiment with a Mira-like character, though he would go on to write and direct the 1950 Hindi hit film *Jogan* (cited already for its depiction of a community of Mira-esque women renouncers and opening with the main character, a woman renouncer named Mira Devi, singing bhajans of the saint), and also a short educational film on the saint's life produced in 1960.[116] *Armaan* tells the story of a scientist who in 1910 "invents a ray that records pain and pleasure photographically... [whose] experiments render him blind."[117] He is nursed back to health by the heroine Meera, a village girl, and a romance grows between the two. However, she ends up murdering a holy man to get his healing potion—an elixir that can cure her beloved's blindness but whose price is beyond her reach. She rushes back to bring it to him, but "all nature protests her actions," and the potion is stolen by a villain who then takes the credit for healing the scientist. In a tragic turn of events, her beloved does not recognize her with his newfound sight and accuses her of murder. The dangers of modernization and technology that may blind one to one's own world are balanced against the idealization yet also limitations of rural and traditional feminine sensibilities (embodied by the saint's namesake), even as the potential healing power but also heartless exploitation of religion converge in the story.

Though her beloved eventually learns the truth, opening up the possibility for reconciliation, the film raises particularly serious questions about this woman's willingness to kill to save him. All of nature recoils at her action, as the audience undoubtedly would, the shock magnified by her association with the saintly Mira. Yet if the absolute devotion to God (embodied by the saint) is deployed to inspire absolute devotion to a human beloved—or to the nation or even to the wider pursuit of justice and peace—does such devotion mean that one would, or should, be willing to die but also to kill? And is such killing ever justifiable, even in the face of tremendous evil or dire need? Or is it murder—the immoral and unnatural taking of a life in the desire to obtain what one wants, whether for self, beloved, family, or nation? And can one ever really return home after such killing and resume ordinary life?

Both *Apna Ghar* and *Armaan* were released in 1942. The Japanese had bombed Calcutta and the east coast of India, and India was being drawn directly into World War II, though initially divided over which side to take amid shifting internal alliances. The Quit India movement was launched in August, as the Independence struggle intensified and grew more militant. Gandhi was in prison, and the resistance movement—"by far the most serious rebellion since that of 1857," in the words of the viceroy—was violently suppressed by combined British and Indian troops.[118] Women had increasingly gotten involved in direct violent resistance over the preceding decade, evoking a strong counterreaction of revulsion in public discourse.[119] It is against this backdrop of noncooperation, violence, and turmoil that these films were released. Mira's story and character inflected into the contemporary world is part of the imaginary used to present and wrestle with the internal and external conflicts of fighting for social justice, for Independence, and within this larger global conflict, whether with nonviolent or violent means.

Between 1936 and 1947, following Bose's *Meerabai/Rajrani Meera*, eight other features specifically focused on the saint Mira's life would be produced in Hindi, Tamil, Marathi, Telegu, Gujarati, and Punjabi.[120] Among these, it is *Meera*, directed by Ellis S. Duncan and starring the Karnatic singer M. S. Subbulakshmi (1916–2004), that would have the greatest impact on perceptions of the saint and on the nation.[121] The impetus for this film came from Subbulakshmi's husband, Sadasivam, who saw film as a premier vehicle for recognition of his wife's talent as well as for the uplift of the common people via bhakti. Subbulakshmi herself is said to have chosen Mira as a subject (Figure 6.1).[122] An avid Gandhian activist, Sadasivam had married Subbulakshmi in 1940, avowedly so that he might be able to fully dedicate himself to guide and develop her talent, and he established his own production company, Chandraprabha Cinetone, to ensure his wife's meteoric rise from the concert stage to the screen.

An American Hollywood cinematographer, Ellis Duncan, who had arrived in India in 1935 and subsequently became a major director of Tamil

Figure 6.1 M. S. Subbulakshmi as Mirabai in a promotional picture for the film *Meera* (1945 Tamil/1947 Hindi) by Chandraprabha Cinetone. Wikimedia, accessed January 13, 2023, https://commons.wikimedia.org/w/index.php?curid=55982.

films, directed this film as well as Subbulakshmi's earlier film appearance in *Shakunthalai* (1940). Sadasivam cowrote the plot with his close friend and colleague, famed journalist, fiction writer, and Gandhian freedom fighter "Kalki" R. Krishnamurthy, who was also an outspoken proponent of the political power of film and an advocate for its responsible use.[123] Filmed primarily on location in the stunning landscape of Rajasthan, as well as in Vrindavan and Dwarka, *Meera* was released first in Tamil in 1945 and then in Hindi in 1947 and was immediately a tremendous popular hit (though critics were not always so kind).[124] The subsequent playback recording of Subbulakshmi's Mira songs became a standard, and for many, Subbulakshmi would come to *be* Mira.[125] When they imagined the saint, it was the young Subbulakshmi they saw and her voice that they heard. Even during the filming in Vrindavan, people flocked to follow her, spontaneously creating the immense crowd needed for the scene.

This cinematic portrayal fills the narrative with song and celebrates the exquisite beauty of these compositions and the immense depth and sweetness of Mira's devotion—and Subbulakshmi's voice. Fully half of the film is dedicated to Subbulakshmi singing as Mira while engaged in acts of devotion, sometimes in private, sometimes surrounded by enraptured devotees. The camera lingers on her face and on Krishna, invoking the same devotion in those who hear her within the film, as the viewing audience is drawn into Mira's presence and into this extended community of the saint in characteristically bhakti ways. Mira is not portrayed as rebellious in any sense but rather as one so strong in her love of God that she can do no other—the embodiment of bhakti itself and of the feminine spirituality expected of both women and men in Vaishnava devotion and of truly "Indian" women in an idealized Indian nation, past and present.

Mira's childhood devotion is portrayed with innocent purity (by Subbulakshmi's step-daughter Radha), the lively child inextricably and irresistibly drawn to Krishna, dancing as Radha in the opening children's dramatic performance, spontaneously breaking into song and embarrassed to find herself singing solo out loud and in public in the temple, dancing with the Divine Cowherd again as Radha in her dreams, waking to run down to the palace temple to embrace his image (later given to her by the visiting sadhu to whom it belonged and who is none other than Rup Goswami), impishly declaring to her mother that Girdhar Gopal will be her bridegroom when she sees a wedding party, and dancing before Krishna's image, until suddenly she is years older and a young woman (in a scene acclaimed for its cinematic innovation). She does not want to marry another, but does not resist. She is portrayed with eyes lowered during the marriage ceremony but as fulfilling her ritual obligations within it and mirroring the shyness and emotions of other young brides preparing to leave their natal homes to enter into patrilocal arranged marriages.

The rana is ever understanding and supportive of Mira's private nightly devotion in the palace. The two stroll through the beautiful palace grounds singing a bhajan together, and he promises to build a Krishna temple for her. He does so, and they go to the temple together for darshan, the rana visibly caught up in the emotion as Mira sings before all those gathered. She begins to attract followers; sadhus and ordinary men and women as well as members of the royal family listen with rapt attention and sing her songs. She spends more and more time in the temple and even wanders the streets singing in ecstasy, with larger and larger crowds gathering around her (bringing to mind Dutt's earlier portrayal of her companionate marriage to the rana and the growing distance between the couple).

Women are shown singing her songs as they work, carrying water and churning butter, little girls playing and adolescent young women dancing, potters molding their clay and farmers driving oxen to separate grain or turn waterwheels for irrigation, cowherds and boatmen, women returning with fuel and farmers coming home in the evening, musicians and pilgrims—even the birds and streams seem to sing her songs. She is clearly beloved by the common people of every walk of life, caste, and class, culminating in a stunning scene of her singing in the street accompanied by an immense, ecstatic crowd.

The rana observes all this and appears painfully disturbed, though not angry, and he talks gently to Mira, telling her that she may bring disgrace to Mewar, not because of her own behavior but because of all the renouncers and poor people in the streets (seemingly reflecting a more twentieth-century concern of the emerging nation but also removing even the faintest hint of possible blemish from Mira's reputation). When she innocently points out that God knows no difference between the poor and the powerful, he becomes exasperated with her, but she agrees to comply with his request that she fulfill her ceremonial responsibilities as the wife of a maharana at an upcoming festival. He is clearly longing for her presence, but when he asks her to join him once again in the gardens, she plainly feels the pull of the waiting devotees in the temple, and he turns away in disappointment, letting her go.

Beautifully arrayed in finery—silks, jewels, flowers, and ornaments—and on her way to join him in court as she had promised, she hears Krishna's flute echoing in the halls of the palace and, unable to resist, runs to the temple. Singing bhajans with deep devotion, she is portrayed in stark contrast to the dancing girls performing for the maharana, who becomes increasingly agitated in the presence of all the waiting courtiers, as the scene cuts back and forth between Mira and the waiting rana. Initially reassured that women take a long time to dress, he is finally informed of what is delaying his wife and strides into the temple to find her surrounded by the masses, who are singing and playing drums and cymbals in a devotional frenzy. She faints just as he seems ready to draw his sword, truly angry now.

In the next scene, her husband's younger brother Vikram emerges from the shadows and pours poison into a cup he then gives to his frightened and reluctant sister Uda to take to Mira. Mira must die to protect the honor of Mewar. Uda delivers it to Mira, who is worshiping in her private temple. Praying to Krishna, Mira brings the cup to her lips. Her sister-in-law cries out, trying to stop her, but Mira drinks it down. At that very moment, as Rup Goswami worships in Krishna's temple in Dwarka, the image changes color (echoing the story from Mahipati), and the doors allowing his darshan snap shut on their own.[126] But Mira is unharmed and reassures her sister-in-law, breaking into another song and playing kartals. As her sister-in-law runs out, Mira starts to dance.

Tansen comes to hear her sing in the temple in the usual disguise, accompanied not by Akbar but by the Kachvaha prince of Amer (Jaipur), Man Singh, who, as we have noted, was a trusted military commander in the Mughul court and who would lead Akbar's attack on the famed Rana Pratap in the Battle of Haldighati.[127] Hearing Mira sing, they are clearly swept up in devotion. The rana's younger brother and his advisor enter and grow suspicious of the two, especially after the respectful strangers talk to Mira and give her a pearl necklace on behalf of their guru. There is no question of Akbar himself coming or of a Muslim touching Mira here. When Mira asks their guru's name, Man Singh says only that he will come soon to hear her sing.

The deep appreciation for the saint expressed by these two men who come on behalf of Akbar troubles conceptions of polarized opposition along religious lines and affirms a shared cultural heritage, with the dialogue declaring Mira's fame throughout "Hindustan." Yet these emissaries of the emperor do still come in disguise into the heart of Mewar, and Man Singh himself was viewed by some as a collaborator with the enemy, even as Mewar was lauded in nationalist rhetoric for never submitting to Mughal rule.[128] An ambivalence toward Hindu-Muslim relations thus remains, albeit attenuated.

The rana's brother and his advisor follow the two men out of the temple and confront them rudely, accusing them of being thieves. In the ensuing fistfight, the intruders get away but drop a box marked with Akbar's seal that had held the jewels. When his brother reports this to the rana, the rana is finally truly enraged, and under his brother's influence orders the destruction of the temple where his wife worships so publicly and that he had built for her but which the enemies of Mewar have now defiled. His brother is dispatched to carry out the order, but when he confronts Mira, she refuses to leave the temple that is her only refuge, though she tries to persuade others to do so until he insults Krishna, denying her Lord's power to save his devotees. Then she stands her ground, encouraging the continued public singing as others pledge to remain with her. This is the only time she speaks with such conviction and strength, but she does so only in defense of Krishna and not to her husband but to his evil brother, whose divisive behavior is creating conflict where there was none.

Derisively laughing with his advisor and the gathered soldiers, the rana's brother has a cannon loaded and aimed at the temple, though Mira is standing in front of its closed doors to protect those singing within—the epitome of a Gandhian satyagrahi. Mira's sister-in-law Uda bursts in before the rana, confessing their earlier failed attempt to poison Mira and, now as her supporter, begging him to stop his brother from firing on the temple and killing her, as do others in his court. Persuaded, the rana rides out to stop them. All the soldiers have refused to fire on Mirabai, so Vikram's advisor does it himself. Mira is not hurt, though the arriving rana himself appears injured, in heart if not in body, clearly caring nothing for his own life in his effort to save her. Mirabai asks her husband, with the same sweet innocence, if indeed he had ordered the destruction of the very temple he had built for her. When he does not answer, she realizes that she must leave the palace, having driven her husband to such an act and unable to fulfill her role as a rajput queen. She must go in search of her Lord. She kneels before the rana before setting off for Vrindavan; he is clearly heartbroken, though he does not try to stop her. People prostrate themselves before her as she walks slowly away, singing and playing the vina as she goes.

Mira then appears climbing alone to the top of a mountain over boulders, wearing simple dark clothing, her hair loose, and singing with poignant sorrow of the pain that the absence of Krishna's darshan brings. A vast empty countryside stretches below her, as we see her small figure silhouetted against the immensity of the sky, the wind riffling her clothing (reminiscent of Kanu Desai's portrait of her "quest"). She walks alone across wastelands and sand dunes (mirroring the sentiments evoked in the refrain of the low-caste epic *Mira Janam Patri*: "Come Sanvariya, Girdhari come quickly—having put her trust in you, Mira is alone"). Parched and at the end of her strength, she sees a pool of water but falls unconscious at its edge, unable even to drink. Krishna appears as a young goatherd and pours water into her mouth to revive her. The scene cuts back briefly to the rana, pining away in his silent, empty courtyards, crushing a flower that clearly no longer holds any fragrance for him, the sounds of their former devotional duets haunting him and bringing him to tears.

Mira struggles on, through forests and jungle, isolated, pelted by rain and buffeted by wind, her vina smashed by a falling branch in the storm. Finally she reaches the shores of the Jamuna River and Vrindavan. She starts to sing, and people flock to her—holy men, women, pilgrims—as she walks through idyllic pastoral scenes until she reaches Rup Goswami's ashram. His disciples try to turn away this woman, but when he hears her wise response, he runs out to meet her himself, calling her "guru" even as she does him (as in Dutt's telling). She reminds him that he gave her an image of Krishna when she was a child.

Meanwhile back in Mewar, the people are in an uproar because Mira has gone. Then news comes that she has reached Vrindavan and is now on her way to Dwarka. The rana sets out with a party of armed horsemen to find her and bring her back, galloping through the desert hills. She is shown calmly riding in a palanquin on a camel (again à la Kanu Desai) with a large entourage on her way to Dwarka and then walking across the dunes, dressed in white, with Rup Goswami and a small band of his disciples, all the while singing. Having reached the temple, she sings with tragic longing, her eyes fixed on the closed inner doors. The rana arrives, hears her singing, and comes running through the temple complex. Suddenly the inner doors of the temple open on their own, and the image of Krishna comes alive, his arms reaching out toward Mira.

At that moment, as she begins to run toward Krishna, the rana enters, calling out, "Mira, Mira." He reaches her, touching her shoulder just as her body collapses to the ground, her spirit leaving her body and joining her Lord. The rana is depicted tragically cradling her head and stroking her hair, but she is gone. The scene shifts, and he is alone in her temple in his palace, a handful of flowers in his hands. Suddenly all the lights are aflame, the bells are ringing, and he can hear Mira singing. The doors here, too, open on their own, and Krishna is visible through the rising smoke of incense. As the film closes, the rana places his offering at Krishna's feet in much the way Mira had done in so many earlier scenes. There is a dignity and refined beauty to the portrayal of Mira here, both reflecting and shaping many people's perceptions of the saint, and the rehabilitation of Mira's husband Bhojraj, begun by Dutt, reaches its culmination, for he is ever supportive of his wife and an immensely sympathetic character, his only "fault" that he loved her so much.

The acclaimed English poet and highly respected nationalist orator and activist Sarojini Naidu (1879–1949) was selected by Sadasivam to introduce

Subbulakshmi to North Indian audiences at the Hindi release of the film. Merging the two women, Naidu praised both Subbulakshmi's artistic excellence and Mira's appeal and significance as a cultural icon. Indeed she declared, "Mira rightly belongs to the North though she indeed belongs to the whole world."[129] In such a context her words carried great weight. An advocate of Hindu-Muslim unity, imprisoned by the British multiple times and known for her abilities as a political organizer, she played an instrumental role in founding the All India Women's Congress and was elected the first Indian woman president of the Indian National Congress in 1925.[130] Though she rejected his asceticism and was known for her glamorous dress and enjoyment of life's pleasures, she worked closely with Gandhi for many years, and he sent her on a lecture tour of the United States in the wake of Mayo's *Mother India*, an Indian woman speaking for Indian women, her charm, fiery character, and eloquence a compelling counter to such racist imperialism.[131]

At this crucial moment in India's struggle for Independence, Sadasivam invited her to speak to and for the nation, asserting and affirming Mira as a truly all-India and indeed global saint (and his wife as a cultural treasure, the pride of the new nation). Clearly Mira could bridge North and South, and even Hindu and Muslim, and this film, released in both Hindi and Tamil at this time, bolstered an emerging Indian national and cultural identity. Naidu spoke in English, as she almost always did, here strategically sidestepping South Indian and other opposition to Hindi as a national language as she addressed people across linguistic regions of India and beyond its borders.[132] The Hindi film was released on August 15, 1947, to coincide with the formal declaration of national Independence, and a gala screening only a few months later, in November, in the wake of the devastating violence of the Partition, was attended by the new prime minister Jawaharlal Nehru and former viceroy Lord Mountbatten and his wife as well as other national leaders.[133] That this film was screened by Doordarshan on national television decades later in 1991, in the aftermath of Rajiv Gandhi's assassination in Tamil Nadu by a Tamil Tiger suicide bomber, confirms a wide recognition of Mira's, and the film's, powerful unifying potential for the nation.[134] At the time of its release, it also contributed significantly to increasing awareness of Mira outside of India, with a European premiere in the Netherlands in 1951.[135]

The portrayal of Mira here belongs to the narrative family of the rajput-nationalist-devotional synthesis represented by Dutt, Deviprasad, and Behari, with Mira's husband an even more sympathetic character and Mira strong in her devotion but always loved and respected by him and ever the loving companion, her character marked by an innocent sweetness. The human story is tragic: the rana loves her, and she clearly cares deeply for him, though her love of God is essential to her very being and at times causes him distress. In the end it is his brother's enmity, rather than Akbar's coming, and the rana's inability initially to see the situation clearly and control his anger that tip the balance toward seemingly unnecessary but perhaps ultimately unavoidable tragedy, particularly for him.

India as a nation suffered similarly in the communal violence that marred the Independence struggle. The film seems to traverse the emotional landscape of such conflict even as it fosters national unity, evoking the beauty and richness of India's shared cultural and religious heritage, which stands in stark contrast to the deep sorrow and pain caused by a divisiveness so unfounded but tragic in its consequences. Politics enters the film even more overtly when Mira stands before the temple doors in the face of the loaded cannon, a paragon of Gandhian noncooperation and nonviolent resistance—willing to die but not to kill and not wanting to be the cause of further conflict. At the same time the film also reflects many people's understanding of and deep affection for Mira as a bhakti saint, and stands in continuity with earlier visual representations of the saint and conceptions of femininity. Mira's activism here does not address social inequities, exploitation, land rights, and the like but is safely spiritualized and redefined as loyalty.

In many ways the film also resonated with Subbulakshmi's own life. She was born into the female lineage of devadasis of Madurai, though this fact remained a "public secret," not widely acknowledged until after her death and not part of her official public persona.[136] This is not surprising given the anti-nautch campaigns that began in the nineteenth century and intensified in the 1920s and 1930s, with these temple performers labeled as prostitutes and disenfranchised economically, socially, and religiously.[137] During this same period, the dance and musical traditions of the devadasis were lauded as authentic Indian traditions and allegedly "rescued from the hands of degenerate devadasis and taken up by women from respectable (that is, Brahmin) families."[138]

Her voice was truly extraordinary, and guided by her mother, who was an accomplished vina player, Subbulakshmi moved readily from singing in the temples of Madurai into the realm of recording and then of public classical music performance, when even this was still largely not considered proper for women. Her mother would also seek to secure her own and her daughters' future through marriages to wealthy patrons, but Subbulakshmi exhibited a quiet strength of character and independence from an early age, gently refusing her mother's first proposal and affirming her desire to develop her musical talents.[139] By seventeen she had already become a highly acclaimed singer. She met the brahman Sadasivam in 1936 in Madras—she nineteen, he thirty-four—when he interviewed her for a magazine article. He became a daily visitor, assisting her in arranging concerts and the like. Concerned about the growing relationship, her mother took her back to Madurai and found a second wealthy marriage partner for her, but once again demonstrating courage and determination, Subbulakshmi fled under cover of darkness and returned to Madras, finding refuge ultimately in Sadasivam's home. Though he had a wife and two daughters, Sadasivam was more than willing to assist the young woman and threw himself into promoting her career and arranging for her to act in her first film, *Sevasadanam* (1938). Directed by K. Subramanyam, the film combined song with a message-oriented story "challenging British colonialism and Brahmanic oppression at that same time," in which a poor brahman girl without a dowry is forced to marry a much older man and tormented by her in-laws, eventually running away to try to support herself singing, her husband ultimately setting her free.[140]

Subbulakshmi and Sadasivam's relationship gave rise to gossip, and conflict with her mother and brother erupted after her departure. They tried first to persuade Subbulakshmi to return and even allegedly abducted her at one point, but she ultimately chose to stay. Subbulakshmi would fall in love with her sophisticated and extremely musically talented costar G. N. Balasubramaniam during the filming of her second film, *Shakuntalai*, her passionate feelings expressed in letters he kept hidden away for decades. Sadasivam did everything he could to disrupt their relationship and after his wife's death married Subbulakshmi himself in 1940, some would say all too soon.[141]

Their marriage followed the companionate model of Mira and the rana in the film, he supportive (though also highly controlling) of her musical career and she reserved, deferential, and humble, exhibiting an inner strength and dignity coupled with innocent purity—the perfect embodiment of a virtuous brahman middle-class wife. She spoke of him as her "friend, guide and philosopher" and as her parent and preceptor. It was commonly assumed that their relationship was not sexual, and some speculated that her husband stood in for the father she never knew. He was "rana" to her "Mira," on the model of the sympathetic celluloid king, whose cinematic rehabilitation would also validate and valorize Sadasivam's relationship with his illustrious wife. Their marriage would be lifted up as exemplary of "a new type of ideal marriage [in which music was the bonding agent that] . . . had the advantage of being able to appear both voluntary and deeply traditional, private as well as public," as other middle-class women were also being encouraged to engage in the "spiritually uplifting domestic activity" of learning classical music to fill their newly acquired leisure time.[142]

A close family friend, Lakshmi Vishwanathan, drawing parallels between the lives of the saint and the singer, reports, "Subbulakshmi's only love has been her music. Realising this, perhaps, Sadasivam did not burden her with any of the duties or responsibilities of a traditional Indian wife. She put her heart and soul into music and gradually devoted all her energy to purely devotional music. Above all, she readily donated most of her earnings to charity, helping with every worthy cause and needy institutions."[143] Sadasivam would build her the twentieth-century equivalent of a temple for her musical devotion, in ensuring her entry into film, founding his own production company, and writing and producing *Meera* (after her success starring in *Sevasadanam*, his own production *Shakuntalai*, and Y. V. Rao's *Savithri*). As Amanda Weiden observes, Subbulakshmi "became a larger-than-life figure not simply by her musical talent but also by Sadasivam's careful cultivation of her persona as a singer of pan-Indian and international appeal."[144]

Yet Subbulakshmi's life was also marked by sorrow—in having to essentially leave her mother behind in her marriage; in the misfortunes of her step-daughter and disciple Radha, whom she felt powerless to help; in the loss of her material wealth; and even, according to some, in her marital relations, with Sadasivam rumored to have been jealous of her male admirers as her fame grew, even as he had earlier thwarted her budding romance with her costar.[145] Yet this sorrow and loss are said to have led to a deepening of her devotion and the emotional power of her exquisite singing, again paralleling the rajput historians' portrayal of Mira. She was at once traditional and thoroughly modern, performing and promoting classical musical traditions as she achieved national and international fame, traveling the world and being the first musician to be honored by the national Bharat Ratna award, yet always compliant and reverential to her husband. And her filmic portrayal of Mirabai, it seems, was the crown jewel in her mature identity, crafted jointly by husband and wife and importantly allowing her to negotiate the transformation from devadasi to brahman wife, just as the art forms once the purview of these female ritual specialists were transformed into the classical arts of India suitable for upper-caste and upper-class society. Both she and the devadasi art forms she perfected were thereby given a brahman stamp of approval, a transformation facilitated at least in part by Mira. As Kumkum Sangari also notes, her story "[a]s a reformed 'daughter' of a devadasi ... mov[ing] from transgression to restraint" demonstrated the "'uplift' and (self) brahmanisation" advocated by "colonial and national male reformism."[146]

In life and on screen, Subbulakshmi embodied devotional, nationalist, and upper-caste images of the saint and ideals of feminine spirituality at this crucial juncture, and her performance brought solace and offered a fragile spark of unity in this dark and tumultuous time. Gandhi asked her to sing a well-known Mira bhajan of *vinaya*, or request, for what would be his last birthday in 1947, the bhajan in which Mira asks for help as Krishna's servant, recounting how he rescued past devotees—Prahlad, Draupadi, and the drowning elephant—and knowing that when she suffers, he feels her pain.[147] Subbulakshmi's rendition of this song was played across the country as news of Gandhi's assassination was broadcast only a few months later—hers the voice of the grieving nation and Mira's words their collective outcry, even as they had been for the Mahatma himself.

That two other Mirabai features were also released in 1947 in Gujarati and Hindi and two more in Hindi in 1949 and 1956 suggests that the saint had indeed come of age as a pan-Indian cultural icon.[148] The fact that none of these was particularly memorable and that no further feature films about Mira's life were made until the 1970s confirms the power and perceived completeness of Subbulakshmi's particular portrayal and embodiment of the saint in this film as in life. Mira became Subbulakshmi even as Subbulakshmi became Mira, both transformed into this domesticated national saint. As the new nation was born, the saint served as a rallying point for what was good and true and authentic about India, epitomized in Subbulakshmi's cinematic portrayal, in dramatic contrast to the unspeakable violence of Partition that attended that birth. And Mira's voice, particularly in songs of *viraha* (love in separation), also articulated the intense suffering, loss, and longing that marked this turbulent time for so many others, in addition to Gandhi.[149]

Conclusion

Having examined the earliest available information about Mirabai—the written artifacts of stories people told about her in the sixteenth, seventeenth, and eighteenth centuries—we find the saint Mira made and remade, elements of her character emerging and episodes that will mark later tellings of her life set out. Clearly these hagiographic tellers have great admiration for this great devotee, yet they also have agendas and interests of their own, addressing particular audiences and sociopolitical contexts and employing performed narrative strategically to get a number of things done—to expand the constituency of their own sampraday and garner patronage, to draw this well-loved saint into the orbit of their own lineage or to expel her, to create a transregional and transsectarian spiritual, ethical, and aesthetic bhakti sensibility, to school women in how to balance bhakti and domestic life, to reinforce social hierarchies even while relativizing them, and much more. Even so, it is they (and others whose words have gone unrecorded) who must be credited with crafting Mirabai the saint, with telling the story of her life along with other beloved bhaktas, demonstrating her great love for Krishna and his for her, the power of her songs and example to draw others into such love, and the incredible opposition that she had to overcome to do so. And they remain the foundation of what we know of her life, with the verses of Nabhadas and Priyadas, Mahipati and the Pushtimargi *Vartas* still being read and recited for personal and communal devotion and commented on and incorporated into didactic kathas and kirtans into our own time.

However, as we have seen, the dominant story that informs scholarly and popular writing on who Mirabai was harkens back to her nineteenth-century and early twentieth-century alleged "historical biography," drafted by elite nationalists and rajput historians, standing on the shoulders of these earlier hagiographers but deploying a wholly different set of narrative conventions, drawn from tales of female heroines, and writing in a historical docudrama mode. The tale they tell is of an educated, strong, intelligent, and creative woman, embodying Indian cultural and religious ideals—but also one who always defers to her husband and other males who direct her actions, neither rebel nor memsahib, and who could embody Indian femininity and spirituality in the face of British material and technological dominance. These elite men would be largely successful in disseminating this "historical biography" of the saint (though even here there is variation), at least for a time. But freed from the tyranny of their claims to exclusionary historical veracity and dismissal of so much else as distortion and falsification, we are able to appreciate this and other tellings for what they are: stories speaking of the past but also to the present, memories interwoven with creative imaginings, both collective and individual, the artifacts of relationships with the saint and all she represents, reflecting a river of circulating traditions about her and a wide array of communities and individuals' contexts and concerns. And we are able to hear the truths of many other tellings—for example, the brutal realities of caste and gender oppression, the struggles and negotiations, triumphs and tragedies of those who live under them, as we heard in *Mira Janma Patri,* and the challenges of arranged marriage and the power and danger of love but also of constraining social norms in the *Mira Mangal* khyals of Lacchiram of Kuchaman and Punamchand Sikhwal.

In the twentieth century leading up to India's Independence, we have also seen how key events, specific individuals, and new media significantly impacted perceptions of the saint as she was fully transformed into an Indian cultural heroine with pan-Indian appeal who could rally especially women in the fight for Independence, their own as well as that of the nation. The particulars of these relationships reveal how people experience the saint, her impact as they negotiate their individual lives and identities, and the ways this ripples out into the wider circulating traditions that swirl around her, in particularly dramatic ways in the cases of Tagore, Mahadevi, Gandhi, Behari, and Subbulakshmi, but also by more ordinary women and men. And despite efforts to propagate a more socially conservative Mira, many would find in her inspiration and precedent for quite unorthodox lives and for personal and social transformation.

We have followed many threads that together offer a multidimensional portrait of the saint—who Mirabai has been and is to so many. Yet this is not the end but rather only a beginning. In the decades following Independence people in India turned to Mira again and again as they wrestled with what it means to be Indian, to be modern in an Indian mode, to be a woman of substance in a man's world, to be a Hindu, to be a member of a global interspiritual community, to be empowered to live a life of dignity and fulfillment, to find one's voice as a writer or an artist, to be a true human being. She continues to be a vital part of the cultural imaginary and of multidimensional understandings of the feminine in India and beyond, and her life story continues to be used strategically to speak many truths and, sometimes, to

Figure C.1 Images of Mirabai and Krishna installed in 2002 in the Meera Temple within the Chittor Fort.

suppress others that might nevertheless erupt once again in another telling. Many continue to emerge transformed from engagement with the saint, some in ongoing relationships that last throughout their lives. And so there is much more we can learn about who she has become in postcolonial and global contexts (see Figure C.1).

As a saint Mira is known also for her voice, the songs sung in her name, and her appropriateness as a cultural icon rests not only on her embodiment of Indian spirituality and femininity but also on her being the greatest premodern poetess of what has been advocated (at least by some) as the Indian national/civilization language of Hindi. But there is no agreement on which songs sung in her name were indeed composed by her, and among them are certainly a great number that do not conform to a strict Vaishnava orthodoxy or to the nationalist-rajput-devotional image of the saint. Coming to terms with this vast body of song would be a project for the scholars of the new nation and an increasingly interested international scholarly community. Yet, even as some have tried to close down the abundance of tellings of Mira's life, others have sought to circumscribe Mira's "authentic" works. Though they, like other elite nationalists and advocates of a generalized Hindu orthodoxy, might have some measure of success in propagating their views, Mira's voice cannot be so easily corralled. She will go global, carried wherever Indian people migrated and picked up by others, captivated by stories of her and songs sung in her name, translated into new cultural and religious contexts, the floodgates opened by new electronic media.

Armed with the knowledge of how she has come to us across earlier centuries, we are now in a better position to understand something of this immense diversity, her ongoing relevance, and the continuing inspirational and transformative power of her life, character, and voice. Even as we should not accept her alleged "historical biography" as the final and objective record of her life, neither can we assume that songs sung in her name give us access to an individual sixteenth-century woman's thoughts and words. But there is much we can say about the importance of such an archetypal figure in the minds and hearts of people across South Asia and now around the world and of participation in singing and co-authoring her voice. Accordingly, we are now poised to explore the dynamic song tradition that bears her name and postcolonial and global invocations and incarnations of this incredible woman saint and cultural heroine into our own time.

Notes

Introduction

1. Nancy M. Martin, "Mirabai Comes to America: The Translation and Transformation of a Saint," *Journal of Hindu Studies* 3 (2010): 12-35.
2. Marzia Balzani and Varsha Joshi, "The Death of a Concubine's Daughter: Palace Manuscripts as a Source for the Study of the Rajput Elite," *South Asia Research* 14, no. 2 (1994): 137-139.
3. For such an inscription dated 1497 praising Rama Bai, daughter of Rana Kumbha, see R. C. Agarwal, "An Inscription from Javar, Rajasthan," *Indian Historical Quarterly* 34 (1958): 215-225.
4. Aditya Behl, *Love's Subtle Magic: An Indian Islamic Literary Tradition, 1379-1545*, ed. Wendy Doniger (New York: Oxford University Press, 2012), 177-217.
5. For an introduction to these women saints, see Madhu Kishwar and Ruth Vanita, eds., *Women Bhakta Poets, Manushi 50-52* (1989).
6. A. K. Ramanujan, "Three Hundred *Rāmāyaṇas*: Five Examples and Three Thoughts on Translation" (1991), in *The Collected Essays of A. K. Ramanujan*, general editor Vinay Dharwadker (New Delhi: Oxford University Press, 1999), 158.
7. Ramanujan, "Three Hundred *Rāmāyaṇa*," 134.
8. Kirin Narayan and Kenneth M. George, "Stories about Getting Stories: Interactional Dimensions in Folk and Personal Narrative Research," in *The Sage Handbook of Interview Research: The Complexity of the Craft*, 2nd edition, ed. Jaber F. Gubrium, James A. Holstein, Amir B. Marvasti, and Karyn D. McKinney (Thousand Oaks, CA: Sage, 2012), 514.
9. Paula Richman, ed., *Many Rāmāyaṇas: The Diversity of a Narrative Tradition in South Asia* (Berkeley: University of California Press, 1991).
10. Julius Lipner, "A Hindu View of Life," in *The Meaning of Life in the World Religions*, ed. J. Runzo and N. M. Martin (Oxford: Oneworld, 1999), 118.
11. Philip Lutgendorf, *The Life of a Text: Performing the Rāmcaritmānas of Tulsidas* (Berkeley: University of California Press, 1981).
12. Wendy Doniger [O'Flaherty], *Other People's Myths: The Cave of Echoes* (Chicago: University of Chicago Press, 1995), 25-44.
13. Vecheru Narayana Rao, David Shulman, and Sanjay Subrahmanyam, *Textures of Time: Writing History in South India 1600-1800* (Delhi: Permanent Black, 2001), 11.
14. Richard H. Davis, *Lives of Indian Images* (Princeton, NJ: Princeton University Press, 1997), 9.
15. A. K. Ramanujan, "On Women Saints" (1982), in *Collected Essays*, 272-275.
16. Davis, *Lives of Indian Images*, 261, 263.
17. John Stratton Hawley, "Author and Authority" (1988), in *Three Bhakti Voices: Mirabai, Surdas and Kabir in Their Times and Ours* (New York: Oxford University Press, 2005), 21-47.
18. *Mahabharata* 17: 3: 15, trans. John D. Smith, *The Mahābhārata: An Abridged Translation* (New York: Penguin, 2009), 776.

19. Kumkum Sangari details the historical and social situation in fifteenth- and sixteenth-century Rajasthan in connection to Mira in "Mirabai and the Spiritual Economy of Bhakti," *Economic and Political Weekly,* July 7 and 14, 1990, 1464–1475, 1537–1552.
20. Alan W. Entwistle, *Braj: Center of Krishna Pilgrimage* (Groningen: Egbert Forsten, 1987), 136–157.
21. David L. Haberman, *Acting as a Way of Salvation: A Study of Rāgānugā Bhakti Sādhana* (New York: Oxford University Press, 1988), 82–87.
22. Christian Lee Novetzke, *Religion and Public Memory: A Cultural History of the Saint Namdev in India* (New York: Columbia University Press, 2008), 13–23.
23. Parita Mukta, *Upholding the Common Life: The Community of Mirabai* (New Delhi: Oxford University Press, 1994).
24. Diana L. Eck, *Darshan: Seeing the Divine Image in India*, 3rd edition (New York: Columbia University Press, 1998).
25. Karl Smith, "From Dividual and Individual Selves to Porous Subjects," *Australian Journal of Anthropology* 23 (2012): 50–64.
26. Robert A. Orsi, *Between Heaven and Earth: The Religious Worlds People Make and the Scholars Who Study Them* (Princeton, NJ: Princeton University Press, 2005), 6.
27. Patton Burchett, "Agradās and Rām *Rasik Bhakti* Community: The Politics of Remembrance and the Authority of the Hindu Saint," *International Journal of Hindu Studies* 22 (2018): 432.

Chapter 1

1. In this section I offer an introduction to bhakti for purposes of understanding Mirabai—her story, her songs, the context of their performance. Understandings of bhakti have varied immensely across time and region, and its meaning and forms have developed in interaction with yogic and tantric traditions, integrated with meditation, asceticism, and temple worship, and in the presence of Buddhism, Jainism, and Sufism. Scholarship on bhakti (as well as other dimensions of what we have come to call Hinduism) from the nineteenth century to the present has been deeply impacted by nationalist and other interests, and characterizations of this strand of Hindu tradition as a distinct movement and a separate religious path have masked much of this variability, integration, and interaction. John Stratton Hawley and Patton E. Burchett offer much-needed correctives in their nuanced historical studies. See Hawley, *A Storm of Songs: India and the Idea of the Bhakti Movement* (Cambridge, MA: Harvard University Press, 2015) and Burchett, *A Genealogy of Devotion: Bhakti, Tantra, Yoga and Sufism in North India* (New York: Columbia University Press, 2019).
2. A. K. Ramanujan, "Afterword," in *Hymns for the Drowning: Poems for Viṣṇu by Nammāḻvār* (New York: Penguin Books, 1993), 103–104, n2.
3. Karen Pechilis [Prentiss], *The Embodiment of Bhakti* (New York: Oxford University Press, 1999), 24.
4. For a discussion of the term "sant," see Karine Schomer, "Introduction," in *The Sants: Studies in a Devotional Tradition of India*, ed. Karine Schomer and W. H. McLeod (Delhi: Motilal Banarsidass, 1987), 2–9. I have chosen to follow the convention of referring to these exemplary figures with the English word "saint" to capture their special status.
5. John Stratton Hawley, "Introduction: Saints and Virtues," in *Saints and Virtues*, ed. John Stratton Hawley (Berkeley: University of California Press, 1987), xi–xxiv.

6. James P. Hare, "Garland of Devotees: Nābhādās' *Bhaktamāl* and Modern Hinduism" (PhD diss., Columbia University, 2011), 4–6. He notes the twelfth-century Tamil Shaiva *Periya Purāṇam* by Cēkkiḻār and the thirteenth-century Virashaiva *Basava Purāṇa* of Palkāriki Somanātha as examples of compendiums limited by sectarian affiliation.
7. Most of the hagiographic references to Mira we will examine in this chapter and the next have been noted by Indian scholars writing in Hindi. The earliest comprehensive study was done by Vrajaratnadās, *Mīrā-Mādhurī* (Vāraṇsī: Hindī Sāhitya Kuṭīr, 1948), who offers full texts as well as some discussion. Many subsequent authors will reprise these passages and add to them. C. L. Prabhāt recaps all these hagiographic materials in Hindi, incorporating Vrajaratnadās and subsequent additions as well as his own, in his *Mīrā Jīvan aur Kāvya* (Jodhpur: Rājasthānī Granthāgār, 1999), 21–93.
8. Nābhādās, *Śrī Bhaktamāl*, with the *Bhaktirasabodhinī* commentary of Priyādās (Lucknow: Tejkumar Press, 1969), 713–723; Vrajaratnadās, *Mīrā-Mādhurī*, 28–32. This Tejkumar edition is the most widely available and used version. No critical edition or full English translation of either Nabhadas's *Bhaktamal* or Priyadas's commentary are currently available. Hawley has translated Nabhadas's verse and paraphrased Priyadas's commentary on Mira in John Stratton Hawley and Mark Juergensmeyer, *Songs of the Saints of India*, revised ed. (Delhi: Oxford University Press, 2004), 122–127. For a detailed discussion of the bhaktamal, including dates, manuscripts, etc. and its author, see Hare, "Garland of Devotees," especially chapter 2.
9. See Hare, "Garland of Devotees," for discussion of the full range of figures portrayed.
10. Charlotte Vaudeville, "The Govardhan Myth in Northern India," *Indo-Iranian Journal* 20 (1980): 1–15.
11. This manifestation of Krishna may have Shaiva origins as well as deep roots in folk traditions centering on the importance of mountains and cattle. See Charlotte Vaudeville, "Govardhan, the Eater Hill," in *Devotional Literature in South Asia, Current Research, 1985–1988*, ed. R. S. McGregor (Cambridge: Cambridge University Press, 1992), 3–4. Alan Entwistle notes that the term "Giridhar" or "Girdhari" is used not only for images of Krishna holding Mount Govardhan aloft or raising his hand as if to do so but also more generally for flute-playing images. Entwistle, *Braj*, 79.
12. Braj or Vraj is the region where Krishna spent his childhood among the cowherding people to whom his foster parents belonged.
13. Hare notes this location for her story, her position supporting his general contention that Nabhadas privileges devotion and patronage rather than political power in his presentation of royalty. Hare, "Garland of Devotees," 59–60, 79–83. Further evidence that Mira's lineage as a Rathor might have been well-known in this time is brought forward by Heidi Pauwels citing Hariram Vyas's coupling of a line remembering Mirabai with a line about Jaimal Rathor, in a poem we will examine shortly. Heidi R. M. Pauwels, "Rāṭhaurī Mīrā: Two Neglected Rāṭhaur Connections to Mīrā—Jaimal Mertīyo and Nāgrīdās," *International Journal of Hindu Studies* 14, nos. 2–3 (2010): 182.
14. Hawley describes this caste (*ḍom*) as "corpse-handling" (Hawley, *A Storm of Songs*, 118). However, while this is true of communities so-named in other regions, it does not necessarily appear to be the case in Rajasthan. See K. S. Singh, *The Scheduled Castes*, revised ed. (New Delhi: Oxford University Press, 1995), 470–501; Munshi Hardyal Singh, *The Castes of Marwar: Census Report of 1891* (1894), 2nd ed. (Jodhpur: Books Treasure, 1990),124. Cf. Kshitimohan Sen, *Medieval Mysticism in India*, trans. Manomohan Ghosh (London: Luzac, 1936), 77.

15. William R. Pinch, "History, Devotion and the Search for Nabhadas of Galta," in *Invoking the Past: The Uses of History in South Asia*, ed. Daud Ali (New Delhi: Oxford University Press, 1999), 367–399; Hare, "Garland of Devotees," 25–44; Hawley, *A Storm of Songs*, 117–118.
16. Richard Burghart, "The Founding of the Ramanandi Sect," *Ethnohistory* 25, no. 2 (1978): 121–139. He notes that other heterodox ascetic orders also had such open admission practices, notably Buddhism (137n2).
17. Burghart, "Founding of the Ramanandi Sect," 126.
18. Burchett, *A Genealogy of Devotion*, 195–236.
19. Burchett, *A Genealogy of Devotion*, 111.
20. Burchett, *A Genealogy of Devotion*, 115–121.
21. Hawley, *A Storm of Songs*, 151; Entwistle, *Braj*, 159–160, 180–197, 190–194.
22. Hawley, *A Storm of Songs*, 150–157.
23. Sheldon Pollock, *The Language of the Gods in the World of Men: Sanskrit, Culture and Power in Premodern India* (Berkeley: University of California Press, 2006); Tyler Williams, "Sacred Sounds and Sacred Books: A History of Writing in Hindi" (PhD diss., Columbia University, 2014); Burchett, *A Genealogy of Devotion*, 218–220.
24. Burchett, *A Genealogy of Devotion*, 204.
25. Monika Horstmann, "The Rāmānandīs of Galtā (Jaipur, Rajasthan)," in *Multiple Histories: Culture and Society in the Study of Rajasthan*, ed. Lawrence A. Babb, Varsha Joshi, and Michael W. Meister (Jaipur: Rawat, 2002), 141.
26. Noting the absence of Muslim devotees as well as followers of Dadu and Nanak, Hare describes Nabhadas's inclusive community as broadly Vaishnava with Shaiva bhaktas included only because Shiva himself is portrayed as a Krishna bhakta ("The Garland of Devotees," 250–251). Hawley too observes the distinct absence of Nanak and other Sikhs as well as Muslim saints and the predominantly North Indian perspective in Nabhadas's work (*A Storm of Songs*, 120, 136–139, 290). Burchett suggests that the exclusion of Gorakhnath as well as Dadu and Nanak and their followers was likely related to "competition, self-definition, and social status," with all three teaching an exclusive nirgun path, denouncing sagun devotion, as Sufis would, who were also excluded. The Naths would be deployed by many in this period in contrast to both bhakti and Sufi devotion, and Burchett cites the Dadupanthi and Sikh blurring of the lines between Hindu and Muslim and their associations with Naths as possible additional reasons for their exclusion (*A Genealogy of Devotion*, 229–232). Dadu and his followers may well have also been perceived as competitors in the Kachvaha court, with members of the royal family subsequently part of its lineage, including Man Singh's younger brother who would come to be called Haridas. See James M. Hastings, "Poets, Warriors and Brothers: The Shifting Identities of Rajput Dadupanthis, circa 1660–1860," in *Culture, Community and Change*, ed. Varsha Joshi (Jaipur: Rawat, 2002), 86–87.
27. Pinch, "History, Devotion and the Search for Nabhadas," 377.
28. Heidi R. M. Pauwels, *In Praise of Holy Men: Hagiographic Poems by and about Harirām Vyās* (Groningben: Egbert Forsten, 2002), 24–33.
29. Pauwels, *In Praise of Holy Men*, 85; Hawley, "Mirabai in Manuscript" in *Three Bhakti Voices*, 94. The available manuscript is dated 1737, but I agree with Hawley that Pauwels makes a convincing argument that this poem dates to his life. This song is also referenced in Indian academic sources, including by Bankey Behari, though he translates it as referring to "parents" rather than simply "father," in keeping with his

presentation of Mirabai as adhering to normative dharmic expectations for women and girls. See *Minstrels of God*, part 1, 2nd ed. (Bombay: Bhartiya Vidya Bhavan, 1970), 104. Male renouncers are similarly urged to treat women as their mothers, suggesting that Vyas's praise may indicate her revered status as a female renouncer. See Monika Horstmann, *Bhakti and Yoga: A Discourse in Seventeenth-Century Codices* (Delhi: Primus Books, 2021), 10.

30. This song appears in multiple Hindi sources, including Vrajaratnadas, *Mīrā-Mādhurī*, 24–26, and is translated by Heidi Pauwels in "The Early Bhakti Milieu as Mirrored in the Poetry of Harirām Vyās," in *Studies in South Asian Devotional Literature*, ed. Alan Entwistle and Françoise Mallison (Delhi: Manohar, 1994), 27. Pauwels discusses this poem and the broad religious family to which Vyas belonged in this essay (27–33) and in *In Praise of Holy Men*, 104–105. As she notes, Vyas was not seeking to found a new sect and so is not necessarily motivated to be exclusionary in his presentation of his religious lineage.

31. Winand M. Callewaert, in collaboration with Swapna Sharma, provides a critical edition of the texts of Anantadas's parchai, together with English translations and an introduction, in *The Hagiographies of Anantadās: The Bhakti Poets of North India* (Richmond, Surrey: Curzon, 2000). Callewaert dates his composition of the parchai as "sometime before or around 1600 CE" (1).

32. See Vikram Singh Gūndoj, "Rājasthānī Paracī Kāvya—Ek Paricay," in *Mīrābāī rī Paracī va Paracī Kāvya, Paramparā 69–70*, ed. Nārāyan Singh Bhāṭī (Caupasani, Jodhpur: Rājāsthānī Shodh Sansthān, 1984), 72n3.

33. Callewaert, *The Hagiographies of Anantadās*, 1, 3.

34. *Pīpā Paracaī*, chapter 35, verse 16, translated by Callewaert and Sharma, *The Hagiographies of Anantadās*, 224. Though her name is linked to that of Trilochan in this verse, surrounding verses mention Kabir, Raidas, Namdev, Dhana, Bithal, Sen, Chauhan Bhuvan, Ranka and Banka, and Chaturbhuj and his wife. This text is noted by Hawley, *Three Bhakti Voices*, 98.

35. John Stratton Hawley and Gurinder Singh Mann make this argument for a circulation rather than diffusion model in their essay "Mirabai at the Court of Guru Gobind Singh," in *Culture and Circulation: Literatures in Motion in Early Modern India*, ed. Allison Busch and Thomas de Bruijn (Leiden: E. J. Brill, 2014), 107–138.

36. Nabhadas, *Śrī Bhaktamāl*, with the *Bhaktirasabodhinī* commentary of Priyādās, 713–723; Vrajaratnadas, *Mīrā-Mādhurī*, 28–32. Priyadas was a disciple of Manohar Das of the Gaudiya Sampraday and lived in Vrindavan by his own admission. Otherwise little is known (though much is posited) about him, save that he was renowned for reciting and commenting on Nabhadas's bhaktamal. See R. D. Gupta, "Priyā Dās, Author of the 'Bhaktirasabodhinī,'" *Bulletin of the School of Oriental and African Studies, University of London* 32, no. 1 (1969): 57–70. As noted above, Hawley paraphrased Priyadas's commentary on Mira in *Songs of the Saints*, 123–128, as have many other authors. Monika Horstmann offers a full translation in *Banasa: A Spiritual Autobiography* (Wiesbaden: Harraassowitz Verlag, 2003), 12–14. Priyadas's poetic lines allow for alternative readings, and within the tradition itself, commentary, both oral and written, is a key part of understanding and appreciating the text. However, in an effort to disentangle these layers of tradition, I have tried to follow the actual text as closely as possible in translating here and to resist imposing later commentarial interpretations on difficult passages, choosing to retain ambiguity and preserve potential multiple meanings as

much as possible where I find them present. The parenthetical numbers (1–10) at end of each verse indicate their position in Priyadas's extended telling.
37. Hawley notes the lack of clarity in Priyadas's account but suggests that it is perhaps more likely a reference in this telling to her father-in-law as the ruling rana at the time. Hawley and Juergensmeyer, *Songs of the Saints*, 125.
38. The meaning of the final two lines of this stanza is particularly obscure. I have offered one possible translation. Horstmann translates the same lines: "Though he had seen [God's] power on her, his mood was unbending. Tell me, what can you do without Hari's grace?" (*Banasa*, 14).
39. Rana Sanga (Mira's father-in-law in some accounts) was himself poisoned, according to historical sources. For an example of familial poisoning in women's songs, see Gloria Goodwin Raheja and Ann Grodzins Gold, *Listen to the Heron's Words: Reimagining Gender and Kinship in North India* (Berkeley: University of California Press, 1994), 132.
40. *Ranchor* is often said to mean "one who flees from battle," referring to Krishna's decision to leave his father's kingdom and establish his own court in Dwarka, when the brother-in-law of the slain demon Kansa and his allies laid siege to Mathura (Entwistle, *Braj*, 41). However, Françoise Mallison suggests that this popular epithet might more accurately be understood to mean "the one who takes away debt" or "fault," as it is a name attached to images of four-armed Vishnu in Gujarat, particularly associated with merchant castes, and may refer to the inborn debts of the three higher castes—to forefathers, guests, teachers, humanity at large, and all living beings—that can be waived through bhakti. Françoise Mallison, "Development of Early Krishnaism in Gujarāt: Viṣṇu—Raṇchoḍ—Kṛṣṇa," in *Bhakti in Current Research, 1979-1982*, ed. Monika Horstmann (Berlin: Dietrich Reimer Verlag, 1983), 247–248. The name is one of several associated with Krishna in Dwarka and exclusively with the "Lord of Dakor." A flute placed in the hand of the images further establishes identification with Krishna. Mira is commonly said to be particularly devoted to Krishna in this form as well as Girdhar Nagar.
41. A. K. Ramanujan, "On Women Saints" (1982) in *Collected Essays*, 270–278. See also his article "Talking to God in the Mother Tongue" in Kishwar and Vanita, *Women Bhakta Poets*, 9–14. Kumkum Sangari notes Ramanujan's categories in passing in "Mirabai and the Spiritual Economy of *Bhakti*" but does not explore hagiographic portrayals of Mira further.
42. The encounters of male saints with kings or emperors, particularly Akbar, are discussed by W. L. Smith in *Patterns in North Indian Hagiography* (Stockholm: University of Stockholm Press, 2000), 159–176.
43. Ramanujan, "On Women Saints," 272–274. David Lorenzen discusses Ramanujan's typology and develops a male model for *nirgun* saints in "The Lives of *Nirguni* Saints," in *Bhakti Religion in North India: Community Identity and Political Action*, ed. David Lorenzen (Albany: SUNY Press, 1995), 185–193.
44. Tukaram, *Says Tuka*, trans. Dilip Chitre (New Delhi: Penguin Books, 1991), 42–49.
45. Ramanujan offers a concise diagram of the stages of life of women saints that makes the range of these choices and their consequences very clear. See "On Women Saints," 272–273, or "Talking to God in the Mother Tongue," 12. The following examples are drawn from Ramanujan and other essays from Kishwar and Vanita, *Women Bhakta Poets*, particularly Uma Chakravarti, "The World of the Bhaktin in South Indian Traditions—The Body and Beyond" (23–26) and Ruth Vanita, "Three Women Saints of Maharashtra: Muktabai, Janabai, Bahinabai" (45–61).

46. Sati (*satī*) is a practice in which a highly virtuous wife would choose to make a vow at the death of her husband to accompany him to the next life by ascending the funeral pyre with him and lighting the pyre by the inner heat of her virtue. Though never commonly practiced, sati nevertheless constituted an ideal of wifely devotion, and temples were built and festivals held honoring women who performed this act. Because of the potential for abuse, the practice has been outlawed and its glorification discouraged. See Catherine Neinberger-Thomas, *Ashes of Immortality: Widow Burning in India* (New Delhi: Oxford University Press, 2000).
47. For example, see A. K. Ramanujan, trans., *Speaking of Śiva* (New York: Penguin Books, 1973), 135.
48. For example, see Sanjukta Gupta, "Women in the Shaiva/Shakta Ethos," in *Roles and Rituals for Hindu Women*, ed. Julia Leslie (Delhi: Motilal Banarsidass, 1991), 202–204.
49. In popular culture there is also a measure of suspicion directed at holy men because of the sadhus' power and privileged access to women as spiritual teachers—saffron robes a ready disguise for a man still driven by lust.
50. Ramanujan, "Talking to God in the Mother Tongue," 13.
51. Callewaert, "The Parchaī of Pīpā," in *The Hagiographies of Anantadās*, 141–226.
52. Ram Vallabh Somani, *History of Mewar from Earliest Times to 1751 A.D.* (Jaipur: C. L. Ranka, 1976), 206–217.
53. Pauwels discusses such confrontations between kings and holy men in *In Praise of Holy Men*, as a conflict between mundane and spiritual power (233–239). See also Smith, *Patterns in North Indian Hagiography*, 159–176.
54. John Stratton Hawley, *Sur Das: Poet, Singer, Saint* (Seattle: University of Washington Press, 1984), 10–11.
55. Winand M. Callewaert, *The Hindī Biography of Dādū Dayāl* (Delhi: Motilal Banarsidass, 1988), 41–55.
56. Sarojini Mehta, "Gauribai," in *Women Saints of East and West*, ed. Swami Ghanananda and John Stewart-Wallace (London: Ramakrishna Vedanta Centre, 1955), 73–79.
57. Ramanujan, *Speaking of Śiva*, 112.
58. Callewaert, *The Hindī Biography of Dādū Dayāl*, 43.
59. Winand M. Callewaert and Peter Friedlander, *The Life and Works of Raidās* (Delhi: Manohar, 1992), 31–32.
60. David Lorenzen, *Kabir Legends and Ananta-Das's* Kabir Paracai (Albany: SUNY Press, 1991), 32–35.
61. Ramanujan, *Speaking of Śiva*, 93.
62. There are strong associations between snakes and goddesses and between the god Shiva and safely consuming poison. Shakta (goddess) priestesses like Yogeshvari Devi (June McDaniel, *The Madness of the Saints: Ecstatic Religion in Bengal* [Chicago: University of Chicago Press, 1989], 220–228) and tantric healers (Burchett, *The Genealogy of Devotion*, 58) are said to be able to handle both snakes and poison. Taming lions similarly is a standard mark of a yogi's advanced spiritual powers (Horstmann, *Bhakti and Yoga*, 44, 131). Burchett argues that both Shakta worshipers and tantric Nath yogis were the rhetorical "others" against whom bhaktas defined themselves at least from the seventeenth century, suggesting that bhaktas' reported abilities in this regard might also be an assertion of their equal power. Other religious traditions also attest to spiritual powers manifesting in similar ways, as in Mark 16:17–18 of the New Testament.

63. See John Stratton Hawley, "Krishna and the Gender of Longing" in *Three Bhakti Voices*, 165–178.
64. Ramanujan, *Speaking of Śiva*, 113.
65. Ramanujan, "On Women Saints" in *Collected Essays*, 275.
66. For example, in S. S. Gulzar's 1979 film *Meera*, starring Hema Malini.
67. Chaitanya himself is said to have advocated the practice of male devotees shunning women in order to control desire in Kṛṣṇadās Kavirāj's *Caitanya-caritāmṛt* (1581 CE). Jadunath Sarkar, trans., *Chaitanya's Life and Teachings* (Calcutta: Orient Longman, 1988), 210–217.
68. A. K. Ramanujan, "Men, Women and Saints" in *Collected Essays*, 291.
69. Madhu Kishwar and Ruth Vanita, "Poison to Nectar: The Life and Work of Mirabai," in Kishwar and Vanita, *Women Bhakta Poets*, 85.
70. Kishwar and Vanita, "Poison to Nectar," 86–87.
71. Linda Hess with Sukhdev Singh, *The Bijak of Kabir* (1983), 2nd ed. (Delhi: Oxford University Press, 2002).
72. Ākiñcana-dāsa, *Vivarta vilāsa* (Calcutta: Taracand Dās, 1948), 107–108, translated and quoted in Edward C. Dimock Jr., *The Place of the Hidden Moon: Erotic Mysticism in the Vaiṣṇava-sahajiyā Cult of Bengal* (Delhi: Motilal Banarsidass, 1991), 216. References to Mira as the disciple of Haridas of the Ramavat sampraday appear in at least two illustrated *Mira ki Katha* manuscripts: manuscript 30029 of the Rajasthan Oriental Research Institute, Jodhpur, assigned the date nineteenth century vs (c. 1750–1850 CE) and a similar illustrated manuscript from the private collection of Narendra Parson (see Figure 1.2). The Ramavat community is a Ram rasik sampraday developing out of the Ramanandis in seventeenth-century Rajasthan. See Ronald Stuart McGregor, *Hindi Literature from Its Beginnings to the Nineteenth Century* (Weisbaden: Otto Harrassowitz, 1984), 167–171.
73. The *Prem Ambodh* is cited in Callewaert and Friedlander, *Raidās*, 13, drawing on J. S. Sābar, *Bhagat Ravidas Srodha Pustak*, 1984 (69–81), and they note that in this text Mirabai (rather than the Jhali Rani) is mentioned as Raidas's disciple (26n113) and that Raidas (also known as Ravidas, Rohidas, or Rivdas) probably lived from 1450 to 1520 CE. A much more detailed discussion of the dates and authorship of the *Prem Ambodh* together with a full translation and analysis of the passage on Mirabai are offered by John Stratton Hawley and Gurinder Singh Mann in "Mirabai in the *Pothi Prem Ambodh*," *Journal of Punjab Studies* 15, nos. 1–2 (2008): 199–226 and in "Mirabai at the Court of Guru Gobind Singh," 107–138.
74. Gurinder Singh Mann, *The Making of Sikh Scriptures* (New York: Oxford University Press, 2001), 9.
75. Winand Callewaert, "The 'Earliest' Song of Mira (1503–1546)," *Orientalia Lovaniensia Periodica* 22 (1991): 201–214.
76. For a detailed discussion of Anantadas's *Raidas Parchai* and comparison to Priyadas's account, see Callewaert and Friedlander, *Raidās*, 15–16, 30–35. For a critical edition and translation, see Callewaert, *The Hagiographies of Anantadās*, 303–356. Callewaert notes that an extended second section on the Jhali Rani where she invites Raidas to Chittor is variable and not present in all manuscripts (306). A similar story is still told about Mirabai and Raidas in the folk epic *Kumbha Rana ri Bhat* performed in the Sirohi region of Rajasthan (see chapter 4). See also Hare's analysis of the implications of Priyadas's particular telling in "The Garland of Devotees," 103–110, 125–128.

77. A shalagram (śālagrām) is a particular type of black stone, understood to be an aniconic image of Vishnu and a common focus for devotional practice among Vaishnavas, treated with the same reverence as a more iconic image would be. More specifically it is "a kind of smooth and rounded black stone, usually marked with fossilized ammonites and other mollusks, that is found in the bed of the Gandak river, which flows through Nepal and joins the Ganges at Patna" (Entwistle, *Braj*, 81).
78. Callewaert and Friedlander, *Raidās*, 29.
79. Peter Friedlander, "The Struggle for Salvation in the Hagiographies of Ravidās," in *Myth and Mythmaking*, ed. Julia Leslie (Richmond, Surrey: Curzon, 1996), 116–117.
80. Burchett, *A Genealogy of Devotion*, 230–232.
81. Hawley notes that Sanga's mother was of the Jhala clan in "Mirabai in Manuscript" in *Three Bhakti Voices*, 92.
82. Callewaert, *The Hagiographies of Anantadās*, 11–17, 20–21.
83. R. Nath, "Śrī Govindadeva's Itinerary from Vṛndāvana to Jayapura c. 1534–1727," in *Govindeva: A Dialogue in Stone*, ed. Margaret Case (New Delhi: Indira Gandhi National Centre for the Arts, 1996), 161–183.
84. Horstmann, "The Rāmānandīs of Galtā," 158–159. In this article, Horstmann discusses this period in detail, including its ramification on the present. See also Hawley, *A Storm of Songs*, 99–147.
85. Kiyokazu Okita, *Hindu Theology in Early Modern South Asia: The Rise of Devotionalism and the Politics of Genealogy* (New York: Oxford University Press, 2014), 21–40.
86. Burghart, "The Founding of the Ramanandi Sect"; Horstmann, "The Rāmānandīs of Galtā"; William Pinch, *Peasants and Monks in British India* (Berkeley: University of California Press, 1996), 53–54.
87. John Stratton Hawley, "The Four *Sampradāys*: Ordering the Religious Past in Mughal North India," *South Asian History and Culture* 2, no. 2 (2011): 170–171.
88. Okita, *Hindu Theology in Early Modern South Asia*, 35.
89. Monika Horstmann, "Theology and Statecraft," *South Asian History and Culture* 2, no. 2 (2011): 184–204.
90. Hare, "The Garland of Devotees," 135.
91. Hare, "The Garland of Devotees," 117–119, drawing on Pinch, "History, Devotion and the Search for Nabhadas," 391–394.
92. Joseph Schaller, "Raidas and Mira: Tales of Power and Devotion," paper presented at the international conference Mirabai: Hindu Saint for a Global World, Los Angeles, California, October 2002; Mukta, *Upholding the Common Life*, 105–114.
93. Hawley, *Songs of the Saints*, 177n18.
94. Hermann Goetz, *Mirabai, Her Life and Times* (Bombay: Bharatiya Vidya Bhavan, 1966), 6–7, first published in *Journal of the Gujarat Research Society* 18 (April 1956).
95. The dates of the individual poets' lifetimes are contested and whether such songs were actually composed by them uncertain, but the assignment of these works to them is of interest even so. A number are presented and discussed in detail by Vrajaratnadas, *Mīrā-Mādhurī*, 23–71; Hiralal Maheshwari, *Rājasthānī Bhāṣā aur Sāhitya* (Calcutta: Adhunik Pustak Bhavan, 1960), 302–310; Prabhat, *Mīrā Jīvan aur Kāvya*, 22–34.
96. Richard K. Barz, *The Bhakti Sect of Vallabhācārya* (1976; Delhi: Munshiram Manoharlal, 1992), 100–103. This text is attributed to Gokulnath, a son of Vitthalnath, whose oral teachings were recorded by his disciple Hariray in the mid-seventeenth century. Hariray added his own commentary to his guru's words as he recorded them. For an initial

complete discussion of the dates identifying the earliest verifiable manuscript as 1695, see Hawley, "Mirabai in Manuscript," 95, with his revised evaluation accepting the 1640 date in *A Storm of Songs*, 365n105.

97. These three vartas are presented and discussed in numerous Hindi texts on Mira, including Hukam Singh Bhāṭī, *Mīrābāī: Aitihāsik va Sāmājik Vivecan* (Jodhpur: Rājasthānī Sāhitya Sansthān, 1987), 52.

98. "Three Vartas of Govind Dube the Sacora Brahman." For a discussion of versions of the text, see Richard K. Barz, "The *Caurāsī Vaiṣṇavan kī Vārtā* and the Hagiography of the Puṣṭimārg," in *According to Tradition: Hagiographic Writing in India*, ed. Winand M. Callewaert and Rupert Snell (Wiesbaden: Harrassowitz, 1994), 58–62. At least two printed versions exist: (1) *Caurāsī Bārttā (Eighty-four Accounts)* published in Mathura in 1883 and in six subsequent editions, which is favored by more conservative members of the Pushtimarg, and (2) *Caurāsī Vaiṣṇavan kī Vārtā (Tin Janm kī Līlā Bhāvnā Vālī) (The Accounts of the Eighty-four Vaishnavas (Containing the Appreciation of the Lila of the Three Lives)* (1948; Mathura: Śrī Govarddhan Granthamālā Karyalay, 1970), which includes the commentary of Hariray and is the standard text used in the Vallabh sect today, according to Barz. This varta is number 34 in the *Chaurasi Bartta* (165–166) and varta 40 in the *Chaurasi Vaishnavan ki Varta* (214–215).

99. The damning contents of the note do not appear in the *Chaurasi Bartta* but do in the *Chaurasi Vaishnavan ki Varta* (the message appearing within the portion of the text attributed to Gokulnath himself, not in Hariray's commentary). The wording is particularly ironic in light of the fact that Mira is known to use this same comparison when she refuses to exchange the Lord of the Universe for some human husband. The *Chaurasi Bartta* is not quite so critical of Mira, but it is difficult to tell which reading might be earlier, and the note is sent, and Govind Dube leaves in both instances.

100. "Three Vartas of Mirabai's Purohit Ramdas." *Chaurasi Bartta*, varta 47, 211–212; *Chaurasi Vaishnavan ki Varta*, varta 54, 269–270.

101. Although Ramdas is less violent in his reaction in the *Chaurasi Bartta*, he is no less unwavering in his decision to leave.

102. "The Three Vartas of Krishnadas Adhikari." *Chaurasi Vaishnavan ki Varta*, varta 92. Translated in full with Hariray's commentary by Barz, *The Bhakti Sect of Vallabhācārya*, 213–215.

103. Hawley, "The Four *Sampradāys*," 169.

104. For further discussion of this theme in the *Vartas* as well as in passages on Mira, see Vasudha Dalmia, "The 'Other' in the World of the Faithful," in Horstmann, *Bhakti in Current Research*, 115–138; Galina Rousseva-Sokolova, "Sainthood Revisited: Two Printed Versions of the *Lives of the Eighty-four Vaishnavas* by Gokulnath," in *Bhakti beyond the Forest: Current Research on Early Modern Literatures of North India, 2003–2009*, ed. Imre Bangha (New Delhi: Manohar, 2013), 96, 98–99.

105. Hawley, "Mirabai in Manuscript," 95–98.

106. Mallison, "Development of Early Krishnaism in Gujarāt," 248.

107. Heidi R. M. Pauwels, "Hagiography and Reception History: The Case of Mīrā's Padas in Nāgrīdās's *Pada-prasaṅga-mālā*," in Horstmann, *Bhakti in Current Research*, 226n16.

108. Hawley, *Three Bhakti Voices*, 97.

109. Barz, *The Bhakti Sect of Vallabhācārya*, 40–41.

110. The central manifestation of Krishna venerated by the Vallabhites is Shri Nathji, his hand held high as the lifter of Mount Govardhan, now enshrined in Nathdwara, Rajasthan.

111. Jon Keune importantly points out that the pedagogical discursive use of an "other" cannot automatically be assumed to correspond to actual attitudes in a given historical period. Jon Keune, "Pedagogical Otherness: The Use of Muslims and Untouchables in Some Hindu Devotional Literature," *Journal of the American Academy of Religion* 84, no. 3 (2015): 729.
112. Ramanujan, "On Women Saints," 271.
113. Ramanujan, *Speaking of Śiva*, 113–114.
114. This song appears in many collections and in translation in A. J. Alston, *The Devotional Poems of Mira Bai* (Delhi: Motilal Banarsidass, 1980), 44–45.
115. Krishnadas Kaviraj's *Chaitanya-carit-amrita* contains a wealth of examples (*Chaitanya's Life and Teachings*, trans. Sarkar).
116. The following discussion is entirely dependent on the translation of the passage from the *Prem Ambodh* about Mira published by Hawley and Mann in "Mirabai in the *Pothi Prem Ambodh*," and is indebted to their detailed discussion of the text, including the uncertainty of its authorship, the context of its composition and performance, and its theological agenda, there and in Hawley and Mann, "Mirabai at the Court of Guru Gobind Singh." They acknowledge their own debt to the only scholarship available on the *Prem Ambodh* at the time they embarked on their research: Davindar Singh Osahan's *Prem Ambodh Pothī* (Patiala: Punjabi University Publication Bureau, 1989). All English translations of the text herein are theirs.
117. In Mira's case, see Hawley and Mann, "Mirabai in the *Prem Ambodh*," 204–205, 210–211.
118. Braj Bhasha is the vernacular language spoken in the Braj region, often employed in both literary works and bhakti songs and texts in North India.
119. Francesca Orsini notes that Hindavi kathas in the fifteenth and sixteenth centuries similarly were written both to teach and to entertain and incorporated considerable humor into the tales, much like the *Prem Ambodh*. See her "Texts and Tellings: Kathas in the Fifteenth and Sixteenth Centuries," in *Tellings and Texts: Music, Literature and Performance in North India*, ed. Francesca Orsini and Katherine Butler Schofield (Cambridge, UK: Open Book, 2015), 328.
120. Hawley and Mann, "Mirabai at the Court," 115–116.
121. Hawley and Mann, "Mirabai at the Court," 109; Hawley and Mann, "Mirabai in the *Prem Ambodh*," 202.
122. Hawley and Mann, "Mirabai in the *Prem Ambodh*," 121.
123. Hawley and Mann, "Mirabai in the *Prem Ambodh*," 204; Hawley and Mann, "Mirabai at the Court," 119–120.
124. Hawley and Mann, "Mirabai in the *Prem Ambodh*, 205.
125. Hawley and Mann, "Mirabai in the *Prem Ambodh*," 204–206; Hawley and Mann, "Mirabai at the Court," 123–124.
126. Hawley and Mann, "Mirabai at the Court," 121.
127. Hawley and Mann, "Mirabai in the *Prem Ambodh*," 206–207.
128. Hawley and Mann, "Mirabai in the *Prem Ambodh*," 207–211.
129. Mann, *The Making of Sikh Scriptures*, 111.
130. Hawley and Mann, "Mirabai in the *Prem Ambodh*," 211–213.
131. Hawley and Mann, "Mirabai in the *Prem Ambodh*," 213–216; Hawley and Mann, "Mirabai at the Court," 109–110.
132. Hawley and Mann, "Mirabai at the Court," 134–135.
133. Hawley and Mann, "Mirabai at the Court," 136.

134. Gobind Singh's predecessor Tegh Bahadur was executed in imperial custody in 1675 in response to political unrest in the Punjab and alleged Sikh opposition to Aurangzeb's sovereignty, as "an enemy of the state." Audrey Truschke, *Aurangzeb: The Life and Legacy of India's Most Controversial King* (Stanford, CA: Stanford University Press, 2017), 54–55.
135. Hawley and Mann, "Mirabai at the Court," 110–113, 121, 131–136. The authors explore the relationship between these two texts in detail in this essay.
136. Gurcharan Das, *Three Plays: Larins Sahib, Mira, 9 Jakhoo Hill* (New Delhi: Penguin, 2001), 15–23, 107–146.
137. Hawley and Mann, "Mirabai at the Court," 129.
138. Callewaert, *The Hagiographies of Anantadās*, 2–3.
139. Hawley and Mann, "Mirabai at the Court," especially 128–136.
140. Prabhat identifies this text for the first time in the Hindi literature and reads it as the correct interpretation of Priyadas's text in *Mīrābāī* (Bombay: Hindi Granth Ratnakar, 1965), 42–50. He presents Vaishnavdas's full text, including the text of Tansen's song, drawing on a manuscript from the collection of Prachya Vidya Mandir, Baroda, dated 1767 and composed in Banaras. Available manuscripts are discussed in detail by Hare, "The Garland of Devotees," 147–148, drawing on Kailāśacandra Śarmā, *Bhaktamāl aur Hindī Kāvya meṁ Uskī Paramparā* (Delhi: Manthan, 1983). Hare also cites subcommentaries by Balakram, Laldas, Sevahitdas, and Hulasdas that warrant further investigation. Vaishnavdas is said to have lived in Vrindavan, and Prabhat identifies him as a member of the Nimbarka sampraday, while other sources identify him as belonging to the Gaudiya sampraday. For further discussion, see Pauwels, "Hagiography and Reception History," 232.
141. Rupert Snell, "Bhakti in the Poetry of Dhruvdās," in McGregor, *Devotional Literature in South Asia*, 248. McGregor dates his works from 1593 to 1641 CE in his *Hindi Literature Beginnings*, 160, and Vrajaratnadas gives the time of the creation of this work as between 1623 and 1643 CE in *Mīrā-Mādhurī*, 32.
142. Dhruvdas's verse is given by Vrajaratnadas, *Mīrā-Mādhurī*, 32–33. The problematic line is as follows: *lalitā hū lai boli ke tāsoṇ ho ati het*. Mira is also sometimes said to be an incarnation of the *sakhi* Lalita.
143. Hawley and Mann, "Mirabai at the Court," 112.
144. Mira is also said to have visited Miradatta in Gujarat, which is in fact associated with a Muslim pir. It seems likely that the similarity with Mira's name and the popularity of this pilgrimage site among those who sing Mira's songs generated stories about her visit there.
145. M. Corcoran, "Vrindavan and Its Role in Divine Activity," in *Early Hindi Devotional Literature in Current Research*, ed. Winand Callewaert (Leuven: Katholieke Universiteit, 1980), 40–47. McGregor supports the reading that this line in Dhruvdas is a figurative rather than physical reference to Vrindavan (*Hindi Literature from Its Beginnings*, 81n164).
146. Rāghavdās, *Bhaktamāl*, ed. and introduction by Agarcand Nāhṭa (Jodhpur: Rajasthan Oriental Research Institute, 1965), 99. Raghavdas's portrayal of Mirabai is discussed by (among others) Vrajaratnadas, *Mīrā-Mādhurī*, 39–41; Prabhat, *Mīrā Jīvan aura Kāvya*, 48–50; and Bhati, *Mīrābāī: Aitihāsik va Sāmājik Vivecan*, 44–45. The date of this text is debated, though Horstmann and Hawley (drawing on her work) give a compelling argument for its 1660 composition. Others give it an early eighteenth-century date of 1713 or 1720 CE. See Hawley, *A Storm of Songs*, 129–130, drawing on Monika Horstmann, "The Flow of Grace: Food and Feast in the Hagiography and History of the Dādūpanth," *Zeitschrift der Deutschen Morgenländischen Gesellschaft* 150 (2000): 515n9. Raghavdas's Mira passage is translated in full in Nancy M. Martin, "Dyed in the Color

of Her Lord: Multiple Representations in the Mirabai Tradition" (PhD diss., Graduate Theological Union, 1995), 69.

147. Hastings, "Poets, Warriors and Brothers," 86. Hastings details the rajput origins and continuing involvement in the Naga branch of the Dadupanth to which Raghavdas belonged, initiated by a former warrior from Bikaner Sundardas and including within their lineage royal Kachvaha rajputs of Amer (Jaipur), including Man Singh's younger brother Haridas.
148. Hawley discusses Raghavdas's larger agenda (particularly his transformation of the notion of the four sampradays) in *A Storm of Songs*, 127–138.
149. Hawley, *A Storm of Songs*, 134.
150. Pauwels finds potential evidence a century earlier of a possible Vallabhite connection or appreciation of Mira in Hariram Vyas's incorporation of Mira in a line following a grouping of Surdas, Paramanand, and Meha, identified by Raghavdas's time as Vallabhites ("Rāṭhaurī Mīrā," 182). However, as Hawley's careful study of early works of Surdas reveals, it is unlikely that Surdas was affiliated with Vallabha or his followers in Vyas's time, though the *Vartas* would later lay claim to him as one of their most highly regarded poet-saints (*Sur Das*, 25–28).
151. Chaturdas's full Hindi text is given by Vrajaratnadas, *Mīrā-Mādhurī*, 41–42. W. G. Orr discusses both Chaturdas's commentary and Raghavdas's bhaktamal in *A Sixteenth-Century Indian Mystic: Dadu and His Followers* (London: Lutterworth Press, 1947), 207.
152. For a list of some additional bhaktamals, commentaries, etc., see Agarcand Nāhṭa's introduction to Rāghavdās's *Bhaktamāl*, which he edited, and Prabhāt, *Mīrābāī*, 33–35.
153. Hawley cites the work of Francesca Orsini and Stefano Pellò ("Bhakti in Persian," paper presented at the 21st European Conference on Modern South Asian Studies, Bonn, July 27, 2010) in his discussion of Rām Soni's bhaktamal in *A Storm of Songs*, 138–139. Hawley notes Mira's presence there but gives no details of the content of the telling (138). Burchett also cites Hawley's raising of the possibility that Nabhadas might have been influenced by the Sufi genre of tazkira in *A Genealogy of Devotion*, 227.

Chapter 2

1. Novetzke, *Religion and Public Memory*, 39, 40.
2. Ramanujan, *Hymns for the Drowning*, 4.
3. Ramanujan, *Hymns for the Drowning*, 33–36.
4. Linda Hess, "Lovers' Doubts: Questioning the Tulsi Rāmāyaṇ," in *Questioning Ramayanas: A South Asian Tradition*, ed. Paula Richman (Berkeley: University of California Press, 2001), 25–47.
5. On katha, see Lutgendorf, *The Life of a Text*, 115–117.
6. Nagridas's passage on Mira's composition of six songs is presented and discussed extensively in the Hindi literature. See, for example, Vrajaratnadas, *Mīrā-Mādhurī*, 42–48; Bhati, *Mīrābāī: Aitihāsik va Sāmājik Vivecan*, 45–47; Prabhat, *Mīrā Jīvan aur Kāvya*, 52–54. Heidi Pauwels offers detailed analysis in her essays "Hagiography and Reception History" (including full translations of the relevant narrative passages on Mira together with annotated original texts of the songs with variants and translations in an appendix) and "Rāṭhaurī Mīrā."
7. Pauwels discusses this largely overlooked seventh song of Mira, providing Nagridas's original text and a full translation of the passage as well as this same story in Nabhadas's

bhaktamal, though without the full song or attribution to Mira ("Hagiography and Reception History," 229–230, 243–244; "Rāṭhaurī Mīrā," 192–194). This Mira song within the *Padaprasangmala* had earlier been noted by Harinarāyan Śarmā, *Mīrā Brihatpadavalī*, vol. 1, ed. Kalyāṇ Singh Śekhāvat (Jodhpur: Rājasthān Prācyavidyā Patiṣṭhān, 1967), 261, as Pauwels acknowledges ("Hagiography and Reception History," 229).

8. Mira is speaking of Krishna, who is sometimes called "Ghana Shyam," the blue-black cloud heavy with rain, both in reference to his dark complexion and to the coming clouds that mark the season of both rain and love.

9. Pauwels's careful metric analysis of this song reveals that the references to the rana stand outside the metric unity of the poem, perhaps attached to an earlier song which did not include them and thus offered a more general critique of stridharm (women's dharma or duty) in contrast to Mira's embrace of the bhakti path. Pauwels does not suggest necessarily that Nagridas himself inserted the references to the rana; in all likelihood he records the form in which the song was popularly known, as others before him assumed that these words of Mira were addressed to the rana based on the references to the relation of brother-in-law and sister-in-law and to sati. Pauwels, "Hagiography and Reception History," 227–228.

10. In the *Mahabharata*, Draupadi was saved from the attempts of the evil Kaurava brothers to publicly disrobe her after the eldest of their cousins the five Pandava brothers (her husbands) had lost her in a dice game. When she called on Krishna, he made her *sari* endless so that no matter how much they pulled off, she was still fully clothed, her modesty and honor preserved. Vishnu in the form of Narasimha, the man-lion *avatar*, killed the demon Hirankasyapa (father of the famous devotee Prahlad) when he threatened his son and because he had usurped the place of the gods. The drowning elephant was also rescued from a crocodile by Vishnu after he had been caught in the act of plucking a lotus to offer to his Lord.

11. This Mira song employs standard images and metaphors from both classical and folk love songs to speak of love and longing in separation (*viraha*): the sleepless woman waiting for an absent lover gazing down the road for his return; the thirsty *chatak* bird who notoriously drinks only raindrops that fall during a specific season; and the dying fish out of water.

12. Pauwels, "Hagiography and Reception History," 242.

13. The tribhanga (thrice-bent) pose is a lively curving stance with the hips and shoulders swinging in opposite directions, the head cocked, and the right leg bent at the knee and crossing over the left. This is the posture taken by Krishna as he plays his flute in standard representations.

14. Heidi R. M. Pauwels, *Mobilizing Krishna's World: The Writings of Prince Sāvant Singh of Kishangarh* (Seattle: University of Washington Press, 2017), 115.

15. Pauwels, "Hagiography and Reception History," 223.

16. Pauwels, *Mobilizing Krishna's World*, 116.

17. Pauwels, *Mobilizing Krishna's World*, 147.

18. Pauwels, *Mobilizing Krishna's World*, 144–145.

19. Pauwels notes that the painting is attributed to Nihalchand, painter of the Kishangarh style who was attached to Savant Singh and to his son during Savant Singh's lifetime even after he renounced the throne, so that the painting might reasonably have been commissioned by Savant Singh himself (*Mobilizing Krishna's World*, 145, 232n50).

20. Pauwels, *Mobilizing Krishna's World*, 145–146. A full reproduction of the painting appears in Prabhat, *Mīrā Jīvan aur Kāvya*, 472. Prabhat includes another picture allegedly of Mira

21. For example, Vrajaratnadas, *Mīrā-Mādhurī*, 48.
22. Pauwels, *Mobilizing Krishna's World*, 144–146.
23. Pauwels argues further that he may have had little affection for Merta, as a rival kingdom to his own in his time. See Pauwels, "Rāṭhauṛī Mīrā," 190.
24. Pauwels, *Mobilizing Krishna's World*, 187.
25. Kishwar and Vanita, "Poison to Nectar," 84. Sundar Kunwarbai is also cited by Varsha Joshi as an example of royal rajput women's literary production, noting "[s]he was a great follower of the Radha Vallabh Panth . . . [who] was well versed in religion and wrote eleven granths (works)," though Joshi says nothing of her persecution. Varsha Joshi, *Polygamy and Purdah: Women and Society among Rajputs* (Jaipur: Rawat, 1995), 129.
26. Pauwels, *Mobilizing Krishna's World*, 47.
27. Pauwels, *Mobilizing Krishna's World*, 200.
28. For details of these counterclaims by followers of Nimbarka and of Vallabha, see Pauwels, "Hagiography and Reception History," 224–226; Pauwels, "Rāṭhauṛī Mīrā," 185.
29. The fifteenth varta reports that Jaimal's entire family became Vaishnava as a result of this correspondence, and the forty-seventh varta identifies Mira's husband's younger brother's wife as Ajab Kumarbai. Vrajaratnadas, *Mīrā-Mādhurī*, 34–35; McGregor, *Hindi Literature from Its Beginnings*, 209; Maheshwari, *Rājāsthānī Bhāṣā aur Sāhitya*, 306–307; Prabhat, *Mīrā Jīvan aur Kāvya*, 60–61. For other possible connections between Mira and Jaimal, see Pauwels, "Rāṭhauṛī Mīrā," 178–183.
30. This text and its reference to Mirabai are discussed by Heidi Pauwels and Emilia Bachrach, "Aurangzeb as Iconoclast? Vaishnava Accounts of the Krishna Images' Exodus from Braj," *Journal of the Royal Asiatic Society*, series 3, 28, no. 3 (2018): 492–493.
31. For further discussion of contemporary Pushtimargi engagement with the *Varta* literature, see Emilia Bachrach, *Religious Reading and Everyday Lives in Devotional Hinduism* (New York: Oxford University Press, 2022). Bachrach reports that she found attitudes toward Mira to be variable among those she interviewed but notes one woman's condemnation of the saint, not because Mira was not a formal disciple of Vallabhacarya but because she selfishly ended her life rather than continuing appropriate *seva* (ritual service) to Krishna (54).
32. Pauwels gives a detailed description of this political and religious milieu in chapters 1 and 2 of *Mobilizing Krishna's World*, 13–70.
33. Pauwels, *Mobilizing Krishna's World*, 148. Pauwel's argument, outlined herein, that Nagridas is responding to the reforms of Jai Singh II is detailed on pages 157–161.
34. *Varna-ashrama-dharma* refers to orthodox norms for behavior based on social position or caste (*varna*), life stage (*ashrama*) and gender as prescribed in the *dharma-shastra* and *dharma-sutra* texts, such as the *Laws of Manu*.
35. Pauwels, "Hagiography and Reception History," 235.
36. Pauwels, *Mobilizing Krishna's World*, 148.
37. Pauwels, *Mobilizing Krishna's World*, 113–116.
38. Pauwels also concedes that the shorter version might reflect the simple fact that songs of Mira (and presumably the other omitted saints) are not regularly sung in the Kishangarh Shri Kalyanaraya temple (*Mobilizing Krishna's World*, 146).

39. Pauwels, Tyler Williams, and others are undertaking precisely this kind of careful study in their ongoing work on this crucial transition into print.
40. Mukta, *Upholding the Common Life*.
41. Pauwels, "Rāṭhaurī Mīrā"; Frances Taft, "The Elusive Historical Mira: A Note," in Babb, Joshi, and Meister, *Multiple Histories*, 313–335; Frances Taft, "Six Incarnations of Mirabai," in *Culture, Politics and Economy*, ed. Varsha Joshi and Surjit Singh (Jaipur: Rawat, 2009), 163–172.
42. Pauwels discusses this pilgrimage narrative in detail in *Mobilizing Krishna's World*, chapter 3.
43. For this discussion I am drawing on Justin E. Abbott and Narhar R. Godbole, trans., *Stories of Indian Saints: Translation of Mahipati's Marathi* Bhaktavijaya, 4th edition (Delhi: Motilal Banarsidass, 1988), first published in Pune, 1933. It is in the 133 verses of chapter 38 that Mirabai is described (vol. 2, 66–77), and all quoted English translations of Mahapati's work herein are theirs. Christian Lee Novetzke asserts that this text, composed in writing, has come down through the nineteenth and twentieth centuries without significant change (*Religion and Public Memory*, 53), and Shankar Gopal Tulpule provides a summary of Mahipati's life and works in *Classical Marathi Literature: From the Beginning to A.D. 1818* (Wiesbaden: Otto Harrassowitz, 1979), 430–431.
44. The word *kirtan* generally refers to a devotional performance, the particular nature of which varies in different regions and religious traditions. See Novetzke's *Religion and Public Memory* for further discussion of this regionally specific tradition and Mahipati.
45. *Bhaktavijaya* 1:37–38, 2:248–249 (Abbott and Godbole, *Stories of Indian Saints*, vol. 1, 4, 29). Here Mahipati indicates he is drawing from Nabhaji (though he identifies him as a brahman from Gwailor) and from another hagiographer in Mandesh named Uddhvachidghan. However, Tulpule observes that Mahipati appears to have accessed the works of Nabhadas (and Priyadas) through an interpreter (*Classical Marathi Literature*, 430–431). See also Novetzke, *Religion and Public Memory*, 53.
46. Godbole and Abbott (*Stories of Indian Saints*, xxvii) identify Mahipati's source for his tale of Mira as Namdev's *Mirabai che Caritra*. This work was likely composed by the eighteenth-century Shimpi Nama, one of a line of kirtankar "Namas" who performed the works of Namdev but also added to them, both in the saint's name and in their own, who is indeed credited with composing a biography of Mira (Novetzke, *Religion and Public Memory*, 152). C. L. Prabhat gives the text of Shimpi Nama's *Mira Caritra* in *Mīrā Jīvan aur Kāvya* (62–65), which corresponds to the main plotline of Mahipati's telling, though Shimpi Nama's dates are uncertain, and conceivably he might actually be drawing on Mahipati and/or on preexisting oral traditions in the region.
47. S. G. Tulpule, "Hagiography in Medieval Marathi Literature," in Callewaert and Snell, *According to Tradition*, 166.
48. Stewart Gordon, *The New Cambridge History of India II 4: The Marathas 1600–1818* (Cambridge: Cambridge University Press, 1993), 146.
49. Jon Keune notes the particular northern orientation of Varkari tradition in "Emphatically Ignoring the Neighbors: The Selective Geographic Orientation of Marathi Bhakti," *Journal of Hindu Studies* 8 (2015): 296–314. He raises the possibility that the maratha expansion may have impacted this orientation but notes that the stories of the northward travels of Namdev, Jnandev, and Eknath predate this (309). While ignoring saints from farther south, Mahipati does include Naths and Muslim devotees, categories excluded by Nabhadas, reflecting the differing relations between these communities in these different regions and in

the histories of the sampradays. Jon Keune, "Gathering of Bhaktas in Marāṭhī," *Journal of Vaishnava Studies* 15, no. 2 (Spring 2007): 178–179.

50. This appears to be the first such written reference to Mira playing the vina, though this instrument is commonly mentioned in songs attributed to Namdev (Novetzke, *Religion and Public Memory*, 88).
51. Erik Reenberg Sand, "*Matapitribhakti*: Some Aspects of the Development of the *Pandalika* Legend in Marathi Literature," in McGregor, *Devotional Literature in South Asia,* 139. See also Christian Lee Novetzke, "A Family Affair: Krishna Comes to Paṇḍharpūr and Makes Himself at Home," in *Alternative Krishnas: Regional and Vernacular Variations on a Hindu Deity*, ed. Guy L. Beck (Albany: State University of New York Press, 2005), 113–114.
52. Charlotte Vaudeville, "The Shaiva-Vaishnava Synthesis in Maharashtrian Santism," in Schomer and McLeod, *The Sants*, 223–224.
53. Vaudeville, "The Shaiva-Vaishnava Synthesis," 224.
54. See Burchett, *The Genealogy of Devotion*, especially chapter 1.
55. Vaudeville, "The Shaiva-Vaishnava Synthesis," 116, 222; McGregor, *Hindi Literature Beginnings*, 39; Tulpule, *Classical Marathi Literature*, 329–334.
56. Novetzke, "A Family Affair," 116. See also Vaudeville, "The Shaiva-Vaishnava Synthesis," 223.
57. Vanita, "Three Women Sants of Maharashtra," 47.
58. The specific designation that it is Udaipur (rather than the earlier capital of Chittor) where she is born may reflect a lack of historical knowledge or importance of such detail in a land so far away from Rajasthan, and Udaipur would have been the capital of Mewar in Mahipati's time.
59. Abbott and Godbole, *Stories of Indian Saints*, vol. 2, 771.
60. This turning color of Krishna as he saves Mira from the poison marked the culminating scene of a Mirabai lila performed at Phogala Ashram on August 9, 1993, in Vrindavan, likely influenced by this Maharashtrian tradition, though conceivably via the 1945/1947 film starring Subbulakshmi (discussed in chapter 6). Seeing Krishna in this changed state for the sake of his devotee evoked a mixture of love and sorrow, and it was before Krishna in this iconic form that the final *arati* of the lila was carried out. Arati is a ritual offering of light made to the deity and then offered to worshipers who draw the light into themselves with a ritual gesture.
61. This myth appears in the *Mahabharata* and in the *Matsya, Vayu,* and *Brahmanda Puranas*, as noted in Wendy Doniger [O'Flaherty], *The Origins of Evil in Hindu Mythology* (Berkeley: University of California Press, 1976), 283.
62. Abbott and Godbole, *Stories of Indian Saints*, vol. 1, 330.
63. See Novetzke, *Religion and Public Memory*, 52–73.
64. Keune, "Gathering of Bhaktas in Marāṭhī," 169–187.
65. Keune develops this notion of "strategic ambiguity" with regard to equality and caste in Jon Keune, *Shared Devotion, Shared Food: Equality and the Bhakti-Caste Question in Western India* (New York: Oxford University Press, 2021).
66. Abbott and Godbole, *Stories of Indian Saints*, vol. 1, 401–405.
67. Abbott and Godbole, *Stories of Indian Saints*, vol. 1, 338–357. See also Keune, "Gathering of Bhaktas in Marāṭhī," 174–175.
68. The following account of Sukhsaran's work is based exclusively on an edition of this text published by Rājāsthānī Shodh Sansthān (Caupasani, Jodhpur, 1984) in volumes 69–70 of the *Paramparā* series titled *Mīrābāī rī Paracī va Paracī Kāvya*, ed. Nārāyan Singh Bhāṭī, including an essay by V. S. Gūndoj, "Rājasthānī Paracī Kāvya," 71–115.

69. Prabhat, *Mīrā Jīvan aur Kāvya*, 65–67. Though some textual evidence would support the assertion that the author belonged to the Ramsnehi sect, Prabhat admits that the date of the text's composition is uncertain. Agarcand Nahṭa mentions a Ramsnehi sampraday hagiographical work by a person named Sukhśāraṇ of 1735 ślokas, giving the date as vs 1900 (1844 CE) in his introduction to Rāghavdās, *Bhaktamāl*, 78, as noted in Winand Callewaert, "Bhagatmāls and Parchaīs of Rajasthan," in Callewaert and Snell, *According to Tradition*, 89.
70. See Hiralal Maheshwari, *History of Rajasthani Literature* (Delhi: Sahitya Adademi, 1980), 133–145.
71. This edition draws on Rajasthan Shodh Sansthan manuscripts 12268(7) (dated vs 1934) and 7191(13) (dated vs 1939), with padas incorporated into a third (Rajasthan Oriental Research Institute, Jodhpur, manuscript 12585) included in an appendix. Bhati, *Mīrābāī rī Paracī va Paracī Kāvya*, 15.
72. The name of this village is properly transliterated as Kuḍkī.
73. The debate over where Mira was born focuses on when Ratan Singh (Mira's supposed father) received the land grant including the village of Kurki. See Bhati, *Mīrābāī: Aitihāsik va Sāmājik Vivecan*, 10–12.
74. Taft notes that this story appears in information collected on caste for the 1891 census in Marwar and was published in the 1896 *Report Mardunshumārī Rājmārwāḍ* (reprinted, Jodhpur: Shri Jagdish Singh Gahlot Research Institute, 1997), 439–440. The story includes that Mira cursed him and predicted that members of his caste would have either offspring or success but not both. Taft, "The Elusive Historical Mirabai," 330. Regarding this caste, see also Munshi Hardyal Singh, *The Castes of Marwar*, 153–154.
75. When I visited this temple in 1993, those overseeing it readily reported this connection to Mira, and she is also depicted on the outside of the complex above the entry door.
76. There are shared elements with Nagridas's account, where Mira is described as accompanied by brahmans and her husband's older brother threatens her, though in Sukhsaran's account her husband also does. Given the uncertainty of the dates of Sukhsaran's work and other significant differences, there is no direct evidence of influence either way.
77. *Bhagavata Purana* 10.23. Book 10 of this purana contains the stories of Krishna's incarnation, and it is a foundational religious text among Vaishnava sects.
78. Callewaert and Friedlander, *Raidās*, 30.
79. Hawley and Juergensmeyer, *Songs of the Saints*, 15–16; David Lorenzen, "The Kabir Panth and Social Protest," in Schomer and McLeod, *The Sants*, 288–289.
80. For example, see Bankey Behari, *The Story of Mira Bai* (1935; Gorakhpur: Gita Press, 2008), 26.
81. The *kanti mala* of *tulsi* (basil) beads that Mira wears is commonly worn by Vaishnava devotees and used as a rosary in the recitation of the name of God.
82. Gangaur is a name for Parvati, the wife of Shiva, and a women's festival honoring her is a major annual event in the ritual year in Rajasthan. Women worship her in the hopes that they, too, will have a husband like Shiva who is immortal.
83. Anne Mackenzie Pearson, *"Because It Gives Me Peace of Mind": Ritual Fasts in the Religious Lives of Hindu Women* (Albany: State University of New York Press, 1996).
84. *Sannyas* or renunciation is the ideal final stage of life (the fourth of the ashramas discussed in note 32), though few actually undertake it. The person who vows to do this performs their own ritual funeral, thereby breaking with past identity and all social relations to focus solely on spiritual realization. Such renunciation may also be taken at an earlier stage of life,

but there are arguments against doing so, claiming that a person must first fully experience life to be able to truly renounce it.

85. *Moksha* is release from the cycle of birth and death through spiritual liberation and enlightenment. The *Laws of Manu*, a dharmic text composed by and for brahman men, makes such a claim: "Though he may be bereft of virtue, given to lust, and totally devoid of good qualities, a good woman should always worship her husband like a god. For women, there is not independent sacrifice, vow or fast; a woman will be exalted in heaven by the mere fact that she has obediently served her husband" (5.154–155). Patrick Olivelle, trans., *The Law Code of Manu* (New York: Oxford University Press, 2009), 96.

86. See the discussions in chapter 1 regarding the Punjabi 1693 *Prem Ambodh* and the Bengali Sahajiya *Vivarta vilāsa* of Ākiñcana-dāsa, identified as late seventeenth century by Edward Dimock.

87. See, for example, Fateh Lal Mehta, *Handbook of Meywar and Guide to Its Principal Objects of Interest* (Bombay: Times of Indian Steam Press, 1888), 6 and F. Spratt and John Murray, *A Handbook for Travellers in India and Ceylon* (London: John Murray, Thacker, Spink, 1892), 84.

88. Rājā Rāghurāj Singh, *Bhaktamāla Rāmarasikāvalī* (Bombay: Lakṣmī Veṅkateśvar Steam Press, vs 1971/1914 CE), 860–879. The original publication date is not noted in this edition, edited by Khemrāj Śrīkṛṣṇadās; however, McGregor gives the date for the text as 1864 in *Hindi Literature from Its Beginnings*, 171. A member of the Ramavat sampraday, Raghuraj Singh was a poet in his own right and a prolific writer as well as a patron of the *Ramcharitmanas*, following in the footsteps of his father. For further information on his life and works, see B. P. Singh, *Rāmabhakti mem Rasik Sampradāya* (Balarāmpur: Avadha-Sāhitya-Mandir, 1957), 469–474. Vrajaratnadas includes a paraphrase of Raghuraj Singh's passage from the *Ramarasikavali* on Mira in *Mīrā-Mādhurī*, 61–63.

89. Pandit Ram Gharib Chaube, "The Legend of Mirabai," *North Indian Notes and Queries* 2, no. 2 (February 1893): 184.

90. With respect to Namdev, see Mahipati, *Bhaktavijaya*, 4:38–62 (Abbott and Godbole, *Stories of Indian Saints*, vol. 1, 60–61). In relation to Mira, a version of this milk test also appears in *Saang Mira Bai* composed and performed by Lakhmi Chand (1901–1945), the most famous of the composers of this type of folk drama found in Hariyana. See Krishna Chandra Sharma, *The Luminous Bard of Haryana Lakhmi Chand: A Study in the Indian Culture, Life and the Folk Theatre* (New Delhi: Siddharth Publications, 1990), 68–69, 117–124, 178–182, 203–205. Such a milk test has also been recounted to me repeatedly in oral contexts and has been incorporated into a play composed by Pandit Purushottamdās Purohit, *Ādarś Bhakt arthāt Mīrābāī* (Merta City: Sri Charbhuja Jagaran Mandal, 1980) for performance in the Merta Temple. This latter drama also includes an explanation for why, if Mira was devoted to Charbhuja there, she did not take this image with her when she left Merta. Charbhuja himself suggests that she take the image of Girdhar Gopal so that he might remain in Merta to continue to protect and bless her natal family.

91. This version of the snake-in-the-basket story is very common, and this very shalagram is said to be present in the Mirabai temple in Vrindavan, among other places.

92. M. A. Macauliffe reports this episode, attributing it to "the Bhagat Mala" in "The Legend of Mirabai," *Indian Antiquary*, August 1903, 332, and to "Nabhaji" in the reprinted and slightly revised version of this essay incorporated into *The Sikh Religion: Its Gurus, Sacred Writings and Authors* (Oxford: Clarendon Press, 1909), vol. 6, 348.

93. This interchange appears in full translated by Macauliffe, "The Legend of Mirabai," 332–333. Hawley notes that this exchange also appears in *Mūl Gusāīn Carit*, attributed to Beṇi Mādhavdās and said to have been written in 1630, though this date is highly suspect and it is more likely a late nineteenth-century text. Hawley, "The Saints Subdued in *Amar Chitra Katha*" (1995) in *Three Bhakti Voices*, 146; Philip Lutgendorf, "The Quest for the Legendary Tulsidas," in Callewaert and Snell, *According to Tradition*, 68–69.
94. Krishnalal Mohanlal Jhaveri does mention a woman renouncer poet-saint named Radhabai (d. 1857) who allegedly composed a biography of Mirabai. Krishnalal Mohanlal Jhaveri, *Milestones in Gujarati Literature* (Bombay: Gujarati Printing Press, 1914), 212. C. L. Prabhat includes a brief discussion of this text but finds no distinctive differences from other accounts beyond female authorship (*Mīrā Jīvan aur Kāvya*, 69).
95. A. K. Ramanujan, "Where Mirrors Are Windows: Toward an Anthology of Reflections" (1989), in *Collected Essays*, 8–9.
96. Narayan and George, "Stories about Getting Stories," 514.

Chapter 3

1. Portions of this argument appear in my earlier essay Nancy M. Martin[-Kershaw], "Mirabai in the Academy and the Politics of Identity" in *Faces of the Feminine from Ancient, Medieval and Modern India*, ed. Mandakranta Bose (New York: Oxford University Press, 2000), 162–182. Rekha Pande has drawn directly on this published work, largely word for word and without proper attribution in her presentation of Mirabai in *Divine Sounds from the Heart—Singing Unfettered in Their Own Voices: The Bhakti Movement and its Women Saints* (Newcastle upon Tyne: Cambridge Scholars Publishing, 2010), 157.
2. Muhnot Nainsi, *Munhatā Naiṇsī rī Khyāt*, vol. 1, ed. Badariprasad Sakariya (Jodhpur: Rājasthān Prācyavidyā Pratiṣṭhān, 1960), 21. Nainsi's reference has been discussed extensively in the Hindi and English scholarship on Mirabai.
3. Richard Saran and Norman Zeigler, *The Meṛtīyo Rāṭhoṛs of Meṛto, Rājasthān: Selected Translations Bearing on the History of a Rajpūt Family, 1462–1660* (Ann Arbor: Centers for South and Southeast Asian Studies, University of Michigan, 2001), vol. 1, 8–24.
4. Hukam Singh Bhati cites *Meḍiyā Khāp Khulāsā* (100/1) 850, Abhliekhāgār, Bīkāner, as the source for the marriage date of Bhojraj (*Mīrābāī: Aitihāsik va Sāmājik Vivecan*, 14n37). However, Frances Taft contends that this text does not include this date ("The Elusive Historical Mira," 333n6).
5. Taft, "Six Incarnations of Mirabai," 166–167, drawing on the work of Manohar Singh Ranawat, *Muhnot Nainsi ki Khyat* (Sitamau: Shri Natnagar Shodh Sansthan, 1987), 5.
6. The prominent sign stating this in the temple is quoted in full by Hawley, *Songs of the Saints*, 128–129. Like Merta, the Bikaner kingdom was established by one of the sons of Rathor Maharaja Jodha, founder of the kingdom of Marwar.
7. Taft, "Six Incarnations of Mirabai," 165–168.
8. Hawley, "The Saints Subdued in *Amar Chitra Katha*" in *Three Bhakti Voices*, 141.
9. Saran and Ziegler, *The Mertiyo Rathors*, vol. 2, 34.
10. See, for example, G. N. Sharma, *Bhakta Mirabai* (Udaipur: Mira Kala Mandir, 1990), 46.
11. Rao, Shulman, and Subrahmanyam, *Textures of Time*, 1–23; Christian Lee Novetzke, "The Theographic and the Historiographic in an Indian Sacred Life Story," in *Time, History and*

the Religious Imaginary in South Asia, ed. Anne Murphey (New York: Routledge, 2011), 113–132.
12. Burchett, "Agradās and Rām Rasik Bhakti Community," 432.
13. Tarinee Churun Mitra and William Price, eds., *Hindee and Hindustanee Selections: To Which Are Prefaced the Rudiments of Hindoostanee and Bruj Bhakha Grammar* (Calcutta: Hindustanee Press, 1927). This text was compiled by Mitra under the guidance of Price as a practical guide for teaching vernacular Indian languages to military personnel. James Hare discusses this text at length and reports that Mira's story is included in "Selections from the Bhukta Mal, or Lives of the Principal Hindoo Saints" ("Garland of Devotees," 185–186). Pauwels notes that these particular songs found in Nagridas's *Padaprasangmala* appear in almost identical form in Vaishnavadas's roughly contemporary works ("Hagiography and Reception History," 232–233), drawing on Prabhat, *Mīrā: Jīvan aur Kāvya*, 44. McGregor reports the additional song attributed to Mira in the section of Mitra and Price's work containing "a lithographed collection of some 200 poems" titled *sādhāran hindī gān* in the 1830 edition (223–250) and concludes that these songs represent "early nineteenth-century popular poetry in the form of songs." He notes that the song attributed to Mira here "describes the *sakhīs* weighing Kṛṣṇa on the scale of their love." Ronald Stuart McGregor, "An Early Nineteenth-Century Collection of Hindi Devotional Poems," in *Studies in South Asian Devotional Literature: Research Papers 1988–1991*, ed. Alan W. Entwistle and Françoise Mallison (New Delhi: Manohar, 1994), 514–515, 517.
14. H. H. Wilson, "Religious Sects of the Hindus," *Asiatic Researches* 16 (1928): 98–100. Wilson's essay was republished in 1846 (in Calcutta by Bishops College Press) under the title *Sketch of the Religious Sects of the Hindus* and in his posthumously collected works edited by Ernst Reinhold Rost as volume 1 of *Essays and Lectures Chiefly on the Religion of the Hindus* (London: Trubner, 1862; reprinted Calcutta: Susil Gupta, 1958). Rost confirms in a footnote that the translated Mirabai poems in Wilson's text came from Price and Mitra (138).
15. Mitra and Price, *Hindee and Hindustanee Selections*, ix, cited by Hare, "Garland of Devotees," 192.
16. James Tod, *Annals and Antiquities of Rajasthan (1829–1832)*, 3 vols., ed. William Crooke (Delhi: Low Price Publications, 1990). The *Annals* have been reprinted many times.
17. Bernard S. Cohn, *Colonialism and Its Forms of Knowledge: The British in India* (Princeton, NJ: Princeton University Press, 1996), 4–5.
18. Cohn, *Colonialism and Its Forms of Knowledge*, 49.
19. Cohn, *Colonialism and Its Forms of Knowledge*, 51.
20. See "On the Study of the Native Languages, Hindi and Hindustani Selection—Asiatic Lith. Comp. Press 2nd edition, 1830, Gulistan," *Calcutta Review* 4, no. 7 (1845): xii–xxiii, and "William Price," in *Dictionary of National Biography*, ed. Sidney Lee, vol. 46 (London: Smith, Elder, 1896), 343–44. A second citation attributes this volume to Price, Mitra, and Catarbhuja Misra.
21. "Horace Hayman Wilson," in Lee, *Dictionary of National Biography*, vol. 42 (1900), 97–99.
22. Hare, "Garland of Devotees," 134–159, 175–182.
23. Hare, "Garland of Devotees," 187.
24. Vasudha Dalmia, *The Nationalization of Hindu Traditions: Bhāratendu Hariśchandra and Nineteenth-Century Banaras* (New Delhi: Oxford University Press, 1999), 183–184, 274–275n43; Ulrike Stark, *An Empire of Books: The Naval Kishore Press and the Diffusion of the*

Printed World in Colonial India (New Delhi: Permanent Black, 2008), 424–425, cited by Hare, "Garland of Devotees," 186.
25. Wilson, "Religious Sects of the Hindus" (1928), 98–100.
26. E. Eckford Luard, *Census of India*, 1901, vol. 19-A: *Central India*, part 2 (Lucknow: Nawal Kishore, 1902), 304; R. E. Enthoven, *Census of India*, 1901, vol. 9: *Bombay*, part 1 (Bombay: Government of India Press, 1902), 78.
27. Regarding the Udasis, see Wilson, *Sketch of the Religious Sects of the Hindus* (1846), 174.
28. Wilson, "Religious Sects of the Hindus" (1928), 99.
29. More recently Mira images have been installed or identified in several temples. The Vrindavan temple discussed earlier in this chapter has an image of Mira on Krishna's right, with Radha on his left. Supposedly there is also an image of Mira enshrined in Sri Jagat Shiromaniji Temple in Amer, the former Kachvaha capital. Though identified by the Archeological Survey of India as a Radha Krishna temple built over the period 1599 to 1608 by Rani Kankawati, wife of Raja Man Singh, in memory of her son Jagat Singh, the *pujari* (priest) in the temple assures visitors proudly that the image at Krishna's left is not Radha but Mira. Images of Mira can also be found facing the central deity from some distance in the Charbhuja Temple associated with her childhood devotion in Merta, and in two temples in Pushkar constructed by jinghar mochi and vijavaragi communities in the twentieth century. Only very recently marble images of Mira and Krishna have also been installed in the temple identified with Mira at the Chittor Fort (see Figure 7.1) and in a temple built especially for the saint in Udaipur in conjunction with a research and arts center named for her, Mira Kala Mandir.
30. Hare notes that Wilson did not particularly appreciate the bhaktamal, describing it as "insipid and extravagant" even as he notes its overwhelming influence in North India (*Sketch of the Religious Sects*, 6–7); cited by Hare, "Garland of Devotees," 192–193.
31. William Crooke, "Introduction," in Tod, *Annals and Antiquities of Rajasthan*, edited by Crooke and first published in 1920. See also Jason Freitag, *Serving Empire, Serving Nation: James Tod and the Rajputs of Rajasthan* (Leiden: Brill, 2009), 33–50.
32. Freitag, *Serving Empire, Serving Nation*, 51–74.
33. Lloyd I. Rudolph and Susanne Hoeber Rudolph, *Romanticism's Child: An Intellectual History of James Tod's Influence on Indian History and Historiography* (New Delhi: Oxford University Press, 2017), 39n4. See also Florence D'Souza, *Knowledge, Mediation, and Empire: James Tod's Journeys among the Rajputs* (Manchester: Manchester University Press, 2015), 142–148.
34. Freitag, *Serving Empire, Serving Nation*, 46–47.
35. Rudolph and Rudolph, *Romanticism's Child*, 15. D'Souza suggests Tod may have employed these metaphors in order to make his subject matter comprehensible to "an elite London readership," modeled after the travel writing of Bishop Reginald Heber (*Knowledge, Mediation and Empire*, 82).
36. Rudolph and Rudolph, *Romanticism's Child*, 123.
37. Isaiah Berlin, *The Roots of Romanticism*, ed. Henry Hardy (Princeton, NJ: Princeton University Press, 1999), 8–9, quoted by Freitag, *Serving Empire, Serving Nation*, 115.
38. Rudolph and Rudolph, *Romanticism's Child*, 18–19.
39. Rudolph and Rudolph, *Romanticism's Child*, 21–27.
40. Tod, *Annals and Antiquities of Rajasthan*, 337–338, 951. Identifying Mira as the daughter of Duda and Jaimal as his grandson (951), Tod also notes that they accompanied Mira when she married Kumbha and their descendants found refuge in Badnor in Mewar (567).

41. Tod, *Annals and Antiquities of Rajasthan* (1990), 1818.
42. James Tod, *Travels in Western India* (London: William H. Allen, 1839; reprinted Delhi: Munshiram Manoharlal, 1997), 435–436, originally published in 1839 with the subtitle *Embracing a Visit the Sacred Mounts of the Jains and the Most Celebrated Shrines of the Hindu Faith between Raputana and the Indus; with an Account of the Ancient City of Nehrwalla.*
43. In *Annals and Antiquities of Rajasthan* (360–367), Tod is considerably less sympathetic to Bikramajit and nowhere mentions such devotion on his part.
44. Joseph Heliodore Garcin de Tassy, *Histoire de la Litterature Hindouie et Hindoustanie*, vol. 2 (Paris: Oriental Translation Committee of Great Britain and Ireland, 1847), 21–26. Mira also appears in a second edition (Paris: Adolphe Labitte, 1870) in vol. 2, 322–328.
45. Aamir R. Mufti, *Forget English! Orientalisms and World Literatures* (Cambridge, MA: Harvard University Press, 2016), 135.
46. George A. Grierson, *The Mediaeval Vernacular Literature of Hindustan* (Vienna: Alfred Holder, 1888), 12–13.
47. Shiv Singh Sengar, *Sivsimh Saroj* (1878), ed. Swaroop Narayan Pandey (Lucknow: Naval Kishore, 1926), 475. Vrajaratnadas presents and discusses relevant passages in *Mīrā-Mādhurī*, 59–61. Acknowledging that there are differing stories about her, Sengar presents Mira as the wife of Rana Kumbha, details the nature of her devotion, and describes her temple in Chittor. *Sivsimh Saroj* was the culmination of an ongoing effort to formalize Hindi literature initiated by Harishchandra (Dalmia, *The Nationalization of Hindu Traditions*, 274–275). Ulrike Stark details published sources Sengar drew on, including English works, and the impact of this popular work (reprinted seven times already by 1926) in narrowing Hindi literature to Hindu literature (*An Empire of Books*, 425–427).
48. Alfred Comyn Lyall, "The Religion of an Indian Province," *Fortnightly Review* (London), 1872, 136.
49. Michael Altman, *Heathen, Hindoo, Hindu: American Representations of India, 1721–1893* (New York: Oxford University Press, 2017), 30–36, 68–70.
50. Rajendralal Mitra, *The Antiquities of Orissa*, vol. 2 (1880), 137 (reprint, Calcutta: Indian Studies Past and Present, 1963), 226. In referring to Mira as the daughter of "Surya Rana," Mitra is likely referring to the Suryavansh or Sun lineage of rajputs, which includes the Kachvahas of Amer/Jaipur as well as the Sisodiyas, Rathors, and others.
51. Wilson, *Essays and Lectures Chiefly on the Religion of the Hindus*, vol. 2, 74, cited by Mitra, *Antiquities of Orissa*, vol. 2 (1880), 137. Here, in a lecture originally delivered at the University of Oxford on February 27, 1840, Wilson does refer to Mira as "princess of Jaypur."
52. William Simpson, "The Lord of the World," *Fraser's Magazine* (London) 26 (July–October 1882), new series: 80 and *Frank Leslie's Popular Monthly* (New York) 14 (July–December 1882): 558.
53. Auguste Barth, *The Religions of India*, trans., J. Wood (London: Trubner, 1882), 236–237 (explicitly drawing on Wilson); William Samuel Lilly, *India and Its Problems* (London: Sands, 1902), 137 (drawing on Barth).
54. For example, Robert W. Frazer, *A Literary History of India* (New York: Charles Scribner's Sons, 1898), 347–348.
55. Vijay Pinch, "Bhakti and the British Empire," *Past and Present* 179 (May 2003): 173–180.
56. Anindita Ghosh, *Power in Print: Popular Publishing and the Politics of Language and Culture in Colonial Society 1778–1905* (New Delhi: Oxford University Press, 2006), 4.

57. C. A. Bayly, *Empire and Information: Intelligence Gathering and Social Communication in India, 1780–1870* (Cambridge: Cambridge University Press, 1996), 355.
58. Bayly, *Empire and Information*, 355.
59. Rājā Raghurāj Singh, *Bhaktamāla Rāmarasikāvalī*. For further details see chapter 2, note 82. Macauliffe explicitly draws on this work in "The Legend of Mira Bai" (1903).
60. Chaube, "The Legend of Mirabai," 184. From a scholarly family in Gorakhpur district (U.P.), Chaube worked intimately with William Crooke on the collection and publication of Indian folktales and with G. A. Grierson in his *Linguistic Survey of India*. He was also the tutor of Ram Chandra Shukla (who became a towering figure in shaping the history of Hindi literature) and worked with G. H. Ojha to translate Tod's *Annals and Antiquities of Rajasthan* into Hindi (though Ojha did not credit him in print, just as Crooke often did not). See Sadhana Naithani, *In Quest of Indian Folktales: Pandit Ram Gharib Chaube and William Crooke* (Bloomington: Indiana University Press, 2006), 5–20. For Chaube's specific contribution with respect to recording popular traditions of Mirabai, see chapter 2.
61. Ashis Nandy, *The Intimate Enemy: Loss and Recovery of Self under Colonialism* (Delhi: Oxford University Press, 1983), 4–5.
62. Nandy, *The Intimate Enemy*, 7–8. See also Thomas R. Metcalf, *The New Cambridge History of India*, vol. 3, part 4: *Ideologies of the Raj* (Cambridge: Cambridge University Press, 1994); Mrinalini Sinha, *Colonial Masculinity: The "Manly Englishman" and the "Effeminate Bengali" in the Late Nineteenth Century* (New Delhi: Kali for Women, 1997).
63. Bayly, *Empire and Information*, 360.
64. The following description is largely drawn from Uma Chakravarti, "Whatever Happened to the Vedic Dasi?," in *Recasting Women: Essays in Indian Colonial History*, ed. Kumkum Sangari and Sudesh Vaid (New Brunswick, NJ: Rutgers University Press, 1990), 47–48. See also Partha Chatterjee, *Nationalist Thought and the Colonial World: A Derivative Discourse?* (London: Zed Books for United Nations University, 1986) and *The Nation and Its Fragments: Colonial and Postcolonial Histories* (Princeton, NJ: Princeton University Press, 1993).
65. Chakravarti, "Whatever Happened to the Vedic Dasi?," 42–46.
66. "East Indian Poetry—Female Poets," *National Magazine: Devoted to Literature, Art, and Religion*, 7 (July–December 1855): 546–550. The magazine is published in New York and edited by Abel Stevens, and the anonymous author of the essay indicates that it is a translation of a portion of Garcin de Tassy's work. The editor states his intentions for the magazine in the first pages of the first edition (July 1852).
67. Sangeeta Ray, *En-Gendering India: Woman and the Nation in Colonial and Postcolonial Narratives* (Durham, NC: Duke University Press, 2000), 9.
68. Barbara D. Metcalf and Thomas R. Metcalf, *A Concise History of India* (Cambridge: Cambridge University Press, 2002), 104–105, 111.
69. Tod, *Annals and Antiquities of Rajasthan*; J. D. Cunningham, *History of the Sikhs* (London: John Murray, 1849); Grant Duff, *History of the Marathas* (London: Longmans Green, 1826).
70. This claim may have had to be made all the more vehemently given that in Rajasthan all but the maharaja of Bundi sided with the British in 1857. Sisir Kumar Das, *A History of Indian Literature: 1800–1910 Western Impact: Indian Response* (Delhi: Sahitya Akademi, 1991), 127.
71. Dalmia, *The Nationalization of Hindu Traditions*, 32–42; Metcalf and Metcalf, *A Concise Indian History*, 3–8. The Indus River runs through what is now Pakistan, offering a northwest boundary to the Indian subcontinent.

72. Chakravarti, "Whatever Happened to the Vedic Dasi?," 48.
73. Bankimchandra Chatterji, "*Kṛṣṇacaritra*" (1886), in *Rancanavali* (Calcutta: Sahitya Samsad, 1958), vol. 2, 407–583, cited by Nandy, *The Intimate Enemy*, 23. See also Partha Chatterjee, *Nationalist Thought and the Colonial World*, 54–84; Sudipta Kaviraj, *The Unhappy Conscience: Bankimchandra Chattopadhyay and the Formation of Nationalist Discourse in India* (Delhi: Oxford University Press, 1995).
74. Nandy, *The Intimate Enemy*, 23–24.
75. Chakravarti, "Whatever Happened to the Vedic Dasi?," 49. Such an ideal also had precedence in the Dadupanthi, Ramanandi, Dasnami, and Nimbarka bands of warrior ascetics of the eighteenth century, with rajputs among them. See Hastings, "Poets, Warriors and Brothers."
76. Partha Chatterjee, "Colonialism, Nationalism, and Colonialized Women: The Contest in India," *American Ethnologist* 16, no. 4 (1989): 622–633.
77. See Kathryn Hansen, "Heroic Modes of Women in Indian Myth, Ritual and History: The *Tapasvini* and the *Virangana*," in *The Annual Review of Women in World Religions*, vol. 2: *Heroic Women*, ed. Arvind Sharma and Katherine K. Young (Albany: SUNY Press, 1992), 20–52.
78. The nineteenth-century editors of the *Calcutta Review* were British and Christian, and its contributors, whether British or Bengali, were generally also "either Christian converts or students or followers of Alexander Dutt," who served as the journal's editor from 1845 to 1848 ("The Calcutta Review," University of Calcutta, https://www.caluniv.ac.in/publication/CR.html, accessed May 20, 2020). Dalmia identifies Dutt as "one of the most militant representatives of the Christian faith on the subcontinent" (*The Nationalization of Hindu Traditions*, 345); examples of his anti-Hindu diatribes are quoted at length by John N. Gray, "Bengal and Britain: Culture Contact and the Reinterpretation of Hinduism in the Nineteenth Century," in *Aspects of Bengali History and Society*, ed. Rachel Van M. Baumer (Honolulu: University of Hawaii Press, 1975), 111. The Rudolphs note Dutt's specific choice to evangelize middle- and upper-caste and -class Indians via English education, whereas earlier missionaries had primarily targeted lower-caste communities (*Romanticism's Child*, 63–64, 78–79n15).
79. "Hindoo Female Celebrities [Part 1]," *Calcutta Review* 48, no. 95 (1869): 54.
80. "Hindoo Female Celebrities [Part 2]," *Calcutta Review* 48, no. 96 (1869): 7.
81. Keshub Chunder Sen, "Native Female Improvement," address delivered to the Social Sciences Association on February 24, 1871, published in Keshub Chunder Sen, *Discourses and Writings* (Calcutta: Brahmo Tract Society, 1904), 90.
82. Anonymous, "The Development of the Female Mind in India," *Calcutta Review* 55, no. 109 (1872), 59. The author appears to be drawing on both Tod and Wilson, though with considerable license.
83. John A. Weisse, *Origin, Progress and Destiny of the English Language* (New York: J. W. Bouton, 1879), 517–518.
84. Dalmia, *The Nationalization of Hindu Traditions*, 354.
85. Dalmia, *The Nationalization of Hindu Traditions*, 390.
86. B. C. Chatterji, "Dharmmatattva," in *Bankim Racaniibali*, vol. 2 (Calcutta: Sahitya Samsad, 1959), 661, translated and quoted by Rachel Van M. Baumer, "The Reinterpretation of Dharma in Nineteenth-Century Bengal: Righteous Conduct for Man in the Modern World," in Baumer, *Aspects of Bengali History and Society*, 93.
87. Baumer, "The Reinterpretation of Dharma, 95.

88. Chatterji, "Dharmmatattva," trans. Rachel Van M. Baumer, in Baumer, "The Reinterpretation of Dharma," 94–95.
89. Bankimchandra Chatterji, *Anandamath or The Sacred Brotherhood*, trans. with critical apparatus and introduction by Julius J. Lipner (New York: Oxford University Press, 2005); Chakravarti, "Whatever Happened to the Vedic Dasi?," 52–54; Tanika Sarkar, *Rebels, Wives and Saints: Designating Selves and Nations in Colonial Times* (London: Seagull Books, 2009), 192–228.
90. Respected judge, historian, and social reformer Mahadev Govind Ranade would similarly claim Mirabai for Marthati literature in a 1898 communication, published posthumously as "A Note on the Growth of Marathi Literature," *Journal of Asiatic Society Bombay* 20 (1902): 87–88.
91. G. M. Tripathi, *The Classical Poets of Gujarat and Their Influence on Society and Morals* (Bombay: N. M. Tripathi, 1916). First published in 1894, this work was republished in its exact original form in 1916 in response to popular demand, according to its publisher Ramaniyaram Govardhanram Tripathi (v).
92. G. M. Tripathi, from *Govardhanram Madhavram Tripathi's Scrap Book 1888–1894*, ed. K. C. Pandya, R. P. Bakshi, and S. J. Pandya (Bombay: MN Tripathi & Sons, 1959), 29, quoted by Sudhir Chandra, "A Nineteenth-Century View of the Hindu Joint Family: Notes from Govardhanram Tripathi's *Scrap Book*," in *Continuing Dilemmas: Understanding Social Consciousness* (New Delhi: Tulika, 2002), 191. See also Sudhir Chandra, "Salvaging the 'Immediate' Past: Govardhanram Tripathi's' *The Classical Poets of Gujarat and Their Influence on Society and Morals*," in *Continuing Dilemmas*, 218.
93. Rachel Dwyer, *The Poetics of Devotion: The Gujarati Lyrics of Dayārām* (Richmond, Surrey: Curzon, 2001), 72.
94. Chandra, *Continuing Dilemmas*, 222, 192.
95. Dwyer, *Poetics of Devotion*, 73.
96. Tripathi, *Scrap Book 1888–1894*, 28, quoted by Chandra, *Continuing Dilemmas*, 219.
97. Chandra, *Continuing Dilemmas*, 228.
98. Tripathi, *The Classical Poets of Gujarat*, 9–11; Chandra, *Continuing Dilemmas*, 222.
99. Tripathi, *The Classical Poets of Gujarat*, 65.
100. Tripathi, *The Classical Poets of Gujarat*, 31.
101. Chandra, *Continuing Dilemmas*, 222.
102. Tripathi follows this song directly for much of his information about her leaving for Gujarat. For a translation of the full song, see Jhaveri, *Milestones in Gujarati Literature*, 32–33; Dwyer, *The Poetics of Devotion*, 64–65.
103. Tripathi, *The Classical Poets of Gujarat*, 19–21, 27, 76.
104. Tripathi, *The Classical Poets of Gujarat*, 65. The rana's attempt to poison Mira is mentioned in the song on which Tripathi relies so heavily for his presentation (see note 102), making his omission appear deliberate.
105. Tripathi, *The Classical Poets of Gujarat*, 28.
106. Tripathi, *The Classical Poets of Gujarat*, 56.
107. Tripathi, *The Classical Poets of Gujarat*, 21.
108. Tripathi, *The Classical Poets of Gujarat*, 3, 19. See also Chandra, *Continuing Dilemmas*, 191–192.
109. Tripathi, *The Classical Poets of Gujarat*, 72.
110. Manmatha Nath Dutt, "The Heroines of Ind," in Dutt, *Gleanings from Indian Classics*, vol. 2, 169–183. Dutt is well known for his many excellent translations of key Sanskrit works,

including the *Ramayana and Mahabharata*, as well as a number of puranas and dharma shastras and also for his scholarly works on Hindu metaphysics, Buddhism, and a number of other subjects. With respect to the genre of biography, Durgadas Lahari wrote of the legendary heroines Ahalyabai, Rasmani, Rani Bhavani, and Kashmibai in his *Dvādaś Nārī* in Bengali in 1885, but as far as I know Dutt's 1893 telling is the first story of Mirabai in this mode (Das, *History of Indian Literature*, 175). A possible exception might by Kartikprasad Khatri's *Mīrābāī ka Jīvan Charit,* also published in 1893, but it is not clear which one was published first, and I have not been able to locate a copy of Khatri's work for comparative examination. Nalini Mohan Sanyal reports that Khatri identifies Mirabai as married to Kumbha in this work. Nalini Mohan Sanyal, "Mira Bai," *Kalyana-Kalaptaru* 1, no. 1: 245.

111. Dutt, "The Heroines of Ind," i–xvi.
112. Dutt, "The Heroines of Ind," 183.
113. Dutt, "The Heroines of Ind," 169–170.
114. Indira Chowdhury-Sengupta, "Reconstructing Spiritual Heroism: The Evolution of the Swadeshi Sannyasi in Bengal," in *Myth and Mythmaking*, ed. Julia Leslie (Surrey: Curzon, 1996), 128; Freitag, *Serving Empire, Serving Nation*, 176.
115. The following account, including all quotations, is drawn from Dutt, "The Heroines of Ind," 170–182.
116. Chatterjee, *The Nation and Its Fragments*; 116–134; Judith E. Walsh, *Domesticity in Colonial India: What Women Learned When Men Gave Them Advice* (New York: Rowan & Littlefield, 2004), 51–62.
117. Tanika Sarkar, *Hindu Nation, Hindu Wife: Community, Religion, and Cultural Nationalism* (Delhi: Permanent Black, 2001), 39.
118. Sarkar, *Hindu Nation, Hindu Wife*, 39–43.
119. Metcalf and Metcalf, *A Concise History of India*, 148–153.
120. Das, *History of Indian Literature*, 509.
121. Pratap Narayan Mishra, translated and quoted from Vijay Shankar Mall, ed., *Pratapnarain-Granthavali* (Kashi: Samvat 2014), 181 by Sudhir Chandra in "Communal Consciousness in Late 19th Century Hindi Literature," in *Communal and Pan-Islamic Trends in Colonial India*, ed. Mushirul Hasan (Delhi: Manohar, 1981), 173–174.
122. Akshaya Mukul, *Gita Press and the Making of India* (New Delhi: Harper Collins India, 2015), 17. Mukul notes that "Mishra castigated readers of his journal *Brahman* for not being serious in their commitment to [this] goal."
123. Ākiñcana-dāsa, *Vivarta vilāsa*, noted by Dimock, *The Place of the Hidden Moon*, 216. "Mirabai's Notebook" is discussed by Rebecca Manring in her forthcoming essay "Mirabai in Bengal." References to Rup rather than Jiv Goswami also appear in later accounts, such as Shishir Kumar Ghose's *Lord Gauranga or Salvation for All*, vol. 1 (Calcutta: Golap Lal Ghose, 1897), xl.
124. Dutt, "The Heroines of Ind," 182–183.
125. Das, *History of Indian Literature*, 498; Francesca Orsini, "Pandits, Printers and Others: Publishing in Nineteenth-Century Benares," in *Print Areas: Book History in India*, ed. Abhijit Gupta and Swapan Chakravorty (Delhi: Permanent Black, 2004), 120. The Kashi Nagari Pracharini Sabha was founded as a society dedicated to the promotion of the devanagari script and the publication of works in Hindi and about Hindi literary history.
126. Khatri's biography is cited in multiple editions as published in 1893 by Thakur Prasad & Sons, Calcutta (Callewaert, "The 'Earliest' Song of Mira," 209) and by Narayan Press, Muzaffarpur (Munshi Deviprasad, *Mīrābāī kā Jīvan Caritra* [1898; Calcutta: Bangiya

Hindi-Parishad, 1954], 1–2) and in 1920 by Lahari Press, Benaras (Nalini Mohan Sanyal, "Mira Bai," *Kalyana-Kalpataru* 1, no. 1 [January 1934]: 245).

127. Ronald Stuart McGregor, *Hindi Literature Nineteenth and Early Twentieth Centuries* (Wiesbaden: Otto Harrassowitz, 1974), 90, 96.

128. Baldevprasad Mishra, *Mirabai (Dharmamulak Aitihasik Natak)* (Bombay: n.p., 1897).

129. Kaviraj, *The Unhappy Conscience*, 104, 116–117, 125.

130. Ranajit Guha, *An Indian Historiography of India: A Nineteenth-Century Agenda and Its Implications* (Calcutta: K. P. Bagchi, 1988); Chatterjee, *A Nation and Its Fragments*.

131. Shyamaldas's text is available now as *Vīr Vinod: Mewār kā Itihās* (Delhi: Motilal Banarsidass, 1986).

132. On Tod's impact, see Freitag, *Serving Empire, Serving Nation*, including a table of translations and publications (174–179).

133. Nina Sharma and Indu Shekhar, *Becoming a Modern Historian in Princely India: An Intellectual History of Shyamal Das and His* Vir Vinod (London: Olympia, 2015), 20–36.

134. Rudolph and Rudolph, *Romanticism's Child*, 115.

135. Sharma and Shekhar, *Becoming a Modern Historian*, 37.

136. Rima Hooja, *A History of Rajasthan* (Delhi: Rupa, 2006), 810–816; Rudolph and Rudolph, *Romanticism's Child*, 110–113.

137. Hooja, *A History of Rajasthan*, 815–819, 1008–1009; Rudolph and Rudolph, *Romanticism's Child*, 110–113. Photo exhibit documentation in the Udaipur City Palace Museum (April 2015) identified him as a "staunch traditionalist," conspicuous in his absence from photos of British mandatory durbars called in Delhi and for a decided lack of photographs with foreign dignitaries.

138. Rudolph and Rudolph, *Romanticism's Child*, 87–100.

139. Kaviraj Shyamaldas, "The Antiquity, Authenticity and Genuineness of the Epic Called *The Prithvir Raj Raso*, and Commonly Ascribed to Chand Bardai," *Journal of the Asiatic Society of Bengal* 55, part I (1886), discussed in detail by Rudolph and Rudolph, *Romanticism's Child*, 128–134. See also Sharma and Shekhar, *Becoming a Modern Historian*, 213–243.

140. Rudolph and Rudolph, *Romanticism's Child*, 125–127.

141. Sharma and Shekhar, *Becoming a Modern Historian*, 262.

142. Shyamaldas, *Vir Vinod*, part 1; 362, 371; part 2, vol. 1, 1–2.

143. Hooja, *A History of Rajasthan*, 935. Hooja indicates that Shyamaldas did so without acknowledging them directly, but Sharma and Shekhar contest this portrayal, citing a number of direct references and praise of these sources and their authors (in addition to his citations of European authors) (*Becoming a Modern Historian*, 152–154).

144. Frances Taft confirms in "The Elusive Historical Mirabai" (318) that though Shymaldas evidently drew on traditional records kept by the Mewar bhats or barwas (a caste group responsible for recording the ruling family's genealogy), the present location of those records is unknown.

145. According to Padmavati Shabnam, Keshari Singh first composed his *Jaimal Vansha Prakash* in 1884, and his son published a second edition under the title *Govinda Kul Ratnakar*. However only his grandson Gopal Singh's 1932 third edition of the family chronicles, again under the title *Jaimal Vansa Prakash*, is currently available. Padmavati Shabnam, *Mīrā: Vyaktitva aur Kṛtitva* (Varanasi: Hindī Pracārak Sansthān, 1973), 37–38.

146. Sharma and Shekhar, *Becoming a Modern Historian*, 181–182.

147. Sharma and Shekhar note that he does not mention having sisters nor his wife by name even in his will, and elsewhere writes of women being "less intelligent than men," despite his more progressive views in other areas (*Becoming a Modern Historian*, 73).

148. Sharma and Shekhar, *Becoming a Modern Historian*, 42–50.

149. Rudolph and Rudolph, *Romanticism's Child*, 118–119; see also Sharma and Shekhar, *Becoming a Modern Historian*, 38–42.
150. Sharma and Shekhar, *Becoming a Modern Historian*, 41–42, 273.
151. Rudolph and Rudolph, *Romanticism's Child*, 134.
152. For example, Har Bilas Sarda, *Maharana Sāngā* (Ajmer: Scottish Missions Industries Company, 1918), 95–96.
153. Sharma and Shekhar, *Becoming a Modern Historian*, 141–180.
154. Shyamaldas, *Vir Vinod*, part 2, vol. 2, 881, translated by Sharma and Shekhar, *Becoming a Modern Historian*, 153–154. The edition of Deviprasad's *Mīrābāī kā Jīvan Charitra* I have been able to examine is a reissue edited by Lalitā Prasād Sukul and published by Bangīya Hindī Pariśad in Calcutta in 1954.
155. Komal Kothari, "Introduction," in *The Castes of Marwar*, by Singh, vol. 1; Taft, "The Elusive Historical Mira," 330.
156. Kaviraj, *The Unhappy Conscience*, 73.
157. Kaviraj, *The Unhappy Conscience*, 80.
158. Kaviraj, *The Unhappy Conscience*, 80.
159. Kaviraj, *The Unhappy Conscience*, 73.
160. Deviprasad, *Mīrābāī kā Jīvan Charitra*, 2nn.
161. This information is in Sukhsaran's account, as we noted in chapter 2. Deviprasad reports it as being "said," so he could have drawn it from this source, or he may have come across the story in his data collection for the 1891 census in Marwar, a possibility raised by Taft, "The Elusive Historical Mirabai," 330.
162. This temple was discussed in chapter 1 in connection with the Vallabhite rejection of Mira (see chapter 1, note 107). However, the dominant legend is that the image in this temple was brought from Dwarka in the twelfth century and kept in hiding until a Krishna temple was built at this formerly Shaiva site in 1556, when it was installed. It was said that Shiva continued to reside there and indeed to have insisted that Krishna join him there. The Vallabha sampraday displaced the previous brahman priests after Hariray's visit in 1625, and the current temple was built in 1772. Mallison, "Development of Early Krishnaism in Gujarāt," 248; Françoise Mallison, "Lorsque Ranachodaraya quitte Dwarka pour Dakor, ou comment Dvarakanatha prit la succession de Dankanatha," in *Devotion Divine: Bhakti Traditions from the Regions of India*, ed. Diana L. Eck and Mallison (Groningen: Egbert Forster. 1991), 197–207. It is possible that there is a particular rajput affinity for this temple, as the devotee on behalf of whom Ranchorji is said to have originally come from Dwarka was a rajput, and the temple was within rajput-controlled territory though the region was ruled by Muslim sultans. Pacified rajputs began to draw on Vaishnavism for legitimation in the fifteenth century, according to Samira Sheikh, *Forging a Region: Sultans, Traders, and Pilgrims in Gujarat 1200–1500* (New Delhi: Oxford University Press, 2010), 136, 139, 172–173.
163. The songs he includes are "No one knows my pain," "I bought the Dark One in the market," and "I married Gopal in a dream."
164. A portion of Harinarayan's correspondence has been published, and the original documents are available at the Rajasthan Oriental Research Institute, Jaipur. See Nārāyan Singh Bhāṭī, ed., *Vidhyābūṣan Purohit Harinārāyan, Paramparā 63-64* (Caupasani, Jodhpur: Rājāsthānī Shodh Sansthān, 1982).
165. Ojha refers to Mira in his *Udaipur Rajya ka Itihas*, 358 and *Rajputane ka Itihas*, vol. 2, 672. See Shabnam, *Mira: Vyaktitva aur Krititva*, 36–37.

166. Chatur Singh, *Caturkul Caritra* (Nasīrābād: Edward Printing Press, 1902), 78–80; Thakur Gopal Singh Rathor Mertiya, *Jaimal Vansa Prakasa or the History of Badnore*, vol. 1 (Ajmer: Vedic Yantralaya, 1932), 71–73.
167. Chatur Singh, letters to Harinarayan dated January 21, 1940 (85) and February 28, 1940 (89) in Bhati, *Vidhyābūṣan Purohit Harinārāyan*.
168. Padmavati Shabnam gives J. S. Gahlot's edited version of Kavivar Umardan's *Umar Kavya* (1930) (75–76) as the source for his real contribution to the conversation on Mira (rather than his *Rajputane ka Itihas* [1937]), giving the passage in full in *Mīrā: Vyaktitva aur Kṛtitva*, 37–38. Harinarayan identifies further information from Gahlot's *Marwar ka Itihas* (1925) (255) in his discussion of these materials in Bhati, *Vidhyābūṣan Purohit Harinārāyan*, 68.
169. Gopal Singh, *Jaimal Vansh Prakash*, 71–73. The edition I was able to examine included the passage on Mira in the first pages of volume 2, published in 1975 (i–ix).
170. Vidyananda Sharma writing in 1954 and K. S. Shekhawat writing in 2001 each claim to have been given this 1498 date by Mertiya bhats (traditional genealogists of the Mertiya Rathors), leading Frances Taft to posit that this was also Chatur Singh's likely source. Others were given different dates by Mertiya bhats: Harinaryan Sharma reports 1505 from such a source, and 1504 is reported by Jagdish Singh Gahlot in 1955, allegedly drawn from a Jodhpur ranimanga bhat source.
171. See Taft, "Six Incarnations of Mira" for a complete review of all the claims and available information about Mira's dates.
172. Harinarayan's notes from his conversations with Chatur Singh and Gopal Singh appear in Bhati, *Vidhyābūṣan Purohit Harinārāyan*, 66–83.
173. This information was communicated to Harinarayan by Chatur Singh in a letter dated February 28, 1940, and said to be included in *Chaturkul Charitra*, though Harinarayan appears not to have personally examined a copy of this work, and it did not appear in the copy of the text I was able to examine (graciously provided to me by Frances Taft). Bhati, *Vidhyābūṣan Purohit Harinārāyan*, 91.
174. Lindsey Harlan, *Religion and Rajput Women: The Ethic of Protection in Contemporary Narratives* (Berkeley: University of California Press, 1992), 205–222.
175. Lindsey Harlan, "Abandoning Shame: Mīrā and the Margins of Marriage," in *From the Margins of Hindu Marriage: Essays on Gender, Religion, and Culture*, ed. Lindsey Harlan and Paul B. Courtright (New York: Oxford University Press, 1995), 208.
176. Mukta, *Upholding the Common Life*, 69–70, 178–181.
177. M. L. Menaria, letter to Harinaryan, July 1, 1938, preserved in the Vidya Bhūṣaṇ Saṅgrah, Jaipur, translated by Callewaert, "The 'Earliest' Song of Mira," 201.
178. Lakshmi Vishwanathan, *Kunjamma . . . Ode to a Nightingale: M. S. Subbulakshmi* (New Delhi: Roli Books, 2003), 62.
179. Chaturvedi, personal correspondence with Padmavati Shabnam, quoted in her 1973 *Mīrā: Vyaktitva aur Kṛtitva*, 500; cited and translated by V. K. Sethi in *Mira the Divine Lover* (Beas: Radha Soami Satsang, 1979), 27.
180. During my own initial fieldwork in Rajasthan in 1992–1993 and subsequently I have encountered precisely this type of ambivalence about her behavior as a woman and a wife, and elsewhere my inquiries have simply been met with indifference but not with hostility. It seems likely, however, that attitudes were undergoing rapid change in this period.

181. Chatur Singh, letter to Harinarayan, January 21, 1940, and Harinarayan's notes from his conversations with Chatur Singh and Gopal Singh in Bhati, *Vidhyābūṣan Purohit Harinārāyan*, 85, 72–73.
182. Bhati, *Vidhyābūṣan Purohit Harinārāyan*, 78.
183. See, for example, Ghosh, *Power in Print*.
184. Goetz, *Mirabai, Her Life and Times* (1966, first published 1956); Kalyan Singh Shekhavat, *Mīrābāī kā Jīvanvrit evam Kāvya* (Jodhpur: Hindi Sahitya Bhavan, 1974), filed as his PhD dissertation in 1969.
185. This information is drawn from the 1967 correspondence of Dilip Kumar Roy and Hermann Goetz in Dilip Kumar Roy, *The Rounding Off* (Bombay: Bharatiya Vidya Bhavan, 1983), 63–67.
186. Goetz, *Mirabai: Her Life and Times*, iii, 1.
187. Goetz, *Mirabai: Her Life and Times*, iii.
188. Goetz, *Mirabai: Her Life and Times*, 8.
189. David Gordan White, *Sinister Yogis* (Chicago: University of Chicago Press, 2009), 220–221; William Pinch, *Warrior Ascetics and Indian Empires* (Cambridge: Cambridge University Press, 2006).
190. Goetz, *Mirabai: Her Life and Times*, 22–23.
191. For example, Hooja, *A History of Rajasthan*, 458–460.
192. Goetz, *Mirabai: Her Life and Times*, 29.
193. This temple allegedly enshrining Mira's Krishna image in Amer is the Sri Jagat Shiromaniji Temple. (For further details, see note 29). That Man Singh brought Mira's image of Girdhar Nagar here from Chittor is reported in earlier sources, including the *Archaeology Progress Report* of the Archeological Survey of India, Western Circle, 1897, 47.
194. Goetz, *Mirabai: Her Life and Times*, 38.
195. Hawley has brilliantly laid out these developing characterizations of bhakti in *A Storm of Songs*.
196. Shekhavat, *Mīrābāī kā Jīvanvrit evam Kāvya*, 50–51.
197. For a recent example, see B. V. Ramana, "Mirabai: Devotee of a Noble Order," in *Bhakti Movement and Literature: Re-forming a Tradition*, ed. M. Rajagopalachary and K. Damodar Rao (Jaipur: Rawat, 2016), 99–106.
198. Madhav Hada, *Pachrang Cholā Pahar Sakhī Rī* (New Delhi: Vani Prakashan, 2015), translated by Pradeep Trikha as *Meera vs. Meera: Devoted Saint-Poet or Determined Queen?* (New Delhi: Vani Prakashan, 2020). Hada offers an impressive and wide-ranging analysis of the traditions that surround Mirabai, though his attempt to present a clearer view of the woman herself draws heavily on songs attributed to her, with the underlying assumption that selected songs offer direct access to her words, thoughts, and feelings. Attractive as it may be, such an assumption is clearly unwarranted given the inability to confirm her individual authorship or even an early corpus of songs associated with her and the immense number of songs composed by others in her name across the centuries. Hada lays particular responsibility on Tod for the image of Mirabai as "a romantic and mystic poet" that he is trying to counter (*Meera vs. Meera*, 182), even as he accuses more contemporary "Marxist critics" and "neo-feminists" (most especially Parita Mukta and Kumkum Sangari) of presenting her as "a helpless, ill-fated figure against the backdrop of a suppressive society" (75).
199. Kathryn Hansen gives the specifics of these heroines' stories in "Heroic Modes of Women in India" (28–34), where she analyzes this genre in detail.

Chapter 4

1. Milton Singer, "The Rādhā-Krishna Bhajanas of Madras City," in *Krishna: Myths, Rites, and Attitudes*, ed. Milton Singer (Chicago: University of Chicago Press, 1966), 110-111.
2. Dutt, "The Heroines of Ind," 183. Dutt and company's telling of Mira's story is discussed in detail in chapter 3.
3. A. K. Ramanujan, "Where Mirrors Are Windows," in *Collected Essays*, 9.
4. *Bombay Gazetteer*, Poona District, vol. 15, part 1 (1885): 384.
5. Many examples of these conversational songs can be found in Harinarayan Sharma's collection *Mīrā Brihatpadavalī*, vol. 1.
6. One such *byāvlo* was recorded as sung by a Nath *baba* in the village of Ghanerao in 1971 by Rupayam Sansthan; it resembles the *Mira Janma Patri* we will discuss in detail. Harinarayan Sharma includes a shorter *byāhulo* in his *Mīrā Brihatpadavalī*, vol. 1, 180-182, which also includes Mira's conflict with the rana and his attempt to poison her. A commercial cassette has also been released, titled *Mirabai ro Byav*, which tells of Mira's birth, its singer identified as "Jogiram" and the recording released by Yuki Transistor Company (Delhi, 1989).
7. The designation *janma patri* is also found for sections within other epics, for example in the tales of King Bharthari and King Gopi Chand (Ann Grodzins Gold, *A Carnival of Parting* [Berkeley: University of California Press, 1992]) and the epic of Pabuji (John D. Smith, *The Epic of Pābūjī: A Study, Transcription, and Translation* [Cambridge: Cambridge University Press, 1991]). This term was also initially used for what are now called *janam-sakhis* (birth testimonies) of the life of Nanak in the Sikh tradition. See W. H. McLeod, *The Evolution of the Sikh Community* (Oxford: Clarendon Press, 1976), 21.
8. Ramanujan, "Where Mirrors are Windows," 8.
9. Goetz, "Preface," in *Mira Bai: Her Life and Times*, iii.
10. Mukta, *Upholding the Common Life*, 98-100.
11. Arjun Appadurai, "Afterword," in *Gender, Genre, and Power in South Asian Expressive Traditions*, ed. Arjun Appadurai, Frank J. Korom, and Margaret A. Mills (Philadelphia: University of Pennsylvania Press, 1991), 468.
12. Hansen, "Heroic Modes of Women in India," 41; Charu Gupta, *Sexuality, Obscenity, Community: Women, Muslims, and the Hindu Public in Colonial India* (New York: Palgrave, 2002), 102-103.
13. Devilal Samar gives Lacchiram's death date as 1937, saying he acted until he died at seventy, in *Rājasthānī Lok-Nātya* (Udaipur: Bharatiya Lok-Kala Kendra Mandal, 1957), 19. Madan Mohan Mathur gives his dates as 1847-1938 and indicates that he began performing professionally in the 1870s: "Kuchamani Khyal: A Vibrant Folk Theatre of Rajasthan," *Sangeet Natak* 40, no. 3 (2006): 35.
14. Kathryn Hansen, *Grounds for Play: The Nautanki Theatre of North India* (Berkeley: University of California Press, 1992), 56-85.
15. John Robson, *A Selection of Khyals or Marwari Plays with an Introduction and Glossary* (Beawar, Rajasthan: Beawar Mission Press, 1866), iv-v. Robson is quoted and discussed by both Hansen, *Grounds for Play*, 63-64 and Cecil Thomas Ault Jr., *Folk Theatre of Rajasthan: Introducing Three Marwari Khyal Plays Translated into English* (Gurgaon: Partridge India, 2017), 3-7.

16. Devilal Samar, "The Dance Dramas of Rajasthan," *Cultural Forum* 6, no. 3 (May 1964), cited by Hansen, *Grounds for Play*, 65.
17. Samar, *Rājasthānī Lok-Nāṭya*, 20.
18. Komal Kothari, personal communication, January 1995.
19. Mathur, "Kuchamani Khyal," 35.
20. Samar reports that *Mira Mangal* was one of ten or twelve published plays by Lacchiram (*Rājasthānī Lok-Nāṭya*, 19–20.) A copy (without date, place of publication or publisher) is available in the library of Bharatiya Lok Kala Mandal in Udaipur, as is a copy of Punamchand Sikhwal's text published by Banṣīdhar Śarmā Booksellers of Kishangar, Rajasthan (n.d.) which indicates the author was from Denda. Lacchiram's text is illustrated (see Figure 4.1). Though not mentioned by Samar, Mahendra Bhanawat does list a Punamchand Dolataram Sikhwal among the composers of khyals: *Lokraṅg* (Udaipur: Bharatiya Lok Kala Mandal, 1971), 210.
21. In *A Selection of Khyals,* Robson makes no mention of Mira, giving the texts of only four, two blatantly political and anti-British and two related tales of renouncer kings Gopichand and Ranja. Lakhmi Chand (1901–1945) of Hariyana did compose a *sang* (*sāṅg*) folk drama of Mira performed in the early decades of the twentieth century which is quite different from the Marwari dramas. Here, Mira is the daughter of a King Midat of Jodhpur. Her question to her mother about who her own bridegroom will be when she sees a wedding procession is recounted, though her mother does not answer and Mira decides on her own that it will be Krishna. Her father tests her devotion by demanding she make Krishna drink milk she offers, and he does—a test more often associated with Namdev, as noted in chapter 2. Her marriage to the rana of Udaipur occurs after hunters see the beautiful Mira sitting at the edge of a water tank and describe her to Mewar's ruler. The rana will not take no for an answer, and Mira's family is forced to accept the marriage. Even so, Mira treats the rana as a brother and appears as one lost in mystical love, unaware of the world and with an extraordinary devotion since childhood. The composer praises the saint effusively and also makes it clear that she is a sati, or virtuous woman, wife of God, and paragon of virgin perfection. See Sharma, *The Luminous Bard of Hariyana Lakhmi Chand,* 68–69, 74, 117–124, 178–182, 198–199, 203–206. Hansen also notes an All India Radio (Mathura) recording produced by Tribhuvan Sharma of a *nautanki* performance titled *Bhakta Mirabai,* a Hindi/Urdu folk drama form from Uttar Pradesh (*Grounds for Play*, 304).
22. Ault notes that he could readily find scripts of khyals in the bookstalls in cities across Rajasthan in 1986 when he began his research but that by 1997 he could find only a few old and tattered copies in Jodhpur (*Folk Theatre of Rajasthan*, 6). I was unable to find any of *Mira Mangal* even by 1993, except in the possession of singers and in the library of Bharatiya Lok Kala Mandal in Udaipur.
23. Ault, *Folk Theatre of Rajasthan*, 27–34.
24. Ault, *Folk Theatre of Rajasthan*, 39–42.
25. The following description is drawn from Thomas Ault, "Tonight Amar Singh Rathore: Marwari *Khyal* in Transition," *Asian Theatre Journal* 8, no. 2 (Fall 1991): 145–148 and Ault, *Folk Theatre of Rajasthan*, 12–21. Robson notes that during the mid-nineteenth century they were particularly popular in the weeks after Holi (*A Selection of Khyals*, vi). Mathur claims that such village performances occurred "until the late 1950s" ("Kuchamani Khyal," 35).
26. Ault reports that drama troupe members might be invited to the homes of village elites on the morning after the performance to perform a particular scene and might receive

additional remuneration, but that this type of performance was not supported by "old courts or wealthy patrons" but was a theater of the people, though key figures in the dramas are kings and queens (*Folk Theatre of Rajasthan*, 14).

27. Ault, *Folk Theatre of Rajasthan*, 21.
28. Ault, *Folk Theatre of Rajasthan*, 18–19.
29. Mathur, "Kuchamani Khyal," 36, 40.
30. Which khyals are most popular varies regionally (Komal Kothari, personal communication, January 1995). Ault gives Amar Singh Rathor and Harishchand as the most popular khyals in the regions around Jodhpur and Merta City when he did his field research ("Tonight Amar Singh Rathore," 152).
31. I have been assured that a performance of *Mira Mangal* could be staged, although I have not yet been able to make the necessary arrangements to serve as patron for such a performance. One khyal troupe I interviewed in the 1990s sang some of Lacchiram's text for me, a copy of which they had among their collection of scripts.
32. Again, I draw this general description from Ault's "Tonight Amar Singh Rathore" and *Folk Theatre of Rajasthan*, supplemented by my observations of khyal performances in the 1990s.
33. Ault, "Tonight Amar Singh Rathore," 144. See also Hansen, *Grounds for Play*, 66.
34. Ayad Ashtar, "On Reading Plays," in *Disgraced: A Play* (New York: Little, Brown, 2013), vii.
35. For example, see Bhanawat, *Lokraṅg*, 203–208. Bhanawat's categories include historical, romantic, social, and dharmic (religious) khyals.
36. Hansen, *Grounds for Play*, 65–66.
37. In this Rajasthani khyal this form of Vishnu/Krishna is called Cyārbhujā (Lacchīrām, *Khyāl Mīrā Mangal Ko*, 12) or Cārbhujā (Pūnamcand Sikhwāl, *Mīrāṃ Mangal kā Mārwāḍī Khyāl*, 11), and the temple in Merta is referred to in this way. Elsewhere this four-armed form is generally referred to as Chaturbhuj.
38. Frances Taft identifies Rao Duda Jodhavat as the one who constructed the Charbhuja Temple in Merta in "Six Incarnations of Mirabai," 165. A plaque on the wall of the temple commemorates its renovation in 1948 and credits the jingar mochis. Chloe A. Martinez has further interviewed the priest of the temple, reporting the jingar mochis' privileges of making the first offerings, in "A Family of Bhakti: Poems from the Charbhuja Temple, Merta, Rajasthan," senior thesis, Barnard College, Columbia University, 2000. Komal Kothari also reports that in Rajasthan, Charbhuja temples are generally associated with lower castes and Lakshmi-Narayan temples with rajputs (personal communication, 1993).
39. Members of the jingar community were known as makers of saddles (*jin*) for horses and elephants as well as shields, sheaths for swords and knives (and for sharpening them), bags for coins, and other riding equipment and are also reported to have engaged variously in print work on fabric, embroidery on leather items, the making of faux leather crafts, and agricultural labor. They claim rajput descent from the Rathors and the Sankhla branch of the Panwar, who do not recognize them as such, and they have been included among the "scheduled castes," those communities officially recognized by the Government of India as socially and economically disadvantaged and stigmatized. However, Mandira Nanda reports that they had congenial relations with other communities because of the goods they provided. Mandira Nanda, "Jingar," in *Rajasthan, Part 1, People of India*, vol. 38, gen. ed. K. S. Singh (Mumbai: Anthropological Survey of India, 1998), 451–454; Rukhvir Singh Gahlot and Banshi Dhar, *Castes and Tribes of Rajasthan* (Jodhpur: Jain Brothers, 1989), 180. The

same sources also indicate that the Mertiya Rathors venerated Charbhuja, as evidenced by this same Merta temple.
40. Divya Cherian, "Fall from Grace? Caste, Bhakti, and Politics in Late Eighteenth-Century Marwar," in *Bhakti and Power: Debating India's Religion of the Heart*, ed. John Stratton Hawley, Christian Lee Novetzke, and Swapna Sharma (Seattle: University of Washington Press, 2019), 184–186.
41. The *haṃs* is actually a bar-headed goose (*Anser indicus*) that breeds high in the Himalayas, said to eat pearls and to be able to separate milk from water, symbolizing "the discerning person having reached a high spiritual level." Winand M. Callewaert and Swapna Sharma, *Dictionary of Bhakti: North-Indian Bhakti Texts into Khaṛi Bolī Hindī and English* (New Delhi: DK Printworld, 2009), 2145–2146. In English these connotations are more accurately conveyed by "swan," and I have chosen to follow this convention.
42. Rashmi Bhatnagar, Renu Dube, and Reena Dube, *Female Infanticide in India: A Feminist Cultural History* (Albany: SUNY Press, 2005), 90–96.
43. Ralph W. Nicholas, "The Effectiveness of the Hindu Sacrament (*Saṃskāra*): Caste, Marriage, and Divorce in Bengali Culture," in Harlan and Courtright, *From the Margins of Hindu Marriage*, 137–159.
44. Tod (1973), *Annals and Antiquities of Rajasthan*, 359; Aditya Malik, "Avatāra, Avenger and King: Narrative Themes in the Rājasthānī Oral Epic of Devnārāyaṇ" in *Flags of Fame: Studies in South Asian Folk Culture*, ed. Heidrun Bruckner, Lothar Lutze, and Aditya Malik (Delhi: Manohar, 1993), 383; Frances Taft [Plunkett], "Royal Marriages in Rajasthan," *Contributions to Indian Sociology: New Series* 7 (1973): 79. Ann Gold also notes a tale about a woman tricked into marrying a sword in "The 'Jungli Rani' and Other Troubled Wives in Rajasthani Oral Traditions," in Harlan and Courtright, *From the Margins of Hindu Marriage*, 129, 132.
45. William Crooke, *The Popular Religion and Folk-lore of Northern India*, vol. 2 (1896; Delhi: Munshiram Manoharlal, 1968), 185. On Ram Gharib Chaube and his collaboration with Crooke, see chapter 3, note 60.
46. Ault, *Folk Theatre of Rajasthan*, 24.
47. Crooke, *The Popular Religion and Folk-lore*, 115. Crooke reports this practice from Kangra in the Punjab as well as a whole range of other types of "pseudo-marriages" to trees and other plants, in some cases to stave off misfortune or to allow for time to find an appropriate human groom for a "second marriage" but also, he suggests, in some cases to invoke the fertility and longevity of the tree (115–121).
48. In the *Ramayana*, Sita is abducted by the demon king Ravana, who seeks her love even though she is the wife of Rama, and she refuses him again and again. Ravana for his part has vowed not to take a woman by force or will not because his love is genuine, and so he must win her over, an utterly impossible task. Within the khyal there are many other references to wider narrative traditions which could not be included in this brief review of the drama.
49. Hansen, *Grounds for Play*, 145.
50. Hansen, *Grounds for Play*, 149.
51. In this comparison, I am drawing on Hansen's presentation of romantic dramas in *Grounds for Play*, 144–170.
52. This motif is common in Sufi romances as well. For example, in Kutuban's *Miragāvatī*, composed in Hindi in 1503, the prince goes in search of the heroine Miragavati (who "represents divine beauty on earth") in the guise of a Nath jogi. S. M. Pandey, "Kutuban's Miragāvatī: Its Content and Interpretation," in McGregor, *Devotional Literature in South Asia*, 179–189.

See also Pandey's discussion of the character Bajir in Maulāna Dāūd's *Candāyan* in "Bājir as a Lover and a Yogi," in Horstmann, *Bhakti in Current Research*, 209–220; Burchett, *A Genealogy of Devotion*, 277–282.

53. Hansen, *Grounds for Play*, 188–198; Hansen, "Heroic Modes of Women in India," 40–45.
54. Hansen, *Grounds for Play*, 153.
55. Kiran Nagarkar, *Cuckold* (New Delhi: Harper Collins, 1997); J. A. Joshi, *Follow the Cowherd Boy* (Victoria, Canada: Trafford, 2006); Shashi Deshpande, *The Binding Vine* (1993; New York: Feminist Press, 2001). The avant-garde San Francisco theater company Contraband took up dimensions of the violence against and denigration of women in a 1991 Mira cycle, interweaving songs of Mirabai (versions by Robert Bly) with the tale of an abandoned girl in Tennessee, reflecting and transforming childhood experiences of artistic director and choreographer Sara Shelton Mann through the collective improvisation of the dancers. Michael Fox, "'Mira, Cycle 1': Contraband Melds Poetry and Personal Pain," *San Francisco Chronicle*, June 9, 1991.
56. Hansen, *Grounds for Play*, 119–127.
57. Hansen, *Grounds for Play*, 33–55.
58. Portions of the following discussion of *Mira Janma Patri* first appeared in my earlier essay, Nancy M. Martin, "*Mira Janma Patri* and Other Tales of Resistance and Appropriation," in *Religion, Ritual, and Royalty*, ed. Rajendra Joshi and N. K. Singhi (Jaipur: Rawat Press, 1999), 227–261.
59. Parita Mukta has noted the lack of specificity regarding the use of the term *rana* also in songs attributed to Mira sung in the low-caste communities she studied and the consequent sense of Mira offering a general critique of rajput dominance and feudal authority and exploitation (*Upholding the Common Life*, 84).
60. I personally recorded all of this material except the 1975 recording done by Rupayan Sansthan. The 1996 recording was done in conjunction with Komal Kothari, and copies of all these recordings are in the Rupayan Sansthan archive. Parita Mukta summarized and briefly discussed the 1975 recording in *Upholding the Common Life* (112–114, 136, 233–234). There is sometimes considerable variation between different performers' *Janma Patris*; the boundaries between this and other circulating Mira epics like *Mirabai ro Byavlo* and *Kumbha Rana ri Bat* seem to be permeable, such that what we find may more accurately be described as a family of related epics than a singular one.
61. K. S. Singh, *Scheduled Castes*, rev. ed. (New Delhi: Oxford University Press, 1995), 186–187; L. N. Soni, "Bawaria," in Singh, *People of India: Rajasthan*, 119–122.
62. Dominique Sila Khan, *Conversions and Shifting Identities: Ramdev Pir and the Ismailis of Rajasthan* (Delhi: Manohar, 1997); Singh, *The Scheduled Castes*, 937–942; D. P. Biswas, "Meghwal," in Singh, *People of India: Rajasthan*, 629–632; Singh, *The Castes of Marwar*, 196–198.
63. Singh, *The Castes of Marwar*, 162–163. See also Neeladri Bhattacharya, "Predicaments of Mobility: Peddlers and Itinerants in Nineteenth-Century Northwestern India," in *Society and Circulation: Mobile People and Itinerant Cultures in South Asia, 1750–1950*, ed. Claude Markovits, Jacques Pouchepadass, and Sanjay Subrahmanyam (New Delhi: Permanent Black, 2003), 187–188.
64. Singh, *The Castes of Marwar*, 38–41. The jats are reputed to be hardworking and claim rajput status; nineteenth-century British writers, including Tod, designated them as such.
65. Komal Kothari reports that portions of some other epics have also taken on a kind of independent life and are more widely performed by more singers than the full epics. A similar

alternation between song and speech occurs in many epic performances as well, and the spoken sections are used to repeat, explain, and expand sung portions. For example, see Stuart Blackburn, Peter Claus, Joyce Flueckiger, and Susan Wadley, eds., *Oral Epics in India* (Berkeley: University of California Press, 1989). In the performance of the *Janma Patri*, the sung portions are repeated verbatim in prose, although there is also considerable freedom to add material in the prose sections, and much of the narrative detail appears here.

66. For example, a version of "What Can the Mewari Rana Do?" is incorporated into the narrative, and this full performance concludes with a set of popular Mira songs. Smith reports that wedding songs are incorporated in a similar way into the performance of the Pabuji epic, although many more of the incorporated songs in the *Mira Janma Patri* actually contain narrative material specific to the story of Mira. See Smith, *The Epic of Pābūjī*, 20.

67. The text does not specify whether Mira is Duda's daughter or his granddaughter, only that she is a daughter of his house.

68. Regarding ritual practices relating to the handling of the umbilical cord, see Sahab Lal Srivastava, *Folk Culture and Oral Tradition* (New Delhi: Abhinav, 1974), 71–72.

69. For an example, see William G. Archer, *Songs for the Bride: Wedding Rites in Rural India*, ed. Barbara Stoller Miller and Mildred Archer (New York: Columbia University Press, 1985), 141–142.

70. Srivastava, *Folk Culture*, 208–209.

71. L. Winifred Bryce, *Women's Folk-songs of Rajputana* (Delhi: Ministry of Information and Broadcasting, Government of India, 1961), 70–72.

72. Smith, *The Epic of Pābūjī*, 460, 328.

73. The motifs of calling the astrologer and of describing the child's cradle also have a place in bhakti poetry, appearing in Sur's songs of *vatsalya*, or parental love, for the child Krishna. See Kenneth Bryant, *Poems to the Child-God: Structures and Strategies in the Poetry of Sūrdās* (Berkeley: University of California Press, 1978), 152, 158–159.

74. Many birth songs recount such birth rituals for sons, but such a celebration of a daughter is definitely unusual. See, for example, Bryce, *Women's Folk-songs of Rajputana*, 127–135, which includes a song chastising a woman for having a daughter rather than a son. Ann Gold notes one song in honor of Hadi Rani, a famed heroine who cuts off her own head when her husband hesitates to leave her on their wedding night when he is called to the rescue of another queen and hesitates again at the gate essentially to ask if she will perform sati if he should die. She does so in order to spur him on to act with honor as a man, and he ties her head to his saddle as he rides into battle. In the song Gold translates, when her mother hears what she has done, she cries, "How joyful a daughter's birth!" Gold further notes that in the story of Karni-Ma, "the baby incarnate-goddess quickly punish[es] a family member who laments the birth of a girl." Ann Gold, "Gender, Violence and Power: Rajasthani Stories of Shakti," in *Women as Subjects: South Asian Histories*, ed. Nita Kumar (Charlottesville: University Press of Virginia, 1994), 37, 42, 45n28. But both of these are special cases—an adult woman who takes her own life to uphold rajput honor being praised after her death and a goddess who demands respect.

75. Parita Mukta translates a popular bhajan in Saurashtra that recounts a similar conversation between Mira and Rohidas and is sung in the voice of Rohidas. He begs Mira to return home because she is a Rathor princess and he a chamar; because the rana will be angry, will kill him and revile Mira; and because people will slander them both. It is clear in this popular song that Mira has already become his disciple, and at issue is whether she should return to Chittor or continue her life of wandering. Mukta, *Upholding the Common Life*, 110.

76. For further information on the Naths, see Gold, *A Carnival of Parting*, 35–53; David Lorenzen and Adrian Munoz, eds., *Yogi Heroes and Poets: Histories and Legends of the Naths* (Albany: State University of New York Press, 2011); Burchett, *Genealogy of Devotion*, 169–172.
77. Burchett, *Genealogy of Devotion*; Monika Horstmann, *Bhakti and Yoga: A Discourse in Seventeenth-Century Codices* (New Delhi: Primus Books, 2021). As we noted in chapter 1, Nabhadas appears to have quite intentionally excluded Naths and also Dadupanthis and Sikhs from his bhaktamal, but the Ramanandis did affirm yogic ascetic practice (see especially note 26). In contrast, the Varkari tradition had a quite different relationship, with Mahipati including Naths in his *Bhaktavijaya* (discussed in chapter 2).
78. Horstmann, *Bhakti and Yoga*, 101, 123.
79. Hawley, *Three Bhakti Voices*, 119–127.
80. This telling was recorded in 1993 in a village halfway between Chittor and Udaipur and combines elements from the *Janma Patri* as recorded in 1975 with elements from another epic. The singers were jats and spoke of the song as *Mira Janma Patri*, although it had also previously been referred to as *Mira ki Phali* (the "beans" or episodes of Mira). When the hero of the sixteenth-century Sufi romance *Madhumalati*, Manohar, takes on the guise of a yogi in search of his beloved, he is also described as having all the accoutrements of a Nath as well as a rosary of basil wood beads (Burchett, *A Genealogy of Devotion*, 279). Lorenzen and Munoz note the presence of Naths who are also Vaishnava in orientation in *Yogi Heroes and Poets*, x.
81. It is also the case that Naths were revered by rajputs, some rising to positions of great power as advisors to the rulers, most notably during the reign of Man Singh of Jodhpur. See Daniel Gold, "The Instability of the King: Magical Insanity and the Yogis' Power in the Politics of Jodhpur, 1803–1843," in Lorenzen, *Bhakti Religion in North India*, 120–132.
82. Entwistle, *Braj*, 81.
83. Mukta, *Upholding the Common Life*, 136.
84. A. K. Ramanujan, *Folktales from India* (New York: Pantheon Books, 1991), xxvii.
85. Ann Grodzins Gold, "Devotional Power or Dangerous Magic? The Jungli Rani's Case" in Raheja and Gold, *Listen to the Heron's Words*, 149–163; Gold, "The 'Jungli Rani' and Other Troubled Wives."
86. Gold, "The 'Jungli Rani' and Other Troubled Wives," 122. Gold offers a full translation of this tale as she recorded it and detailed analysis in both this essay and "Devotional Power or Dangerous Magic?"
87. Kirin Narayan with Urmila Devi Sood, *Mondays on the Dark Side of the Moon: Himalayan Foothill Folktales* (New York: Oxford University Press, 1997), 41–49, 236–237. Narayan lists a number of variants, and the ritual context of reciting the tale is also varied. Gold records it as told by a rajput woman in connection to Holi in Rajasthan and Narayan in connection to "the Five Days of Fasting" kept during the middle of the month of Karttik by upper-caste women in Kangra.
88. Harlan, "Abandoning Shame," 215–217.
89. Gold, "Devotional Power or Dangerous Magic?," 163.
90. Gloria Goodwin Raheja discusses this broader range of caste relationships beyond hierarchies of purity, including "mutuality" and "centrality," in *The Poison in the Gift: Protestation and the Dominant Caste in a North Indian Village* (Chicago: University of Chicago Press, 1988).
91. Edward O. Henry makes similar observations about the singing of nirgun bhajans which teach the inevitability of suffering and the assurance that no one suffers alone as well

as that all are equal in the face of death in *Chant the Names of God: Musical Culture in Bhojpuri-Speaking India* (San Diego, CA: San Diego State University Press, 1988).
92. Margaret Trawick addresses this relationship between art and life in her poignant study of a hymn to a goddess and a narrative sung and told by a young agricultural woman laborer in Tamil Nadu of her sister's life: "Wandering Lost: A Landless Laborer's Sense of Place and Self," in Appadurai, Korom, and Mills, *Gender, Genre, and Power*, 224–266.
93. Mukta, *Upholding the Common Life*, 87–105, 112–114.
94. Sharankumar Limbale, *Towards an Aesthetic of Dalit Literature*, trans. Alok Mukherjee (New Delhi: Orient Longman, 2004), 19, 32, quoted by Laura R. Bruick, *Writing Resistance: The Rhetorical Imagination of Hindi Dalit Literature* (New York: Columbia University Press, 2014), 38, 48.
95. Bruick, *Writing Resistance*, 62; Eleanor Zelliot, *From Untouchable to Dalit: Essays on the Ambedkar Movement*, 3rd ed. (Delhi: Manohar, 2001).
96. Bruick, *Writing Resistance*, 39.
97. Again this reference to clasping a tree may refer to ritual understandings of trees as generative and able to remove misfortune, particularly with regard to marriage, and of marrying trees as a way of affirming and restoring human relations with nature, restoring balance, and reestablishing the world as it should be. Vijaya Nagarajan, *Feeding a Thousand Souls: Women, Ritual and Ecology—An Exploration of the Kōlam* (New York: Oxford University Press, 2018), 225–242.
98. Mukta, *Upholding the Common Life*, 98. Restrictions imposed on members of the lower castes included prohibitions on wearing various types of jewelry and clothing reserved only for higher-caste communities as visible markers of status and privilege.
99. Crooke, *The Popular Religion and Folklore of Northern India*, vol. 2, 3, 28–29, 50.
100. Jhaveri, *Milestones in Gujarati Literature*, 33. Rachel Dwyer identifies this as a reference specifically to a Sufi's black blanket (*The Poetics of Devotion*, 65).
101. James Tod, "Personal Narrative," in *Annals and Antiquities of Rajasthan*, vol. 3, 1734.
102. Such black clothing and ornaments may also be related to possession by the Devi (Goddess). Susan Wadley records the text of a song speaking of a woman's black sari and bracelets worn in such a context, from the William and Charlotte Wiser Collection of Folklore from Karimpur, U.P., 1925–1930. Susan Wadley, *Essays on North Indian Folk Traditions* (New Delhi: Chronicle Books, 2005), 116.
103. This song also is sung as a separate bhajan, sometimes addressed directly to Sanvara, the Dark Lover, rather than her guru. It was probably also incorporated into the *Janma Patri* from the wider tradition since it contains no narrative content specific to the epic. The bullock endlessly circling a grinding stone is widely used to signify a miserable enslaved existence. The reference to her making a parrot from the "dirt" of her own body also has precedence in puranic literature; Parvati is said to give substance to her son Ganesh in a similar way, as she is bathing while Shiva is away.
104. Mukta, *Upholding the Common Life*, 87–90.
105. Bhatnagar, Dube, and Dube discuss in detail the resistance to rajput patriarchal values in songs attributed to Mira, including not only female infanticide but also arranged, patrilocal, and hypergamous marriage and much more in *Female Infanticide in India*, 171–233. They go so far as to argue that "a Meera lyric is always an oppositional argument explicitly opposing Rajput patriarchal values" (184), and more specifically that "at the heart of Meera's rejection of her Rajput heritage is a refusal of the practice of female infanticide" (172).

106. Though castes are defined as "closed endogamous groups," there are complex rules within them regarding which sub-castes may marry, and thus marrying "up" is possible in terms of sub-caste status but also wealth and prestige, and even outside of caste per se, as when ruling families intermarry to cement alliances. See Bhatnagar, Dube, and Dube, *Female Infanticide in India*, 186–196.
107. Douglas Haynes and Gyan Prakash, "Introduction: The Entanglement of Power and Resistance," in *Contesting Power: Resistance and Everyday Social Relations in South Asia*, ed. Douglas Haynes and Gyan Prakash (Berkeley: University of California Press, 1991), 16. See also Gyan Prakash, "Becoming a *Bhuinya*: Oral Traditions and Contested Domination in Eastern India" in Haynes and Prakash, *Contesting Power*, 145–174; Debjani Ganguly, *Caste and Dalit Lifeworlds: Postcolonial Perspectives* (New Delhi: Orient Blackswan, 2005), 117–126.
108. *Mira ri Janma Patri*, cassette produced by Target and copyrighted by Senior Systems, Delhi, 1987.
109. The refrain is also limited only to the lines asking Sanvariya Girdhari to come quickly because, having put her faith in him, Mira is alone. See further discussion of the impact of cassettes on both devotional and folk music traditions in Peter Manuel's *Cassette Culture: Popular Music and Technology in North India* (Chicago: University of Chicago Press, 1993), especially 183–186, which focus on Rajasthan.
110. The following account is drawn from a performance of this epic recorded as sung by turi bhat singers (who perform for meghwals) in the Sirohi district in January 1997, which I recorded together with Komal Kothari and which is now archived at Rupayan Sansthan in Jodhpur. The only earlier recording of this epic was made in 1976 by Rupayan Sansthan but covers only the episode of Raidas reported here rather than the full epic. However, filmmaker Anjali Panjabi has undertaken a documentary on this epic tradition.
111. Indeed in spite of the fact that Komal Kothari knew exactly whom to ask, based on his 1976 recording of a fragment of the epic, it still took us a number of trips over nearly five years before singers would consent to perform it for us.
112. There are a number of kings in various regions and periods named "Bhoj." No specificity is given in the epic except that he is reincarnated as Rana Kumbha.
113. This motif of being sawed in half by neem leaves appears in other stories as well. See, for example, Dominique Sila Khan, "Ramdeo Pir and the Kamadiya Panth," in *Folk, Faith, and Feudalism*, ed. N. K. Singhi and Rajendra Joshi (Jaipur: Rawat, 2005), 307. The neem tree (*Azadirachta indica*) is widely known for its medicinal qualities. Its small twigs are commonly chewed to clean teeth, and neem leaves and oil are used as a pest deterrent.
114. See Callewaert and Friedlander, *The Life and Works of Raidas*, 31–32.
115. Lila Abu-Lughod, "The Romance of Resistance: Tracing Transformations of Power through Bedouin Women," *American Ethnologist* 17, no. 2 (1990): 47. See also, for example, James C. Scott, *Domination and the Arts of Resistance: Hidden Transcripts* (New Haven, CT: Yale University Press, 1990), especially 136–182; Gold and Raheja, *Listen to the Heron's Words*; Haynes and Prakash, *Contesting Power*.
116. See, for example, Kirin Naryanan, *Storytellers, Saints and Scoundrels: Folk Narrative in Hindu Religious Teaching* (Philadelphia: University of Pennsylvania Press, 1989), 39–40.
117. See Jacob Srampickal, *Voice of the Voiceless: The Power of People's Theatre in India* (New Delhi: Manohar, 1994).
118. "Sheetal Sathe Sings Song on Govind Pansare, Penned in Prison by Sachin Mali," Kabir Kala Manch Defence Committee, May 12, 2015, https://kabirkalamanch.wordpress.com/.

The Naxalites are a Maoist-inspired insurgency that began in 1967 in northeast India and continues to engage Indian security forces.

119. See Henry Schwarz, *Constructing the Criminal Tribe in Colonial India: Acting Like a Thief* (Chichester: Blackwell, 2010); Budhan Theatre's website, http://www.budhantheatre.org/ ; the documentary film *Acting Like a Thief*, directed and produced by Kerim Fiedman and Shashwati Talukdar, 2005, https://www.youtube.com/watch?v=vpbL1UfxnzI.

120. Nandi Bhatia, *Acts of Authority/Acts of Resistance: Theater and Politics in Colonial and Postcolonial India* (Ann Arbor: University of Michigan Press, 2004), 111–119.

121. Mallika Sarabhai is responsible for the concept, script, and artistic direction of *An Idea Named Mira*, as well as choreographing the dance in collaboration with Daksha Mashruwala. This work was commissioned for and first performed as part of a Mirabai festival in Los Angeles in 2002, for which I was a principal organizer.

122. Bhatia, *Acts of Authority/Acts of Resistance*, 119.

123. B. R. Ambedkar, "Untouchables or The Children of India's Ghetto," in *Dr. Babasaheb Ambedkar Writings and Speeches*, vol. 5, compiled by Vasant Moon (Bombay: Government of Maharashtra, 1989), 101–102, quoted by Christophe Jaffrelot, "The Politics of Caste Identities," in *The Cambridge Companion to Modern Indian Culture*, ed. Vasudha Dalmia and Rashmi Sadana (Cambridge: Cambridge University Press, 2012), 89–90.

124. Jaffrelot, "The Politics of Caste Identities," 80–81.

125. Michael R. Schwartz, "Indian Untouchable Texts of Resistance: Symbolic Domination and Historical Knowledge," in *Identity, Consciousness and the Past: Forging Caste and Community in India and Sri Lanka*, ed. H. L. Seneviratne (Delhi: Oxford University Press, 1997), 177–191. On Jyotirao Phule (1827–1890) specifically, see Jaffrelot, "The Politics of Caste Identities," 83–84.

126. B. K. Sharma, *Peasant Movements in Rajasthan* (Jaipur: Pointer Publishers, 1990); P. C. Mathur, ed., *Social and Economic Dynamics of Rajasthan Politics: Before and after 1947* (Jaipur: Aalekh, 1996).

127. For a discussion of the notion of "making a way out of no way" modeled by both the biblical figure Hagar and newly freed African American slave women who identified with her, see Delores S. Williams, *Sisters in the Wilderness: The Challenge of Womanist God-Talk* (Maryknoll, NY: Orbis, 1995).

128. Parita Mukta offers one photograph of images of Mira for sale along with others of Shivaji and Krishna in Maharashtra, and she acknowledges the co-opting of bhakti by forces of Hindu revivalism but offers no further details (*Upholding the Common Life*, plate XV). I have so far not found any direct evidence of Mira's having a central place in the rhetoric of such movements, though her bhajans—along with those of other saints—may be sung to rally people to action. However, she is depicted in the popular 2013 television serial *Bharat ka Veer Putra—Maharana Pratap* (Heroic Son of India: Rana Pratap), created by Abhimanyu Raj Singh. There she gives her blessing and Krishna's to the young Pratap in his violent campaign to defend the "motherland." He is represented as virulently anti-Muslim and Akbar portrayed as unremittingly evil and depraved. There were significant protests against these portrayals of Pratap and Akbar, and Mira's portrayal here is not consistent with any found elsewhere, yet there was evidently no public protest on her behalf.

129. Sangari, "Mirabai and the Spiritual Economy of Bhakti," 1551.

130. Sangari, "Mirabai and the Spiritual Economy of Bhakti," 1468.

131. Abu-Lughod, "The Romance of Resistance," 42.

334 Notes

132. Scott, *Domination and the Arts of Resistance*, 136–137; Haynes and Prakash, "Introduction," in *Contesting Power*, 16.
133. Robert Orsi, *History and Presence* (Cambridge, MA: Harvard University Press, 2016), 92.
134. Karen McCarthy Brown makes a similar observation with regard to Haitians and the Vodou spirits in comparison to the Catholic saints with which they are identified in *Mama Lola: A Vodou Priestess in Brooklyn* (Berkeley: University of California Press, 1991), 98.
135. Sumi Madhok, "Action, Agency, Coercion: Reformatting Agency for Oppressive Contexts," in *Gender, Agency and Coercion*, ed. Sumi Madhok, Anne Phillips, and Kalpana Wilson (New York: Palgrave Macmillan, 2013), 102–121.
136. The notion of lifestyle choice itself as resistance is explored in detail by Veena Talwar Oldenburg, "Lifestyle as Resistance: The Case of the Courtesans of Lucknow," in Haynes and Prakash, *Contesting Power*, 23–61. See also Romila Thapar, "Renunciation: The Making of a Counter-Culture?," in *Ancient Indian Social History: Some Interpretations*, 2nd ed. (New Delhi: Orient Black Swan, 2010), 56–93 (cited in an earlier edition by Oldenburg, 23). Madhok warns against an "action bias" in looking at "agency in oppressive contexts," encouraging us to privilege speech rather than action and move away even from focusing on "choice." Working with low-caste women development workers in Rajasthan being trained by urban women activists to be agents of the state, she observes that they "negotiate elements of their subject formation, all the while self-consciously crafting creative strategies, both conceptual and practical, in order to define their new roles and make sense of their new and existing identities" ("Action, Agency, Coercion," 109).
137. Stuart Blackburn, "Life Histories as Narrative Strategy: Prophecy, Song, and Truth-Telling in Tamil Tales and Legends," in *Telling Lives in India: Biography, Autobiography, and Life History*, ed. David Arnold and Stuart Blackburn (Bloomington: Indiana University Press, 2004), 208. These tellings of Mira's life also correspond to the folktale pattern of "the innocent persecuted heroine" noted by Blackburn (217).

Chapter 5

1. Jhaveri, *Milestones in Gujarati Literature*, 29–35. Jhaveri references Tod and acknowledges Deviprasad and Shyamaldas but still assigns her to the fifteenth century.
2. F. E. Keay, *A History of Hindi Literature* (Calcutta: Association Press, Oxford University Press, 1920), 29–30. The Association Press is affiliated with the Indian YMCA (Hawley, *A Storm of Songs*, 55).
3. I am indebted to John Stratton Hawley for his discussion of Kshitimohan Sen's work on Mirabai, particularly Sen's essay "Mira's Songs and the Spring Festival" (Mīrār Gān o Vasantotsav) (1935), included in *Kṣhitimohan Sen Sādhak o Sādhanā*, ed. Praṇati Mukhopādhyāy (Kokata: Punaśca, 2009), 194–208. As Hawley further details, Sen's understanding of bhakti is presented in his *Medieval Mysticism of India* (1936), first delivered in lectures in 1929, though Mirabai remains peripheral to this discussion. Hawley, *A Storm of Songs*, 243–245.
4. Vasudha Dalmiya details how this conception of bhakti, initially propagated by Vallabhacharya, was instrumental in attempts to craft a united Hindu identity from the latter decades of nineteenth century in *The Nationalization of Hindu Traditions*, 338–429.
5. This assertion would be developed by a number of authors, including Ishwari Prasad in his *History of Medieval India*, published in Allahabad in 1925, as detailed by Hawley,

A Storm of Songs, 56. Prasad makes reference to Mira in a single sentence: "[T]he Mewar Princess Mīrābāī expressed her love for Kṛṣṇa in exquisite verse and moved the hearts of millions by her pathetic tenderness, the sincerity and earnestness of her devotion and the sweet melody of her songs" (508).

6. Agrawal, "The Naths in Hindi Literature," in Lorenzen and Munoz, *Yogi Heroes and Poets*, 6.
7. See Hawley's extraordinary study of the development of the notion of "the bhakti movement," especially in the writing of Hazariprasad Dvivedi, in *A Storm of Songs*. See also Agrawal, "The Naths in Hindi Literature," 3–17.
8. Missionary scholar J. N. Farquhar writes of her in *An Outline of the Religious Literature of India* (1920), describing Mira's "Radha-Krishna lyrics in Braj [as] very famous but rather disappointing," her Gujarati lyrics marked by a disturbing eroticism (306).
9. Reported by Hawley, *A Storm of Song*, 242, citing Sen's 1935 essay on the saint, "Mira's Songs and the Spring Festival," 194.
10. Sharma, *Mīrā Brihatpadavalī*, vol. 1, ed. Shekhawat; Bhati, *Vidhyābūṣan Purohit Harinārāyan*. Sharma's work was completed in 1944, though not published until 1967, while his correspondence was published in 1982.
11. U. N. Mukhopadhyay, *Mirabai of Udaipur* (Calcutta: 1901); Mirabai, *Mirabai ki Shabdavali* (Allahabad: Belvedere Press, 1909). For a more extensive list of early song publications, see Callewaert, "The 'Earliest' Song of Mīrā," 205, 209.
12. Narottamdas Swami, *Mīrā Mandākinī* (Agra: Gaya Prasad and Sons, 1930); Parashuram Chaturvedi, *Mīrābāī kī Padāvalī* (1932), 18th ed. (Prayāg: Hindī Sāhitya Sammelan, 1989).
13. R. C. Tandon, trans., *Songs of Mirabai: Translated from the Original Hindi* (Allahabad: Hindī Mandir, 1934); Anath Nath Basu, *Mirabai: Saint and Singer of India, Her Life and Writings* (London: George Allen & Unwin, 1934). Tandon explicitly thanks his friends Parashuram Chaturvedi and Sriyut Dhirendra Varma (then head of the Hindi Department at the University of Allahabad) as well as Dr. P. E. Dastoor of the English Department for their guidance. Basu indicates that he drew his original songs from manuscripts "kept in sacred temples" and oral traditions from rural Rajasthan as well as earlier publications. In his bibliography he lists a number of earlier publications as well as a general reference to manuscripts in his possession as well as works of Munshi Deviprasad and Purohit Harinarayan Sharma. Each author published a set of fifty poems.
14. Among them, J. P. Gulrajani (1916), B. N. Mehta (1918), S. S. Mehta (1919), G. Karlekar (1922), B. N. Mishra Madhva (1934), M. Shrivastav (1934), R. L. Sharma (1936), V. S. Manju (1938), J. C. Jain (1945), R. N. Thakur (1945), and M. S. Gahalot (1945). For a selected list of such early publications, see Callewaert, "The 'Earliest' Song of Mira," 209–210.
15. Rabindranath Tagore, *The Oxford India Tagore: Selected Writings on Education and Nationalism*, ed. Uma Das Gupta (Delhi: Oxford University Press, 2009), viii, 436–437 (chronology of his life).
16. Rabindranath Tagore, *Selected Letters of Rabindranath Tagore*, ed. Krishna Dutta and Andrew Robinson (Cambridge: Cambridge University Press, 1997), 57, 65–67, 82, 84, 92–93, 113–114, 120–121, 179, 213–214, 226–227, 231–235, 238–243, 301–302, 383–384, 409–411. Much of this information about his relationship with his daughter appears in introductions provided to the letters and footnotes as well as his letters to her, her husband, and others.

17. In the following discussion I draw on Kalpana Bardhan's translation "Letter from a Wife" in her *Of Women, Outcastes, Peasants, and Rebels: A Selection of Bengali Short Stories* (Berkeley: University of California Press, 1990), 96–109. For an alternative translation, see Supriya Chaudhuri's "A Wife's Letter" in Rabindranath Tagore, *Selected Short Stories*, ed. Sukanta Chaudhuri (New Delhi: Oxford University Press, 2000), 205–218. Chaudhuri's translation suggests further resonances of imagery with Mirabai's poetry and a more deeply devotional dimension to Mrinal's description of her realization.
18. Tagore, "Letter from a Wife," trans. Bardhan, 102.
19. Tagore, "Letter from a Wife," trans. Bardhan, 109.
20. Tagore, "Letter from a Wife," trans. Bardhan, 109.
21. Tagore, "Letter from a Wife," trans. Bardhan, 106. Hawley has identified "fearlessness" as Mira's defining characteristic (*Three Bhakti Voices*, 51–55).
22. Tagore, "Letter from a Wife," trans. Bardhan, 108.
23. Letter to Rathindranath, August/September 1919, in Tagore, *Selected* Letters, 226–227. Portions of this letter are also quoted and Tagore's relationship with his daughter Mira mentioned by Sabhyasachi Bhattacharya in his discussion of *Strir Patra* (The Wife's Letter) in *Rabindranath Tagore: An Interpretation* (New Delhi: Penguin, Viking, 2012), 124–125.
24. Tanika Sarkar, "Many Faces of Love: Country, Woman and God in *The Home and the World*," in *Rabindranath Tagore's* The Home and the World: *A Critical Companion*, ed. Pradip Kumar Datta (Delhi: Permanent Black, 2002; London: Anthem Press, 2005), 30. Sarkar notes the long-standing bhakti practice of composing in a woman's voice and nineteenth-century Bengali novelists, including Bankimchandra, who do this before this time as precedents for this move by Tagore.
25. Bhattacharya, *Rabindranath Tagore*, 124–125.
26. This passage from Tagore is quoted and translated by Datta, "Introduction," in *Rabindranath Tagore's* The Home and the World, 2.
27. Datta, "Introduction," 7, 9.
28. Datta, "Introduction," 8.
29. Santosh Chakrabarti, *Studies in Tagore: Critical Essays* (New Delhi: Atlantic Publishers, 2004), 1–2 (see also 61 and 96).
30. Kishwar and Vanita, "Poison to Nectar," 85.
31. Supriya Chaudhuri, "A Sentimental Education: Love and Marriage in *The Home and the World*," in Datta, *Rabindranath Tagore's* The Home and the World, 50.
32. Bhattacharya, *Rabindranath Tagore*, 69–73.
33. See, for example, Mukta, *Upholding the Common Life*, 229–231.
34. Chaudhuri, "A Sentimental Education," 50.
35. Bardhan, "Introduction," in *Of Women, Outcastes, Peasants, and Rebels*, 14.
36. For example, Martha Craven Nussbaum, "In Defense of Universal Values," *Idaho Law Review* 36, no. 2 (2000): 379–447.
37. Sarkar, "Many Faces of Love," 30.
38. Bhattacharya, *Rabindranath Tagore*, 164.
39. Supriya Chaudhuri, "Introduction," in Rabindranath Tagore, *Relationships: Jogajog*, trans. Supriya Chaudhuri (New Delhi: Oxford University Press, 2006), 1, 13. The novel was first serialized from September–October 1927 to March–April 1929 in *Bichitra*, then published in novel form in June–July 1929 (1).
40. Chaudhuri discusses its meaning in her "Introduction," in Tagore, *Relationships: Jogajog*, 1; Hiten Bhaya's translation "Yogayog (Nexus)" appears in *The Tagore Ominbus*, vol. 1 (New

Delhi: Penguin Books, 2005), 465–672. The first two segments of the story were published under the title "Three Generations," but Tagore changed it in the next installment as the novel took on a life of its own. See Chaudhuri, "Introduction," 1–3 and "Appendix: Change of Name" (256–258), written by Tagore and originally published in *Bichitra* (November–December 1927) with the third installment of the serial, translated by Chaudhuri.

41. Tagore, "Yogayog," trans. Bhaya, 474–475.
42. Tagore, "Yogayog," trans. Bhaya, 524.
43. Letter to Radharani Debi, 14 Bhadra 1335 (1928), quoted by Chaudhuri, "Introduction," in Tagore, *Relationships*, 5.
44. Tagore, *Relationships*, trans. Chaudhuri, 69, 98–101; Olivelle, *The Law Code of Manu*, 96.
45. Walsh discusses the life and work of Nagendrabala Dasi in *Domesticity in Colonial India*, chapter 7 (141–161), and I am indebted to her for the information presented herein. It is striking that this is the only reference to Mira noted by Walsh in domestic manuals from this period (149). She translates chapter 2 (7–19) of Nagendrabala Dasi's *Women's Dharma* (Calcutta, 1900) in Appendix E (195–201); the reference to Mira appears on 198.
46. Nagendrabala Dasi, *Women's Dharma*, in Walsh, *Domesticity in Colonial India*, 198.
47. Walsh, *Domesticity in Colonial India*, 153.
48. Bhattacharya, *Rabindranath Tagore*, 164–165.
49. Rabindranath Tagore, "The Indian Ideal of Marriage" (1925), in *The English Writings of Rabindranath Tagore*, vol. 3: *A Miscellany*, ed. Sisir Kumar Das (New Delhi: Sahitya Akademi, 1996), 532.
50. Walsh, *Domesticity in Colonial India*, 145–146.
51. Walsh, *Domesticity in Colonial India*, 153–154.
52. Walsh, *Domesticity in Colonial India*, 148–151.
53. Walsh, *Domesticity in Colonial India*, 145.
54. *Mahānirvāṇa tantra*, quoted by Dasi, *Women's Dharma*, 57, translated and discussed by Walsh, *Domesticity in Colonial India*, 150, italics added.
55. Walsh, *Domesticity in Colonial India*, 159.
56. Nagendrabala Dasi recounts this information in the preface to her supplementary *Household Dharma*, published in 1904, as noted by Walsh, *Domesticity in Colonial India*, 146.
57. Walsh, *Domesticity in Colonial India*, 141–161.
58. Tagore, "Yogayog," trans. Bhaya, 527.
59. Bhattacharya, *Rabindranath Tagore*, 164, paraphrasing from the same letter of Tagore to Radharani Devi, 1928, referenced above (Rabindranath Tagore Archives, no. 2479).
60. Tagore, "Yogayog," trans. Bhaya, 622.
61. Chaudhuri, "Introduction," in Tagore, *Relationships*, 25–26.
62. Tagore, "Yogayog," trans. Bhaya, 642–643.
63. Tagore, "Yogayog," trans. Bhaya, 643–644. I have inserted Supirya Chaudhuri's translation "tenderness" in addition to Bhaya's "possessiveness," which add different dimensions to the meaning (Tagore, *Relationships*, 229).
64. Tagore, "Yogayog," trans. Bhaya, 644.
65. Tagore, "Yogayog," trans. Bhaya, 660.
66. Bhattacharya, *Rabindranath Tagore*, 164–165, quoting Tagore, "The Indian Ideal of Marriage," 537.
67. Tagore, "Yogayog," trans. Bhaya, 666.
68. Chaudhuri, "Introduction," in Tagore, *Relationships*, 28–29.

69. Radha Chakravarty reviews a number of such responses in *Novelist Tagore: Gender and Modernity in Selected Texts* (New Delhi: Routledge, 2013), 120–121. See also Chaudhari, "Introduction," in Tagore, *Relationships*, 14.
70. Chaudhari, "Introduction," in Tagore, *Relationships*, 26–28.
71. Amartya Sen, "Introduction," in Rabindranath Tagore, *Boyhood Days*, trans. Radha Chakravarty (New Delhi: Penguin, 2007), xx; Amit Chaudhari, "Foreword," in *The Essential Tagore*, ed. Fakrul Alam and Radha Chakravarty (Cambridge, MA: Harvard University Press, 2011), xxvi, both quoted by R. Chakravarty, *Novelist Tagore*, 41–42.
72. Chaudhari, "Introduction," in Tagore, *Relationships*, 7.
73. See Tagore, "Religion of Man" (1930), in Das, *The English Writings of Rabindranath Tagore*, vol. 3, 83–189; Amiya P. Sen, trans., *Religion and Rabindranath Tagore: Selected Discourses, Addresses, and Letters in Translation* (New Delhi: Oxford University Press, 2014). Tagore credits Sen with introducing him to the medieval poets, and they mutually influence each other's thoughts, with several essays by Kshitimohan Sen appended to Tagore's essay "Religion of Man."
74. For an alternative comparison of Mrinal and Kumudini, see Chaudhuri, "Introduction," in Tagore, *Relationships*, 13.
75. Gandhi would also sometimes speak of her or address her simply as "Mirabai" or "Mira," as did others. See, for example, Mohandas K. Gandhi, *The Collected Works of Mahatma Gandhi*, vol. 33 (Delhi: Publications Division, Ministry of Information and Broadcasting, Government of India, 1969), 269.
76. Numerous references to Mira can be found in Gandhi, *The Collected Works* from 1907. For further discussion of Gandhi's use of Mira, see Madhu Kishwar and Ruth Vanita, "Gandhi's Mira," in *Women Bhakta Poets*, 86–87; Mukta, *Upholding the Common Life*, 182–200; Martin, "Dyed in the Color of Her Lord," 241–245.
77. This is reported in "Talks to Ashram Women" (1926), in *Collected Works*, 32:486, and noted by Mukta in her comprehensive analysis of Gandhi's references to Mira therein (*Upholding the Common Life*, 183).
78. Neelima Shukla-Bhatt, "Performance as Translation: Mira in Gujarat," *International Journal of Hindu Studies* 11, no. 3 (2007): 279. The song she mentions refers to Mira as the daughter of Jaimal Rathor also. Gandhi's family were followers of Vallabhacharya, his mother a member of the Pranami sect, and he grew up surrounded by bhajans and religious stories, particularly the *Ramayana*, and with Jains and Muslims also frequently in their home. Margaret Chatterjee, *Gandhi's Religious Thought* (Notre Dame, IN: University of Notre Dame Press, 1983), 15–16. Though Gandhi invoked Tod's work elsewhere, there is no indication that his portrayal of Mira was influenced by him. Rudolph and Rudolph, *Romanticism's Child*, 97–98.
79. Gandhi, "From the Report of the Commissioners Appointed by the Punjab Subcommittee of the Indian National Congress" (March 25, 1920), in *Collected Works*, 17:152–153.
80. Kishwar and Vanita, *Women Bhakta Poets*, 86–87. See, for example, Gandhi, *Collected Works*, 12:425, 14:506, 18:116, 31:512, 32:486, 78:392.
81. Chatterjee, *Gandhi's Religious Thought*, 27–28, 136–137.
82. Chatterjee, *Gandhi's Religious Thought*, 27, 178.
83. Neelima Shukla-Bhatt, *Narasinha Mehta of Gujarat: A Legacy of Bhakti Songs and Stories* (New York: Oxford University Press, 2015), 173–206.
84. These lines appear, for example, in a speech Gandhi delivered at Belur Math, January 30, 1921 (*Collected Works*, 19:306), but also in many other places including 24:167, 25:61, 32:147, 32:187, 39:177, 56:350, 62:170, 63:388, 81:59, 88:219, 88:261.

85. String puppets are a lively part of Indian folk culture, so this image would have invoked childhood memories of the magic of traveling puppet shows.
86. Mukta, *Upholding the Common Life*, 182–200. See also Pamela Sue Anderson, *A Feminist Philosophy of Religion: The Rationality and Myths of Religious Belief* (Oxford: Blackwell, 1998), drawing on Mukta.
87. Tanika Sarkar, "Gandhi and Social Relations," in *The Cambridge Companion to Gandhi*, ed. Judith M. Brown and Anthony Parel (Cambridge: Cambridge University Press, 2011), 183.
88. Gandhi, "Deputation Notes (after September 3, 1909)," in *Collected Works*, 9:386; Vishwanathan, *Kunjamma*, 50–51.
89. Sarkar, "Gandhi and Social Relations," 184–187.
90. Sarkar, "Gandhi and Social Relations," 185–186.
91. Gandhi, "Talks to Ashram Women," in *Collected Works* 32:485–486.
92. Gandhi, "A Twentieth Century Sati?," *Young India*, May 21, 1931, in *Collected Works*, 46:73–74.
93. Gandhi, *Collected Works*, 46:75.
94. Sarkar, "Gandhi and Social Relations," 187.
95. Sarkar, "Gandhi and Social Relations," 185.
96. Sarkar, "Gandhi and Social Relations," 178, 189, with reference to Mohandas K. Gandhi, *An Autobiography: The Story of My Experiments with Truth* (Ahmedabad: Navjivan Trust, 1927), 255.
97. Gandhi, "More Questions," *Navajivan*, August 23, 1925, in *Collected Works*, 28:105.
98. Gandhi, "Letter to Ramachandra Trivedi" [on or after December 14, 1930], in *Collected Works*, 44:385. See letter to Ramachandra, December 13, 1930 (379), that makes it clear Gandhi is addressing Ramachandra's mother's stance on untouchability in relation to his father's attitude.
99. Sarkar, "Gandhi and Social Relations," 182; Shukla-Bhatt, *Narasinha Mehta*, 173–206.
100. Joel Lee, "Bhakti, Dalits, and the Nation," paper presented at the American Academy of Religion National Meeting, Chicago, 2012; Joel Lee, "Recognition and Its Shadows: Dalits and the Politics of Religion in India" (Ph.D. diss., Columbia University, 2015), 179. Lee discusses this process of the Hinduizing of "untouchables" in detail in chapter 4 (129–183).
101. Gandhi, "Message to All-India Women's Conference [before December 22, 1938]," in *Collected Works* 68:230; Mohandas K. Gandhi, *Gandhi on Women (Collection of Mahatma Gandhi's Writings and Speeches on Women)*, ed. Pushpa Joshi (Ahmedabad: Navajivan Publishing House, Centre for Women's Development Studies, 1988), 306; Gandhi, *Navajivan*, June 7, 1931, quoted by Shukla-Bhatt, *Narasinha Mehta*, 201.
102. Shukla-Bhatt, *Narasinha Mehta*, 173–206.
103. Mrinalini Sinha, "Refashioning Mother India: Feminism and Nationalism in Late-Colonial India," *Feminist Studies* 26, no. 3 (2000): 636–638.
104. Sinha, "Refashioning Mother India," 634.
105. Sinha, "Refashioning Mother India," 635, 636–638.
106. The following information on Gadge Maharaj is drawn primarily from Anna Schultz's presentation of his life and illuminating analysis of his work in *Singing a Hindu Nation: Marathi Devotional Performance and Nationalism* (New York: Oxford University Press, 2013), especially 60–64, 73–75. In addition, I have drawn on Eleanor Zelliot and Maxine Berntsen's "Editors' Introduction" to G. N. Dandekar, "The Last Kīrtan of Gadge Baba," trans. Maxine Berntsen with Jayant Karve, in *Essays on Religion in Maharashtra*, ed.

Eleanor Zelliot and Maxine Berntsen (Albany: State University of New York Press, 1988), 223–224.
107. Schultz, *Singing a Hindu Nation*, 62, 64.
108. Schultz, *Singing a Hindu Nation*, 74–75.
109. Dandekar, "The Last Kīrtan of Gadge Baba," 242.
110. Schultz, *Singing a Hindu Nation*, 63.
111. I do not know whether this was her birth name or an assumed name. Schultz, *Singing a Hindu Nation*, 73–74. But she had left her husband to join the movement (124).
112. *Bombay Gazetteer*, Poona District, vol. 15, part 1 (1885): 384. This source indicates that her name was among the most popular women's names among the tribal Dhangar shepherds in the Pune district, and Gadge Maharaj does actually mention Dhangars in his final kirtan, though in the context of its being acceptable to call a man who does not provide for his family "a Dhangar's sheep" (Dandekar, "The Last Kīrtan of Gadge Baba," 247).
113. Joel Lee details the overlapping Hinduization campaigns of Gandhi's Harijan Sevak Sangh and the Arya Samaj in "Recognition and Its Shadows," 129–183.
114. Though this analysis is based on a single kirtan performance, issues related specifically to women are not mentioned by either Schultz (*Singing a Hindu Nation*) or Zelliot and Berntsen ("Editors' Introduction") as being a part of his broad-ranging reform agenda. It is, however, also worth noting that in this final kirtan, Gadge Maharaj does not employ Tukaram and Kabir directly in support of eliminating casteism, though he invokes lines from songs attributed to them on a number of other issues, including the efficacy of bhajan singing, the nature of God, the excesses and uselessness of ritual worship, and the dangers of egocentric pride. Instead he addresses his audience directly, in a manner reminiscent of Kabir, challenging them to change their lives and serve the common good, with Gandhi as his principal ideal exemplar.
115. Akeel Bilgrami, "Gandhi's Religion and Its Relation to His Politics," in Brown and Parel, *The Cambridge Companion to Gandhi*, 93.
116. Veena R. Howard, *Gandhi's Ascetic Activism: Renunciation and Social Action* (Albany: State University of New York Press, 2013), 183. The internal quotes reflect Gandhi's own writing on how he viewed the *Mahabharata* in "On the Verge of It," *Young India*, May 21, 1925, in *Collected Works*, 31:373; quoted at length by Howard on 183.
117. Howard, *Gandhi's Ascetic Activism*, 180. Gandhi speaks of characters like Harishchandra as "living realities" whether or not they were actual historical figures in *An Autobiography: The Story of My Experiments with Truth*, trans. Mahadev Desai (Boston: Beacon Press, 1957), 7–8 (quoted by Howard). He writes of "salvation through the service and salvation of the nation and humanity" in, among other places, "Speech at Prabartak Ashram, Chandernagore," *Amrita Bazar Patrika*, May 8, 1925, in *Collected Works*, 31:279 (quoted by Howard).
118. Howard, *Gandhi's Ascetic Activism*, 184.
119. Sarkar, "Gandhi and Social Relations," 186.
120. Mirabehn (Madeleine Slade) is one such woman, but there were and are many others. Gandhi lauded such a choice, though acknowledging that not all people were capable of making it and therefore marriage remained a social necessity, though with a tendency to draw one's attention away from service to humanity, narrowing one's focus to family alone. I met a number of such women in 1989 when I participated in a joint delegation of Indian and American grassroots women activists sponsored by the Gandhi Peace Foundation.

121. Madhu Kishwar, "Traditional Female Moral Exemplars in India," *Teaching about Asia* 6, no. 3 (Winter 2001): 30.
122. Madhu Kishwar, "Gandhi on Women," *Economic and Political Weekly* 20, no. 41 (October 12, 1985): 1756.
123. Parita Mukta discusses Ravishankar Rawal in *Upholding the Common Life*, 206–207, reproducing his painting of Mirabai as Illustration IX, noting that it was used by the Government of Gujarat on a calendar after Independence: "It shows a Mira more akin to the figure of a chaste housewife-widow, who is immersed in *murti-puja* within the household." An ektara is a one stringed musical instrument and kartals are handheld rhythm instruments of wood with metal jingles (resembling the edge of a tambourine in structure and also making a similar sound), both commonly used to accompany bhajan singing.
124. Kanu Desai, *Mirabai: Ten Pictures from the Life of India's Greatest Poetess of the Past* (Bombay: D. B. Taraporevala Sons, 1943). She is either dressed in white or portrayed in a line drawing, with the exception of the first two paintings, when she is still the rani. In the first only her face is portrayed, her headcovering white but trimmed in orange, and in the second she is gazing into the distance at the moon through a window of the palace. This collection includes a foreword by Madame Sophia Wadia, addressed to those outside Gujarat and even India to give them some background. The life of Mirabai presented is largely that of Deviprasad, though she suggests, "The real story of Mirabai is the story of her soul struggles and her self-purification." Kanu Desai's portraits of Mira are discussed in detail by Mukta, *Upholding the Common Life*, 206–207 and by Shukla-Bhatt in response, "Performance as Translation," 287–290.
125. Partha Mitter, *Art and Nationalism in Colonial India 1850–1922: Occidental Orientations* (Cambridge: Cambridge University Press, 1995), 332. See chapter 3, note 102 regarding the Gujarati song describing Mira's departure by camel.
126. J. P. Vaswani, ed., *Born to Serve* [An Interpretation of the Life, Thought and Work of Sri T. L. Vaswani] (Poona: Gita Publishing House, 1965), 19. T. L. Vaswani's extensive publications include *Saint Mira* (Poona: St. Mira's English Medium School, n.d.) and *The Call of Mira Education* (Poona: Mira Publications, n.d.), published sometime in the 1950s or 1960s.
127. The centrality of Mira at the school was very evident when I visited in 1996 and was earlier documented at both the school and college by John Stratton Hawley, who visited both and interviewed Mrs. R. A. Vaswani and Mr. Atma Vaswani in 1985 (*Songs of the Saints*, 120–121, 202n4, 6). By 2022, however, a review of their web presence suggests that Swami Vaswani himself has largely displaced Mira in imagery and pageantry of these institutions, though the Mira College for Girls continues to acknowledge her as their patron saint on their website and as a source of inspiration in the "What Is Special about St. Mira's" section of their prospectus. The primary school continues to follow the founding philosophy, at least in principle, though no images of Mira appear in any of the photos posted for this now coeducational school. The Swami Vaswani Foundation has also founded the coeducational Swami Vaswani International School, with state-of-the-art facilities in Pune and elsewhere (grades nursery–11) and established a college of nursing (2006), an institute for training pre-primary teachers (2009), and an Institute for Management Studies for Girls (2010), the last with a page titled "Mira Legacy" that references the saint and the Mira Movement for Education. It is not clear how much the students themselves at any of these institutions continue to identify with the saint.
128. T. L. Vaswani, *The Call of New Education* (Poona: Mira, 1968), 33.

129. Mukta, *Upholding the Common Life*, 191–192. The second quotation here is drawn by Mukta from "Ashram Bhajanavali," November 11, 1930, in Gandhi, *Collected Works*, 44:449–50. It is worth noting also, however, that Gandhi translated these bhajans specifically for his disciple Mirabehn while in Yerba prison.
130. Howard, *Gandhi's Ascetic Activism*.
131. Shukla-Bhatt, "Performance as Translation," 282–283. Shukla-Bhatt found both versions of this song in multiple published collections of Mira songs, so whether Gandhi or someone in his circle actively improvised their own version of this popular song or selected an existing version rather than the more prevalent one that speaks directly to the issue of widowhood warrants further investigation.
132. The following discussion of Mahadevi Varma is drawn primarily from Karine Schomer's wonderful study of her life and work, *Mahadevi Varma and the Chhayavad Age of Modern Hindi Poetry* (Delhi: Oxford University Press, 1998; first published by University of California Press, 1983). I have supplemented this material with Mahadevi's lectures on Mira published under the title *Mīrā Śraddhānjali* (Udaipur: Mira Pratishtan Mahila Mandal, 1975). Schomer gives her birth year as 1902 based on the day March 24 and the memory of her family that it was Holi, which occurred in 1902 and not in 1907.
133. Varma, "Dedication," in *Nīrajā* (1934), quoted and translated by Schomer, *Mahadevi Varma*, 243.
134. This story is related by Mahadevi in *Mīrā Śraddhānjali*, 17. Schomer discusses the early influence of her mother's bhakti on the young Mahadevi in *Mahadevi Varma*, 163–164. Francesca Orsini notes that Mahadevi's mother was steeped in the Vallabha tradition, which if true would give further evidence that Mirabai was embraced by at least some women in the tradition. Francesca Orsini, *The Hindi Public Sphere 1920–1914: Language and Literature in the Age of Nationalism* (New York: Oxford University Press, 2002), 446.
135. Schomer discusses the Chhayavad poetic movement (1918–1938) in detail in *Mahadevi Varma*. For a short summary, see Anita Anantharam, *Bodies That Remember: Indigenous Women's Knowledge and Cosmopolitanism in South Asian Poetry* (Syracuse, NY: Syracuse University Press, 2012), 39–40.
136. Schomer, *Mahadevi Varma*.
137. Varma, *Sāndhya-gīt*, 7–8, translated and quoted by Schomer, *Mahadevi Varma*, 285.
138. Varma, *Sāhityakār kī Āsthā*, 27, translated and quoted by Schomer, *Mahadevi Varma*, 286, italics in original translation.
139. Schomer, *Mahadevi Varma*, 43–45.
140. Schomer, *Mahadevi Varma*, 43.
141. See Mahadevi Varma, "Our Country and Our National Language," trans. Vasudha Dalmia, in *Mahadevi Varma: Political Essays on Women, Culture, and Nation*, ed. Anita Anantharam (Amherst, NY: Cambria Press, 2010), 183–192.
142. Schomer, *Mahadevi Varma*, 262–263.
143. Anantharam, *Bodies That Remember*, 51. Schomer discusses Mahadevi's kayashta background in detail, noting that this relatively small group was probably the result of intercaste marriage within Hindu courts. Members of the community tended to be highly literate, serving in a number of writing capacities and included many great literary figures. They were also known for their adaptability and in the modern period were progressive, many embracing the Arya Samaj and instituting social reforms and women's education ahead of many other sections of North Indian society. Schomer, *Mahadevi Varma*, 150–153.

144. Schomer, *Mahadevi Varma*, 166-169.
145. The following discussion of Allahabad in this time is drawn from Schomer, *Mahadevi Varma*, 124-149.
146. Schomer, *Mahadevi Varma*, 135.
147. Schomer, *Mahadevi Varma*, 137.
148. Hawley, *A Storm of Songs*, 244. Regarding the press, see also Vinay Dharwadker, *Kabir: The Weaver's Song* (New Delhi: Penguin, 2003), 40, 71-72.
149. Schomer, *Mahadevi Varma*, 198-199.
150. Schomer, *Mahadevi Varma*, 201-202.
151. Schomer, *Mahadevi Varma*, 205.
152. Anantharam, *Bodies That Remember*, 80-82. Anantharam quotes extensively from Varma, "My Childhood Days." See this full essay, translated by Anantharam, as well as "Our Country and Our National Language," translated by Dalmia, in Anantharam, *Mahadevi Varma: Political Essays*.
153. Schomer, *Mahadevi Varma*, 220.
154. Schomer, *Mahadevi Varma*, 236.
155. Orsini, *The Hindi Public Sphere*, 307.
156. Orsini, *The Hindi Public Sphere*, 267.
157. Orsini, *The Hindi Public Sphere*, 268, 273-274.
158. Orsini, *The Hindi Public Sphere*, 273.
159. Schomer, *Mahadevi Varma*, 228.
160. Varma, "The Links in Our Chain," trans. Shobna Nijhawan, in Anantharam, *Mahadevi Varma: Political Essays*, 71-72.
161. Schomer, *Mahadevi Varma*, 228.
162. For example, see Varma, "The Links in Our Chains," 82. See also Anantharam's "Introduction," in *Mahadevi Varma: Political Essays*, 20.
163. Varma, *Śṛnkhalā kī Kaṛiyāṅ* (Links in the Chain) (1943), noted by Schomer, *Mahadevi Varma*, 228; Anantharam, *Bodies That Remember*, 18.
164. On the differences between Mahadevi's use of poetry and prose, see Schomer, *Mahadevi Varma*; Anantharam, *Bodies That Remember*; Francesca Orsini, "The Reticent Autobiographer: Mahadevi Varma's Writings," in *Telling Lives in India: Biography, Autobiography, and Life History*, ed. David Arnold and Stuart Blackburn (Bloomington: Indiana University Press, Permanent Black, 2004), 54-82.
165. Schomer, *Mahadevi Varma*, 286.
166. Schomer, *Mahadevi Varma*, 287.
167. Anantharam, *Bodies That Remember*, 67, 79.
168. On the "right to feel," see Orsini, *The Hindi Public Sphere*, 274-289.
169. Schomer, *Mahadevi Varma*, 287-288; Orsini, *The Hindi Public Sphere*, 307.
170. Orsini, *The Hindi Public Sphere*, 307.
171. Orsini, "The Reticent Autobiographer," 60.
172. Schomer, *Mahadevi Varma*, 98.
173. Varma, *Ādhunik Kavi*, translated and quoted by Schomer, *Mahadevi Varma*, 266.
174. Anantharam reports that she did continue to write some poetry in later years (*Bodies That Remember*, 78).
175. Schomer, *Mahadevi Varma*, 306-307; Anantharam, *Bodies That Remember*, 49-50, 79.
176. Anantharam, *Bodies That Remember*, 18.
177. These works are discussed in detail by Orsini, "The Reticent Autobiographer."

178. Orsini, "The Reticent Autobiographer," 67.
179. Orsini, "The Reticent Autobiographer," 80.
180. Anantharam notes the importance of Gandhi in this regard in *Bodies That Remember*, 56. Orsini posits that the identification of Mahadevi's intensely passionate poetry as mystical and like Mirabai's helped to mitigate the sense of her poems being autobiographical ("The Reticent Autobiographer," 55).
181. Schomer, *Mahadevi Varma*, 262–263; Mahadevi, *Mīrā Śraddhāñjali*.
182. Schomer, *Mahadevi Varma*, 197.
183. Schomer, *Mahadevi Varma*, 251–252.
184. Varma, "Ādhunik nārī kī sthiti par ek dṛṣṭi," translated and quoted by Orsini, *The Hindi Public Sphere*, 304.
185. Orsini, *The Hindi Public Sphere*, 304.
186. Varma, "The Home and the World," trans. Sujata Mody, in Anantharam, *Mahadevi Varma: Political Essays*, 45.

Chapter 6

1. Annie Besant, *Children of the Motherland* (Banaras: Central Hindu College, 1906), 212–220.
2. Joanne Stafford Mortimer, "Annie Besant and India 1913–1917," *Journal of Contemporary History* 18, no. 1 (1983): 61–78. Besant also made reference to Mirabai in her 1917 presidential address to the thirty-second Indian National Congress, "The Case for India," in a section titled "The Awakening of Indian Womanhood" (Calcutta: Home Rule for India League, 1917), 30.
3. Mortimer, "Annie Besant and India," 61–62.
4. Arvind Sharma, *Gandhi: A Spiritual Autobiography* (New Haven, CT: Yale University Press, 2013), 38–40; Gandhi, *Collected Works*, vol. 13, 519–520; Dutta and Robinson, *Selected Letters of Rabindranath Tagore*, 182–185, 211–212; Mortimer, "Annie Besant and India," 75–76.
5. For Besant's broader conception of Hinduism presented in her 1903 *Sanātana Dharma: An Elementary Text-Book of Hindu Religion and Ethics*, see J. S. Hawley, "Sanātana Dharma as the Twentieth Century Began: Two Textbooks, Two Languages," in *Ancient to Modern: Religion, Power, and Community in India*, ed. Ishita Banerjee-Dube and Saurabh Dube (New Delhi: Oxford University Press, 2009), 312–336.
6. Josephine Maria Davies Ransom, *Indian Tales of Love and Beauty* (Adyar, Madras: Theosophical Publishing House, 1912), 42–52.
7. Ransom, *Indian Tales of Love and Beauty*, x.
8. James H. Cousins, *The King's Wife* (Madras: Ganesh, 1919).
9. Cousins, *The King's Wife*, 4.
10. Cousins, *The King's Wife*, 79–84.
11. James H. Cousins and Margaret E. Cousins, *We Two Together* (Madras: Ganesh, 1950), 290, 318.
12. Cousins and Cousins, *We Two Together*, 321.
13. Cousins and Cousins, *We Two Together*, 325.
14. Margaret Cousins, *The Awakening of Asian Womanhood* (Madras: Ganesh, 1922), 85.
15. Cousins and Cousins, *We Two Together*, 377–380.

16. R. Srinivasan, *Mīrā Pāy = Meera Bai: An Interesting and Instructive Tamil Drama* (Madurai: "Kalvi" Publishing House, 1919).
17. For example, see Singer, "The Rādhā-Krishna Bhajanas of Madras City."
18. Hazrat Inayat Khan, *The Complete Works of Pir-O-Murshid Hazrat Inayat Khan; Original Texts: Lectures on Sufism 1925 1: January to May 24, 1925 and Six Plays c. 1912 to 1926*, editors-in-chief Donald Avery Graham and Anne Louise Wirgman (Suresnes, France: Nekbakht Foundation, 2011), 249–255. The play was first published in *The Sufi, a Quarterly Magazine* 1, no. 2 (1916): 18–23.
19. Donald Avery Graham and Anne Louise Wirgman, "Preface to Plays," in Khan, *Complete Works*, 183.
20. Khan, *Complete Works*, 255.
21. Though published in 1916, it is not clear whether this play was ever actually produced during Khan's lifetime. In the "Preface to Plays" in Khan, *Complete Works*, Graham and Wirgman indicate that to their knowledge it was never produced (183). However, it was staged at least once, in Amsterdam on November 14, 1954, as noted by Rokus de Groot in "The Reception in the Netherlands of an Indian Singing Saint: Meerabai in Film, in Translation and in Concert," *Tijdschrift van de Koninklijke Vereniging voor Nederlandse Muziekgeschiedenis* 56, no. 1 (2006): 46.
22. Eleanor Lucia Turnbull and R. Watkins, *Little Plays from Indian History, First Series* (Bombay: Oxford University Press, 1931).
23. J. G. Covernton, *Occasional Reports No. 2: Vernacular Reading Books in the Bombay Presidency* (Calcutta: Office of the Superintendent, Government Printing, India, 1906), 77, 81.
24. Turnbull and Watkins, *Little Plays from Indian History*, iv.
25. Turnbull and Watkins, *Little Plays from Indian History*, 23. The full play spans pages 23–40.
26. Turnbull and Watkins, *Little Plays from Indian History*, 24.
27. Turnbull and Watkins, *Little Plays from Indian History*, 24–25.
28. This description of the interwar period and of the publication of and response to Mayo's book in the next paragraph is drawn from Mrinalini Sinha's "Refashioning Mother India," 625–626.
29. Sinha, "Refashioning Mother India," 628.
30. Sumita Mukherjee, "Using the Legislative Assembly for Social Reform: The Sarda Act of 1929," *South Asia Research* 26, no. 3 (2006): 219–233.
31. Sinha, "Refashioning Mother India," 632.
32. For example, a portion of the drama appeared in May 2019 as a text for studying "English 1" on the online platform TutorVista.com, noted as an excerpt from "Scenes from the Life of Saint Mirabai" by Turnbull. TutorVista was originally an Indian-based company and provided web content globally, though it was acquired and has now been subsumed in BJYU's Learning platform.
33. The following biographical account is drawn from Chhaganlal Lala, *Bhakti in Religions of the World [With Special Reference to Dr. Sri Bankey Behariji]* (Delhi: B. R. Publishing, 1986), 67–83, supplemented by Deborah Baker, *A Blue Hand: The Beats in India* (New York: Penguin, 2008), 192–194. However, it must be noted that Lala's work has a hagiographic character, praising a revered teacher and spiritual guru. Some of this information also appears on covers of editions of Behari's biography of Mira.
34. Devendra Singh, *Meerut Conspiracy Case and the Communist Movement in India, 1929-35* (Meerut: Research India, 1990), 73.

35. Lala, *Bhakti in Religions of the World*, 69–70.
36. Sri Krishnaji, interview, August 11, 1993.
37. Baker, *A Blue Hand*, 192–194.
38. Bankey Behari, *The Story of Mira Bai*, reprinted at least a dozen times between 1935 and 2009. Based on a comparison of the 1937 second edition and the 2008 twelfth edition, though the pagination differs, the text appears to be stable across these multiple printings. The titles of illustrations are the same, but there appears to be some variability, and a line drawing of a seated Mira gazing at Krishna's image and clasping his feet that opens the bhajan collection following the narrative in the 1937 edition is not present in the 2008 edition. The edition referenced herein is the twelfth Gita Press reprinting in 2008.
39. Tandon, *Songs of Mirabai*, 5.
40. Behari, *The Story of Mira Bai*, iii–iv.
41. His presentation aligns with Radhasoami beliefs which count Jesus and Buddha among the enlightened gurus of the past, as teaching the same eternal truth as the nirgun bhakti saints. The leader of the Beas branch Charan Singh (1916–1990) also specifically gives Mirabai as an example to show that women can reach the highest levels of spiritual realization, despite their allegedly heavier karma. Charan Singh, *The Master Answers to Audiences in America* (1966), 3rd. ed., rev. (Beas: Radhasoami Satsang, 1973), 15, noted by Mark Juergensmeyer, *Radhasoami Reality: The Logic of a Modern Faith* (Princeton, NJ: Princeton University Press, 1991), 122.
42. Behari, *The Story of Mirabai*, iii; Lala, *Bhakti in Religions of the World*, 69. Behari does say that he was asked to write about her by "Buchun," but gives no more identifying information.
43. Behari, *The Story of Mirabai*, 7.
44. Behari, *The Story of Mirabai*, 68.
45. Behari, *The Story of Mirabai*, 70, 42. This emphasis on the essential guidance of the guru, the universal nature of the highest teachings of all religions, and the disregard for caste on the spiritual path are consistent with Radhasoami teachings from its inception.
46. Lala, *Bhakti in Religions of the World*, 67.
47. Behari, *The Story of Mirabai*, 51.
48. Behari, *The Story of Mirabai*, iii. He details this path especially in chapters 5 and 6.
49. Behari, *The Story of Mirabai*, 35.
50. God and guru/master as parent is also consistent with Radhasoami understandings of the devotee or initiate as a "child."
51. The following discussion on Gita Press and these two key figures is drawn from Monika Horstmann, "Towards a Universal Dharma: *Kalyāṇ* and the Tracts of the Gītā Press," in *Representing Hinduism: The Construction of Religious Traditions and National Identity*, ed. Vasudha Dalmia and Heinrich von Stietencron (London: Sage, 1995), 294–305, with much more detailed information provided by Akshaya Mukul, *Gita Press and the Making of India* (New Delhi: Harper Collins India, 2015).
52. Horstmann, "Towards a Universal Dharma," 296–297, 299.
53. Horstmann, "Towards a Universal Dharma," 304.
54. Monika Freier, "Cultivating Emotions: The Gita Press and Its Agenda of Social and Spiritual Reform," *South Asian History and Culture* 3, no. 3 (2012): 400.
55. Horstmann, "Towards a Universal Dharma," 302.
56. Mukul, *Gita Press*, 227–343; identified earlier by Horstmann, "Towards a Universal Dharma," 300–301.

57. Mukul, *Gita Press*, 169–224.
58. Mukul, *Gita Press*, 50–59.
59. Mukul, *Gita Press*, 224.
60. Horstmann, "Towards a Universal Dharma," 297; Freier, "Cultivating Emotions," 397–413.
61. Horstmann, "Towards a Universal Dharma," 297; see also Freier, "Cultivating Emotions," 401.
62. Freier, "Cultivating Emotions," 398, 402.
63. Anne Elizabeth Hardgrove, *Community as Public Culture in Modern India: The Marwaris in Calcutta, 1897-1997* (New York: Columbia University Press, 2004), 162, quoted by Freier, "Cultivating Emotions," 406.
64. Lutgendorf, *The Life of a Text*, 421–425.
65. Freier, "Cultivating Emotions," 405.
66. Mukul, *Gita Press,* 350–351.
67. Freier, "Cultivating Emotions," 406.
68. Goyandka, *Strīdharm praśnottari*, 4, quoted by Freier, "Cultivating Emotions," 407.
69. Freier, "Cultivating Emotions," 406; Orsini, *The Hindi Public Sphere*, 274–289.
70. Hanumān Prasād Poddār, "Mīrābāī," in *Bhakt Nārī*, 13th ed., ed. Hanumān Prasād Poddār (1930; Gorakhpur: Gītā Press, 1950), 22–47. The introduction suggests that this is a second volume portraying select women devotees.
71. Hada, *Meera vs. Meera*, trans. Trikha, 204.
72. Nalini Mohan Sanyal, "Mira Bai," *Kalyan Kalpataru* 1 (God Number) (January 1934): 242–258.
73. The author makes multiple citations of Parasuram Chaturvedi, "Mira Bai," *Hindustani*, January 1931, as well as referencing Tod, Jhaveri, Sivsingh Sengar, and Kartikprasad Khatri (edition published by Lahari Press, Banaras City, 1920), among many others.
74. This illustration appears as the opening color plate in the *Bhakt Nari*, with a second picture in black and white accompanying Poddar's Mira essay, illustrating Mira's reception of the snake in the basket that becomes a shalagram. Mira would also be presented in a line drawing worshiping Krishna on the *Bhakt Nari* cover of at least the 1950 edition, though some later additions sport a full-color portrayal of Janabai instead. The same illustration of Mira worshiping alone in the palace also graces the cover of Behari's *The Story of Mira Bai* (both 1937 and 2008 editions).
75. In "Mira Bai," Sanyal indicates (252) that the songs presented are drawn from the Belvedere Press collection as well as one by Viyogi Hari (Sahitya Bhavan Press, Allahabad), and also includes a translation from Macauliffe (of the earliest known documented song of Mira dated to 1604, discussed in chapter 1) (255). He includes the devanagri texts of the songs in the footnotes.
76. Mira is mentioned in many other essays across the decades in both *Kalyan* and *Kalyana-Kalapataru*, though often with little detail. In the 882-page comprehensive special issue of *Kalyāṇ* on women, *Nārī-Aṇk* 22, no. 9 (1948), "Rani Mira" is pictured in a black-and-white drawing worshiping in private, together with four other female exemplars of bhakti—Anasuya, Shabari, Gopijan, and Vidurani—on an inserted page between 552 and 553. A short article, "Rajrani Mira," written by Sriramlalji is buried far back in the volume on 624–626. See Mukul's discussion of this volume on women in *Gita Press*, 356ff. In *Kalyana-Kalapataru*'s much later "Women Number" (new series, 41, no. 1 [October 1995]), the saint is mentioned briefly in a boxed paragraph by Swami Sivananda on women's education, in which he indicates that he supports only "such education and culture as will make them

immortal and glorious, that will make them ideal women, ideal wives like Sulabhā, Mīrā, Sāvitrī, and Damayanī" (277). She is also mentioned in passing in this same volume by G. R. Vijayakumar in "The Indian Ideal of Womanhood" as exemplary of historical "women who had attained peace and poise and fulness through their spiritual life" (273).
77. For an example of Behari's differences of opinion with the Press's editors, see Mukul, *Gita Press*, 210.
78. Horstmann, "Towards a Universal Dharma," 297.
79. Māṁ Banasa [Banārsīdevī Lath], *Merā Anubhav* [My Experiences] (Maṇḍrelā: Bābā Baldev Vāṇī Mandir, vs 2047), translated with introduction by Monika Horstmann, *Banasa*. The following description of Banasa's life is drawn from Horstmann's "Introduction," 1–22. Horstmann notes that Banasa is described as an avatar of Mirabai in Sāgarmar Śarmā, *Śekhāvāṭī ke Sant*, vol. 1 (Ciṛāvā: Śekhāvāṭī Śodh Pratiṣṭān, 1995), 110–114.
80. Horstmann, "Introduction," *Banasa*, 4.
81. Banasa, "My Experiences," trans. Horstmann, *Banasa*, 48.
82. Horstmann, "Introduction," *Banasa*, 11.
83. Horstmann, "Introduction," *Banasa*, 19.
84. Jhaveri, *Milestones of Gujarati Literature*, 212.
85. Nancy M. Martin, "Mīrābāī: Inscribed in Text, Embodied in Life," in *Vaisnavi: Women and the Worship of Krishna*, ed. Steven Rosen (Delhi: Motilal Banarsidass, 1996), 7–46.
86. *Jogan*, directed by Kidar Nath Sharma (1950); Monika Horstmann, "The Bhajan Repertoire of the Present-Day Dādūpanth," in *Bhakti in Current Research, 1979–1982*, ed. Monika Horstmann (Berlin: Dietrich Reimer, 1983), 395–396.
87. Antoinette DeNapoli, "'Crossing over the Ocean of Existence': Performing 'Mysticism' and Exerting Power by Female Sādhus in Rajasthan," *Journal of Hindu Studies* 3 (2010): 315–320.
88. G. N. Sharma provided this clarification of his reference in *Bhakta Mirabai* (52) in a personal communication, April 30, 1993.
89. Banasa, "My Experiences," trans. Horstmann, *Banasa*, 79.
90. Horstmann, "Introduction," *Banasa*, 15.
91. The explicit aim of Bhartiya Vidya Bhavan (Institute for Indian Culture in Bombay) is "the reintegration of the Indian culture in the light of modern knowledge and to suit our present-day needs and the resuscitation of its fundamental values in their pristine vigour." K. M. Munshi, "General Editor's Preface," in Behari, *Bhakta Mira*, v.
92. Behari, *Bhakta Mira*, 1–32, drawing on *Sri Braj Chandra Chakori Mira* (Vrindavan: Sri Radhika Library, 1951). Behari attributes this six-hundred-page work solely to Krishnaji, though Callewaert lists it as jointly authored by Krishna Prabhakar and Bankey Bihari ("The 'Earliest' Song of Mira," 210).
93. Kamala Chandrakant, "Mirabai," *Amar Chitra Katha*, #36 (Bombay: India Book House, 1972), later reprinted as vol. 535. See also J. S. Hawley, "The Saints Subdued in *Amar Chitra Katha*," in *Three Bhakti Voices*, 139–164.
94. Kumkum Sangari, "Love's Repertoire: Qurratulain Hyder's *River of Fire*," in *Love in South Asia: A Cultural History*, ed. Francesca Orsini (New Delhi: Cambridge University Press, 2007), 272–273.
95. Sandria B. Freitag, "Visions of the Nation: Theorizing the Nexus between Creation, Consumption and Participation in the Public Sphere," in *Pleasure and the Nation: The History, Politics and Consumption of Public Culture in India*, ed. Rachel Dwyer and Christopher Pinney (New Delhi: Oxford University Press, 2001), 35–75.

96. Ravi S. Vasudevan, "Shifting Codes, Dissolving Identities: The Hindi Social Film of the 1950s as Popular Culture," in *Making Meaning in Indian Cinema*, ed. R. S. Vasudevan (Delhi: Oxford University Press, 2000), 108.
97. M. S. S. Pandian, "Tamil Cultural Elites and Cinema: Outline of an Argument," *Economic and Political Weekly* 31, no. 15 (April 13, 1996): 950.
98. For an example of the variety of ways Mira songs have been used in a film, see Heidi Pauwels, "*Bhakti* Songs Recast: Gulzar's *Meera* Movie," in *Indian Literature and Popular Cinema: Recasting Classics*, ed. H. R. M. Pauwels (Abingdon: Routledge, 2007), 99–120.
99. Arjun Appadurai and Carol A. Breckenridge, "Why Public Culture?," *Public Culture* 1, no. 1 (Fall 1988): 5–9.
100. Rosie Thomas, "Melodrama and the Negotiation of Morality," in *Consuming Modernity: Public Culture in a South Asian World*, ed. Carol Breckenridge (Minneapolis: University of Minnesota Press, 1995), 158.
101. Ashish Rajadhyaksha and Paul Willemen, *Encyclopedia of Indian Cinema*, 2nd ed. (London: Fitzroy Dearborn, 1999), 350.
102. Debakti Bose's 1933 *Meerabai/Rajrani Meera* would be preceded by films by Ramnik Desai and Chaturbhuj Doshi, both titled *Meerabai*, in Hindi and released in 1932. The first is cited by Rajadhyaksha and Willemen, *Encyclopedia of Indian Cinema*, 618 and the second by Rachel Dwyer in *Filming the Gods: Religion in Indian Cinema* (New York: Routledge, 2006), 87. Madhuja Mukherjee includes an advertisement for "Sagar's Super Talkies" with a photo from this second film, originally in *The Cinema* 5, no. 8 (April 1932): 8 in *Aural Films Oral Cultures: Essays on Cinema from the Early Sound Era* (Kolkata: Jadavpur University Press, 2012), 211.
103. Rajadhyaksha and Willemen, *Encyclopedia of Indian Cinema*, 68, 119, 257.
104. Madhuja Mukherjee discusses New Theatres studio's self-representation as a "cathedral of culture" in detail and reproduces one such advertisement for its distributor Aurora Film Corporation, touting both Mira films, in *New Theatres Ltd.: The Emblem of Art, The Picture of Success* (Pune: National Film Archive of India, 2009), 79.
105. Sarmistha Goopta, *Bengali Cinema: "The Other Nation"* (New York: Routledge, 2011), 42–44; Mukherjee, *New Theatres*, 12–13.
106. Dwyer, *Filming the Gods*, 69.
107. Beyond a brief mention by Rajadhyaksha and Willemen (*Encyclopedia of Indian Cinema*, 257), I could locate only a set of lobby cards that might be associated with the film (from an undated Bengali film, though listed as Bharat Laxmi Studios), among samples provided by the Media Lab at Jadvapur University at www.medialabju.org/archive_slideshow.php?id=12 (accessed December 2021).
108. Rajadhyaksha and Willemen, *Encyclopedia of Indian Cinema*, 257.
109. Rajadhyaksha and Willemen, *Encyclopedia of Indian Cinema*, 255.
110. Goopta, *Bengali Cinema*, 42; Mukherjee, *New Theatres*, 12.
111. Madhuja Mukherjee, "Rethinking Popular Cinema in Bengal (1930s–1950s): Of Literariness, Comic Mode, Mythological and Other Avatars," *South Asian History and Culture* 8, no. 2 (2017): 131.
112. Goopta, *Bengali Cinema*, 42–43.
113. Ashis Nandy, "Invitation to an Antique Death: The Journey of Bramathesh Barua as the Origin of the Terribly Effeminate, Maudlin, Self-Destructive Heroes of Indian Cinema,"

in Dwyer and Pinney, *Pleasure and the Nation*, 144, quoted by Goopta in author's discussion of the impact of Chattopadhyay (*Bengali Cinema*, 44–46).
114. See Indira Chowdhury, *The Frail Hero and Virile History: Gender and the Politics of Culture in Bengal* (Delhi: Oxford University Press, 1998); Sinha, *Colonial Masculinity*.
115. Rajadhyaksha and Willemen, *Encyclopedia of Indian Cinema*, 292–293. The following description is drawn from their synopsis. Debaki Bose wrote and directed this film, produced by CIRCO, Cine Industries & Recording Company.
116. Rajadhyaksha and Willemen, *Encyclopedia of Indian Cinema*, 215, 293, 318.
117. Rajadhyaksha and Willemen, *Encyclopedia of Indian Cinema*, 293. This description, including the quotations, are taken from their film synopsis.
118. Metcalf and Metcalf, *A Concise History of India*, 200–206; Rajadhyaksha and Willemen, *Encyclopedia of Indian Cinema*, 21.
119. Tanika Sarkar, "Politics and Women in Bengal—The Conditions and Meaning of Participation," in *Women in Colonial India: Essays on Survival, Work and the State*, ed. J. Krishnamurty (Delhi: Oxford University Press, 1989), 239–241. Sarkar notes a decided shift in 1931 when "two teenage schoolgirls assassinated the District Magistrate of Comilla," spurring many more women to follow in their footsteps, and she details counterreactions, including by Tagore in his novel *Char Adhyaya* (1934).
120. These films include the following:

1936	*Meerabai*	A. Narayanan/ T. C. Vadivdlu Naicker	Tamil
1937	*Sadhvi Meerabai*	Baburao Painter	Marathi
1938	*Bhakta Meera*	Y. V. Rao	Tamil
1940	*Meerabai*	Bhimavarapu Narasimha Rao	Telegu
1940	*Matwali Meera*/aka *Mirabai*	Prafulla Roy/K. Sharma	Punjabi
1945/1947	*Meera*	Ellis Duncan	Tamil/Hindi
1947	*Meerabai*	Nanabhai Bhatt	Gujarati
1947	*Meerabai*	W. Z. Ahmed	Hindi

Listed in Rajadhyaksha and Willemen, *Encyclopedia of Indian Cinema*.
121. Portions of the 1947 Hindi version of this film are intermittently viewable on YouTube, and film archivist Nivedita Ramakrishnan has published a synopsis with embedded clips of songs in "M. S. Subbulakshmi's Hindi Meera (1947)" on her blog *The Cinema Corridor*, December 4, 2009, http://cinemacorridor.blogspot.com/2009/12/m-s-subbulakshmis-hindi-meera-1947.html. Copies of the full-length Tamil film, sometimes with subtitles, have periodically appeared on YouTube since at least 2014, for example, https://www.youtube.com/watch?v=V8rHt1ES2QI (viewable through at least December 2021). The following description is based on these resources and Ramakrishnan's synopsis. The film is discussed by Rajadhyaksha and Willemen, *Encyclopedia of Indian Cinema*, 304, and Parita Mukta analyzes it briefly in *Upholding the Common Life*, 203–204.
122. Vishwanathan, *Kunjamma*, 59.
123. According to Rajadhyaksha and Willemen, Kalki also composed the Tamil dialogue and lyrics, and the script and dialogue for the Hindi version were written by Amritlal Nagar,

with lyrics by Narendra Sharma (*Encyclopedia of Indian Cinema*, 115, 304). The Hindi film credits list Sadasivam and Kalki as cowriting the plot.

124. For example, a review in *Picturepost*, November 15, 1945, 47–50 criticizes Subbulakshmi's acting ability or lack thereof, as well as the inappropriateness of her South Indian origins and even her physical appearance (paraphrased by Dwyer, *Filming the Gods*, 89).
125. Ramakrishnan, "Subbulakshmi's Hindi Meera."
126. Ramakrishnan notes this detail of Krishna turning "blue" in "Subbulakshmi's Hindi Meera," though the film is black and white. Mahipati's telling of Mira's story is detailed in chapter 3.
127. Hooja, *A History of Rajasthan*, 465–475, 485–497.
128. Orsini, *The Hindi Public Sphere*, 211.
129. Naidu's introduction, much of it unfortunately overdubbed in Hindi, is available at https://www.youtube.com/watch?v=O05QUww2u7Q (accessed December 2021).
130. Susie Tharu and K. Lalita, eds., *Women Writing in India: 600 B.C. to the Present*, vol. 1: *600 B.C. to the Early Twentieth Century* (New York: Feminist Press, 1991), 331.
131. Parama Roy, *Indian Traffic: Identities in Question in Colonial and Postcolonial India* (Berkeley: University of California Press, 1998), 145.
132. Naidu always wrote her poetry and delivered her speeches in English and decidedly not in Hindi—in dramatic contrast to Mahadevi, who did the opposite.
133. *Times of India*, August 17, 1947, reported by Sangari, "Love's Repertoire," 284–285; Viswanathan, *Kunjamma*, 59–65; de Groot, "The Reception in the Netherlands of an Indian Singing Saint," 34–36.
134. Reported by Ramakrishnan, whose clips for the 1947 Hindi film (posted on her blog *Subbulakshmi's Hindi Meera*) were originally recorded at that time. Rajiv Gandhi was assassinated on May 21, 1991, by a member of the Liberation Tigers of Tamil Eelam (LTTE), a militant group fighting for a separate Tamil homeland in Sri Lanka, during a campaign stop in Tamil Nadu, in retaliation for his failed attempt as prime minister to force a peaceful settlement of the civil war in Sri Lanka in 1990.
135. De Groot, "The Reception in the Netherlands of an Indian Singing Saint," 25–26.
136. Amanda J. Weiden, *Singing the Classical, Voicing the Modern: The Postcolonial Politics of Music in South India* (Durham, NC: Duke University Press, 2006), 304n17. T. J. S. George did not publish his biography of her under the title *M. S.: A Life in Music* (New Delhi: Harper Collins India, 2004) until after her death that year (republished under the title *M. S. Subbulakshmi: The Definitive Biography* [New Delhi: Aleph, 2016]), and there is no mention of this, for example, in family friend Lakshmi Vishwanathan's *Kunjamma* (2003) nor in later popular works eulogizing her.
137. Weiden, *Singing the Classical, Voicing the Modern*, 115–121.
138. Weiden, *Singing the Classical, Voicing the Modern*, 120.
139. George, *Subbulakshmi*, 54–55.
140. George, *Subbulakshmi*, 98–99.
141. George, *Subbulakshmi*, 85–116, 239–243.
142. Weiden, *Singing the Classical, Voicing the Modern*, 138.
143. Vishwanathan, *Kunjamma*, 63.
144. Weiden, *Singing the Classical, Voicing the Modern*, 127.
145. Vishwanathan, *Kunjamma*, 43. Sadasivaram was even reported to have accused her of infidelity and low character based on her devadasi origins (recorded by Weiden, *Singing*

the Classical, Voicing the Modern, 113). In contrast, George writes, "Sadasivam seemed determined to end any distress his wife would encounter on account of her background. The criticisms he heard and the resistance he faced at different levels hardened his stand. Orthodox as he was in his Brahminical ways, he set out to ensure that his wife fitted into his socio-religious hierarchy as an equal and that the Brahmin establishment accepted her as such. He would pursue that goal relentlessly, using music and cinema, religion and charity, political connections and social contacts, journalism and every other avenue open to him for the purpose" (*Subbulakshmi*, 123).

146. Kumkum Sangari, "Viraha: A Trajectory in the Nehruvian Era," in *Poetics and Politics of Sufism and Bhakti in South Asia: Love, Loss and Liberation*, ed. Kavita Panjabi (Hyderabad: Orient BlackSwan, 2011), 257.
147. Vishwanathan, *Kunjamma*, 50. The bhajan he requested was "*Hari tum haro*." A version of this bhajan appears in Nagridas, Vaishnavdas, and many subsequent publications, as we have noted. See Pauwels, "Hagiography and Reception History," 240; Chaturvedi, *Mīrābāī kī Padāvalī* (fifteenth ed., 1973), 118, translated by Alston, *Devotional Poems of Mīrā Bāī*, 59 (poem 61).
148. These include director Nanbhai Bhatt's *Meerabai* (1947, Gujarati); W. Z. Ahmed's *Meerabai* (1947, Hindi); Prafulla Roy's *Girdhar Gopal ki Meera* (1949, Hindi); and G. P. Pawar's *Rajrani Meera* (1956, Hindi) (cited in Rajadhyaksha and Willemen, *Encyclopedia of Indian Cinema*).
149. Sangari, "Viraha," 256–258.

Selected Bibliography

Abbott, Justin E., and Narhar R. Godbole, trans. *Stories of Indian Saints: Translation of Mahipati's Marathi Bhaktavijaya.* 4th edition. Delhi: Motilal Banarsidass, 1988. Originally published in Pune, 1933.

Abu-Lughod, Lila. "The Romance of Resistance: Tracing Transformations of Power through Bedouin Women." *American Ethnologist* 17, no. 2 (1990): 41–55.

Agrawal, Purushottam. "The Naths in Hindi Literature." In *Yogi Heroes and Poets: Histories and Legends of the Naths,* edited by David Lorenzen and Adrian Munoz, 3–18. Albany: State University of New York Press, 2011.

Alston, A. J. *The Devotional Poems of Mira Bai.* Delhi: Motilal Banarsidass, 1980.

Anantharam, Anita. *Bodies That Remember: Indigenous Women's Knowledge and Cosmopolitanism in South Asian Poetry.* Syracuse, NY: Syracuse University Press, 2012.

Appadurai, Arjun, Frank J. Korom, and Margaret A. Mills, eds. *Gender, Genre, and Power in South Asian Expressive Traditions.* Philadelphia: University of Pennsylvania Press, 1991.

Arnold, David, and Stuart Blackburn, eds. *Telling Lives in India: Biography, Autobiography, and Life History.* Bloomington: Indiana University Press, 2004.

Ault, Cecil Thomas, Jr. *Folk Theatre of Rajasthan: Introducing Three Marwari Khyal Plays Translated into English.* Gurgaon: Partridge India, 2017.

Ault, Thomas. "Tonight Amar Singh Rathore: Marwari *Khyal* in Transition." *Asian Theatre Journal* 8, no. 2 (1991): 142–167.

Baker, Deborah. *A Blue Hand: The Beats in India.* New York: Penguin Press, 2008.

Bardhan, Kalpana, trans. *Of Women, Outcastes, Peasants and Rebels: A Selection of Bengali Short Stories.* Berkeley: University of California Press, 1990.

Barz, Richard K. *The Bhakti Sect of Vallabhācārya.* Delhi: Munshiram Manoharlal, 1992. Originally published in 1976.

Baumer, Rachel Van M. "The Reinterpretation of Dharma in Nineteenth-Century Bengal: Righteous Conduct for Man in the Modern World." In *Aspects of Bengali History and Society,* edited by R. V. M. Baumer, 82–98. Honolulu: University Press of Hawaii, 1975.

Bayly, C. A. *Empire and Information: Intelligence Gathering and Social Communication in India, 1780–1870.* Cambridge: Cambridge University Press, 1996.

Behari, Bankey. *Bhakta Mira.* 1961. 2nd edition. Bombay: Bharatiya Vidya Bhavan, 1971.

Behari, Bankey. *The Story of Mira Bai.* 1935. Reprint, Gorakhpur: Gita Press, 2008.

Bhanawat, Mahendra. *Lokraṅg.* Udaipur: Bharatiya Lok Kala Mandal, 1971.

Bhati, Hukam Singh. *Mīrābāī: Aitihāsik va Sāmājik Vivecan.* Jodhpur: Rājasthānī Sāhitya Sansthān, 1987.

Bhati, Narayan Singh, ed. *Mīrābāī rī Paracī va Paracī Kāvya: Paramparā 69–70.* Caupasani, Jodhpur: Rājasthānī Shodh Sansthān, 1984.

Bhati, Narayan Singh, ed. *Vidhyābūṣan Purohit Harinārāyan, Paramparā 63–64.* Caupasani, Jodhpur: Rājasthānī Shodh Sansthān, 1982.

Bhatia, Nandi. *Acts of Authority/Acts of Resistance: Theater and Politics in Colonial and Postcolonial India.* Ann Arbor: University of Michigan Press, 2004.

Bhatnagar, Rashmi, Renu Dube, and Reena Dube. *Female Infanticide in India: A Feminist Cultural History.* Albany: State University of New York Press, 2005.

Bhattacharya, Sabhyasachi. *Rabindranath Tagore: An Interpretation.* New Delhi: Penguin/Viking, 2012.

Bruick, Laura R. *Writing Resistance: The Rhetorical Imagination of Hindi Dalit Literature.* New York: Columbia University Press, 2014.

Bryce, L. Winifred. *Women's Folk-Songs of Rajputana.* Delhi: Ministry of Information and Broadcasting, Government of India, 1961.

Burchett, Patton. "Agradās and Rām *Rasik Bhakti* Community: The Politics of Remembrance and the Authority of the Hindu Saint." *International Journal of Hindu Studies* 22 (2018): 431–449.

Burchett, Patton E. *A Genealogy of Devotion: Bhakti, Tantra, Yoga, and Sufism in North India.* New York: Columbia University Press, 2019.

Burghart, Richard. "The Founding of the Ramanandi Sect." *Ethnohistory* 25, no. 2 (Spring 1978): 121–139.

Callewaert, Winand. "The 'Earliest' Song of Mira (1503–1546)." *Orientalia Lovaniensia Periodica* 22 (1991): 201–214.

Callewaert, Winand M. *The Hindī Biography of Dādū Dayāl.* Delhi: Motilal Banarsidass, 1988.

Callewaert, Winand M., and Peter Friedlander. *The Life and Works of Raidas.* Delhi: Manohar, 1992.

Callewaert, Winand M., with Swapna Sharma. *The Hagiographies of Anantadās: The Bhakti Poets of North India.* Richmond, Surrey: Curzon, 2000.

Callewaert, Winand M., and Rupert Snell, eds. *According to Tradition: Hagiographic Writing in India.* Wiesbaden: Harrassowitz, 1994.

Chakravarti, Uma. "Whatever Happened to the Vedic Dasi?" In *Recasting Women: Essays in Indian Colonial History*, edited by Kumkum Sangari and Sudesh Vaid, 27–87. Brunswick, NJ: Rutgers University Press, 1990.

Chakravarty, Radha. *Novelist Tagore: Gender and Modernity in Selected Texts.* New Delhi: Routledge, 2013.

Chandra, Sudhir. *Continuing Dilemmas: Understanding Social Consciousness.* New Delhi: Tulika, 2002.

Chatterjee, Margaret. *Gandhi's Religious Thought.* Notre Dame, IN: University of Notre Dame Press, 1983.

Chatterjee, Partha. *Nationalist Thought and the Colonial World: A Derivative Discourse?* London: Zed Books for the United Nations University, 1986.

Chatterjee, Partha. *The Nation and Its Fragments: Colonial and Postcolonial Histories.* Princeton, NJ: Princeton University Press, 1993.

Chaturvedi, Parashuram. *Mīrābāī kī Padāvalī.* 1932. 18th edition. Prayāg: Hindī Sāhitya Sammelan, 1989.

Chaube, Ram Gharib. "The Legend of Mirabai." *North Indian Notes and Queries* 2, no. 2 (February 1893): 184.

Chaudhuri, Supriya. "A Sentimental Education: Love and Marriage in *The Home and the World*." In *Rabindranath Tagore's* The Home and the World: *A Critical Companion*, edited by Pradip Kumar Datta, 45–65. Delhi: Anthem Press, 2005.

Cohn, Bernard S. *Colonialism and Its Forms of Knowledge: The British in India.* Princeton, NJ: Princeton University Press, 1996.

Cousins, James H. *The King's Wife.* Madras: Ganesh, 1919.

Cousins, James H., and Margaret E. Cousins. *We Two Together.* Madras: Ganesh, 1950.

Crooke, William. *The Popular Religion and Folk-lore of Northern India.* Vol. 2. Revised and illustrated edition. 1896. Reprint, Delhi: Munshiram Manoharlal, 1968.

Dalmia, Vasudha. *The Nationalization of Hindu Traditions: Bhāratendu Hariśchandra and Nineteenth-Century Banaras.* New Delhi: Oxford University Press, 1999.

Dandekar, G. N. "The Last Kīrtan of Gadge Baba." Trans. Maxine Berntsen with Jayant Karve. In *The Experience of Hinduism: Essays on Religion in Maharashtra*, edited by Eleanor Zelliot and Maxine Bernstein, 223–250. Albany: State University of New York Press, 1988.

Das, Sisir Kumar. *A History of Indian Literature: 1800-1910 Western Impact: Indian Response*. Delhi: Sahitya Akademi, 1991.

Datta, Pradip Kumar, ed. *Rabindranath Tagore's* The Home and the World: *A Critical Companion*. Delhi: Permanent Black, Anthem Press, 2005.

Davis, Richard H. *Lives of Indian Images*. Princeton, NJ: Princeton University Press, 1997.

de Groot, Rokus. "The Reception in the Netherlands of an Indian Singing Saint: Meerabai in Film, in Translation and in Concert." *Tijdschrift van de Koninklijke Vereniging voor Nederlandse Muziekgeschiedenis* 56, no. 1 (2006): 25-65.

Desai, Kanu. *Mirabai: Ten Pictures from the Life of India's Greatest Poetess of the Past*. Bombay: D. B. Taraporevala Sons, 1943.

Deviprasad, Munshi. *Mīrābāī kā Jīvan Charitra*. Edited by Lalitā Prasād Sukul. Calcutta: Bangīya Hindī Pariśad, 1954. Originally published in 1898.

Dimock, Edward C., Jr. *The Place of the Hidden Moon: Erotic Mysticism in the Vaisnava-sahajiya Cult of Bengal*. Delhi: Motilal Banarsidass, 1991. Originally published in 1966.

D'Souza, Florence. *Knowledge, Mediation, and Empire: James Tod's Journeys among the Rajputs*. Manchester: Manchester University Press, 2015.

Dutt, Manmatha Nath. *The Heroines of Ind: Gleanings from Indian Classics*. Vol. 2. Calcutta: R. K. Bhatta, 1893.

Dwyer, Rachel. *Filming the Gods: Religion in Indian Cinema*. New York: Routledge, 2006.

Dwyer, Rachel. *The Poetics of Devotion: The Gujarati Lyrics of Dayaram*. Richmond, Surrey: Curzon, 2001.

Dwyer, Rachel, and Christopher Pinney, eds. *Pleasure and the Nation: The History, Politics and Consumption of Public Culture in India*. New Delhi: Oxford University Press, 2001.

Entwistle, Alan W. *Braj: Center of Krishna Pilgrimage*. Groningen: Egbert Forsten, 1987.

Freier, Monika. "Cultivating Emotions: The Gita Press and Its Agenda of Social and Spiritual Reform." *South Asian History and Culture* 3, no. 3 (2012): 397-413.

Freitag, Jason. *Serving Empire, Serving Nation: James Tod and the Rajputs of Rajasthan*. Leiden: Brill, 2009.

Gandhi, Mohandas K. *The Collected Works of Mahatma Gandhi*. Delhi: Publications Division, Ministry of Information and Broadcasting. Government of India, 1959-1983.

Garcin de Tassy, Joseph Heliodore. *Histoire de la Litterature Hindouie et Hindoustanie*. Vol. 2. Paris: Oriental Translation Committee of Great Britain and Ireland, 1847.

George, T. J. S. *M. S. Subbulakshmi: The Definitive Biography*. New Delhi: Aleph, 2016.

Ghosh, Anindita. *Power in Print: Popular Publishing and the Politics of Language and Culture in Colonial Society 1778-1905*. New Delhi: Oxford University Press, 2006.

Goetz, Hermann. *Mirabai, Her Life and Times*. Bombay: Bharatiya Vidya Bhavan, 1966. Originally published in *Journal of the Gujarat Research Society* 18 (April 1956): 87-113.

Gold, Ann Grodzins. "Devotional Power or Dangerous Magic?" In *Listen to the Heron's Words: Reimagining Gender and Kinship in North India*, edited by Gloria Raheja and Ann Grodzins Gold, 149-163. Berkeley: University of California Press, 1994.

Gold, Ann Grodzins. "The 'Jungli Rani' and Other Troubled Wives in Rajasthani Oral Traditions." In *From the Margins of Hindu Marriage: Essays on Gender, Religion and Culture*, edited by Lindsey Harlan and Paul B. Courtright, 119-136. New York: Oxford University Press, 1995.

Goopta, Sarmistha. *Bengali Cinema: "The Other Nation*." New York: Routledge, 2011.

Grierson, George A. *The Medieval Vernacular Literature of Hindustan*. Vienna: Alfred Holder, 1888.

Gundoj, Vikram Singh. "Rājasthānī Paracī Kāvya-Ek Paricay." In *Mīrābāī rī Paracī va Paracī Kāvya: Paramparā 69-70*, edited by Nārāyan Singh Bhāṭī, 71-115. Caupasani, Jodhpur: Rājasthānī Shodh Sansthān. 1984.

Hansen, Kathryn. *Grounds for Play: The Nautanki Theatre of North India*. Berkeley: University of California Press, 1992.

Hansen, Kathryn. "Heroic Modes of Women in Indian Myth, Ritual, and History: The *Tapasvini* and the *Virangana*." In *The Annual Review of Women in World Religions*, Vol. 2:

Heroic Women, edited by Arvind Sharma and Katherine K. Young, 20–52. Albany: SUNY Press, 1992.

Hare, James P. "Garland of Devotees: Nābhādās' *Bhaktamāl* and Modern Hinduism." PhD diss., Columbia University, 2011.

Harlan, Lindsey. "Abandoning Shame: Mira and the Margins of Marriage." In *From the Margins of Hindu Marriage: Essays on Gender, Religion, and Culture*, edited by Lindsey Harlan and Paul B. Courtright, 204–227. New York: Oxford University Press, 1995.

Harlan, Lindsey. *Religion and Rajput Women: The Ethic of Protection in Contemporary Narratives*. Berkeley: University of California Press, 1992.

Hastings, James M. "Poets, Warriors and Brothers: The Shifting Identities of Rajput Dadupanthis, circa 1660–1860." In *Culture, Community and Change*, edited by Varsha Joshi, 85–103. Jaipur: Rawat, 2002.

Hawley, John Stratton. "The Four *Sampradāys*: Ordering the Religious Past in Mughal North India." *South Asian History and Culture* 2, no. 2 (April 2011): 160–183.

Hawley, John Stratton. *A Storm of Songs: India and the Idea of the Bhakti Movement*. Cambridge, MA: Harvard University Press, 2015.

Hawley, John Stratton. *Sur Das: Poet, Singer, Saint*. Seattle: University of Washington Press, 1984.

Hawley, John Stratton. *Three Bhakti Voices: Mirabai, Surdas and Kabir in Their Times and Ours*. New York: Oxford University Press, 2005.

Hawley, John Stratton, and Mark Juergensmeyer. *Songs of the Saints of India*. Revised edition. Delhi: Oxford University Press, 2004. Originally published in 1988.

Hawley, John Stratton, and Gurinder Singh Mann. "Mirabai at the Court of Guru Gobind Singh." In *Culture and Circulation: Literatures in Motion in Early Modern India*, edited by Allison Busch and Thomas de Bruijn, 107–138. Leiden: E. J. Brill, 2014.

Hawley, John Stratton, and Gurinder Singh Mann. "Mirabai in the *Pothi Prem Ambodh*." *Journal of Punjab Studies* 15, nos. 1–2 (2008): 199–226.

Hawley, John Stratton, Christian Lee Novetzke, and Swapna Sharma, eds. *Bhakti and Power: Debating India's Religion of the Heart*. Seattle: University of Washington Press, 2019.

Haynes, Douglas, and Gyan Prakash, eds. *Contesting Power: Resistance and Everyday Social Relations in South Asia*. Berkeley: University of California Press, 1991.

Hess, Linda, with Sukhdev Singh. *The Bijak of Kabir*. 2nd edition. Delhi: Oxford University Press, 2002. Originally published in 1983.

Hooja, Rima. *A History of Rajasthan*. Delhi: Rupa, 2006.

Horstmann, Monika, trans. *Banasa: A Spiritual Autobiography*. Wiesbaden: Harrassowitz Verlag, 2003.

Horstmann, Monika. *Bhakti and Yoga: A Discourse in Seventeenth-Century Codices*. Delhi: Primus Books, 2021.

Horstmann, Monika, ed. *Bhakti in Current Research, 2001–2003*. New Delhi: Manohar, 2006.

Horstmann, Monika. "The Rāmānandīs of Galtā (Jaipur, Rajasthan)." In *Multiple Histories: Culture and Society in the Study of Rajasthan*, edited by Lawrence A. Babb, Varsha Joshi, and Michael W. Meister, 141–197. Jaipur: Rawat, 2002.

Horstmann, Monika. "Towards a Universal Dharma: *Kalyāṇ* and the Tracts of the Gītā Press." In *Representing Hinduism: The Construction of Religious Traditions and National Identity*, edited by Vasudha Dalmia and Heinrich von Stietencron, 294–305. New Delhi: Sage, 1995.

Howard, Veena R. *Gandhi's Ascetic Activism: Renunciation and Social Action*. Albany: State University of New York Press, 2013.

Jaffrelot, Christophe. "The Politics of Caste Identities." In *The Cambridge Companion to Modern Indian Culture*, edited by Vasudha Dalmia and Rashmi Sadana, 80–81. Cambridge: Cambridge University Press, 2012.

Jhaveri, Krishnalal Mohanlal. *Milestones in Gujarati Literature*. Bombay: Gujarati Printing Press, 1914.
Kaviraj, Sudipta. *The Unhappy Conscience: Bankimchandra Chattopadhyay and the Formation of Nationalist Discourse in India*. Delhi: Oxford University Press, 1995.
Keune, Jon. "Gathering of Bhaktas in Marāṭhī." *Journal of Vaishnava Studies* 15, no. 2 (Spring 2007): 169–187.
Khan, Hazrat Inayat. *The Complete Works of Pir-O-Murshid Hazrat Inayat Khan; Original Texts: Lectures on Sufism 1925 1: January to May 24, 1925 and Six Plays c. 1912 to 1926*. Editors-in-chief Donald Avery Graham and Anne Louise Wirgman. Suresnes: Nekbakht Foundation, 2011.
Khatri, Kartikprasad. *Mīrābāī ka Jīvan Charit*. Muzaffarpur: Narayan Press, Thakur Prasad & Sons, 1893.
Kishwar, Madhu, and Ruth Vanita. "Poison to Nectar: The Life and Work of Mirabai." *Manushi* nos. 50–52 (January–June 1989): 74–93.
Kishwar, Madhu, and Ruth Vanita, eds. *Women Bhakta Poets, Manushi* nos. 50–52 (January–June 1989).
Lacchiram. *Khyāl Mīrāṃ Mangal Ko*. Jodhpur: Khatri Mikamchand Bookseller, n.d.
Lala, Chhaganlal. *Bhakti in Religions of the World: With Special Reference to Dr. Sri Bankey Behariji*. Delhi: B. R. Publishing, 1986.
Lee, Joel. "Recognition and Its Shadows: Dalits and the Politics of Religion in India." Ph.D. diss., Columbia University, 2015.
Lorenzen, David, ed. *Bhakti Religion in North India: Community Identity and Political Action*. Albany: State University of New York Press, 1995.
Lorenzen, David, and Adrian Munoz, eds. *Yogi Heroes and Poets: Histories and Legends of the Naths*. Albany: State University of New York Press, 2011.
Lutgendorf, Philip. *The Life of a Text: Performing the Rāmcaritmānas of Tulsidas*. Berkeley: University of California Press, 1981.
Macauliffe, Max Arthur. "The Legend of Mīrā Bāī, the Rajput Poetess." *Indian Antiquary* 32 (August 1903): 329–335.
Madhok, Sumi. "Action, Agency, Coercion: Reformatting Agency for Oppressive Contexts." In *Gender, Agency and Coercion*, edited by Sumi Madhok, Anne Phillips, and Kalpana Wilson, 102–121. New York: Palgrave Macmillan, 2013.
Maheshwari, Hiralal. *Rajāsthānī Bhāṣā aur Sāhitya*. Calcutta: Adhunik Pustak Bhavan, 1960.
Mallison, Françoise. "Development of Early Krishnaism in Gujarāt: Viṣṇu—Raṇchoḍ—Kṛṣṇa." In *Bhakti in Current Research, 1979–1982*, edited by Monika Thiel-Horstmann, 245–255. Berlin: Dietrich Reimer Verlag, 1983.
Mann, Gurinder Singh. *The Making of Sikh Scripture*. New York: Oxford University Press, 2001.
Martin, Nancy M. "Dyed in the Color of Her Lord: Multiple Representations in the Mirabai Tradition." PhD diss., Graduate Theological Union, 1995.
Martin, Nancy M. "Mirabai Comes to America: The Translation and Transformation of a Saint." *Journal of Hindu Studies* 3 (2010): 12–35.
Martin, Nancy M. "Mirabai: Inscribed in Text, Embodied in Life." In *Vaisnavi: Women and the Worship of Krishna*, edited by Stephen Rosen, 7–46. Delhi: Motilal Banarsidass, 1996.
Martin, Nancy M. "Mirabai in the Academy and the Politics of Identity." In *Faces of the Feminine from Ancient, Medieval and Modern India*, edited by Mandakranta Bose, 162–182. New York: Oxford University Press, 2000.
Martin, Nancy M. "*Mira Janma Patri* and Other Tales of Resistance and Appropriation." In *Religion, Ritual, and Royalty*, edited by Rajendra Joshi and N. K. Singhi, 227–261. Jaipur: Rawat Press, 1999.
Mathur, Madan Mohan. "Kuchamani Khyal: A Vibrant Folk Theatre of Rajasthan." *Sangeet Natak* 40, no. 3 (2006): 36–40.

McGregor, Ronald Stuart, ed. *Devotional Literature in South Asia, Current Research, 1985–1988.* Cambridge: Cambridge University Press, 1992.

McGregor, Ronald Stuart. *Hindi Literature from Its Beginnings to the Nineteenth Century.* Weisbaden: Otto Harrassowitz, 1984.

McGregor, Ronald Stuart. *Hindi Literature of the Nineteenth and Early Twentieth Centuries.* Wiesbaden: Otto Harrassowitz, 1974.

Metcalf, Barbara D., and Thomas R. Metcalf. *A Concise History of India.* Cambridge: Cambridge University Press, 2002.

Mirabai. *Mīrābāī kī Śabdavali.* Anonymous translator. Allahabad: Belvedere Press, 1909.

Mitra, Rajendralal. *The Antiquities of Orissa.* Vol. 2. Calcutta: Indian Studies Past and Present, 1963. Originally published in 1880.

Mitra, Tarinee Churun, and William Price, eds. *Hindee and Hindustanee Selections: To Which Are Prefaced the Rudiments of Hindoostanee and Bruj Bhakha Grammar.* Calcutta: Hindustanee Press, 1927.

Mortimer, Joanne Stafford. "Annie Besant and India 1913–1917." *Journal of Contemporary History* 18, no. 1 (1983): 61–78.

Mukherjee, Madhuja. *New Theatres Ltd.: The Emblem of Art, the Picture of Success.* Pune: National Film Archive of India, 2009.

Mukta, Parita. *Upholding the Common Life: The Community of Mirabai.* New Delhi: Oxford University Press, 1994.

Mukul, Akshaya. *Gita Press and the Making of India.* New Delhi: Harper Collins India, 2015.

Nabhadas. *Śrī Bhaktamāl,* with the *Bhaktirasabodhinī* Commentary of Priyādās. Lucknow: Tejkumar Press, 1969.

Nagarkar, Kiran. *Cuckold.* New Delhi: Harper Collins, 1997.

Nainsi, Munhata. *Muṅhatā Naiṇsī rī Khyāt.* Edited by Badariprasad Sakariya. Jodhpur: Rājasthān Prācyavidyā Pratiṣṭhān, Rajasthan Oriental Research Institute, 1960.

Nandy, Ashis. *The Intimate Enemy: Loss and Recovery of Self under Colonialism.* Delhi: Oxford University Press, 1983.

Narayan, Kirin, and Kenneth M. George. "Stories about Getting Stories: Interactional Dimensions in Folk and Personal Narrative Research." In *The Sage Handbook of Interview Research: The Complexity of the Craft,* 2nd edition, edited by Jaber F. Gubrium, James A. Holstein, Amir B. Marvasti, and Karyn D. McKinney, 511–524. Thousand Oaks, CA: Sage, 2012.

Novetzke, Christian Lee. "A Family Affair: Krishna Comes to Paṇḍharpūr and Makes Himself at Home." In *Alternative Krishnas: Regional and Vernacular Variations on a Hindu Deity,* edited by Guy L. Beck, 113–138. Albany: State University of New York Press, 2005.

Novetzke, Christian Lee. *Religion and Public Memory: A Cultural History of the Saint Namdev in India.* New York: Columbia University Press, 2008.

Okita, Kiyokazu. *Hindu Theology in Early Modern South Asia: The Rise of Devotionalism and the Politics of Genealogy.* New York: Oxford University Press, 2014.

Olivelle, Patrick, trans. *The Law Code of Manu.* New York: Oxford University Press, 2009.

Orsini, Francesca. *The Hindi Public Sphere 1920–1940: Language and Literature in the Age of Nationalism.* New Delhi: Oxford University Press, 2002.

Orsini, Francesca. "The Reticent Autobiographer: Mahadevi Varma's Writings." In *Telling Lives in India: Biography, Autobiography, and Life History,* edited by David Arnold and Stuart Blackburn, 54–82. Bloomington: Indiana University Press, Permanent Black, 2004.

Pauwels, Heidi R. M. "Hagiography and Reception History: The Case of Mīrā's *Padas* in Nāgrīdās's *Pada-prasaṅga-mālā.*" In *Bhakti in Current Research, 2001–2003,* edited by Monika Horstmann, 221–244. Delhi: Manohar, 2006.

Pauwels, Heidi R. M. *In Praise of Holy Men: Hagiographic Poems by and about Harirām Vyās.* Groningen: Egbert Forsten, 2002.

Pauwels, Heidi R. M. *Mobilizing Krishna's World: The Writings of Prince Sāvant Singh of Kishangarh*. Seattle: University of Washington Press, 2017.

Pauwels, Heidi R. M. "Rāṭhaurī Mīrā: Two Neglected Rāṭhauṛ Connections to Mīrā—Jaimal Meṛtīyo and Nāgrīdās." *International Journal of Hindu Studies* 14, nos. 2-3 (2010): 177-200.

Pinch, William R. "History, Devotion and the Search for Nabhadas of Galta." In *Invoking the Past: The Uses of History in South Asia*, edited by Daud Ali, 367-399. New Delhi: Oxford University Press, 1999.

Pollock, Sheldon. *The Language of the Gods in the World of Men: Sanskrit, Culture and Power in Premodern India*. Berkeley: University of California Press, 2006.

Prabhat, C. L. *Mīrābāī*. Bombay: Hindi Granth Ratnakar, 1965.

Prabhat, C. L. *Mīrā Jīvan aur Kāvya*. 2 vols. Jodhpur: Rājasthānī Granthāgār, 1999.

Raghavdas. *Bhaktamāl*. Edited and introduction by Agarcand Nāhṭa. Jodhpur: Rajasthan Oriental Research Institute, 1965.

Raheja, Gloria Goodwin, and Ann Grodzins Gold. *Listen to the Heron's Words: Reimagining Gender and Kinship in North India*. Berkeley: University of California Press, 1994.

Rajadhyaksha, Ashish, and Paul Willemen. *Encyclopedia of Indian Cinema*. Revised edition. London: Fitzroy Dearborn, 1999.

Ramakrishnan, Nivedita. "M. S. Subbulakshmi's Hindi Meera (1947)." *The Cinema Corridor*, December 4, 2009. http://cinemacorridor.blogspot.com/2009/12/m-s-subbulakshmis-hindi-meera-1947.html.

Ramanujan, A. K. *The Collected Essays of A. K. Ramanujan*. General editor Vinay Dharwadker. New Delhi: Oxford, 1999.

Ramanujan, A. K., trans. *Hymns for the Drowning: Poems for Viṣṇu by Nammāḻvār*. New York: Penguin Books, 1993. Originally published by Princeton University Press, 1981.

Ramanujan, A. K., trans. *Speaking of Śiva*. New York: Penguin Books, 1973.

Ramanujan, A. K. "Talking to God in the Mother Tongue." *Women Bhakta Poets, Manushi* nos. 50-52 (January-June 1989): 9-14.

Ransom, Josephine Maria Davies. *Indian Tales of Love and Beauty*. Adyar, Madras: Theosophical Publishing House, 1912.

Rao, Vecheru Narayana, David Shulman, and Sanjay Subrahmanyam. *Textures of Time: Writing History in South India 1600-1800*. Delhi: Permanent Black, 2001.

Robson, John. *A Selection of Khyals or Marwari Plays with an Introduction and Glossary*. Beawar, Rajasthan: Beawar Mission Press, 1866.

Rudolph, Lloyd I., and Susanne Hoeber Rudolph. *Romanticism's Child: An Intellectual History of James Tod's Influence on Indian History and Historiography*. New Delhi: Oxford University Press, 2017.

Samar, Devilal. *Rājasthānī Lok Nāṭya*. Udaipur: Bharatiya Lok Kala Mandal, 1957.

Sangari, Kumkum. "Love's Repertoire: Qurratulain Hyder's *River of Fire*." In *Love in South Asia: A Cultural History*, edited by Francesca Orsini, 259-285. New Delhi: Cambridge University Press, 2007.

Sangari, Kumkum. "Mirabai and the Spiritual Economy of Bhakti." *Economic and Political Weekly*, July 7 and 14, 1990, 1464-1475, 1537-1552.

Sangari, Kumkum. "Viraha: A Trajectory in the Nehruvian Era." In *Poetics and Politics of Sufism and Bhakti in South Asia: Love, Loss and Liberation*, edited by Kavita Panjabi, 256-287. Hyderabad: Orient BlackSwan, 2011.

Saran, Richard D., and Norman P. Ziegler. *The Meṛtīyo Rāṭhoṛs of Meṛto, Rājasthān: Select Translations Bearing on the History of a Rajpūt Family, 1462-1660*. Ann Arbor: Centers for South and Southeast Asian Studies, University of Michigan, 2001.

Sarkar, Jadunath, trans. *Chaitanya's Life and Teachings*. Calcutta: Orient Longman, 1988. Originally published in 1913.

Sarkar, Tanika. "Gandhi and Social Relations." In *The Cambridge Companion to Gandhi*, edited by Judith M. Brown and Anthony Parel, 173–195. Cambridge: Cambridge University Press, 2011.

Sarkar, Tanika. *Hindu Nation, Hindu Wife: Community, Religion, and Cultural Nationalism.* Delhi: Permanent Black, 2001.

Sarkar, Tanika. "Many Faces of Love: Country, Woman and God in *The Home and the World*." In *Rabindranath Tagore's The Home and the World: A Critical Companion*, edited by Pradip Kumar Datta, 27–44. Delhi: Permanent Black, Anthem Press, 2005.

Schomer, Karine. *Mahadevi Varma and the Chhayavad Age of Modern Hindi Poetry.* Berkeley: University of California Press, 1983.

Schomer, Karine, and W. H. McLeod, eds. *The Sants: Studies in a Devotional Tradition of India.* Delhi: Motilal Banarsidass, 1987.

Schultz, Anna. *Singing a Hindu Nation: Marathi Devotional Performance and Nationalism.* New York: Oxford University Press, 2013.

Scott, James C. *Domination and the Arts of Resistance: Hidden Transcripts.* New Haven, CT: Yale University Press, 1990.

Sen, Kshitimohan. *Medieval Mysticism in India.* Trans. Manomohan Ghosh. London: Luzac, 1936.

Shabnam, Padmavati. *Mīrā: Vyaktitva aur Kṛtitva.* Varanasi: Hindī Pracārak Sansthān, 1973.

Sharma, G. N. *Bhakta Mirabai.* Udaipur: Mira Kala Mandir, 1990.

Sharma, Krishna Chander. *The Luminous Bard of Hariyana Lakhmi Chand: A Study in the Indian Culture, Life, and Folk Theatre.* New Delhi: Siddarth, 1988.

Sharma, Nina, and Indu Shekhar. *Becoming a Modern Historian in Princely India: An Intellectual History of Shyamal Das and His Vir Vinod.* London: Olympia, 2015.

Sharma, Purohit Harinarayan. *Mīrāṃ Bṛhatpadāvalī.* Vol. 1. Edited by Kalyāṇ Singh Śekhāvat. Jodhpur: Rājasthān Prācyavidyā Pratiṣṭhān, 1967.

Shekhavat, Kalyan Singh. *Mīrābāī kā Jīvanvrit evam Kāvya.* Jodhpur: Hindī Sāhitya Mandir, 1974.

Shukla-Bhatt, Neelima. *Narasinha Mehta of Gujarat: A Legacy of Bhakti Songs and Stories.* New York: Oxford University Press, 2015.

Shyamaldas. *Vīr Vinod: Mewār kā Itihās.* Delhi: Motilal Banarsidass, 1986.

Sikhwal, Punamchand. *Bhakt Siromaṇi Mīrāṃ Mangal kā Mārwaḍī Khyāl.* Kishangar: Bansīghar Śarma Booksellers, n.d.

Singer, Milton. "The Rādhā-Krishna Bhajanas of Madras City." In *Krishna: Myths, Rites, and Attitudes*, edited by Milton Singer, 90–138. Chicago: University of Chicago Press, 1966.

Singh, Chatur. *Caturkul Caritra.* Nasīrābād: Edward Printing Press, 1902.

Singh K. S., gen. ed. *People of India: Rajasthan.* Part 1, vol. 38. Mumbai: Popular Prakashan, 1998.

Singh, K. S. *The Scheduled Castes.* Revised edition. New Delhi: Oxford University Press, 1995.

Singh, Munshi Hardyal. *The Castes of Marwar: Census Report of 1891.* 2nd edition. Jodhpur: Books Treasure, 1991. English summary of the full report *Marchumshumari Raj Marwar* originally published in 1894.

Singh, Raja Raghuraj. *Bhaktamāla athart Rāmarasikāvalī.* 1914. Edited by Khemrāj Śrīkṛṣṇadās. Bombay: Lakṣmī Veṅkateśvar Steam Press, vs 1971.

Singh Rathor Mertiya, Thakur Gopāl. *Jayamal Vansa Prakasha or the History of Badnore.* Vol. 1. Ajmer: Vedic Yantralaya, 1932.

Sinha, Mrinalini. *Colonial Masculinity: The "Manly Englishman" and the "Effeminate Bengali" in the Late Nineteenth Century.* New Delhi: Kali for Women, 1997. Originally published by University of Manchester Press, 1995.

Sinha, Mrinalini. "Refashioning Mother India: Feminism and Nationalism in Late-Colonial India." *Feminist Studies* 26, no. 3 (2000): 623–644.

Smith, John D. *The Epic of Pābūjī: A Study, Transcription, and Translation.* Cambridge: Cambridge University Press, 1991.
Smith, William L. *Patterns in North Indian Hagiography.* Stockholm: University of Stockholm Press, 2000.
Srivastava, Sahab Lal. *Folk Culture and Oral Tradition.* New Delhi: Abhinav, 1974.
Stark, Ulrike. *An Empire of Books: The Naval Kishore Press and the Diffusion of the Printed World in Colonial India.* New Delhi: Permanent Black, 2008.
Swami, Narottamdas. *Mīrā Mandākinī.* Agra: Gaya Prasad and Sons, 1930.
Taft, Frances. "The Elusive Historical Mira: A Note." In *Multiple Histories: Culture and Society in the Study of Rajasthan,* edited by Lawrence A. Babb, Varsha Joshi, and Michael W. Meister, 313–335. Jaipur: Rawat, 2002.
Taft, Frances. "Six Incarnations of Mirabai." In *Culture, Polity, and Economy,* edited by Varsha Joshi and Surjit Singh, 163–172. Jaipur: Institute of Rajasthan Studies, Rawat Publications, 2009.
Tagore, Rabindranath. "The Indian Ideal of Marriage" (1925). In *The English Writings of Rabindranath Tagore,* Vol. 3: *A Miscellany,* edited by Sisir Kumar Das, 524–537. New Delhi: Sahitya Akademi, 1996.
Tagore, Rabindranath. "Letter from a Wife." In *Of Women, Outcastes, Peasants, and Rebels: A Selection of Bengali Short Stories,* trans. and introduction by Kalpana Bardhan, 96–109. Berkeley: University of California Press, 1990.
Tagore, Rabindranath. *Relationships: Jogajog.* Trans. and introduction by Supriya Chaudhuri. New Delhi: Oxford University Press, 2006.
Tagore, Rabindranath. *Selected Letters of Rabindranath Tagore.* Edited by Krishna Dutta and Andrew Robinson. Cambridge: Cambridge University Press, 1997.
Tagore, Rabindranath. "Yogayog (Nexus)." Translated by Hiten Bhaya. In *The Tagore Omnibus,* vol. 1, 465–672. New Delhi: Penguin Books, 2005.
Tandon, R. C. *Songs of Mirabai: Translated from the Original Hindi.* Allahabad: Hindi Mandir, 1934.
Tod, James. *Annals and Antiquities of Rajasthan (1829–1832).* 3 vols. Edited by William Crooke. Reprint, Delhi: Low Price Publications, 1990.
Tod, James. *Travels in Western India.* Delhi: Munshiram Manoharlal, 1997. Originally published by William H. Allen in 1839.
Tripathi, G. M. *The Classical Poets of Gujarat and Their Influence on Society and Morals.* Bombay: N. M. Tripathi, 1916. Originally published in 1894.
Tulpule, Shankar Gopal. *Classical Marathi Literature: From the Beginning to A.D. 1818.* Wiesbaden: Otto Harrassowitz, 1979.
Turnbull, Eleanor Lucia, and R. Watkins. *Little Plays from Indian History, First Series.* Bombay: Oxford University Press, 1931.
Vanita, Ruth. "Three Women Saints of Maharashtra: Muktabai, Janabai, Bahinabai." *Women Bhakta Poets: Manushi* nos. 50–52 (January–June 1989): 45–61.
Varma, Mahadevi. *Mahadevi Varma: Political Essays on Women, Culture, and Nation.* Edited by Anita Anantharam. Amherst, NY: Cambria Press, 2010.
Varma, Mahadevi. *Mīrā Śraddhāñjali.* Udaipur: Mira Pratishtan Mahila Mandal, 1975.
Vaudeville, Charlotte. "The Shaiva-Vaishnava Synthesis in Maharashtrian Santism." In *The Sants: Studies in a Devotional Tradition of India,* edited by Karine Schomer and W. H. McLeod, 215–228. Delhi: Motilal Banarsidass, 1987.
Vishwanathan, Lakshmi. *Kunjamma . . . Ode to a Nightingale: M. S. Subbulakshmi.* New Delhi: Roli Books, 2003.
Vrajaratnadās. *Mīrā-Mādhurī.* 3rd edition. Vārṇasī: Hindī Sāhitya Kuṭīr, 1970. Originally published in 1948.

Walsh, Judith E. *Domesticity in Colonial India: What Women Learned When Men Gave Them Advice*. New York: Rowan & Littlefield, 2004.

Weiden, Amanda J. *Singing the Classical, Voicing the Modern: The Postcolonial Politics of Music in South India*. Durham, NC: Duke University Press, 2006.

Williams, Tyler W. "Sacred Sounds and Sacred Books: A History of Writing in Hindi." PhD diss., Columbia University, 2014.

Wilson, H. H. "Religious Sects of the Hindus." *Asiatic Researches* 16 (1928): 1–136, and 17 (1832): 169–314.

Filmography

Bose, Debaki, director. 1933. *Meerabai/Rajrani Meera*.
Bose, Debaki, director. 1942. *Apna Ghar/Aple Ghar*.
Duncan, Ellis, director. 1945 (Tamil)/1947 (Hindi). *Meera*.
Sharma, Kidar Nath, director. 1942. *Armaan*.
Sharma, Kidar Nath, director. 1950. *Jogan*.
Gulzar, S. S., director. 1970. *Meera*.

Index

For the benefit of digital users, indexed terms that span two pages (e.g., 52–53) may, on occasion, appear on only one of those pages.

Figures are indicated by *f* following the page number

Adi Granth, 48–49
advaita, 128, 203–4. *See also* nondual shudhadvaita, 204–5
advice manuals. *See* domestic advice manuals
agency, 131, 199–200, 210, 214–16, 257
Agarwal, Baleshvar Prasad, 238–39
Agradas, 28–29, 51–52
Agrawal, Purushottam, 205
Ahalya, 127
Ahalyabai, 127–28, 141–42, 159–60
Aiyer, S. V., 163
Ajab Kumarbai, 82–83
Akbar
   Annie Besant, 248–49
   Baldevprasad Mishra, 141–42
   Bankey Behari, 258
   Bharat ka Veer Putra—Maharana Pratap 2013 television serial, 333n.130
   James Cousins's *The King's Wife*, 249
   Deviprasad, 149
   Hermann Goetz, 158
   hagiography of bhakti saints, 43–44, 45
   "Heroines of Ind" 135–36, 137, 139
   Kachvaha alliance, 28–29
   Inayat Khan's *Tansen*, 251–52
   Meera (1945/1947), 280–81, 283–84
   Meerabai/Rajrani Meera (1945/1947), 275
   Mira as source of Akbar's liberal tolerance, 158, 258
   Hanuman Prasad Poddar, 264–65
   Priyadas, 37–39, 42, 47, 52–53, 116
   Raghuraj Singh, 105
   Vaishnavadas, 66–67
Allahabad, 205–6, 238–39, 240, 255–57
Allama Prabhu, 46
All-India Women's Congress, 228, 282–83
Amar Chitra Katha, 270–71

Ambedkar, Bhimrao, 188, 197, 261
Amer (Jaipur), 27, 28–29, 50–51, 280
American popular literature, 120, 124, 252–53
Anandamayi Ma, 255–56
Anantadas, 30–31, 64–65
   chatur sampraday, 50–51, 68
   Jhali Rani, 49, 50
   Raidas, 49, 50, 97
Anantharam, Anita, 239–40, 242–43
Andal, 5–6, 40–41, 57
Andrews, C. F., 261–62
Angad, 30–31
Anti-cow slaughter. *See* cow-protection
Anti-nautch campaigns, 120, 284
Apna Ghar/Aple Ghar (1942), 275, 276–77
Appadurai, Arjun, 167
Arjuna, 100–1
Armaan (1942), 275–77
Aryan, 122–23, 125, 128, 213
Arya Samaj, 128, 260–61, 340n.115, 343n.145
astachaps, 128
Ault, Thomas, 170
Aurobindo, Shri, 255–56
authenticity, 13–14, 33, 121–22, 166, 250, 291–92
Ayodhya, 171, 261

Badnor, 144–45, 149–51
Bahinabai, 5–6, 40–41, 219
Banaras (Kashi)
   Hindi literary activity, 128, 141–42, 205, 238
   Hindu University, 248
   pilgrimage, 67–68, 171
   Raidas, 49–50, 53
Banasa, 267–70, 274

Barth, Auguste, 120–21
Basu, Anath Nath, 205–6
Bauls, 220–21
bavari, 179–80
Bayly, Christopher Alan, 121, 123, 124
Behari, Bankey, 16–17, 247, 255–71, 283–84, 290
Belvedere Press, 205–6, 238–39, 256–57
Bengal, 48, 101–2, 134, 138–39, 163, 207
Bengali. *See also* Shantiniketan
    domestic manuals, 213–16
    elite nationalists, 124–25, 142, 155–56, 166
    film, 271, 272–73, 274
    language and literature, 114–15, 129–30, 141–42, 205–6, 210, 211, 215, 247
    Mira tradition, 48, 140–41
    translations of James Tod, 135, 142–43
Besant, Annie, 248–49, 251, 252–53, 254
    Children of the Motherland, 248–49
bhadralok, 126–27, 274
Bahadur Shah of Gujarat, 148–49
Bhagavad Gita, 89–90, 128, 157–58, 248, 260–61, 262, 266
Bhagavata Purana, 73, 96, 97, 98
bhajan. *See also* Mira songs
    singing, 12–13, 22–23, 87–88, 174–75, 229–31, 263–64
bhaktamal, 25, 69, 113–14, 116
    Dhruvdas, 67–68
    in films, 275–76, 277–78, 279–80
    Nabhadas, 25–26, 27–28, 30, 31, 113–14, 115
    Raghavdas, 68
    Raghuraj Singh, 104, 105–6, 121–22, 163
Bhaktamal ki Drishtant, 66–67, 113–14
Bhaktavijaya, 86–92
Bhaktirasabodhini Tika, 32–38, 52, 58–59, 65
Bhardhan, Kalpana, 211
Bhatt, Gangal, 30
Bhattacharya, Sabyasachi, 210, 211–12, 213–14
Bhaya, Hiten, 211–12
Bhils, 143, 197
Bhojraj
    historical biography of Mirabai, 110–12, 144, 148, 156–57, 160
    Raja Bhoj in *Mira Janma Patri*, 194
    rehabilitation, 137–38, 144, 148–49, 151, 257–59, 264–65, 282
Bhudan Theatre, 195–97
Bhupal Singh, Rana, 154
Bihar, 114, 119, 163

Bikaner, 111, 144–45
Bombay, 64, 115–16, 129–30, 131, 139–40, 168, 271
    Bombay Gazetteer, 164
    Bombay Talkies, 272–73
Bose, Debaki, 272–74, 275, 277
brahman
    female renouncers, 269
    Gajadhar (Mira's teacher), 151–52
    hagiography, 28, 43–44, 49, 86, 91–92, 94–95, 194
    heroines, 126, 159–60
    Mira in Dwarka, 38, 77–78, 81, 95–96, 116, 152–53, 157–58
    Rajasthani folk traditions, 168, 169–70, 194, 196–97
    saints, 89–90, 227–28
    woman of Barsana, 96–97, 102–3, 258
brahmanization, 27, 53, 96–98, 137–38, 168, 284–85, 286
Brahmo Marriage Act, 138–39
Brahmo Samaj, 127–28
Braj, 15, 26–27, 38, 67–68, 81–82, 85–86
    removal of images, 50–51, 82
Braj Bhasha, 21, 59, 236–37, 239–40
Buddhism, 3, 130–31, 188, 239, 249, 260–61
    Buddha, 147
Burchett, Patton, 19, 28
Burghart, Richard, 28, 51

Calcutta, 114, 116–17, 134, 168, 205–6, 268, 272–73, 276–77
Calcutta Review, 126–28
Callewaert, Winand, 30–31, 50, 64–65
caste. *See also* bavari; brahman; chamar; charan; Dalit; dholi; equality; garoliya lohar; jat; jingar mochi; kayastha; marwari; meghwal; rajput; vijavaragi; untouchable
    bhakti, 22–23, 44–45, 47, 69–70, 130–31
    British identification with upper-caste Indian women, 123, 124
    equality (*see* equality)
    in film, 271, 275, 279
    Gandhi, 225, 226–138, 231–32, 234–35
    Mahipati, 91–92
    Nabhadas, 27–28, 29–30
    Nagridas, 79
    nationalist writing, 122, 125, 126, 129, 130–31, 132–33, 134, 139–40, 155–56, 163–64, 205, 228–31, 247, 259–60, 261, 266–67
    Prem Ambodh, 62–63

Priyadas, 34, 44–45, 47, 48–49, 50–53
Rajasthani folk traditions, 164–205
resistance to oppression (*see* resistance)
Sukhsaran, 96–98, 102–4
varna-ashrama-dharma (*see* varna-ashrama-dharma)
census, 115–16, 124–25, 146
Chaitanya, 15, 28–29, 46, 48, 50–51, 52, 58–59
Chakravarti, Uma, 123–24
Chakravarty, Radha, 220–21
chamar, 44, 49, 53, 97, 179, 182, 187–89, 194, 204–5, 259
Chand (Hindi women's journal), 240–41, 263
Chandidas (1932), 273–74
Chandra, Sudhir, 130, 131–33
charan, 143, 145
Charandas, 54
Charbhuja, 171–72
   Merta Temple, 172, 314n.30
Chatterjee, Margaret, 222–23
Chatterjee, Partha, 123
Chatterji, Bankimchandra, 125–26, 128–30, 146–48, 155–56, 157–58, 160, 161
   Anandamath, 129
Chaturdas, 68–69, 96
chatur sampraday, 50–51, 54, 56, 68, 84
Chatur Singh of Rupaheli, 149–52, 153, 155
Chaturvedi, Parashuram, 154, 205–6, 238–39, 256–57
Chaube, Ram Gharib, 104, 121–22, 174
Chaudhuri, Amit, 220
Chaudhuri, Supriya, 211–12, 217–18, 220
Chaurasi Vaishnavan ki Varta, 54–57, 68, 82–83, 115–16
Chennai. *See* Madras
Chhayavad, 235–37, 242–44
Chittor
   history, 43, 62–63, 148–49, 158
   Jhali Rani, 49, 50, 53–54
   Mira's marital home, 34–35, 94, 100–1, 135–36, 137, 154, 155, 158–59, 160, 175, 177–78, 191–92, 258–59
   Mira temple, 101–2, 118, 250, 291f, 314n.30, 315n.48
   singers from region, 179–80
choice. *See also* agency
   brahmacharya, 232, 269
   Mira and, 21, 47, 153, 190–91, 192–93, 200–1, 213, 224
   women and, 211, 213, 214–15, 216, 222, 226–27, 235–36, 242, 246, 298n.45, 324n.2

Christian/Christianity, 125–27, 128, 137–38, 158, 222–23, 260–61
   missionaries, 120–21
   mystics, 120–21, 270–71
cinema. *See* film
coercion, 163–64, 165, 174–75, 184–85, 193, 199–200, 218–19, 223, 258
Cohn, Bernard, 114
comic book, 109, 247, 270–71
Cousins, James H., 249–51, 252, 258
Cousins, Margaret, 249, 250–51
cow protection, 139–40, 261
Crooke, William, 104, 121–22, 174
Cuckold, 8–9. *See also* Kiran Nagarkar
Cunningham, J.D., 125

Dadu, 43, 44, 68, 204–5
Dadupanth, 15, 68
   warrior ascetics, 83, 317n.76
   women renouncers, 269
Dakor, 56, 67–68, 149
Dalit, 166–67, 195–96, 201–2, 229
   literary theorists, 188–89
Dalmia, Vasudha, 128
darshan, 17, 36–37, 43, 82–83, 94–95, 152–53, 175, 256, 272
   Akbar and Mira, 38, 58–59, 66–67
   Meera (1945/1947), 229–30, 279, 280, 281–82
Das, Gurcharan, 64
Das, Sisir Kumar, 140
Dasi, Nagendrabala, 213–16, 269
Dasnamis
   warrior ascetics, 50–51, 317n.76
   women renouncers, 269
Davis, Richard H., 9, 12
Dayaldas, 144–45
Dayaram, 94–95, 148–49, 152–53
Delhi, 57, 143, 168
Delhi Sultanate, 125
De Napoli, Antoinette, 269
Desai, Kanu, 232–33, 261–62, 281–82
devadasi, 120, 158, 284, 286
Devara Dasimayya, 45
devi. *See* Goddess; goddesses
Deviprasad, Munshi, 146–53, 155–56, 159, 161
   combined with Dutt, 203–4, 247, 253
   influence, 248–49, 256–57
   rajput historical biography of Mira, 142–59
   rajput-nationalist-devotional synthesis, 257, 283–84
Devnarayan ro Byavlo, 174

Dhana, 28, 30–31, 59
dharma, 141–42, 147, 165, 171, 186, 226–27, 249, 260
  bhakti and, 128–29, 157–58
  Jai Singh II, 50–51, 83–84, 85–86
  Prem Ambodh, 32, 62–63
  rajput, 136, 187
  sanatan dharma, 260–61, 262, 267
  See also stridharm; varna-ashrama-dharma
dholi, 169–70
Dhruv (Dhruhi), 59
Dhruvdas, 67–68
diaspora, 109, 260
Doniger, Wendy, 8
Do Sau Bavan Vaishnavan ki Varta, 82–83
domestic advice manuals, 213, 214–16. *See also Kalyan*
dowry, 207–8, 210–11, 260, 284–85
Draupadi, 77–78, 95, 127, 286–87
drum, 26, 27, 169–70
Dube, Govind, 55
Duda, Rao, 93, 111–12, 118, 122, 144, 148, 156–57
  Mira Janma Patri, 181, 182, 184, 191–93, 199–200
  Mira Mangal, 171–72, 173–74
Duff, Grant, 125
Duncan, Ellis S., 277–78
Durgavati, 127, 159–60
Dutt, Manmatha Nath, 134–42, 156, 163, 189, 221–22, 256, 282
  influence of, 247, 248–49, 258
  integration with Deviprasad, 203–4, 253
  rajput-nationalist-devotional synthesis, 257, 283–84
Dvivedi, Hazariprasad, 205
Dvivedi, Mahavirprasad, 236–37, 238, 244
Dwarka
  Bankey Behari, 258
  Chaturdas, 33
  Deviprasad, 149
  Hermann Goetz, 157–59
  Meera (1945/1947), 277–78, 280, 282
  Mira Mangal, 171, 175, 176, 178
  Mira temple, 118–19, 152
  Nagridas, 77–78
  pilgrimage destination, 55
  Priyadas, 38–39
  Raghuraj Singh, 105–6
  Sukhsaran, 95–96, 100–2

James Tod, 118–19
H. H. Wilson, 116

East India Company, 110, 114, 116–17, 124–25
Eknath, 54
ektara, 232–33
England, 116–17, 209, 248, 252–53
English
  accounts of Mira, 113–22, 134–42, 203–4, 247, 253–54, 255–71
  Arts and Crafts movement, 121
  education, 126–27, 132–33, 141–42, 207, 215, 237–38, 274, 282–83
  publications, 110, 127, 141–42, 205–6, 209
  superiority of, 127–28
  translation, 3, 22, 59, 134, 205–6, 211–12, 294n.4
equality
  bhakti, 15–16, 29, 58–59, 84–86, 131, 134, 205, 266–67
  caste, 8–9, 48–49, 91–92, 190, 197
  formal, 227–28
  gender, 8–9, 20, 48–49, 124, 130, 226, 227, 235, 241–42
  Hinduism with Christianity, 136
  Shantiniketan, 207
eroticism, 11, 63–65, 89, 147, 205, 244–45
Europe/European
  claims of superiority, 142–43
  colonialism, 126–27, 254
  conjugality, 138–39, 213–14
  historians, 143–44, 145
  Inayat Khan, 251
  materialism, 128
  premiere of *Meera* (1945/1947), 283
exogamy, 192

Fateh Singh, Rana, 143–44, 145–46
feminine
  Gandhi and, 224–25, 235
  heroism, 155–56, 176 (*see also* heroines)
  Indian concepts, 11, 69–70, 132, 284 (*see also* shakti)
  Mahadevi Varma and, 246
  sensibilities, 275–76
  spiritual identity, 15, 46
  spirituality, 263–64, 268–69, 278, 286–87
  virtue, 141, 224, 226, 231–32, 258–59, 264–65
feminist, 3, 211
film in India
  condemnation of, 260

devotional saint films, 271, 273, 274, 275
  Mira in, 232–33, 247, 269, 271–87
  mythologicals, 271
  silent, 271
  song in, 12–13, 272, 277–79, 280, 282
folk traditions, 163–64, 167, 252–53
  drama, 8–9, 164–65, 167–78, 272
  epic, 164, 174, 179–91 (see also *Mira Janma Patri*)
Fort William College, 114–15
four sampradays. *See* chatur sampraday
France, 251
  Garcin de Tassy, 76
Freier, Monika, 262, 263
Friedlander, Peter, 49–50

Gadge Maharaj, 228–31, 269–70
Gahlot, Jagdish Singh, 149–52, 153
Gajadhar (Mira's teacher), 151–52
Gandhi, Mohandas K. *See also* caste; feminine; marriage; Parita Mukta; Narsi Mehta; patriarchy; untouchability; women's political activism
  Bankey Behari and, 256
  Annie Besant and, 248
  James Cousins and, 250
  Mahadevi Varma and, 235–36, 239–40, 243, 244–45
  Meera (1945/1947), 280–78, 281, 284
  Mira and, 155, 207, 221–35, 274, 275
  Sarojini Naidu and, 282–83
  Hanuman Prasad Poddar and, 260–62
  political leadership of, 254, 256–57, 273, 276–77
  Subbulakshmi and, 286–87
Gandhi, Rajiv, 283
Ganesh, 139–40
Gangaur (Parvati), 98
Gangaur festival, 181
Ganges, 44, 67–68, 77, 84, 191
Garcin de Tassy, J. H., 119, 124
Gargi, 127–28
garoliya lohar, 179
Gaudiya sampraday, 28–29, 32, 46, 50–51, 52–53, 54, 65, 101–2
Gauribai, 41, 43–44
Ginsberg, Allen, 256
Girdhar (Giridhar), 26, 33, 66–67, 105, 173, 180, 184–85, 217–18, 259, 278–79, 323n.199
  "Mine is Girdhar Gopal" bhajan, 212, 213, 216
  Mira's husband in *Prem Ambodh*, 60–62, 63

Gita Press, 247, 260–66, 267, 270–71
Gobind Singh, Guru, 59–60, 64–65
Goddess (Devi, Mahadevi), 22–23, 72
goddesses, 11, 95, 184–85, 213–14, 299n.62.
  See also kuldevi; Mari; Parvati; Sita
Goetz, Hermann, 156–59, 160, 166–67
Gokulnath, 54
Gold, Ann Grodzins, 185–86
Gopichand (renouncer king), 178, 325n.22
gopis, 26–27, 31, 97, 100–1, 102–3, 147
Goswami, Chimanlal, 260
Goswami, Jiv
  Gaudiya sampraday theologian, 15
  Mira and, 38–39, 42, 45–47, 48, 50–51, 53, 55, 65, 84, 104, 105, 111, 221–22, 239, 264–65
Goswami, Rup
  Gaudiya sampraday theologian, 15, 28–29, 30
  Meera (1945/1947), 278–79, 280, 282
  Mira and, 46, 48, 137–38, 140–42, 186, 256
  Sahajiya Vaishnava guru, 48, 140–41
Goswami, Sanatan, 15, 30
Govardhan, 26, 57, 89
Government of India Act, 124–25
Govindevji Temple, 28–29
Goyandka, Jaydayal, 260–63, 266
Grierson, George A., 76, 104, 120–21, 163
Growse, Frederic Salmon, 120–21
Gujarat, 129–30, 131–34, 148–49, 221–22, 227
Gujarati, 129–30, 132, 134, 142–43, 204, 205–6, 226–28, 232–33, 247
  film, 271, 277, 287
Gulzar, S. S., 273
guru
  Agradas (*see* Agradas)
  of Banasa, 268–69
  bhakti saints as, 23, 256–57
  Chaitanya (*see* Chaitanya)
  Gobind Singh (*see* Gobind Singh)
  hagiography, 28, 45–47, 48–57, 258–60
  Jiv Goswami (*see* Jiv Goswami)
  Mira as, 28, 62–63, 251–52, 256–57
  Mira's, 48–57, 140–41 (*see also* Jiv Goswami; Rup Goswami; Raidas)
  Raidas (*see* Raidas)
  Ramananda (*see* Ramananda)
  Rup Goswami (*see* Rup Goswami)
  Sikh, 48–50
  Vallabha sampraday, 54–55, 56, 57

Hada, Madhav, 159, 264

Index

hagiography
  male saints' lives, 30–31, 40, 42–43
  women saints' lives, 39–58
  See also Chaturdas; Dhruvdas; Mahipati; Nabhadas; Nagridas; Priyadas; Raghavdas; Raghuraj Singh; Sukhsaran; Vaishnavdas
Hansen, Kathryn, 168, 176, 177, 178
Hare, James, 52
Haridas Niranjani, 68
Haridas (Ramavat), 48
Haridwar, 171
Hariray, 54
Harishchand (renouncer king), 170, 178
Harishchandra, Bharatendu, 128, 143
Harlan, Lindsey, 153–54, 164
Hawley, John Stratton, 52, 55–56, 59–65, 67–68, 111–12
heroines
  Anandamath, 129
  clever-bride, 185–87
  legendary, 5, 26, 126–28, 134, 141–42, 159–60, 176, 195, 211, 217, 231, 249, 289–90
  Mirabai as, 19–20, 134–42, 148, 152, 153–54, 159–60, 206–7, 234–35, 275
  romantic, 171, 176
Hindi
  civilizational and national language, 19–20, 28–29, 109, 120, 128, 135, 140, 145, 163–64, 239–41, 260
  film, 20, 260, 272–77
  literature, 10, 109, 115, 141–42, 149–51, 154, 159, 204, 205–6, 238–39, 244–45
  poetry, 128, 235–37, 238–39, 244 (*see also* Chhayavad)
Hindi Sahitya Bhavan, 270–71
Hindi Sahitya Sammelan, 238–39
Hindu
  identity, 125–27
  nationalism, 139–34, 261–62
  orthodoxy, 248, 255, 257, 260–62, 263–64, 266, 267
  religion, 119–20, 123, 128, 139
historiography, 8–9, 110, 112, 125–26, 129–34, 142–59
Hit Harivamsh, 30, 67
Holi, 169–70, 330n.89
honor
  heroism and, 117–18, 134, 142–43, 159–60
  national, 155–56, 195, 201–2
  rajput (*see* rajput honor)
  shame and, 26–27, 29–30, 47–48, 95, 106, 137, 171, 176
  women's, 77, 94, 99, 154, 157, 177–78, 213–14
Hooja, Rima, 144–45
Horstmann, Monika, 51, 260–61, 262, 268–70
Howard, Veena, 231, 234–35
hypermasculinity, 123, 124–25, 129, 160

imaginative subjectivity, 242–43
independence
  heroines, 126, 161
  Indian, 109, 126, 201–2, 206–7, 239, 247, 255, 271, 276–77, 283, 284
  Mahadevi Varma, 235–36, 239–40, 241–42, 243–46
  Mira, 53, 100–1, 105–6, 129–30, 133–34, 135, 138, 190, 191, 205, 211, 222, 223, 230–31, 259–60, 265–66
  Subbulakshmi, 246, 284–85
  women's, 109, 131, 133–34, 138, 140, 159–60, 185–87, 222, 223
Indian National Congress, 143–44, 240, 248, 255, 282–83
infanticide, 191–92
initiation, 46, 48–57, 82, 105–6, 182–83, 192–93, 264–65
interreligious spirituality, 3
Ireland, 249, 252–53
Ishmailis, 44
ishtadev, 21
Islam. *See* Mughal; Muslim; Sufi

Jaganath, 120
Jaidev, 59
Jaimal, 74f, 82–83, 105, 144–45, 148–51, 156–57, 253
  Jaimal family chronicles, 144–45, 149–51
Jaipur. *See* Amer
Jai Singh II (r. 1699–1743), 50–51, 52–53, 58–59, 83–86
Janabai, 92
jankhi, 272
Japan, 252–53, 276–77
Jasvant Singh, Maharaja of Jodhpur 110–11
jat, 83, 124–25, 179–80, 193–94
jauhar, 136, 148–49
Jesus, 147, 156, 222, 258, 266
Jews, 260–61

Jhali Rani, 49, 50, 53–54
Jhaveri, Krishnalal Mahanlal, 204, 269
jingar mochi, 172, 314n.29
Jnanadev, 89–90
Jodhpur, 110–12, 144, 146, 148–49, 151
Jogan (1950), 269, 275–76
John of the Cross, 120–21
jungle, 174, 185, 190–91
jungli rani, 185–87, 191

Kabir
   brahmanization, 97
   hagiography, 28, 30–31, 44–45, 52, 54, 59, 83–84, 87
   Hindi literature, 205
   Hindu and Muslim followers, 95
   Indian spirituality, 204–5, 220–21
   nirgun saint, 68
   songs of, 47, 236
Kabir Kala Manch, 195–97
Kabirpanth, 97, 116
Kachvaha rajputs, 28–29, 50–51, 52–53, 280
Kali, 11
Kali Yug, 97
Kalyan (journal), 260–62, 265–66
Kalyana-Kalpataru (journal), 260, 265
Karaikkal Ammaiyar, 5–6, 40–41
Karmabai, 49–50, 58–59, 62–63, 93
Karmaitibai, 93
kartals, 67, 232–33, 265–66
Kashi Nagari Pracharini Sabha. *See* Nagari Pracharini Sabha
katha, 73, 92–93, 96, 231
Kaviraj, Sudipta, 142, 146
kayastha, 237–38
Keay, F. E., 204
Keune, Jon, 91–92
khadi, 231–32, 239–40
Khan, Pir-o-Murshid Hazrat Inayat, 251–52
Khatri, Kartikprasad, 141–42, 146
khyal (folk drama). *See* folk tradition
khyat, 110–11, 145–46, 151–52. See also *Nainsi ri Khyat*
kirtan, 86, 87, 90, 92–93, 228–31, 256
Kishangarh, 75, 80–81, 82, 84–85
Kishwar, Madhu, 81–82, 222, 232
Kisturabai, 93
Krishnajanambhumi, 261
Krishnaji, Shri (disciple of Bankey Behari), 256, 270–71
Krishnamurthy, "Kalki" R., 277–78

Krishnamurti, 248, 255–56
kshatriya, 97, 125, 129
kuldevi, 28–29, 33–34, 105–6, 116, 185
Kumbha Mela, 239
Kumbha, Rana, 110, 118–19, 122, 132, 135, 144, 221–22, 249, 265
Kumbha Rana ri Bat, 164–65, 193, 194–95, 196–97
Kunwaribai, Sundar, 81–82
Kurki (Kurḍi), 93, 101–2, 148, 152–53
Kurur Amma, 46

Lacchiram of Kuchaman, 167–69, 169*f*, 171, 175
Lakha, Rana, 118–19
Lakshmibai. *See* Rani of Jhansi
Lala, Chhaganlal, 256
Lalita, 67–68, 97
Lalla, 40–41, 42
lila, 8–9, 15, 17–18, 168, 272
Lilly, William Samuel, 120–21
Limbale, Sharankumar, 188
lion, 44
Lipner, Julius, 6–7
Lodi, Sikandar, 44–45
Lyall, Alfred Comyn, 120

Macauliffe, M. A., 203–4, 221–22, 247, 248–49, 256–57
Madhav Das, 44, 45
Madhvacharya, 50–51
Madhya Pradesh, 163, 269
Madras, 163, 248, 251, 284–85
Mahabharata, 14, 125, 147, 215, 257
Mahadevi. *See* Goddess
Mahadeviyakka, 5–6, 40–41, 42, 44, 46, 57
Maharaj Libel Case, 131
Maharashtra, 54, 89, 92, 101–2, 171, 228–29
Maharshi, 255–56
Mahipati, 86–92, 101–2, 103–4, 106, 203–4, 230, 280
Maitreyi, 127, 249
Malaviya, Madan Mohan, 155
Malayalam, 271
Maldeo, Rao, 111–12, 144–45, 148–49
Mann, Gurinder Singh, 59–65, 67–68
Man Singh, Raja (r. 1589-1614), 28–29, 158, 280
Manu, Laws of, 11, 127, 215
Manushastras, 263
marathas, 83, 110, 116–17, 125, 128, 140–41

Index

Marathi, 114–15, 142–43, 205–6, 247, 271, 275, 277
Mari (cholera goddess), 189–90
Marriage. *See also* Nagendrabala Devi
  arranged, 47–48, 127, 138–39, 148, 171, 173, 177, 183–85, 207–10, 212, 214, 226–27, 235–36, 237–38, 239, 242, 253, 258–59, 268, 275, 278–79
  bhakti and, 40–41, 96–97, 98–100, 154, 267–70
  child, 127, 138–39, 207–8, 209–10, 214, 226, 235–36, 245, 254, 255
  Gandhi, 223, 225–27
  hypergamy, 173, 186
  Mira's (*see* Mirabai's marriage)
  Tagore, 207–10, 211–12, 213–18, 219–20
  women saints and, 40–41, 57–58
Marriage Restraint Act, 278–79
martial races, 124–25
Marwar, 32, 57–58, 110–12, 164, 185
marwari, 260, 262–63, 264–65, 267, 268, 270
  Marwari Agarwal Sabha, 260
masculine, 129, 133, 160
masculinity, 126, 160. *See also* hypermasculinity
Mathur, Madan Mohan, 168, 170
maya, 11
Mayo, Katherine, 254, 282–83
McDermott, Rachel, 273
McGregor, Ronald Stewart, 141–42
Meera (1945/1947), 277–84
Meerabai/Rajrani Meera (1933), 272–75
Meerut Conspiracy Case, 255, 256
meghwal, 168, 179–80, 187–89, 194
Meha, 30
Mehta, Narsi, 54, 68, 130, 131, 132–33
  and Gandhi, 222–24, 227–28
Menaria, M. L., 154
Merta, 32, 65, 81–82, 93, 101–2, 111–12, 116, 118, 144–45, 148–49, 155, 156–58, 175, 190–91
Mewar. *See also* Chittor
  history of, 43, 62–63, 110–12, 113, 142–43, 144–45, 148, 152, 153
  kingdom of, 279, 280–81, 282
  Mira's marital family, 38, 101–2, 137–38, 153–54, 155, 232–33
  Mira's natal home, 65, 88–89, 90
  rana (*see* rana)
  James Tod and, 116–17, 118–19
  women renouncers, 269

Mirabai
  birth, 32, 93–94, 96, 106, 148, 149, 151, 181–82, 191–92
  childhood, 32, 38–39, 40, 86–94, 98, 104, 159, 172, 183, 253–54, 259–60, 278–79
  education, 115, 121–22, 138, 148, 151–52, 156–57, 159–60
  guru (*see* guru; Raidas; Jiv Goswami; Rup Goswami)
  marriage (*see* Mirabai's marriage)
  previous birth, 92–93, 96, 100–1, 258
  Akbar and (*see* Akbar)
Mirabai's marriage, 41, 47–48, 57–58, 104–5, 120, 151–52, 153, 159–60, 164–65, 196–97, 198, 253, 264
  Behari, 258–59
  Bhojraj (*see* Bhojraj)
  Deviprasad, 148
  Dutt, 135–36, 137–39
  Gandhi and, 221–22, 226–27
  Hermann Goetz, 156–57
  Kumbha (*see* Kumbha, Rana)
  Mahapati, 87–88
  Meera (1945/1947), 278–79
  Mira Janma Patri, 183–85, 189, 192
  Mira Mangal, 167–78
  Nagridas, 76
  Priyadas, 32, 57–58
  Prem Ambodh, 60–61, 63–64
  Sukhsaran, 94
  Tripathi, 132–33
Mirabais (sect), 115–16
Mira Janma Patri, 8–9, 10, 164–65, 171, 179–91, 227, 274, 275
Mira Mangal, 164–65, 167–78
Mira Movement for Education. *See* Swami T. L. Vaswani
Mira ri Parachi, 92–101, 171
St. Mira School for Girls, 233, 234f, 265–66
Mira songs, 12–16, 21, 74–86, 102, 154, 163, 191, 217–18, 223–24, 232–33, 234–35, 236, 237, 244, 250, 264–65, 266, 286–87, 289–90, 291–92
  "*Mere to Girdhar Gopal, dusara na koi*" ("Mine is Girdhar Gopal—there is no other"), 213, 216, 269
  "*Suni main Hari ki avaz*" ("I heard the sound/voice/call of Hari"), 236
Mishra, Pratap Narayan, 140
Mitra, Rajendralal, 120
Mitra, Tarinee Charun, 113–15, 116

moksha, 96, 100, 171, 173
Monier-Williams, Monier, 119–21
Mother India (*Bharat Mata*) (1957), 272
Mughal Empire, 28–29, 50–51, 52–53, 280
    Mughal court, 114, 280
    Mughal emperor, 139, 258 (*see also* Akbar)
    Mughal gazetteer, 145
    Mughal-rajput alliance and patronage, 28–29, 83
    Mughals, 83, 117–18, 203–4
Mukhopadhyay, U. N., 205–6
Mukta, Parita, 16, 166–67, 188–89, 227
    Gandhi, 223, 226, 234–35
    rajput suppression of Mira's memory, 154
Muktabai, 93
Mukul, Akshaya, 261–62, 263
Murraham, 139–40
music
    devadasi traditions, 284
    film and, 272, 274
    Inayat Khan, 251
    Indian classical, 284–85, 286
    Mira and, 2–3, 12–13, 90, 105, 151–52
    musician, 27, 135, 154, 170, 251, 279 (*see also* Tansen)
    Subbulakshmi, 284–86
    Tagore, 217–18
    unifying power of, 252
Muslim. *See also* Akbar
    anti-Muslim rhetoric, 117–18, 125, 126–27, 129, 131–32, 139–40, 158–59, 207, 261–62, 280
    Hindu as not Muslim, 126, 260–61
    Kabir, 44, 47, 95, 97
    Mughal (*see* Mughal)
    mutual appreciation between Hindus and, 45, 47, 66–67, 170, 179–80, 181
    nationalist ambivalence, 91, 139–40, 280
    Sufism (*see* Sufism)
    unified spiritual and cultural heritage of Hindus and, 28, 140, 170, 179–80, 181, 207, 248–49, 252, 261–62, 282–83

Nabhadas
    bhaktamal, 50, 61
    influence on bhaktamal tradition and hagiographers, 67–68, 69, 86–87, 102, 105
    influence on scholarship, 113–14, 115, 119, 263–64
    Mira, 25–27, 29–30

    Ramanandis and, 27–29, 51–52
Nagari Pracharini Sabha, 141–42, 205, 238
Nagarkar, Kiran, 8–9, 178
Nagridas (Savant Singh), 73, 74–86, 101–2, 103–4, 106
    influence of, 113–14, 144–45
Naidu, Sarojini, 282–83
Nainsi, Muhnot, 110–11, 122, 144–45, 154–55
    Nainsi ri Khyat, 80, 110–12, 118, 151
Namdev, 16, 30–31, 59, 71, 87, 92, 95, 104
Nammalvar, 21–72
Nanak, 68, 116, 141–42, 204–5, 248–49
Nandy, Ashis, 122–23, 125–26
Narasimha, 94, 105
Narayan, Kirin, 6, 186
Narayandas Natava, 74–75, 79–80, 84–86, 102
Nath, 89–90, 168, 182–83, 269
Nathdwara, 67–68
National Council of Women in India, 228
nautanki (folk drama), 168
Nehrus, 155, 207, 238, 239–40, 283
New India, 248
New Theatres, 272–73, 274
Nimbarka sampraday, 15, 28–29, 50–51, 75, 82, 304n.140
    warrior ascetics, 83, 317n.76
nirgun
    bhajans, 238–39, 331n.93
    Dadupanth, 68
    devotion, 48, 93
    saints, 22–23, 44, 53, 83–85, 204–5, 220–21, 238–39 (*see also* Kabir; Namdev; Nammalvar; Raidas; Tukaram)
    sampradays, 35, 53, 68–69
    understanding of God as beyond form, 35, 53, 63, 69–70, 89–90, 204–5, 237, 266
    Radhasoami, 346n.46
    Sikhs, 35, 59–60, 63–65
nondual, 61–62, 63, 203–5
nonviolence
    Mira as embodiment of, 221–35, 246, 254, 256–57, 274, 281
    resistance, 221, 223–24, 228–29, 231–32
    satyagraha (*see* satyagraha)
    women and, 206–7, 221–22, 224, 226, 231–32
Novetzke, Christian Lee, 16, 71

obscenity, 155–56, 168

Index

Ojha, Gaurishankar, 148, 149–52, 153
Okita, Kyokazu, 52
oral epics of Rajasthan. *See* folk traditions
orality, 6, 166
Orissa, 120
Orsi, Robert, 18, 199
Orsini, Francesca, 240–41, 243–45

Pabuji, 182
Padaprasangmala, 74–86, 101–2, 103, 105, 113–14, 152–53, 165. *See also* Nagridas
Padmavati, 28
Padmini, 5, 127
Pandharpur, 87, 89, 229
parchai, 30–31, 49, 50, 59, 64–65, 92–101
Parmanand, 30
Parsi theater, 168, 251, 272
Partition, 233, 283, 287
Parvati, 98
pativrata
   ideal for women, 129, 134, 213–14, 217, 218–19, 224, 235
   Mira as alternative, 242
   Mira as counter example, 226–27, 229–30, 275
   Mira of human husband and model for women, 135, 138, 147–48, 160, 249, 263, 266–67
   Mira of Krishna, 94, 100–1, 103–4, 134, 213
   rajput women question Mira's pativrata status, 153–54
patriarchy, 155–56, 163–64, 195, 205, 209–10, 214–16, 228, 263
   and Gandhi, 223, 224, 225, 226–27
   new patriarchy, 134, 138–39, 163–64, 178, 195, 197, 210, 213, 215, 230, 242, 263
patronage, 112, 121–22, 143, 169–70, 272
Pauwels, Heidi, 30, 56, 80–82
Payahari, Krishnadas, 28–29
Pechilis, Karen, 22
Persian, 114, 128, 239–40, 255–56
Phalke, Dhundiraj Govind, 271
Phulibai, 93
pilgrimage, 2–3, 50–51, 81–82, 83, 87, 171, 188–89, 229–30, 267, 270, 279
   Banaras, 87, 171
   Ganges, 67–68, 84
   Mira's, 38, 67–68, 81, 84, 95, 118, 136–37, 138, 149, 151–52, 175, 176, 190–91, 251–52, 258–59, 265, 281, 282

Nagridas, 81–82, 83–84, 85–86
Pandharpur, 87, 89–90, 229
Pushkar, 94–95, 172, 175, 190–91
Vrindavan, 67, 81–82, 213–14, 277–78
Pinch, Vijay, 120–21
Pipa, 30–31, 59, 95
   Pipa's wife Sita, 42, 50
Pipa Parchai, 30
pirs, 44
Poddar, Hanuman Prasad, 260–65, 266–67
poetry, 129–32, 144, 147, 208
   bhakti, 128, 130, 131
   Mahadevi Varma, 235–46
   Mira, 118–20, 122, 128, 130, 133–34, 135, 138, 149, 154, 205–7 (*see also* Mira Songs)
   women and, 124, 208, 213
poison
   royal rajput weapon, 36–37
   spiritual power, 29–30
   women's songs, 36–37
Prabhat, C. L., 93
Prahlad, 59, 77–78, 94, 95, 222, 286–87
prakriti, 11
Pratap, Rana, 141–42, 280, 333n.130
Prayag Mahila Vidhyapith, 240
Prem Ambodh, 31, 48–50, 58–66, 106, 177, 212
Price, William, 113–15, 116, 122–23
Prithviraj (r. 1502-1527), 28–29
Priyadas, 27, 31, 32–59, 62, 63–69, 72–73, 86–87, 94–95, 106
   influence of, 105, 113–14, 115, 116, 119, 203–4, 263–64
Punamchand Sikhwal of Denda, 168–69, 175
Pune, 164, 168, 233
   Prabhat Studios, 272–73
Punjab
   Punjabi film, 271, 277
puranas, 23, 96–97
purdah, 2, 42, 47–48, 82–83, 154
Pushkar, 94–95, 171–72, 175, 190–91
Pushtimarg. *See* Vallabha sampraday

Quit India movement, 229–30, 276–77

Radha, 15, 52, 64–65, 67–68, 75, 118, 127, 278–79
   allegorical interpretation, 147
   Mira as incarnation, 97, 258
   M.S. Subbulakshmi's step-daughter, 278–79, 286

Index

Radhabai, 106n.94, 269
Radhakrishnan, S., 261–62
Radhasoami Satsang, 238–39, 256, 346n.46
Radhavallabh sampraday, 15, 30, 67
Raghavdas, 68–69, 82–83
Raghuraj Singh, Raja, 104, 105–6, 121–22, 163, 203–4
Rai, Lala Lajput, 155
Raidas (Rohidas, Ravidas)
　brahminization, 97
　inclusion in hagiographic texts, 28, 30–31, 44, 83–84, 87, 91–92, 97
　Mira's guru, 10, 47, 48–54, 59–60, 63–64, 84, 104, 106, 165, 182–83, 187, 191, 194, 258–59, 264–65
　scholarly debates about connection to Mira, 204–5, 266
Raidas Parchai, 49, 97
Raj, Sangeeta, 76
Rajasthan, 85–86, 88, 250, 262, 267, 269–70, 277–78
Rajasthani, 205–6, 247, 268–69, 273–74
rajput
　formation, 14–15
　hero deity, 179–80, 182
　heroines (*see* Ahalyabai; heroines; Padmini; Tarabai)
　historians' biography of Mira, 10, 64, 109, 110–13, 142–59, 161, 197, 198–99, 201–2, 286
　honor (*see* rajput honor)
　memory/honoring of Mira, 80–82, 85–86, 153–54
　Mira as, 73, 103–4, 165, 194, 249, 281
　Nagridas as, 73, 103
　nationalist embrace of valor/heroism, 109, 110–11, 117–18, 124–25, 135–36, 248, 254, 257–58
　nationalist synthesis of Mira's life, 203–6, 211, 231–32, 234–35, 245, 255–71, 275, 283–84
　Raghavdas as, 68
　shifting alliances with Mughals, marathas, Afghans, jats, 28–29, 83
　suppression of memory of Mira by, 85–86, 154–55
　sword marriages, 174
　thakur, 267–68
　women's normative behavior, 39, 41–42, 118–19, 122, 184, 270 (*see also* sati)
　women renouncers, 269

rajput honor, 14–15, 41–42, 76, 136, 137–38, 141, 155–56, 163–64, 172–73, 178, 184, 192, 195, 210–11, 258, 279, 280
Ram Singh, Raja of Jodhpur, 168
Ram Soni, 69
Rama, 22–23, 73, 83–84, 93, 168, 272
Ramananda, 28, 29–30, 48, 51, 83–84
Ramanandi sampraday, 15, 27–29, 30, 50–52, 54, 93, 101–2
　warrior ascetics, 83, 317n.76
Ramanuja, 28, 50–51
Ramanujan, A.K., 6, 22, 40, 41–42, 46–47, 48, 57, 59–60, 104, 107, 164
Ramavat sampraday, 48, 267–68
Ramayana, 6, 73, 95, 174–75, 190–91, 215, 257
Ramcharitmanas, 7, 73, 260
Ramdas varta, 55
Ramdev, 179–80
Ramjanambhumi agitation in Ayodhya, 261
Ramsnehi sampradays, 93
rana, 32, 44–45, 58–59, 65, 68, 104–6, 116, 136. *See also* Bhojraj; Bhupal Singh; Fateh Singh; Kumbha; Lakha; Sanga; Sajjan Singh; Shambhu Singh
　Dutt, 136, 137, 138–39, 140–41
　Mahipati, 88, 90, 92–93
　Mira Mangal, 172–75, 177–78
　Mira Janma Patri, 179–80, 183–84, 185, 187–93, 199–200, 201
　Nagridas, 75–76, 77–78, 79, 81, 84
　Priyadas, 32, 34–37, 38–39, 44
　Prem Ambodh, 62–63
　Sukhsaran, 94–95, 96, 99, 100–1
　symbol of patriarchal, feudal, and/or social oppressor, 179, 196, 197–98, 273–74
　Tripathi, 133–34
Ranabai, 93
Ranchor, 38–39, 104, 115–16, 149, 204
Rani of Jhansi (Lakshmibai), 126, 127, 135, 141–42, 159–60
Ransom, Josephine Maria Davies, 249
rape, 178, 216
Rasik Bihari (Bani Thani), 79
Ratan Singh (Mira's father), 93, 144, 148, 171
Ratan Singh, Rana (r. 1528-1531), 148–49, 157, 171, 258, 265–66
Rathor, Amar Singh, 141–42, 170
Rathor, Kanjibhai, 271
Rathor rajputs
　as devotees, 27 (*see also* Duda; Jaimal)

Rathor rajputs (*cont.*)
  genealogist of, 149, 158–59
  historical sources for Mira, 110–11, 144
  marriage alliances with Sisodiyas, 148
  Mira as, 97, 111–12, 118, 171, 173, 179, 185
  Nagridas as, 75, 80–82
  pride in Mira, 151
  Amar Singh (see *Amar Singh Rathor*)
Ravana, 95, 174–75
Rawal, Ravishankar, 232–33
renunciation, 28, 33, 42, 79, 81–82, 99, 101, 138–39, 189, 190–91
  alternative for women, 232, 269, 275–76
  Mira's, 74–75, 76, 81–82, 132–33, 137, 144, 149, 152, 157–58, 197–98
  Mira Mangal, 171, 175, 176, 182, 183–84, 187
renouncer, 27, 37, 50, 68, 87–88, 125–26, 129, 148–49, 171, 184, 228–29, 231–32, 251–52, 268, 272 (*see also* Gopichand; Harishchand; sadhu)
  lover as renouncer (jogi), 176
  Mira as renouncer, 45, 68, 166, 173, 178, 187, 251–52, 274
resistance
  to caste oppression, 15–16, 164–65, 166–67, 191–202
  familial to women's non-normative behavior, 41–42, 208, 268
  Mira's resistance, 2, 74–75, 184, 210, 265–66, 275
  Mira's songs and story as a language of, 8–9, 164–65, 191–202, 235, 284
  to missionary education, 123–24
  nonviolent, 16–17, 221–22, 223–24, 226, 228–29
  rajputs to Mughals, 117–18
  to use of violence in freedom struggle, 276–77
revolt of 1857, 121, 124–25, 126, 238, 276–77
Robson, John, 168
romance, 167–68, 171, 175–77, 265, 286
  in film, 271, 272, 274, 275–76
romanticism, 117–18
romanticization, 118, 122, 123, 124, 144, 244–45, 248–49, 250
Royal Asiatic Society, 117–18, 143–44
Rudolph, Lloyd and Susanne, 117–18, 144, 145
Rukmini, 127

Sabarmati Ashram, 250, 255–56
Sadasivam, 277–78, 282–83, 284–86
sadhana, 24, 71
sadhu, 34–35, 37, 42, 58–59, 132, 182–83, 204, 231, 263, 267–68, 278–79 (*see also* renouncer)
  female, 269
  lustful sadhu episode, 37, 42, 62, 153, 264–65
  Mira Mangal, 171, 172, 173
saffron, 183–84, 189
Saghal, Ramrakh Singh, 241, 263
sagun
  devotion, 28, 63–64, 69–70, 89–90, 93, 120–21, 204–5
  experience of God through form, 22–23, 64–65, 205, 237, 266
Sahajiya Vaishnava sampraday, 48, 140–41
Sajjan Singh, Rana, 143–44
sakhi, 67–68, 97
Salt March, 254
Sammelan Patrika (journal), 238
Samudragupta, 252–53
sang (folk drama), 168
Sanga, Rana, 110–11, 118–19, 144, 151–52, 157, 253
Sangari, Kumkum, 198–99, 271, 274, 286
sannyas. *See* renouncer; renunciation
Sanskrit, 23, 114–15, 119, 122–23, 128, 134, 145, 204–5, 210, 215, 237–38, 239–40
sant, 23, 35
Sanyal, Nalini Mohan, 265–67
Sarasvati (journal), 238
Sarda Act (Child Marriage Restraint Act), 255
Sarkar, Tanika, 211, 223–24, 225, 231–32
sati, 41, 75, 76, 137–39, 213–14, 217, 218–19, 225, 253
satsang, 71, 86–87, 268–69
satyagraha, 221, 223, 226. *See also* nonviolence
satyagrahi. *See also* nonviolence
  Mira as, 2–3, 221–35, 246, 254, 256–57, 274, 281
Savant Singh. *See* Nagridas
Savitri, 213–14, 217, 249
Savithri (1941), 286
Schomer, Karine, 237, 239, 241, 242–43, 244, 245
Schultz, Anna, 229
scorpion, 95
Self-Respect movement, 228

self-rule (swaraj), 248, 249, 254, 255
Sen, 28, 30
Sen, Amartya, 220
Sen, Keshub Chunder, 127-28, 242
Sen, Kshitimohan, 204-6, 220-21, 261-62
Sengar, Shiv Singh, 120
Sevasadanam (1938), 284-85, 286
Shabnam, Padmavati, 144-45
Shaiva, 22-23, 89-91, 322n.166
    Dasnami ascetics, 50-51, 269, 317n.76
    Virashaiva, 45, 57
    See also Shiva
Shaktas, 22-23
shakti, 11, 190, 219
Shakuntala, 127
Shakuntalai (1940), 285, 286
shalagram, 49, 53, 91-92, 98, 105, 171, 183, 184, 185, 187, 191, 212, 224-25
Shambhu Singh, Rana, 143
shankavalis, 73
Shantiniketan, 205, 207-8, 209, 219, 232-33, 261-62
Sharma, G. N., 269-70
Sharma, Kidar Nath, 273, 275-76
Sharma, Nina, 145
Sharma, Harinarayan, 149-52, 154, 155, 205-6
Shekhar, Indu, 145
Shekhavat, Kalyan Singh, 156, 158-59, 160
Sher Shah, 252-53
Shiva, 5-6, 46, 72, 89-91, 98, 134, 181, 213-14, 322n.166
Shivaji, 140, 248-49, 252-53, 333n.130
Shri Vaishnava, 28, 51, 57
shudhadvaita, 204-5
shudras, 28, 43
Shukla-Bhatt, Neelima, 221-23, 234-35
Shyamaldas, Kaviraj, 142-46
Sikhs, 15, 48-50, 53, 86, 89, 110, 116, 124-25, 222-23, 260-61
Sindhi, 141-42, 205-6, 247
Sinha, Mrinalini, 228, 255
Sisodiyas
    marriage alliance with Rathors, 148, 173
    Mira's behavior as insult to, 153, 154, 177-78
    rana, 94, 172-73, 190
Sita
    heroine of *Ramayana*, 73, 95, 120, 174-75, 190-91
    role model for women, 127-28, 129, 133, 196, 213-14, 217, 225

Sita-Ram image and Kachvaha dynasty, 28-29
Sita (Pipa's wife), 50
Slade, Madeleine (Mira Behn), 221
snakes
    handling as mark of spiritual power, 45
    sent to kill Mira, 95, 105, 157, 175, 190, 224-25, 248-49, 348n.79
sorcery, 185, 186, 193
Srinivasan, R., 251
stridharm (women's dharma), 98-101, 129, 133, 152, 213, 215, 221-22, 225, 229, 249, 258. *See also* Nagendrabala Dasi
Subbulakshmi, M. S., 16-17, 20, 154, 247, 273, 277-79, 282-83, 284-87
Sufi, 3, 44, 222-23, 255-56, 328n.53, 330n.81, 331n.102
    International Sufi Movement, 251-52
    saints, 267, 270-71
suhag, 34
suicide, 171, 208-9, 210-11, 250, 283
    attempted, 253, 258, 265
Sukhdev, 59-60
Sukhla, Ramchandra, 205
Sukhsaran, 73, 92-104, 106, 165, 229
Sundar Kunwaribai, 81-82
Surdas, 30, 43, 54, 236
Sursuranand and Sursuri, 28
Swami, Nattotamdas, 205-6
sword 94, 173-74, 175, 177-78

Taft, Frances, 111, 144-45, 149-51
Tagore, Rabindranath, 155, 207-21, 236-37, 248, 254, 259-60, 261-62, 266-67
    Shantiniketan (*see* Shantiniketan)
    "Streer Patra" (Letter from a Wife), 208-11, 219, 235-36, 247
    Yogayog, 211-12, 216-21, 235, 250, 269
Tamil, 20, 22-23, 141-42, 247, 251
    film, 271, 277-78, 283
Tamil Nadu, 251, 283
Tamil Tigers, 283
Tandon, R. C., 205-6, 256-57
Tansen, 37-39, 42, 43, 58-59, 66-67, 98-99, 251-52, 280
Tarabai, 127, 159-60
tazkira, 33
Telegu, 141-42, 247, 271, 277
television, 201-2, 333n.130
Temple, Richard, 121
Teresa of Avila, 120-21

textbooks/school lessons, 10–11, 13, 109, 252–53
Theosophical Society, 248–50, 251–8, 252–53
Thomas, Rosie, 272
Tilak, Bal Gangadhar, 139–40, 155–56
Tod, James, 16–17, 113–14, 116–19, 122–23, 163, 167–68, 189, 256–57
  influence of, 119–20, 121–22, 125, 127, 135, 140–41, 232, 265
  Shyamaldas and, 143–44, 145, 146
  translations, 135, 142–43
Trilochan, 30–31, 59
Tripathi, Govardhanram Madhavram, 129–34, 146, 158, 159, 204, 205, 221–22, 226–27, 232–33, 248–49
Tukaram, 40, 54
Tulpule, S. G., 86–87
tulsi, 182–83, 232–33
Tulsidas, 7, 73, 141–42, 205, 260
  letter exchange with Mira, 105–6, 149, 203–4, 258–59, 264–66
  Ramcharitmanas (see *Ramcharitmanas*)
Turnbull, Eleanor Lucia, 252–53

Uda (Udabai, Mira's sister-in-law), 95, 98–99, 100, 175, 258, 280, 281
Udaipur, 63, 65, 87, 88–89, 101–2, 116, 151, 153, 154, 179, 185
Udaisingh, 144
United States, 211, 251, 254, 282–83. *See also* American popular literature
untouchability, 28, 97, 166–67, 187, 188–89, 192–93, 195–96, 230
  Gandhi and, 223–24, 226–30, 261–62
Upanishads, 23, 127, 237–38, 256, 257–58
  women in (*see* Gargi; Maitreyi)
uplift campaigns, 230, 286
Urdu, 128, 141–42, 143, 239–40, 255–56

Vaikunth, 175, 191
Vaishnava
  devotees, 22–23, 44, 48, 68–26, 78, 83–84, 87, 146
  devotion, 60, 64–65, 71–72, 73, 85–86, 96, 182–83
  inclusive bhakti sensibility, 28–29, 30, 53
  Indian spiritual heritage, 128, 204–5, 220–22
  orthodoxy, 50–51, 53, 54, 57 (*see also* chatur sampradaya)
  pilgrimage centers (*see* Dwarka; Vrindavan)

  universal and unifying Hinduism, 256–67
  See also chatur sampradaya; *Chaurasi Vaishnavan ki Varta*; Gaudiya sampraday; Radhavallabh sampraday; Ramanandi sampraday; Ramavat sampraday; Sahajiya Vaishnava sampraday; Shri Vaishnava; Vallabha sampraday; Varkari sampraday; Vrindavan
Vaishnavdas, 66–67, 113–14
Vallabhacharya, 15, 28–29, 50–51, 54–57, 68
Vallabha sampraday, 75, 128, 131
  astachaps (see astachaps)
  Mira, 54–57, 82–83, 84–85, 115–16
  Padaprasangmala, 80, 82–83, 84–85
  Vallabhites, 50–51, 52, 54–57, 59–60, 68
  Vartas (see *Vartas*)
Valmiki (Balmik), 59
Vamana, 71–72
vamshavalis (family chronicles), 110, 144–45, 149–51
Vanita, Ruth, 81–82, 222
Varkari sampraday, 54, 73, 86–92, 101–2, 103, 228–29, 230
Varma, Mahadevi, 16–17, 20, 235–46, 247, 252–53, 254, 256–57, 260–61, 266–67
  "Links in Our Chain" 241–43
varna-ashrama-dharma, 83–84, 85–86, 96, 204–5, 235, 262
Vartas
  Chaurasi Vaishnavan ki Varta, 54–57, 68, 82–83, 115–16
  Do Sau Bavan Vaishnavan ki Varta, 82–83
Vaswani, Swami T. L., 233, 261–62
Vaudeville, Charlotte, 89
Vedanta, 255–56
Vedas, 23, 96–97, 130–31, 237–38
Vedic reforms, 128, 130–31
Vedic ritual, 83–84, 85–86
vernacular, 119, 121, 124–25, 155–56
  history, 143
  literization and literaturization, 28–29
  press, 124–25, 127, 155–56
Victorian devotionalism, 120–21
vijavaragi, 94–95, 148–49, 314n.30
Vikramajit (Vikramaditya, Bikramajit), 118–19, 144, 148–49, 152, 157, 158–59, 160, 265–66
Vikram, 280–81
Vilvamangal, 46

vina, 87, 265–66, 284–85
virag, 144
viraha, 198, 287, 306n.11
virahini, 237–38
Viramdev, 94, 144, 148–49, 158–59
viranganas. *See* heroines
Virashaiva, 45, 57
Vir Vinod, 142–46
Vishnu, 22–23, 49, 71–72
Vishnuswami, 50–51, 68
Vishwanathan, Lakshmi, 286
Vitthal, 89–91
Vitthalnath, 82–83
Vivekananda, 155
vote, 228, 266–67
Vrindavan
   Bankey Behari, 256, 258–59
   inner, 67–68, 249–50
   Meera (1945/1947), 277–78, 281, 282
   Meera Temple, 111
   Mira, 38, 66–67, 77, 84, 96, 105–6, 111, 136–37, 175, 253, 264–65 (*see also* Jiv Goswami)
   Nagridas, 75, 81–82
   pilgrimage, 171, 213–14
   removal of images, 82
   Vaishnavism, 28–29, 30, 32, 50, 56, 66–67, 86, 89–90
   women renouncers, 269
Vyas, Hariram, 30, 54, 137

Walsh, Judith, 215
war, 252–53, 254, 276–77
warrior ascetics, 50–51, 83, 317n.76
Watkins, R., 252–53, 254, 255
Weiden, Amanda, 286
Weisse, John A., 127–28
West, 251, 252
   Western audiences, 251, 252
   Western ideas, 270
widowhood, 40–41, 81, 127, 138–39, 189, 218, 226, 270
Wilson, Horace Hayman, 113–16, 163
   influence of, 119–20, 121–23, 135, 140–41, 203–4
   Mira, 41, 75–76, 149, 156–57, 197, 198, 223, 234–35, 253, 266, 269–70
   Wilson College Literary Society, 129–30
women saints, 39–58. *See also* Andal; Bahinabai; Gauribai; Lalla; Mahadeviyakka
women's seclusion and veiling. *See* purdah
women's education, 109, 123–24, 126–28, 138, 159–60, 207–8, 209–10, 215, 233
   Mahadevi Varma, 239, 240, 241
Women's Indian Association, 228, 249
women's political activism, 248, 249, 255, 275, 276–77
   Gandhi, 221, 222, 224, 231–33, 235
   Mahadevi Varma, 235–36, 239–42, 244
women's songs, 36–37, 182, 191–92
women's worship tales, 185–87, 191–92, 275

Yashoda, 127

Zoroastrians, 260–61